ODGERS ON HI
PLEADING AND

AUSTRALIA AND NEW ZEALAND
The Law Book Company Ltd.,
Sydney: Melbourne: Perth: Brisbane

CANADA
The Carswell Company Ltd.
Agincourt, Ontario

INDIA
N.M. Tripathi Private Ltd.
Bombay
and
Eastern Law House Private Ltd.
Calcutta and Delhi
M.P.P. House
Bangalore

ISRAEL
Steimatzky's Agency Ltd.
Jerusalem: Tel-Aviv: Haifa

PAKISTAN
Pakistan Law House
Karachi

ODGERS
ON HIGH COURT
PLEADING AND PRACTICE

TWENTY-THIRD EDITION

BY

D. B. CASSON, LL.B., J.D., F.R.S.A.

of Gray's Inn, Barrister,
Rank Foundation Professor of Law
at the University of Buckingham,
formerly Reader in Law
at the Inns of Court
School of Law

LONDON
SWEET & MAXWELL/STEVENS
1991

First Edition	*(1891) By William Blake Odgers*
Second Edition	*(1894) By William Blake Odgers, Q.C.*
Third Edition	*(1897)*
Fourth Edition	*(1900)*
Fifth Edition	*(1903)*
Sixth Edition	*(1906)*
Seventh Edition	*(1912)*
Eighth Edition	*(1919)*
Revised	*(1922) By Walter Blake Odgers*
Ninth Edition	*(1926)*
Tenth Edition	*(1930) By Walter Blake Odgers and A. H. Armstrong*
Eleventh Edition	*(1934) By Walter Blake Odgers and B. A. Harwood*
Twelfth Edition	*(1939) By Walter Blake Odgers, K.C., and B.A. Harwood*
Thirteenth Edition	*(1946) By Walter Blake Odgers, K.C., and Lewis F. Sturge*
Fourteenth Edition	*(1952) By Lewis F. Sturge*
Fifteenth Edition	*(1955) By Master B. A. Harwood*
Sixteenth Edition	*(1957)*
Seventeenth Edition	*(1960) By Master B. A. Harwood and G. F. Harwood*
Eighteenth Edition	*(1963) By G. F. Harwood*
Nineteenth Edition	*(1966) By G. F. Harwood*
Twentieth Edition	*(1971) By G. F. Harwood*
Twenty-First Edition	*(1975) By D. B. Casson and I. H. Dennis*
First Impression	*(1977)*
Twenty-Second Edition	*(1981) By D. B. Casson and I. H. Dennis*
First Impression	*(1988)*
Twenty-Third Edition	*(1991) By D. B. Casson*

Published by Sweet & Maxwell/Stevens
of South Quay Plaza, 183 Marsh Wall, London E14 9FT
Computerset by LBJ Enterprises Limited
Chilcompton, Somerset
Printed in Great Britain by
Richard Clay Limited, Bungay, Suffolk

British Library Cataloguing in Publication Data
A CIP catalogue record for this book is available from
the British Library

PREFACE

The centenary edition of *Odgers* appears at a time of exceptional activity in the law of civil procedure. In February 1985 the Lord Chancellor, Lord Hailsham of St. Marylebone, set up a Review Body on Civil Justice—the Civil Justice Review—with the following terms of reference:—

> To improve the machinery of civil justice in England and Wales by means of reforms in jurisdiction, procedure and court administration and in particular to reduce delay, cost and complexity.

The Review Body reported in 1988. Its recommendations are set out in Appendix 3 of this book. They cover many aspects of procedure and practice. Some have already been implemented; others are given statutory basis in the Courts and Legal Services Act 1990, which will provide the machinery for major innovations in procedural law and in the provision of legal services. The Act is inspired not only by the Civil Justice Review, but also by the views of the present Lord Chancellor, Lord Mackay of Clashfern, in relation to legal services generally. This edition of *Odgers* has been prepared during the parliamentary progress of the Act, and I express my warmest thanks to Mr. L. C. Oates and to Mr. J. A. C. Watherston of the Lord Chancellor's Department for their kindness in keeping me informed of the progress of the Bill.

I express my warmest thanks also to Mr. Richard Field Q.C. who very kindly read the proofs of the chapter on Trial and made many valuable comments based upon his great experience of High Court litigation.

Professor Ian Dennis, who collaborated with me in the preparation of the 21st and 22nd editions, has turned his attention to other matters, and has not been involved in the preparation of this edition. Instead, I have had the advantage of contributions from several colleagues and friends. Mr. Stephen Worthington, Barrister, and Miss Freya Newbury, Barrister, undertook the very considerable task of revising the chapters on Pleading and the associated precedents set out in Appendix 1. Mr. Timothy Evans, Barrister, undertook a similar role in relation to the chapters on Chancery Procedure and the associated precedents. Mr. Simon Goulding LL.M., Barrister, has made a significant contribution by revising the chapters on Costs, Discovery and the major sections in Chapter 4 on Mareva Injunctions, Anton Piller Orders, and Interlocutory Injunctions, the last of which appears for the first time in

Odgers, having been first published in *Modern Developments in the Law of Civil Procedure* by Professor Dennis and myself. Mr. Goulding helped also with the chapter on Interrogatories. I was very fortunate in securing the co-operation of Mrs. Helen Helston LL.M., Barrister, who very kindly agreed to revise the section on Jurisdiction of the High Court (and managed to correct the proofs despite the need to serve them out of the jurisdiction) and of Mr. Barry Hough LL.M., who has greatly expanded the section on Representative Actions in the light of his researches into this interesting and increasingly important topic. Mr. Andrew Hodge LL.M., Barrister, was good enough to help with the chapter on Appeals. In expressing my gratitude to these contributors, it is, of course, necessary to say that responsibility for the final state of the text and for any imperfections, errors or infelicities that appear, is mine.

I would like to express my thanks also to the staff of the publishers who have been tolerant and helpful in the light of the delays to which I have necessarily subjected them in the presentation of the manuscript.

Finally, it will be noted that the title of the book has undergone a minor change and is now a little less ponderous than for the last century. I have little doubt that the next edition of the book will appear with a more significant alteration to its title, to reflect the changes that will take place in procedure and practice in the years to come.

D. B. Casson

October 1990

CONTENTS

Contents

Contents

TABLE OF CASES

TABLE OF STATUTES

TABLE OF RULES AND ORDERS

[References to the text of Rules are shown in **bold** type.]

xlvii

CHAPTER 1

AN INTRODUCTORY SURVEY

The High Court of Justice

Civil actions in England and Wales may be commenced either in the High Court or the county court. The High Court is one part of the Supreme Court of Judicature, which was created originally by the Judicature Act 1873.[1] Following the Supreme Court Act 1981, the Supreme Court now consists of the Court of Appeal, the High Court of Justice and the Crown Court.[2] The modern county courts date from 1846 when Parliament set up a system of courts to deal with small civil cases.[3] In essence the procedure of a civil action in the High Court and the county court is similar; the main distinguishing feature of the two courts is that of jurisdiction. It is proposed to describe the jurisdiction of the respective courts and to clarify the relationship between them, before dealing in detail with the structure and organisation of the High Court, the court with which this book is principally concerned.

Jurisdiction and the County Courts

The jurisdiction of the High Court used to be set out in sections 18–25 of the Judicature Act 1925. The scheme of this consolidating legislation was to vest in the High Court the jurisdiction of various courts which were in existence in 1875 and which were merged into the new High Court on November 1 of that year. Hence section 18 provided that the High Court now had the jurisdiction formerly exercised by the High Court of Chancery, the Court of Queen's Bench, the Court of Common Pleas, the Court of Exchequer, the Court of Common Pleas at Lancaster and the Court of Pleas at Durham. In addition the Judicature Act 1925 vested in the High Court jurisdiction in probate matters,[4] matrimonial causes,[5] legitimacy declarations[6] and Admiralty[7] and prize[8] cases.

---

[1] This Act came into force on November 1, 1875. It was merged with later amending Acts in the Supreme Court of Judicature (Consolidation) Act 1925, referred to in this book for convenience as the Judicature Act 1925.
[2] s.1(1). The Crown Court has mainly criminal jurisdiction and is therefore outside the scope of this book.
[3] The governing statute is now the County Courts Act 1984.
[4] s.20.
[5] s.21(*a*).
[6] s.21(*b*).
[7] s.22 (repealed by the Administration of Justice Act 1956, s.57, Sched. II and replaced by s.1 of that Act). Detailed provisions concerning the Admiralty jurisdiction of the High Court are now set out in the Supreme Court Act 1981, ss.20–24.
[8] s.23.

1

The Judicature Act 1925 was repealed by the Supreme Court Act 1981. However, section 19(2) of the Supreme Court Act 1981 provides that "there shall be exercisable by the High Court—(a) all such jurisdiction (whether civil or criminal) as is conferred on it by this or any other Act; and (b) all such other jurisdiction (whether civil or criminal) as was exercisable by it immediately before the commencement of this Act (including jurisdiction conferred on a judge of the High Court by any statutory provision)." Sections 20–31 of the Supreme Court Act then make further provision with regard to a number of specific matters of jurisdiction, for example, Admiralty cases, and applications for judicial review. Thus the jurisdiction vested in the High Court by the Judicature Act 1925 is preserved, subject to some amendments, but the 1925 Act has been replaced as the source of the jurisdiction.

In recent years original jurisdiction over new statutory types of civil claim, such as those of employees for unfair dismissal, has sometimes been assigned to specialist tribunals rather than to the High Court; however, the latter is often given an appellate jurisdiction on points of law in these cases.

When the High Court does have original jurisdiction over a civil proceeding, that jurisdiction is unlimited in amount. The jurisdiction of the county court, on the other hand, is limited in amount by statute.[9] These limits may be increased by Order in Council. The current jurisdiction of the county court is as follows[10]:

(i) Actions founded on contract or tort, where the amount claimed does not exceed £5,000[11];

(ii) Actions for the recovery of land, where the net annual value for rating of the land on March 31, 1990 did not exceed £1,000.[12] In respect of property in London, the relevant value is £1500[13];

(iii) Certain proceedings in equity, where the value of the property or fund in question does not exceed £30,000[14];

(iv) Applications for new tenancies of business premises, where the net annual value for rating of the premises does not exceed £5,000[15];

---

[9] The County Courts Act 1984 is the principal statute.

[10] In addition, under ss.18 and 24 of the County Courts Act the parties to most common law and some equity proceedings which would otherwise be outside the limit of the jurisdiction may consent to trial in the county court.

[11] County Courts Act 1984. The amount is £15,000 in Consumer Credit Act cases.

[12] County Courts Act 1984, s.21.

[13] Rent Act 1977, s.141. Housing Act 1985, s.110. See also Housing Act 1988, s.40.

[14] County Courts Act 1984, s.23.

[15] Landlord and Tenant Act 1954, s.38(4).

(v) Admiralty proceedings, where the amount does not exceed £15,000 in a claim in the nature of salvage, and in other cases £30,000.[16] Only those county courts appointed for the purpose by the Lord Chancellor have Admiralty jurisdiction.

It follows that within these limits there is concurrent jurisdiction and the plaintiff in such a case will have a choice between the High Court and the county court. However, the County Courts Act also contains provisions bearing directly on the question of the appropriate forum, and the plaintiff's choice is by no means free or indefeasible. First, there is power to transfer actions from the High Court to the county court,[17] for example, where the amount claimed or remaining in dispute on the claim is within the monetary limit of the jurisdiction of the county court, or where the proceedings are not likely to raise any important question of law or fact and are suitable for determination by a county court. Similarly, actions may be transferred the other way,[18] for example, an action begun in the county court where the amount of the claim is within the limit, but the claim itself is likely to involve an important question of law or fact. Provisions for transfer of actions are discussed more fully later.[19] Secondly, sections 19 and 20 of the County Courts Act 1984 contain important provisions relating to the costs recoverable by a plaintiff who has brought in the High Court an action founded on contract or tort which could have been commenced in the county court. If such a plaintiff recovers less than £3,000 in his action, he will only be entitled to costs on the county court scale, and if he recovers less than £600 he will receive no costs at all.[20] These provisions are designed to ensure that, as far as possible, smaller civil claims which present no particular difficulties of law or fact are disposed of more quickly and cheaply in the county court.

The Civil Justice Review[21] recommended in 1988 that there should be major changes in the civil justice system. With a view to increasing efficiency and reducing delay in litigation it proposed a significant transfer of workload from the High Court to the county courts. The Review recommended that there should be no upper limit of county court jurisdiction and

---

[16] County Courts Act 1984, ss.26–31. Some courts also have divorce and insolvency jurisdiction, and matters under the Race Relations Act 1976.
[17] County Courts Act 1984, s.40.
[18] County Courts Act 1984, ss.41, 42.
[19] *Post*, Chap. 18.
[20] s.20.
[21] Cm. 394. See Appendix 3.

that the High Court should in future handle and try only public law cases, other specialist cases and general list cases of importance, complexity and substance. "Cases of substance" mean those where the amount in issue exceeds £25,000; and that there should be a flexible financial band between £25,000 and £50,000 within which cases may be tried in the county court or the High Court. The Review recommended also that there should be a single point of entry in the county court for all personal injury cases. The Courts and Legal Services Act 1990 contains provisions conferring power on the Lord Chancellor to make orders allocating and transferring business between the High Court and county courts. When brought into effect, the Act will permit implementation of the recommendations of the Civil Justice Review, with the resulting necessity of a fundamental reconsideration of the traditional understanding of the relationship between and the jurisdiction of the High Court and the county courts.

Structure of the High Court

The High Court consists of the Lord Chancellor, the Lord Chief Justice, the President of the Family Division, the Vice-Chancellor, and not more than 80[22] puisne judges (Supreme Court Act 1981, s.4(1)). The court is organised into three Divisions.[23] These Divisions are:

(i) the Chancery Division, consisting of the Lord Chancellor and the Vice-Chancellor, who are the president and vice-president of the Division respectively, and such of the puisne judges as are attached to the Division in accordance with section 5 of the Supreme Court Act 1981;

(ii) the Queen's Bench Division, consisting of the Lord Chief Justice as president of the Division, and such of the puisne judges as are attached to the Division;

(iii) the Family Division,[24] consisting of a President, and such of the puisne judges as are attached to the Division.[25]

---

[22] The number is subject to increase (see below). The current number is 82.

[23] Supreme Court Act 1981, s.5(1).

[24] Formerly the Probate, Divorce and Admiralty Division, which was renamed and reorganised as the Family Division by the Administration of Justice Act 1970, s.1, Sched. 1. Under the reorganisation some former jurisdiction was reassigned: probate business, except for non-contentious or common form probate business, to the Chancery Division; Admiralty, prize court and commercial list business to the Queen's Bench Division.

[25] The maximum number of puisne judges of the High Court may be increased from time to time by Order in Council (Supreme Court Act 1981, s.4(4)). Suitably qualified persons may be requested to assist in the transaction of business by acting as judges of the High Court (*ibid.*, s.9(1)), or, as a temporary measure, may be appointed deputy High Court judges (s.9(4)).

The Supreme Court Act 1981 provides that all jurisdiction vested in the High Court under the Act shall belong to all the Divisions alike,[26] although this is stated to be without prejudice to the provisions of the Act relating to the distribution of business in the High Court. In order to clarify the scope of this book it will be helpful to describe briefly the distribution of business in the High Court and the different procedures used in the three Divisions for dealing with the work allocated. The distribution is made in terms of a mixture of types of action (for example, the execution of a trust), historical jurisdiction (for example, actions within the exclusive cognisance of the old Court of Common Pleas) and particular assignment (for example, under any other statute, or by order of the Lord Chancellor, who has a general power under section 61 of the Supreme Court Act 1981 to redistribute business among the Divisions of the High Court). There is some overlap between the work done in the three Divisions, and it is for the plaintiff to choose the Division in which to bring his action.[27] It is not fatal to his claim to select a Division other than the one to which the case ought to have been assigned, although the action may later be transferred to the appropriate Division.[28]

The Chancery Division has been assigned[29] jurisdiction over all causes and matters relating to the sale, exchange or partition of land, or the raising of charges on land; the redemption or foreclosure of mortgages; the execution of trusts; the administration of the estates of deceased persons; bankruptcy; partnerships; the rectification, setting aside or cancellation of deeds or other written instruments; contentious probate business[30]; patents, trade marks, registered designs, copyright; the appointment of guardians of the estates of minors; companies. Chancery jurisdiction is discussed further in Chapter 21, but in general the Chancery Division is largely concerned with the numerous aspects of property law and allied technical matters.

The Queen's Bench Division has a more heterogeneous jurisdiction. First, it has inherited the jurisdiction formerly possessed by the old common law courts of Queen's Bench, Common Pleas at Westminster and Exchequer.[31] The Queen's

---

[26] s.5(5). It follows that any judge of the High Court has jurisdiction to try any action which has been wrongly assigned to the Division in which he sits: see *Russian Commercial Bank* v. *British Bank for Foreign Trade* [1921] A.C. 438.

[27] Supreme Court Act 1981, s.64.

[28] See generally *ibid.*, ss.64, 65, and R.S.C., Ord. 4, r. 3.

[29] Supreme Court Act 1981, Sched. 1, s.1. The Companies Court and Patents Court are within the Chancery Division.

[30] See *ante*, note 24.

[31] Judicature Act 1925, s.56(2)(*a*).

Bench Division is thus the appropriate forum for original proceedings in contract and tort, the vast majority of which consist of claims for contract debts and actions for damages for personal injuries.[32] The inheritance also includes the supervisory jurisdiction exercised by the Court of Queen's Bench over the activities of inferior courts and tribunals. This jurisdiction now takes the form of the issue of declarations, injunctions and the judicial orders of mandamus, prohibition or certiorari, and may be invoked by an application for judicial review under R.S.C., Ord. 53.[33] Secondly, the Queen's Bench Division has been assigned the Admiralty and prize jurisdiction of the High Court.[34] The Administration of Justice Act 1970 transferred this jurisdiction from the former Probate, Divorce and Admiralty Division, and provided for the constitution, as part of the Queen's Bench Division, of an Admiralty Court.[35] This court takes the Admiralty and prize business of the High Court and is staffed by puisne High Court judges nominated by the Lord Chancellor. A similar special court, called the "Commercial Court," was constituted at the same time to deal with causes and matters entered in the commercial list.[36] Thirdly, particular matters may be assigned to the Queen's Bench Division from time to time by other statutes.[37]

The jurisdiction of the Family Division was first set out in the Administration of Justice Act 1970.[38] It consists, as the name of the Division suggests, of all causes and matters connected with the status and welfare of families. Thus it embraces matri-

---

[32] For example, in 1989 some 288,000 writs were issued in the Queen's Bench Division. Of these, 206,000 were for moneys payable under contract and a further 56,000 were personal injuries cases. Personal injuries actions are by far the largest group of actions which actually come to trial; approximately two-thirds of all actions tried in the Queen's Bench Division. Approximately 2·5 million cases were started in the county courts in 1986 (see Judicial Statistics, 1989 (Cm 1154)).

[33] Ord. 53 was completely revised in 1977 (by R.S.C. (Amendment No. 3) 1977) following a report by the Law Commission (Law Com. No. 73: Remedies in Administrative Law (1976)). The Law Commission recommended the introduction of a new form of procedure, to be known as an "Application for Judicial Review," for persons seeking to challenge an administrative act or omission in the High Court. The new procedure eliminates the difficulty and technicality formerly involved in applications for administrative law remedies. See further Supreme Court Act 1981, ss.29–31, Sched. I, s.2(*b*).

[34] *Ibid.*, ss.20–24, 27, Sched. 1, s.2(*c*).

[35] See s.2, and the Supreme Court Act 1981, s.6(1)(*b*).

[36] Administration of Justice Act 1970, s.3, and the Supreme Court Act 1981, s.6(1)(*b*). The commercial list had existed as part of the practice of the Queen's Bench Division since 1895, but had not been taken consistently by specialist judges. A further feature of the reorganisation in 1970 was the empowering of Commercial Court judges to take arbitrations: *ibid.*, s.4.

[37] Judicature Act 1925, s.56(2)(*b*). This provision is not expressly restated in the Supreme Court Act 1981, but its continued operation seems to be envisaged by sections 19(2) and 61(1).

[38] s.1(2); Sched. 1. See now the Supreme Court Act 1981, Sched. 1, s.3.

monial causes such as petitions for divorce and annulment, proceedings for declarations of legitimacy or matrimonial status, wardship, adoption and guardianship of minors. In addition the Family Division has been assigned the non-contentious or common form probate business of the High Court,[39] although in practice this administrative work is dealt with by the various probate registries. The Family Division also has an extensive appellate jurisdiction, dealing with proceedings on appeal from magistrates' courts.

There are a number of methods of beginning proceedings in the High Court, namely by writ of summons, by originating summons, by originating motion or by petition.[40] It is not the purpose of this book to deal in detail with all these methods, since a full treatment would necessitate discussion of many specific provisions in statutes or the Rules of the Supreme Court dealing with particular types of civil proceedings, which are fully dealt with in specialist works on those topics. Instead this book concentrates on the procedure in an action commenced by writ of summons (usually abbreviated to "writ") in the Queen's Bench Division. This procedure is appropriate, *inter alia*, for virtually all actions founded on the common law, and is thus the procedure used to transact by far the greatest part of business in the Queen's Bench Division. The procedure in an action begun by writ in the Chancery Division is dealt with in a separate chapter, although it is not now very different from that in the Queen's Bench Division. The Chancery Division also deals with a large number of matters begun by originating summons, and an outline of this procedure is given in a second separate chapter. Proceedings by originating motion or by petition are not covered except in the most general terms, and the particular procedures of the Family Division are not covered at all. The Civil Justice Review recommended that, subject to a very few essential exceptions, all civil proceedings should be commenced by a writ.

The Queen's Bench Division

Organisation and Personnel

Before the reorganisation of the courts effected by the Courts Act 1971, the Queen's Bench Division as part of the Supreme Court had its main sittings at the Royal Courts of Justice in

---

[39] Supreme Court Act 1981, Sched. 1, s.3(*b*)(iv).
[40] R.S.C., Ord. 5, r. 1.

London. The judges of the Queen's Bench Division and the Family Division also sat from time to time at various provincial towns throughout England and Wales at "Assizes." The Queen's Bench Division judges tried mainly criminal cases at Assizes, but they also tried some civil actions and, when so doing, constituted a court of the High Court.

The Courts Act 1971 abolished all courts of assize,[41] and provided instead that the sittings and any other business of the High Court might be held and conducted at any place in England and Wales authorised by the Lord Chancellor.[42] In fact the Lord Chancellor has directed the establishment of 26 permanent trial centres in the main provincial towns in England and Wales for the trial of Queen's Bench Division actions outside London.[43] These centres are visited regularly by the Queen's Bench Division judges for the hearing of such actions. In addition, of course, the Supreme Court continues to sit as before in London.

Proceedings in the Queen's Bench Division are heard either in public by a judge sitting robed in open court,[44] or in private by a master (or district registrar) or a judge sitting in chambers and not robed. A master, who will have been a practising barrister or solicitor[45] before his appointment, is an officer of the court who has power to decide, subject to a right of appeal to a judge, nearly all the preliminary (interlocutory) questions which arise in an action before the trial. A district registrar is the provincial equivalent of a master. A civil action in the Queen's Bench Division may be commenced in a District Registry outside London, and in such a case the proceedings are under the control of a district registrar who has, in general, the same powers and jurisdiction as a master.[46] The masters sit every day in term time to hear lists of short non-counsel summonses in the morning and of counsel summonses at noon and to deal with longer matters by special appointment. Lists of the more urgent cases are also taken in the vacation.

The administrative business of the Supreme Court, that is to say, such matters as the issue of writs, acknowledgments of

---

[41] s.1(2).

[42] s.2. See now the Supreme Court Act 1981, s.71.

[43] Ord. 33, r. 1. For Chancery proceedings outside London, see *Practice Directions* [1972] 1 W.L.R. 1; [1982] 1 W.L.R. 1189; [1983] 1 W.L.R. 1211.

[44] In exceptional cases the judge may order trial *in camera*: see Chap. 20.

[45] Supreme Court Act 1981, Sched. 2.

[46] Accordingly, the word "master" in this book will include "district registrar." In effect a district registrar may not except by consent deal with cases to which the Crown is a party (see Ord. 77, r. 2); nor, save in certain district registries, with originating summonses in Chancery proceedings (see Ord. 7, r. 5(2)); except that originating summonses and writs in mortgage actions may be issued out of the district registry of the district where the property is situated (Ord. 88, r. 3).

service, the entry of judgments, the issue of summonses and the drawing up of orders in the Queen's Bench Division, and the filing of affidavits and other documents, is performed by the "Central Office,"[47] which is divided into various departments and the business of whichh is superintended by the masters of the Queen's Bench Division. One of those masters in rotation sits as "Practice Master" and is always present to give any necessary directions to the staff, to help with any procedural difficulties encountered by litigants and their advisers, and to deal with the numerous and varied applications which are made *ex parte*, that is to say, without notice to the other side and usually by lodging an affidavit verifying the grounds of the application.

Orders made on these preliminary questions are called interlocutory,[48] as opposed to final orders which are usually made at the trial of the action and which finally dispose of the dispute between the parties subject to any right of appeal.

The Rules of the Supreme Court

The procedure in actions in the Queen's Bench Division (as also in the Chancery Division and to some extent in the Family Division) is regulated by "Rules of the Supreme Court" which are divided according to their subject-matter into "Orders." They have statutory effect, having been made by the Rule Committee under powers now contained in the Supreme Court Act 1981.[49] Rules of particular use to students are referred to throughout this book. The remainder can be found in *The Rules of the Supreme Court 1965* as amended or in *The Supreme Court Practice* (usually called the "White Book").

The rules provide, *inter alia*, how an action shall be commenced and how any application is to be made during the course of the action. An application may be made either in chambers (when it is made by a summons served on the other parties to the action unless the rules permit it to be made *ex parte*[50]) or in open court (when it is made by motion, notice of which must usually be given to the other parties affected).[51] A summons is a document calling on the parties to the action to

---

[47] Ord. 63, rr. 1, 2.
[48] The vast majority of interlocutory matters are dealt with by application in chambers but a few are heard on motion, that is to say, in open court. Occasionally, a summons which raises matter of general interest is adjourned into court for argument and decision.
[49] s.84.
[50] Ord. 32, r. 1.
[51] Ord. 8, r. 2.

attend. It is prepared by the applicant in proper form and taken to the summons room in the Central Office of the Royal Courts of Justice, where after payment of a fee it is sealed and is thereupon deemed to be issued. A return day is allotted according to the state of the list, and the summons is then served upon the opposite party.

In the rules before they were revised the expression "the court or a judge" constantly occurred and "the court" meant one or more judges sitting upon the bench in open court, and "a judge" meant a judge sitting in chambers. In the current rules the expression "the court" is constantly used. This includes, according to the context, the High Court, any one or more judges thereof whether sitting in court or in chambers, masters of the Queen's Bench and Chancery Divisions, registrars of the Family Division and district registrars.[52] The jurisdiction of these officers and what matters are reserved to the judges are defined in Order 32, rr. 11, 14 and 23. Interlocutory applications are now generally heard and disposed of by a master or registrar; in the Queen's Bench Division most of them only come before a judge on appeal from a master. Throughout this volume, therefore, "the master" is usually substituted for "the court." In the Chancery Division interlocutory matters are frequently referred by the master to the judge.

The Modes of Beginning Proceedings

Civil proceedings in the High Court may be begun by writ, originating summons, originating motion or petition.[53] Most actions in the Queen's Bench Division are begun by writ and it is with such actions that the rest of the book is mainly concerned. In some cases, however, an originating summons is appropriate. As its name indicates, this is a mode of actually commencing proceedings as opposed to an ordinary summons in a pending action.

The following proceedings by a plaintiff *must* ordinarily be begun by writ[54]:

    (a) claims for any relief or remedy for a tort, other than trespass to land;

    (b) claims based on an allegation of fraud[55];

---

[52] Ord. 1, r. 4(2).
[53] Ord. 5, r. 1.
[54] Ord. 5, r. 2.
[55] Where an allegation of fraud arises in the course of an action begun by originating summons, it may be continued under Ord. 28, r. 8, as though it had been begun by writ. See *Re Deadman decd., Smith* v. *Garland* [1971] 1 W.L.R. 426. *Semble*, Ord. 28, r. 8, may also apply where the action is based on fraud in the first instance. But see *Re 462 Green Lanes, Ilford, Gooding* v. *Borland* [1971] 1 W.L.R. 138, doubted and not followed in *Re Deadman.*

(c) claims for damages for breach of duty (whether contractual, statutory or otherwise) resulting in death, personal injury (including disease and mental impairment) or damage to property; and

(d) claims in respect of the infringement of a patent.

A claim for the possession of land in occupation by a trespasser may be begun by writ or by originating summons. It may be to the plaintiff's advantage to adopt the summary procedure under Order 113 in such a case by commencing proceedings with an originating summons.[56]

The following proceedings *must* be begun by originating summons, except where the application is expressly required or authorised by the rules or a statute to be made otherwise.[57]

Proceedings by which an application is to be made to the High Court or a judge thereof under any Act. This does not apply to an application made in pending proceedings. Nor, for example, does it apply to proceedings under the Fatal Accidents Act 1976, for these must under paragraph (c) above be begun by writ. The commonest examples in the Family Division are summonses under the Married Women's Property Act 1882, s.17, concerning disputes between spouses as to the ownership or possession of property.[58]

All other proceedings *may* be begun either by writ or by originating summons,[59] except where the proceedings are by the rules or a statute required to be begun in one or the other manner or are authorised to be begun by motion or petitions. But proceedings:

(a) where the sole or principal question at issue is, or is likely to be, one of the construction of an Act or of any instrument made under an Act, or of any deed, will, contract or other document, or some other question of law, or

(b) in which there is unlikely to be any substantial dispute of fact,

are both ordinarily appropriate to be begun by originating summons unless the plaintiff intends to apply for summary judgment under Order 14 or 86 (see Chapters 5 and 21).

The summons must include a statement of the questions on which the plaintiff seeks the determination or direction of the court or a concise statement of the relief or remedy claimed,

[56] See Chap. 5.
[57] Ord. 5, r. 3.
[58] Such summonses were formerly heard in the Queen's Bench Division.
[59] Ord. 5, r. 4.

with sufficient particulars to identify the cause or causes of action.[60] The procedure upon an originating summons is briefly described for the purpose of proceedings in the Queen's Bench Division at the end of this chapter. It is governed by Order 28 which applies irrespective of the Division in which the proceedings are begun, and the reader is referred to Chapter 22 for further details.

Bodies corporate and the representatives of minors and patients must generally sue and defend through a solicitor and cannot act in person.[61] All other persons may begin and carry on proceedings in the High Court by a solicitor or in person.[62]

An Action in the Queen's Bench Division

A preliminary outline of the more important steps in an ordinary Queen's Bench action may be of assistance to the student. In subsequent chapters the practice and procedure in such actions is considered in detail.

The Writ

A writ is a formal document by which an action is commenced. Until 1980 the prescribed form included a command by the Queen to the defendant to "enter an appearance" within so many days, if he wished to dispute the plaintiff's claim; otherwise judgment might be signed against him. The issue of this old form of writ was then "witnessed" by the Lord Chancellor. However, important and far-reaching changes in the procedure for the issue, service and acknowledgment of proceedings were introduced[63] with effect from June 3, 1980, and apply to proceedings commenced after that date. The current form of writ omits the Royal Command and the Teste of the Lord Chancellor, although the Queen's association with the administration of justice is maintained by a replica of the Royal Arms at the top of the writ, and the writ's authenticity will be vouched by the requirement that every copy of a writ for service on a defendant must be sealed with the seal of the office of the Supreme Court at which the writ is issued.[64]

---

[60] Ord. 7, r. 3.
[61] Ord. 5, r. 6; Ord. 80, r. 2. However, a body corporate is expressly empowered by Ord. 12, r. 1(2) and Ord. 12, r. 9(3), to acknowledge service of a writ of summons and an originating summons and to give notice of intention to defend by a person duly authorised to act on its behalf, instead of acting by a solicitor.
[62] Ord. 5, r. 6.
[63] By R.S.C. (Writ and Appearances) 1979 (S.I. 1979 No. 1716).
[64] Ord. 10, r. 1(6).

The writ states the plaintiff's name, followed by the defendant's name and address, then calls upon the defendant, in imperative terms, either to satisfy the plaintiff's claim, or to return to the specified Court Office within a prescribed time (usually 14 days) an accompanying acknowledgment of service stating therein whether he intends to contest the proceedings. The defendant is then warned that if he fails to satisfy the claim, or fails to return the acknowledgment of service in due time, or does return the acknowledgment but fails to state therein an intention to contest the proceedings, the plaintiff may proceed with the action and may enter judgment against him without further notice. The plaintiff's claim is set out or "indorsed" on the back of the writ, and the indorsement may take the form of a short indication of the general nature of the claim (a "general indorsement") or of a full statement of claim (a "special indorsement").[65]

Issuing the Writ

As soon as the writ is prepared and its indorsement duly drafted, the next step is to "issue" it; that is, to make it an official document emanating from the court. In former times issuing a writ was regarded as a judicial, not a ministerial act; the officer of the court drafted, or at all events settled, the plaintiff's writ for him, and would not allow any writ to issue which, in his opinion, was not in proper form. This often caused an eager litigant trouble and delay, though it might save him costs in the end. But there is no longer any difficulty of this kind. The plaintiff now settles his indorsement as he pleases; and the officers of the court raise no formal objection as to its sufficiency in law although it is within their discretion to call attention to any apparent defect. It is for the defendant to take objection subsequently, if it is not as it should be.

There are, however, some cases in which leave to issue a writ is still sometimes necessary, for example, where the defendant is beyond the jurisdiction of the court. In many such cases the writ will not be issued unless the plaintiff first obtains the leave of a judge or master under the provisions of Order 11.[66]

Normally issuing a writ is a straightforward process. The plaintiff or his solicitor takes[67] a sufficient number of copies of

---

[65] For examples, see Precedents Nos. 1 and 2 in Appendix 1.

[66] The provisions of Ord. 11 are considered more fully in Chap. 2. See also Ords. 73 and 76, dealing with arbitrations and probate actions respectively.

[67] A plaintiff may also issue a writ by post, whether he is suing by a solicitor or acting in person: *Practice Direction* [1971] 1 W.L.R. 75, as amended by *Practice Direction* [1980] 3 All E.R. 822.

the proposed writ to the Writ Department of the Central Office of the High Court in London, or to a district registry, signs one copy, and pays the fee.[68] The issuing officer impresses a stamp on the signed copy and files it. He stamps the other copies with the official seal of the issuing office, marks them with the year, letter and number of the action[69] and hands them back. Under the current procedure the plaintiff must prepare and have sealed as many copies of the writ as there are defendants to be served[70] and he must also produce to the issuing officer a form of acknowledgment of service for each defendant on whom the writ is to be served.[71] In addition the plaintiff must complete the formal parts of these latter forms, that is, the Division of the High Court, the district registry, if any, out of which the writ is being issued, and the names of the parties. Copies of the writ will not be sealed unless the corresponding number of duly completed forms of acknowledgment of service are produced at the same time.

Service of the Writ

The next step is for the plaintiff to "serve" a copy of the writ on each defendant. Until recently the generally prescribed method of effecting service of originating process was by "personal service." This procedure required the plaintiff or his agent to hand to or leave with the defendant in person a copy of the writ, and, if asked, to show the defendant the original. Under the rules introduced in 1980[72] the duly sealed copy may be served on the defendant personally, or it may be served by sending it to him by first-class post to his usual or last-known address, or it may be served by inserting it through the letter-box for that address. Often, however, the defendant's solicitor accepts service of the writ on his behalf, and the solicitor will then indorse a statement on the writ to that effect. When none of these courses is practicable the master may in certain circumstances make an order for what is called "substituted service."[73]

Acknowledgment of Service

In early days, a defendant who wished to contest the action had physically to appear before the court, and submit to or

---

[68] Currently £70. Fees were increased by the Supreme Court Fees (Amendment) Order 1990 (S.I. 1990 No. 1460).
[69] For example, "1991–D.—No. 123," the letter being the initial of the first plaintiff's surname.
[70] Ord. 10, r. 1(6).
[71] *Ibid.*
[72] Ord. 10, r. 1, as amended.
[73] See Ord. 65, r. 4, and Chap. 4.

protest against its jurisdiction, and state publicly that he intended to defend the action and on what grounds. In the course of time physical appearance as a method of responding to the service of proceedings was replaced by the formal procedure of "entry of appearance," whereby a defendant on whom a writ had been served and who wished to defend the action would lodge a "memorandum of appearance" in the office of the court. This procedure was itself replaced by the procedure entitled "acknowledgment of service." Under the provisions of Order 12 a defendant who wishes to defend the action should complete the acknowledgment of service, which accompanied the writ served on him, and return it within the prescribed time (ordinarily 14 days) to the court office out of which the writ was issued.[74] The acknowledgment should contain a statement by the defendant of his intention to contest the proceedings, and if it does, the plaintiff will be precluded from entering a judgment in default of acknowledgment of service (see below) and the action will proceed. If the defendant wishes to object to any irregularity in the writ, or in the issue or service thereof, or if he wishes to dispute the jurisdiction of the court, he should complete and return the acknowledgment of service in the normal way and then apply to the court within 14 days of the acknowledgment for an appropriate order.[75]

Failure to Give Notice of Intention to Defend

If the defendant does not give notice of intention to defend (that is, by acknowledging service of the writ with a statement of his intention to contest the action) within the prescribed time (14 days after the service of the writ on him, inclusive of the day of service[76]), the plaintiff is, as a rule, entitled to judgment in default of notice of intention to defend. Where the writ claims a liquidated, that is an ascertained, sum of money and the defendant fails to give notice of intention to defend, the plaintiff may enter *final* judgment for the amount claimed on the writ, interest and costs (Order 13, r. 1(1)). If the action is for the recovery of land, the plaintiff is entitled to a judgment that the defendant do give him possession of the land, but the plaintiff may not, without leave, enter judgment for possession

---

[74] Ord. 12, r. 1(1), (3).
[75] Ord. 12, rr. 7, 8, terminating the former practice of "conditional appearance" in such a case. See Chap. 4.
[76] Ord. 12, r. 5.

of land unless he produces a certificate by his solicitor or (if he sues in person) an affidavit, stating either that the claim does not relate to a dwelling-house or that the claim relates to a dwelling-house of which the rateable value on every day specified by the Rent Act 1977, s.4(2), in relation to the premises exceeds the sum so specified or of which the rent payable in respect of the premises exceeds the sum specified in section 4(4)(*b*) of the Act. (Order 13, r. 4(2)). The object of this requirement is to ensure that judgment is not signed for possession of land if the defendant is entitled to the protection of the Rent Acts. If the action is for unliquidated damages, the plaintiff is not entitled to final judgment; he can only have what is called an *interlocutory* judgment—a judgment, that is, in his favour but with no amount stated; the amount of damages must subsequently be assessed by a master unless another mode of assessment is ordered.[77] The defendant, although he has not given notice of intention to defend, may attend and argue and call evidence at the assessment. And then the plaintiff may enter final judgment for the amount assessed.

A judgment in default of notice of intention to defend may, in the discretion of the court, be set aside upon terms.[78]

Summary Judgment

After acknowledgment of service with notice of intention to defend, Queen's Bench actions fall broadly into three classes: (a) those in which summary judgment is obtained under Order 14; (b) those which proceed to trial without pleadings; and (c) those which proceed to trial in the normal way. After the defendant has given notice of intention to defend the action, the plaintiff may apply by summons to a master for what is called "summary judgment." He or someone with knowledge of the facts swears an affidavit that he believes there is no defence to the whole or part of the plaintiff's claim. The defendant must then show by affidavit or otherwise satisfy the master that he has some genuine triable defence to raise. If he fails to do this, the plaintiff is given leave to sign judgment, either for the whole or part of his claim. A defendant may be given leave to defend the whole or part of the case. (See Chapter 5).

---

[77] *e.g.* by an official referee (a circuit judge or recorder who decides questions of accounts and tries actions which are unsuited for trial by judge alone or by judge and jury). See Chap. 18.

[78] Ord. 13, r. 9. See Chap. 4.

Pleadings

Either party may, after notice of intention to defend, apply for trial without further pleadings. In that case he must issue a summons (see Chapter 6). If summary judgment or trial without pleadings was not asked for or has been refused wholly or in part, the next stage in the action will normally be the service of pleadings or further pleadings, as the case may be. Pleadings are statements in writing served by each party alternately on his opponent, stating the facts relied on to support his case, and giving all such details as his opponent needs to know in order to prepare his case in answer. They are now served under a timetable prescribed by the rules: the usual pleadings in an action are:

(a) A Statement of Claim, in which the plaintiff sets out the facts relied on to support his cause of action with all necessary particulars as to his injuries and losses.

(b) A Defence, in which the defendant deals with every material fact alleged by the plaintiff in his statement of claim and also states any new facts on which he intends to rely. A defendant may also set up a cross-claim known as a Counterclaim.

(c) A Reply in which the plaintiff deals with fresh facts raised by the defendant in his defence. A reply is unusual except where the defendant sets up a counterclaim.

Although the plaintiff may have indorsed his statement of claim upon the writ, it sometimes happens, especially in apparently simple debt cases, that leave to defend is given upon an application for summary judgment and a fuller pleading is desirable. This the master may order to be served by way of amendment.

The nature and object of the various pleadings is explained in Chapters 12 to 15.

Summons for Directions

After the close of pleadings the parties must in many cases without order disclose to each other all relevant documents which they have (see Order 24, Chapter 16). Thereafter the plaintiff must generally take out a Summons for Directions before a master (Order 25) (see Chapter 18). But if he applies for summary judgment and fails to obtain it, the master proceeds then to give necessary directions just as though the summons had been taken out under Order 25.

The master has power to decide whether there shall, or shall not, be any further pleading or particulars served, whether any pleading should be amended, whether there shall be further discovery and inspection of documents, whether ordered interrogatories shall be served and how certain facts, if not admitted, shall be proved at the trial, in which list the action is to be entered, where it shall be tried, and whether by a judge alone or by a judge and jury or by an official referee; and practically all other questions which arise in the action before final judgment is entered, save only those that arise at the actual trial. The decision of some of these matters may if necessary be postponed to an adjourned hearing of the summons. In personal injury cases, however, it is provided that certain directions take effect automatically, and a summons for directions will not therefore be necessary.

Discovery

If either party has not yet, or not sufficiently, disclosed his documents, the master may order him to make an affidavit or a list of all documents which are or have been in his possession and are material to any question in issue in the action; and to permit his opponent to inspect and take copies of them before the trial. This process is technically known as "discovery of documents"; it often tends to save expense and shorten litigation. What is more, the master has power to order either party to answer on oath before the trial certain questions submitted by his opponent. These questions are called "interrogatories." Many "interrogatories" may now be served without leave, but the parties may wish to serve additional interrogatories. The master goes through the proposed questions first to see if they ought to be allowed in the interests of justice. There are, of course, limits to the power of a party thus to extract evidence in his favour from his opponent before the trial (see Chapters 16 and 19).

Trial

After the order giving directions, the plaintiff (or in some cases the defendant) sets down the action for trial in the appropriate list at the Royal Courts of Justice, *i.e.* "Jury," "Non-jury" or "Short cause," or for trial at a provincial centre. In due course or on a fixed date the case will be scheduled for trial. Then the parties must attend in court with their counsel and witnesses, and bring with them all necessary books and papers. The procedure at an ordinary trial is described in Chapter 20. The plaintiff's counsel generally begins. He opens his case, calls his witnesses and examines them, and hands in his documents to the officer of the court. The defendant's counsel cross-examines the plaintiff's witnesses, and then at the close of the evidence for the plaintiff he proceeds to meet it by stating what his defence is and, generally, but not always, by calling witnesses and putting in any documents upon which he relies. In a non-jury case counsel then in turn address the judge who delivers a reasoned judgment. If there is a jury, counsel's speeches are addressed to them, the judge sums up and the jury return their verdict; and the judge orders the appropriate judgment to be entered thereupon. In either case the judge makes an order for costs.

Execution

After judgment has been entered there follows execution, that is, proceedings to enforce the judgment (see Chapter 24) unless the defendant pays up voluntarily; though execution is sometimes stayed pending an appeal.

This execution of High Court judgments is the responsibility of the sheriff of each county, though in practice the actual work is done by the under-sheriff and his servants. The High Court, unlike the county court, has never had officers of its own to serve process or to execute judgment; it merely issues at the request of the judgment creditor a command in the form of a writ directed to the sheriff of the county where the person or property of the judgment debtor may be. The most usual form of execution is that of *fi. fa.* (*fieri facias*) whereby the judgment debtor's goods are seized and sold. A High Court judgment may, however, be enforced in the county court.

Appeal

Either party may ordinarily appeal to the Court of Appeal against the decision on the law or the facts or both. The Court of Appeal studies the documents and reviews the oral evidence by reading the transcript. It does not, as a rule, see the actual witnesses but relies on the note of their evidence. Consequently it will seldom interfere with the judge's findings of fact so far as these depend on the credibility of the witnesses.[79] But

---

[79] See Chap. 23.

with this important qualification the appeal is in name and in fact a rehearing. The powers of the court, which are freely exercised, include those of varying or reversing the judgment or sending the case back for a new trial. It can, though it seldom does, hear fresh evidence.

From the Court of Appeal a further appeal lies to the House of Lords, but the appellant must have leave either of that House or of the Court of Appeal and such leave is somewhat sparingly given, sometimes on terms as to costs.

Originating Summons in the Queen's Bench Division

In general the rules as to issue, service and acknowledgment of service of an originating summons are the same as those for a writ. Exceptions are an *ex parte* originating summons, and an originating summons under Order 113 (summary proceedings for the possession of land). Originating summons procedure is considered more fully in Chapter 22, and Order 113 is discussed in Chapter 5.

CHAPTER 2

MATTERS TO BE CONSIDERED BEFORE WRIT

Before beginning proceedings the plaintiff must decide whether he should issue a writ or an originating summons.[1] The following matters may also arise for consideration:

   I. —Parties.

   II. —Joinder of Causes of Action.

   III. —Jurisdiction of the High Court of Justice.

To make a false start in any of these respects will cause the plaintiff trouble, expense and delay at some stage or other of the action.

I. Parties

There must be set out at the head of every writ the name of every plaintiff and every defendant whom it is proposed to make a party to the proceedings. These names form the title of the action. And in the selection of these parties there is a twofold chance of error. A plaintiff may omit parties whose presence is essential; or he may add parties whose presence is improper. Hence you must learn what parties are necessary and what unnecessary, who *must* be joined, and who *may* be joined or not, as the plaintiff chooses. In the case of an originating summons the party taking it out is described as the plaintiff and the other parties as defendants.[2]

Formerly the law and practice as to "parties" was of the utmost importance, misjoinder of a plaintiff being ground of nonsuit, while non-joinder of a necessary plaintiff was the subject of a plea in abatement.[3] But now "no cause or matter shall be defeated by reason of the misjoinder or nonjoinder of any party; and the court may in any cause or matter determine the issues and questions in dispute so far as they affect the rights and interests of the persons who are parties to the cause or matter" (Order 15, r.6(1)). And "at any stage of the proceedings in any cause or matter the court may on such

---

[1] See Chap. 1. The Civil Justice Review recommended that, with some essential exceptions, all proceedings should be commenced by a writ.

[2] Ord. 7, r. 2(2).

[3] Pleas in abatement were abolished in 1875. The modern rules do not alter the legal principles with regard to actions, and it is still necessary to have before the court the proper parties necessary for determining the point at issue: see, for illustrative purposes, *Performing Right Society Ltd.* v. *London Theatre of Varieties Ltd.* [1924] A.C. 1; *Walter & Sullivan Ltd.* v. *J. Murphy & Sons Ltd.* [1955] 2 Q.B. 584.

terms as it thinks just and either of its own motion or on application:

(*a*) Order any person who has been improperly or unnecessarily made a party or who has for any reason ceased to be a proper or necessary party to cease to be a party; (*b*) order any of the following persons to be added as a party, namely—(i) any person who ought to have been joined as a party or whose presence before the court is necessary to ensure that all matters in dispute in the cause or matter may be effectually and completely determined and adjudicated upon, or (ii) any person between whom and any party to the cause or matter there may exist a question or issue arising out of or relating to or connected with any relief or remedy claimed in the cause or matter which in the opinion of the court it would be just and convenient to determine as between him and that party as well as between the parties to the cause or matter; but no person shall be added as a plaintiff without his consent signified in writing or in such other manner as may be authorised" (rule 6(2) and (4)). A plaintiff may be substituted although the original plaintiff had no cause of action.[4] But where an action is commenced in the name of a man already dead, his representative cannot be substituted as plaintiff.[5] And where the plaintiff did not exist as a legal entity at the time the writ was issued, the proceedings were and always had been a nullity and should be struck out. The court has no jurisdiction to join a valid plaintiff in such a case (except in the case of a misnomer within Order 20, r. 5(3).[6] In addition, where a relevant period of limitation has expired, a person may not be added or substituted as a party except in the restricted circumstances set out in Order 15, r. 6(5), (6). No one can appear on the record both as a plaintiff and as a defendant, even though he does so in different capacities.[7] All plaintiffs must normally appear by the same counsel,[8] and cannot set up conflicting cases *inter se.*

It is now possible, since the passing of the Crown Proceedings Act 1947, to sue the Crown both in contract and in tort. The defendant will be the appropriate government department, *e.g.* the *Department of the Environment* or *Home Office*; the

---

[4] *Hughes* v. *The Pump House Hotel Co. Ltd. (No. 2)* [1902] 2 K.B. 485.

[5] *Tetlow* v. *Orela Ltd.* [1920] 2 Ch. 24.

[6] See *Lazard Bros. & Co.* v. *Midland Bank Ltd.* [1933] A.C. 289, H.L., applied in *Dubai Bank Ltd.* v. *Galadari (No. 4), The Times,* February 23, 1990. *Evans Construction Co. Ltd.* v. *Charrington & Co. Ltd.* [1983] Q.B. 810, C.A.

[7] *Re Phillips, Public Trustee* v. *Meyer* (1931) 101 L.J. Ch. 338.

[8] *Lewis* v.*Daily Telegraph (No. 2)* [1964] 2 Q.B. 601.

writ is served upon the solicitor to the department or, in some cases, the Treasury Solicitor. The procedure differs from that in ordinary actions in certain respects. The department sued may, before acknowledging service of the writ, call upon the plaintiff to amplify the indorsement to the writ, which must state the circumstances in which the Crown's liability arises and the government department and officers of the Crown concerned.[9] Judgment in default of notice of intention to defend or pleading cannot be entered without leave,[10] nor can summary judgment be obtained under Order 14.[11] Discovery of documents does not automatically follow the close of pleadings as in other actions but must be achieved as directed by the court.[12] The action cannot be ordered to be tried outside London except with consent of the Crown.[13] And, finally, execution cannot be levied against the Crown.[14] Set-off and counterclaim against the Crown are considered in Chapter 14. There are other special rules, but these are the most important.

Foreign sovereigns[15] and states,[16] ambassadors and Ministers and their staff,[17] High Commissioners representing Commonwealth countries and the Republic of Ireland,[18] certain international organisations and their representatives and officers,[19] and representatives and staff (included in an authorised list) of certain governments represented at conferences in the United Kingdom,[20] cannot be sued in the courts of this country unless they submit to the jurisdiction. The agent of a foreign government cannot be sued here without his principal.[21] Moreover, where a foreign government, though not a defendant, is

---

[9] Ord. 77, r. 3.
[10] Ord. 77, r. 9.
[11] Ord. 77, r. 7.
[12] See Chap. 16.
[13] Ord. 77, r. 13.
[14] Ord. 77, rr. 15, 16.
[15] State Immunity Act 1978, s.20, applying to Heads of State the provisions of the Diplomatic Privileges Act 1964.
[16] The law on state immunity was codified in the State Immunity Act 1978. The Act gives statutory force to the doctrine of restrictive immunity, whereby immunity of a foreign state is restricted to acts of a governmental nature and does not extend to acts of a commercial nature. See further, *Trendtex Trading Corp.* v. *Central Bank of Nigeria* [1977] Q.B. 529; *Hispano Americana Mercantil S.A.* v. *Central Bank of Nigeria* [1979] 2 Lloyd's Rep. 277.
[17] Diplomatic Privileges Act 1964, ss.1, 2, Sched. 1.
[18] Diplomatic Immunities (Commonwealth Countries and Republic of Ireland) Act 1952.
[19] International Organisations Act 1968.
[20] Diplomatic Immunities (Commonwealth Countries and Republic of Ireland) Act 1961. And see Sierra Leone Independence Act 1961 and any other particular Acts of a like nature which may from time to time be passed.
[21] *Twycross* v. *Dreyfus* (1877) 5 Ch.D. 605.

indirectly impleaded because the action affects property to which it has some substantial claim, the action may be stayed.[22]

Contract

In actions founded on contract it is important to state the parties correctly; a false start may well incur the delay and expense of an application to amend the proceedings.

The law relating to parties depends largely on whether the contract sued on is joint, or several, or joint and several. This is a question which turns primarily on the language of the contract itself. Still, it is a question of the intention of the parties, and the judge will also have regard to all the surrounding circumstances, to the respective interests of the parties and to their conduct. Thus, a contract made by the executors of a will, the trustees of a settlement, or the partners in a firm, acting as such, will generally be construed a joint and not a several contract, unless there is something in the language of the contract which forbids this construction. The distinction is one of importance; as, on the bankruptcy of one joint contractor the other contractors may sue or be sued in respect of the contract without the joinder of the bankrupt (Insolvency Act 1986, s.285). In addition, a release given to one joint contractor releases all[23]; however, this common law rule no longer applies in respect of a judgment against one joint contractor. Such judgment is not a bar to an action, or to the continuance of an action, against any other person jointly liable in respect of the same debt or damage.[24]

In any action for breach of a contract made by or with several persons *jointly* all persons jointly entitled to relief who are alive must join as plaintiffs or, if they will not do so, be made defendants, unless the master gives leave to omit them.[25] However, the personal representatives of a deceased joint creditor should not be joined as plaintiffs, nor should the representatives of a deceased joint debtor be joined as defendants; the right to sue and the liability on the contract vest in the survivors, and therefore only the survivors should be made parties.

In relation to joinder of defendants, the rule was formerly that all persons jointly, but not severally, liable had ordinarily

---

[22] *Juan Ysmael & Co.* v. *Govt. of Indonesia* [1955] A.C. 72; *Rahimtoola* v. *Nizam of Hyderabad* [1958] A.C. 379; *I Congreso del Partido* [1981] 1 All E.R. 1092.
[23] *Re E.W.A.* [1901] 2 K.B. 642; *cf. Gardiner* v. *Moore* [1969] 1 Q.B. 55.
[24] Civil Liability (Contribution) Act 1978, s.3, reversing the rule in *King* v. *Hoare* (1844) 13 M. & W. 494, and *Kendall* v. *Hamilton* (1879) 4 App.Cas. 504.
[25] Ord. 15, r. 4(2).

to be joined as defendants, otherwise the master might be asked to stay the proceedings until they had been added.[26] Where, however, liability was several, or joint and several, the plaintiff had the option of joining as parties to the same action all or any of the persons liable, and a judgment against one person severally liable was no bar to an action against the others.[27] This practice is now applicable to all cases in consequence of section 3 of the Civil Liability (Contribution) Act 1978.[28] Accordingly, where the liability of two or more persons under a contract is joint, several, or joint and several, the plaintiff may choose which person or persons to sue, and he is not obliged to join other persons also liable even if the liability is under a joint contract only. If a defendant wishes to obtain contribution from other persons jointly liable, he may make a claim under the 1978 Act, but this is not a matter of concern to the plaintiff.

Again there may be a contract on which one or other of two persons is liable in the alternative, but not both. If judgment is taken against one of them, that is a conclusive and irrevocable election and a bar to further proceedings against the other.[29] Nor will it avail to set the judgment aside.[30]

If a necessary co-plaintiff refuses to join in the action, the proper course was formerly to tender him an indemnity against costs; and then, if he still refused to be joined as a co-plaintiff, to make him a defendant.[31] Now the master has a discretion to allow him to be left out. He can only be joined as a co-plaintiff if he gives his consent, which he must ordinarily do in writing by signing a consent himself though the master may authorise his solicitor to do so (see Order 15, r. 6). If he is joined without such consent, his name will be struck out, and the solicitor who issued the writ will probably be ordered to pay his costs and also all costs occasioned to the defendant by such improper joinder.[32]

Tort

If several persons are joint-owners or joint-occupiers of any land or premises affected by trespass, nuisance or any other

---

[26] See the 21st edition of this book, p. 19, and authorities there cited.

[27] *King* v. *Hoare* (1844) 13 M. & W. 494; *Blyth* v. *Fladgate* [1891] 1 Ch. 337.

[28] See note 25, *supra*.

[29] *Morel Brothers* v. *Earl of Westmorland* [1904] A.C. 11.

[30] *Hammond* v. *Schofield* [1891] 1 Q.B. 453.

[31] *Cullen* v. *Knowles and Birks* [1898] 2 Q.B. 380; *Johnson* v. *Stephens and Carter* [1923] 2 K.B. 857; *Burnside* v. *Harrison Marks Productions Ltd.* [1968] 1 W.L.R. 782.

[32] Ord. 62, r. 11.

tort, or the joint-owners of any chattel which the defendant has converted or damaged, they should all, as a rule, be joined as co-plaintiffs in the action. Where, however, premises are leased, the tenant only should sue for trespass or nuisance; the landlord can only complain if there is damage to the reversion. In an action for wrongful interference with goods[33] one of several persons having an interest in the goods may sue alone, but he must either have the written authority of every other interested person to sue on the latter's behalf, or indorse his writ with a statement giving particulars of his title and identifying every other person who, to his knowledge, has or claims any interest in the goods.[34]

Where the tort was committed by joint tortfeasors the plaintiff has a free hand. He is not obliged to join as a defendant every joint tortfeasor. He may, if he prefers, sue only one or two; and the liability of the others will be no defence for those sued, and will not mitigate the damages recoverable, for all persons concerned in a common wrongful act are jointly and severally liable for all damage caused by it.[35] And a judgment against these is no bar to a subsequent action for the same tort against anyone else who was jointly liable with them.[36] If, however, the plaintiff obtained from the defendant the whole of the damages awarded, there would be no point in bringing another action against a different defendant, because the plaintiff could not recover further damages from the second defendant, and in any event the plaintiff is not entitled to costs in any successive action for the same damage unless the court is of opinion that there was reasonable ground for bringing the action.[37] Contribution between two or more tortfeasors liable for the same damage may be claimed in accordance with the provisions of the Civil Liability (Contribution) Act 1978.

Recovery of Land

In this action the proper plaintiff is the person who is now entitled to immediate *possession* of the property. He may be the freeholder or only a tenant. If there is no tenancy created by, or

---

[33] Torts (Interference with Goods) Act 1977, s.1.
[34] Ord. 15, r. 10A(1). For the rights of the defendant in such a case, see the Torts (Interference with Goods) Act 1977, s.8, and Ord. 15, r. 10A(2), (3), (4).
[35] *The Koursk* [1924] P. 140.
[36] Civil Liability (Contribution) Act 1978, s.3, replacing and extending s.6 of the Law Reform (Married Women and Tortfeasors) Act 1935.
[37] Civil Liability (Contribution) Act 1978, s.4.

otherwise binding on, the freeholder, then his ownership involves the right to present possession. All joint tenants must join as plaintiffs.

Strictly, all persons who are actually in physical possession of the property should be made defendants. "In ejectment the tenant in possession *must* be sued."[38] It is neither necessary nor proper to join any person who is merely in receipt of the rents and profits of the land. But where a large number of persons are in occupation of the premises who all claim title under the same lessor, the rule is relaxed and the plaintiff is allowed merely to make that lessor defendant.[39] By section 145 of the Law of Property Act 1925 the tenant is bound, under penalty of three years' rent, "forthwith" to give notice to his landlord that a writ in ejectment has been served on him. And the landlord can then at once obtain leave to defend the action under Order 15, r. 10. The master will on an *ex parte* application grant such leave to any person who, by himself or his tenant, is in possession of the land sought to be recovered in the action, although he is not named on the writ.

Classes of Persons

A married woman may sue and be sued, either in contract or tort or otherwise, in all respects as if she were a *feme sole* (Law Reform (Married Women and Tortfeasors) Act 1935, s.1).[40] In this respect marriage or divorce now leaves a woman's position practically unaffected. But actions in tort between spouses may be stayed if it appears that no substantial benefit would accrue to either party from the continuation of the proceedings or that the procedure for settling property disputes under section 17 of the Married Women's Property Act 1882 is appropriate.[41]

A minor sues by his next friend (see Precedent No. 2), who, though not a party to the action, is personally liable for the costs of the suit[42]; but the minor is prima facie liable to indemnify him against costs properly incurred in the interest of the minor.[43] The court has power to dismiss an action brought by a minor in his own name or to allow the proceedings to be amended by adding the next friend.[44] Any money recovered in

---

[38] *Berkeley* v. *Dimery and Another* (1829) 10 B. & C. 113, *per* Lord Tenterden C.J.
[39] *Minet* v. *Johnson* (1890) 63 L.T. 507; *Green* v. *Herring* [1905] 1 K.B. 152.
[40] And see Married Women (Restraint upon Anticipation) Act 1949.
[41] See Law Reform (Husband and Wife) Act 1962; Ord. 89, r. 2.
[42] See *Masling* v. *Motor Hiring Co.* [1919] 2 K.B. 538.
[43] *Steeden* v. *Walden* [1910] 2 Ch. at p. 400.
[44] *Cooper* v. *Dummett* [1930] W.N. 248.

an action by or on behalf of a minor must be paid into court to be held and applied for the benefit of the plaintiff, and no settlement of the action or acceptance of money paid into court is valid unless approved by the court.[45] A minor defends by a guardian *ad litem*[46] who will not be held personally liable for costs unless he has been guilty of some misconduct.[47]

A person who, by reason of mental disorder, is incapable of managing his affairs (generally referred to as a "patient")[48] also sues by a next friend and defends by a guardian *ad litem*. The title on the writ should be, "A.B. by C.D. of——, his next friend [*or guardian ad litem*] (under Order 80, rule 2)." The provisions of Order 80, rr. 10 and 12 (*ante*), apply also to patients. Jurisdiction in the management of the property and affairs of such persons is ordinarily exercised by the Court of Protection.

A person voluntarily resident in an enemy or enemy-controlled country cannot sue.[49]

Partners carrying on business within the jurisdiction may sue and be sued in the name of their firm; but if they sue in the firm name they can be compelled to disclose the name and address of every member of the firm.[50] If they are sued in the firm name they must acknowledge service in their own names individually, but the subsequent proceedings nevertheless continue in the name of the firm.[51] An individual carrying on business within the jurisdiction under a trade name may be sued in that name as though he were a member of a firm.[52]

A corporation and a company registered under the Companies Acts sue and are sued in their corporate name; they are legal persons. And a trade union, though not a body corporate, may sue and be sued in its own name.[53]

In any action concerning trust property, all the trustees within the jurisdiction must as a rule be joined; in any action concerning the estate of a deceased person all administrators, or all executors who have proved the will, must be joined.[54] In

---

[45] Ord. 80, rr. 10, 12. Nor should any interim payment on account of damages in respect of personal injuries be made without the approval of the court.

[46] Ord. 80, r. 2; *John* v. *John* [1965] P. 289.

[47] *Hooper* v. *Mackenzie, The Times*, January 23, 1901.

[48] Ord. 80, r. 1.

[49] *Porter* v. *Freudenberg* [1915] 1 K.B. 857. And see Trading with the Enemy Act 1939 as to vesting of enemy property.

[50] Ord. 81, rr. 1, 2.

[51] Ord. 81, r. 4(1); and see *Ellis* v. *Wadeson* [1899] 1 Q.B. 714.

[52] Ord. 81, r. 9.

[53] Trade Union and Labour Relations Act 1974, s.2(1)(*h*). The same applies to an unincorporated employers' association (s.3(1)(*b*)).

[54] See *Latch* v. *Latch* (1875) L.R. 10 Ch. 464.

neither case is it necessary to add any of the persons beneficially interested in the trust or estate (Order 15, r. 14). But in
any action relating to the estate of a deceased person or to
property subject to a trust, Order 15, r. 13A permits the court
to direct that notice of the action be served on any person who
is not a party but who may be affected by the judgment. A
person served may acknowledge service and thereby become a
party to the action, but in default of acknowledgment he will
be bound by any judgment given as if he were a party. Rule
13A, made pursuant to the Administration of Justice Act 1985,
s.47, constituted a significant exception to the general rule that
judgments bind only parties.

Under the Law Reform (Miscellaneous Provisions) Act 1934
many causes of action vested in or subsisting against a person
who dies survive for the benefit of, or against, his estate. If
there is no administrator, the court has power to appoint some
person to represent the estate at the instance of a claimant
under Order 15, r. 15(1),[55] for example, the official solicitor if he
consents to act. In the event of the death or bankruptcy of a
party after writ issued the action does not abate, if the cause of
action is one that survives, and the personal representative
may be made a party (Order 15, r. 7). A writ issued after the
death but before letters of administration are granted to the
plaintiff may be amended with leave pursuant to Order 20, r. 5
even after the period of limitation has expired if the court
thinks it just to do so.[56]

Order 15, r. 7 (*supra*) provides for the necessity, in an action
already brought, to change parties by reason of a death, and
Order 15, r. 15 (*supra*) deals with the representation of a
deceased person involved in existing proceedings. The problem of instituting proceedings where the proposed defendant
has died but no personal representatives have been appointed,
and where the defendant named in the writ has in fact died
before its issue, are now met by the Supreme Court Act 1981,
s.87(2). Order 15, r. 6A, gives effect to the Act as follows:

(1) Where any person against whom an action would have
    lain has died but the cause of action survives, the action
    may, if no grant of probate or administration has been
    made, be brought against the estate of the deceased.
(2) An action brought against "the personal representatives
    of A.B. deceased" shall be treated as having been
    brought against his estate.

---

[55] See *Lean* v. *Alston* [1947] K.B. 467 and cases there cited. The proposed representative
must be willing to act but the court may appoint any person who consents to act.
[56] Negativing *Finnegan* v. *Cementation Co. Ltd.* [1953] 1 Q.B. 688.

(3) An action purporting to have been commenced against a person shall be treated, if he was dead at its commencement, as having been commenced against his estate, whether or not a grant of probate or administration was made before its commencement.[57]

Before service of the writ or originating summons the plaintiff must apply to the court for an order appointing a person to represent the estate (or, where personal representatives have in fact been appointed since the writ was issued, for an order that they be made a party to the proceedings) and for an order that the proceedings be carried on accordingly (rule 6A (4)).

The judgment or order in the proceedings binds the estate as if a grant of probate or administration had been made (rule 6A (7)).

Representative Proceedings

The general rule with respect to parties is that all persons interested in the subject of the litigation should be made parties to the record[58] since this ensures that a "final end might be made of the controversy."[59] But it was recognised at an early date that injustice could result from a strict application of the rule, where the persons interested were very numerous. The practice of the old Court of Chancery was that, where the persons interested in the suit were too numerous to be joined as parties, the plaintiff was allowed to proceed in a representative capacity on behalf of himself and others with whom he shared a common interest in the suit or against a named defendant as representing a class where the defence was common to all.[60] The joinder of only as many parties as was necessary to ensure a fair trial of the action would be required.[61] Following the Judicature Act 1873, Rule of the Supreme Court, Order 16 was introduced in order to apply the practice of the old Court of Chancery to all Divisions of the High Court.[62]

---

[57] Ord. 15, r. 6A(3), in effect reverses *Dawson (Bradford) Ltd.* v. *Dove* [1971] 1 Q.B. 330, which held that an action commenced against a deceased person was a nullity and could not be cured by substituting his executors as defendants.

[58] *Per* Sir L. Shadwell V.-C. in *Longe* v. *Yonge* (1830) 2 Sim. 369, 385; also *per* Lord Eldon in *Cockburn* v. *Thompson* (1809) 16 Ves.Jun. 321, 325.

[59] *Per* Lord Macnaghten in *Bedford (Duke of)* v. *Ellis* [1901] A.C. 1 at 8.

[60] For a modern example, see *Michaels (Furriers) (M)* v. *Askew* (1983) 127 S.J. 597, C.A.

[61] *Adair* v. *New River Co.* (1805) 11 Ves.Jun. 429.

[62] *Bedford (Duke of)* v. *Ellis* [1901] A.C. 1, at p. 8 (*per* Lord Macnaghten) and at p. 14 (*per* Lord Shand). For a contrary view that the Order brought into existence a new statutory jurisdiction, see Cozens-Hardy L.J. in *Dyson* v. *A.-G.* [1911] 1 K.B. 410, 417; also *Markt & Co. Ltd.* v. *Knight Steamship Co. Ltd.* [1910] 2 K.B. 1021.

A representative action is one brought by a self-appointed[63] representative plaintiff or plaintiffs on behalf of himself and some[64] or all other members of a group having the same interest in the proceedings for the vindication of a common right or the redress of a common grievance. Alternatively, the proceedings may be instituted against a named defendant or defendants as representing a class of others who have a common interest in resisting the suit.[65] It is essential that the person named as a representative of the class should have the same interest in the matter as the persons represented.[66] If this unity of interest is present the class representative is at liberty to define the boundaries of the class on behalf of which the suit is brought.[67] Neither the leave of the court nor a representation order is required before a representative action can be instituted.[68] There is no requirement that the class members should be informed about the commencement of the action,[69] nor that they should consent to representation in the manner proposed by the representative plaintiff. Fundamentally, however, absentee class members are bound by any judgment or order made in the proceedings.[70]

Subject to the rule that the class representative must "fairly represent" the class[71] the safeguards against abuse of this form of proceedings are limited. In certain circumstances, class members who are not content to be represented by the plaintiff

---

[63] Usually the representative of the class is self-elected but it is clearly possible for him to be selected by class members and advance their interests with their consent.

[64] A modern illustration of this is *John* v. *Rees* [1969] 2 All E.R. 274 in which the representative plaintiff was held to be entitled to issue a writ on behalf of himself and all other members of an unincorporated association except the named defendants. See also *Lloyd* v. *Loaring* 6 Ves.Jun. 773.

[65] *Supra*, n. 61.

[66] Ord. 15, r. 12.

[67] *Ibid.*

[68] This contrasts with the U.S. Federal class action where it is regarded as an essential safeguard for the absentee class members that the representative parties should only be able to proceed after obtaining the certificate of the court that the action is properly brought in class form. The certificate must be obtained as soon as practicable after the commencement of the action—Rule 23 of the Federal Rules of Civil Procedure, *infra*. There were signs of similar developments in English law where, in *Morgan's Brewery* v. *Crosskill* [1902] 1 Ch. 898, it was held that before a defendant can be allowed to represent himself and others, the court must be satisfied that he is authorised by the absentee class members to do so.

[69] In the United States the court has a discretion whether to order the notification of class members by the class plaintiff that the latter's rights will be ajudicated on in a class suit. However, Rule 23(c)(2) provides that notification is mandatory in what are known as "damages" class suits; see Bush (1986) C.J.Q. 109, 120. This notification requirement has, however, been subject to different interpretations: see *Hansberry* v. *Lee* 311 US 32 (1940); *Mullane* v. *Central Hanover Bank & Trust Co.* 339 US 306 (1950) and *Eisen* v. *Carlisle & Jacqueline* 417 US 156 (1974).

[70] Ord. 15, r. 12(3).

[71] *Infra.*

may apply to the court to be joined as defendants but this will not always be appropriate.[72] The rule requires, however, that leave must be sought before any judgment or order can be enforced against a member of the class represented who is not a party to the proceedings. But this safeguard is of a limited nature since the class member against whom enforcement of the order is sought is still bound by the result in the case in which liability was settled. Enforcement is a separate question.[73]

As the representative plaintiff is *dominus litis* he may compromise or settle the dispute. The class members represented are not responsible for the costs in the action.

"Community of Interest"

The old Chancery procedure required that all those on behalf of whom the proceedings were instituted should have "one common interest in all the objects of the suit."[74] Order 15, r. 12(1) now requires that:

> "where numerous persons have the *same interest* in any proceedings . . . the proceedings may be begun, and, unless the court otherwise orders, continued, by or against any one or more of them as representing all or as representing all except one or more of them."

It has been stated that before the rule can be satisfied it is essential that all members of the class have a common interest in the proceedings, that all should have a common grievance, and that the relief sought should be beneficial to all.[75] The true scope of these individual requirements has never been judi-

---

[72] An example is *John* v. *Rees* [1969] 2 All E.R. 274 in which the relief sought against the defendants would not be appropriate against class members who were not sympathetic to the action.

[73] See *Michaels (Furriers) (M)* v. *Askew* (1983) 127 S.J. 597, C.A. Auerbach (1987) 16 I.L.J. 227 at pp. 234 *et seq.*

[74] F. Calvert, *Parties to Suits in Equity* (2nd ed., 1847) at p. 42, *Jones* v. *Garcia del Rio* (1823) 1 T. & Russ. 297. In the U.S. the community of interest theory has become less influential. More recent cases seem to interpret the basis of the doctrine as the consent of the class members to be bound by the decision of the court: *Eisen* v. *Carlisle & Jacqueline* 417 US 156 (1974). An alternative "substantive theory" of class litigation has been advanced in the U.S., the essence of which is that the class suit facilitates litigation by victims of unlawful conduct and by assisting them to prosecute their rights it realises public policy: (1976) 89 Harv. Law Rev. 1318.

[75] *Smith* v. *Cardiff Corporation* [1954] 1 Q.B. 210, but even if these requirements are fulfilled the court is not bound to allow the suit to proceed as a representative action: *J. Bollinger S.A.* v. *Goldwell* [1971] R.P.C. 410, 420.

cially defined but it is clear that they are not mutually exclusive and that in most cases there will be some overlap between them. The failure to satisfy these conditions prevented the plaintiffs from suing in a representative capacity in *Smith* v. *Cardiff Corporation*.[76] The representative plaintiffs had issued a writ on behalf of themselves and all other tenants of houses provided by a local authority under the provisions of the Housing Act 1936 to challenge a proposed change in the manner in which their rents would be calculated. The scheme contemplated that some tenants would suffer an increase in rent whereas the rent payable by others would be reduced according to their means. In effect, some tenants would sub-sidise the rents of others. Essentially, therefore, the relief sought would not be beneficial to all class members. The Court of Appeal held that the would-be representative plaintiffs could only proceed in their individual capacities.[77]

The requirement that the relief sought should be beneficial to all may not necessarily prevent representation where a sub-stantial number of class members are in fact hostile to the claim advocated by the representative plaintiff provided that all share a common interest in the action.[78] Moreover, it seems that, provided that there exists a common interest in the suit, a representative action is not necessarily undermined where the class members enjoy different rights *inter se*.[79] The effect is that the "community of interest" requirement does not prevent the representation of a class which includes members with diverse interests in the action brought by the plaintiff provided that a broader common interest can be identified and that the relief sought is beneficial to all.

Some inclination to widen the circumstances in which a representative action may be employed can be detected in *Michaels (Furriers) (M)* v. *Askew*[80] in which an injunction was granted by the Court of Appeal against named defendants representing themselves and all other members of an unincor-porated pressure group to restrain them from picketing the plaintiff's premises. Members of the pressure group neither named nor before the court, some of whom may not even have taken part in the action, were held subject to the injunction.

---

[76] [1954] 1 Q.B. 210.
[77] Unity of interest amongst defendants prevented their being joined in a representative action in *UK Nirex* v. *Barton, The Times*, October 14, 1986.
[78] *John* v. *Rees* [1969] 2 All E.R. 274. Also *Pan Atlantic Insurance Co. Ltd.* v. *Pine Top Insurance Co.* [1988] 2 Lloyds Rep. 505.
[79] *Bedford (Duke of)* v. *Ellis* [1901] A.C. 1.
[80] *Michaels (Furriers) (M)* v. *Askew* (1983) 127 S.J. 597, C.A.

The objection to this was that some members of the association not before the court might have objected to the manner of the picketing which would allow them separate defences and so preclude their having a common interest in the proceedings. Somewhat surprisingly, and construing the unity of interest requirement particularly broadly, the court held that the members of the association could be bound as a class since the required unity of interest could be identified in the common objectives which all members of the group shared in campaigning against the fur trade. The safeguard for absentee class members, it was held, lay in the rule that prevents enforcement of the order against them individually without leave of the court.

The decision, in which a firm reliance was placed on the early Chancery authorities, significantly broadens the circumstances in which the rule will be applicable and may promote more frequent recourse to this form of proceeding.

There is a further requirement that the class representative should fairly represent the class.[81] This is an essential consequence of the *res judicata* effect for absentee class members.

The idea of "fair representation" is neither settled nor precise. The paramount consideration is probably that the class representatives should be competent to furnish the court with a comprehensive presentation of the dispute as it affects the class. This broadly represents the position in the United States federal class action where the rule is a facet of the constitutional guarantee of "due process."[82] In English law, however, the case law has failed to focus with any clarity on the fair representation principle.[83] The true position was probably stated by Lord Eldon in *Adair* v. *New River Co.*[84] in which he emphasised that the class representatives must together, by their presentation of the issues, permit the court "fairly and honestly (to) try the legal right."

This, however, imposes a burden upon judges hearing representative actions to ensure that fair representation is

---

[81] *Taff Vale Rly. Co.* v. *Amalgamated Society of Railway Servants* [1901] A.C. 426, 438, *per* Lord Macnaghten.

[82] Rule 23(a)(4) Fed. Rules of Civil Procedure provides that the class representatives should "fairly and adequately represent the interests of the class." In *Hansberry* v. *Lee* 311 US 32 (1940) this was held to be satisfied provided that the proceedings ensured the protection of the interests of absentee class members. The implications of the rule remain controversial: *Mullane* v. *Central Hanover Bank & Trust Co.* 339 US 306 (1950) and *Eisen* v. *Carlisle & Jacqueline* 417 US 156 (1974).

[83] Compare *Taff Vale Rly. Co.* v. *Amalgamated Society of Railway Servants* [1901] A.C. 426, 438–439; *John* v.*Rees* [1969] 2 All E.R. 274; *Bedford (Duke of)* v. *Ellis* [1901] A.C. 1.

[84] (1805) 11 Ves.Jun. 429 at 445.

achieved. This may necessitate an inquiry into the composition of the class in order to ascertain the named plaintiff's competence to provide fair representation. The court's knowledge can only be gleaned from information made available through the representative plaintiff.

Inadequate information as to the composition of the class would be likely to prejudice the interests of absentee class members[85] because there will remain the possibility that pertinent issues are not before the court. The judge must then ensure that fundamental differences within the class will be eradicated either by the redefinition of the class or, ultimately, by preventing representation altogether.[86]

Limitations on Availability of Representative Proceedings

Strict adherence to the community of interest requirement has placed important limitations upon the availability of the representative action. It has, for example, prevented a representative action based upon separate contracts.[87] Fundamentally, an action for damages on behalf of individuals holding separate rights cannot be brought as a representative action since the claim of each individual has to be established separately.[88] Damages are a form of personal relief in the recovery of which no other individual than the plaintiff could have an interest.[89] But an individual action for damages in tort may be brought against named defendants as representing all the members of an unincorporated association.[90] Generally, the only remedy that will be appropriate in this form of proceeding will be declaratory.[91]

---

[85] In *Michaels (Furriers) (M)* v. *Askew* (1983) 127 S.J. 597, C.A., a common interest was apparently assumed to exist without serious inquiry. For analysis, see Auerbach (1987) 16 I.L.J. 227 at pp. 231 *et seq.*

[86] *e.g. Smith* v. *Cardiff Corpn.* [1954] 1 Q.B. 210 where representation was not permitted.

[87] *Markt & Co. Ltd.* v. *Knight Steamship Co. Ltd.* [1910] 2 K.B. 1021 although this may require qualification in the light of the decision of Hirst J. in *Pan Atlantic Insurance Co. Ltd.* v. *Pine Top Insurance Co.* [1988] 2 Lloyds Rep. 505 and of the Court of Appeal in *Irish Shipping Ltd.* v. *Commercial Union* [1989] 3 All E.R. 853.

[88] *Ibid.*

[89] Per Fletcher-Moulton L.J. in *Markt & Co. Ltd.* v. *Knight Steamship Co. Ltd.* [1910] 2 K.B. 1021, 1035. This proposition must now be read subject to the *Prudential Assurance* case, *infra*, in which it was held that damages in tort may be obtained in representative proceedings in a two-stage procedure by which a declaration as to entitlement of the class might be awarded followed by proof of loss by individual class members.

[90] *Campbell* v. *Thompson* [1953] 1 Q.B. 445.

[91] *Prudential Assurance Co. Ltd.* v. *Newman Industries Ltd.* [1981] Ch. 257. But see *Irish Shipping Ltd.* v. *Commercial Union, supra.* n. 87. Controversy surrounds the availability of an injunction since there the relief may be barred (*e.g.* because of laches) as to some members of the class but not others, *ibid.*

This principle has prevented the use of the representative action in cases in which compensation is sought by a large number of individuals who claim that they have sustained damage as a result of allegedly tortious conduct by the defendant. The consequences of this limitation have recently received prominent attention in such well-publicised cases as *Thalidomide* and *Opren*. In a class action for damages, as in the United States, compensation might have been sought on behalf of all of the victims in a single action.[92]

In English law the general restriction on the availability of the representative action has been somewhat qualified in *Prudential Assurance* v. *Newman Industries Ltd.*[93] in which it was held that, subject to important limitations,[94] the court may award a declaratory judgment that members of the class are entitled to damages in tort, leaving it to each class member separately to establish his individual entitlement. As Uff suggests,[95] the *Prudential Assurance* case, if rightly decided, may mark a significant step forward in English law since, to employ his example, in a case where a group hired a coach to take them on an outing and they were injured in an accident en route, one member of the group could bring a single action on

---

[92] An example of this was *Re "Agent Orange" Product Liability Litigation* 100 F.R.D. 718 (E.D.N.Y. 1983) in which a class action for damages was brought on behalf of tens of thousands of servicemen against six chemical companies for compensation for injuries caused from contact with chemical defoliants used in the Vietnam war. The matter was compromised before the court had the opportunity to consider issues of liability.

In English law, in a case like *Opren* involving a powerful defendant, the overwhelming difficulty for individual plaintiffs in seeking damages is the costs involved. This was exacerbated by the complexity of the litigation and in particular the fact that the drug concerned was alleged to have caused not one typical side effect but a range of possible side effects. At one stage in the *Opren* case it was likely that the burden of costs might have forced at least some of the non-legally aided victims to withdraw. The problem flowed from the decision of the Court of Appeal in *Davies* v. *Eli Lilly & Co.* [1987] 1 W.L.R. 1136 in which all 1,500 plaintiffs were ordered to contribute to the costs of those selected plaintiffs who would bring "lead actions" in which certain preliminary issues would be resolved.

Even the legally aided might have faced difficulties under the legal aid rules which require that the prospects of success should be such that an imaginary privately-funded litigant of "sufficient but not superabundant means" would continue with the action. At that stage of the case, this was not at all clear, raising at least the possibility that legal aid funding might have been withdrawn. Following the *Davies* case the intervention of a wealthy philanthropist who offered to underwrite the costs of the non-legally-aided allowed the case to proceed.

[93] [1981] Ch. 257.

[94] It was held that no order could be made in favour of the representative plaintiff unless there was an interest common to the claims of all members of the class; the representative action must not confer a right on any individual class member which he could not have asserted in a separate action, or to bar a defence which might have been available to the defendant in a separate action; and that it should be for the benefit of the class that the plaintiff be permitted to sue in a representative capacity.

[95] [1986] C.J.Q. 50.

behalf of all the others for a declaration as to the issue of liability. Thereafter each group member would only be required to establish his personal entitlement to damages. Where the harm is inflicted on a wider scale, however, there is an increased likelihood that different legal issues would arise as between some class members and the defendant preventing representation. Where it is alleged that a number of individuals have been injured as a result of taking a drug, the question of causation may well arise thereby preventing them from enjoying a common interest in the litigation sufficient to enable an order to be obtained in a representative capacity. The decision of the Chancery Division in *EMI Records* v. *Riley*[96] demonstrates, however, that in those cases in which the losses sustained by each class member can readily be ascertained the two-stage procedure may be circumvented so that the court may order an inquiry into the damages sustained by each member of the class.

Reform of Representative Proceedings

Where a class action for damages is permitted, a principal advantage for the class is an economic one. The high cost of litigation tends to prohibit in particular the judicial determination of relatively small claims; only persons suffering more serious harm generally find the cost/benefit analysis sufficiently advantageous to justify proceedings. In cases where private individuals seek to prosecute claims against multi-national companies such as in the *Opren* case, the expense involved may threaten to preclude an effective remedy. The class action offers an opportunity to lower this financial barrier to the proceedings where the injury is suffered in common with a number of individuals. The issues common to the class members can be tried in a single action so as to prevent a multiplicity of litigation. Costs may be borne by all those who are in a position to benefit in the action.[97] Where widespread slight damage is caused this may be the only means by which an action will come to court.[98] But for the availability of a class

---

[96] [1981] 2 All E.R. 838.

[97] In the light of the decision of the Court of Appeal in *Davies* v. *Eli Lilly & Co.* [1987] 1 W.L.R. 1136 (*supra*, n. 92) this may not be a controversial development. See also the decision of Steyn J. in *Chrzanowska* v. *Glaxo Laboratories Ltd.*, *The Times*, March 16, 1990.

[98] In *Hackett* v. *General Host Corpn.* 45 F. Ed. 618 (3rd Cir.) six million Philadelphia residents were joined in a class action in which the class representative sought to recover about nine dollars as representing her individual loss and similarly small amounts for class members.

action, in some cases, the unlawful behaviour of the defendant would never be challenged.[99] Furthermore, and regardless of whether damages are sought, where the defence succeeds in a class suit, the issue of liability having been resolved against the class, no further claims by class members can be brought. This not only acts in the interest of the defendant in reducing his costs in defeating claims, but also operates in the public interest by saving judicial time. Inconsistency as to the results of claims is also avoided.

In the United States, however, the class action for damages has been criticised for permitting claims which would not have been individually viable.[1] Moreover, there seems to be no means of filtering out class actions for damages brought on behalf of groups of such size that the suit is not capable of judicial resolution.[2] Class actions have also been questioned as being potentially oppressive of the defendant. One manifestation of the possible inequity is that it may invite forms of "blackmail" since the threat to the defendant of a heavy bill in damages can result in unfair pressure to settle.[3] Alternatively, the defendant may be unfairly prejudiced since, if the class suit is capable of lowering the financial threshold to litigation where large numbers of class members are represented, he is exposed to an action in cases in which, but for the class action, he would never have been sued at all. For some organisations acting on a large scale the damages awarded could be destructive of their commercial venture. And this would have implications for the wider public interest by, for example, the possible loss of employment opportunities.

It is now judicially accepted that the question of reform of the English representative action must be addressed. In *Davies* v. *Eli Lilly & Co.*[4] Donaldson M.R. invited the "responsible authorities" to consider the desirability of introducing a class action for damages, possibly on the United States model, so as to permit a single action for damages to be brought on behalf of a class of victims. Donaldson M.R. was no doubt aware that there is some urgency in this inquiry as mass tort litigation is certain to become more common.

---

[99] *Ibid.* But this need not only apply where damages are sought. Some individuals who might have standing to seek an injunction might be reluctant to prosecute a case individually because of the expense involved.

[1] *e.g. Hackett* v. *General Host Corpn., supra,* n. 98.

[2] *e.g. Diamond* v. *General Motors* 47 A.L.R. 759.

[3] As a safeguard against this there seems to be some authority in the United States that certification is only possible if there is a substantial possibility of prevailing on the merits: *Dolgow* v. *Anderson* 43 F.R.D. 472 but an inquiry into the merits may not be desirable at the pre-trial stage.

[4] *Davies* v. *Eli Lilly & Co.* [1987] 3 All E.R. 94.

The mechanism for introducing a class action for damages would be the amendment of Order 15, r. 12 and in particular the common interest requirement since, as has been indicated, many of the limitations on representative proceedings flow from this part of the rule. In such a process, however, one of the central difficulties which would have to be resolved would be the means by which damages for individual class members might be assessed. If the *Prudential Assurance* case is good law it is already possible to permit full individual trial as to quantum following a declaratory judgment as to liability.[5] Alternatively, it might be possible to examine alternatives such as to allow summary judgment on proof of loss by individual class members, or to permit recovery on a class-wide basis with subsequent distribution amongst individuals.[6] However, the latter possibility might not permit accurate assessment of damages relative to the harm suffered by each individual. Questions of injustice might arise since the claimant might assert that his legal right to compensation has been compromised if he received less than he might have done if suing in his individual capacity or, alternatively, the defendant might claim that, *vis-à-vis* some claimants, he has been ordered to pay in excess of what might have been claimed individually. It is a policy decision as to whether an approximation of damages to the harm suffered is outweighed by the advantages of permitting one single action to be brought.

A further issue to be addressed would be the rules as to costs. Although under the English system the award of costs is in the discretion of the court, costs normally "follow the event."[7] The representative plaintiff is therefore bound to pay the defendant's costs if his action is unsuccessful. He is not entitled to a contribution towards meeting this liability from the absentee class members, nor can the representative claim as of right a contribution from class members towards his own costs in instituting the litigation. Possible reforms should focus upon the desirability of sharing the cost burden amongst those likely to benefit from the successful prosecution of the claim.[8]

It must be recognised, however, that if it was sought to facilitate the claims of victims in cases such as *Opren*, the reformed law must not act inequitably by permitting the class to cause the defendant, by means of unfair pressure, to settle

---

[5] As in the *Prudential Assurance* case, *supra*, n. 93.
[6] None of these methods has been found to be without problems in the United States: 89 Harv. Law Rev. 1516 *et seq*.
[7] Supreme Court Act 1981, s.51, Ord. 62, r. 3(3). See Chap. 25.
[8] *Supra*, n. 97.

the claim. A possible solution, adopted in the United States, would be to prevent settlement without the approval of the court.[9]

The reform of Order 15, r. 12, necessary before a class action for damages could be introduced into English law, might invite the provision of further safeguards against abuse of the representative action. Reforms might target the need to incorporate protections for the judicial process, class members and the defendants in order to eliminate vexatious or oppressive class suits. The introduction of a requirement to seek the leave of the court before instituting proceedings could serve as a filter against the abuse of the judicial process and might perform a similar role to the certification requirement in the United States.[10]

Possible reform might also concentrate upon the very limited safeguards at present available to class members. Primary amongst these might be the introduction of a right for absentee class members to receive notification of the suit and possibly a right to "opt out" of it.[11] Under existing rules their legal rights may be adjudicated upon without their knowledge and if this occurs their dispute with the defendant will be *res judicata*.

It is now recognised[12] that at present the position of victims of widespread unlawful action perpetrated by institutional defendants requires examination. The English representative action provides a focus for the possible reforms and it is likely that the restructuring of the rule, or, possibly, statutory intervention, will take place in order to extend the availability and utility of the representative action in English law.

Legal Aid

Special provision has been made to enable persons of small means to bring or defend actions without incurring heavy

---

[9] Rule 23e of the Federal Rules of Civil Procedure provides: "A class action shall not be dismissed or compromised without the approval of the court, and notice of the proposed dismissal or compromise shall be given to all members of the class in such manner as the court directs."

[10] *Supra*, n. 68.

[11] Preservation of the individual's right to sue opens the possibility of relitigation of the issue. In the United States, in "damages" class actions, rule 23 provides a right to "opt out." The burden is on the individual class member to do so; and if this right is not exercised the decision in the class action will bind him.

[12] *Per* Sir John Donaldson M.R. in *Davies* v. *Eli Lilly & Co.*, *supra*, n. 97 at p. 96, who invited "the appropriate authorities" to conduct an examination to see whether the US class action has anything to offer and to make the necessary procedural changes if it was found to do so. See also the Civil Justice Review, Recommendation 27. *Chrzanowska* v. *Glaxo Laboratories Ltd.*, *The Times*, March 16, 1990, *per* Steyn J.

liability as to costs. This is achieved under the Legal Aid Act 1988. It would be beyond the scope of this book to describe in detail the working of legal assistance under the Act and the regulations made thereunder. But, broadly speaking, persons whose "disposable" income (*i.e.* income as assessed after making certain deductions) and whose "disposable" capital do not exceed specified limits, are eligible for legal aid.[13] Administration of the scheme is the responsibility of the Legal Aid Board acting through area directors and area committees of practising lawyers. Applications for legal aid are made to the area director, and means are assessed by the Department of Social Security so that the applicant's contribution can be assessed. Thereafter he employs his own solicitor and counsel and the case proceeds in most respects as though he were an ordinary litigant. But an assisted person, even though unsuccessful, may be relieved wholly or partly from liability for his opponent's costs.

II. Joinder of Causes of Action

The Rules of the Supreme Court give a plaintiff a very extensive power of joining on one writ several different causes of action. And in a proper case the plaintiff should certainly avail himself of this power. For if he brings two actions where one would have sufficed he will probably have to pay the costs of one action. Section 49(2) of the Supreme Court Act 1981 provides that the court " . . . shall so exercise its jurisdiction in every cause or matter before it as to secure that, as far as possible, all matters in dispute between the parties are completely and finally determined, and all multiplicity of legal proceedings with respect to any of these matters is avoided." The avoidance of unnecessary proceedings is thus a major factor in the application of the rules of court concerned with joinder of causes of action.

The key rules are Order 15, rr. 1, 4(1) and 5(1). By rule 1 it is provided that: "(1) Subject to rule 5(1), a plaintiff may in one action claim relief against the same defendant in respect of more than one cause of action—(*a*) if the plaintiff claims, and the defendant is alleged to be liable, in the same capacity in respect of all the causes of action, or (*b*) if the plaintiff claims or

---

[13] The legislation also provides for legal *advice* to a maximum cost which may not be exceeded without approval by a solicitor and, where necessary, counsel, to persons not exceeding certain disposable income and capital limits. See generally Legal Aid Handbook, 1990.

the defendant is alleged to be liable in the capacity of executor or administrator of an estate in respect of one or more of the causes of action and in his personal capacity but with reference to the same estate in respect of all the others, or (*c*) with the leave of the court. (2) An application for leave under this rule must be made *ex parte* by affidavit before the issue of the writ or originating summons, as the case may be, and the affidavit must state the grounds of the application." Although rule 4 is headed "Joinder of Parties" it falls to be considered here in so far as the causes of action of the various parties may differ: "Subject to rule 5(1), two or more persons may be joined together in one action as plaintiffs or as defendants with the leave of the court or where—(*a*) if separate actions were brought by or against each of them, as the case may be, some common question of law or fact would arise in all the actions, and (*b*) all rights to relief claimed in the action (whether they are joint, several or alternative) are in respect of or arise out of the same transaction or series of transactions" (rule 4(1)). But, "If claims in respect of two or more causes of action are included by a plaintiff in the same action or by a defendant in a counterclaim, or if two or more plaintiffs or defendants are parties to the same action, and it appears to the court that the joinder of causes of action or of parties, as the case may be, may embarrass or delay the trial or is otherwise inconvenient, the court may order separate trials or make such other order as may be expedient" (rule 5(1)).

Joinder is not necessarily final, and on an application by summons, the master has a discretion to order severance. For although the joinder may be within the terms of the rules, or although he (or a different master) may on prima facie grounds have given leave for joinder on an *ex parte* application, he may, nevertheless, at a later stage order severance after hearing argument upon a summons, if it appears that embarrassment, delay or inconvenience may be caused by the joinder of causes of action or of parties.[14]

The plaintiff's application for leave under rule 1 must, by the terms of the rule, be made *ex parte* by affidavit before the writ is issued.

The following sections show how joint, several or alternative claims may be included in the same writ and the principles on which the master's discretion may be likely to be exercised. In

---

[14] As expressed in a former rule, he might make "such order as may be just to prevent any defendant from being embarrassed or put to expense by being required to attend any proceeding in which he may have no interest."

many of the old cases the joinder was permissible within the terms of the rules as they then stood, but nevertheless the court refused to allow it as a matter of discretion. The principle of these cases presumably still holds good.

Take the simplest case first:

1. Same plaintiff: same defendant

Here the parties are the same in all the causes of action which it is sought to join.

The plaintiff may without leave join on one writ any number of different causes of action against the same person or persons provided that "the plaintiff claims, and the defendant is alleged to be liable, in the same capacity in respect of all the causes of action" (Order 15, r. 1(1)(*a*)). To this proviso there is one exception, namely, that a person may sue or be sued both as executor or administrator and in his personal capacity if the personal claims have reference to the same estate. In all other cases leave is required (rule 1(1)(*b*) and (*c*)).

Now we come to cases of more difficulty, where not every plaintiff, or not every defendant, is interested in every cause of action joined.

2. Different plaintiffs: same defendant

When may two or more plaintiffs join on one writ distinct and separate causes of action against the same defendant or defendants?

They may do so without leave on two conditions; first, that if each brought a separate action some common question of law or fact would arise in all the actions; and secondly, that all rights to relief claimed in the action (whether they are joint, several or alternative) are in respect of, or arise out of, the same transaction or series of transactions. In other cases leave is necessary (Order 15, r. 4). This will not be granted if the joinder may embarrass or delay the trial or is otherwise inconvenient; and even if the joinder has lawfully been made without leave, the master may on the same grounds order separate trials or make such other order as may be expedient (rule 5).

Joinder of plaintiffs without leave according to these principles is illustrated by *Universities of Oxford and Cambridge* v. *Gill*,[15] where the Universities of Oxford and Cambridge were

---

[15] [1899] 1 Ch. 55.

allowed to join in one action to restrain a publisher from selling books under such titles as "The Oxford and Cambridge Publications." Joinder has also been permitted to a group of eight trustees libelled collectively in respect of the performance of their duties,[16] to six market gardeners claiming on behalf of themselves and of other fruit growers in respect of both individual and general class claims under a statute regulating Covent Garden Market,[17] and to a group of eight plaintiffs claiming jointly for conspiracy and severally for separate slanders against a group of six defendants.[18]

3. Same plaintiff: different defendants

When may the same plaintiff or plaintiffs join on one writ separate and distinct causes of action against different defendants?

Here, too, Order 15, rr. 4 and 5, apply and the joinder may be made without leave if the two conditions in rule 4(1) are satisfied. In other cases leave is necessary and the master has the same power to order severance or otherwise so as to avoid embarrassment, delay or inconvenience, as he has in the cases of joint plaintiffs.

(i) *Claims in the alternative*

Where a plaintiff has but one cause of action, which entitles him to judgment against either A or B but not against both, he may without leave join A and B on the same writ as defendants in the alternative, and so determine the question which of them is liable. For example, a plaintiff may join in one action a claim against a principal on a contract made by his alleged agent, and an alternative claim against the alleged agent for contracting without authority.[19]

(ii) *Joint and several claims*

When a plaintiff alleges that two or more persons are *all* jointly liable to him on different causes of action, whether

---

[16] *Booth v. Briscoe* (1877) 2 Q.B.D. 496.
[17] *Duke of Bedford v. Ellis* [1901] A.C. 1.
[18] *Thomas v. Moore* [1918] 1 K.B. 555.
[19] *Bennetts v. McIlwraith* [1896] 2 Q.B. 464. See also *Child v. Stenning* (1877) 5 Ch.D. 695 (alternative claims by a tenant against a trespasser claiming grant of a right of way and against the landlord for breach of covenant in granting any such alleged right).

sounding in tort or contract, he may without leave join them all on one writ. This has always been so and is still so under the present rules, not necessarily by virtue of Order 15, r. 4 (for the claims may arise out of totally different transactions), but by virtue of Order 15, r. 1, "Subject to rule 5(1), a plaintiff may in one action claim against the same defendant in respect of more than one cause of action . . . if the plaintiff claims and the defendant is alleged to be liable in the same capacity in respect of all the causes of action . . . ," so long as there is no change of capacity. (The Interpretation Act 1978 applies for the inter-pretation of the rules[20] so that here "defendants" may be read for "defendant.") Where, however, the plaintiff wishes to add any separate cause of action against one or more of the defendants severally, he should first consider whether the two conditions laid down by Order 15, r. 4 are satisfied. If they are, there is no difficulty and he may issue his writ without leave; if they are not, he would be wise to apply for leave, for it does not seem likely that an individual defendant would be held to be the "same defendant" as himself together with another or others jointly.

So, for example, if A and B are both jointly liable to X on two different contracts, whether connected or unconnected in their subject-matter, X may without leave bring one action against them jointly on both contracts. On the other hand, if A and B are jointly and severally liable on unconnected contracts and X wishes to pursue his rights against them individually as well as jointly, he should seek leave for the joinder. Similarly, if A, B and C are all three liable to X on a bill of exchange, and A and B are also liable to X on a promissory note, and C alone on a cheque and the transactions are unconnected, X will probably have to bring three actions. In this case leave for joinder might well be refused if it would involve A and B in sitting idle in court while the claim on the cheque was being tried, and C would also be wasting his time while the claim on the prom-issory note was being considered.[21]

(iii) *Separate claims*

Where a plaintiff seeks to recover judgment against A on one cause of action and at the same time to recover judgment against B on a separate and distinct cause of action, he can only

---

[20] See Ord. 1, r. 3.
[21] See also *Walters* v. *Green* [1899] 2 Ch. 696; *Re Beck* (1918) 87 L.J.Ch. 335.

join the two on one writ if *some* common question of law or fact
arises *and* the causes of action arise out of the same transaction
or series of transactions. If these two conditions are fulfilled it
matters not that the causes of action may not be identical or
that the respective liabilities of the defendants may to some
extent be based on different grounds.

For example, in *Compania Sansinena* v. *Houlder Brothers & Co.
Ltd.*[22] D1 contracted to carry meat to be exported by the
plaintiffs, and procured the carriage of the plaintiffs' meat on a
ship belonging to D2. The master of the ship signed a bill of
lading. The plaintiffs alleged damage to the meat caused by the
ship being unseaworthy, and they were permitted to claim in
one action against D1 on the contract of carriage and against
D2 on the bill of lading. Similarly, in *Oesterreichische Export A.G.*
v. *British Indemnity Insurance Co. Ltd.*,[23] in an action on policies
of marine insurance, the Court of Appeal allowed joinder of
two insurance companies who were each liable for half the
total amount of the goods insured, the liability of each company depending on the same facts.

4. Different plaintiffs: different defendants

It is not likely that cases with different plaintiffs and different
defendants will be suitable for joinder. But where two or more
cases are pending in the same Division and some common
question of law or fact arises, or the relief claimed arises out of
the same transaction or series of transactions, Order 4, rule 9
permits the master to order that the actions be consolidated or
tried at the same time or in sequence or that one of the actions
be stayed until the other is determined. An application for a
ruling under rule 9 is normally considered at the summons for
directions. (See Chapter 18).

III. Jurisdiction of the High Court of Justice

On January 1, 1987 the Civil Jurisdiction and Judgments Act
1982 came into force. This Act gives the force of law to the 1968
Brussels Convention on Jurisdiction and the Recognition and
Enforcement of Judgments in Civil and Commercial Matters,
the 1971 Protocol and the 1978 Luxembourg Accession Convention. It is therefore necessary to consider the jurisdiction of the

---

[22] [1910] 2 K.B. 354.
[23] [1914] 2 K.B. 747.

High Court not only under the traditional rules but also in relation to the 1982 Act and the Conventions. The main distinction lies between jurisdiction outside the European Community (traditional rules) and jurisdiction within the European Community (1982 Act and Convention).

Traditional Rules

The High Court of Justice has jurisdiction over the whole of England and Wales, but not over Scotland, the Isle of Man or the Channel Islands or anywhere beyond the territorial waters.[24] The court will allow unrestricted right of suit only in cases in which the defendant is properly served with process within the jurisdiction. However, the court has an inherent discretion to set aside proceedings as an abuse of the process of the court or to stay proceedings on the basis that there is another more appropriate forum.[25] It is not an abuse of process for the defendant to be served with the writ while temporarily present in the jurisdiction,[26] unless he was induced to enter the jurisdiction by fraud.[27] In exercising its discretion to stay proceedings in favour of a more appropriate forum, the court must take into consideration all relevant factors including the locality of the parties and witnesses, the locality of the transaction (if any) or wrongful event and the law governing any transaction. The fact that the plaintiff may be deprived of a legitimate advantage should a stay be granted is relevant but not conclusive provided that it is in the interests of the parties and justice that trial should take place in the more appropriate forum.[28]

If the defendant is out of the jurisdiction, it is not permissible for the plaintiff to serve a writ on him except by leave or by virtue of an enactment (Order 6, rule 7(1)) giving the High Court power to hear the action.

Leave

Leave can only be granted in the cases specified by Order 11, rule 1(1) and is subject to the discretion of the court.

---

[24] By a legal fiction a British man-of-war is deemed to be within the parish of Stepney and so within the jurisdiction. *Seagrove* v. *Parks* [1891] 1 Q.B. 551.

[25] *Spiliada Maritime Corporation* v. *Cansulex Ltd.* (*The Spiliada*) (1987) A.C. 460; [1986] 3 All E.R. 843, H.L.

[26] *Maharanee of Baroda* v. *Wildenstein* [1972] 2 Q.B. 283. See also *The Atlantic Star* [1974] A.C. 436.

[27] *Watkins* v. *North American, etc. Co.* (1904) 20 T.L.R. 534.

[28] *The Spiliada. Ante,* n. 25.

Under Order 11, rule 1(1)(*a*) leave may be granted if the defendant is domiciled within the jurisdiction. According to Order 11 rule 1(1)(4) "domicile" is to be determined in this context by reference to the Civil Jurisdiction and Judgments Act 1982, ss.41–46.[29] In the case of individuals this can be summarised as: (i) residence in the United Kingdom or part thereof, and (ii) the nature and circumstances of the residence indicate a substantial connection with the United Kingdom or part thereof. Substantial connection can be presumed from residence for the preceding three months.[30] The seat of a company, legal person or association of natural or legal persons will be treated as its domicile.[31] A company or association will have its seat in the United Kingdom if, and only if: (i) it was incorporated or formed under a part of the law of the United Kingdom, and (ii) it has its registered office or some other official address in the United Kingdom or its central management and control is exercised in the United Kingdom.[32] The plaintiff may obtain leave under rule 1(1)(*b*) if his writ includes a bona fide claim for an injunction as to any thing to be done or refrained from within the jurisdiction. The injunction must not be merely incidental to the relief which the plaintiff is in fact seeking.[33] It can apply to injunctions to prevent future wrongs which are threatened to be committed within the jurisdiction.[34] It does not, however, extend to interim injunctions against a defendant who would not otherwise be subject to the jurisdiction of the court.[35] It cannot therefore be used to obtain a Mareva injunction, for example in a case where the substantive proceedings against the defendant do not fall within the court's jurisdiction.[36] The Civil Jurisdiction and Judgments Act 1982, s.25(3) allows the extension of section 25(1)[37] by Order in Council to proceedings which do not fall within the scheme of the European Convention on Civil Jurisdiction and Judgments. No such Order has been made. Under rule 1(1)(*c*) where a writ has already been duly served on a defendant within, or out of the jurisdiction, leave

---

[29] *Infra.*
[30] Civil Jurisdiction and Judgments Act 1982, s.41(6).
[31] 1968 Brussels Convention, Art. 53.
[32] 1982 Act, ss.42–43.
[33] *Rosler* v. *Hilbery* [1925] Ch. 250.
[34] *James North Ltd.* v. *North Cape Ltd.* [1984] 1 W.L.R. 1428.
[35] *The Siskina (Owners of Cargo lately laden on board)* v. *Distos Compania Naviera SA* [1979] A.C. 210.
[36] *Mareva Compania Naviera SA* v. *International Bulk Carriers SA* (1975) 119 S.J. 660; Supreme Court Act 1981, s.37.
[37] *Infra.*

will be given in a proper case to serve another defendant who is outside the jurisdiction provided he is a necessary and proper party to the action. Where two defendants are out of the jurisdiction one cannot by submitting to the jurisdiction confer jurisdiction as against the other.[38] By Order 11, rule 4(1)(*d*) the affidavit in support of the application for leave must show grounds for believing that there is between the deponent and the person on whom the writ has already been served a real issue to be tried. Therefore the writ must have been properly served on a principal or real and substantial defendant and not merely a nominal one.[39]

Where the subject-matter of the action is a contract which is either: (i) made within the jurisdiction; (ii) made by or through an agent trading or residing within the jurisdiction on behalf of a principal trading or residing out of the jurisdiction; (iii) by its terms or by implication to be governed by English law; or which (iv) contains a term to the effect that the High Court shall have jurisdiction; then leave may be obtained under rule 1(1)(*d*). The postal acceptance rule will apply to rule 1(1)(*d*)(i).[40] In relation to rule 1(1)(*d*)(iii) the choice of English law may be express, or it may be inferred from the surrounding circumstances. Alternatively, the contract may be governed by that system of law with which it has its closest and most real connection. Under rule 1(1)(*e*) leave may be granted if a claim is brought in respect of a breach committed within the jurisdiction of a contract wherever made. Leave may be granted irrespective of the fact that the breach committed within the jurisdiction was preceded or accompanied by a breach committed out of the jurisdiction that rendered performance within the jurisdiction impossible. This sub-rule does not apply to anticipated breaches.[41]

Under rule 1(1)(*f*) leave may be granted where an action is founded on tort and the damage was sustained, or resulted from an act committed, within the jurisdiction. The formulation of this sub-rule appears to be in accordance with the interpretation by the European Court of Article 5(3)[42] of the Brussels Convention in *Handelswerkerij GJ Bier* v. *Mines de*

---

[38] *John Russell & Co. Ltd.* v. *Cayzer Irvine and Co. Ltd.* [1916] 2 A.C. 298; *Amanuel* v. *Alexandros Shipping Co.* [1986] Q.B. 464.

[39] *The Brabo* [1949] A.C. 326 and see Dicey and Morris, *Conflict of Laws*, p. 217.

[40] *Wansborough Paper Co. Ltd.* v. *Laughland* [1920] W.N. 344. The postal acceptance rule does not apply to instantaneous communications; *Brinkibon Ltd.* v. *Stahag Stahl GmbH* [1983] 2 A.C. 34.

[41] *The Siskina* (*supra*, note 35). Rather, a claim for an injunction to restrain future breaches would fall within sub-rule 1(1)(*b*).

[42] *Infra*, p. 57.

Potasse d'Alsace.[43] According to *Bier's* case, the plaintiff has the option to commence proceedings either at the place where damage occurred or at the place of the event giving rise to the damage. Where the damage occurred, or the acts giving rise to the damage were committed, in more than one jurisdiction, the court will assume jurisdiction under this rule if significant damage occurred, or substantial acts were committed, within the jurisdiction.[44]

Where land is situated within the jurisdiction and the whole of the subject-matter of the action relates to that land or the perpetuation of testimony relating to that land, rule 1(1)(g) provides for leave to be granted. This covers, for example, an action for the recovery of the possession of land and for mesne profits.[45] Under rule 1(1)(h) leave may be obtained if the claim is brought to construe, rectify, set aside or enforce an act, deed, will, contract obligation or liability affecting land situate within the jurisdiction. This would appear to cover any action in respect of any matter affecting land in England and Wales.[46] Leave may also be obtained under rule 1(1)(i) in an action for a claim for a debt secured on immovable property or where the claim is made to assert, declare or determine proprietary or possessory rights or rights of security in or over movable property, or to obtain authority to dispose of movable property, situate within the jurisdiction. In relation to immovable property, issues arising from a mortgage itself will fall within rule 1(1)(g) or (h), whilst actions for the recovery of a mortgage debt come under rule 1(1)(i). The main application of rule 1(1)(i) to movable property will be in respect of interpleader proceedings.[47]

Rule 1(1)(j) applies to an action where a claim is brought to execute the trusts of a written instrument where those trusts ought to be executed according to English law and of which the person to be served is a trustee. It extends to any claim for any relief or remedy which might be obtained in any such action. However, since it refers to written instruments it does not appear to apply to resulting or constructive trusts nor to unwritten trusts arising under the Administration of Estates Act 1925, s.33 and Law of Property Act 1925, ss.34–36.[48] It is no longer necessary that the property forming the subject-matter

---

[43] [1976] E.C.R. 1735.
[44] *Metall und Rohstoff AG Donaldson Lufkin* v. *Jenrette Inc.* [1989] 3 W.L.R. 563.
[45] *Agnew* v. *Usher* (1884) 14 Q.B.D. 78.
[46] Dicey and Morris, p. 200.
[47] See Jacob, *Private International Litigation*, p. 41.
[48] Jacob, *ibid.* at pp. 41–42.

of the trust be situate within the jurisdiction. Where a person dies domiciled within the jurisdiction and a claim is made for the administration of the deceased's estate or for any relief or remedy which may be obtained in such an action, then leave may be obtained under rule 1(1)(*k*). As with rule 1(1)(*a*) "domicile" is to be determined according to the 1982 Act.[49] Order 11 rule 1(1)(*l*) covers probate actions as defined by Order 76.

Order 11 rule 1(1)(*m*) introduces a new head of jurisdiction relating to a claim to enforce any judgment or arbitral award.[50] It will extend to an action brought at common law on a foreign judgment or arbitral award against a judgment debtor who remains out of the jurisdiction but who has assets within the jurisdiction. This new sub-rule does not affect the common law or statutory principles governing the recognition and enforcement of foreign judgments. It is merely a procedural device whereby the plaintiff can begin proceedings to establish whether the award can be enforced in a case where the judgment debtor is out of the jurisdiction.

Claims by the Inland Revenue Commissioners for, or in relation to, any of the duties or taxes which have been, or are, under their care and management are covered by rule 1(1)(*n*). This sub-rule does not apply where the defendant is domiciled in Scotland or Northern Ireland.

Where leave is required under (i) an enactment dealing with proceedings brought in respect of liability for damage caused by nuclear installations or (ii) in respect of contributions under the Social Security Act 1975, then rule 1(1)(*o*) applies. Rule 1(1)(*p*) allows for leave to be obtained where a claim is brought in pursuance of E.C. Directive 76/308/EEC[51] and where service is to be made in a Member State of the EEC. Leave to serve process out of the jurisdiction for a claim under the Drug Trafficking Offenders Act 1986 can be obtained under rule 1(1)(*q*); rule 1(1)(*r*) applies when the claim is made under the Banking Act 1987, and rule 1(1)(*s*) when the claim is made under Part VI of the Criminal Justice Act 1988. The new rule 1(1)(*t*) relates to claims for money had and received or for an account or other relief against a defendant as constructive trustee arising out of acts committed within the jurisdiction.

---

[49] Ord. 1, r. 1(4).

[50] Ord. 11, r. 1(1)(*m*) applies to an action commenced by writ to enforce an arbitral award but not to a summons for leave to enforce an arbitral award as a judgment under Arbitration Act 1950, s.26. See further, Jacob at p. 44.

[51] *e.g.* in actions to recover sums arising from operations of the EAGGF (European Agricultural Guidance and Guarantee Fund).

Where leave is required under Order 11 the plaintiff applies *ex parte* with an affidavit in support. Order 11, rule 4(1) sets out what must be contained in the affidavit. The primary consideration for the court in its exercise of discretion under Order 11 is whether the English court is the most appropriate forum for the trial of the action.[52] The assessment of the most appropriate forum involves a consideration of all the relevant factors. The burden of proof lies initially with the plaintiff to establish that England is the most appropriate forum. The fact that the plaintiff may be deprived of a legitimate advantage if leave is refused is relevant but not conclusive.

No Leave

Leave of the High Court is not required if the Civil Jurisdiction and Judgments Act 1982 applies or if any other enactment conferring jurisdiction applies notwithstanding the absence of the defendant or the place of the actionable event.[53] Other enactments conferring such jurisdiction are the Carriage by Air Act 1961, the Carriage by Air (Supplementary Provisions) Act 1962, the Carriage of Goods by Road Act 1965, the Protection of Trading Interests Act 1980 and the Civil Aviation Act 1982. Leave to serve out of the jurisdiction should not be sought where these enactments apply.

Civil Jurisdiction and Judgments Act 1982

By section 2(1) of the 1982 Act the force of law is given to the 1968 Brussels Convention, 1971 Protocol and 1978 Accession Convention. The Conventions are set out in the Schedules to the 1982 Act.[54] The Brussels Convention establishes the jurisdictional rules whilst the 1971 Protocol provides for questions concerning the Convention's interpretation to be referred to the European Court of Justice.[55] The Accession Convention not only provides for the accession of the United Kingdom, Denmark and Ireland to the 1968 Convention, it also amends certain aspects of that Convention[56] to take into account the accession of two countries with common law systems.

---

[52] *The Spiliada, supra,* note 25.

[53] Ord. 6, r. 7 and Ord. 11, r. 1(2). *Infra,* at p. 62.

[54] Schedule 1: 1968 Convention on Jurisdiction and the Enforcements of Judgments in Civil and Commercial Matters; Schedule 2: 1971 Protocol; Schedule 3: 1978 Accession Convention; Schedule 4: Title II of 1968 Convention as Modified for Allocation of Jurisdiction within UK.

[55] The procedure for referring questions concerning the interpretation of the Conventions is much the same as that laid down by Art. 177 of the Treaty of Rome. The principal difference is that the power to refer is limited to appellate courts.

[56] These amendments are contained in Part II of the 1982 Act (Schedule 4 to the Act). Part II allocates jurisdiction as between the courts of England and Wales, Scotland and Northern Ireland in accordance with the rules contained in the 1968 Convention. However, the rules in Part II of the 1982 Act operate subject to the 1968 Convention.

The jurisdictional rules contained within the 1968 Convention only apply in civil and commercial matters. The law by which these are to be classified is not specified. However, the European court has interpreted the concept of civil and commercial matters as an independent one based on the objectives of the 1968 Brussels Convention and the general principles which emerge from the totality of the national legal systems of Member States.[57] The Convention specifically excludes the following from its scope: revenue, customs and administrative matters; issues concerning status and legal capacity, matrimonial property, wills and succession; bankruptcy and related proceedings; matters concerning social security and arbitration.[58]

Assuming an action to be within the scope of the Convention, Article 2 provides the basic rule as to jurisdiction. This rule turns on domicile in a contracting state so that persons should be sued in the courts of the contracting state in which they are domiciled. There is no independent concept of domicile. The courts of the contracting states are required to refer to their own internal law of domicile.[59] In order to bring English law into line with that of the other contracting states, the 1982 Act, ss.41–46 provides a statutory definition of domicile for the purposes of the jurisdiction. By section 41 an individual is domiciled:

(a) in the United Kingdom, if, and only if, he is resident in the United Kingdom and the nature and circumstances of his residence indicate that he has a substantial connection with the United Kingdom;

(b) in a particular part of the United Kingdom if, and only if, he is resident in that part and the nature and circumstances of his residence indicate a substantial connection with that part. If an individual satisfies the test as to domicile within the United Kingdom, but fails to satisfy the test as to domicile in a particular part, he will be treated as domiciled in the part in which he is resident;

(c) in a particular place in the United Kingdom, if, and only if, he is domiciled in the part of the United Kingdom in which the place is situated and is resident in that place;

(d) in a state other than a contracting state if, and only if, he is resident in that state and the nature and circum-

---

[57] *LTV Lufttransportunternehmung GmbH & Co. KG* v. *Eurocontrol* [1976] E.C.R. 1541; *Henri Gourdain* v. *Franz Nadler* [1979] E.C.R. 733 and *Netherlands State* v. *Reinhold Rüffer* [1980] E.C.R. 3807.

[58] Brussels Convention, Art. 1.

[59] Brussels Convention, Art. 52(1).

stances of his residence indicate that he has a substantial connection with that state.

Neither "residence" nor "substantial connection" is defined. However, "substantial connection" may be presumed if the individual is resident for at least the last three months in the United Kingdom or part thereof.

Article 53 of the Convention provides that the seat of a company or other legal person or association of natural or legal persons will be its domicile. When defining "seat" the court is referred to its national law[60]; the rules of which as far as the United Kingdom courts are concerned, are contained in sections 42 and 43 of the Act. A corporation or association will have its seat in the United Kingdom if, and only if, it was incorporated or formed under the law of a part of the United Kingdom and has its registered office or some other official address in the United Kingdom, or its central management and control is exercised in the United Kingdom. It will have its seat in a particular part of the United Kingdom if, and only if, it has a seat in the United Kingdom and either it has its registered office or some other official address in that part or its central management and control is exercised in that part or it has a place of business in that part. It has its seat in a particular place in the United Kingdom if, and only if, it has its seat in the part of the United Kingdom in which that place is situated and the registered office or other official address, central management and control or a place of business is in that place. A corporation or association will have its seat in a state other than the United Kingdom if, and only if, it was incorporated or formed under the law of that state and it has its registered office or some other official address there, or its central management and control is exercised in that state, unless the courts of that state would not regard it as having its seat there.

Since, under these provisions, a corporation or association may have its seat in two or more states, any jurisdictional conflicts which arise as a result thereof will be settled according to Articles 21–23 of the Convention.[61] Section 43 of the 1982 Act contains the rules for determining the seat of a corporation or association for the purposes of Article 16(2) and Articles 5A and 16(2) in Schedule 4 to the Act.[62] The distinguishing feature between these provisions and the rules mentioned above is that (with the exception of Scotland or where the law of more

---

[60] Brussels Convention, Art. 53.
[61] *Infra.*
[62] *Infra.*

than one part of the United Kingdom is involved) the "registered office" or some other official address is not a relevant factor. It will have its seat in a particular place in Scotland if, and only if, it has its seat there and has its registered office or some other official address in that place or, having no registered office or other official address in Scotland, its central management and control is exercised in that place.[63] Where the corporation or association is incorporated or formed under an enactment forming part of the law of more than one part of the United Kingdom it will, if it has a registered office, be taken to have its seat in the part of the United Kingdom in which that office is situated. A corporation or association has its seat in a contracting state other than the United Kingdom if, and only if, it was incorporated or formed under the law of that state or its central management and control is exercised in that state.

Section 44 of the 1982 Act deals with the domicile of a person for the purposes of proceedings arising out of the operations of a branch or agency or other establishment in the United Kingdom. Section 45 contains the rules for determining the domicile of a trust. A trust will be domiciled in the United Kingdom if it is domiciled in a part thereof. It will be so domiciled if, and only if, the system of law of that part is the system of law with which the trust has its closest and most real connection. Under section 46 the seat of the trust is to be treated as its domicile. The Convention provides for various qualifications to the general rule contained in Article 2. Article 16 specifies the courts which will have exclusive jurisdiction in certain proceedings regardless of the defendant's domicile or any jurisdiction clause[64] or an implied submission under Article 18. In order for the matters listed in Article 16 to be the subject of exclusive jurisdiction, they must form the principal subject-matter of the proceedings brought.[65] Once Article 16 applies any court seised of proceedings which does not have exclusive jurisdiction under that Article must declare that it has no jurisdiction. Article 16 applies to the following proceedings. Proceedings which have as their objects rights *in rem* in, or tenancies of, immovable property. In such proceedings the courts of the contracting state in which the property is situated shall have jurisdiction.[66] The *lex situs* of the immovable property will determine whether the action is concerned with a

---

[63] Civil Jurisdiction and Judgments Act 1982, s.43(2).
[64] The effect of which is dealt with by Article 17 of the Convention (*infra*).
[65] Jenard Report (OJ 1979 No. C59/1), p. 34.
[66] Art. 16(1) of the Convention.

right *in rem*.[67] Where proceedings are brought which have as their object the validity of the constitution, the nullity or the dissolution of companies or other legal persons or associations of natural or legal persons, or the decisions of their organs, the courts of the contracting state in which the corporation or association has its seat shall have exclusive jurisdiction.[68] "Seat" is defined for Article 16 by section 43 of the 1982 Act. Where the national law of a contracting state which is applicable by virtue of Article 53 allows for a corporation to have two seats, then the plaintiff probably has an option where to commence proceedings.[69] Proceedings having as their object the validity of entries in public registers should be commenced in the courts of the contracting state in which the register is kept.[70] The courts of the contracting state in which the deposit or registration of patents, trademarks, designs or other similar rights has been applied for shall have exclusive jurisdiction in proceedings concerned with the registration or validity of such rights.[71]

Articles 5 and 6 of the Convention describe the situations in which a defendant may be sued in a contracting state other than that of his domicile. Articles 5 and 6, unlike Article 16, do not provide for exclusive jurisdiction. Where they apply the plaintiff may choose to commence proceedings in the court of the defendant's domicile or in the courts of the contracting state provided for by those Articles. By Article 5(1) in matters relating to a contract the defendant may be sued in the courts of the place of performance of the obligation in question. In relation to an exclusive sales concession "obligation in question" has been interpreted to mean the obligation forming the basis of the legal proceedings,[72] whilst in relation to employment contracts it has been interpreted to mean the obligation which characterises the contract.[73] In determining the place of performance of the obligation the court must apply its own conflict of laws rules.[74] The parties may agree on the place of performance.[75] Article 5(1) may apply even though the existence of the contract itself is disputed.[76]

---

[67] Schlosser Report (OJ 1979 No. C59/71) para. 168.

[68] Art. 16(2).

[69] Jacob, *Private International Litigation*, p. 143.

[70] Art. 16(3).

[71] Art. 16(4).

[72] *Ets. A. de Bloos* v. *Ets. Boyer SA* [1976] E.C.R. 1497 and see *Shenavai* v. *Kreischer* [1987] 3 C.M.L.R. 782.

[73] *Ivenel* v. *Schwab* [1982] E.C.R. 1891.

[74] *Tessili* v. *Dunlop* [1976] E.C.R. 1473.

[75] *Zelger* v. *Salinitri* [1980] E.C.R. 89.

[76] *Effer* v. *Kantner* [1982] E.C.R. 825.

Article 5(2) provides that in matters relating to maintenance the defendant may be sued either in the courts of the place where the maintenance creditor is domiciled or habitually resident; or, if the matter is ancillary to the proceedings concerning the status of a person, in the courts of the place which according to its own law has jurisdiction to entertain those proceedings, unless that jurisdiction is based solely on the nationality of one of the parties. By Article 5(3) in matters relating to tort, delict or quasi-delict, the defendant may be sued in the courts of the place where the harmful event occurred. According to the European Court's interpretation of Article 5(3) the plaintiff has the option of commencing proceedings thereunder either in the courts of the contracting state where the damage was suffered or in the courts of the contracting state where the event causing the damage occurred.[77] The European Court has also ruled that tort, delict and quasi-delict are autonomous concepts which seek to question the defendant's liability other than in relation to a contract.[78] It is not clear whether the courts specified in this Article have jurisdiction to grant injunctions against threatened torts.[79] In a civil action for damages or restitution which is based on an act giving rise to criminal proceedings, the defendant may be sued in the court seised of those proceedings provided that that court has jurisdiction under its own law to entertain civil proceedings.[80] Where a dispute arises out of the operation of a branch, agency or other establishment, the defendant may be sued in the courts of the place where the branch, agency or other establishment is situated.[81] If the defendant is being sued in his capacity as settlor, trustee or beneficiary of a trust created by written instrument, or created orally and evidenced in writing or created by operation of a statute, he may be sued in the courts of the contracting state where the trust is domiciled.[82] In the event of a conflict between this provision and Article 16, the latter will prevail.[83] Article 5(7) deals with claims for salvage or freight and limitation of actions in Admiralty claims.

Article 6 specifies the courts in which the defendant may be sued where there are a number of defendants, a third party or

[77] *Handelswerkerij GJ Bier BV* v. *Mines de Potasse d'Alsace* [1976] E.C.R. 1735.
[78] *Kalfelis* v. *Schroder, Munchmeyer Hengst & Co., The Times*, October 5, 1988.
[79] Schlosser Report (OJ 1979 No. C59/71), para. 134, considers they should. See also Jacob, *Private International Litigation*, p. 152 where it is suggested that the proper course would be to apply for such an injunction under Art. 24.
[80] Art. 5(4).
[81] Art. 5(5).
[82] Art. 5(6).
[83] See Jacob, *Private International Litigation*, p. 154.

a counterclaim. By Article 6(1) if the defendant is one of many defendants then he may be sued in the courts of the place where any one of them is domiciled. Where the defendant is a third party he may be sued in the court seised of the original proceedings unless such proceedings were brought solely with the object of ousting him from the jurisdiction. By Article 6(3) a person domiciled in a contracting state may be sued, on a counterclaim arising from the same contract or facts on which the original claim was based, in the courts in which the original claim is pending. It is not clear whether this would apply to "set-offs."[84]

By Article 17 of the Convention the parties, one or more of whom being resident in a contracting state, may expressly provide that the courts of a contracting state shall have jurisdiction. Such an agreement must not be contrary to Articles 12 and 15 and must not be for the benefit of one party only.[85] If the courts whose jurisdiction the agreement purports to exclude have exclusive jurisdiction under Article 16 then the latter jurisdiction will prevail.[86] It appears that "parties" refers to the original parties to the agreement rather than parties in the proceedings.[87] Where a jurisdiction agreement submitting to the courts of a contracting state is concluded by parties none of whom is domiciled in a contracting state, the court of other contracting states will have no jurisdiction over the dispute unless the courts chosen have declined jurisdiction. Whilst Article 17 refers to the chosen courts having "exclusive jurisdiction" this does not mean that such courts must in any event have jurisdiction. Therefore if the defendant has submitted to the jurisdiction of a court other than the chosen court, the former court can validly found jurisdiction upon Article 18.[88] However, Article 17 *will* take precedence over Articles 5 and 6.[89] Reciprocal jurisdiction agreements are within the scope of Article 17.[90] For any jurisdiction agreement to be valid for the purposes of Article 17, it must either be in writing, or be evidenced in writing; or, in relation to international trade or commerce, be in a form which accords with the practices in that trade or commerce of which the parties are or ought to have been aware. The European Court adopts a strict approach

---

[84] See further, *Jacob, ibid.* p. 156.
[85] Art. 17(4).
[86] Art. 17(3).
[87] See Jacob, *ibid.* pp. 157–158.
[88] *Elefanten Schuh GmbH* v. *Pierre Jacqmain* [1981] E.C.R. 1671.
[89] See Jacob, *ibid.* p. 57.
[90] *Meeth* v. *Glacetal* [1978] E.C.R. 2133.

to these formal requirements of Article 17.[91] However, since the parties are free to specify the place of performance of an obligation in any manner acceptable under the law governing the contract, they may effectively select the jurisdiction for the resolution of their disputes without adhering to Article 17's formalities.[92] Where the parties agree to confer jurisdiction on the courts of a non-contracting state, these courts may declare themselves competent. It is not clear whether such an agreement will deprive the courts of contracting states of jurisdiction.[93]

Finally, where the parties to a dispute concerning a contract had agreed in writing before the entry into force of the 1978 Accession Convention that the contract was to be governed by the law of a part of the United Kingdom or of Ireland, the courts of that part of the United Kingdom or of Ireland will retain the right to exercise jurisdiction.[94]

Under Article 18, notwithstanding jurisdiction derived from the other provisions of the Convention, the court of a contracting state before which a defendant has entered an appearance will have jurisdiction. Article 18 will not apply if the defendant enters such an appearance merely to contest jurisdiction nor where another court has exclusive jurisdiction under Article 16. In order to determine whether or not there has been an appearance reference must be made to the rules of procedure in the contracting state. (See Order 12, rules 7, 8 and 10). Section 4 of Title II of the Convention deals specifically with consumer contracts. By Article 14 where proceedings are brought against a consumer, those proceedings are to be brought only in the courts of the contracting state in which the consumer is domiciled. The consumer may bring proceedings either in the courts of the contracting state in which the other party to the contract is domiciled or in the courts of the contracting state in which the consumer himself is domiciled. Article 15 of the Convention provides for a restricted jurisdiction agreement to operate in relation to consumer contracts. Such a jurisdiction agreement must be entered into after the dispute has arisen; or it must be one which allows the consumer to bring proceedings in courts other than those specified by the Convention; or it is entered into by the parties to the contract both of whom are at the time of the conclusion

---

91 In *Estasis Salotti di Colzani Aimo Gianmario Colzani* v. *Rüwa Polstereimaschinen GmbH* [1976] E.C.R. 1831; *Galeries Segoura Sprl* v. *Rahim Bonakdarian* [1976] E.C.R. 1851.
92 See Jacob, *loc. cit.* p. 160.
93 *Ibid.* p. 162.
94 Accession Convention, Title V, Art. 35.

of the contract domiciled or habitually resident in the same contracting state and it confers jurisdiction on the courts of that state. Section 3 of Title II of the Convention deals specifically with insurance contracts. By Article 8, actions brought against an insurer which relate to insurance may be brought either in the courts of the contracting state where the insurer is domiciled; or in another contracting state in the courts of the place where the policy-holder is domiciled; or if he is a co-insurer, in the courts of the contracting state in which proceedings are brought against the same leading insurer. By Article 9 where the proceedings relate to the insurance of immovable property or liability insurance, the insurer may also be sued in the courts of the place where the harmful event occurred. Article 10(2) provides for Articles 7–9 to apply to actions brought by the injured party directly against the insurer. By Article 11 actions by the insurer may only be brought in the courts of the contracting state where the defendant is domiciled. Article 12 provides that the special jurisdiction rules contained in section 3 of Title II of the Convention may only be departed from where there is a jurisdiction agreement. Such a jurisdiction agreement must be entered into after the dispute has arisen; or it must allow the policy-holder, insured or beneficiary to bring proceedings in courts other than those specified in section 3 Title II; or it must be concluded between a policy-holder and an insurer domiciled or habitually resident in the same contracting state and it confers jurisdiction on the courts of that state; or it must be concluded with a policy-holder who is not domiciled in a contracting state; or it must relate to a contract of insurance covering one of the risks set out in Article 12A.

An application may be made to the courts of a contracting state for such provisional, including protective, measures as may be available under the law of that state even if under the Convention the courts of another contracting state have jurisdiction over the main issue.[95] In order that England could give effect to this provision, sections 24 and 25 of the 1982 Act were enacted. By section 24 of the Act the powers of a court in England are extended to grant interim relief pending trial or determination of an appeal to cases where the issue to be tried relates to the jurisdiction of the court to entertain the proceedings. By section 25 the court in England has power to grant interim relief where proceedings have been or are to be

---

[95] 1968 Convention, Art. 24.

commenced in a contracting state other than the United Kingdom.[96]

Since concurrent jurisdictions are possible under the 1968 Convention, courts in different contracting states may all be properly seised of the matter. Articles 21–23 cover such a situation. By Article 21 where proceedings are brought in the courts of different contracting states involving the same cause of action and between the same parties,[97] any court other than the court first seised of the proceedings must of its own motion decline jurisdiction in favour of that court. As a general rule in continental countries a claim becomes pending when the document instituting the proceedings is served. In the United Kingdom it becomes pending as soon as the originating document is issued. By Article 22 of the Convention, where there are related actions, any court other than the court first seised may either stay its proceedings; or it may on the application of one of the parties decline jurisdiction if the law of that court permits the consolidation of related actions and the court first seised has jurisdiction over both actions. Related actions are those which are so closely connected that it is expedient to hear and determine them together to avoid the risk of irreconcilable judgments resulting from separate proceedings.[98] In deciding whether to decline jurisdiction under Article 21 or whether to stay proceedings under Article 22, the question as to which court would be the more appropriate does not arise.[99] By section 49 of the 1982 Act, a United Kingdom court may stay, strike out or dismiss any proceedings before it on the ground of *forum non conveniens* or otherwise where to do so is not inconsistent with the 1968 Convention. Where the English court has jurisdiction under Article 8, it cannot rely on section 49 to stay its proceedings.[1]

Where every claim contained in the writ is one which the High Court has power to hear and determine according to the 1982 Act and there are no proceedings between the parties concerning the same cause of action pending in the courts of a contracting state and either the defendant is domiciled in a

---

[96] The effect of this provision is to reverse the decision in *The Siskina* (*supra*) in situations where the Brussels Convention applies.

[97] Where the plaintiff commences proceedings in one contracting state and then the roles are reversed, so that this plaintiff becomes a defendant to proceedings commenced in another contracting state, the parties in both sets of proceedings are to be treated as the same parties for the purposes of Art. 21. See *The Linda* [1988] 1 Lloyds L.R. 175.

[98] 1968 Brussels Convention, Art. 22(3).

[99] *The Linda* (*supra*).

[1] *S. & W. Berisford plc* v. *New Hampshire Insurance Co.* [1990] 2 All E.R. 321; *Arkwright Mutual Insurance Co.* v. *Bryanston Insurance Co. Ltd.* [1990] 2 All E.R. 335.

contracting state, or Article 16 of Schedule 1 or of Schedule 4 to the 1982 Act refers to the proceedings; or the defendant is a party to the jurisdiction agreement under Article 17 of Schedule 1 or of Schedule 4 to the 1982 Act, then by Order 11, rule 1(2) no leave is required to serve the writ out of the jurisdiction. The plaintiff should determine whether the claims in the writ can be so classified and should indorse the writ with a statement to the effect that the court has power under the 1982 Act to hear and determine the claim. Article IV of the Protocol provides that service of the documents may be effected by the documents being sent by the appropriate public officers of the state in which the documents have been drawn up directly to the appropriate public officers of the state in which the addressee is to be found. Order 11, rule 1(2) complements Order 6, rule 7. Order 10, rule 3(2) was consequently amended and now provides that service pursuant to a special mode prescribed by contract outside the jurisdiction will be good service if service of the writ is permitted without leave under Order 11, rule 1(2). Acknowledgment of service should take place within 21 days if the writ is for service in the European territory of a contracting state and within 31 days in any other territory of a contracting state.[2] If the defendant wishes to dispute jurisdiction an application should be made under Order 12, rule 8 within the time limited for service of a defence.

[2] Ord. 11, r. 1(3).

CHAPTER 3

THE WRIT AND ITS INDORSEMENT

Having carefully considered all the matters set out in the previous chapter and more particularly who are the proper parties to sue and be sued, the plaintiff will now be in a position to issue the writ of summons, commonly called "the writ," which begins the action.

The form of writ now in use dates from June 3, 1980. It omits the former reference to the Sovereign and the Royal Command addressed to the defendant to cause an appearance to be entered for him in the action as well as the "Teste" or witnessing of the issue of the writ by the Lord Chancellor. This change has not in any way diminished the authority of the writ since the continuing association of the Sovereign is indicated by a replica of the Royal Arms at the top of the writ and by the requirement that every copy of the writ for service on a defendant must be sealed with the seal of the office of the Supreme Court out of which the writ is issued (Order 10, r. 1(6)).

The writ now informs the defendant, to whom it is addressed, that "this writ of summons has been issued against you by the above-named plaintiff in respect of the claim set out on the back" and calls upon him either to satisfy the claim or to return to the specified Court office the accompanying Acknowledgement of service stating therein whether he intends to contest the proceedings; warning him that if he fails to satisfy the claim or to return the Acknowledgment within the time stated (normally 14 days after service counting the day of service) or if he returns the Acknowledgment without stating therein an intention to contest the proceedings, the plaintiff may proceed with the action and judgment may be entered against him forthwith without further notice.

Until 1980 differing forms of writ were prescribed for issue out of the Central Office or a district registry; for indorsement with the statement of Claim; for a Probate action; and for actions where the writ or notice of it was to be served out of the jurisdiction. Order 6, r. 1 now provides, however, that every writ must be in the form prescribed (as set out in Appendix 1 of this book). The new form is a single, multi-purpose form of writ and it is the responsibility of the plaintiff's solicitor (or the plaintiff himself if he is acting in person) to complete and adapt it to suit the purpose of the action and to indicate whether it is to be brought in the Queen's Bench Division or the Chancery Division.

The writ is issued by being sealed by an officer of the Court. The plaintiff must prepare a sufficient number of copies of the writ to correspond with the number of defendants to be served, as every copy for service must be sealed with the Court seal. Two further copies are required, one of which will be sealed with the word "Original" and will be retained by the plaintiff, and the other, which must be signed by or on behalf of the plaintiff's solicitor, or by the plaintiff himself if suing in person (Order 6, r. 7(5)) will be retained by the issuing officer as the Court copy of the writ.

A writ may also be issued by post, whether the plaintiff is acting in person or suing by a solicitor.[1]

On issue the writ is marked with the plaintiff's initial letter and a serial number for that year, thus "1990 B. No. 540." The parties to the action must be correctly set out. If any of them sue or are sued in a representative capacity, in the Queen's Bench Division this fact is commonly stated when setting out the parties at the head of the writ, *i.e.* the "title" of the action. It *must* always be stated in the indorsement.[2] The body of the writ contains its date of issue which marks the commencement of the action. On the back of the writ are stated the name and address of the plaintiff's solicitor (if any) and also the plaintiff's place of residence. This is done for a variety of reasons: so that the defendant may know where to find his creditor and pay him, where to serve notices, summonses and other documents, and so that he may ask for security for costs (see Chapter 18) if the plaintiff lives abroad. The plaintiff must also make on the writ before it is issued an "indorsement of claim" (Order 6, r. 2).

The Indorsement of Claim

Before a writ is issued it must be indorsed *either* with a full statement of the plaintiff's claim (formerly called a "special indorsement"), to which all the rules of pleading apply, *or* with a concise statement of the nature of the claim made, *or* with a concise statement of the relief or remedy required in the action (Order 6, r. 2(1)). Despite the wording of this rule, however, the indorsement should state the nature of the claim made *and* the relief or remedy required.[3] The purpose of this is to let the defendant know why he is sued. And if the claim is for a debt

---

[1] Practice Direction [1980] 3 All E.R. 822.
[2] Ord. 6, r. 3; *Bowler* v. *John Mowlem Ltd*. [1954] 1 W.L.R. 1445.
[3] *Sterman* v. *E.W. & W.J. Moore* [1970] 1 Q.B. 596.

or liquidated demand only the writ must further state the amount claimed in respect of the debt or demand and for costs and must inform the defendant that further proceedings will be stayed if within the time limited for acknowledging service[4] he pays the whole amount.[5]

If the writ is indorsed merely with a concise statement as above (formerly called a "general indorsement") the plaintiff must subsequently serve upon the defendant a full statement of claim because the former is intended merely as a label to show to what class of action the suit belongs and to let the defendant know in very general terms the reason why he is being sued. An indorsement merely claiming "damages for breach of contract" or "damages for negligence" is insufficient; the defendant should be given some indication of the contract which he is alleged to have broken or the duty which he failed to perform.[6] The defect may, however, be remedied by the service of a statement of claim.[7] In actions of libel the indorsement must state sufficient particulars of the publications in respect of which the action is brought to enable them to be identified (Order 82, r. 2). Where the plaintiff claims possession of land, the writ must be indorsed with a statement showing whether the claim relates to a dwelling-house, and if so, whether the rateable value of the premises on every day specified by section 4(2) of the Rent Act 1977, in relation to the premises exceeds the sum so specified.[8]

The exact wording of the general indorsement may become important if the defendant does not give notice of his intention to contest the proceedings. But if he does, a statement of claim will be served in due course, stating everything in proper form. The plaintiff may not introduce in his statement of claim a fresh cause of action distinct from anything mentioned on his writ.[9] But apart from this the indorsement on the writ in no way fetters or limits the statement of claim. For by Order 18, r. 15(2), "a plaintiff may in his statement of claim alter, modify, or extend any claim made by him in the indorsement of the writ without amending the indorsement." For example in an action for slander the writ will be indorsed with the words

---

[4] Fourteen days after service, including the day of service (see Ord. 12, r. 5).

[5] Ord. 6, r. 2(1)(*b*).

[6] *Marshall* v. *L.P.T.B.* [1936] 3 All E.R. 83; *Batting* v. *L.P.T.B.* [1941] 1 All E.R. 228.

[7] *Hill* v. *Luton Corporation* [1951] 2 K.B. 387; *Grounsell* v. *Cuthell* [1952] 2 Q.B. 673.

[8] Ord. 6, r. 2(1)(*c*), and see Chap. 2. Ord. 6 also imposes special requirements when the action is brought to enforce a right to recover possession of goods or when it relates to a consumer credit agreement.

[9] Ord. 18, r. 15(2); *Cave* v. *Crew* (1893) 62 L.J.Ch. 530; *Sterman* v. *E.W. & W.J. Moore* [1970] 1 Q.B. 596; *Brickfield Properties Ltd.* v. *Newton* [1971] 1 W.L.R. 862.

"The plaintiff's claim is for damages for slander." In the statement of claim the plaintiff may also claim "an injunction restraining the defendant from repeating the alleged slander." But this rule does not apply where the defendant has not given notice of his intention to contest the proceedings.[10]

Whether the plaintiff's claim comes within the definition of a "debt or liquidated demand" affects not only the question whether the plaintiff should indorse his writ with a claim for fixed costs, but also the form of judgment which can be obtained in default of acknowledgment of service or defence (see Chapter 4). When the amount to which the plaintiff is entitled can be ascertained by calculation, or fixed by any scale of charges or other positive *data*,[11] it is said to be "liquidated" or made clear. The House of Lords held in *Miliangos* v. *George Frank (Textiles) Ltd.*,[12] departing from previous authority, that the court has power to give judgment in a foreign currency annd that a claim for a debt or liquidated demand may therefore be made in a foreign currency. But when the amount to be recovered depends upon the circumstances of the case and is fixed by opinion or by assessment or by what might be judged reasonable, the claim is generally unliquidated. It has, however, been clearly decided that a claim upon a *quantum meruit*, where the plaintiff states the precise sum which he claims as the value of his services, is a liquidated demand.[13] But if the claim is in its nature a claim for damages at large, it is not in law treated as a "liquidated demand" even if the plaintiff puts a figure on the damages which he is claiming. A contract may, however, provide for the payment of a fixed sum by way of damages in certain events; and if such a sum is a true pre-estimate of the damage likely to flow from the breach and is not a "penalty"[14] it may properly be claimed as liquidated damages.

Statement of Claim Indorsed on Writ

Formerly the cases where the writ could be "specially indorsed" with a statement of claim were provided for by rule and unless the writ was so indorsed the plaintiff could not

---

[10] *Gee* v. *Bell* (1887) 35 Ch.D. 160; *Kingdon* v. *Kirk* (1887) 37 Ch.D. 141.
[11] See, for example, *G.L. Baker Ltd.* v. *Barclays Bank Ltd.* [1956] 1 W.L.R. 1409; [1956] 3 All E.R. 519.
[12] [1976] A.C. 443. *Practice Directions* [1976] 1 W.L.R. 83 and [1977] 1 W.L.R. 197.
[13] *Lagos* v. *Grunwaldt* [1910] 1 K.B. 41.
[14] See, among many other cases, *Dunlop Pneumatic Tyre Co. Ltd.* v. *New Garage & Motor Co.* [1915] A.C. 79.

apply for summary judgment. The statement of claim can now be indorsed on the writ in all cases. If it is drafted and served separately the action is delayed; moreover, if the plaintiff does not indorse it on the writ when it is reasonable and proper that he should, he may be penalised in respect of any extra costs thereby occasioned.[15]

A statement of claim so indorsed is the statement of claim in the action[16] and no further statement of claim can be served except by way of amendment. It must be so headed[17] and be signed by counsel, if settled by him, otherwise by the plaintiff's solicitor[18] or by the plaintiff himself if acting in person (Order 18, r. 6(5)). It must comply with all the rules applicable to a pleading and in particular must give dates and items sufficient to inform the defendant specifically what is the claim made against him, so that he may be able to make up his mind whether he will pay or fight.[19] If he fights, he must (unless other steps are taken) plead to it within 14 days after the time limited for acknowledging service of the writ (Order 18, r. 2). It must also state all material facts necessary to constitute a complete cause of action. The more concisely such material facts are stated the better. "But if a man employs the machinery of a specially indorsed writ, he must make his indorsement a full and complete statement of his cause of action."[20]

In the absence of sufficient particulars of the claim it may not be clear whether it is truly liquidated and the plaintiff may not be able to enter judgment by default.

Claim for Interest

Any claim for interest must be specifically pleaded[21] and should therefore be included in a statement of claim indorsed on the writ. Interest may be payable by agreement, express or implied, or by virtue of some statute. In such cases the agreement to pay interest at the rate claimed, or the facts from which such an agreement can be implied, or the statute in question must be sufficiently alleged on the writ.

In the case of a bill of exchange, promissory note, cheque or any other negotiable instrument to which the Bills of Exchange

---

[15] See Ord. 62, r. 10.
[16] *Anlaby* v. *Praetorius* (1888) 20 Q.B.D. 764.
[17] Ord. 18, r. 6(1)(*d*).
[18] The solicitor's signature by the hand of a duly authorised clerk is sufficient (*France* v. *Dutton* [1891] 2 Q.B. 208).
[19] See Chap. 6.
[20] *Per* Lord Coleridge C.J. in *Fruhauf* v. *Grosvenor & Co.* (1892) 67 L.T. at p. 351.
[21] Ord. 18, r. 8(4).

Act 1882 applies, interest may be claimed till payment or judgment. And the expenses of noting and protesting the bill may also be claimed on a writ. The Act expressly declares that such claims for interest and expenses are to be "deemed to be liquidated damages."[22]

The Supreme Court Act 1981, section 35A(1), confers on the High Court a general power to award simple interest in any proceedings for the recovery of a debt or damages. The interest may relate to all or any part of the period between the date when the cause of action arose and the date of judgment and may cover all or any part of the debt or damages in respect of which judgment is given. The Act provides by section 35A(2), however, that the power to award interest must be exercised in favour of a plaintiff who sues for personal injuries or death and who recovers damage exceeding £200, unless the court is satisfied that there are special reasons to the contrary.

[22] ss.9(3), 57; see *London and Universal Bank* v. *Clancarty* [1892] 1 Q.B. 689; *Dando* v. *Boden* [1893] 1 Q.B. 318.

CHAPTER 4

MATTERS TO BE CONSIDERED AFTER WRIT

Service

After the writ has been issued, it must be served on the defendant or defendants. Until 1980 the long-standing general rule was that each defendant must be served with the writ personally by the plaintiff or his agent. This is still the basic rule contained in Order 10. But by a major departure from the previous practice, rule 1(2) now provides that as an alternative to personal service, a defendant who is within the jurisdiction may be served by sending a copy of the writ (which must in every case be sealed with the court seal and be accompanied by a form of acknowledgment of service) by ordinary first-class post to the defendant at his usual or last known address, or if there is a letter box for that address, by inserting through the letter box a copy of the writ enclosed in a sealed envelope addressed to the defendant.[1] These methods must be adhered to strictly, so that posting by registered or recorded delivery post, or handing the writ to a person who answers the door at the defendant's premises, do not constitute effective service.[1a]

Where a writ is served by post or through a letter box the date of service will, unless the contrary is shown, be deemed to be the seventh day after the date on which the writ was sent to or inserted through the letter box. In calculating the period of seven days, holidays and Sundays are included (rule 1(3)(*a*)).

A partnership or firm may be served by personal service on a partner or other person having the control or management of the business at its principal place of business, or by post (Order 81, r. 3). But a partnership may not be served by insertion of the writ through the letter box.

The State Immunity Act 1978, section 12, provides that a writ for service on a State must be transmitted through the Foreign and Commonwealth Office to the Ministry of Foreign Affairs of that State, unless the State has agreed to some other method of service. The Act does not obviate the need to obtain leave to

---

[1] In *Barclays Bank of Swaziland* v. *Hahn* [1989] 1 W.L.R. 506 the House of Lords held that the alternatives to personal service are effective only when the defendant is physically present within the jurisdiction at the time of service, and that the deemed date of service under rule 1(3)(*a*) may be displaced on proof that the defendant acquired knowledge of the writ at some other date.

[1a] See *Kenneth Allison Ltd. (in liq) and others* v. *A. E. Limehouse & Co. (a firm)* [1990] 2 All E.R. 723, C.A.

serve process out of the jurisdiction when that is otherwise necessary under Order 11. Rule 7 governs the procedure for service.

A solicitor for a defendant may indorse on the writ a statement that he accepts service of the writ on behalf of the defendant, and in such case the writ shall be deemed to have been duly served on that defendant on the date the indorsement was made (Order 10, r. 1(4)).

Where personal service or service in any other manner is impracticable for any reason the plaintiff may apply to the court on affidavit for an order for "Substituted Service" (Order 65, r. 4). The master may then order service by some other means such as advertisement or upon the defendant's partner or agent or upon a solicitor acting for him but not instructed to accept service. The modern provision for ordinary service by post means that applications for an order for substituted service where the defendant is evading service are less frequent than previously since the form of substituted service most frequently ordered in the past was service by post.

A company registered under the present or former Companies Acts may be served with a writ (or any other process) by leaving it at or sending it by post to the registered office of the company.[2] This method of effecting service is frequently adopted even when the company has a solicitor acting for it. A registered trade union may be served in like manner. Other bodies corporate, in respect of which no special statutory provision is made, are served by personally serving the appropriate officer or by first-class post or by insertion through the letter box (Order 65, r. 3).

Order 12, r. 8A deals with the situation where a person has been named as a defendant in a writ which has not been served on him. In such a case the defendant may serve a notice on the plaintiff requiring him either to serve the writ or to discontinue the action. If the plaintiff fails to comply with the notice the defendant may apply by summons for the action to be dismissed.

Duration and Extension of Validity of Writ

Order 6, r. 8 provides that for the purpose of service a writ issued after June 4, 1990 is valid in the first instance for four months beginning with the date of its issue, or for six months

---

[2] Companies Act 1985, s.725. But see *Singh* v. *Atombrook Ltd.* [1989] 1 W.L.R. 810.

where leave to serve the writ out of the jurisdiction is required under Order 11. These periods implement a recommendation of the Civil Justice Review that the previously operative period of 12 months from the date of issue be reduced.

If the writ is served more than the specified period from the date of issue[3] it is deemed to have been irregularly served and may be set aside; but the irregularity may be waived if the defendant fails to acknowledge service or fails to give notice of intention to defend the proceedings. The plaintiff may, before the specified period has expired, apply to the master to extend the validity of the writ. If the master thinks it proper to do so either because the defendant cannot be found or for some other good reason, he will do so for successive periods not exceeding four months each (or, exceptionally, under rule 8(2A) for up to 12 months) (Order 6, r. 8). The application to extend can by leave be made after the expiration of the original or of the extended period.

The importance of the application will be greatly enhanced if the limitation period has expired before the writ has been served. The principles applicable to the exercise of the court's discretion on application for extension of the validity of a writ in such cases were laid down by the House of Lords in *Kleinwort Benson Ltd.* v. *Barbrak Ltd., The Myrto (No. 3),*[4] where the House reviewed the earlier authorities, and again in *Waddon* v. *Whitecroft-Scovill Ltd.*[5] where the House applied the principles stated in the *Kleinwort* case.

In these cases the House stressed that on the true construction of Order 6, r. 8 the power to extend the validity of a writ should only be exercised for good reason, but that it is *not* necessary, as had been suggested in some earlier authorities, for the plaintiff to show exceptional circumstances. The question whether good reason exists in any particular case depends on all the circumstances of that case. Difficulty in effecting service of the writ may well constitute good reason but it is not the only matter which is capable of doing so. The balance of hardship between the parties can be a relevant matter to be taken into account in the exercise of the discretion.[6]

Hardship to the parties, however, is not of itself sufficient to justify a decision to extend. The plaintiff must in all cases show good reason, such as the impossibility of or great difficulty in

---

[3] Including that date (*Trow* v. *Ind Coope Ltd.* [1976] 2 Q.B. 899). All defendants must be served within the prescribed period: *Jones* v. *Jones* [1970] 2 Q.B. 576.

[4] [1987] A.C. 597.

[5] [1988] 1 W.L.R. 309.

[6] *Ibid. per* Lord Brandon.

finding or serving the defendant, or an agreement between the parties that the writ should not be served. On the other hand, the mere fact that negotiations for a settlement are proceeding is unlikely to constitute good reason.[7]

Acknowledgment of Service

The former procedure of entering an appearance to the writ was abolished in 1979. Instead, Order 12 provides that a defendant who wishes to contest the proceedings must complete and return the form of Acknowledgment of Service he will have received with the writ. He must enter his full name and add the words "sued as" if the name set out on the writ is different. He must state whether or not he intends to defend the action, or to apply for a stay of execution against judgment for a debt or liquidated demand, or to transfer the action to another court. He must give his address for service whether he is acting in person or by a solicitor, and the Acknowledgment must be signed by his solicitor or by the defendant if he is acting in person.

The Acknowledgment of Service, once duly completed, must be posted to or handed in at the office of the Supreme Court out of which the writ was issued. If a defendant fails to return the Acknowledgment of Service within the prescribed time (usually 14 days after service of the writ), judgment in default of acknowledgment may be entered against him under Order 13 (*post*). Similarly, if the defendant returns the Acknowledgment of Service stating therein that he does not intend to contest the proceedings, the plaintiff may enter judgment against him forthwith. But if the defendant returns the Acknowledgment in due time stating therein that he intends to contest the proceedings, the action will proceed. A defendant who is an infant or patient may only acknowledge service by his guardian *ad litem* (Order 80, r. 2).

Order 12, r. 4 provides that on receiving an Acknowledgment of Service the officer of the court must stamp it showing the date of receipt, enter it in the cause book with an indication whether the defendant has stated an intention to contest the proceedings or to apply for a stay of execution in respect of any judgment obtained against him, and post a stamped copy to the plaintiff or his solicitor at the address for service.

---

[7] Per Lord Denning M.R. in *Easy* v. *Universal Anchorage Co. Ltd.* [1974] 1 W.L.R. 899, at p. 902. *Aliter* where the defendant's insurers have stated that there is no need to serve the writ during settlement negotiations: *North* v. *Kirk* (1967) 111 S.J. 793.

A defendant who wishes to dispute the jurisdiction of the court or challenge some irregularity in the issue or service or renewal of the writ or notice of the writ should not be deterred thereby from returning the Acknowledgment of Service or stating therein his intention to contest the proceedings, since Order 12, r. 7 provides that acknowledgment shall not be treated as a waiver by the defendant of any such irregularity. Instead, he must give notice of intention to defend and within 14 days, apply to the court for the relief he seeks (r. 8). This procedure replaces the former practice of entering a conditional appearance, which has been abolished.

Failure to give Notice of Intention to Defend

If the defendant does not give notice of intention to defend within the prescribed time, the plaintiff is ordinarily entitled to judgment. There are, however, certain exceptions. When the defendant is an infant or a patient, the plaintiff must apply to the master to appoint a guardian *ad litem* for the defendant. When the claim is for special relief not mentioned in Order 13, rr. 1–4 (usually claims which before the Judicature Act 1873 could only have been given in the Court of Chancery), the procedure is as described later in this section. Leave must be obtained: (i) in actions in tort between husband and wife[8]; (ii) where the defendant is a State, as defined by the State Immunity Act 1978 (Order 13, r. 7A); (iii) where the writ has been served out of the jurisdiction under Order 11, r. 1(2)(*a*) or has been served within the jurisdiction on a defendant domiciled in Scotland or Northern Ireland or in any other Convention territory (Order 13, r. 7B). If the plaintiff omits or delays to enter judgment, the defendant may still acknowledge service and defend the action; but he gains no extra time for his defence or for taking any other step through his delay (Order 12, r. 6(2)).

The procedure on entering judgment on failure to give notice of intention to defend varies according to the nature of the plaintiff's claim. When the writ is indorsed for a liquidated sum the plaintiff may, on filing an affidavit showing that the writ has been duly served, or on producing the writ indorsed with an acceptance of service by the defendant's solicitor, enter *final* judgment for any sum not exceeding the sum indorsed on the writ, together with interest, if properly claimed under the

---

[8] See Ord. 89, r. 2.

Supreme Court Act 1981, section 35A, at the prescribed rate per annum, to the date of the judgment, and costs (Order 13, r. 1). Order 13, r. 8 deals with the case where judgment for a debt or liquidated demand is entered against a defendant who has returned the acknowledgment of service stating that although he does not intend to contest the proceedings he intends to apply for a stay of execution of the judgment. Rule 8 provides that in such a case execution by a writ of *fieri facias* (see Chapter 24) shall be stayed for a period of 14 days from the acknowledgment of service during which time the defendant may issue a summons supported by an affidavit describing his financial circumstances and giving his proposals for payment of the judgment debt by instalments. If he does so the stay will continue until the summons is heard.

If, however, the plaintiff's claim is for unliquidated damages, he cannot immediately obtain final judgment since the damages have to be assessed. He is entitled instead to what is called an *interlocutory* judgment which he can afterwards convert into a final judgment (Order 13, r. 2). If the action is solely for the detention of goods the plaintiff may at his option either enter interlocutory judgment against the defendant for the return of the goods or their value to be assessed and costs, or enter interlocutory judgment for their value to be assessed and costs or apply by summons for delivery of the goods without giving the defendant the alternative of paying their value[9] (Order 13, r. 3). In actions for possession of land only other than mortgage actions[10] he may enter final judgment for possession subject to the provisions and requirements of rule 4.[11] When the writ is indorsed with two or more of the claims so far mentioned (*i.e.* for a liquidated demand or unliquidated damages, or detention of goods or possession of land) and no other, the plaintiff may obtain judgment in respect of any such claim as if it were the only claim indorsed on the writ (rule 5).

But in actions not covered by the preceding rules, including claims for an injunction, specific performance, rectification, an account or a declaration and other claims which before the Judicature Acts could only have been brought in the Court of Chancery, the procedure is different. The plaintiff is not at this stage allowed to enter any judgment, either final or interlocutory, upon the claim, even though the defendant has not given notice of intention to defend. After proving due service of the

---

[9] See *Howard E. Perry & Co. Ltd.* v. *British Railways Board* [1980] 1 W.L.R. 1375.
[10] As to which see Ord. 88.
[11] See p. 16, *supra*.

writ he must, unless the writ is already fully indorsed, prepare a statement of claim and serve it on the defendant either personally, or by leaving it at his address, or by post, or in such other manner as the court may direct (Order 65, r. 5). When this has been done the plaintiff may proceed with the action in the undermentioned way (Order 13, r. 6(1)). If the defendant desires, he may still give notice of intention to defend, and if he does, the action proceeds as if he had done so at the proper time, and he must serve a defence. But if he does not give notice, he cannot serve a defence, and the plaintiff, after waiting 14 days, can apply by summons[12] for judgment in default of defence. The statement of claim will stand admitted, and the plaintiff will obtain such judgment as he is entitled to thereon (Order 19, r. 7(1)). No evidence is necessary or, indeed, admissible.[13] But the court has a discretion as to the order it will make,[14] and also over the costs of the action.[15] If, however, the defendant has satisfied or complied with the claim—*e.g.* by abating a nuisance complained of—so that it becomes unnecessary for the plaintiff to proceed further with the action, then, if the defendant fails to give notice of intention to defend, the plaintiff may apply by summons for leave to enter judgment against him for costs (Order 13, r. 6(2)). If one of several defendants defaults, the plaintiff may proceed in accordance with Order 19, r. 7(2). The court can, if need be, give leave to amend the statement of claim; if so, it may in its discretion order re-service and adjourn the application meanwhile.

An interlocutory judgment does not specify what amount is due to the plaintiff, since this has still to be determined. The amount of damages or the value of the chattel must subsequently be assessed by a master, unless reference to an official or special referee, or trial before a judge is specially ordered, or unless there are other defendants against whom the action is proceeding to trial. The defendant is given notice of the hearing and the defendant, although he has not appeared, may attend it in person or by solicitor or counsel. He is entitled to cross-examine the witnesses called on behalf of the plaintiff, call evidence himself on the issue of *quantum* and address the court. When the damages (or value of the chattel) have been

---

[12] This alternative to application by motion has been possible since 1958. A motion or, when appropriate, a summons before a judge in chambers, is necessary where relief is claimed which a master has no power to grant, such as an injunction.

[13] *Webster & Co. Ltd.* v. *Vincent* (1897) 77 L.T. 167; *Young* v. *Thomas* [1892] 2 Ch. 134.

[14] *Charles* v. *Shepherd* [1892] 2 Q.B. 622.

[15] *Young* v. *Thomas* (*supra*).

assessed, then the plaintiff can enter *final* judgment for the amount assessed.[16]

Where provisional damages for personal injuries are part of the relief claimed pursuant to section 32A of the Supreme Court Act 1981, entry of judgment with or without leave is not permissible for failure to give notice of intention to defend under Order 13 or on default of pleadings under Order 19 (Order 37, r. 8(5)). Instead, a special procedure is laid down.[17] At the trial, there will be in issue both quantum of damages and the question whether the case is an appropriate one for an award of provisional damages and if so, upon what terms.

A judgment in default of notice of intention to defend or defence may be set aside or varied unconditionally or upon terms. (Order 13, r. 9; Order 19, r. 9; "The principle obviously is that unless and until the court has pronounced a judgment upon the merits or by consent, it is to have the power to revoke the expression of its coercive power where that has only been obtained by a failure to follow any of the rules of procedure.")[18]

Where a judgment is irregularly obtained, the defendant is entitled as of right to have it set aside on application by summons or by motion (under Order 2, rr. 1, 2).[19] The irregularities relied on must be specified in the summons and the application must be made within a reasonable time and before any fresh step is taken after knowledge of the irregularity. But before granting any application to set aside a judgment regularly obtained (*i.e.* strictly in compliance with the rules), the court will require to be satisfied not only that the defendant had some reasonable excuse, *e.g.* illness, for failing to give notice of intention to defend but also as to his "merits," *i.e.* that in the action itself there is some prospect of his being at least partly successful. An affidavit is usually necessary for this purpose. If a judgment has been set aside on conditions and the defendant does not comply with the conditions, the judgment stands and the plaintiff may proceed upon it unless the master otherwise directs (Order 45, r. 10; see also r. 9), or unless the defendant obtains an extension of time.[20]

---

[16] See Ord. 37, rr. 1–5.

[17] See *Practice Note* [1988] 1 W.L.R. 654, [1988] 2 All E.R. 102: Claims for Provisional Damages—Default Judgments.

[18] *Evans* v. *Bartlam* [1937] A.C. at p. 480, *per* Lord Atkin. See also *Alpine Bulk Transport Co. Inc.* v. *Saudi Eagle Shipping Co. Inc., The Saudi Eagle* [1986] 2 Lloyd's Rep. 221, C.A., where the unconditional nature of the discretionary power to set aside a default judgment is indicated.

[19] And see *Anlaby* v. *Praetorius* (1888) 20 Q.B.D. 764; *White* v. *Weston* [1968] 2 Q.B. 647.

[20] *Manley Estates Ltd.* v. *Benedek* [1941] 1 All E.R. 248, 461; *Reading Trust Ltd.* v. *Spero* [1930] 1 K.B. 492.

A judgment for an amount larger than is due at the time it is entered is bad and will be set aside or reduced.[21] In the case of genuine mistake the plaintiff may get leave *ex parte* to amend, provided he applies before communicating the contents of the judgment to the defendant or taking any steps to enforce it. In other cases where there has been a clerical mistake in the judgment or an error arising from some accidental slip or omission the application must be made on summons under the "slip rule" (Order 20, r. 11, and see Chapter 11).

Interim Payments

The Supreme Court Act 1981, section 32, provides that, as regards proceedings pending in the High Court, rules may enable the court to order interim payments.

Order 29, r. 10, provides that the plaintiff may, at any time after the writ has been served on the defendant and the time limited for him to acknowledge service has expired, apply for an order requiring the defendant to make an interim payment, meaning a payment on account of damages, debt or other sum (but not costs) which the defendant may be held liable to pay to the plaintiff. The procedure originally applied to personal injuries actions only but in 1980 was extended so as to apply to actions of any kind.

The application must be made by summons (or as part of a summons for summary judgment) supported by an affidavit verifying the amount of damages and giving the grounds of the application with any documentary evidence relied on, and these documents must be served on the defendant not less than 10 clear days before the return day.

Where the application is made in an action for damages the court may order an interim payment where the defendant has admitted liability, or the plaintiff has obtained judgment for damages to be assessed, or the court is satisfied that if the action proceeded to trial the plaintiff would obtain judgment for substantial damages. The amount of the interim payment will be such as the court thinks just, not exceeding a reasonable proportion of the damages the plaintiff would be likely to recover. But in a personal injuries action, no interim payment can be awarded unless the defendant is either insured against the claim, or is a public authority or is a person whose means

---

[21] *Muir* v. *Jenks* [1913] 2 K.B. 412.

are such as to enable him to make the interim payment (rule 11).[22]

The hearing of the application may be treated as a convenient opportunity for the giving of certain directions for the further conduct of the action, and in particular, the court may order an early trial of the action (rule 14).

The fact that an interim payment has been ordered may not be mentioned in the pleadings, nor should it be mentioned to the trial judge until all questions of liability and the amount of damages have been decided (rule 15). The judge must then be so informed in order that the final judgment can be tailored to meet the financial obligations resulting between the parties. It may, for example, be necessary to order the plaintiff to repay to the defendant so much of an interim payment as exceeds the judge's award.

Interlocutory Injunctions

The power of the High Court to grant injunctions is now contained in section 37 of the Supreme Court Act 1981.[23] This provides:

"(1) The High Court may by order (whether interlocutory or final) grant an injunction or appoint a receiver in all cases in which it appears to the court to be just and convenient to do so.

(2) Any such order may be made either unconditionally or on such terms and conditions as the court thinks just."

Until 1975 the generally accepted view of the profession was that a plaintiff who wished to obtain an interlocutory injunction had to make out a prima facie case.[24] A judge hearing a motion to restrain the defendant from doing acts which either infringed or threatened to infringe the plaintiff's legal rights would determine the relative strength of the cases for the plaintiff and the defendant, and would require to be satisfied that, on the affidavit evidence sworn in the action, the plaintiff had proved a probability of entitlement to success at the trial. The remedy of injunction is discretionary, and the judge would

---

[22] In *Ricci Burns Ltd.* v. *Toole and Another* [1989] 3 All E.R. 478, the Court of Appeal held that there is power to make an interim payment order under Order 29 against a defendant even though it had been held that he was entitled to unconditional leave to defend the action under Order 14. See Chap. 5.

[23] This section is derived from, and replaces, s.45 of the Judicature Act 1925.

[24] See, *e.g. Preston* v. *Luck* (1884) 27 Ch.D. 497, 505–506 (Cotton L.J.) *J.T. Stratford & Son Ltd.* v. *Lindley* [1965] A.C. 269, 338 (Lord Upjohn); *F. Hoffmann-La Roche & Co. AG* v. *Secretary of State for Trade and Industry* [1975] A.C. 295, 360 (Lord Diplock).

then apply a test of the balance of convenience in deciding whether to grant the relief sought. In particular, the plaintiff would have to satisfy the judge that any award of damages made in his favour at the trial of the action would not provide adequate compensation for the injury he was likely to sustain from the defendant's unrestrained acts before trial.

The problem with the requirement of proof of a prima facie case was that in order to determine the issue, in many cases the court would have to conduct a kind of preliminary trial on conflicting affidavits, where it was clear that there were substantial disputes of fact to be resolved. At the same time, as Lord Denning M.R. pointed out,[25] this procedure did have the advantage that where injunctive relief was the main object of the action, its grant or refusal or an interlocutory application would often dispose of the matter. In *American Cyanamid Co.* v. *Ethicon Ltd.*[26] the House of Lords was faced with the prospect of an appeal in an interlocutory application in a patent action, where the appeal was estimated to last 12 days and involved a mass of conflicting affidavit evidence. In the event, the House, in the person of Lord Diplock, with whose speech the other Law Lords concurred, took the opportunity to restate the principles which should govern the granting of interlocutory injunctions.

The plaintiff must show first that there is a serious issue to be tried.[27] That is, he must adduce sufficiently precise factual, supporting evidence to satisfy the court that his claim is not frivolous or vexatious, and that he has a real prospect of succeeding in his claim for a permanent injunction at the trial.[28] Lord Diplock stated that this principle applied to all cases, including patent actions. There was no rule of law that the plaintiff had to do more at this stage by way of showing a prima facie case of entitlement to success at the trial.[29] Once the plaintiff has shown that there is a serious issue to be tried, the

---

[25] In *Fellowes and Son* v. *Fisher* [1976] Q.B. 122. See also *Office Overload Ltd.* v. *Gunn* [1977] F.S.R. 39; *Newsweek Inc.* v. *B.B.C.* [1979] R.P.C. 441.

[26] [1975] A.C. 396.

[27] *Ibid.* at p. 407.

[28] See *Re Lord Cable (deceased), Garratt* v. *Waters* [1976] 3 All E.R. 417, a case in which the plaintiff failed to surmount this first hurdle. "Frivolous or vexatious" in this context is not to be understood in the restricted sense in which it is used as the test for striking out under Ord. 18, r. 19. An injunction will be refused if the plaintiff's case is hopeless, even though it might not be frivolous or vexatious in the restricted sense: *Mothercare Ltd.* v. *Robson Books Ltd.* [1979] F.S.R. 464, *per* Megarry V.-C.

[29] [1975] A.C. 396, 407. In *Cayne* v. *Global Natural Resources plc* [1984] 1 All E.R. 225 Eveleigh L.J. held that it is sufficient if there is a serious question to be tried, that is to say there is some supporting material for the plaintiff's case, and the outcome of the eventual trial on that issue is in doubt.

test to be applied then is the balance of convenience.[30] There are a number of factors to be considered in making this assessment. The first is whether the plaintiff would be adequately compensated by an award of damages at the trial for any loss suffered as a result of the defendant's unrestrained acts. If so, and the defendant would be in a position to pay the damages, then no injunction should normally be granted. If on the other hand, damages would not be an adequate remedy for the plaintiff, then the court should consider what would happen if the injunction were granted but the defendant succeeded at the trial. If then the defendant could be adequately compensated in damages and the plaintiff would be able to pay, then an injunction should normally be granted.[31]

So where the plaintiff is granted an interlocutory injunction he will normally be required to give an undertaking as to damages[32] so that the plaintiff will be liable to compensate the defendant for any losses he has suffered by the grant of the injunction if the plaintiff's action subsequently fails.[33]

In other cases where the adequacy of damages or the solvency of the parties is in doubt, the balance of convenience will involve the weighing up of many factors. In *American Cyanamid Co.* v. *Ethicon Ltd.* Lord Diplock said that it would not be appropriate to list them all, although he noted that individual cases might have "special factors" which would tip the

---

[30] This expression has received some criticism from the Court of Appeal recently. For instance, in *Cayne* v. *Global Natural Resources plc (supra)* at 237, May L.J. preferred the phrase "the balance of the risk of doing an injustice" because this better described the process involved. And in *Francome* v. *Mirror Group Newspapers Ltd.* [1984] 1 W.L.R. 892, Sir John Donaldson M.R. at 898 said that the balance of convenience was an unfortunate expression since the business of the court was justice not convenience. He continued "we must contemplate the possibility that either party may succeed and must do our best to ensure that nothing occurs pending the trial which will prejudice his rights. Since the parties are usually asserting wholly inconsistent claims, this is difficult, but we have to do our best. In doing so we are seeking a balance of justice, not of convenience." See also *Films Rover International Ltd.* v. *Cannon Film Sales Ltd.* [1987] 1 W.L.R. 670.

[31] For examples of uncompensatable damage to the plaintiff where injunctions were granted, see *Alfred Dunhill Ltd.* v. *Sunoptic S.A.* [1979] F.S.R. 337 (injury to goodwill and reputation); *Laws* v. *Florinplace Ltd.* [1981] 1 All E.R. 659 (pollution of the neighbourhood). For a case where an injunction was refused on the ground that the defendants would be likely to suffer substantial damage for which the plaintiffs would be likely to be unable to pay, and the plaintiffs had no real prospect of success, see *Morning Star Co-Operative Society Ltd.* v. *Express Newspapers Ltd.* [1979] F.S.R. 113.

[32] This has become automatic as the "price" to be paid for obtaining an interlocutory injunction and if it is accidentally omitted from the order the court can subsequently add such an undertaking: *Colledge* v. *Crossley, The Times,* March 18, 1975.

[33] Where the applicant for an interlocutory injunction is the Crown which is seeking to enforce the law it will not be required to give an undertaking unless the person against whom it is sought shows some very good reason why it should be given: *Hoffmann-La Roche A.G.* v. *Secretary of State for Trade and Industry* [1975] A.C. 295.

balance of convenience one way or the other.[34] He went on to
say that if other factors appeared to be equally balanced, then it
would be appropriate to preserve the status quo pending trial
by granting an injunction.[35] Where the hardship likely to be
suffered from the grant or refusal of the injunction was roughly
equal then it would be appropriate to consider the relative
strength of the parties' case, although this should be done on
evidence not in dispute. Lastly, Lord Diplock indicated that the
matter is one of discretion of the judge who hears the motion
for the injunction, and that an appeal court should hesitate to
interfere with the exercise of the discretion unless satisfied that
the judge had gone wrong in law.[36]

Although Lord Diplock expressed the view that the
principles he enunciated in *American Cyanamid* were applicable
to all cases, later authorities have introduced some modifications to the generality of these principles.

First, the principles have no application where the interlocutory injunction will effectively dispose of the action.[37] If the
effect of granting the injunction will be to give the plaintiff
substantially the whole of the relief he is seeking, thus making
it unnecessary for him to ever proceed to trial, then it will be
unfair to the defendant who is then prevented from presenting
his case.[38] Therefore, in this type of case the court will look at
the strength of the plaintiff's case and in *N.W.L. Ltd.* v. *Woods*[39]
Lord Diplock stated that the likelihood that the plaintiff would
have succeeded in establishing his right to an injunction if the
action had gone to trial is a factor to be brought into the
balance of convenience.[40] In *Office Overload Ltd.* v. *Gunn*[41] Lord
Denning M.R. said that the plaintiff should establish a strong

---

[34] [1975] A.C. 396, 409.

[35] See, *e.g. Hubbard* v. *Pitt* [1975] 3 All E.R. 1; *News Group Newspapers Ltd.* v. *The Rocket
Record Co. Ltd.* [1981] F.S.R. 89.

[36] [1975] A.C. 396, 409; *Duport Steels Ltd.* v. *Sirs* [1980] 1 All E.R. 529.

[37] In fact, Lord Diplock himself subsequently stated that *American Cyanamid* "was not
dealing with a case in which the grant or refusal of an injunction at that stage would, in
effect, dispose of the action . . . " and that there was nothing in the decision which
prevented the judge from giving full weight to the practical realities of the situation to
which the injunction will apply: *N.W.L. Ltd.* v. *Woods* [1979] 1 W.L.R. 1294.

[38] As was noted by the Court of Appeal in *Cayne* v. *Global Natural Resources plc* [1984] 1 All
E.R. 225 this would in certain circumstances amount to giving summary judgment for
the plaintiff.

[39] [1979] 1 W.L.R. 1294.

[40] *Supra*, at 1307.

[41] [1977] F.S.R. 39.

prima facie case.[42] However, in *Cayne* v. *Global Natural Resources plc*[43] the Court of Appeal was of the opinion that it was not appropriate to refer to the balance of convenience, and the court should approach a case such as this on the broad principle of what it can do in its best endeavour to avoid injustice. It would only be in an exceptional case where the plaintiff had an overwhelming case that it would be proper to grant an injunction.

Secondly, where a plaintiff is seeking an interlocutory injunction to prevent the publication of allegedly defamatory material the court will not normally grant the injunction where the defendant shows that he will be pleading justification or qualified privilege at the trial.[44] To do so would interfere with the right to free speech and encourage the use of "gagging writs."

Thirdly, where an action is brought against a defendant who is likely to succeed in establishing a defence under sections 13 or 15 of the Trade Union and Labour Relations Act 1974 (*i.e.* that the act complained of was done in contemplation or furtherance of a trade dispute) then the court shall, in exercising its discretion whether or not to grant an interlocutory injunction, take this factor into account in deciding where the balance of convenience lies.[45] This factor is not, however, a paramount or overriding consideration so if the court considers that the defendant is virtually certain to establish the trade dispute defence it will naturally give more weight to this factor, and therefore be more likely not to grant the injunction, than if it considers the prospect of successfully establishing the defence is more doubtful.[46]

Fourthly, in circumstances where the law and the facts are clear and undisputed then the court can properly take into account the relative strengths of the parties' claims. This has

---

[42] This was applied in *John Michael Design plc* v. *Cooke* [1987] 2 All E.R. 332 which involved a dispute arising out of a restraint of trade covenant (where the grant of an injunction will usually dispose of the action because of the relatively short duration of the covenants) where it was held that the court should consider whether the covenant is prima facie valid and if it is then it should ordinarily grant an injunction restraining the defendant.

[43] [1984] 1 All E.R. 225.

[44] *Quartz Hill Consolidated Gold Mining Co.* v. *Beall* (1882) 20 Ch.D. 501; *Harakas* v. *Baltic Mercantile and Shipping Exchange Ltd.* [1982] 1 W.L.R. 958. However, an injunction might be granted where the plaintiff can show malice on the part of the defendant or where there is clear evidence of a conspiracy to injure the plaintiff: see, *e.g.*, *Gulf Oil (Great Britain) Ltd.* v. *Page* [1987] Ch. 327.

[45] Trade Union and Labour Relations Act 1974, s.17(2) which was inserted by the Employment Act 1975 to take account of the *American Cyanamid* decision.

[46] *N.W.L. Ltd.* v. *Woods* [1979] 1 W.L.R. 1294.

happened particularly in actions for passing off and breaches of restrictive covenants.[47]

Where a plaintiff asks the court to grant a mandatory as opposed to a prohibitory interlocutory injunction the court is normally required to feel a high degree of assurance that the plaintiff will succeed at trial before it grants the injunction.[48] This is because there is a higher risk of injustice if a mandatory injunction is granted and the plaintiff subsequently fails to establish that he was entitled to it at the trial. These orders usually go further than the preservation of the status quo and require the defendant to take some positive steps or undo what he has already done (for example, remove a fence).[49] They are, as a result, more likely to cause a greater waste of time and money than a prohibiting order if it transpires that they have been "wrongly" granted.

This is not always the case though.[50] There are exceptional cases where the court can grant such an injunction even though it does not feel a high degree of assurance that the plaintiff will succeed at trial if the withholding of the injunction carried with it a greater risk of injustice than granting it. So a mandatory injunction could be granted where it is needed to preserve the status quo, for example to prevent the owner of a vessel using a ship otherwise than in accordance with the terms of a charterparty agreement.[51]

Finally, in certain circumstances it should not be overlooked that there are public interest considerations to be taken into account when the court is deciding where the balance of convenience lies. So, for example, in cases involving the press, one of the "special factors" to be considered is the consequence to the public of granting or refusing an injunction, namely whether the public will be deprived of information in which it

[47] *Newsweek Inc.* v. *B.B.C.* [1979] R.P.C. 441; *Alfred Dunhill Ltd.* v. *Sunoptic S.A.* [1979] F.S.R. 337; *B.B.C.* v. *Talbot Motor Co. Ltd.* [1981] F.S.R. 228; *Office Overload* v. *Gunn* [1977] F.S.R. 39.

[48] *Shepherd Homes Ltd.* v. *Sandham* [1971] Ch. 340 at 351 (Megarry J.); *Leisure Data* v. *Bell* [1988] F.S.R. 367.

[49] *Shepherd Homes Ltd.* v. *Sandham* (*supra*).

[50] As Hoffman J. stated in *Films Rover International Ltd.* v. *Cannon Film Sales Ltd.* [1987] 1 W.L.R. 670 at 680.

[51] *Associated Portland Cement Manufacturers Ltd.* v. *Teigland Shipping A/S, The Oakworth* [1975] 1 Lloyd's Rep. 581, *per* Lord Denning M.R.

has an interest.[52] Similarly, where the defendant is a public authority performing duties to the public the court must take into account the interests of the public in general to whom these duties are owed and should not grant an injunction unless the plaintiff shows that he has a real prospect of obtaining a permanent injunction at the trial.[53] The problem of conflicting public interests was considered in *Att.-Gen.* v. *Guardian Newspapers Ltd. & Others*[53a] where the House of Lords, by a majority, thought that interlocutory injunctions had been properly granted restraining certain newspapers from disclosing or publishing any information obtained by a former member of the British Security Services in his capacity as such despite the fact that the latter's book containing the information in question was published in the United States and was circulating in Britain. The majority thought that the injunctions were necessary in the public interest to maintain the efficiency of the Security Service, which should prevail over the right of the public to be fully informed.

The Mareva Injunction

A clear danger faced by a creditor suing for recovery of a debt is that the debtor may dispose of his assets or transfer them abroad in the inevitable interval between the cause of action arising or issue of writ and judgment, and so prevent the creditor from satisfying any judgment the court may give in his favour. Civil law jurisdictions are familiar with the procedure known as *saisie conservatoire* whereby the assets of a debtor may be impounded before judgment, but English law has had until relatively recently no comparable procedure. The view was that the creditor must await judgment before he could seek to restrain the debtor in the use of his assets, and that view appeared to be supported by *Lister* v. *Stubbs*[54] where Cotton L.J. said:

---

[52] See *Schering Chemicals Ltd.* v. *Falkman Ltd.* [1981] 2 W.L.R. 848 at 881 (Templeman L.J.). However, see *Att.-Gen.* v. *Guardian Newspapers Ltd. & Others* [1987] 1 W.L.R. 1248 where the House of Lords, by a majority, held that interlocutory injunctions had been properly granted restraining certain newspapers from disclosing or publishing any information obtained by a former member of the British Security Services in his capacity as such despite the fact that the information was contained in the latter's book which was published in the United States and was circulating in Britain. The majority thought that the injunctions were necessary in the public interest to maintain the efficiency of the Security Service.

[53] *Smith* v. *Inner London Education Authority* [1978] 1 All E.R. 411, 422 (Browne L.J.). See *R.* v. *Westminster City Council ex p. Sierbien, The Independent*, March 26, 1987.

[53a] See note 52.

[54] (1890) 45 Ch.D. 1, 13.

"I know of no case where, because it was highly probable
that if the action were brought to a hearing the plaintiff
could establish that a debt was due to him from the
defendant, the defendant has been ordered to give
security until that has been established by the judgment
or decree."

The development since 1975 of the Mareva injunction, in
what Lord Denning has described[55] as "the greatest piece of
judicial law reform in my time," has produced a means
whereby a debtor may be prevented from disposing of his
assets before judgment either by the debtor removing them
from the jurisdiction or by dissipating them within the jurisdiction. The Mareva injunction takes its name from *Mareva Compania Naviera S.A.* v. *International Bulkcarriers S.A.*[56] where
charterers of a ship, the Mareva, defaulted on the third
instalment of hire due to the shipowners. The charterers had
money standing to their credit in a London bank, and the
shipowners applied *ex parte* for an injunction restraining the
charterers from removing the money or disposing of it out of
the jurisdiction. The Court of Appeal held that, notwithstanding *Lister* v. *Stubbs* (*ante*), jurisdiction to confer the injunction
was conferred by section 45 of the Judicature Act 1925, which
provided that an injunction may be granted ". . . by an
interlocutory Order of the Court in all cases in which it shall
appear to the court to be just or convenient . . ." Lord Denning
M.R. thought that the grant of the injunction in these circumstances was "only just and right."[57]

The procedure is now well established and the statutory
authority for granting a Mareva injunction is currently contained in section 37(1) of the Supreme Court Act 1981 whenever it is "just and convenient" to do so. Section 37(3) goes on
to provide:

"The power of the High Court under subsection (1) to
grant an interlocutory injunction restraining a party to
any proceedings from removing from the jurisdiction of
the High Court, or otherwise dealing with, assets located
within that jurisdiction shall be exercisable in cases where

---

[55] In *The Due Process of Law* (London, Butterworths, 1980), p. 134.
[56] [1975] 2 Lloyd's Rep. 509; [1980] 1 All E.R. 213, C.A. The Court of Appeal had granted a
Mareva injunction a month previously in *Nippon Yusen Kaisha* v. *Karageorgis* [1975] 1
W.L.R. 1093, but had not there been referred to *Lister* v. *Stubbs, ante*.
[57] [1975] 2 Lloyd's Rep. 509 at 511; [1980] 1 All E.R. 213, 215.

that party is, as well as in cases where he is not, domiciled, resident or present within that jurisdiction."

Thus, it is no longer uncertain whether an order can be granted against an English-based defendant as opposed to only a foreign-based one.[58]

The plaintiff has to have a cause of action against the defendant when he applies for the order. The right to apply for any interlocutory injunction is dependent on there being a pre-existing cause of action arising out of an actual or threatened invasion by the defendant of legal or equitable rights of the plaintiff.[59]

The Mareva injunction can be, and usually is, granted *ex parte* before the issue of the writ with the applicant giving an undertaking to issue it forthwith.[60] If the matter is one of extreme urgency and the court is not sitting then an application can be made to a judge at his home. A Mareva injunction can also be granted after final judgment to assist the plaintiff in executing his order.[61]

To be able to obtain a Mareva the plaintiff will have to show that he has "a good arguable case"[62] and since the defendant will not normally be represented at the hearing the Court of Appeal in *Third Chandris Shipping Corporation* v. *Unimarine S.A.*[63] has held that an applicant must observe the following guidelines:

    1. The plaintiff is under a duty to make full and frank disclosure of all material facts known to him or which should have been known to him had he made all such inquiries as were reasonable and proper in the circumstances[64];

---

[58] *Rahman (Prince Abdul) bin Turki al Sudairy* v. *Abu-Taha* [1980] 1 W.L.R. 1268; *Barclay-Johnson* v. *Yuill* [1980] 1 W.L.R. 1259; *Siskina (Owners of cargo lately laden on board)* v. *Distos Compania Naviera S.A.* [1979] A.C. 216 at 261.

[59] *Siskina* v. *Distos Compania Naviera S.A. (supra)*, per Lord Diplock at p. 256.

[60] *P.S. Refson & Co. Ltd.* v. *Saggars* [1984] 1 W.L.R. 1025. A Mareva injunction is not a substitute for the relief to be granted at trial so if a plaintiff obtains a Mareva and then does not take steps to have the action set down for trial the Mareva can be discharged: *Lloyd's Bowmaker Ltd.* v. *Britannia Arrow Holdings plc* [1988] 1 W.L.R. 1337.

[61] *Orwell Steel (Erection and Fabrication) Ltd.* v. *Asphalt and Tarmac (UK) Ltd.* [1985] 3 All E.R. 747.

[62] *Ninemia Maritime Corporation* v. *Trave Schiffahrtsgesellschaft mbH* [1983] 1 W.L.R. 1412, per Kerr L.J. at 1422.

[63] [1979] Q.B. 645.

[64] *Brink's-Mat Ltd.* v. *Elcombe* [1986] 1 W.L.R. 1350. If there was a material non-disclosure by an applicant when he obtained a Mareva injunction the defendant can seek a discharge of the injunction on that ground despite the fact that the defendant has delayed the bringing of the application for a discharge: *Lloyd's Bowmaker Ltd.* v. *Britannia Arrow Holding plc* [1988] 1 W.L.R. 1337 where the defendant successfully discharged the injunction after a two-year delay.

The extent of the inquiries which will be held to be proper and as such necessary for the plaintiff to carry out will depend on all the circumstances of the case. In order to determine this question the court is likely to look at the nature of the case and the effect of granting the injunction on the defendant and also the urgency and the time available to the plaintiff to make inquiries.[65] Where a defendant can establish that the plaintiff obtained the order without making full disclosure then the court will be "astute to ensure that the plaintiff is deprived of any advantage he may have derived from that breach of duty."[66] However, the court will not discharge the order in every case where a material non-disclosure is proved. The court has a discretion to continue the order or to make a new order on different terms.[67]

2. He must give particulars of his claim and state fairly the points made against it by the defendant;
3. He must give some grounds for believing that the defendant has assets within the jurisdiction[68];
4. That there is a real risk of the assets being dissipated within the jurisdiction or removed from it before the judgment or award is satisfied[69];

A bare assertion by the plaintiff which is not supported by any evidence that the defendant is likely to dissipate or remove his assets and is unlikely to honour any judgment or award will be insufficient.[70] The plaintiff does not have to prove that the defendant intends to dissipate his assets in order to obtain a Mareva injunction; merely that there is a real risk that he will do so and that a judgment in favour of the plaintiff would then remain unsatisfied. A Mareva injunction; should not be used simply as a device to give the plaintiff a security for his claim over the defendant's other creditors.[71]

---

[65] *Bank Mellat* v. *Nikpour* [1985] F.S.R. 87 *per* Slade L.J. at 92, 93.

[66] *Bank Mellat* v. *Nikpour* (*supra*), *per* Donaldson L.J. at 91. See also *Siporex Trade S.A.* v. *Comdel Commodities Ltd.* [1986] 2 Lloyd's Rep. 428.

[67] *Lloyd's Bowmaker Ltd.* v. *Britannia Arrow Holdings plc* [1988] 1 W.L.R. 1337, *per* Glidewell L.J. at 1343, 1344. The appropriate time for a defendant to apply to the court to have an injunction discharged on the grounds that there was a material non-disclosure by the plaintiff is at the trial and not during the interlocutory proceedings because these are not appropriate for the court to hear evidence and determine allegations: *Dormeuil Frères S.A.* v. *Nicolian International (Textiles) Ltd.* [1988] 1 W.L.R. 1362. See also *Behbehani & Others* v. *Salem & Others* [1989] 2 All E.R. 143 and *Ali & Fahd Shobokshi Group Ltd.* v. *Monheim* [1989] 2 All E.R. 404.

[68] For these purposes the existence of a bank account is sufficient even if it is currently overdrawn.

[69] *Ninemia Maritime Corporation* v. *Trave Schiffahrtsgesellschaft mbH* [1983] 1 W.L.R. 1412, *per* Kerr L.J. at p. 1419.

[70] *Z Ltd.* v. *A-Z and AA-LL* [1982] 1 Q.B. 558.

[71] *Ninemia Corporation* v. *Trave Schiffahrtsgesellschaft mbH* (*supra*), *per* Kerr L.J. at 1422.

5. He must give an undertaking in damages in case the claim fails or the grant of the injunction turns out to be unjustified.[72]

In *Z Ltd*. v. *A-Z*[73] Kerr L.J. took the view that normally a Mareva injunction should be a "maximum sum" type of order rather than an order which applied to all the defendant's assets. This type of order then only freezes the defendant's assets up to the level of the plaintiff's prima facie justifiable claim leaving him free to deal with the balance. Despite this, many orders restraining the defendant's assets generally are still made.

The assets which are to be the subject of a Mareva injunction must be owned by the defendant in the same capacity as that in which he is sued. If the plaintiff has reason to believe that assets are being held by a nominee or third party for the defendant, then these assets could be included in the order as well. The principles upon which an order will be made against a third party were considered and enunciated by the Court of Appeal in *SCF Finance Co. Ltd*. v. *Masri*.[74] They are broadly as follows:

1. Where a plaintiff asks the court to make a Mareva injunction which includes in its scope assets which on their face appear to belong to another party, the court should not accede to the request without good reason for supposing that the assets are in truth the assets of the defendant.

2. Where the defendant or the third party asserts that the assets in question properly belong to the third party the court is not bound to accept that assertion without inquiry.

3. In deciding whether to accept the assertion of the defendant or the third party without further inquiry, the court will be guided by what is just and convenient between the parties concerned.

4. The court can decide to order the issue to be tried between the plaintiff and the third party in advance of the main action.

It was held in this case that it was correct for the judge to order a further inquiry before he decided the issue of whether to

---

[72] The judge can require a bond or other security to support this undertaking. However, a Mareva injunction will not necessarily be denied to a plaintiff where the plaintiff is poor and legally aided and therefore the undertaking is not worth very much: *Allen* v. *Jambo Holdings Ltd*. [1980] 1 W.L.R. 1252.
[73] [1982] 1 Q.B. 558.
[74] [1985] 1 W.L.R. 876.

make an order so as to include funds in the bank account of the wife of the defendant. Similarly, a Mareva injunction should not be extended so as to include the assets of a defendant's spouse unless the court has good reason to suppose that these assets were in reality the assets of the defendant.[75]

Although the Mareva injunction has the effect of temporarily freezing the assets of the defendant it has become the normal practice to include in the order a provision allowing the defendant to have his ordinary living expenses and to be able to discharge his ordinary debts and liabilities as they become due.[76] What constitutes ordinary living expenses in this context will depend on the circumstances of the individual case, for example the wealth of the defendant and his lifestyle. If the order does not originally contain such a provision then the courts will insist on one being included.[77]

Apart from this concession, an injunction in an otherwise unqualified form may still be capable of causing hardship both to the defendant and his other creditors. For instance, in *Iraqi Ministry of Defence* v. *Arcepey Shipping Co. S.A.*[78] the defendant's only asset, the proceeds of insurance of the single ship of a one-ship company, was made subject to a Mareva injunction. There were no other funds from which the defendants could make bona fide payments in the ordinary course of business, and the court permitted the release of money to permit such payments to be made. As Robert Goff J. stated:

> "it does not follow that, having established the injunction, the court should not thereafter permit a qualification to it to allow a transfer of assets by the defendant if the defendant satisfies the court that he requires the money for a purpose which does not conflict with the policy underlying the Mareva jurisdiction."[79]

It is not enough though for the defendant to say simply: "I owe somebody some money," and if, as in *A.* v. *C. (No. 2)*[80] he has, or may have, other assets from which the relevant payment can be made, the injunction will not be qualified

---

[75] *Allied Arab Bank Ltd.* v. *Hajjar* [1988] Q.B. 944.
[76] *Z Ltd.* v. *A-Z* [1982] 1 Q.B. 558, 576; *PCW (Underwriting Agencies) Ltd.* v. *Dixon* [1983] 2 All E.R. 697.
[77] *Law Society* v. *Shanks* (1987) 131 S.J. 1626.
[78] [1980] 2 W.L.R. 488.
[79] *Ibid.* at p. 494. See also Sir Robert Megarry V.-C. in *Barclay-Johnson* v. *Yuill* [1980] 1 W.L.R. 1259 at 1264.
[80] [1981] 2 W.L.R. 634.

unless he can satisfy the court that to do so will not conflict with the underlying policy of the jurisdiction.

The Mareva injunction is an order made *in personam* against the defendant. It can, however, also have an effect *in rem* on third parties.[80a] The order takes immediate effect on all the assets of the defendants which are covered by the order and so everyone who is holding any of these assets and who has knowledge of the order becomes bound by it. The third parties are bound as soon as they have notice of the order even if this is before the defendant himself has notice.[81] Third parties will be in contempt of court if, with notice of the order, they then proceed to assist the defendant to dispose of or dissipate the assets. The third parties which are most commonly affected here are banks which, when served with notice of the order, may be placed in a difficult situation. This is because to protect themselves they may have to institute a very costly and elaborate search throughout all their branches to see whether they are holding any assets belonging to the defendant.[82] Of course, it should ultimately be the plaintiff who has to bear the cost of this search as a result of the undertaking which he is required to give, but he may be unaware of the extent of the liability he is incurring.[83] Generally, therefore, orders which are likely to affect third parties and will be served upon them should have careful attention paid to the terms in which they are drawn up. It is the duty of the plaintiff to consider very carefully the extent of the injunction necessary to safeguard his prima facie justified claim and to the extent to which the assets are known or suspected to exist. These should be identified even if the value is unknown.

If it is known or suspected that assets are in the hands of third parties, especially if the third party is a bank, every effort should be made to define the location of them. Therefore, the plaintiff should attempt to indicate which bank holds the accounts in question specifying, if possible, the branches and account numbers. Where a defendant has a joint account with another person or persons, a bank will generally not know in what proportion the amounts standing to the credit of the

---

[80a] But see the discussion and disapproval of the use of this phrase by Lord Donaldson M.R. in *Derby & Co. Ltd.* v. *Weldon (Nos. 3 & 4)* [1989] 2 W.L.R. 412 at 425.

[81] *Z Ltd.* v. *A-Z* (*supra*), *per* Kerr L.J. at p. 586.

[82] Evidence given in *Z Ltd.* v. *A-Z* (*supra*) suggested that a "full trawl" through all the branches of a clearing bank could cost as much as £2,000.

[83] The undertaking which the plaintiff must give to pay the expenses of a bank or other third party which they incur in complying with a Mareva injunction is called a "Seatrain" proviso from the case *Searose Ltd.* v. *Seatrain (UK) Ltd.* [1981] 1 W.L.R. 894.

account have been provided by the defendant and the other account holders respectively. Therefore, as the other account holders cannot be subjected to such orders any notice of a Mareva injunction served on a bank should not be applicable to joint accounts unless the order unequivocally so provides. Such an order will rarely be justified.[84]

The Mareva injunction originated as a means by which a foreign-based defendant could be prevented from dissipating or removing his assets overseas to defeat an order of an English court.[85] As we have seen, subsequent development and clarification of the injunction has meant that it will lie equally against an English-based defendant who is likely to dissipate his assets within the jurisdiction. For some time, however, it was unclear whether the English courts had the ability to make an order which has effect on assets of the defendant which are located abroad.[86] It is now clear, however, that English courts can grant a Mareva injunction covering a defendant's assets located in any part of the world but only in exceptional cases.[87] In the words of Kerr L.J.:

> "some situations . . . cry out—as a matter of justice to plaintiffs—for . . . Mareva type injunctions covering foreign assets of defendants even before judgment."[88]

The kind of circumstances which would lead a court to conclude that a case is an exceptional one and that such an order should be made are where for instance there is a very large sum involved, there are no or insufficient assets located in England whereas there is evidence of substantial assets existing abroad and where there are grounds for believing that the defendants may have acted dishonestly and that they have the ability to lock away assets in inaccessible overseas companies.

A worldwide Mareva injunction or one purporting to freeze assets outside the jurisdiction will not be made uncondi-

---

[84] See the judgment of Kerr L.J. in *Z Ltd.* v. *A-Z supra* at 586 *et seq.* generally for the position of banks in relation to Mareva injunctions.

[85] See *Iraqi Ministry of Defence* v. *Arcepey Shipping Co. S.A.* [1980] 2 W.L.R. 488 at 493.

[86] See, *e.g., Ashtiani* v. *Kashi* [1987] Q.B. 888.

[87] *Babanaft International Co. S.A.* v. *Bassatne* [1989] 2 W.L.R. 232; *Republic of Haiti* v. *Duvalier* [1989] 2 W.L.R. 261; *Derby & Co. Ltd.* v. *Weldon* [1989] 2 W.L.R. 276 and *Derby & Co. Ltd.* v. *Weldon (Nos. 3 & 4)* [1989] 2 W.L.R. 412. There had been some doubts as to whether this type of order could be made both before and after judgment, there being perhaps a stronger argument for a restraint order after judgment when the plaintiff has fully established his claim. However, it was held in *Republic of Haiti* v. *Duvalier* following *dicta* in *Babanaft* that the court also has jurisdiction to make a pre-judgment order. See also the discussion of the power of the courts to make "disclosure" orders ancillary to Mareva injunctions below.

[88] *Babanaft International Co. S.A.* v. *Bassatne (supra)* at 247.

tionally. This is because a Mareva injunction can have an effect on persons other than the defendant and it would be an exorbitant and improper assertion of extra-territorial jurisdiction for an English court to purport to make an order affecting third parties outside the jurisdiction. The court could insist that a proviso is inserted into the order which restricts its effect to the defendant only and expressly excludes third parties from its scope. The problem with a clause of this type is clearly that it substantially reduces the practical usefulness of the order. As an alternative, the following proviso formulated by Lord Donaldson M.R. in *Derby & Co. Ltd.* v. *Weldon (Nos. 3 & 4)*[89] could be inserted.

> "Provided that, in so far as this order purports to have any extra-territorial effect, no person shall be affected thereby or concerned with the terms thereof *until it shall be declared enforceable or be enforced by a foreign court* and then it shall only affect them to the extent of such declaration or enforcement *unless* they are: (*a*) a person to whom this order is addressed or an officer of or an agent appointed by a power of attorney of such a person or (*b*) persons who are subject to the jurisdiction of this court and (i) have been given written notice of this order at their residence or place of business within the jurisdiction, and (ii) are able to prevent acts or omissions outside the jurisdiction of this court which assist in the breach of the terms of this order."[89a]

Part (b) of this clause is directed towards clarifying the position of English banks with branches abroad and foreign banks with branches in England both of whom are subject to the jurisdiction of the English court.[89b]

To increase the effectiveness of the Mareva injunction the court can order that the defendant make disclosure of the whereabouts and extent of his assets.[90] Orders for this type of disclosure are not made under Order 24, rule 1 because the documents which can be made the subject of discovery under that Order must relate "to matters in question in the action." Instead, the power to make this sort of ancillary order for disclosure is inherent and implicit in the power to grant an

---

[89] *Supra.*
[89a] *Supra* at 425 (emphasis added). Lord Donaldson M.R. was of the opinion that this was a preferable clause to the "Babanaft proviso" suggested in *Babanaft International Co. S.A.* v. *Bassatne (supra)*.
[89b] See *Derby & Co. Ltd.* v. *Weldon (Nos. 3 & 4) (supra)* at 425.
[90] See *A* v. *C (Note)* [1981] 2 W.L.R. 629.

injunction contained in section 37(1) of the Supreme Court Act 1981 from which the Mareva jurisdiction is itself derived.[91] The disclosure can be ordered either before[92] or after[93] judgment and it can be made against a defendant who has assets outside England and Wales as well as in those cases where he has assets within the jurisdiction.[94] The defendant can be required to attend for cross-examination on his affidavit and produce such books and documents as are in his possession and relevant to discovering the extent of his assets.[95]

Finally, in an appropriate case another ancillary order which a court might make is an injunction to restrain the defendant from leaving the jurisdiction.[96] However, since this form of order constitutes an interference with the liberty of the subject it should not run for longer than is necessary to give effect to the orders of the court.[97] For instance, an order might be appropriate restraining the defendant from leaving the jurisdiction until he has served an affidavit on the plaintiff's solicitors disclosing the nature and extent of his assets.[97a]

The courts have on occasion issued a writ *ne exeat regno* which can require the defendant to pay a stated sum and if he refuses or is unable to pay he can be arrested, detained and brought before the court.[98]

But following *Allied Arab Bank Ltd.* v. *Hajjar*[98a] it is unlikely that such orders will be made in the future. The court can only make this order if the absence of the defendant from England will materially prejudice the plaintiff in the prosecution of his action.[99] Leggatt J. held that this condition would not be

---

[91] *Bekhor & Co. Ltd.* v. *Bilton* [1981] Q.B. 923.

[92] *Republic of Haiti* v. *Duvalier* [1989] 2 W.L.R. 261.

[93] *Interpool Ltd.* v. *Galani* [1988] Q.B. 738 (although in this case the order for the examination of the defendant about his assets outside the jurisdiction was made under Order 48, see Chap. 24) *Maclaine Watson & Co. Ltd.* v. *International Tin Council (No. 2)* [1988] 3 W.L.R. 1190).

[94] The Court of Appeal has even held that this type of order can be made even though it is not ancillary to a Mareva injunction to aid execution where Order 48 could not apply: *Maclaine Watson Co. Ltd.* v. *ITC (No. 2)* (*supra*). See (1989) L.M.C.L.Q. 465 (P. Kaye).

[95] *House of Spring Gardens* v. *Waite* [1985] S.J. 64. The defendant will only enjoy the privilege against self-incrimination in respect of offences and penalties provided for by United Kingdom law as s.14(1) of the Civil Evidence Act 1968 makes clear. But the fact that certain disclosure may incriminate the defendant under the criminal law of a foreign state is a factor which can be taken into account in deciding whether and, if so, in what terms a disclosure order should be made: *Arab Monetary Fund* v. *Hashim* [1989] 3 All E.R. 466.

[96] *Bayer A.G.* v. *Winter* [1986] 1 W.L.R. 497; *Allied Arab Bank Ltd.* v. *Hajjar* [1988] Q.B. 787.

[97] *Allied Arab Bank Ltd.* v. *Hajjar* (*supra*), per Leggatt J. at 795.

[97a] *Arab Monetary Fund* v. *Hashim* [1989] 3 All E.R. 466.

[98] *Al Nahkel for Contracting and Trading Ltd.* v. *Lowe* [1986] Q.B. 235.

[98a] [1988] 1 Q.B. 787.

[99] See s.6 of the Debtors Act 1869 summarised by Megarry J. in *Felton* v. *Callis* [1969] 1 Q.B. 200.

satisfied where a plaintiff was seeking the order primarily for the purpose of enforcing the Mareva injunction and compelling the defendant to identify assets. A Mareva injunction is a remedy in aid of execution and not part of the prosecution of the action.

Anton Piller Orders

Under Order 29, rules 2 and 3, the High Court has the power to make an order for the detention, preservation or inspection of any property which is the subject of a dispute or about which questions may arise during the action and the court can authorise the person applying for such an order to enter upon the land of the defendant to carry out the order. A major limitation on this type of order is, however, that it can only be made following an *inter partes* application. It became clear that what a plaintiff needed was an effective interlocutory remedy against the danger that the defendant might destroy vital material in his possession before the action reached the stages of discovery or trial. Such a remedy appeared in 1974 when the courts exercised their inherent jurisdiction to develop a procedure whereby the defendant is prevented from frustrating the process of justice by destroying the subject-matter of an action or documents or other evidence relating thereto.[1]

This relief is known as the Anton Piller order after the case in which the Court of Appeal first gave consideration to the conditions under which such an order could be granted.[2] Broadly, it is an order which empowers the plaintiff to enter the defendant's premises and search for material relevant to his action. As such it is a mandatory interlocutory injunction which may now be granted pursuant to section 37 of the Supreme Court Act 1981. Although Anton Piller orders originated and are most common in the context of intellectual property disputes, the courts can grant them in any appropriate case.[3]

The order will usually be sought on an *ex parte* application by the plaintiff and quite possibly before the writ has even been

---

[1] *E.M.I. Ltd.* v. *Pandit* [1976] R.P.C. 333; *Anton Piller K.G.* v. *Manufacturing Processes Ltd.* [1976] 1 Ch. 55; *Universal City Studios Inc.* v. *Mukhtar & Sons Ltd.* [1976] 1 W.L.R. 568.

[2] *Anton Piller K.G.* v. *Manufacturing Processes Ltd.* (*supra*).

[3] *e.g.* in *Emanuel* v. *Emanuel* [1982] 1 W.L.R. 669 where an Anton Piller order was granted in the Family Division to assist a wife in her application for ancillary relief. The order was used to obtain details and documents relating to the husband's property and income where it was clear that the husband was ready to flout the authority of the court and to mislead it. Again, in *Yousif* v. *Salama* [1980] 1 W.L.R. 1540 an Anton Piller order was granted to obtain vital evidence in an agency dispute.

issued. The court will normally sit *in camera* when the application is heard since it is essential to the effectiveness of the remedy that the defendant should not have advance notice of the application or the order and so be able to destroy the relevant material before the order can be executed.[4]

To obtain the order the plaintiff must satisfy the court that he has an extremely strong prima facie case on the merits of his claim, that he is likely to suffer very serious actual or potential damage from the defendant's actions, that there is clear evidence that the defendant has incriminating documents or articles in his possession and that there is a grave danger that the defendant will smuggle away or destroy this material before an application *inter partes* can be made.[5] The plaintiff must state his case to the court when applying for the order since he should not use this procedure as a "fishing expedition" to enable him to find out what charges and allegations he can make against the defendant.[6]

If the plaintiff can satisfy these conditions the court will grant appropriate relief in the form of injunctions directed to the defendant, breach of which will put the defendant in contempt of court and so make him liable to committal.

The order will include a direction to the defendant that he permit the plaintiff to enter the defendant's premises, to search for goods or documents belonging to the plaintiff or which are relevant to his claim, and to remove, inspect, photograph or make copies of such material according to the circumstances of the case. In addition the defendant may be ordered to disclose to the plaintiff the names and addresses of his suppliers (for example of goods which infringe the plaintiff's patent or copyright),[7] or customers (including persons to whom the defendant has passed on confidential information belonging to the plaintiff),[8] and to give inspection of documents relevant to such transactions.

---

[4] See *Vapormatic Co. Ltd.* v. *Sparex Ltd.* [1976] 1 W.L.R. 939.

[5] *Anton Piller* (*supra*), *per* Ormrod L.J. at p. 62; *Vapormatic Co. Ltd.* v. *Sparex Ltd.* (*supra*). And if the plaintiff on an *ex parte* application fails to make full disclosure to the court of all material facts he knew or should have known, the order may be discharged without investigation of the merits and even if the failure to disclose resulted from an error of judgment and was not deliberate: *Thermax Ltd.* v. *Schott Industrial Glass Ltd.* [1981] F.S.R. 289. See also the corresponding cases on the effects of non-disclosure in the context of *Mareva* injunctions: *Brink's-Mat Ltd.* v. *Elcombe* [1988] 1 W.L.R. 1350.

[6] *Hytrac Conveyors* v. *Conveyors International Ltd.* [1983] 1 W.L.R. 44.

[7] *E.M.I.* v. *Sarwar* [1977] F.S.R. 146.

[8] *Vapormatic Co. Ltd.* v. *Sparex Ltd.* (*supra*).

Clearly this is a draconian power[9] and proper safeguards for the defendant should be insisted upon by the courts.[10] The order must specify precisely what the defendant is required to do,[11] what premises are to be entered[12] and the persons to whom articles or documents are to be delivered up. The order should be drawn so as to extend no further than the minimum extent necessary to achieve the proper purpose for which it was granted, namely the preservation of documents or articles which might otherwise be destroyed or concealed.[13] The order should be executed with circumspection by the plaintiff's solicitor who is an officer of the court. He should explain the order to the defendant who should be given an opportunity to contact his solicitor. It is clear that if the defendant refuses entry, the plaintiff is not entitled to use force. In that sense the order is not a search warrant.[14] The defendant will be in contempt of court by refusing permission to enter but, if he applies subsequently on an *inter partes* application for the order to be discharged and succeeds, it appears that he will not be liable to any penalty.[15] Donaldson M.R. has indicated with clarity the dilemma in which defendants may find themselves:

" . . . defendants who take this line do so very much at their peril. If they succeed in getting the order discharged, all well and good. But if they fail, they will render themselves liable to penalties for contempt of court."[16]

The problem for the defendant is that to allow the execution of an Anton Piller order and then to challenge it may not serve

---

[9] *Per* Donaldson L.J. in *Yousif* v. *Salama* [1980] 1 W.L.R. 1540, 1544.

[10] See Scott J. in *Columbia Picture Industries Inc.* v. *Robinson* [1986] 3 W.L.R. 542 who considers the Anton Piller jurisdiction and the consequences of making an order generally. He expresses some disquiet concerning the frequency with which Anton Piller orders are applied for and granted bearing in mind that in the *Anton Piller* case itself Ormrod L.J. had stated that these orders were at the extremity of the court's powers and bearing in mind also the damaging and irreversible consequences they can have on a defendant and his business following an *ex parte* application.

[11] See generally *Anton Piller* (*supra*); *Universal City Studios* v. *Mukhtar* (*supra*) at 571.

[12] An order will not generally be made for entry to premises described only in general terms, *e.g.* "any other premises under the control of the defendant," because the lack of precision may lead to argument and a danger of a breach of the peace: *Protector Alarms Ltd.* v. *Maxim Alarms Ltd.* [1978] F.S.R. 442 (Goulding J.).

[13] *Per* Scott J. in *Columbia Picture Industries Inc.* v. *Robinson* (*supra*) at 371.

[14] *Anton Piller* (*supra*).

[15] *Per* Buckley L.J. in *Hallmark Cards Inc.* v. *Image Arts Ltd.* [1977] F.S.R. 150, 153. The judge granting the order should not normally discharge it on an application *ex parte* by the defendant, particularly where the application is unsupported by sworn evidence: *ibid.*

[16] *W.E.A. Records Ltd.* v. *Visions Channel 4 Ltd.* [1983] 1 W.L.R. 721, 724.

any useful purpose since the defendant will have already suffered the harm and the courts may be reluctant in any case to revoke the order if this would be pointless and an empty gesture.[17] The defendant may nevertheless wish to challenge the granting of the order if he seeks to retrieve any material which was retained by the plaintiff.[18]

An Anton Piller order should not purport to authorise the plaintiff's solicitors to take and retain all relevant documentary material. Further, the procedure should be that stated by Scott J. in *Columbia Picture Industries* v. *Robinson*:[19]

> "[o]nce the plaintiff's solicitors have satisfied themselves what material exists and have had an opportunity to take copies thereof, the material ought in my opinion, to be returned to its owner. The material need be retained no more than a relatively short period for that purpose."

In addition a detailed record should be kept of any material that is removed from the defendant's premises.[20]

Where material is seized, the ownership of which is in dispute,[21] it is not appropriate that the property should be held by the plaintiff's solicitors pending trial. The reason is that the plaintiff's solicitors, although officers of the court, are engaged to act in the best interests of the plaintiffs. It follows that, if the proper administration of justice does require the material to be withheld from the defendants under an Anton Piller order it should be delivered to the defendant's solicitors on their giving an undertaking to keep it in safe custody and to produce it when necessary in court.[22]

When obtaining the order the plaintiff will normally be required to give an undertaking in damages to compensate the

---

[17] *Per* Scott J. in *Columbia Picture Industries Inc.* v. *Robinson* (*supra*) at 379.

[18] The proper procedure for challenging an Anton Piller order, since it is made *ex parte*, is that laid down in Order 32, r. 6. Any application for a discharge or variation should be made first to the judge who originally made the order so he can review his decision in the light of argument put forward by the defendant. If an appeal is then made to the Court of Appeal this will normally be heard in open court unless counsel is of the opinion that a hearing *in camera* is necessary in the interests of justice. In this case he can apply to the registrar in writing and a preliminary decision will be made on this issue: Practice Note [1982] 1 W.L.R. 1420.

In determining whether the Anton Piller order was properly granted the court can take into account not only the evidence put before the court at the *ex parte* stage but also material obtained as a result of the search in the execution of the order: *W.E.A. Records Ltd.* v. *Visions Channel 4 Ltd.*, *supra.*

[19] [1986] 3 W.L.R. 542.

[20] *Ibid.* at 371.

[21] Such as allegedly pirate video or audio tapes.

[22] *Columbia Picture Industries Inc.* v. *Robinson* (*supra*) at 371, 372.

defendant for any loss caused should the plaintiff's claim fail. Although the damages awarded under this undertaking will be primarily compensatory the court can, if it feels that the Anton Piller order has been executed in an excessive or oppressive manner, award aggravated damages. Further, even exemplary damages may be appropriate since the solicitor executing the order is an officer of the court and therefore analogous to a servant of the government against whom such damages are awarded if they act in an oppressive, arbitrary or unconstitutional manner.[23]

There will also be an undertaking which may be express but, if not, will in any case be implied, that material or information gained in consequence of the order will not be used by the plaintiff for any purpose other than the action in which the order is given. This principle is derived from cases on discovery.[24] The plaintiff's undertaking, which is given to the court, can, however, be discharged in appropriate circumstances at the discretion of the court.[25]

An Anton Piller order can be obtained for a similar purpose to that of a *Norwich Pharmacal* order, *i.e.* for the purpose of obtaining information which is to be used subsequently to pursue actions against third parties. These are in essence actions for discovery and are a different species of action. Here it seems that there can be no implied undertaking to the court that the information obtained will only be used for the purpose of an existing action and so the plaintiff can use the material and information without first seeking the leave of the court.[26]

As regards the rights of third parties to use or inspect material obtained under an Anton Piller order, especially with a view to pursuing possible criminal offences, the position is still largely governed by the express or implied undertakings of the plaintiffs or their solicitors. Therefore, in *General Nutrition Ltd.* v. *Pradip Pattni*[27] the plaintiffs asked the court for leave to make available to the police copies of documents which came to light following an Anton Piller search. This request was refused. The fact that an offence may have been committed did not justify a departure from the general rule. However, in *Customs & Excise Commissioners* v. *A.E. Hamlin & Co.*,[28] solicitors

---

[23] *Ibid.* at 379. See also Lord Devlin in *Rookes* v. *Barnard* [1964] A.C. 1129.
[24] *Riddick* v. *Thames Board Mills Ltd.* [1977] Q.B. 881.
[25] *Crest Homes plc* v. *Marks* [1987] A.C. 829.
[26] *Sony Corporation* v. *Anand* [1981] F.S.R. 398. The distinction was also observed in *Roberts* v. *Jump Knitwear Ltd.* [1981] F.S.R. 527.
[27] [1984] F.S.R. 403.
[28] [1984] 1 W.L.R. 509.

who were holding documents which had been obtained on the execution of an Anton Piller order were compelled to allow the Customs and Excise Commissioners to examine and take copies of the documents in connection with the Commissioners' investigation of the defendants' liability to value added tax. Although the Commissioners could not examine and copy the documents under their statutory rights of inspection without the leave of the court, Falconer J. was of the opinion that such leave would normally be given in a case such as this. In *EMI Records Ltd.* v. *Spillane*[29], however, Sir Nicolas Browne-Wilkinson V.-C., in a similar case, disagreed and expressed the better view that it would be quite wrong to authorise the use of documents obtained under an Anton Piller order "in criminal proceedings brought under fiscal laws and having no connection with the original cause of action."

In 1981, the decision in *Rank Film Distributors Ltd.* v. *Video Information Centre*[30] revealed an important defect in the Anton Piller procedure. At common law, generally speaking, a person cannot be compelled to produce documents or to answer questions in civil proceedings, if such production or answers would have a tendency to expose him to a real risk of prosecution for a criminal offence or to proceedings for a penalty. In this case the defendants to an action for breach of copyright successfully sought the discharge of that part of an Anton Piller order which ordered them to disclose the names and addresses of their suppliers of and customers for illicit copies of the plaintiffs' films, and to produce documents relating to such illicit copies, on the ground that compliance would tend to expose them to proceedings for a criminal offence, namely conspiracy to defraud at common law. The House of Lords held that the privilege against self-incrimination was capable of being invoked in such a case, and accordingly it appeared that the court should not make an *ex parte* order compelling disclosure of documents or the answering of interrogatories where the plaintiffs' evidence indicated that such an order would put the defendant in danger of self-incrimination.

This decision had serious implications for a plaintiff, since a large part of the utility of the Anton Piller procedure is that it can enable him to track down the supply and distribution networks of articles and material which infringe his rights.[31]

---

[29] [1986] 1 W.L.R. 967.
[30] [1981] 2 W.L.R. 668; [1982] A.C. 380.
[31] See *Rank Film Distributors Ltd.* v. *Video Information Centre* (*supra*) at pp. 668 and 672 (Lord Wilberforce), 677 (Lord Fraser); *Sony Corporation* v. *Anand* (*supra*).

Where the defendant is privileged from disclosing the relevant information, on the ground that he is entitled to protect himself from possible criminal charges of conspiracy, the plaintiff is left simply with the power to inspect the defendant's premises and to remove, photograph, etc., any infringing material he may find. This may stop only one outlet for what may be an extensive operation of piracy of the plaintiff's patent, copyright, registered design and so on.

The full efficiency of the Anton Piller order was, however, almost immediately restored by section 72 of the Supreme Court Act 1981. This provides as follows:

(1) In any proceedings to which this subsection applies a person shall not be excused, by reason that to do so would tend to expose that person, or his or her spouse, to proceedings for a related offence or for the recovery of a related penalty—

    (*a*) from answering any question put to that person in the first-mentioned proceedings; or

    (*b*) from complying with any order made in those proceedings.

(2) Subsection (1) applies to the following civil proceedings in the High Court, namely—

    (*a*) proceedings for infringement of rights pertaining to any intellectual property or for passing off;

    (*b*) proceedings brought to obtain disclosure of information relating to any infringement of such rights to any passing off; and

    (*c*) proceedings brought to prevent any apprehended infringement of such rights or any apprehended passing off.

The effect of this provision is thus to withdraw the privilege against self-incrimination in the proceedings to which the section applies and it will cover any order for the discovery and production of relevant information and documents concerning the defendant's suppliers and customers.

The offences which the defendant may be exposed to and which are described in subsection (1) as "related offences" and in respect of which the privilege against self-incrimination is removed are defined in subsection (5) as:

    (*a*) in the case of proceedings within subsection (2)(*a*) or (*b*)—

    (i) any offence committed by or in the course of the infringement or passing off to which those proceedings relate; or

    (ii) any offence not within sub-paragraph (i) committed in connection with that infringement or passing off, being an offence involving fraud or dishonesty;

  (*b*) in the case of proceedings within subsection (2)(*c*), any offence revealed by the facts on which the plaintiff relies in those proceedings;

The scope of this definition was considered by the Court of Appeal in *Universal City Studios Inc.* v. *Hubbard*.[32] Here the plaintiffs' solicitors removed certain documents and other material from the defendant's premises during the execution of an Anton Piller order. It was alleged that the defendant had infringed the plaintiffs' copyright in a number of films. The defendant then applied for the Anton Piller order to be set aside and for all the material to be returned to him. The defendant's argument was that the material which had been taken and the answers which he would be required to give to the plaintiffs about it would tend to incriminate him in the offence of manufacturing pornographic films under the Obscene Publications Act 1959 as opposed to an intellectual property or a "related offence" within subsection (5) and that therefore section 72 did not operate to remove his privilege against self-incrimination. The Court of Appeal rejected this argument and favoured a wide interpretation of "any offence" in subsection (5)(*b*) in relation to any proceedings brought to prevent any *apprehended* infringement of intellectual property rights. This was because it was the policy of Parliament to deny the defendant the privilege against self-incrimination for offences not committed by or in the course of or in connection with the alleged infringement (for example the alleged Obscene Publications offences here) where there was a risk of further damage to a plaintiff.

    The defendant is protected to some extent from the consequences of withdrawal of the privilege by section 72(3) and (4), which provide in effect that no statement or admission made by him in response to an order of the court in the relevant civil proceedings shall be admissible in evidence against him in criminal proceedings for a related offence,

---

[32] [1984] Ch. 225.

unless the criminal proceedings are for perjury or contempt of court.

References to the European Court

A question may arise in an action in the High Court[33] as to the interpretation of any of the provisions of the Treaty of Rome, or as to the validity or interpretation of any acts of the institutions of the European Economic Community. In such a case the Treaty of Rome, which has direct legal effect in the United Kingdom [34] provides for a reference to be made to the European Court of Justice in Luxembourg for a ruling on the question. The relevant provision of the EEC Treaty is Article 177.[35]

> "(1) The Court of Justice shall have jurisdiction to give preliminary rulings concerning:
>   (a) the interpretation of this Treaty;
>   (b) the validity and interpretation of acts of the institutions of the Community;
>   (c) the interpretation of the statutes of bodies established by an act of the Council, where those statutes so provide.
> (2) Where such a question is raised before any court or tribunal of a Member State, that court or tribunal may, if it considers that a decision on the question is necessary to enable it to give judgment, request the Court of Justice to give a ruling thereon.
> (3) Where any such question is raised in a case pending before a court or tribunal of a Member State, against whose decisions there is no judicial remedy under national law, that court or tribunal shall bring the matter before the Court of Justice."

The procedure for the making of references by the High Court, or the Court of Appeal, is set out in Order 114. The order referring a question to the European Court may be made by the Court in England[36] at any stage of the cause or matter, and it

---

33 Such questions may of course arise in other courts also, and the power to refer questions extends to any court or tribunal of the U.K. (Article 177(2), *infra*).
34 European Communities Act 1972, s.2(1).
35 Requests for rulings may also be made in respect of the Treaties establishing the European Atomic Energy Community (Article 150 of the Euratom Treaty) and the European Coal and Steel Community (Article 41 of the ECSC Treaty).
36 In the High Court the order may only be made by a judge in person: r. 2(3).

can be made either on the Court's own motion or on the application of a party before or at the trial of the action.[37] The order making the reference will set out in a schedule the request for the preliminary ruling, and the schedule is prepared under the directions of the Court.[38] The Senior Master acts as the channel of communication with the European Court for sending the request and receiving the ruling.[39] Where a reference is made in any proceedings, those proceedings are stayed[40] until the European Court has given a preliminary ruling on the question referred to it. An order by the High Court making a reference is deemed to be a final decision, so that an appeal will lie to the Court of Appeal without leave, but notice of appeal must be served within 14 days.[41] However, a refusal to make a reference is regarded as an interlocutory order, and leave is then needed to appeal against the judge's decision.[42]

Article 177 creates both a power and a duty to refer questions within the scope of sub-article (1) to the European Court. A discretionary *power* is given by sub-article (2) to all courts and tribunals of the Member State, but this power appears to be subject to sub-article (3), which imposes a mandatory *duty* to refer on any court or tribunal against whose decisions there is no judicial remedy under national law. In *H.P. Bulmer Ltd.* v. *J. Bollinger SA*[43] Lord Denning M.R. expressed the view that sub-article (3) applied solely to the House of Lords as the final court of appeal in England, and that no other English court was bound to refer a question to the European Court.[44] However, since there is no *right* of appeal without leave to the House of Lords from the Court of Appeal, it might be argued that, at least in cases where leave to appeal is refused, the Court of Appeal is itself the final court for the purposes of sub-article (3). Stephenson L.J., with whom Stamp L.J. agreed, preferred not to decide this point without further argument.[45] Accordingly, it may be premature to regard the point as settled, and one writer has suggested[46] that it would itself be an appropriate

[37] r. 2(1).
[38] r. 3.
[39] r. 5.
[40] Unless the English Court orders otherwise; see r. 4.
[41] r. 6.
[42] *H.P. Bulmer Ltd.* v. *J. Bollinger SA* [1974] Ch. 401, 402, *per* Lord Denning M.R.; *Supreme Court Practice 1991*, para. 114/1–6/8, 20.
[43] *Supra.*
[44] [1974] Ch. 401, at p. 420.
[45] *Ibid.* p. 430.
[46] E. Freeman, "References to the Court of Justice under Article 177" [1975] C.L.P. 176 at p. 186.

question for the European Court whether the Court of Appeal falls within sub-article (3).

The principles governing the exercise of the discretionary power to make or refuse an order of reference were fully considered by Lord Denning M.R. in *H.P. Bulmer Ltd.* v. *J. Bollinger SA.* He emphasised that before a reference could be made a condition precedent under Article 177 had to be fulfilled. This condition was that the English court had power to refer only if it considered that a ruling on the question arising was *necessary* to enable it to give judgment. A number of factors were then said to be relevant in considering whether a ruling was "necessary."

It was important that first of all the facts of the case should either have been determined or else not be in dispute. Otherwise it might turn out, when the facts were investigated later, that it was unnecessary to decide the community law question, or that other questions arose. Thus in *DDSA Pharmaceuticals Ltd.* v. *Farbwerke Hoechst AG*[47] Whitford J. held that an application to refer a question concerning the validity of conditions in certain licences, the application having been made on the same day as the originating summons in the action was issued, was premature; it was unclear at that stage, before the exchange of pleadings, what the facts and questions in issue between the parties were.

Secondly, the question to be referred should be conclusive of the case before the English court. That is, the case should not be capable of being decided without a ruling on the question, and the ruling should be decisive one way or the other, so that nothing would remain except for the English court to give judgment. In *Van Duyn* v. *Home Office*[48] Pennycuick V.-C. referred a question concerned with the free movement of workers within the EEC, saying that without a ruling on the question, it would be "quite impossible" to give judgment. Similarly, on an interlocutory application in proceedings for the infringement of a trade mark,[49] Graham J. referred a point to the European Court, saying that if the defendants succeeded in their argument on the point they would have a complete defence, whereas, if they failed, the plaintiffs would be entitled to succeed on the admitted facts.

A third factor indicated by Lord Denning M.R. was that a ruling would not be "necessary" where the English court

---

[47] [1975] 2 C.M.L.R. 50.
[48] [1974] 1 W.L.R. 1107.
[49] *E.M.I. Records Ltd.* v. *C.B.S. United Kingdom Ltd.* [1976] R.P.C. 1. *R.* v. *Plymouth Justices, ex p. Rogers* [1982] 3 C.M.L.R. 221. *Polydor* v. *Harlequin Record Shops Ltd.* [1982] 3 C.M.L.R. 413, C.A.

considered the point to be reasonably clear and free from doubt. In such a case there was no need to interpret the Treaty but only to apply it, and the latter task was exclusively one for the national court. This doctrine originated in France under the name "acte claire"[50]; it has been criticised[51] as being unduly restrictive of the operation of Article 177, which seeks to minimise the possibilities of inconsistent interpretations of community law by national courts. However, the doctrine now seems to be accepted as one of the principles guiding English courts in their use of the power under Article 177.[52]

Lord Denning M.R. indicated a fourth and final guideline on whether a ruling was necessary, namely whether there was a previous ruling of the European Court on substantially the same point. If the point had been previously decided, then the English court could follow the ruling even though it was not obliged to do so. The English court could follow the ruling even though it was necessary to re-submit the point to the European Court for further consideration; this could happen where the earlier decision was thought to be wrong, or where new factors had arisen since the earlier decision.

The discretion of the English Court does not end with the decision on whether a ruling is "necessary" to enable the court to give judgment. In *H.P. Bulmer Ltd.* v. *J. Bollinger SA*[53] Lord Denning M.R. made it clear that, even where the "necessary" condition is fulfilled, the English court has a discretion whether to decide the point of validity or interpretation itself or to refer it to the European Court. He then suggested that in exercising this discretion the courts should take into account such matters as (i) the delay involved in obtaining a ruling from the European Court; (ii) the importance of not overloading the court with references; (iii) the need for clarity in the formulation of the question for the court; (iv) the difficulty and importance of the point to be referred; (v) the expense involved, and (vi) the wishes of the parties. This list of factors does not command universal assent as being either entirely correct or complete. In *Van Duyn* v. *Home Office*[54] Pennycuick V.-C. doubted whether overburdening the European Court was a legitimate consideration, and the European Court itself has made it clear that it does not regard itself as tied by the

---

[50] See the cases cited at [1974] Ch. 401, p. 423.
[51] See Freeman, *op. cit.*, pp. 188, 195.
[52] In the *E.M.I. Records* case Graham J. was careful to say that the point at issue was not a simple one, and did not fall within the principle of "acte claire."
[53] *Supra.*
[54] [1974] 3 All E.R. 178, 187.

form of the question referred to it.[55] A further factor, which weighed heavily with Graham J. in *EMI Records Ltd.* v. *CBS United Kingdom Ltd.*,[56] is the existence of parallel actions in other EEC countries. The learned judge in that case thought that it was desirable to obtain a ruling on the point at issue as soon as possible to avoid posible conflicting decisions in the various national courts. This factor is likely to be of particular importance in other cases concerned with industrial and intellectual property in the EEC.

As Order 114, r. 2(1) makes clear, the English court may make an order of reference at any stage of the proceedings. However, given the principle that a reference should not be ordered until the facts have been determined, this will mean in practice that applications for a reference will rarely be appropriate before the trial of the action has taken place. In some cases, though, it may emerge well before trial that there are no outstanding issues of fact or national law between the parties, for example, after close of pleadings or in interlocutory proceedings for discretionary relief such as an injunction. In these exceptional cases the parties and their advisors should consider an early application for a reference to the European Court if the ruling on the point at issue will be decisive.

In *Factortame Ltd. and others* v. *Secretary of State for Transport*[57] the House of Lords held that a national court has no power to make an order postponing the coming into force of a statute pending a reference to the European Court to determine its validity or to grant an interim injunction against the Crown which would have the effect of restraining enforcement of the statute. The House referred to the European Court the question whether, irrespective of the position under national law, there was an overriding principle of community law that a national court is under an obligation to provide an effective interlocutory remedy to protect rights having direct effect under community law. The European Court ruled[58] that when a national court is seised of a case concerning community law and considers that it is precluded from granting interim relief in the case solely because of a rule of national law, the national court is obliged to set aside the rule of national law.[59]

---

[55] *Bosch* v. *de Geus* [1962] C.M.L.R. 1; *Deutsche Grammophon Gesellschaft* v. *Metro-SB-Grossmärkte GmbH & Co. KG* [1971] C.M.L.R. 631.
[56] [1976] R.P.C. 1.
[57] [1990] 2 A.C. 85.
[58] See *The Times*, June 20, 1990.
[59] Following this ruling, the House of Lords granted an interim injunction: see *The Times*, October 12, 1990.

CHAPTER 5

SUMMARY PROCEEDINGS

Two types of summary proceedings will be dealt with in this chapter, summary judgment under Order 14, and summary proceedings for the possession of land under Order 113.

Procedure under Order 14

Order 14 makes provision for a plaintiff to obtain summary judgment upon his claim or part of his claim without the delay and expense of a trial and its preliminaries if he can show to the satisfaction of a master or a judge that there can be no answer to his case. The nature of Order 14 proceedings has been described with clarity by Parker L.J. in the recent decision of the Court of Appeal in *Home and Overseas Insurance Co. Ltd. v. Mentor Insurance Co. (U.K.) Ltd. (in liq.)*[1]:

> "The purpose of Order 14 is to enable a plaintiff to obtain a quick judgment where there is plainly no defence to the claim. If the defendant's only suggested defence is a point of law and the court can see at once that the point is misconceived the plaintiff is entitled to judgment. If at first sight the point appears to be arguable but with a relatively short argument can be shown to be plainly unsustainable the plaintiff is also entitled to judgment. But Order 14 proceedings should not . . . be allowed to become, in effect, an immediate trial of an action, which will be the case if the court lends itself to determining on Order 14 applications points of law which may take hours or even days and the citation of many authorities before the court is in a position to arrive at a final decision."

The importance of order 14 is indicated by the fact that in 1989 more than 5,000 cases were disposed of under the procedure in the Queen's Bench Division.

Origin and Present Scope of Order 14

The object of a debtor in a vast number of cases is not necessarily to defeat his creditor altogether but to gain time,

---

[1] [1989] 3 All E.R. 74 at p. 77. Lloyd and Balcombe L.JJ. agreed. See also the informative judgment of Neill L.J. in *C. E. Heath plc* v. *Ceram Holding Co. and Others* [1989] 1 All E.R. 203 C.A., the decision in which is negatived by Ord. 15, r. 3(5A), added in 1989. In *British and Commonwealth Holdings plc* v. *Quadrex Holdings Inc.* [1989] 3 All E.R. 492 at p. 512, Browne-Wilkinson V.-C. said: "Order 14 procedure is for clear cases and not for complicated cases which absorb many days to unravel."

which may work grave injustice to the creditor. Before the middle of the nineteenth century a defendant sued in the plainest of plain cases—*e.g.* for the price of goods sold and delivered or upon a dishonoured cheque—had merely to put upon the record a plea, no matter how devoid of merits or remote from the actual facts, and the case had to go for trial with all the delay and expense necessarily involved. At the trial the defendant very often did not appear. Eventually the bankers and other holders of bills in the City of London complained so vigorously that in 1855 the Summary Procedure on Bills of Exchange Act ("Keating's Act") was passed. In cases to which that Act applied the defendant had to get leave to appear, which he could only do by paying the money into court or setting out his defence in an affidavit. By the Judicature Act 1873 and later by the Rules of the Supreme Court 1883 the procedure was extended to cover cases where the plaintiff sought to recover a debt or liquidated demand in money and actions for the recovery of land. In 1937 the procedure became additionally applicable so far as the Queen's Bench Division only is concerned to all actions except libel, slander, malicious prosecution, false imprisonment, and actions in which fraud is alleged by the plaintiff. Since January 1, 1964, the procedure has been available with the same exceptions in all actions commenced by writ in the Queen's Bench or Chancery Division,[2] and is available not only to a plaintiff but also to a counterclaiming defendant. It was then also extended so as to enable application to be made for judgment on part only of a claim or counterclaim. This was a radical departure from the old rule, which presupposed that if the plaintiff succeeded the expense of a trial would be avoided altogether.

It is only after a defendant has given notice of intention to defend the action that a plaintiff can ask for summary judgment. And there are many cases in which he should not ask for it. He should remember that Order 14 is only intended to apply to cases where there is no substantial dispute as to the facts or

---

[2] Except actions for specific performance, etc. for which an analogous procedure is provided by Ord. 86. Order 14 does apply to a claim for an injunction (see, *e.g. Cadogan* v. *Muscatt, The Times,* May 15, 1990, where a mandatory injunction was granted) but the summons for summary judgment must be issued before the Judge in Chambers. The master has no power normally to grant an injunction except in terms agreed by the parties (Ord. 32, rr. 11, 14). The procedure is applicable to an action for damages for breach of contract or breach of fiduciary duty in which the allegations against the defendant carry an implication of fraud or deceit, provided there is no specific claim for fraud. See *Newton Chemical Ltd.* v. *Anseris,* [1989] 1 W.L.R. 1297, C.A. Order 14 is not applicable to an Admiralty action *in rem* (r. 1(2)(c)), but see *The August 8* [1983] 2 A.C. 450.

the law. Actions for damages for negligence are not normally suitable for the procedure unless it is clearly established that there is no defence as to liability.[3] If he applies for summary judgment where there is an obvious defence, his summons may be dismissed with costs. And seeing that he is applying for judgment without a trial it behoves him to have his case strictly in order in all respects.

Before applying for judgment on part of a claim or on a counterclaim it is wise to consider carefully not only whether the application can technically succeed but also whether, if successful, it will produce any substantially useful result. If there is bound to be a trial of the major issues in dispute, the small advantage of obtaining a preliminary judgment upon some unimportant part of the claim may not be worth the expense of the application. Again, although a defendant may be entitled to summary judgment on a counterclaim, justice may require that execution thereon be stayed until the plaintiff's claim is tried. In some cases the claim of the plaintiff may afford a good defence by way of set–off to the defendant's counterclaim. Useless applications may be discouraged by the appropriate exercise of the master's discretion as to costs.

The procedure under Order 14 is as follows:

After the defendant, or any particular defendant against whom the application is intended to be made, has given notice of intention to defend the action and the plaintiff has served a statement of claim upon him, the plaintiff takes out a summons[4] before a master for leave to enter judgment either for the whole claim or for some particular part of the claim. The application should be made promptly; but it may be made even after service of a defence, if the plaintiff can satisfactorily explain the delay[5] and show that the defence cannot hold water. A defendant who has served a counterclaim on the plaintiff may make a similar application against the plaintiff under Order 14, r. 5 or, since 1989, against a co-defendant or additional party under Order 15, r. 3(5A). The summons in either case must be supported by an affidavit verifying the facts on which the claim (or part) is based and stating that in the deponent's belief there is no defence to it (except as to the amount of damages, if damages are claimed[6]). Formerly the

---

[3] See *Dummer v. Brown* [1953] 1 Q.B. 710, where in somewhat exceptional circumstances the plaintiff was allowed to sign judgment for damages to be assessed in an action under the Fatal Accidents Acts.

[4] See Precedent No. 52.

[5] *McLardy v. Slateum* (1890) 24 Q.B.D. 504.

[6] See *Dummer v. Brown (ante)*. Precedent No. 53.

affidavit had to be made by the plaintiff or some other person who could swear positively to the facts. Since 1964 it has become permissible for it to contain statements of information or belief, provided that the sources of the information and the grounds of belief are stated; but it is within the master's discretion to require a further affidavit based on actual knowledge before he will give judgment. A copy of the affidavit and of any exhibits to it must be served with the summons and at least 10 clear days[7] must elapse between the day of service and the return day.

If the affidavit is sworn by an officer or servant of a limited company or by some other person on behalf of the plaintiff, it should show how far the facts are within the deponent's own knowledge and that he is authorised to make it.[8] It may verify the claim in general terms: it need not explicitly repeat every allegation made on the writ.[9] But all material facts (for example, an assignment) must be verified, a joint affidavit or more than one affidavit being made if necessary.[10] Defects in an affidavit may be cured by the filing of a further affidavit at the hearing[11]; but statements in an affidavit will not cure a defect in the statement of claim.[12]

The defendant may show cause against the application by stating his defence to the claim and showing that there is a real issue which ought to be tried. This is usually done by affidavit, though it is not absolutely essential if the master can be satisfied otherwise (Order 14, r. 4). He must state whether the defence alleged goes to the whole or to part only, and (if so) to what part, of the plaintiff's claim. If you appear against a dishonest defendant who puts in a vague affidavit admitting that something is due but seeking to evade a judgment against him by avoiding any actual mention of figures, your proper course is to ask the master to adjourn the matter for the defendant to file a further affidavit specifying in figures how much he admits. The master may, if he thinks fit, order the defendant, or in the case of a body corporate, any officer thereof, to produce any documents, or if there are special circumstances, to attend and be examined on oath (Order 14, r. 4(4)), though such orders are rarely made.[13]

[7] For the meaning of "clear days" see Chap. 6. The time for service of a summons under Ord. 14 is never abridged.

[8] *Chirgwin* v. *Russell* (1910) 27 T.L.R. 21; *Pathé Frères* v. *United Electric Theatres* [1914] 3 K.B. 1253.

[9] *May* v. *Chidley* [1894] 1 Q.B. 451.

[10] *Les Fils Dreyfus* v. *Clarke* [1958] 1 W.L.R. 300; [1958] 1 All E.R. 459.

[11] *Ibid.*

[12] *Gold Ores Reduction Co. Ltd.* v. *Pain* [1892] 2 Q.B. 14.

[13] See *Sullivan* v. *Henderson* [1973] 1 W.L.R. 333; [1973] 1 All E.R. 48.

At the hearing the master may give judgment; and he has a wide choice of other orders, the most common of which are often referred to by number; such as: Order No. 2 (unconditional leave to defend)[14]; Order No. 2A (leave to defend as short cause, see Chap. 18); Order No. 3 (leave to defend conditional upon payment of the whole claim into court, otherwise judgment for the amount claimed); Order No. 4 (leave to defend whole claim on bringing part into court; in default, judgment for that part; in any event leave to defend as to balance); Order No. 8 (leave to defend and trial before master by consent). The master may give leave to defend, either unconditionally, or subject to such terms as to payment into court of the whole or part of the claim, security for costs, time or mode of trial or otherwise as he may think fit (Order 14, r. 4(3)). Leave to defend ought to be given whenever there is an issue to be tried, even though the master may think the defendant will fail.[15] In such a case, however, he is not bound to give unconditional leave: he may impose conditions and has power to order an interim payment under Order 29, r. 10 when granting conditional leave to defend if the case is an appropriate one.[16] Where the conditions merely deal with matters of procedure, such as time and mode of trial, his discretion may be freely exercised; but where they deal with other matters, such as payment into court or giving security, they must not be prohibitive or have the practical effect of debarring the defendant from raising any triable issue which he may bona fide be entitled to raise, even though the master may think the circumstances are suspicious. In *M. V. Yorke Motors (a firm)* v. *Edwards*[17] the House of Lords held that the financial circumstances of the defendant are among the factors to be considered so that it would be a wrong exercise of discretion to grant the defendant leave to defend on condition that he should pay into court a sum that it would not be possible for him to obtain. If, however, there is a good ground on the evidence for believing that the so-called defence is a sham and it is a borderline case whether the plaintiff should not have judgment forthwith, it is proper to give leave to defend conditionally

---

[14] Where unconditional leave to defend is given the court has no power to make an order for an interim payment under Ord. 29, r. 10. (See *British and Commonwealth Holdings plc* v. *Quadrex Holdings Inc.* [1989] 3 All E.R. 492, C.A.; *Ricci Burns Ltd.* v. *Toole and Another* [1989] 3 All E.R. 478, C.A., not followed; *Shanning International Ltd.* v. *George Wimpey International Ltd.* [1988] 3 All E.R. 475, C.A., applied).

[15] *Codd* v. *Delap* (1905) 92 L.T. 510 (H.L.).

[16] See the *British and Commonwealth Holdings* case, *supra*.

[17] [1982] 1 W.L.R. 444; and see *Fieldrank Ltd.* v. *E. Stein* [1961] 1 W.L.R. 1287.

upon a payment into court of the amount claimed,[18] especially if it is clear that the defendant's assets will be dissipated and injustice done to the plaintiff if there is any delay. Such an order if complied with by the defendant places the plaintiff in the position of a secured creditor.[19] If the facts alleged by the defendant do not amount to a defence to the action, either in fact or law, the master will, as a rule, make an order that judgment be entered for the amount endorsed on the writ and, where pleaded, with interest. And as soon as the judgment is entered accordingly the plaintiff becomes a judgment creditor.[20]

Defendant Showing Cause

The defendant is not bound to show a good defence on the merits. He must however satisfy the master that "there is an issue or question in dispute which ought to be tried or that there ought for some other reason to be a trial" of the claim (rule 3). "If, therefore, the defendant shows such a state of facts as leads to the inference that at the trial of the action he may be able to establish a defence to the plaintiff's claim, he ought not to be debarred of all power to defeat the demand made upon him . . . and leave to defend may be granted either unconditionally or upon such terms as may be thought just."[21] Where a defence of a kind is set up by the defendant, but the master has good reason to doubt its good faith, he may order the defendant to pay money into court. But whenever a genuine defence, either in fact or law, sufficiently appears, the defendant is entitled to unconditional leave to defend.[22]

The defence must be stated with sufficient particularity to appear to be genuine. "You do not get leave to defend by putting forward a case that is all surmise and Micawberism."[23] A general statement, "I do not owe the money," or a vague suggestion of fraud or other misconduct on the part of the plaintiff, will not suffice. "General allegations, however strong may be the words in which they are stated, are insufficient to amount to an averment of fraud of which any court ought to take notice."[24] A technical defence, such as the Limitation Act

---

[18] See, *e.g. Ionian Bank Ltd.* v. *Couvreur* [1969] 1 W.L.R. 781.

[19] *Re Ford* [1900] 2 Q.B. 211.

[20] See *Re Gurney* [1896] 2 Ch. 863, decided under the former rule.

[21] *Per* Brett L.J. in *Ray* v. *Barker* (1879) 4 Ex.D. at p. 283.

[22] *Ward* v. *Plumbley* (1890) 6 T.L.R. 198; *Electric Corporation* v. *Thomson-Houston* (1893) 10 T.L.R. 103.

[23] *Per* Megarry V.-C. in *The Lady Anne Tennant* v. *Associated Newspapers Group Ltd.* [1979] F.S.R. 298.

[24] *Wallingford* v. *Mutual Society* (1880) 5 App.Cas. at p. 697; and see pp. 701, 704.

is sufficient. But it must be a defence. An affidavit merely pleading poverty, or showing hardship, or a remedy over against a third person, will not avail, though it may be a ground for a stay of execution (see Chapter 24).

The defendant may in answer to the plaintiff's claim rely upon a set-off or a counterclaim.[25] A true set-off is a defence to the action (see Chapter 14). Where the defendant relies upon a counterclaim various matters have to be considered. If the counterclaim arises out of the subject-matter of the action or may be treated as an equitable set-off,[26] leave to defend *pro tanto* should be given[27]; and if such a counterclaim overtops or may probably overtop the amount of the plaintiff's claim there will be leave to defend as to the whole, even though part of the plaintiff's claim is admitted. If the counterclaim has no connection with the plaintiff's cause of action, the plaintiff may be given leave to sign judgment on the claim, provided that he is clearly entitled to succeed upon it and would be put to unnecessary expense in having to prove it[28]; but it is within the discretion of the court to stay execution up to the anticipated amount of the counterclaim pending the trial of the counterclaim or further order. This it will ordinarily do if the counterclaim appears to be genuine; but it will not necessarily do so, particularly where the plaintiff is suing on a dishonoured bill of exchange or cheque or promissory note.[29] In such an action the plaintiff is normally entitled to judgment on his claim without a stay of execution, and the defendant will not be entitled to set up a set-off or counterclaim whether or not it is connected with the transaction in respect of which the bill or note was given. "We have repeatedly said in this court that a bill of exchange or a promissory note is to be treated as cash. It is to be honoured unless there is some good reason to the contrary, *e.g.* if there is an arguable case based on total failure of consideration."[30] But the court always has a discretion in the matter, and in an appropriate case where there appears to be a very real issue to be tried, leave to defend may be given conditionally on a payment into court by the defendant.[31]

---

[25] As has been mentioned (*ante*), it is also possible for a defendant to apply for summary judgment upon a counterclaim. But see *Express Newspapers plc* v. *News (UK) Ltd. and Others*, The Times, February 13, 1990.

[26] Chap. 14; *Morgan & Son Ltd.* v. *S. Martin Johnson & Co. Ltd.* [1949] 1 K.B. 107.

[27] See *Modern Engineering (Bristol) Ltd.* v. *Gilbert-Ash (Northern) Ltd.* [1974] A.C. 689.

[28] *Sheppards & Co.* v. *Wilkinson* (1889) 6 T.L.R. 13 (C.A.).

[29] *James Lamont Co. Ltd.* v. *Hyland Ltd.* [1950] 1 K.B. 585, 588.

[30] Per Lord Denning M.R. in *Fielding and Platt Ltd.* v. *Selim Najjar* [1969] 1 W.L.R. 357, at p. 361 (C.A.). And see *Jade Steel Ltd.* v. *Robert Nicholas (Steel) Ltd.* [1978] Q.B. 917, C.A.

[31] *Saga of Bond Street Ltd.* v. *Avalon Promotions Ltd.* [1972] 2 Q.B. 325.

If it appears that the defence set up by the defendant applies only to a part of the plaintiff's claim, or that any part of his claim is admitted, the plaintiff can have judgment forthwith for such part of his claim as is not covered by the defence or as is admitted, subject to such terms as the master may think fit (Order 14, r. 3); and the defendant may be allowed to defend as to the residue of the plaintiff's claim. If it appears to the master that any defendant has a good defence to the action, and that any other defendant has no good defence, he may give the former defendant leave to defend and give judgment against the latter. The plaintiff may thereupon issue execution upon such judgment without prejudice to his right to proceed with his action against the former defendant (r. 8). He may thus (as in the case of a default judgment) safely take judgment against one of several joint contractors. But this rule does not apply where the right of action can only be in the alternative against one or other of two defendants. In such a case judgment against one of the defendants is conclusive evidence of an election not to proceed against the other[32]; but until the judgment is drawn up and entered it may not be conclusive.[33]

Order 14 applies to actions for possession of land in which a tenant has forfeited his lease through non-payment of rent. But rule 10 of that Order expressly provides that such a tenant shall "have the same right to apply for relief after judgment for possession of land on the ground of forfeiture for non-payment of rent has been given under this Order as if the judgment had been given after trial"; that is, he will have the right to apply under section 210 of the Common Law Procedure Act 1852 if the rent is six months in arrear, to have the judgment set aside on payment of all rent in arrear and costs. Before judgment the tenant may stop the proceedings by tendering or paying into court the rent in arrear and costs (s.212); and relief may be given by the master in a summary manner pursuant to section 38 of the Supreme Court Act 1981 where the rent is not six months in arrear.[34]

Further Powers of the Master

The master has power, pursuant to the County Courts Act 1984, section 40, to order the transfer of the proceedings to the

---

[32] *Morel Brothers* v. *Earl of Westmorland* [1904] A.C. 11; *French* v. *Howie* [1906] 2 K.B. 674; *Moore* v. *Flanagan* [1920] 1 K.B. 919.
[33] Civil Liability (Contribution) Act 1978.
[34] *Standard Pattern Co. Ltd.* v. *Ivey* [1963] Ch. 432.

county court. This may be done of the court's own motion or in the application of any party in any case: (i) where the parties consent to the transfer; (ii) where the amount in issue is or is likely to be within the monetary jurisdiction of the county court; or (iii) where the proceedings are not likely to raise any important question of law or fact and are suitable for determination by a county court.[35]

If leave to defend is given and the action is transferred, the costs are ordinarily in the discretion of the county court.[36]

If the claim is unliquidated and the master is satisfied that there is no defence except as to the amount of damages, he may give the plaintiff interlocutory judgment for damages to be assessed. Unless he orders otherwise they will be assessed by a master; but he may refer them to an official or special referee or allow the action to go to trial as to damages only, giving any necessary directions (Order 37, rr. 1, 4).

When leave, whether conditional or unconditional, is given to defend or judgment is given with a stay of execution pending the trial of a counterclaim, the master will give directions as to the further conduct of the action as though the application were a summons for directions under Order 25 (see Chapter 18), and the provisions of that Order apply with any necessary modifications, save that a counter-notice for directions by the defendant is not required (Order 14, r. 6(1)). A fresh summons for directions at a later stage is then unnecessary; but the master will adjourn or give liberty to apply under the summons for further directions if required. The directions may, if all parties consent, provide for trial of the action by a master, which may enable it to be quickly, cheaply and conveniently disposed of (Order 14, r. 6(2)). In that case an appeal lies direct to the Court of Appeal (Order 58, r. 2(1)(*a*)).

If the point of the defence is a short one, and the trial will last no longer than four hours, the master may direct the case to be tried as a short cause. (See the form of order in Queen's Bench Masters' Practice Forms, No. P.F. 14.) Such an order is advantageous to a plaintiff since the case may be tried and disposed of quickly and with comparatively little expense. Under Order 14, r. 4(3), conditions may be imposed as to giving security or time or mode of trial. It may even be ordered under Order 64, r. 3, to be tried in vacation if there is urgent need of such a speedy trial and if the judge gives leave.

In order to discourage plaintiffs from making unnecessary applications for summary judgment, it is provided that if a

---

[35] A new s. 40 is substituted by the Courts and Legal Services Act 1990.
[36] See *Practice Directions* [1988] 3 All E.R. 95.

plaintiff makes an application under rule 1 where the case is not within the Order, or if it appears to the master that the plaintiff knew that the defendant relied on a contention which would entitle him to unconditional leave to defend, the application may be dismissed (rule 7(1))[37] with costs and, provided that the plaintiff is not an assisted person, order them to be paid forthwith.[38] If the plaintiff obtains summary judgment he will ordinarily be awarded the fixed costs provided by Order 62, Appendix 3, or, if the master certifies for counsel, costs to be taxed.[38a] If he gives leave to defend, the master usually, though not always, orders "costs in the cause" (see Chapter 25). Notwithstanding that the "event" of the summons may be said to have been in favour of the defendant, this is likely to be the fair order to make in cases where the plaintiff had good ground to believe that there was no defence and was suddenly faced with the defendant's affidavit raising an issue. It often happens that the contentions of the defendant, though sufficient to entitle him to leave to defend, are really quite unsubstantial.

On an application under Order 14 the master is not concerned to ascertain the truth of the defence put forward in the defendant's affidavit unless it can be shown from documentary evidence that it *cannot* be true. A counter-affidavit by the plaintiff may be put in if the master gives leave; but if, as often happens, it serves only to emphasise that there is a dispute to be tried he may disallow the costs of it. If the defendant's affidavit discloses facts which, if true, could reasonably be argued to be a defence to the plaintiff's claim, the master *must* give leave to defend either conditionally or unconditionally although he may have his doubts as to its truth.

A judgment given under Order 14, when the defendant or his solicitor has failed to attend at the hearing of the summons, may be set aside or varied on such terms as the master thinks just (rule 11).

Summary Proceedings for Possession of Land

Order 113 was promulgated in 1970 to provide a new procedure for the recovery of possession of land which is occupied

---

[37] And see *Pocock* v. *A.D.A.C. Ltd.* [1952] 1 T.L.R. 29, 34.

[38] Rule 7(1); and see Chap. 25.

[38a] The plaintiff will be entitled to interest on costs under s. 17 of the Judgments Act 1838. This may confer a substantial advantage on the plaintiff in a case such as a personal injuries action, where damages remain to be assessed: see *O'Connor* v. *Amos Bridgman Abattoirs Ltd. The Times*, April 13, 1990, not following *Putty* v. *Hopkinson* [1990] 1 All E.R. 1057.

by trespassers whose identity may or may not be known; to deal, in other words, with squatters. The earlier procedure presented problems when, as often happens, it was not possible to identify every person trespassing. It was also uncertain whether a final order for possession could be made on an interlocutory application. Order 113 was designed to overcome these difficulties and to provide a speedy means for the recovery of possession of land. Its scope is, however, narrowly confined and it does not apply where the person in occupation is a tenant holding over after the termination of the tenancy, but in *Moore Properties (Ilford) Ltd.* v. *McKeon*[39] Fox J. held that a landlord of a flat could obtain possession under Order 113 against an unlawful sub-tenant, when the sub-tenancy had been granted in breach of an absolute prohibition in the tenancy agreement against sub-letting and without the landlord's knowledge or consent.

The order provides by rule 1 that the proceedings may be brought by originating summons where a person claims possession of land which he alleges is occupied solely by a person or persons (not being a tenant or tenant holding over after the termination of the tenancy) who entered into or remained in occupation without his licence or consent or that of any predecessor in title of his. The same form of summons is used whether or not the wrongful occupiers can be identified and whether or not they are named as defendants in the action but since 1989 the summons must state whether possession is claimed in respect of residential premises or in respect of other land (rule 2(2)). No acknowledgment of service of the originating summons is required (rule 2(1)).

The plaintiff must file an affidavit in support of the originating summons stating his interest in the land, the circumstances in which it has been occupied without consent, and stating that he does not know the name of any person in occupation who is not named in the summons (rule 3), but the plaintiff is under no obligation to take reasonable steps to identify occupiers; it is sufficient that he does not in fact know their identity and that his affidavit states that fact.

Where a defendant is named in the summons, it must be served on him personally, together with a copy of the affidavit in support. Alternatively, a copy of the summons and affidavit may be left or sent to him at the premises. But where a person not named as a defendant is in occupation, the summons is to

---

[39] [1976] 1 W.L.R. 1278. The limited availability of the procedure was stressed by the Court of Appeal in *Filemart Ltd.* v. *Avery, The Times*, February 4, 1989.

be served by affixing a copy of it and of the affidavit to the main door or other conspicuous part of the premises and, if practicable, inserting through the letter box copies in a sealed transparent envelope addressed to "the occupiers," or by placing stakes in the ground at conspicuous parts of the land to each of which an envelope containing a copy of the summons and affidavit must be affixed. Copies of the summons served must be sealed with the court seal.[40] The requirement of Order 28, r. 3 that the summons would have to be served not less than four clear days before the day fixed for the hearing is expressly excluded (rule 4 (3)) so that in an urgent case the court may direct an earlier hearing.

A person in occupation but who is not named as a defendant and wishes to be heard on the question whether an order for possession should be made may apply at any stage of the proceedings to be joined as a defendant (rule 5).

Proceedings under Order 113 are normally heard by a master who may refer them to a judge if he thinks they should properly be decided by the judge. (rule 1A), but except in cases of urgency and by leave, a final order for possession will not be made less than five clear days after service in the case of residential premises, or two clear days in the case of other land. (rule 6). The Court of Appeal held in *McPhail* v. *Persons, Names Unknown*[41] that in the absence of consent on the part of the applicant, the court had no power to direct a suspension of the order for possession.

But with effect from 1981, r. 6(3) provides that nothing in the Order shall prevent the court from ordering possession to be given on a specified date, in the exercise of any power which could have been exercised if possession had been claimed in an action begun by writ.

The order for possession may extend to the whole of the owner's property where further occupation is threatened, even though a part only is in actual occupation. In *University of Essex* v. *Djemal and Others*[42] students went into occupation of part of the administrative offices of the university and vacated them after the university obtained an order for possession. But on the same day that the order was executed, the students occupied another part of the university buildings. The university again applied for possession and the students vacated the

---

[40] Ord. 113, r. 4.

[41] [1973] Ch. 447. Applied in *Swordheath Properties Ltd.* v. *Floydd and Others* [1978] 1 W.L.R. 550, C.A.

[42] [1980] 1 W.L.R. 1301. Applied in *Ministry of Agriculture, Fisheries and Food* v. *Heyman and Others* (1990) 59 P. & C.R. 48, D.C.

buildings shortly before the application was due to be heard, leaving behind them a note threatening further direct action. The Court of Appeal held that in these circumstances the university was entitled to an order for possession extending to the whole of its premises, and not limited to the parts which the students had previously occupied.

An order for possession once made may be enforced within three months without leave, since every occupier will have had notice of the proceedings (rule 7). This contrasts with ordinary actions for the possession of land, where leave of the court is required to issue the writ of possession under Order 45, r. 3. Anyone on the premises at the time the writ of possession is executed by the sheriff is liable to be evicted, whether he was there at the time of the hearing or not.

The application for possession under Order 113 may be brought in the Queen's Bench Division or the Chancery Division, and a comparable procedure exists in the county courts, under Order 24 of the County Court Rules, where the rateable value of the premises in question does not exceed the county court limit.[43]

---

[43] See also Prevention from Eviction Act 1977, as amended by Housing Act 1988.

CHAPTER 6

PLEADINGS

A matter which normally occupies the attention of the parties in the early stages is pleading. The student must familiarise himself not only with the theory and the art of pleading but also with the rules of procedure governing the exchange of pleadings, and how a party may be relieved of embarrassment caused by the defective or irregular pleading of his opponent.

Time for Pleading

The time for serving, amending or filing any pleading, answer or other document is governed by a fixed timetable laid down by Orders 18 and 20. But such time may be, and often is, enlarged by consent in writing without application to the court (Order 3, r. 5(3)). Further, the time fixed for doing any act may be enlarged or abridged by the master, who may enlarge it even though it has already expired (Order 3, r. 5(1), (2)); but it is unwise to defer the application till so late a date. This jurisdiction is not affected by the making of an "unless" or conditional order.[1] So where the court orders, for example, that a pleading be struck out unless a certain act is done within a specified time, but the order to do that act is not complied with, the court retains the power to extend the time within which the act should be done. It appears that this power exists even if the plaintiff defaults in serving a statement of a claim where the court has ordered the action to be dismissed for want of prosecution if he does not do so within a specified time.[2] The costs of a summons to extend time will, in default of a special order, fall upon the party applying (Order 62, r. 6(6)).

When the time allowed for doing any act is seven days or less, Saturdays, Sundays, bank holidays, etc., are not counted (Order 3, r. 2(5))[3]; and in any case where an act has to be done at an office of the Supreme Court and time expires on a Sunday, or other day on which the offices of the court are

---

[1] *Samuels* v. *Linzi Dresses Ltd.* [1981] Q.B. 115; But see *Kleinwort Benson Ltd.* v. *Barbrak Ltd.* [1987] A.C. 597 and *Waddon* v. *Whitecroft-Scovill Ltd.* [1988] 1 All E.R. 996 (H.L.).
[2] *Ibid.* For the meaning of default in this connection, see *Reiss* v. *Woolf* [1952] 2 Q.B. 557.
[3] No provision is made for the case where a time exceeding seven days for an act not required to be done at an office of the Supreme Court—*e.g.* the service of particulars—expires on a Sunday, etc. If an act could not reasonably be done on a particular day because, for example, a solicitor's office was not open to receive a document, the court would doubtless deal appropriately with the situation.

closed (which includes Saturday), the time is automatically extended to the next day on which the offices are open (rule 4). Where a document (other than a writ or originating summons) is served personally on (or left at the proper address of) the person to be served between 12 noon on a Saturday and midnight on Sunday, or after 4 in the afternoon on any other weekday, it is deemed to have been served on the next day available for court business (Order 65, r. 7). But no "process" (which includes a writ, petition and originating summons) may be served on a Sunday except, in case of urgency, with leave (Order 65, r. 10). Since 1990, pleadings may be served during the month of August, as in any other month. Similarly, since 1990, the month of August is included in reckoning any period prescribed by the rules or by any order or direction for serving, filing or amending any pleading.[4] In reckoning a period of time for doing an act "after," "from" or "before" a given date, that day is excluded; if "clear days" are mentioned, the day on which the act is to be done is also excluded (rule 2).

Illustrations

If a writ is served within the jurisdiction, acknowledgment of service may, under Order 12, r. 5, be made within "fourteen days after service of the writ (including the day of service)." Therefore if a writ is served on Wednesday 5, a judgment in default of notice of intention to defend can be entered on, but not before, Wednesday 19; but for the words in brackets it would be Thursday 20. If a writ is served on Monday 3, a judgment in default of notice of intention to defend cannot be entered until Tuesday 18 (for the defendant would be able to acknowledge service on Monday 17).

A summons under Order 14 must be served "not less than ten clear days before the return day." As this period is over seven days, Saturdays, Sundays and the other days mentioned in Order 3, r. 2(5) must be included in the reckoning. The calculation of the return day may therefore be affected by the day of the week on which the summons is issued.[5] Hence, if the return day is on Wednesday 19 the summons must be served not later than noon on Saturday 8.

Subject to the above rules, if the plaintiff has not served a statement of claim with his writ, he must do so not more than 14 days after the defendant's notice of intention to defend (Order 18, r. 1); if he fails to do so, he runs the risk of having his action dismissed for want of prosecution (Order 19, r. 1).[6]

Ordinarily a defendant who gives notice of intention to defend must serve his defence not more than 14 days after the time limited for acknowledging service of the writ or from the

---

[4] Ord. 18, r. 5 and Ord. 3, r. 3, which excluded the month of August for these purposes, were revoked in 1990 (R.S.C. (Amendment No. 2. 1990)).

[5] See *Practice Direction* [1970] 1 W.L.R. 258.

[6] He may save himself by serving it before the hearing of the summons to dismiss, but not necessarily so (*Clough* v. *Clough* [1968] 1 W.L.R. 525).

18, r. 2). If the plaintiff serves a summons for judgment under Order 14 or Order 86 and the defendant obtains leave to defend, the master usually directs whether or not a defence shall be served and within what time; failing such a direction, the defence must be served within 14 days after the order giving leave to defend (Order 18, r. 2(2)). A defendant who is served with a summons for judgment may and should hold his hand and serve no defence until the summons is disposed of.[7] Under Order 18, r. 2(2), the time for serving the defence does not run after service of the summons.

If the time expires and no defence is served, the plaintiff may enter judgment by default under Order 19.[8] But, if he delays in doing this, the defendant may put in a defence after time, which will prevent judgment from being entered—though the defendant may be ordered to pay any costs incurred through his delay. The plaintiff is not bound to enter judgment in default. In a proper case, *e.g.* a libel action or where very heavy damages are claimed, he may take out a summons for directions and proceed to trial in the ordinary way.[9]

If the defendant pleads a counterclaim, the plaintiff must within 14 days (unless the time is extended) reply to it as though he were a defendant serving a defence to a statement of claim; otherwise it is deemed to be admitted (Order 18, r. 3(2)). If the defendant by his counterclaim brings in a new party, the latter is subject to a similar rule (Order 15, r. 3). If there is no counterclaim, but the plaintiff nevertheless desires to serve a reply, he may do so without leave within 14 days from the service of the defence (Order 18, r. 3(4)), or later by leave. If the plaintiff wishes to serve both a reply and a defence to counterclaim, they must be combined in the same document (rule 3(3)).

Pleadings subsequent to a reply may occasionally be ordered under Order 18, r. 4. Otherwise the pleadings are deemed to be closed at the expiration of 14 days after the service of the defence, reply, or defence to counterclaim, as the case may be (rule 20). When the pleadings become closed there is an implied joinder of issue on the pleading last served and every material allegation of fact therein is deemed to be denied (rule 14). At any stage *after* service of the defence or defence to counterclaim, as the case may be, a party may, if necessary,

---

[7] *Hobson* v. *Monks* [1884] W.N. 8.
[8] Leave is necessary in actions in tort between husband and wife (Ord. 89) and in certain claims for possession of land (Ord. 13, r. 4).
[9] *Nagy* v. *Co-operative Press* [1949] 2 K.B. 188.

expressly join issue upon the preceding pleading save as to any facts which he may desire to admit (*ibid.*).

The Function of Pleadings

Before judge or jury is asked to decide any question which is in controversy between litigants, it is in all cases desirable, and in most cases necessary, that the matter to be submitted to them for decision should be clearly ascertained. The defendant is entitled to know what it is that the plaintiff alleges against him; the plaintiff in his turn is entitled to know what defence will be raised in answer to his claim. The defendant may dispute every statement made by the plaintiff, or he may be prepared to prove other facts which put a different complexion on the case. He may rely on a point of law, or raise a cross-claim of his own. In any event, before the trial comes on it is highly desirable that the parties should know exactly what they are fighting about, otherwise they may go to great expense in procuring evidence to prove at the trial facts which their opponents will at once concede. It has been found by long experience that the most satisfactory method of attaining this object is to make each party in turn state his own case and answer that of his opponent before the hearing. Such statements and the answers to them are called the *pleadings*.

The plaintiff naturally begins; if he has not already indorsed his writ with a *Statement of Claim*, he serves one separately. The defendant then puts in his *Defence*, which besides answering the plaintiff's claim, may also set up a *Counterclaim*, after which the plaintiff in turn may serve a *Defence to Counterclaim*, or he may *Reply*, or both. Occasionally the defendant then obtains leave to *Rejoin*. It is very seldom that any further pleadings are ordered, but there may be *Surrejoinders, Rebutters,* and *Surrebutters.*[10] Each of these alternate pleadings must in its turn either admit or deny the facts alleged in the last-preceding pleading; it may also allege additional facts, where necessary. The points admitted by either side are thus extracted and distinguished from those in controversy; other matters, though disputed, may prove to be immaterial; and thus the litigation is narrowed down to two or three matters which are the real questions in dispute. The pleadings should always be conducted so as to evolve some clearly defined *issues*, that is, some definite propositions of law or fact, asserted by one party and denied

---

[10] The leave of the court is required to serve any pleading subsequent to a reply or a defence to counterclaim (Ord. 18, r. 4).

by the other, but which both agree to be the points which they
wish to have decided in the action.

When this is properly and fairly done, four advantages
ensue:

  (i) It is a benefit to the parties themselves to know exactly
      what are the matters left in dispute. They may discover
      that they are fighting about nothing at all, *e.g.* when a
      plaintiff in an action of libel finds that the defendant
      does not assert that the words are true, he is often
      willing to accept an apology and costs, and so put an
      end to the action.

 (ii) It is also a boon to the parties to know precisely what
      facts they must prove at the trial; otherwise, they may
      go to great trouble and expense in procuring evidence of
      facts which their opponent does not dispute. On the
      other hand, if they assume that their opponent will not
      raise such and such a point, they may be taken sadly by
      surprise at the trial.

(iii) Moreover, it is necessary to ascertain the nature of the
      controversy in order to determine the most appropriate
      mode of trial. It may turn out to be a pure point of law,
      which should be decided by a judge; it may involve
      investigation of a complicated building dispute in which
      case the action should be referred to an Official Referee;
      or it may be a question proper for a jury.

 (iv) It is desirable to place on record the precise questions
      raised in the action, so that the parties or their suc-
      cessors may not fight the same battle over again.

The function of pleadings then is to ascertain with precision
the matters on which the parties differ and the points on which
they agree; and thus to arrive at certain clear issues on which
both parties desire a judicial decision.[11] In order to attain this
object, it is necessary that the pleadings interchanged between
the parties should be conducted according to certain fixed
rules, which it is our endeavour to state and explain in the
following pages. The main purpose of these rules is to compel
each party to state clearly and intelligibly the material facts on
which he relies, omitting everything immaterial, and then to
insist on his opponent frankly admitting or explicitly denying
every material matter alleged against him. By this method they

---

[11] And see Lord Radcliffe's speech in *Esso Petroleum Co. Ltd.* v. *Southport Corporation* [1956]
A.C. 218, 241. For a reaffirmation of the essential function of pleadings in civil actions,
see the remarks of Lord Edmund-Davies in *Farrell* v. *Secretary of State for Defence* [1980] 1
W.L.R. 172, 180.

must speedily arrive at an issue. Neither party need disclose in his pleading the evidence by which he proposes to establish his case at the trial. But each must give his opponent a sufficient outline of his case. Every pleading in an action commenced by the issue of a writ after June 4, 1990 must contain the necessary particulars of any claim, defence or other matter pleaded (Order 18, r. 12). So for the first time in the history of pleadings a defendant must now plead particulars of any facts upon which he relies in mitigation or reduction of the damages claimed.

History of Pleading

This method of arriving at an issue by alternate allegations has been practised in England from earliest times. It is apparently as ancient as any portion of our law of procedure. It certainly existed in substantially the same form in the reign of Henry II. The word "issue" is to be found at the very commencement of the Year Books, *i.e.* in the first year of Edward II; and the distinction between an *issue en ley* and an *issue en fet* is equally ancient (see the Year Book, 3 Edw. II, 59). And even before the reign of Edward II the production of an issue had been not only the constant effect, but the professed aim and object, of pleading.

At first the pleadings were oral. The parties actually appeared in open court and a *viva voce* altercation took place in the presence of the judges. These oral pleadings were conducted either by the party himself or his pleader (called *narrator* or *advocatus*); and it seems that the rule was then already established that none but a professional advocate could be a pleader in any cause not his own. It was the duty of the judge to superintend, or "moderate," the oral contention thus conducted before him. His aim was to arrive at some specific point or matter affirmed on the one side, and denied on the other, which they both agreed was the question requiring decision. When this result was attained, the parties were said to be "at issue"—*ad exitum*—the pleadings were over, and the parties were ready to go before a jury, if it were an issue of fact, or before the court, if it were an issue of law. And so strict were the judges in those days, that they allowed only one issue in respect of each cause of action; if a defendant had two defences to the same claim, he had to elect between them; it was only in the reign of Queen Victoria that the parties were allowed to raise more than a single issue, either of law or fact. Hence the question for decision came itself to be called *the issue.*

During the parol altercation one of the officers of the court was busy writing on a parchment roll an official report of the allegations of the parties and of the acts of the court itself during the progress of the pleading. This was called *the Record*. As the suit proceeded, similar entries were made from time to time, each successive entry being called a *continuance*, and, when complete, the roll was preserved "as a perpetual intrinsic and exclusively admissible testimony of all the judicial transactions" which it purported to record.

It is not apparently known when the system of oral pleading fell into disuse; but it gradually became the practice for each pleader in turn to borrow the parchment roll, and enter his statements thereon himself. Later (probably in the reign of Edward IV), the plan was adopted of drawing up the pleadings in the first instance on paper, and interchanging them between the parties in that form; then, after an issue had been arrived at, they were transcribed on to a parchment roll. This was called, "entering the proceedings on the record." But though the practice of oral pleading was abandoned, the ancient method of alternative allegations continued. So that the student may understand the reports of cases which turned on the old system of pleading, note that what we now call a Statement of Claim was before 1875 called a *declaration*; a Defence was called a *plea* or *pleas*; and a Reply was called a *replication*. The names of the further pleadings remain unchanged. A declaration often contained more than one *count*, each of which stated a complete and separate cause of action, and would in fact by itself have been a good and valid declaration. So, too, each plea had to be in itself a complete answer to the count to which it was pleaded. The courts of equity had their own methods of pleading.

The principles on which pleadings were framed, and the rules which regulated them, remained substantially the same till 1852. Their practical utility was, however, seriously impaired by the over-subtlety of the pleaders and by the excessive rigour with which the rules were applied; the merits of the case being constantly subordinated to technical questions of form. A determined effort was made to correct these defects by the provisions of the Common Law Procedure Acts 1852–1860. In 1873, however, it was found necessary to adopt a more thorough method of reform; and the Judicature Act substituted in the new High Court of Justice the system of pleading which is still in force.

Till the year 1893 in every action commenced by writ there were pleadings as a matter of course, unless both parties agreed to dispense with them. In 1893, by an Order revoked in 1917, power was given to the plaintiff, if he thought fit, to declare on his writ that he intended to proceed to trial without pleadings. If the plaintiff did so declare, there were no pleadings, unless the defendant could persuade a master to order them. In 1897 the rules were amended, and for the first time in the history of our law a plaintiff who wished to deliver a pleading was not allowed to do so without an order from a master. But in 1933 further alterations were made, the effect of which was in substance to revert to the practice prior to 1893. In 1955 the plaintiff was empowered by Order XIVB to include in his writ, if specially indorsed, a notice of his intention to apply for trial without pleadings. And now since 1964 an improved procedure has been made available on application by either party (see below). As we have seen in Chapter 1 if the real matter for decision is one of the construction of an Act or document, or some other question of law, or if there is not likely to be any substantial dispute of fact, the plaintiff has the option of commencing proceedings by originating summons (Order 5, r. 4).

When Pleadings will be Dispensed With

The whole object of pleadings, as we have seen, is to bring the parties to a clear issue, and thus to secure that they both know, before the action comes on for trial, what is the real point to be discussed and decided. But a master has power to order that service of a statement of claim be dispensed with if he is satisfied that pleadings are unnecessary. Again, where the defendant in answer to a summons for judgment has filed an affidavit or has in some other way stated his defence, any further pleading may be unnecessary, and the master may make an order accordingly (see Order 18, rr. 1 and 21). A similar order will be made if the questions in dispute have already been argued on an application for an *interim* injunction. A special practice as to pleadings is followed in the Commercial Court.[12] A case entered in the commercial list must be pleaded in the form of points of claim or of defence, which must be as brief as possible. In a suitable case the judge may order that pleadings be dispensed with entirely (Order 72, r. 7).

So, too, "the court may order any question or issue arising in a cause or matter, whether of fact or law . . . and whether

---

[12] The "Guide to Commercial Court Practice" issued in March 1990 forms Appendix A of Order 72 and usefully sets out this practice.

raised by pleadings or otherwise, to be tried before, at or after the trial of the cause or matter, and may give directions as to the manner in which the question or issue shall be stated" (Order 33, r. 3). Then, again, a master may direct the parties to prepare a statement of the issues in dispute (see Order 18, r. 21, *infra*). Such issues take the place of pleadings; they are usually directed to determine whether a particular person was or was not a member of the defendant firm at the time the contract sued on was entered into with that firm, or to determine the liability of a person summoned as a garnishee (see Chapter 24), or to decide between rival claimants to property taken in execution by the sheriff or in the hands of a stakeholder.

Apart from these special instances the master now has a general power under Order 18, r. 21, in actions to which the rule applies, to order trial without pleadings or without further pleadings as the case may be. The procedure is not encumbered with the restrictions and risks involved in the rules of 1955 and has proved a useful change. It is available in actions begun by writ with the exception of actions which include a claim by the plaintiff for libel, slander, malicious prosecution or false imprisonment or based on an allegation of fraud. Unlike the procedure under Order 14 it may be adopted although it is clear that there is an issue to be tried; and it may be appropriate in many cases where the nature and compass of the dispute have been made clear in correspondence. After a defendant has given notice of intention to defend the plaintiff or that defendant, whether his opponent consents or not, may take out a summons; and if the master thinks that the issues can be defined, or that the action can properly be tried, without pleadings or further pleadings, he will order accordingly. He may direct the parties to prepare a statement of the issues in dispute and may settle the statement himself if necessary. He will also give appropriate directions as though a summons for directions had been issued, and may do so even though he refuses the application.

The Form of Modern Pleadings

No entries now are made on any parchment roll; the pleadings are written or printed on paper and interchanged between the parties; the solicitor of one party serves his pleading on the solicitor of the other party, or on the party himself, if he does not employ a solicitor. On the summons for directions, after close of pleadings, an order is made to set down the action for trial and two bundles, each containing the writ, the pleadings, any particulars (with the order or request therefor), orders made on the summons for directions and any legal aid documents, are lodged with the office of the court (Order 34, r. 3(1)). One bundle is for the use of the judge; the other, which is marked with the stamp denoting the fee paid on entry, is regarded as the record and, unless it is withdrawn as a result of a settlement, will be filed after the trial and show what the issues were on which judgment was given.

Remember that a pleading is a document which passes between the parties and, unless indorsed on the writ, is not in the possession of the court until it is lodged as above on setting the action down for trial. Therefore while it is correct to assume that the trial judge has the pleadings before him, do not waste time on a summons in chambers by asking the master or judge if he has them, but see that they are handed to him forthwith if it is necessary to refer to them. In the Chancery Division they may have been left with the master to peruse before the hearing.

Every pleading should bear at the top the year in which the writ was issued, the letter and number of the action, the title of the action, the Division of the High Court to which the action is assigned, the description of the pleading and, at the foot, the date on which it was served (Order 18, r. 6). A statement of claim should also bear the words "Writ issued the . . . day of . . . 19 . . . " in order to show that the cause of action pleaded had accrued before the action was commenced. It must be indorsed with the name and place of business of the solicitor and agent (if any) who serves it, or the name and address of the party serving it, if he does not act by a solicitor. It may be either written, typewritten or printed on proper sized paper.[13] Every pleading must be divided into paragraphs numbered consecutively. Dates, sums and numbers should be expressed in figures, and not in words. It is not necessary, though it is generally desirable, that a pleading should be drawn or settled by counsel; where it has been, he must sign his name at the end of it; if not settled by counsel, it must be signed by the solicitor or by the party if he sues or defends in person. (*Ibid.*) Below counsel's signature there should appear the words: "Served the . . . day of . . . 19 . . . by . . . of (*address*), Solicitor for the [Plaintiff] [Defendant]."

---

[13] Type lithography or stencil duplicating is permitted in lieu of printing. Facsimile copies of documents for use in court may be made photographically (Ord. 66, r. 2). All documents for use in the Supreme Court must now be on A4 paper (Ord. 66, r. 1).

Cardinal Rules in Pleading

The allegations in every pleading must be:
    (i) Material.
    (ii) Certain.
The next two chapters are therefore devoted to Materiality and Certainty.

CHAPTER 7

MATERIAL FACTS

The fundamental rule of our present system of pleading is this:
"Every pleading must contain, and contain only, a statement in a summary form of the material facts on which the party pleading relies for his claim or defence, as the case may be, but not the evidence by which those facts are to be proved, and the statement must be as brief as the nature of the case admits" (Order 18, r. 7(1)).

This rule involves and requires four separate things:
  (i) Every pleading must state facts and not law.
 (ii) It must state material facts and material facts only.
(iii) It must state facts and not the evidence by which they are to be proved.
(iv) It must state such facts concisely in a summary form.

(i) Every Pleading must state Facts and not Law

Conclusions of law, or of mixed law and fact, are no longer to be pleaded. It is for the court to declare the law arising upon the facts proved before it. A plaintiff must not merely aver, "I am entitled to recover £100 from the defendant," or "It was the defendant's duty to do so and so." He must state the facts which in his opinion give him that right, or impose on the defendant that duty; and the judge will decide, when those facts are proved, what are the legal rights and duties of the parties respectively. So, too, a defendant must state clearly the facts which in his opinion afford him a defence to the plaintiff's action. He must not say merely, "I do not owe the money"; he must allege facts which show he does not owe it, *e.g.* that the goods were never ordered, or were never delivered, or that they were not equal to sample. He may plead that, even assuming every allegation of fact in the statement of claim to be true, the plaintiff has no cause of action against him. This is called "an objection in point of law." But if he is not prepared to admit them all, he must deal with the facts alleged by his opponent, and deal with each of them clearly and explicitly. If he pleads that he never agreed as alleged, this will be taken to mean that he never in fact made any such contract—not that the contract is bad in law or not binding on him because he is an infant, or because he was induced to enter into it by fraud.

All facts tending to show the insufficiency or illegality of any contract must be specially pleaded. To say, "There never was any contract," is a different thing from saying, "There was a contract but I contend it is invalid." State the facts and prove them, and the judge will then decide the question of validity. He knows the law, and can apply it to the facts of the case without its being stated in the pleadings.

This was one of the greatest improvements introduced by the Judicature Act. Each party was, before 1875, bound to state with reasonable precision the points which he intended to raise; but this he generally did by stating, not the facts which he meant to prove, but the conclusion of law which he sought to draw from them. The other side thus learnt that the party pleading meant to prove *some* set of facts which would sustain a given legal conclusion; but there might be many sets of facts which would sustain that legal conclusion, and which of these would be set up at the trial was not disclosed. For instance, this was a very common form of declaration: "The plaintiff sues the defendant for £——, money payable by the defendant to the plaintiff for money received by the defendant to the use of the plaintiff."[1] That might cover any one of the following cases, and many more besides; and it could not be ascertained from the plaintiff's pleading which would be his case at the trial:

(a) That the defendant was the plaintiff's rent collector, and had received money for him as such.

(b) That the plaintiff was entitled to an office which the defendant also claimed, and under colour of which the defendant had received fees, which the plaintiff sought to recover from him.

(c) That the plaintiff had paid the defendant the price of goods which he was to supply, and the defendant had never supplied them.

(d) That the plaintiff had paid a sum of money to the defendant by mistake, having taken him for another person of similar name or appearance.

Then, again, there were often several alternative legal conclusions which could be drawn from the facts, any one of which would serve the plaintiff's turn; and therefore several "counts" were pleaded in the same declaration, giving various legal aspects of the same transaction, though the evidence given in support of each at the trial would be identical.

---

[1] As to the scope and limits of this form of action, see the excellent speech of Lord Sumner in *Sinclair* v. *Brougham* [1914] A.C. at pp. 453–456.

So, too, with the defence. In an action for goods sold and delivered, the defendant was allowed to plead "the general issue," as it was called, that he "never was indebted as alleged." This is a conclusion of law, and at the trial it was open to him to give in evidence under this plea any one or more of several totally different defences, of which the following may serve as instances:

(i) That he never ordered the goods.
(ii) That they were never delivered to him.
(iii) That they were not of the quality ordered.
(iv) That they were sold on a credit which had not expired at the time that the action was commenced.

But the defendant might not, under this plea, set up the Statute of Limitations, nor allege payment or a set-off, because each of these defences implies that the defendant *was once* indebted to the plaintiff as alleged. He might deny that any express contract of sale was ever made: he might deny all or any of the matters of fact from which such a contract would by law be implied; but he could not under the plea of "never indebted" insist that the contract, though made in fact, was void in law. Now all such ambiguous formulae are abolished, and the actual facts and particulars on which either party relies must be stated as briefly as possible in his pleading. (Order 18, r. 12).

Illustrations

It is unnecessary to state in a pleading the principles of the common law, or to set forth the contents of a public statute. Thus, law need not be pleaded to show that a plaintiff is entitled to sue upon a dishonoured bill of exchange so long as the necessary facts be alleged; and a defendant may plead simply, "the action is not maintainable without special damage and none is alleged." But where a particular statute is relied on as the foundation of a claim or defence, the facts necessary to bring the case within the statute should be pleaded and reference should usually be made to the section relied on.

Contributory negligence must be specifically pleaded by way of defence to a claim for negligence. In the absence of such a plea, the judge may not reduce the plaintiff's damages under the Law Reform (Contributory Negligence) Act 1945, s.1(1).

Fookes v. *Slaytor* [1978] 1 W.L.R. 1293.

"It is said that an implied warranty is not alleged in the pleadings, but all the material facts are alleged, and in these days, so long as those facts are alleged, that is sufficient for the Court to proceed to judgment without putting any particular legal label upon the cause of action."

Per Denning L.J. in *Shaw* v. *Shaw* [1954] 2 Q.B. 429, 441. See also *Re Vandervell's Trusts (No. 2)* [1974] Ch. 269, holding that a party may rely on any legal consequences of the material facts which he has pleaded, and is not limited to any particular legal result which he has alleged.

It is bad pleading to allege merely that a right or a duty or a liability exists; the facts must be set out which give rise to such right or create such duty or liability. Hence, where the facts stated in the pleading disclose no cause of action, the pleading will be held bad in spite of any allegation to the effect that the act was "unlawful," or "wrongful," or "improper," or "done without any justification therefor or right so to do."

Gautret v. *Egerton* (1867) L.R. 2 C.P. 371.

Day v. *Brownrigg* (1878) 10 Ch.D. 294, 302; 48 L.J. Ch. 173.

It is not sufficient for a plaintiff to say, "under and by virtue of a certain deed I am entitled," etc., for that is an inference of law. The limitations of the deed, and all other facts upon which he proposes to rely as showing that he is so entitled must be stated.

Riddell v. *Earl of Strathmore* (1887) 3 T.L.R. 329.

In actions for goods bargained and sold or sold and delivered, a defence *in denial* must deny the order or contract, the delivery, or the amount claimed, and in an action for money had and received, a defence *in denial* must deny the receipt of the money, or the existence of those facts which are alleged to make the receipt by the defendant a receipt to the use of the plaintiff.

See Order 18, r. 13.

In an action of libel or slander, a defendant may not plead merely that "he published the words on a privileged occasion." He must set out the facts and circumstances on which he relies as creating the privilege, and then the judge will decide on the facts proved at the trial whether the occasion was or was not privileged.

Elkington v. *London Association for the Protection of Trade* (1911) 27 T.L.R. 329.

See Precedent No. 45.

If the plaintiff claims to rescind a contract for misrepresentation it is not enough for the defendant merely to deny the claim if his case in fact is that any such claim is barred on the ground that *restitutio in integrum* is no longer possible. This is a matter which must be specifically pleaded.

See Order 18, r. 8, and Precedent No. 37.

Whenever the same legal result can be attained in several different ways it is not sufficient to aver merely that that result has been arrived at, but the facts must be stated showing how and by what means it was attained.

Illustrations

Where A claims that an estate formerly held by B is now vested in himself, he must state in his pleading the date and nature of the conveyance or other transfer from B to A, whether it was by deed or by will, etc.

Com.Dig. Pleader (E. 23), (E. 24).

Similarly a successor in title to a reversioner who claims forfeiture of the lease for breach of the repairing covenant must set out in the statement of claim the conveyance under which he acquired his title.

See Precedent No. 32.

It is not sufficient in an action upon a contract for the defendant to plead that "the contract is rescinded." This may mean that the parties met, and in express terms agreed to put an end to the contract; or it may mean that such an intention is to be collected from a long correspondence or a whole series of transactions; or it may mean that the plaintiff himself has broken the contract in such a way as to amount to actual repudiation. The defendant must show in what manner and by what means he contends that it was rescinded, *e.g.* that goods sold and delivered were rejected by letter for breach of the implied condition of fitness for purpose; see Precedent No. 39.

(ii) Every Pleading must state Material Facts only

What facts are material?

"The word 'material' means necessary for the purpose of formulating a complete cause of action, and if any one 'material' fact is omitted, the statement of claim is bad" (*per* Scott L.J. in *Bruce* v. *Odhams Press Ltd.*).[2] The same principle applies to defences.

Facts which are not necessary to establish either a cause of action or the defence to it are not, speaking generally, "material" within the meaning of Order 18, r. 7, and should, therefore, be omitted from the pleading unless it is clear that evidence will have to be given of them at the trial.[3] All statements which need not be proved should be omitted.

It is obvious, then, that the question whether a particular fact is or is not material depends mainly on the special circumstances of the particular case. It is a question which it is not always easy to answer, and yet it is a very important one: the result of the case often depends on the ruling of the judge at the trial that it is or is not necessary that a particular fact should be proved. Sometimes it is material to allege and prove that the defendant was aware of a certain fact; at other times it is sufficient to aver that he did some act, without inquiring into the state of his mind. In some cases the defendant's intention is material: in a few cases his motives. The pleader must apply his knowledge of the law, and his common sense, to the facts stated in his instructions, and decide for himself which he must plead and which he may safely omit. Precedents may afford him some assistance; but in the end he must rely on his own judgment. No general rule can be laid down.

In early days, when the courts were very strict, they punished either party who pleaded immaterial facts: for if his opponent pleaded to immaterial facts, and issue was joined thereon, they compelled the party who had alleged such facts

[2] [1936] 1 K.B. at p. 712.
[3] *Gaston* v. *United Newspapers, Ltd.* (1915) 32 T.L.R. 143.

to prove them literally, although they were immaterial; otherwise he failed in his action. He had himself raised the issue, so he must prove it or take the consequences.[4]

Subsequently, however, the courts adopted a far better method of preventing the parties from raising immaterial issues. They declared that "immaterial allegations were not traversable," *i.e.* neither party was allowed to plead to any immaterial matter in his opponent's pleading, but must treat it as surplusage and leave it alone. Thus no issue could be raised on it; and the party pleading it was no longer bound to prove it at the trial.[5]

And now the courts never compel either party to prove at the trial more than the substance of his pleading, even though his opponent may have expressly traversed some immaterial averment contained in it lest by the operation of Order 18, r. 13(1) (see Chapter 9), it should be taken to be admitted.

If after consideration you are still in doubt whether a particular fact is or is not material, the safer course is to plead it, if you think you can prove it. For if you omit to plead it, and it is held to be material, you cannot strictly give any evidence of that fact at the trial, unless the judge will give leave to amend, and such leave may be upon terms as to payment of costs.[6]

Illustrations

It is sufficient if a pleading states such facts, as would, if proved or admitted, establish the plaintiff's case.

Here is a statement of claim in which a most material allegation has been omitted. What is it? (Look towards the end of this illustration *after* deciding.)

"The defendant instructed and employed the plaintiff to do certain work (specifying it). The plaintiff's charges for such work amounted to £——, which sum the defendant promised to pay, but has not paid, to the plaintiff."

The consideration for any contract not under seal is always material, and it is advisable to set it out in the statement of claim[7] except in the case of negotiable instruments, where the consideration is presumed. If the contract is under seal, no consideration need be proved.

In an action against a bailee it is material to know whether he was to be paid for his services, as this affects the degree of diligence which the law expects. But the amount of his remuneration is not material; it is sufficient to aver that he was to carry or warehouse the goods "for reward."

[4] See *Wood* v. *Budden* (1617) Hob. 119; *Cudlip* v. *Rundle* (1692) Carth. 202; *Bristow* v. *Wright* (1781) 2 Doug. 665; *Sir Francis Leke's Case* (1580) 3 Dy. 365; 2 Wms. Saund. 206, n. (22).

[5] See *Lane* v. *Alexander* (1608) Yel. 122; *Osborne* v. *Rogers* (1682) 1 Wms. Saund. 267; *Alsager* v. *Currie* (1843) 11 M. & W. 14.

[6] See *Byrd* v. *Nunn* (1877) 5 Ch.D. 781; 7 Ch.D. 284; and *Brook* v. *Brook* (1866) 12 P.D. 19.

[7] See *Cooke* v. *Rickman* [1911] 2 K.B. 1125 at 1129, 1130.

As a rule the precise wording of a document or a conversation is not material, and it is sufficient to state briefly its purport or effect.

Order 18, r. 7(2).

But in an action for libel or slander the precise words complained of are material, and they must be set out verbatim in the statement of claim. If the words taken by themselves are not clearly actionable, the plaintiff must also insert in his statement of claim an averment (with particulars in support) of an actionable meaning which he will contend the words conveyed to those to whom they were published. Such an averment is called an innuendo.

Harris v. *Warre* (1879) 4 C.P.D. 125; 48 L.J.C.P. 310.

Order 82, r. 3(1).

Lewis v. *Daily Telegraph Ltd.* [1964] A.C. 234. And see Precedent No. 29 for the pleading of a "false" or "popular" innuendo.

Answer to the first illustration: that the plaintiff did the work.

Notice

A party should expressly plead that another party had or was given notice of some fact or matter only when such notice is an element of the cause of action.

For example, notice of dishonour must be given to every person who is sought to be made liable on a negotiable instrument except the acceptor. Unless such notice was given no action lies against the drawer or any indorsee. Therefore the statement of claim must contain an allegation that notice of dishonour was given to the defendant, or a statement of the facts relied on as excusing the giving of such notice.

Bills of Exchange Act 1882, s.48.

Fruhauf v. *Grosvenor & Co.* (1892) 61 L.J.Q.B. 717.

Similarly, a lessor cannot enforce a right of re-entry for breach of covenant contained in a lease unless and until he serves on the lessee a notice complying with the terms of section 146(1) of the Law of Property Act 1925 and the lessee fails within a reasonable time thereafter to remedy the breach and to make compensation in money therefor.

See Precedent No. 32.

Intention and Motive

Whenever an injunction is applied for, it is material to allege that the defendant "threatens and intends" to repeat the illegal act complained of unless such an intention can be readily inferred from the nature of the case and the facts are already pleaded.

Stannard v. *Vestry of St. Giles* (1882) 20 Ch.D. at p. 195.

And see Precedent No. 27.

Otherwise a party's intention or motive should not in general be referred to in the pleadings unless it is necessary to establish the cause of action. For example, for a claim under the Occupiers' Liability Act 1957 it is material to aver that the plaintiff was using the premises as a visitor (s.2(2), and see Precedent No. 25). Similarly, where collusion is alleged between A and B, the fact that A knew the improper motives which actuated B is material, and for this purpose those improper motives must be stated.

Briton Medical, etc., Life Association v. *Britannia Fire Association* (1888) 59 L.T. 888.

Fraud

Any allegation of fraud must be expressly pleaded together with the facts, matters and circumstances relied on to support the allegation (Order 18,

r. 12(1)). In practice the acts alleged to be fraudulent should be set out and then it should be stated that those acts were done fraudulently.

See *Re Rica Gold Washing Co.* (1879) 11 Ch.D. 36 and Precedent No. 21.

Each party must state his whole case. He must plead all facts on which he intends to rely, otherwise he cannot strictly give any evidence of them at the trial. "The plaintiff is not entitled to relief except in regard to that which is alleged in the pleadings and proved at the trial."[8] If the plaintiff claims interest it must be pleaded (section 35A, Supreme Court Act 1981). The statement of claim must disclose a good cause of action: the defendant must show a good defence thereto. Omit no averment which is essential to success; do not plead half a defence and leave the rest to be inferred.

Illustrations

A plaintiff seeking to re-enter upon a breach by the defendant of a tenancy agreement alleged in his statement of claim that "it was a term of the said agreement that the said room should be used for office accommodation only" and that the defendant had used it for living accommodation, but omitted to allege a covenant not to use the premises otherwise than for offices and also a proviso for re-entry on breach of such covenant. It was held that the statement of claim disclosed no cause of action.

Whall v. *Bulman* [1953] 2 Q.B. 198.

Similarly, where the defendant is not the original lessee, a plaintiff seeking to enforce a right of re-entry for breach of the repairing covenants in the lease must aver that the defendant is the assignee of the lease and in possession of the demised premises.

See Precedent No. 32.

Although a defendant is not normally required to plead to particulars (*Chapple* v. *Electrical Trades Union* [1961] 1 W.L.R. 1290), he may be at risk in a negligence action if he raises a positive case in disproof of negligence after pleading only a general traverse of negligence. So, where after such a general denial the defendant adduced evidence at the trial of a positive act which the plaintiff's solicitor could not with reasonable diligence have foreseen, but which he subsequently discovered was not true, the Court of Appeal ordered a new trial.

Crook v. *Derbyshire* [1961] 1 W.L.R. 1360.

Do not leap before you come to the Stile

But the pleader should never allege any fact which is not material at the present stage of the action, even though he may reasonably suppose that it may become material hereafter. It is sufficient that each pleading in turn should contain in itself a good prima facie case, without reference to possible objections not yet urged. It is not necessary to anticipate the answer of

---

[8] *Per* Warrington J. in *Re Wrightson* [1908] 1 Ch. at p. 799.

the adversary; to do so, according to Hale C.J., is "like leaping before one comes to the stile."[9]

"It is no part of the statement of claim to anticipate the defence and to state what the plaintiff would have to say in answer to it. That would be a return to the old inconvenient system of pleading in Chancery, which ought certainly not to be encouraged, when the plaintiff used to allege in his bill imaginary defences of the defendant and make charges in reply to them."[10] So, too, it is quite unnecessary for the defendant to excuse himself from matters of which he is not yet accused, or to plead to causes of action which do not appear in the statement of claim.[11]

Illustrations

In an action for an account, it is sufficient for the plaintiff as his first step to allege facts which show that the defendant is prima facie liable to account to the plaintiff for certain moneys. If the defendant in his defence sets up that all accounts up to a certain date were settled between them, it will then be for the plaintiff to state in his reply the facts which may entitle him to have such settled account reopened. Such facts would be immaterial in the original statement of claim.

Similarly, in an action for libel, it would be bad pleading for the plaintiff to allege in the statement of claim that in publishing the words complained of the defendant was actuated by express malice. This allegation is not necessary to establish the cause of the action, but merely anticipates a plea of fair comment or qualified privilege. Express malice need only be pleaded when one or other of these defences has been raised by the defendant on his own initiative and the proper place for such a plea is the reply.

See Order 82, r. 3(3) and Precedent No. 49.

Normally it is for the defendant to plead specifically any relevant period of limitation (Order 18, r. 8), and therefore, the plaintiff usually need not allege facts which, he hopes, will take the case out of the Limitation Act.

Hollis v. *Palmer* (1836) 2 Bing., N.C. 173 (an action of debt). But see now *Ogunsanya* v. *Lambeth Area Health Authority*, July 3, 1985 (unreported).

However in a claim for money due under an agreement which, but for a subsequent acknowledgment, would be statute-barred, it is proper to plead the facts relating to the acknowledgment in the statement of claim rather than in the reply.

Busch v. *Stevens* [1962] 1 All E.R. 412.

Any foreign limitation period which is relied upon in accordance with section 1 of the Foreign Limitation Periods Act 1984 must be expressly pleaded, with necessary particulars identifying the specific provisions relied on. And where the facts relied on show that the cause of action arose outside the current period of limitation and it is clear that the defendant intends to rely on the relevant Limitation Act, and there is nothing before the court to suggest that the plaintiff could escape from the defence, it is open to the court to strike out the statement of claim as disclosing no reasonable cause of action.

---

[9] *Sir Ralph Bovey's Case* (1684) Vent. 217.
[10] *Per* James L.J. in *Hall* v. *Eve* (1876) 4 Ch.D. at p. 345.
[11] *Rassam* v. *Budge* [1893] 1 Q.B. 571.

Riches v. *Director of Public Prosecutions* [1973] 1 W.L.R. 1019 (C.A.), as explained in *Ronex Properties Ltd.* v. *John Laing Construction Ltd.* [1982] 3 All E.R. 961 (C.A.).

"A party need not plead any fact if it is presumed by law to be true or the burden of disproving it lies on the other party, unless the other party has specifically denied it in his pleading" (Order 18, r. 7(3)).

Illustration

A plaintiff need not, in his pleading, set out the consideration for which a bill of exchange was given him, when he sues only on the bill. It will be for the defendant to plead no consideration. It is otherwise when the plaintiff sues on the consideration as a substantive ground of claim; then, of course, he must allege it specifically.

    cf. Bills of Exchange Act 1882, s.30.

Whenever the rule of law applicable to the case has an exception to it (as it generally has), all facts are material which tend to take the case out of the rule and bring it within the exception. And so are all facts which tend to take the case out of the exception and keep it within the rule.

Whenever the right claimed or the defence raised is the creature of statute, being unknown to the common law, every fact must be alleged necessary to bring the case within the statute.

When the right claimed or the defence raised existed at common law, but the common law applicable to the case has been materially altered in its substance by statute, all facts are material which tend to take the case out of the rule at common law and bring it within the statute. And so are all facts which tend to show that the statute does not apply to the particular case.

But where the right claimed or the defence raised existed at common law, and the subsequent statute has not affected its validity, but merely introduced regulations as to the mode of its existence or performance, the statute does not affect the form of pleading. It is sufficient to allege whatever was sufficient before the statute.

Illustrations

At common law the assignee of a debt could not sue at all; in equity he could sue if he made the assignor a party. But by the Law of Property Act 1925, s.136, he can sue alone if the debt is absolutely assigned to him by writing under the hand of the assignor, and express notice in writing of such assignment has been given to the debtor. The statement of claim of such an assignee suing alone must expressly allege—

(a) an absolute assignment
(b) in writing; and
(c) notice of such assignment
(d) given in writing to the debtor before the commencement of the action.

For without these averments the case is not brought within the statute and the plaintiff has no right to bring the action.

Seear v. *Lawson* (1880) 16 Ch.D. 121; 50 L.J. Ch. 139.

By section 146(1) of the Law of Property Act 1925 a landlord cannot eject a tenant for breach of covenant to repair without serving on him, a reasonable time before the writ is issued, a notice in writing specifying the repairs that are needed and other matters. Need a landlord suing for recovery of possession allege in his statement of claim that he did give such a notice a reasonable time before action? No: for he has a perfectly good right of entry without it; the statute merely regulates his exercise of that right; in other words, it imposes a fresh condition precedent to his right of action. His due performance of the requirements of the statute will therefore be presumed until the defendant pleads that he never was served with any such notice.

Order 18, r. 7(4).

Gates v. *W. A. & R.J. Jacobs, Ltd.* [1920] 1 Ch. 567.

And see Precedent No. 32.

Conditions Precedent

Neither party need allege the performance of any condition precedent. The party who desires to contest the performance or occurrence of any condition precedent must raise the point specifically in his pleading. "A statement that a thing has been done or that an event has occurred, being a thing or event the doing or occurrence of which, as the case may be, constitutes a condition precedent necessary for the case of a party is to be implied in his pleading" (Order 18, r. 7(4)).

Note the wording of this rule. It does not say such an averment is immaterial; only that it shall be implied. There is a reason for this. Although it is no longer necessary for a plaintiff to plead the due performance of all conditions precedent to his right of action, yet the burden of *proving* due performance is still on him, if the defendant specially pleads non-performance. In former days it was essential for a plaintiff to set out in his declaration every condition precedent to his right, and to aver the due performance of it with all particularity. Then came the Common Law Procedure Act 1852, s.57 of which provided: "It shall be lawful for the plaintiff or defendant in any action to aver performance of conditions precedent generally, and the opposite party shall not deny such averment generally, but shall specify in his pleading the condition or conditions precedent the performance of which he intends to contest." And now a general averment of the due performance of all conditions precedent is implied in every pleading.[12]

But what is a condition precedent? And how does it differ from the material facts which must be pleaded?

Where everything has happened which would at common law prima facie entitle a man to a certain sum of money, or vest in him a certain right of action, in this particular case there is something further to be done, or something more must happen before he is entitled to sue, either by reason of the provisions of some statute, or because the parties have expressly so agreed—this something more is called a condition precedent. It is not of the essence of such a cause of action; but it has been made essential. It is an additional formality superimposed on what otherwise would have been valid. Hence the plaintiff can draft a perfectly good statement of claim without any reference to it; and it is for the defendant to raise the point if he thinks the plaintiff has not performed all that is required of him. If neither party refers to the condition, it will probably be because it has been duly complied with; anyhow its due performance will in that event be presumed.

Illustrations

The giving of the notice required by section 146(1) of the Law of Property Act 1925 is a condition precedent to the commencement of the action, but, as we have seen (*ante*), it need not be specially pleaded in the statement of claim.

Gates v. *W. A. & R. J. Jacobs Ltd.* [1920] 1 Ch. 567.

In an action for breach of contract an allegation that the plaintiff was ready and willing to perform the contract may be implied (*Jefferson* v. *Paskell* [1916] 1 K.B. 57, 74), although, where there is a claim for specific performance, it is still common practice for the plaintiff to aver that he has done, or is ready and willing to do, as much towards completion as it is possible for him to do.

Matters affecting Damages

A "material fact" has been defined as a fact which is essential to the plaintiff's cause of action or to the defendant's defence. But there are many facts which are not material on the main issue whether the plaintiff ought to succeed or not, and which will yet be proved and discussed at the trial, because they affect the amount of *damages* which he will be entitled to recover. Such facts are called "matters in aggravation of damages" or "matters in mitigation of damages."

---

[12] *Bank of New South Wales* v. *Laing* [1954] A.C. 135 provides a good illustration of the technicalities arising under the old system of pleading.

Much learning has in the past been displayed in discussing whether the plaintiff and defendant respectively should state such facts in their pleading. In the light of the rules in their present form and the decision in *Plato Films Ltd.* v. *Speidel*[13] it seems clear that they should. Lord Denning says so expressly[14] in relation to evidence of the plaintiff's bad character; moreover, Order 18, r. 8(1)(*b*) requires any matter which might take the opposite party by surprise to be specially pleaded. It was, however, formerly the practice for defendants not to plead specifically to damages nor to plead "matter in mitigation of damage" save in actions for libel or slander where the rules specifically required such a pleading. Since June 1990 the position has changed, and by virtue of Order 18, r. 12(1)(*c*) it is no longer the case that allegations as to the amount of damages are deemed to be traversed. Particulars of any facts on which a party relies in mitigation of, or otherwise in relation to, the amount of damages, must be pleaded in all cases.

It is impossible to draw any logical distinction between matters in aggravation and matters in mitigation of damages, and the former also should be pleaded.[16]

In an action of libel or slander the defendant may, by a special plea in mitigation of damages, justify part of the words, provided such part is distinct and severable from the rest.[17] The plea must distinctly identify the portion justified.[18] Without such a plea the defendant can give no evidence that any portion of his words is true.

A claim for exemplary damages must be specifically pleaded together with the facts on which the party pleading relies (Order 18, r. 8(3)).

(iii) Every Pleading must state Facts, and not the Evidence by which they are to be Proved

Facts should be alleged as facts. It is not necessary to state in the pleadings circumstances which merely tend to prove the truth of the facts already alleged.

The fact in issue between the parties is the *factum probandum*, the fact to be proved, and therefore the fact to be alleged. It is unnecessary to tell the other side how it is proposed to prove that fact; such matters are merely evidence, *facta probantia*, facts

---

[13] [1961] A.C. 1090.
[14] *Ibid.* p. 1135.
[16] *Millington* v. *Loring* (1880) 6 Q.B.D. 190.
[17] *Davis* v. *Billing* (1891) 8 T.L.R. 58.
[18] *Vessey* v. *Pike* (1829) 3 C. & P. 512.

by means of which one proves the fact in issue. Such facts will be *relevant* at the trial, but they are not *material facts* for pleading purposes.[19]

This was always a clear rule of the common law. "Evidence shall never be pleaded, because it tends to prove matter in fact, and therefore the matter in fact shall be pleaded."[20]

In the Court of Chancery, however, this rule was never observed: the pleadings there were lengthy narratives which sometimes became intolerably prolix. They stated the evidence on which the party proposed to rely in full detail, with copious extracts from the material documents. They were more like lengthy affidavits than modern pleadings.

This was partly due to the nature of the matters with which equity courts had to deal; for even now an equitable defence or reply is pleaded in the Queen's Bench Division somewhat more in detail than is usual in the case of ordinary legal defences or replies.[21] Moreover, it is not always easy to decide what are the facts to be proved, and what is only evidence of those facts. The question is often one of degree. "There are many cases in which facts and evidence are so mixed up as to be almost indistinguishable."[22] Usually though the line is reasonably clear between the fact in issue and the evidence by which that fact would be proved, and the courts have been content to affirm the principle without trying to elaborate the distinction further.[23]

Illustrations

So, if the plaintiff alleges that he has suffered certain damage in consequence of the defendant's wrongful act, it is not necessary to set out the facts showing the connection between the damage and the wrongful act. These are matters of evidence. It is sufficient to allege the wrongful act, and that the defendant caused it, and then to continue, "The plaintiff has thereby suffered loss and damage, etc." (specifying the damage). "If both the unlawful act and the consequence are stated, it is unnecessary to allege the means by which that act produced that consequence. . . . The means are matters of evidence."

Per Lord Mansfield and Buller J. in *R.* v. *Eccles* (1783) 3 Doug. at p. 337.

If an issue is whether X had authority to make a certain contract on behalf of the defendant, the plaintiff may plead either that "the defendant employed X as agent to make the said contract on his behalf," or that "the defendant held X out as having authority to make the said contract on his behalf." But he should

---

[19] See *Re Dependable Upholstery, Ltd.* [1936] 3 All E.R. at p. 743; *Thompson* v. *Thompson* [1957] P. 19; but *cf. Bruce* v. *Odhams Press, Ltd.* [1936] 1 K.B. 697, where such facts were material.

[20] *Dowman's Case* (1586) 9 Rep. 9b.

[21] See *Heap* v. *Marris* (1877) 2 Q.B.D. 630.

[22] *Smith* v. *West* [1876] W.N. 55.

[23] See, *e.g.* the remarks of Lord Denman C.J. in *Williams* v. *Wilcox* (1838) 8 A. & E. at p. 331, and of Brett L.J. in *Philipps* v. *Philipps* (1878) 4 Q.B.D. at p. 133.

not plead "at the time of making the said contract X represented that he was the defendant's agent and that he had authority from him to make the said contract on his behalf." And it is absurd to plead, as was once done, that X "has all along been regarded by the lessor, the bankers, and the plaintiff himself, as the agent of the defendant."

Similarly, the plaintiff should not plead that he had "been informed by the defendant that . . . " etc. Such a plea will be struck out on the ground that it states evidence by which it is proposed at the trial to prove the facts in issue.

Jones v. *Turner* [1875] W.N. 239.

And for a case where virtually an entire statement of claim was struck out on the ground that it contained a mass of evidence mixed up with the facts in issue and was therefore embarrassing, see *Davy* v. *Garrett* (1878) 7 Ch.D. 473.

It should be noted that Order 18, r. 12 requires that every pleading should contain the necessary particulars of any claim or defence or other matter relied on, *e.g.* any misrepresentation, fraud, breach of trust, etc. Similarly, in an action for libel or slander, Order 82, r. 3(2) requires a party pleading justification to give particulars of the facts and matters relied on in support of the allegation that the words complained of are true. The object of such particulars is "to inform the other side of the nature of the case they have to meet as distinguished from the mode in which that case is to be proved." (*Per* Lindley L.J. in *Duke* v. *Wisden* (1897) 77 L.T. 67.) The particulars should be set out in the pleadings in the same way as the facts in issue.

The general principle that every pleading must state facts and not the evidence by which they are to be proved is subject to an important exception. For any party who intends to adduce evidence of a conviction must include in his pleading a statement of his intention to do so, giving particulars of the conviction and its date, naming the court of trial, and specifying the issue in the proceedings to which the conviction is relevant.[24] Likewise any denial of the conviction, or of its relevance, or an allegation that it was erroneous must be specifically pleaded with due particularity. For a form of pleading reliance on a conviction in a negligence action involving personal injuries (a common type of case) see Precedent No. 24.

(iv) Every Pleading must state Material Facts concisely in a Summary Form

In the first place, material facts must be stated clearly and definitely. Be as concise as you can, provided you do not thereby become obscure. Pleadings are useless unless they state facts with precision. The names of persons and places, if

---

[24] Order 18, r. 7A; a rule which came into force as a necessary adjunct to s.11 of the Civil Evidence Act 1968 whereunder the fact of a conviction is made admissible in evidence at the trial if it is relevant to any issue to prove the commission of the criminal offence. A similar provision with regard to findings of adultery and paternity is to be found in s.12 of the Act to which this rule also applies.

material, must be accurately given. Avoid pronouns; it often is not clear whom you mean by "he." Repeat "the plaintiff," or "Johnson," whenever "he" would be ambiguous. Use relative pronouns as little as possible; when you do use them see that each has its proper antecedent. Call things by their right names, so far as you can, but in any event always allude to the same thing by the same name. Keep to the same phraseology throughout the pleading; a change of phrase suggests a change of meaning. If you are suing on a document, or relying on an Act of Parliament, do not attempt to improve on the language of either (however strong the temptation may be, especially in the latter case).

Illustrations

The plaintiff and the defendant should not be referred to by name in the body of the pleading. They should always be called "the plaintiff" and "the defendant" or, if more than one, "the first plaintiff," "the second defendant" according to the order in which their names appear in the title of the action.

The name of any other person, not a party to the suit, should be given in full, if known, the first time he is mentioned. Afterwards he can be referred to by his surname only, as "Johnson."

It does not matter in the least whether you allude to the cottage claimed by the plaintiff as "the cottage," or "the house," or "the messuage," or "the premises." But whichever phrase you use the first time should be used throughout the pleading. Nor is it necessary to use the word "said."

It will lead to confusion if you refer to the same document sometimes as "the deed of May 20, 1967," sometimes as "the lease," and sometimes as "the agreement between the parties." In fact, it is technically wrong to call a contract under seal an agreement.

A policy of life insurance by its express terms becomes void "if the assured shall die by his own hand." Do not plead that "the assured killed himself," or that he "committed suicide." Plead in the very words of the policy, "the assured died by his own hand."

See *Borradaile* v. *Hunter* (1843) 5 Man. & G. 639.

Facts should be alleged as facts. Use terse, short, curt, blunt sentences, all in the indicative mood. Be positive. Do not beat about the bush. Go straight to the point. If you mean to allege a particular fact, state it boldly, plainly, clearly and concisely. Avoid all "ifs," all introductory averments and all circumlocution. A pleading is not the place for fine writing, but simply for hard, downright, business-like assertion.

Avoid, too, the passive voice: always use the most direct and straightforward construction, and that, as a rule, will be the active voice. It is simpler and clearer to say, "He repaid the money on June 24, 1989," than to say, "The money was repaid by him" on that date.

Above all, avoid participial phrases; never say that the defendant, being so-and-so, did something. Make two sentences of it; say that he was so-and-so, and then that he did something. Avoid all clauses that are introduced by "being" or "having." If a fact is material, it should be stated as a positive fact, and in a separate sentence.

Then again, it is always conducive to clarity to observe the strict order of time. In all but the simplest cases, dates are of great importance. The only way to tell a long or complicated story clearly and intelligently is to keep to strict chronological order.

Illustrations

It is unnecessary to use introductory statements such as "the plaintiff will contend that (*e.g.*) it was an implied term of the agreement. . . . " Say simply, "It was an implied term of the agreement. . . . "

A long-winded form such as "The defendant denies that the goods referred to in paragraph 3 of the statement of claim, and therein alleged to have been delivered by the plaintiff to the defendant, or any of them, were in fact so delivered, and he puts the plaintiff to proof of such delivery" can and should be shortened to one simple statement: "The plaintiff never delivered any of the goods to the defendant."

An example of a badly-drafted statement of claim: "The plaintiffs, being dealers in oil paintings, have suffered loss by the breach of contract of the defendants, who are also dealers in oil paintings, made by their agent by telephone, refusing to deliver a Picasso oil painting to the plaintiffs." This pleading contains at least three distinct allegations depending on participles and there is no reference to either the consideration for the agreement or to the person who made the oral contract on behalf of the plaintiffs.

This, then, is the *first* essential of good pleading—to be *clear*. The next is to be *brief*. The Rules repeatedly insist on the necessity of brevity.

The fundamental rule cited at the head of this chapter requires that "every pleading must contain, and contain only, a statement in a summary form of the material facts on which the party pleading relies . . . and the statement must be as brief as the nature of the case admits" (Order 18, r. 7(1)).

If anything is done improperly or unnecessarily—and this includes unnecessary prolixity—the court has power to give appropriate directions to the Taxing Master as to the costs thereby occasioned (Order 62, r. 10). Under Order 62, r. 28 the Taxing Master may exercise the power conferred on the court by r. 10(1). He will in any case only allow such costs as are proper to be allowed in accordance with Order 62, r. 12.[25]

Yet, as we have seen each party must state his whole case; he cannot, strictly, prove at the trial any material fact which is not alleged in his pleading. How, then, is the necessary brevity to be attained?

---

[25] See *Practice Direction (Costs, etc.)* June 26, 1990.

In two ways:
  I. By omitting every unnecessary allegation.
  II. By omitting all unnecessary detail when alleging mater-
      ial facts.

I. It is Bad Pleading to insert a Single Unnecessary Allegation

Illustrations

Neither party should set out the provisions of public Acts of Parliament; or of private Acts passed since 1850, unless the Act itself makes it necessary to be cited. Nor should he state in his pleading the propositions of law which he proposes to urge upon the court.

Neither party may plead the evidence by which he proposes to prove the facts on which he relies.

See Order 18, r. 7(1).

It is "a rule of law that a man shall never traverse that which the plaintiff has not alleged in his declaration."

Per Holt C.J. in *Powers* v. *Cook* (1696) 1 Ld.Ray. 63.

Rassam v. *Budge* [1893] 1 Q.B. 571; 62 L.J.Q.B. 312.

"A party need not plead any fact if it is presumed by law to be true or the burden of disproving it lies on the other party, unless the other party has specifically denied it in his pleading."

Order 18, r. 7(3).

Neither party need allege the performance of any condition precedent; such an averment is now implied in every pleading.

Order 18, r. 7(4).

Neither party need set out the whole or any part of any conversation or document, unless its precise words are material. It is sufficient to state its purport or effect as briefly as possible.

Order 18, r. 7(2).

It is unnecessary for either party to plead any matter, or to plead to any matter, which merely affects costs.

It is unnecessary for either party to plead to his opponent's prayer or claim or to his particulars. He need only deal with the allegations contained in the body of the preceding pleading.

Neither party need refer in his pleading to any item for which his opponent has given him credit.

It is unnecessary for either party in his pleading to refer to any interlocutory proceeding in the action, or to recount the history of the case since writ.

It is not necessary for either party to plead any fact which is not yet material to his case, though he may reasonably suppose that it may become material at a later stage.

II. When Pleading Material Facts, all Unnecessary Details should be Omitted

A certain amount of detail is essential to ensure clarity and precision. "Although pleadings must now be concise, they must also be precise."[26] Indeed, Order 18, r. 12, expressly

---

[26] *Per* Kay J. in *Re Parton, Townsend* v. *Parton* (1882) 30 W.R. 287; 45 L.T. 756.

requires that "every pleading must contain the necessary particulars of any claim, defence or other matter pleaded."[27] It is sometimes difficult to know what particulars are necessary, or what degree of particularity is expected of the pleader. The modern approach to pleading is to provide more rather than less information so that all parties will know at the earliest possible moment the nature of the case they will have to meet. Order 18, r. 12 gives specific examples of certain particulars which must be pleaded, and rule 12(1A) provides that in personal injury actions a medical report and a schedule of the special damages claimed shall be served with the statement of claim.

---

[27] Necessary particulars of any debt, expenses or damages, if they exceed 3 folios (216 words or figures) must be set out in a separate document referred to in the pleading, and the pleading must state whether the document has already been served, and if so when, or is to be served with the pleading (Ord. 18, r. 12(2)).

CHAPTER 8

CERTAINTY

Material facts must be alleged with certainty. The object of pleadings is to ascertain definitely what is the question at issue between the parties; and this object can only be attained when each party states his case with precision. If vague and general statements were allowed, nothing would be defined; the issue would be "enlarged," as it is called; and neither party would know, when the case came on for trial, what was the real point to be discussed and decided. On the other hand, a party who pleads with unnecessary particularity may thereby fetter his hand at the trial.[1]

The amount of detail necessary to ensure precision naturally varies with the nature of each case. The only general rule that can be laid down is this—that the party pleading must use such particularity as will make it clear to the court and to his opponent what is the precise question which he desires to raise. "What particulars are to be stated must depend on the facts of each case. But in my opinion it is absolutely essential that the pleading, not to be embarrassing to the defendants, should state those facts which will put the defendants on their guard, and tell them what they will have to meet when the case comes on for trial."[2]

The pleader, then, must decide for himself how far it is necessary for him to set out items and go into figures; how far details of time and place and other surrounding circumstances are necessary to make his pleading intelligible and precise. Experience will teach him this; even common sense without experience will help him much, for our law is rapidly degenerating into common sense!

Perhaps the best test is this: after you have drafted your pleading, banish your instructions from your mind for a moment, and imagine yourself a stranger coming fresh to the matter. Would your draft, read by itself, convey to his mind a clear conception of your client's case? If not, you must make your draft more definite: and this object will often be best attained by omitting half of it. Length does not conduce to perspicuity. Half a dozen neat, short sentences, each clear in itself, will tell your story best.

[1] As in *James* v. *Smith* [1891] 1 Ch. 384.
[2] *Per* Cotton L.J. in *Philipps* v. *Philipps* (1878) 4 Q.B.D. 139.

And note this distinction. If you omit a material fact altogether from your pleading, this slip may lose the case for your client,[3] or at the very least involve delay and expense in amendment. If you plead the fact, but with insufficient detail, the worst that can happen is that you have to give particulars—at some small cost to your client.

Illustrations
The Claim for Relief

Where a plaintiff claims a specific sum of money as the total amount due to him on an account containing many items, he must state particulars showing how that figure is arrived at.

Order 18, r. 12(2).

Philipps v. *Philipps* (1878) 4 Q.B.D. at p. 131.

So if a plaintiff in his statement of claim gives the defendant credit for a certain amount, and claims to recover the balance, he must not merely name a lump sum, but state the dates and items of the amounts credited. For without this information the defendant cannot tell whether it is necessary for him to plead payment or set-off, or to counterclaim for the sums which he has paid the plaintiff.

Godden v. *Corsten* (1879) 5 C.P.D. 17; 49 L.J.C.P. 112.

And see Precedent No. 1.

Where the claim is for damages, no particulars will ordinarily be required of general damage except in personal injury cases, where a medical report must be served with the statement of claim. But special damage must be alleged with sufficient particularity to inform the defendant of the nature and extent of the loss sustained and in personal injury actions a schedule of those damages must be served with the statement of claim.

Contract

The pleading should always state the date of the alleged agreement, the names of all parties to it, and whether it was made orally or in writing, in the former case stating by whom it was made and in the latter case identifying the document. If the agreement be not under seal the consideration must also be stated.

Turquand v. *Fearon* (1879) 48 L.J.Q.B. 703. And see Precedents Nos. 16–21 and 23.

Where a contract is alleged to be implied from a series of letters or conversations or otherwise from a number of circumstances, the contract should be alleged as a fact and the letters, conversations or circumstances set out generally.

See Precedent No. 22.

Where the cause of action is misrepresentation inducing a contract, particulars of the alleged misrepresentation must be contained in the pleading (Order 18, r. 12(1)(*a*)). It should be stated when, by whom and to whom the alleged misrepresentations were made, and whether orally or in writing—in the latter case identifying the document.

Seligmann v. *Young* [1884] W.N. 93.

And see Precedent No. 21.

---

[3] See, *e.g. Collette* v. *Goode* (1878) 7 Ch.D. 842; *Byrd* v. *Nunn* (1877) 5 Ch.D. 781; 7 Ch.D. 284.

Time

In an action on any negotiable instrument, its date and amount and the parties thereto should be stated.

Walker v. *Hicks* (1877) 3 Q.B.D. 8; 47 L.J.Q.B. 27.

In an action for goods sold and delivered, the date and amount of each consignment should be stated; or identified by reference to some specific account already rendered.

Parpaite Frères v. *Dickinson* (1878) 38 L.T. 178.

See Precedent No. 1.

A claim for possession of demised premises based on and for non-payment of rent must state the dates at which the rent claimed fell due.

See Precedent No. 31 (a county court form, but the principle applicable is the same in all cases).

Where the defendant has raised the Limitation Acts or any defence of waiver by laches, dates are most material and must therefore be pleaded.

Reeves v. *Butcher* [1891] 2 Q.B. 509; 60 L.J.Q.B. 619.

Place

In an action for the recovery of land the property must be described with sufficient certainty to enable the sheriff to put the plaintiff in possession of it, if he is successful in the action.

Title

Where either party claims to be the owner of any property, real or personal, or of any right or interest to, in or over it, he must state his title to such property, right or interest, with all due particularity. The pleadings must show title.

But very different degrees of particularity are necessary in different cases. In the first place, our law always respects possession. Possession is a physical fact, and generally an obvious one; it is wholly distinct from ownership, which is often a difficult question of law. The true owner of a field or of a chattel may be in possession of it, or he may not. Again, he may be rightfully out of possession, as where he has let it to a tenant, or lent it to a friend; or he may be wrongfully out of possession, as where he has been evicted from the field by a trespasser, or where the chattel has been stolen.

A man may be said to be in possession of land or of a chattel whenever he has full and uncontrolled physical dominion over it. Thus, he is in possession of a house when he is living in it; if he is absent from it, he would still be held to be in possession, if such absence was only temporary, of if he could return and re-enter at any moment, if he chose, without asking anyone's permission and without any preliminary ceremony. But the moment anyone else enters into and remains in possession of the premises without his consent, the former possessor is ousted; for two persons cannot be in possession of the same property at the same time (unless they are partners or joint occupiers).

I. *Where the Person Showing Title is in Possession or was in Possession at the Date of the Wrong Complained of*

As against a wrongdoer, it is usually sufficient to allege a merely possessory title.[4] Thus, in trespass to land it is sufficient to describe the *locus in quo* as the "land of the plaintiff," or to allege that "the plaintiff was lawfully possessed of certain land," describing it. So, with respect to incorporeal hereditaments, it is sufficient to allege that the plaintiff was possessed of the corporeal thing in respect of which the incorporeal right is claimed, *e.g.* "the plaintiff was possessed of certain premises" (stating their name and situation), "and by reason thereof was entitled to common pasture," or to a right of way, etc. However, where a plaintiff in an action for wrongful interference with goods is one of two or more persons having or claiming any interest in the goods, he must now generally give particulars of his title to the goods and identify every other person who, to his knowledge, has or claims any interest in the goods. If the plaintiff does not give[5] such particulars or does not have the written authority of every other such person to sue on the latter's behalf, he will be taken to be asserting sole possessory title to the goods.

Illustrations

In an action of trespass it is sufficient to allege that the defendant entered certain land of the plaintiff, called——(describing it).

In an action for obstructing a right of way it is sufficient to allege that the plaintiff was possessed of certain premises, the occupiers whereof had from time immemorial (*or* for so many years before action) enjoyed as of right and without interruption a way from the said premises across certain land called Blackacre to a public highway, and back again from the said public highway over the said land to the said premises, for themselves and their servants, on foot and with horses, cattle and carriages, at all times of the year.

See Prescription Act 1832.

As to pleading a prescriptive right at common law to an easement, or to any profit or benefit taken or arising out of land, see 2 Wms.Saund. 401a; *Att.-Gen. v. Gauntlett* (1829) 3 Y. & J. 93. As to pleading a period of prescription under the Act, see Prescription Act 1832, s.5. And see Bullen & Leake's *Precedents of Pleadings*.

---

[4] *Armory* v. *Delamirie* (1722) 1 Smith's *Leading Cases*.
[5] Ord. 15, r. 10A.

A defendant to an action for the recovery of land must plead specifically every ground of defence on which he relies, and a plea that he is in possession of the land by himself or his tenant is not sufficient (Order 18, r. 8(2)). In this respect the law was radically altered by a rule in force since 1964. Formerly he was only required to plead specifically if he was in possession by virtue of a lease from the plaintiff or his predecessor in title or if he had an equitable defence; all other defences could be raised under the bare plea that he was in possession. Now he must plead them. The defendant in an action for the recovery of land has never been bound to disclose his title or want of title: the plaintiff must recover on the strength of his own title, not on the weakness of his adversary's title. Therefore the defendant may deny the plaintiff's title, or any particular link in it, and put him to the proof of it. If, however, the defendant intends to allege specifically that the plaintiff's ancestor conveyed the property to him, or to trustees who are not parties to the action, he should so plead, especially if it is a matter which might take the plaintiff by surprise (Order 18, r. 8(1) and (2)).

A defendant who is in possession of a chattel may also, if he thinks fit, content himself with denying that the goods are the plaintiff's, and so put him to proof of his title.[6] But if the defendant claims any right to the possession of the chattel apart from ownership this should be specially pleaded; otherwise, as soon as the plaintiff proves his title, the right to the possession of his own property (which is always inherent in ownership) will at once attach and displace the prima facie title which the defendant derived from its possession. A plaintiff who has proved his title to the property is not a wrongdoer, and mere possession will not avail against him. A defendant to an action for wrongful interference with goods who seeks to rely on the defence of *jus tertii*[7] must follow the special procedure of Order 15, r. 10A, whereby application must be made for joinder of the *tertius* as a party to the action.

Illustrations

In an action for the recovery of a chattel, the defendant must plead specially that it was hired out to him for a definite period not yet expired, or lent to him for a purpose not yet accomplished, or pawned to him, or that he has a lien on it for warehouse rent, or any other lien. For such defences admit the plaintiff's title to the ownership of the goods, and should therefore be specially pleaded by way of "confession and avoidance".

---

6 But note the position where the defendant is a bailee (*post*).
7 See the Torts (Interference with Goods) Act 1977, s.8.

II. *Where the Party pleading is out of Possession and his Opponent is in Possession*

Here, if the title of the party pleading is material, its *basis*, whether ownership in fee simple or a term of years or an equitable interest, must be pleaded. But how far is it necessary to allege its *origin*?

If he claims possession, he must show possession, either in himself or in someone from whom he claims, prior to the alleged wrongful act or possession of his opponent. As to estates in fee simple the old rule was that it was sufficient to state a *seisin* in fee simple without showing the derivation or commencement of the estate; for if that were required the process might be carried back *ad infinitum*. If, however, he was obliged in his pleading to allege seisin in someone other than himself, he was bound to show how the fee passed to him from such other person.[8]

With respect to *particular estates* (which included estates for life, estates tail, terms of years and tenancies at will) the general rule was that he must show the derivation of that title from its commencement, that is to say, from the last seisin in fee simple with all subsequent devolutions, stating the nature and effect of each transfer or conveyance.[9] An exception was, however, permitted in the case of a plea of "*liberum tenementum*" in answer to an action of trespass, where a defendant was (and still is) allowed to allege a general freehold title; the old plea being merely that "the said close was the close, soil and freehold of the defendant," even though he might only have held a particular freehold estate (as was formerly possible).

The Law of Property Act 1925 and the Settled Land Act 1925 reduced the number of legal estates and extended the classes of persons entitled to the fee simple, and a tenant for life or in tail has the legal estate in fee simple vested in him. There are now only two legal estates: a fee simple absolute in possession (which does not necessarily mean physical possession),[10] and a term of years absolute. And of equitable estates conferring a right to immediate possession, a tenancy under an agreement for a lease is alone likely to be met with in practice.

There do not appear to be any reported cases as to the pleading of title since 1925, but it would seem that in the main

---

[8] See *Stephens on Pleading* (6th ed. 1860), p. 232.
[9] *Ibid.* and Co. Litt. 303b; *Pinhorn* v. *Souster* (1853) 8 Ex. 138.
[10] Law of Property Act 1925, s.205(xix).

the old rules are still applicable. Thus, provided that the party
pleading duly traces title from a fee simple absolute with actual
possession, he need go no further. If he has only a term of
years, his pleading must show the commencement and derivation of his title. Cases where he has to rely upon an equitable
estate will be less frequent, since the owner of the legal estate
will usually be the proper party; but if he does, he should
show its origin in like manner.

In the case of a term of years the pleading should state fully:
  (a) the commencement and derivation of title, if that is
      material,[11] giving the number of owners, if more than
      one, at any stage;
  (b) who granted the lease pleaded and to whom, and any
      subsequent steps such as assignment; and
  (c) the length of the term granted and the period of enjoy-
      ment. (Dates are most material in any case of disputed
      title.)

Illustrations

In an action for the recovery of land of which the plaintiff has never been in
possession, the statement of claim must allege the nature of the deeds and
documents upon which he relies in deducing his title from the person under
whom he claims. A general statement, that by assurances, wills, documents
and Crown grants in the possession of the defendants, without further
describing them, the plaintiff is entitled to the land, is embarrassing and liable
to be struck out under Order 18, r. 19(1).

  Philipps v. *Philipps* (1878) 4 Q.B.D. 127; 48 L.J. Q.B. 135.

If a lease is granted by J.S. to the defendant, and the plaintiff, claiming as
assignee of the reversion, sues the lessee on the covenant therein contained for
rent, he must precisely state the conveyances or other transfers of title from
J.S. to himself, whereby he became entitled to the reversion. To say generally
that the reversion came to him by assignment will not be sufficient without
circumstantially alleging all the mesne assignments. The devolution of the
estate to the plaintiff must be shown.

  Davis v. *James* (1884) 26 Ch.D. 778; 53 L.J. Ch. 523.

Where a plaintiff claims as assignee of a debt originally contracted between
the defendant and A, he must show in his pleading how he derives his title; he
must allege an absolute assignment in writing, and that notice in writing of
such assignment was given to the defendant before action, otherwise he would
not be entitled to sue, at all events without joining A as a co-plaintiff. (Law of
Property Act 1925, s.136.)

  Seear v. *Lawson* (1880) 16 Ch.D. 121; 50 L.J. Ch. 139.

Title by Estoppel

There is one case in which this particularity is unnecessary. No
title need be shown at all where the opposite party is estopped

---

[11] In an action by a lessor against his lessee title is not usually material: nor is it material if
alleged merely by way of inducement.

from denying the title. Thus, if a lessor sues the original lessee, or anyone who has attorned tenant to the lessor, *e.g.* by paying rent, he need allege no title to the premises demised, because in those circumstances a tenant is estopped from denying his landlord's title.[12]

But the tenant is not bound to admit title to any extent greater than would authorise the lease. Hence, if the action is brought not by the lessor himself but by his heir, executor, or other representative or assignee, the title of the lessor must be alleged, in order to show that the reversion is now legally vested in the plaintiff in the character in which he sues.[13] The tenant is not bound to admit that his lessor was seised in fee; and a tenant is not estopped from saying that his landlord's title has determined, or from saying that he paid rent to the plaintiff merely as a collector for his landlord.[14]

Pleading Title in Another

So far we have dealt with the case where the party pleading alleges title in himself. The same rules apply with equal strictness where the party pleading sets up title in some third person, from whom he says he derived the authority to do the act complained of. For instance, where a servant exercises a right of way by his master's order, the right must be pleaded with the same particularity as if the master, whose authority he pleads, had been made a defendant.

Next, we must consider the case where a party alleges title in his adversary with the object of making him liable in respect of the property, real or personal.

In this case it is not necessary to allege title more precisely than is sufficient to show a liability in the party charged, or to defeat his present claim. The reason for this difference is that a party may be presumed to be ignorant of the particulars of his adversary's title, though he is bound to know his own.[15] "It lies more properly in the knowledge of the lessor what estate he himself has in the land, which he demises, than of the lessee who is a stranger to it."[16]

---

[12] *Casey* v. *Hellyar* (1886) 17 Q.B.D. 97; *Jones* v. *Stone* [1894] A.C. 122. If the defendant asserts the title to be in himself or a stranger, he thereby incurs a forfeiture; but a mere traverse of the landlord's title, if the title is expressly alleged, does not have this effect. (*Warner* v. *Sampson* [1959] 1 Q.B. 297.)

[13] See *Cuthbertson* v. *Irving* (1860) 4 H. & N. 742; 6 H. & N. 135 (in error); *Thriscutt* v. *Martin* (1849) 3 Ex. 454; and the judgment of Willes J. in *Smith* v. *Scott* (1859) 6 C.B.(N.S.) 771.

[14] *Jones* v. *Stone* [1894] A.C. 122.

[15] See *Rider* v. *Smith* (1790) 3 T.R. 766; *Att.-Gen.* v. *Meller* (1679) Hard. 459.

[16] *Bradshaw's Case* (1613) 9 Rep. 60b; and see *Cudlip* v. *Rundle* (1692) Carth. 202.

In order to show a liability in the party charged, according to the rule here given, it is in most cases sufficient to allege that your adversary is in possession, and to prove that he has some present interest in chattels, or is in actual possession of land. But this form of pleading is *ex hypothesi* inapplicable if the interest he possesses is by way of reversion or remainder. In that event the party pleading must state his opponent's title in detail. Then, again, there are cases in which to charge a party with mere possession would not be sufficient to show his liability. Thus, if the defendant is sued as assignee of a term of years for arrears of rent due under a covenant in the lease creating that term, it is not sufficient to show that he is in possession of the property demised, but it must be further shown that he is in possession as assignee of the term. But even here the party pleading is not expected to plead all the details of the various assignments of the term, though he must show all the assignments of the reversion; for these are within his knowledge.

Pleading Authority

Whenever the party pleading seeks to justify an act prima facie unlawful, he must show his authority or excuse with precision. If he seeks to justify it by virtue of any writ, warrant, precept or other authority, he must set it forth particularly in his pleading. If he pleads that he did the act by the command of A, he must further show that A had legal right and title so to command. If the plaintiff is in possession of any land or goods, or can otherwise make out a prima facie title to them, it is not enough for the defendant to show a better title in some third person; he must also show that he acted as agent for such third person at the time he did the act complained of.

Illustrations

If you trespass on land of which I am in possession, it is immaterial that the land really belongs to A, unless you claim through or under A, or acted by his authority.

With respect to acts valid at common law, but regulated as to the mode of performance by statute, it is sufficient to use such certainty of allegation as was sufficient before the statute.

Where the act complained of was done in the execution of judicial process, it is not sufficient for the defendant to allege generally that he so acted by virtue of a certain writ or warrant directed to him; he must set it forth particularly in his plea.[17] If the party pleading is an officer of the court, he need not also set out the judgment on which such writ or warrant was founded; for it is his duty to execute the process of the court without inquiring into the validity or even the existence of the judgment.[18] But if the party pleading is not an officer of the court, he must set out the judgment as well as the writ.[19] If it is the judgment of a superior court, none of the previous proceedings in that suit need be stated; if it is the judgment of an inferior court, or, it seems, of a foreign court, then so much of the previous proceedings must be pleaded as will show jurisdiction in that court (*e.g.* that the cause of action arose within its jurisdiction); and if it is a court whose jurisdiction is not defined by any public Act of Parliament of which judicial notice will be taken, the nature and extent of its jurisdiction should also be set forth.[20]

Charges of Misconduct and Negligence

Particularity is especially needed where the pleading contains an imputation on the character of your opponent; as then it is only right and fair that he should know definitely before the trial what is the charge which is made against him. Justice requires you to define the accusation you bring against anyone; and this is a very different thing from setting out the evidence by which you intend to establish it. "The court will require of him who makes the charge that he shall state that charge with as much definiteness and particularity as may be done, both as regards time and place."[21] It is no excuse for the omission of such details that the opponent must already be perfectly well aware of the facts.[22] Each party is entitled to know the outline of the case that his adversary is going to make against him, and to bind him down to a definite story.

Illustrations
Misconduct
Every pleading must contain the necessary particulars of any misrepresentation, fraud, breach of trust, wilful default or undue influence on which the party pleading relies.
    Order 18, r. 12(1)(*a*).

---

[17] 1 Wms.Saund. 298, n. 8; Co. Litt. 303b.
[18] *Andrews* v. *Marris* (1841) 1 Q.B. 3; *Dews* v. *Riley* (1851) 11 C.B. 434.
[19] *Per* Holt C.J. in *Britton* v. *Cole* (1698) 1 Ld. Ray. 305; *Barker* v. *Braham* (1773) 3 Wils. 368.
[20] *Moravia* v. *Sloper* (1737) Will. 30; *Morrell* v. *Martin* (1841) 3 M. & G. 581.
[21] *Per* Lord Penzance in *Marriner* v. *Bishop of Bath and Wells* [1893] P. at p. 146.
[22] *B.* v. *B. and G.* [1937] P. 1, at p. 5.

Where a pleader seeks to avoid the Limitation Acts by pleading concealed fraud he must state his case with the utmost particularity or the pleading may be struck out.

Lawrence v. *Lord Norreys* (1890) 15 App.Cas. 210.

Where the plaintiff alleges that the defendant has committed breaches of trust he must give particulars of the alleged breaches of trust and wilful default, or the allegation will be struck out.

Belmont Finance Corporation Ltd. v. *Williams Furniture Ltd.* [1979] 1 All E.R. 118.

See Precedents Nos. 33, 34.

In an action of defamation, the defence of justification, like fraud, should not be pleaded unless there is "clear and sufficient evidence to support it" (*per* Lord Denning M.R. in *Associated Leisure Ltd.* v. *Associated Newspapers Ltd.* [1970] 2 Q.B. 450 at p. 456). If the libel or slander consists of one specific charge, it is sufficient to allege generally that the words are true, "but the defendant must make clear in the particulars the meaning to be attributed to the words that he is seeking to justify." (*Lucas-Box* v. *News Group Newspapers Ltd.* [1986] 1 W.L.R. 147). Where the defendant justifies a general charge of misconduct, (*e.g.* that the plaintiff is a "swindler"), specific instances must be given in the defence, and stated with sufficient particularity to inform the plaintiff precisely what are the facts to be tried, and what is the charge made against him.

Wootton v. *Sievier* [1913] 3 K.B. 449.

Negligence

Particulars must always be given of any alleged negligence, showing in what respects the defendant was negligent. The statement of claim should state the facts on which the supposed duty is founded, the duty to the plaintiff with the breach of which the defendant is charged, the precise breach of that duty of which the plaintiff complains, and, lastly, particulars of the injury and damage sustained.

Bills v. *Roe* [1968] 1 W.L.R. 925.

And see Precedents Nos. 24, 25, 26.

Particulars of any allegation of contributory negligence should be given or will be ordered where necessary.

Atkinson v. *Stewart and Partners Ltd.* [1954] N.I. 146, C.A.

Fookes v. *Slaytor* [1978] 1 W.L.R. 1293.

And see Precedent No. 41.

Where an employee alleges that an accident was due to the failure by his employers to provide a safe system of work, it is not necessary in every case that he should plead and prove what the proper system of work was. "There may be cases in which the plaintiff will not get very far with an allegation of unsafe system of work unless he can show some practicable alternative, but there are also cases . . . in which a plaintiff can fairly say: 'If this is dangerous, then there must be some other way of doing it that can be found by a prudent employer and it is not for me to devise that way or to say what it is.' "

Per Devlin L.J. in *Dixon* v. *Cementation Co.* [1960] 1 W.L.R. 746, considering a dictum of Viscount Simon L.C. in *Colfar* v. *Coggins & Griffith (Liverpool) Ltd.* [1945] A.C. 197 at p. 203.

See Precedent No. 26.

Mental States

Where a party pleading alleges any condition of the mind of any person, whether any disorder or disability of mind or any malice, fraudulent intention or other condition of mind except knowledge, he must state in the pleading particulars of the facts on which he relies.

Order 18, r. 12(1)(*b*).

Where in an action for libel or slander the plaintiff alleges that the defendant maliciously published the words or matters complained of, he need not in his statement of claim give particulars of the facts on which he relies in support of the allegation of malice, but if the defendant pleads that any of those words or matters are fair comment on a matter of public interest or were published on a privileged occasion, and the plaintiff intends to allege that the defendant was actuated by express malice, he must serve a reply giving particulars of the facts and matters from which the malice is to be inferred.

Order 82, r. 3(3).

(For a discussion of what constitutes express malice in this context see *Horrocks* v. *Lowe* [1975] A.C. 135, H.L.)

Where knowledge is pleaded as a fact, particulars of the facts on which a party relies in support of such allegation may, but need not, be contained in the pleading itself, but such particulars should be given on request or the court may order them to be given. Particulars of the facts and circumstances relied on in support of the allegation will also be ordered where it is pleaded that a party "ought to know" or "ought to have known" some fact.

Order 18, r. 12(4).

Fox v. *H. Wood (Harrow) Ltd.* [1963] 2 Q.B. 601.

Uncertainty

We conclude with one practical observation. Counsel often cannot be as precise as they desire, because they cannot obtain definite information. The lay client is abroad, or there is some other reason. Where you cannot be exact, make too broad rather than too narrow an allegation. It is better to claim too much than too little. It is wiser to state your client's right too largely, if you cannot state it exactly; the greater includes the less. Either party will be allowed as a general rule to prove so much of his allegation as is necessary to support his case, although he has alleged more in his pleadings; for, in the language of the old pleaders, "pleadings are construed *distributively*."

Illustrations

If the plaintiff claims £5,000, he will be allowed to recover £1,000 or £2,000; though where the items are divisible and arise out of separate facts, he ought to be made to pay the costs occasioned by his joining the items as to which he has failed.

In cases of claims for unliquidated damages in the High Court it is usual to claim simply "Damages" without specifying the amount. However in the county court it is the practice to plead the County Court limit (currently £5,000) in the prayer: "Damages limited to £5,000." If the claim is for an amount under £500 or under £3,000 (the current scale 1 and scale 2 costs limits) it is the practice to limit the claim to that amount. This is relevant to both the issue of costs and the availability of arbitration for small claims.

If a defendant pleads that he has paid the plaintiff his whole debt, he will be allowed to prove part payment as a defence *pro tanto*, and the plaintiff will recover judgment only for the balance.

CHAPTER 9

ANSWERING YOUR OPPONENT'S PLEADING

So far we have dealt only with the statement by a party of his own case. But after the first pleading each party must do more than state his own case; he must deal with that presented by his opponent.

There are only three ways in which a party who means to fight can deal with his opponent's pleading:

(i) He can deny the whole or some essential part of the averments of fact contained in it. This is called *traversing* an opponent's allegations.

(ii) He can say, "Well, that is true so far as it goes; but it is only half the truth. Here are several other facts which are omitted from your pleading, and which will put a very different complexion on the case." Alleging such facts is called *pleading by way of confession and avoidance*, or, more shortly, *confessing and avoiding*; because the pleader seems to confess that his opponent's statement discloses a good prima facie case—that it is on the face of it good in law and true in fact—and he then goes on to allege new facts by which he hopes to destroy the effect of the allegations admitted.

(iii) He may take a point of law, and say, "Assuming every word contained in this statement to be true, still I say that it is bad in law; it discloses no cause of action" (or "no defence to my action," or "no answer to my plea," as the case may be). This was formerly called *demurring* (from the Latin *demorari*, or French *demorrer*, to "wait" or "stay"); because the party who demurred would not proceed with his pleading, but awaited the judgment of the court whether any case was made out for him to answer. What was formerly a *demurrer* is now called *"an objection in point of law,"* which is a short definition rather than a name. However, it exactly expresses what a demurrer was.[1]

Every objection in point of law asserts or implies that the pleading objected to is sufficient on the face of it; hence it

---

[1] There is, however, this difference between the former demurrer and the present system. Formerly a party who had demurred could always without leave set the demurrer down for argument before the court *in banc*, and thus frequently delay the trial of the action. Nowadays the point of law raised by an objection is disposed of by the judge who tries the cause at or after the trial, unless on a master's order it is argued before the trial (see *Everett* v. *Ribbands* [1952] 2 Q.B. 198, 206).

admits for the moment that the allegations contained in it are true. Thus, it may be said that a traverse denies, and an objection admits. But they are alike in this, that neither of them introduces any fresh matter; whereas a plea in confession and avoidance neither simply admits nor merely denies; it admits the facts alleged in the opponent's pleading, subject, however, to the new facts by which it seeks to destroy their legal effect.

Formerly, the party pleading had to elect which of these three courses he would adopt; he could not both demur and plead, nor could he traverse any allegation to which he also pleaded by way of confession and avoidance. Now, however, he is not restricted in this way; the same allegation may be traversed in point of fact, objected to as bad in law, and at the same time collateral matter may be pleaded to destroy its effect.[2] Remember, however, that it is foolish to multiply the issues needlessly, as your client may be ordered to pay the costs of those which he fails to prove, even though he succeeds on the main issue.

This may be best explained by one or two instances:

Writ issued the 18th day of November, 1988.

STATEMENT OF CLAIM

1. On or about August 18, 1988, the defendant agreed to pay to the plaintiff the sum of £5,100 on November 18, 1988.
2. In breach of the said agreement the defendant failed to pay to the plaintiff the said sum of £5,100, or any part thereof, on November 18, 1988, or at all.
3. Further, the plaintiff claims interest on the said sum at the rate of 15 per cent. per annum from November 18, 1988 until judgment or sooner payment,

And the plaintiff claims:
   (1) £5,100
   (2) Interest as pleaded.

This is a badly drafted claim to which the defendant may, if he wishes, take three objections in point of law; he is not bound to state them in his pleading but he is entitled to do so. (See Order 18, r. 11.) He may also traverse the alleged agreement.

DEFENCE

1. The defendant denies the alleged or any agreement to pay to the plaintiff the said or any sum. (*Traverse.*)
2. The Statement of Claim discloses no consideration for the said agreement.
3. The Statement of Claim discloses no cause of action for interest.

---

[2] For example, see Precedent No. 45.

4. The writ herein was issued prematurely.

This, however, is a technical defence. There probably was an agreement, with consideration, if indeed the contract was not under seal, and probably also some agreement to pay interest; alternatively an entitlement to interest by virtue of section 35A of the Supreme Court Act 1981. In that case the plaintiff could amend his statement of claim and proceed with the action. Paragraph 4 raises a more serious objection, but this can be overcome by the plaintiff discontinuing the action, paying the costs and issuing a second writ. In the second action the defendant would probably have to confess and avoid.

DEFENCE

1. The defendant admits that he agreed to pay to the plaintiff the said sum of £5,100 on November 18, 1988. In consideration of and as a condition of the defendant's said promise the plaintiff agreed to build by the said date a garage for the defendant in accordance with a specification dated August 3, 1988.
2. The plaintiff failed to build the said garage by November 18, 1988, or any other day in accordance with the said specification or at all.

Thus the parties eventually arrive at the real issue between them, although it should be noted that a combination of bad pleading by the plaintiff and tactical pleading by the defendant has already caused much unnecessary delay and expense.

A second illustration of the different methods of answering pleadings is provided by Precedents Nos. 29, 45, 49, showing the development of a libel action.

In No. 45, the last sentence of paragraph 2 is a traverse of the allegation of publication of the letter (see Order 18, r. 13(2)); paragraph 3 objects that the words complained of were not capable of bearing a defamatory meaning as a matter of law; paragraphs 4, 5 and 6 confess the plaintiff's claim but avoid it by pleading further facts which, if proved, will sustain the defences of justification and qualified privilege.

In his reply (No. 49), the plaintiff joins issue with the defendant on his defence; this is a compendious form of traverse permitted in a reply or any subsequent pleading (see Order 18, r. 14(2)). The plaintiff also confesses and avoids paragraphs 6 of the defence by pleading express malice on the part of the defendant.

Besides pleas by way of traverse and pleas by way of confession and avoidance, there were formerly also certain pleas which were called *dilatory pleas*, because they offered a merely formal objection to the proceedings, without presenting any substantial answer to the merits of the action. Such were:

(a) A plea to the jurisdiction, by which the defendant took exception to the jurisdiction of the court to entertain the action. A dispute as to jurisdiction is, of course, still possible. It will now generally be resolved at an early stage of the action on the hearing of an application by the defendant under the provisions of Order 12, r. 8. An acknowledgment of service of a writ, *not* followed by an application under rule 8(1), is to be treated as a submission by the defendant to the jurisdiction of the court in the proceedings (rule 8(7)).

(b) A plea in suspension of the action; a plea which shows some ground for not proceeding in the suit at the present period, and prays that the pleading may be stayed until that ground be removed. The number of these pleas was always small, and none of them was of ordinary occurrence in practice. Their place is now taken by a summons to stay proceedings, on the hearing of which the point is summarily decided.

(c) A plea in abatement; a plea which showed some good reason for abating or quashing the statement of claim on the ground that it was improperly framed, without, at the same time, tending to deny the right of action itself, *e.g.* the misnomer of a defendant, or the non-joinder of a necessary party. But this plea has long been abolished. The defendant must himself correct the misnomer; and he may, if he thinks fit, take out a summons to have the missing plaintiff or defendant made a party.

In contradistinction to these *dilatory* pleas, traverses and pleas in confession and avoidance were called *peremptory* pleas or *pleas in bar*, because they barred or impugned the right of action altogether.

These three things—traverse, confession and avoidance, and objection in point of law—must be kept clear and distinct. The pleader may adopt any one or two or all three of these methods of pleading, so long as he makes it quite clear which he is adopting. The object of a traverse is merely to compel the opposite party to prove his allegations true in fact; it does not dispute their sufficiency in point of law. If either party desires to object to his opponent's pleading in point of law, he must do so clearly and distinctly by way of objection. A plea, which may be either a traverse or an objection, is embarrassing and will be struck out.[3]

Moreover, an objection in point of law can only be raised where the fault of which you desire to take advantage is apparent on the face of the pleading to which you object. You

---

[3] *Stokes* v. *Grant* (1878) 4 C.P.D. 25.

cannot state new facts in your own pleading or on affidavit, and then contend that the result of the combination is to show that your opponent is wrong in his law. It is the province of a plea in confession and avoidance to state new facts which put your opponent out of court.

So, too, a traverse cannot be made to do the work of a plea in confession and avoidance. Its office is to contradict, not to excuse. Matters justifying an act must not be insinuated into a plea which denies the act. "All matters in confession and avoidance shall be pleaded specially."[4]

As a general rule the burden will lie on your opponent to prove at the trial the facts which you have traversed; but the burden will lie on you to prove the facts which you have alleged by way of confession and avoidance. And you will not be allowed to shift the onus of proof by traversing when you should confess and avoid, even where your opponent has given you the opportunity by introducing an unnecessary averment into the preceding pleading.

Illustrations

A statement of claim in libel or slander always alleges that "the defendant falsely and maliciously wrote [*or* 'spoke'] and published the words." Yet the defendant may not plead "the defendant never wrote [*or* 'spoke'] or published the said words falsely or maliciously or at all." For this, while apparently merely a denial of the fact of publication, is also an insinuation that the words are true, and that the occasion of publication is privileged. It is in fact a traverse and two pleas in confession and avoidance all rolled into one. It is for the plaintiff to prove the publication, and for the defendant to prove truth or privilege.

    Belt v. *Lawes* (1882) 51 L.J. Q.B. 539.

So in an action against the master for the dismissal of his servant, the statement of claim will certainly allege that the defendant *wrongfully* dismissed the plaintiff from his employ. But the defendant ought not to traverse this allegation in its entirety. To plead "The defendant never wrongfully dismissed the plaintiff" would be bad pleading; for it is ambiguous. Does it mean "The defendant never in fact dismissed the plaintiff" or "The defendant had a right to dismiss the plaintiff and therefore did so?" The defendant may plead both defences or either, so long as he makes his meaning clear. He may traverse the fact of dismissal, if he wishes. He may go on to justify the dismissal by showing that the plaintiff was guilty of misconduct which entitled the defendant to dismiss him. This would be a plea in confession and avoidance, and it should state the particular acts of misconduct on which the defendant relies as justifying the dismissal. It is for the plaintiff to prove the dismissal; and for the defendant to show that it was justified.

    Lush v. *Russell* (1850) 5 Ex. 203; 19 L.J. Ex. 214.

    Horton v. *McMurtry* (1860) 5 H. & N. 667; 29 L.J. Ex. 260.

    And see Precedents Nos. 17, 35.

---

[4] Pleading Rules of Hilary Term 1853, rr. 12, 17. Now see Ord. 18, r. 8, *infra*.

Traverses

A traverse is the express contradiction of an allegation of fact in an opponent's pleading; it is generally a contradiction in the very terms of the allegation. It is, as a rule, framed in the negative, because the fact which it denies is, as a rule, alleged in the affirmative.

As to traverses, there are two fundamental rules, the object of which is to compel each party in his turn to admit frankly, or deny fully, each allegation of fact in the pleading of his opponent:

I. Any allegation of fact made by a party in his pleading is deemed to be admitted by the opposite party unless it is traversed by that party in his pleading or a joinder of issue under rule 14 operates as a denial of it[5] (Order 18, r. 13(1)).

II. Every allegation of fact made in a statement of claim or counterclaim which the party on whom it is served does not intend to admit must be specifically traversed by him in his defence or defence to counterclaim, as the case may be; and a general denial of such allegations, or a general statement of non-admission of them, is not a sufficient traverse of them (Order 18, r. 13(3)).

Formerly, any other matters which were not fit subjects to traverse were not taken to be admitted by the defendant's "pleading over" (*i.e.* by his omitting all reference to them in his pleading). Now, however, in view of Order 18, r. 13(1), a defendant may be running a risk if he passes over in silence subsidiary allegations which he deems immaterial, or the "matters of inducement" which are often set out in the introductory paragraphs of a long pleading. They may, however, conveniently be dealt with by a denial of the matter "as alleged or at all" or of "each of the allegations in paragraph 1 of the statement of claim," or as the case may be; but the vital allegations must be dealt with specifically, pleading to the point of substance. Damages and their amount are always in issue unless expressly admitted[6] although it has become usual to plead to them specifically by "non-admission" or denial. It is unnecessary to plead to the prayer or claim for relief at the end of your opponent's pleading. Nor need you plead to particulars. Neither party should traverse matter not alleged; he should be content to answer the case that is actually laid

---

[5] An admission is not however to be implied from the pleadding of a person under a disability. (Ord. 80, r. 8.)

[6] Ord. 18, r. 13(4).

against him, not that which he thinks his opponent meant or ought to have raised.

Illustration

To a statement of claim setting out defamatory words, alleged to have been spoken by the defendant of the plaintiff, the defendant pleaded that he "did say the following words," and proceeded to set out his own version of what he had said, which differed materially from the words set out in the statement of claim. The defendant then alleged that the words spoken by him were true in substance and in fact, and were spoken on a privileged occasion. It was held that the defence, as pleaded, was embarrassing, and tended to prejudice the fair trial of the action, and should therefore be struck out.

Rassam v. *Budge* [1893] 1 Q.B. 571.

I. *Any Allegation of Fact unless Traversed is Admitted*

The pleader must either admit or deny every material allegation of fact in the pleading of his opponent: and he must make it absolutely clear which facts he admits and which he denies. To ensure this, rule 13 provides that any allegation of fact is deemed to be admitted unless traversed and that a traverse may be made either by a denial or by a statement of non-admission and either expressly or by necessary implication. There is no difference in effect between a denial and a non-admission of an allegation[7]; the distinction generally observed is that a party denies any matter, which, if it had occurred, would have been within his own knowledge, while he refuses to admit matters which are alleged to have happened behind his back. But he must be just as specific in not admitting as in denying[8]; in either case he must make it perfectly clear how much he disputes and how much he admits.

Illustration

An employer against whom a claim is made by his employee for personal injury allegedly sustained as a result of the employer's negligence may have no knowledge of whether the employee did, in fact, sustain injury as he alleges. In those circumstances the fact and manner of the injury should be "not admitted" and the negligence "denied." If, on the other hand, the employer denies that the employee suffered any injury or contends that it happened in some manner different from that alleged by the employee then he should deny the injury and the circumstances or plead his positive case as to how the injury was sustained.

What is meant by "necessary implication?" Where the traverse of one allegation necessarily and unmistakably traverses another as well, the latter allegation is denied by necessary

---

[7] See *Warner* v. *Sampson* [1959] 1 Q.B. 297 at pp. 319, 324.
[8] *Per* Jessel M.R. in *Thorp* v. *Holdsworth* (1876) 3 Ch.D. at p. 640.

implication. Since rule 13(3) requires that every allegation made in a statement of claim or a counterclaim must be "specifically" traversed, if it is not intended to be admitted, it is safer to deny both expressly if there can possibly be any misconception.

In pleadings subsequent to the defence or defence to counterclaim, as the case may be, instead of dealing specifically with every allegation of fact in the preceding pleading the pleader may say that he "joins issue"; he may do so either generally upon the preceding pleading or with the exception of certain facts which he admits. As we shall see in Chapter 15 upon "close of pleadings" there is an implied joinder of issue on the pleading last served. A joinder of issue operates as a denial of every material allegation of fact in the preceding pleading which is not expressly admitted (Order 18, r. 14). "There can be no joinder of issue on a statement of claim or counterclaim" (r. 14(3)) and "a general denial of such allegations, or a general statement of non-admission of them, is not a sufficient traverse of them" (r. 13(3)). Care must therefore be taken to deal specifically with *every* material allegation of fact in a claim or counterclaim.

It is in the power of the party either to admit or to deny each allegation in his opponent's plea, as he thinks fit. If he decides to deny it, he must do so clearly and explicitly. Any equivocal or ambiguous phrase will be construed into an admission of it. There is no third or intermediary stage. If the judge does not find in the pleading a specific denial or a definite refusal to admit, there is an end of the matter; the fact stands admitted.

Illustrations

Claim for specific performance of a contract. Defence: "The defendant puts the plaintiffs to proof of the several allegations in their statement of claim." *Held*, when the defendant did not appear at the trial, that all the plaintiffs' allegations were admitted.

 Harris v. *Gamble* (1878) 7 Ch.D. 877, 47 L.J. Ch. 344.

Defence: "The defendants do not admit the correctness of" certain allegations in the statement of claim, "and require proof thereof." *Held*, an insufficient denial. The defendants were ordered to state in what respects they disputed these allegations.

 Rutter v. *Tregent* (1879) 12 Ch.D. 758; 48 L.J. Ch. 791.

Although Order 18, r. 13(3) states that a general denial, or a general statement of non-admission, of allegations of facts is not a sufficient traverse of them, it is apparently not necessary for the pleader to copy out each allegation of fact which he denies or refuses to admit. A permissible and common practice is to say that "the defendant denies each of the allegations contained in paragraph 2 of the statement of claim" or "the defendants deny each of the allegations in paragraph 2 save that. . . . " (a particular allegation is admitted).

See *John Lancaster Radiators Ltd.* v. *General Motor Radiator Co. Ltd.* [1946] 2 All E.R. 685, following *Adkins* v. *N. Met. Tramways Co.* (1893) 10 T.L.R. 1731; 63 L.J.K.B. 361.

Formerly it was common practice to include in a defence a general traverse such as: "Save as is hereinbefore specifically admitted or not admitted, the defendant denies each and every allegation contained in the statement of claim as though the same were set out herein and traversed seriatim." Such a traverse is convenient and permissible when dealing with a long and complicated statement of claim to cover all the allegations which are more or less immaterial and those allegations on which counsel has no instructions. But it should not be adopted in dealing with the allegations which are the gist of the action; to these the defendant should plead as precisely as possible. Moreover it is a form of general traverse which has fallen into abeyance in the light of the increasing tendency towards greater simplicity in pleadings.

See *Warner* v. *Sampson* [1959] 1 Q.B. 297 and the *John Lancaster Radiators* case (*supra*) where Morton L.J. said at p. 687, "I do not propose to express any view, unless and until the matter arises, on a defence consisting simply of one paragraph: 'The defendants and each of them deny each and every allegation contained in the statement of claim as fully as if the same were herein set forth and denied seriatim.' "

If I deny that the defendant was ever tenant to the plaintiff of certain premises, I deny by necessary implication that the plaintiff ever demised those premises to the defendant. But the converse does not hold. The defendant may now be tenant to the plaintiff, although the plaintiff never demised the premises to him. *E.g.* the plaintiff's ancestor may have demised the premises to the defendant for a long term which is still unexpired.

How much ought the party pleading to admit, and how much to deny? Clearly it is wrong to deny plain and acknowledged facts, or any fact which it is not to your client's interest to deny. It was intended by the framers of the Judicature Act that each party in his pleading should frankly admit every statement of fact which he does not intend seriously to dispute at the trial. But this intention has not been carried out. Counsel hesitate to make admissions unless they are expressly instructed to do so—which they very seldom are. Solicitors hesitate to instruct counsel to make admissions, because the facts have not yet been thoroughly sifted; they do not feel sure that they have got to the bottom of the case; and they fear something may turn up hereafter which may make them wish to recall the admission.[9] Either party may at any stage of the case apply for judgment on the admissions which have been made by the other side (Order 27, r. 3). You must be careful, therefore, how you admit even introductory paragraphs which may appear immaterial; they were probably inserted for some purpose. Besides, it is sometimes desirable to deny a particular fact so as to compel your opponent to call as *his* witness a person whom you wish to cross-examine, or by whose evidence you hope to prove a particular fact essential to your case; you may thus, perhaps, be able to avoid calling witnesses, and so gain the right to the last word.

[9] This, in a proper case, can be done (*Hollis* v. *Burton* [1892] 3 Ch. 226).

But as a rule each party should admit whatever facts can be proved against him without trouble. Moreover, it looks weak to deny everything in your opponent's pleading. It suggests that you have no substantial defence to it. In addition, "By rashly traversing statements which are obviously true, much unnecessary expense may be caused."[10] There was formerly a useful rule[11] expressly empowering judges and masters to make a special order as to costs occasioned by unreasonable denials. This has been replaced by the general power under Order 62 to deal at any stage with any part of the costs incidental to any proceedings. This power should be remembered. Further, by Order 25, r. 4, at the hearing of the Summons for Directions the master must endeavour to secure that the parties make all admissions which ought reasonably to be made. When faced by what seems to be an unreasonable denial it may be prudent to serve a formal notice to admit facts.

There is one case in which it is shameful not to make a proper admission. If your opponent relies on a written document, he will either set out the words of the document in his pleading, or he will state shortly its effect. In the latter case, as your construction of the document will probably differ from his, it is quite legitimate to traverse his version of its effect. But if he sets out the actual words correctly, it is slovenly work to plead, as was sometimes done: "The defendant does not admit that the terms of the said indenture are sufficiently or correctly set forth in paragraph 4 of the statement of claim, and craves leave to refer to the original thereof at the trial for greater certainty as to its terms and effect." Why "crave leave" to do that which you have now an absolute right to do? "Any party to a cause or matter shall be entitled at any time to serve a notice on any other party in whose pleadings or affidavits reference is made to any document requiring him to produce that document for the inspection of the party giving the notice and to permit him to take copies thereof" (Order 24, r. 10). Obtain a copy of the document under this rule, if you have not one already, and see if its terms are or are not correctly stated by your opponent. If they are, admit that they are, adding such other portions as you yourself rely on. If they are not, then set them out correctly yourself, if you deem them material. One may suspect that the man who "craves leave" is perfectly familiar with the contents of the documents all the time.

---

[10] *Per* Fletcher Moulton L.J. in *Lever Brothers* v. *Associated Newspapers* [1907] 2 K.B. 628.
[11] R.S.C. 1883, Ord. XXI, r. 9.

II. *Denials must be Specific*

It is not sufficient for a defendant in his defence to deny generally the allegations in the statement of claim, or for a plaintiff in his reply to deny generally the allegations in a counterclaim, but each party must traverse specifically each allegation of fact which he does not intend to admit. The party pleading must make it quite clear how much of his opponent's case he disputes. Sometimes, in order to obey the rule and to deal specifically with every allegation of fact of which he does not admit the truth, it is necessary for him to place on the record two or more distinct traverses to one and the same allegation. Merely to deny the allegation in terms will often be ambiguous.

Illustrations

Claim: "The defendant entered the premises of the plaintiff" [*specifying them*]. If the defendant pleads: "The defendant never entered the premises of the plaintiff," the more obvious meaning of this allegation is that he never entered the premises which the plaintiff claims as his; but it may be that his case is that the premises specified do not belong to the plaintiff. The words are capable of that meaning; and if such ambiguity were permitted, pleadings would lose their utility. If the defendant intends at the trial to deny the plaintiff's possession or right to possession of the premises in question, he must say so distinctly. A literal traverse of the words of the claim will be taken to deny merely that the defendant, in fact, entered those premises. If, then, the defendant desires to raise both defences—to deny both the act complained of and the plaintiff's title to the land—he must put on the record two separate paragraphs, *e.g.*:

"1. The defendant never entered the said premises."

"2. The said premises are not the plaintiff's premises."

In an action for wrongful interference with goods, the defendant is similarly required to deny specifically that the goods were the property of the plaintiff. A mere traverse of the conversion, detention or trespass will be taken as denying merely the acts complained of.

See Torts (Interference with Goods) Act 1977.

If either party wishes to deny the right of any other party to claim as executor, or as trustee whether in bankruptcy or otherwise, or in any representative or other alleged capacity, or the alleged constitution of any partnership firm, he should deny the same specifically.

Furthermore (as was explicitly stated in the old rules) a traverse must not be evasive, but must answer the point of substance; otherwise it will be liable to be struck out under Order 18, r. 19[12] as embarrassing. It must be neither too large nor too narrow. The pleader must deny enough and not too much.

Illustrations

If it is alleged that the defendant received a sum of money to the use of the plaintiff (as in Precedent No. 23), it is not sufficient for the defendant to deny

---

[12] See Chap. 10.

that he received that particular sum; he must deny that he received that sum or any part thereof, or else set out how much he received or he must deny the existence of those facts alleged to make the receipt by him a receipt to the use of the plaintiff.

A defence pleaded: "The terms of the arrangement were never definitely agreed upon as alleged." It was held that such a traverse was an evasive denial and that it admitted that an arrangement was in fact made as alleged. Jessel M.R.: "The whole object of pleadings is to bring the parties to an issue, and the meaning of the rules of this Order is to prevent the issue being enlarged, which would prevent either party from knowing, when the cause comes on for trial, what the real point to be discussed and decided was . . . the defendant is bound to deny that any agreement or any term of arrangement were ever come to, if that is what he means: if he does not mean that, he should say that there were no terms of arrangement come to, except the following terms, and then state what those terms were."

Thorp v. *Holdsworth* (1876) 3 Ch.D. 637.

III. *Dangers of a Literal Traverse*

Do not traverse too literally in an effort to be specific. It is sufficient to answer the point of substance. A traverse may become evasive, if it follows too closely the precise language of the allegations traversed.

(i) By traversing too literally you may fall into the vice of pleading "a negative pregnant." A negative pregnant is such a form of negative expression as may imply or carry within it an affirmative proposition. It is therefore evasive and ambiguous, and must not be used.

Illustrations

A statement of claim alleged that the defendant offered the plaintiff a bribe of £5,000. The defendant pleaded "that he had never offered the plaintiff a bribe of £5,000"; which would have been true if he had offered £4,000 or any sum other than £5,000. Such a denial half admits the main allegation that a bribe of some kind had been offered. It is therefore an unfair and evasive denial. The defendant should have pleaded that he never offered a bribe of £5,000 or any other sum.

Tildesley v. *Harper* (1878) 7 Ch.D. 403; 47 L.J. Ch. 263; (C.A.) 10 Ch.D. 393; 48 L.J. Ch. 495.

In an action against a bank for breach of contract, the plaintiff pleaded that the defendants "effected purchases and sales [of securities] without having been authorised so to do." The defendants denied "that they effected purchases or sales without having been authorised by the plaintiff to do so." After the defendants admitted that they intended at the trial to set up an affirmative case and prove the existence of express authority from the plaintiff, the Court of Appeal, by a majority, ordered particulars of the affirmative case to be given. The defendants would have been in no better position had they not made such an admission, since the denial would then have been ambiguous and embarrassing. The plaintiff would not have known whether the defendants denied having made the alleged transactions at all or whether they admitted the transactions but intended to prove the existence of authority from the plaintiff.

Pinson v. *Lloyds & National Provincial Foreign Bank Ltd.* [1941] 2 K.B. 72.

(ii) Again, there may be many details which were properly introduced into your opponent's pleading, but which it is misleading for you to include in your traverse. By so doing you may raise false issues, and so evade the point of substance. To a denial of the main allegation the addition of the words "as alleged or at all" will often cure this defect.

Illustrations

A plaintiff might allege, in an action for arrears of salary, that he had been employed by the defendant as a representative from September 1, 1987 to December 31, 1987, in the county of Kent. It would be a bad traverse for the defendant to plead: "The defendant denies that he employed the plaintiff as a representative from September 1, 1987, to December 31, 1987, in the county of Kent." The defendant must either deny that he employed the plaintiff at all, or else state for how long he did employ the plaintiff and in what capacity. He should not traverse the place of employment unless it is material; but if he does he must say that the plaintiff was not employed by him in the county of Kent "or in any other place."

(iii) If your opponent's allegation be in the *conjunctive*, you must plead to it in the *disjunctive*; otherwise your traverse may be too large; for it is seldom, if ever, necessary for your opponent to prove at the trial the whole of his allegation precisely as he has pleaded it. In other words, when traversing, remember always to turn "and" into "or," and "all" into "any."

Illustrations

Paragraph 3 of Precedent No. 30 reads: "On or about May 1, 1990, the First Defendant wrongfully pledged and delivered the car to the Second Defendant and thereby wrongfully interfered with the same to her own use." If the first defendant wishes to traverse all these allegations he must plead: "The first defendant denies that he pledged *or* delivered the car to the second defendant *or at all*" (the addition of these words avoids the danger of a pregnant negative) "and the first defendant denies that he wrongfully interfered with the car to his own use as alleged or at all." It should be noted that the date in the statement of claim is traversed by necessary implication.

Where two or more defendants are sued jointly and severally, and they serve one defence, any traverse should begin: "The defendants and each of them deny, etc."

How far should the pleader confine himself to merely traversing? Should he not, after denying his opponent's story, go on to add his own version of the matter?

This is sometimes a difficult question. The pleader must use his own discretion. It is sometimes most desirable to do so, in order to show clearly what is the real point in dispute.[14] If, for instance, a plaintiff in his statement of claim sets out or refers

---

[14] See the judgment of Jessel M.R. in *Thorp v. Holdsworth (ante,* p. 174).

to certain clauses of a written contract on which he relies, the defendant should certainly set out or refer to other clauses, if any, which tell in his favour. Again, if the plaintiff gives his version of the effect of a written document, it will certainly tend to clear the matter up if the defendant, instead of merely denying the plaintiff's version, states also his own construction of the document. And in many cases it may be desirable for a defendant thus to state definitely which his exact contention is. But by so doing he necessarily somewhat limits his case at the trial. He has no longer the same free hand. And there is this further danger that if the defendant, instead of merely denying, sets up an affirmative case as well, both judge and jury will expect him to prove his affirmative case, and are apt to find against him if he does not. The onus of proof is not really shifted by such a method of pleading.[15] But if, when accused of a tort, the defendant pleads, "It was A who did it, not I," the judge may be inclined to treat this as an admission that either A or the defendant did it, and to conclude that if the defendant cannot prove his assertion that A did it he must have done it himself.

Matters in Confession and Avoidance

The party pleading is often willing to admit that the facts alleged by his opponent are so far true, and that they make out a good prima facie case or defence. But he desires to destroy the effect of these allegations either by showing some justification or excuse of the matter charged against him, or some discharge or release from it. A defendant, for instance, may seek to show on the one hand that the plaintiff never had any right of action, because the act charged was under the circumstances justifiable; or on the other that, though the plaintiff once had a right of action, it has been discharged or released by some matter subsequent. In either case, he confesses the truth of the allegation which he proceeds to answer or avoid. Hence such defences are called *pleas in confession and avoidance*.

The effect of such admission, if it stands alone, is extremely strong; for it is binding on the party making it, even though the jury should improperly go out of the issue, and find the contrary of what is thus confessed on the record.[16] At the same time, the confession operates only to prevent the fact from being brought into question in the same suit; it is not conclu-

---

[15] *Kilgour* v. *Alexander* (1860) 14 Moo. 177.
[16] *Hewitt* v. *Macquire* (1815) 7 Ex. 80.

sive as to the truth of that fact in any subsequent action between the same parties. And, even in the same suit, it will not be conclusive, if the party pleading also traverses the facts confessed, as he may do now.

Illustrations

Action of assault. Defence that the defendant did the acts complained of in necessary self-defence. This is a plea in confession and avoidance; for it admits the assault while it justifies it.

Similarly, in an action of libel, a plea that the words are true or that they were published on a privileged occasion, if it stands alone, admits that the defendant published the words of the plaintiff, but justifies or excuses the act.

To plead that the defendant has a lien on certain goods admits that the goods are the plaintiff's, and that the defendant detains them from him.

And generally in any action of tort if the defendant admits the act complained of, but desires to show that it was not wrongful or no breach of duty, he must plead such justification specially by way of confession and avoidance.

All matter in confession and avoidance must be pleaded specially. The pleader must not attempt to insinuate it under an apparent traverse; he should state it clearly and distinctly and in a separate paragraph. At the same time, he should not confess and avoid where a mere traverse is sufficient. For he will thus introduce collateral matter which his client may have to prove, instead of putting the plaintiff to proof of his allegations.

The rule on this subject (Order 18, r. 8(1)) is as follows:

"A party must in any pleading subsequent to a statement of claim plead specifically any matter, for example, performance, release; the expiry of the relevant period of limitation, fraud or any fact showing illegality—

    (a) which he alleges makes any claim or defence of the opposite party not maintainable; or

    (b) which, if not specifically pleaded, might take the opposite party by surprise; or

    (c) which raises issues of fact not arising out of the preceding pleading."

This rule, like the corresponding rule of 1883, "is not confined . . . to a case where a statute is the thing to be pleaded; it applies to all cases of grounds of defence or reply which if not raised would be likely to take the opposite party by surprise or raise issues of fact not arising out of the pleadings. Where the defendant ought to plead things of that sort, the rule does not say that if he does not the court shall adjudicate upon the matter as if a ground valid in law did not exist which does exist. If in the course of the proceedings it was proved that the deed sued upon was a forgery and the defendant does not plead it or did not know it was a forgery, the court would not give judgment upon the deed on the footing that it was a valid deed. The effect of the rule is, I think, for reasons of practice and justice and convenience to require the party to tell his opponent what he is coming to the court to prove. If he does not do that, the court will deal with it in one of two ways. It may say that it is not open to him, that he has not raised it and will not be allowed to rely on it; or it may give him leave to amend by raising it, and protect the other party if necessary by letting the case stand over. The rule is not one that excludes from the consideration of the court the relevant subject-matter for decision simply on the ground that it is not pleaded. It leaves the party in mercy and the court will deal with him as is just."[17]

Illustrations

If a defendant merely pleads that "he never agreed as alleged," he cannot insist at the trial that though a contract was made as alleged it is invalid in point of law; for this must form the subject of a special allegation, showing the circumstances out of which the illegality arose.

Order 18, r. 8(1).

The plaintiff alleged the negligent provision of an unsafe tool; the defendant traversed the alleged negligence. The plaintiff came to trial prepared to prove the defects in the tool, when it appeared that the real defence was that it had been bought from a reputable supplier and that there was no duty to test or examine it. *Held*, that this was a matter of surprise which should have been specially pleaded. Leave to amend and an adjournment were granted at the defendant's expense.

Davie v. *New Merton Board Mills* [1956] 1 All E.R. 379; [1956] 1 W.L.R. 233.

Many other matters must similarly be specifically pleaded. These include, for example, contributory negligence (*Fookes* v. *Slaytor* [1978] 1 W.L.R. 1293); fundamental breach of contract (*Hunt & Winterbottam (West of England) Ltd.* v. *B.R.S. (Parcels) Ltd.* [1962] 1 Q.B. 617); any point concerning limitation, this being a matter of procedure (see *Mitchell* v. *Harris Engineering Co. Ltd.* [1967] 2 Q.B. 703) and of course, fraud. However, a qualification of the principle should be noted in connection with fraud. Where facts have to be established by the evidence of a party, it may be permissible to challenge his veracity by cross-examination even to the extent of showing his conduct in the transaction in question to have been fraudulent without having pleaded fraud.

Wintle v. *Nye* [1959] 1 W.L.R. 284 at p. 294.

In confessing and avoiding, as in traversing, the plea must be neither too wide nor too narrow. It must be as broad and as long as the claim to which it is pleaded and justify or excuse the whole of it; or, if it is intended to apply to part only of such claim, it must be limited accordingly by a prefix "As to so much of the statement of claim as alleges, etc.," or "As to paragraph 4 of the statement of claim." Be careful not to make too wide an averment, whereby you will take on your shoulders an unnecessary burden, or too narrow an averment, which will fetter your hands at the trial.

---

[17] *Per* Buckley L.J. in *Re Robinson's Settlement, Grant* v. *Hobbs* [1912] 1 Ch. 717, 728.

Illustrations

In a libel action, where the plaintiff complains of the words "Fraud Squad Probe Firm" and pleads a "popular" innuendo to the effect that the words meant that he was guilty of or was suspected by the police of being guilty of fraud, it would not be sufficient for the defendants to plead that such an inquiry was in fact taking place. They would have to prove the "sting" of the words used.

See *Lewis* v. *Daily Telegraph Ltd.* [1964] A.C. 234. Considered in *Hayward* v. *Thompson* [1982] Q.B. 47.

Pleading with unnecessary particularity, as in the old cases under the Statute of Frauds, may restrict a party's case at the trial.

Hills & Grant Ltd. v. *Hodson* [1934] Ch. 53, 103 L.J. Ch. 17.

Objection in Point of Law

Either party may object to the pleading of the opposite party on the ground that it does not set forth a sufficient ground of action, defence or reply, as the case may be. Such an objection can only be raised where the fault is apparent on the face of the pleading; and the fault must be something more than a mere imperfection, omission or defect in *form*.

Demurrers were abolished in 1883.[18] But it was desirable, and indeed necessary, to preserve some form of objection in point of law, otherwise parties might incur great expense in trying issues of fact which, when decided, would not determine their rights. So it was provided that any party should be entitled to raise by his pleading any point of law (Order 18, r. 11). In some cases this is better left to be disposed of by the judge at the trial. But the master has a discretion to order that such a point[19] (and also any issue of fact) be tried separately (Order 33, rr. 3 and 4(2)). He may order it to be set down as a preliminary point and may, if he thinks it right, stay other proceedings meanwhile, thus saving the parties the expense of a possibly elaborate contest on the facts and the discovery incidental to it. When the point is decided, if it substantially disposes of the action, judgment may be given accordingly or whatever other order is appropriate may be made (rule 7).

When the matter is one of first impression, or when for any other reason the law on the point is not clear, it may be very desirable to argue an objection and settle the point of law

---

[18] *Special demurrers*, as they were called, *i.e.* mere objections to the *form* of an opponent's pleading, were entirely abolished by the Common Law Procedure Act 1852, s.50, which provided that "on such demurrer the court shall proceed and give judgment according as the very right on the cause and matter in law shall appear unto them, without regarding any imperfection, omission, defect in, or lack of, form."

[19] Particularly when the point, if decided in one way, should be decisive of litigation (*Everett* v. *Ribbands* [1952] 2 Q.B. 198, 206; *Carl Zeiss Stiftung* v. *Herbert Smith & Co.* [1969] 1 Ch. 93).

before incurring the expense of a trial with witnesses. But in ordinary cases it is generally wiser to raise the objection on the pleading but not to apply to have it argued before the trial. The usual result of such an argument is that, if the defendant succeeds, the plaintiff obtains leave, on paying the costs of the argument, to amend his statement of claim; and it is better for the defendant that the plaintiff should be driven to such amendment at the trial. Hence, as a rule, it is best not to apply to have any point of law argued before the trial, unless the objection is one which will dispose of the whole action.

You need not be afraid that, by omitting to apply, you are throwing away a chance of success—that the objection, if not taken at once, cannot be taken afterwards. No doubt slight defects, such as slips of the pen, careless omissions, informal pleading, etc., may sometimes be aided by pleading over, and may often be cured by verdict. But it is never worth while in these days to incur the cost of a motion or summons over some purely formal defect. You should always bear in mind the good advice which that great judge, Sir Edward Coke, deduced as a moral from "the first cause that he ever moved in the King's Bench":

"When the matter in fact will clearly serve for your client although your opinion is that the plaintiff has no cause of action, yet take heed you do not hazard the matter upon a demurrer, in which, upon the pleading and otherwise, more perhaps will arise than you thought of; but first take advantage of the matters of fact, and leave matters in law, which always arise upon the matters in fact, *ad ultimum*, and never at first demur in law, when, after trial of the matters in fact, the matters in law (as in this case it was) will be saved to you."[20] This advice, though now 400 years old, is as sound now as it was in the days of Queen Elizabeth I; in fact, owing to the liberal powers of amendment given by the Judicature Acts, its value has increased rather than diminished. Lindley J. laid down the same rule in *Stokes* v. *Grant*[21]: "If the defendant wants to avail himself of his point of law in a summary way, he must demur; but if he does not demur, he does not waive the objection, and may say at the trial that the claim is bad on the face of it." If then the facts are likely to prove in your favour, you should not, as a rule, apply for a preliminary hearing of the point of law. But if at the trial you will be compelled to admit that you have no case on the merits, then by all means take advantage of any point of law you can.

[20] *The Lord Cromwell's Case* (1581) 4 Rep. at p. 14.
[21] (1878) 4 C.P.D. at p. 28.

No one is bound to take an objection in point of law; Order 18, r. 11 merely says that a party *may* raise it by his pleading. At the trial he may urge any point of law he likes, whether raised on the pleadings or not.[22] The provisions of Order 18, r. 8(1) should, however, be borne in mind. Even in cases not within the four corners of that rule the modern tendency in pleading is to avoid taking an opponent by surprise—a course which may cause embarrassment and inconvenience at the trial.

But if either party desires to have any point of law set down for hearing, and disposed of *before* the trial, he should raise it in his pleading by an objection in point of law. Indeed, where the point of law amounts to a plea in bar such as *res judicata*, it would be the correct procedure.[23] And having regard to the words of Order 33, r. 7 it is clearly worth while to raise on the pleadings any point of law which will substantially dispose of the whole action or render the trial unnecessary.[24]

Illustrations

It is a common error to suppose that where a man who has made two wills at different times revokes the second, he thereby revives the first will. Suppose a plaintiff in that belief propounds the first will: the defendant would plead it was revoked by the execution of the second will; the plaintiff would reply that the second will was in its turn revoked. If the defendant joins issue on this, the cause would proceed to trial on an issue of fact which is wholly immaterial: for the revocation of the second will would not (without more) re-establish the first; it would merely leave the testator intestate. The defendant should object that the reply affords no answer to the defence.

Where special damage is essential to the plaintiff's cause of action, an objection which may dispose of the whole action can be taken in the following manner: "The special damage set out in the statement of claim is not sufficient in law to sustain the action." Similarly, if no special damage be alleged, the defendant may object: "The matters disclosed in the Statement of Claim are not actionable without proof of special damage and no special damage is alleged."

When an objection in point of law has been set down for hearing, the party objecting ordinarily has the right to begin.[25] And for the purposes of the argument he is taken to admit all the facts alleged in the pleading to which he objects.[26] The court will, moreover, take the whole record into consideration and give judgment for the party who, on the whole, appears to

---

[22] But it is desirable to plead it, especially when the point is a substantial one which may dispose of the whole action. *Independent Automatic Sales, Ltd.* v. *Knowles & Foster* [1962] 1 W.L.R. 974.

[23] *Workington Harbour Board* v. *Trade Indemnity Co. Ltd.* (1937) 43 Com. Cas. 235.

[24] As in *Mayor, etc., of Manchester* v. *Williams* [1891] 1 Q.B. 94.

[25] *Stevens* v. *Chown* [1901] 1 Ch. at p. 900. But this is subject to the judge's discretion (Ord. 35, r. 7(1)). And see *Seldon* v. *Davidson* [1968] 1 W.L.R. 1083.

[26] *Burrows* v. *Rhodes* [1899] 1 Q.B. at p. 821; *Anderson* v. *Midland Ry.* [1902] 1 Ch. at p. 374.

be entitled to it. Thus, a plaintiff who objects to a defence may find himself called on to defend the sufficiency of his statement of claim; and, if he is unsuccessful, judgment will be given for the defendant.

CHAPTER 10

ATTACKING YOUR OPPONENT'S PLEADING

These, then, are the leading rules of our present system of pleading. They are clear, simple and sensible; and, at the same time, they are elastic. Pleadings are no longer cast all in one mould; there is full scope for individuality. "An application to set aside for irregularity any proceedings, any step taken in any proceedings or any document, judgment or order therein shall not be allowed unless it is made within a reasonable time and before the party applying has taken any fresh step[1] after becoming aware of the irregularity" (Order 2, r. 2(1)). Hence an irregularity[2] may be cured by your opponent's pleading over. And experienced pleaders often break the letter of these rules for the sake of clearness or brevity. Thus, though it is in general unnecessary to allege matter of law, yet it is sometimes convenient to do so, and it may make the statements of fact more intelligible and show their connection with each other. There is no harm in this, if the facts are also stated on which the proposition of law is based.

But what is a pleader to do when he is confronted by some flagrantly bad bit of pleading in flat violation of the rules? Even then, the best thing he can do, as a rule, is to leave it alone. But there are exceptions. As Bowen L.J. said in *Knowles* v. *Roberts*,[3] "It seems to me that the rule that the court is not to dictate to parties how they should frame their case, is one that ought always to be preserved sacred. But that rule is, of course, subject to this modification and limitation, that the parties must not offend against the rules of pleading which have been laid down by the law; and if a party introduces a pleading which is unnecessary, and it tends to prejudice, embarrass and delay the trial of the action, it then becomes a pleading which is beyond his right." His opponent's remedy in such a case is to apply to the master at chambers for an order that the whole or any part of a pleading be struck out or amended under Order 18, r. 19(1), or for an order for particulars under rule 12(3).

---

[1] See Chap. 13.

[2] As contrasted with a defect dealt with under Ord. 18, r. 19 (*post*). A distinction was drawn in such cases as *Craig* v. *Kanssen* [1943] 1 K.B. 256; *Re Pritchard, Decd.* [1963] Ch. 502; *Cooper* v. *Williams* [1963] 2 Q.B. 567 between an irregularity and a nullity. Now by Ord. 2, r. 1 any failure whatsoever to comply with the rules is to be treated as an irregularity and does not nullify the proceedings, which may be set aside, amended or otherwise dealt with as may be just. See *Harkness* v. *Bell's Asbestos & Engineering Co.* [1967] 2 Q.B. 729.

[3] (1888) 38 Ch.D. at p. 270.

But be careful how you advise any such application. You may materially increase the costs of the action, and yet reap no compensating advantage for your client, even though you succeed. You should also be careful which of these alternatives you adopt. If your opponent has omitted a material allegation, the proper course is to apply under Order 18, r. 19(1); if, however, he has pleaded a material allegation with insufficient particularity, the appropriate remedy is to apply for particulars.[4]

In a personal injury action, if the Plaintiff fails to serve a medical report and a schedule of special damages with the Statement of Claim the Defendant may apply to stay the action until those documents have been provided.

(1) Striking out or Amending your Opponent's Pleading

Your attack may be directed at the whole of your opponent's pleading or upon certain objectionable portions of it; the objective may be to expose the entire action or the defence to it as a sham, or one which cannot possibly succeed in law, and to obtain judgment accordingly; or it may be to force your opponent to amend the whole or some part of an embarrassing pleading under pain of having it struck out if he does not.

The provisions of Order 18, r. 19(1) afford a prompt and summary method of disposing of groundless actions and of excluding immaterial issues. Under this rule a master at chambers has power at any stage to strike out or to order the amendment of the whole or part of any pleading or indorsement which discloses no reasonable cause of action or defence, or which is scandalous, frivolous or vexatious, or which may prejudice, embarrass or delay the fair trial of the action, or which is otherwise an abuse of the process of the court. The master also has power on these grounds to stay or dismiss any action or to order judgment to be entered accordingly.

In addition the court has an inherent jurisdiction to stay all proceedings before it which are obviously frivolous or vexatious or an abuse of its process.[5] This power is a valuable adjunct to those conferred on the court by Order 18, r. 19, since, when application is made to the inherent jurisdiction of the court, all the facts can be gone into and affidavits as to the facts are admissible.[6] Under this jurisdiction the master has similar powers to those exercisable under the Rules.

---

[4] *Bruce* v. *Odhams Press Ltd*. [1936] 1 K.B. 697.
[5] *Reichel* v. *Magrath* (1889) App.Cas. 665.
[6] *Willis* v. *Earl Howe* [1893] 2 Ch. 545 at pp. 551, 554.

We shall now consider separately the various types of applications which may be made under Order 18, r. 19 and under the inherent jurisdiction.

(i) *Where no Reasonable Cause of Action or Defence is Disclosed*

On an application based on this ground alone, no evidence is admissible. The application is analogous to a *demurrer* and the master can look only at the pleadings and particulars, not at any affidavit.[7] The master's power is exercisable at any stage of the proceedings, but he should only strike out a pleading in "plain and obvious cases"[8] and where no reasonable amendment would cure the defect. If the point requires substantial argument and careful consideration, it may be more appropriate to set it down for trial under Order 33; the summary procedure of striking out is only appropriate where it is plainly evident that the statement of claim as it stands is insufficient, even if proved, to entitle the plaintiff to what he asks, or that the defence cannot afford any answer in law to the claim.[9] "No exact paraphrase can be given, but I think 'reasonable cause of action' means a cause of action with some chance of success, when (as required by r. 19(2)) only the allegations in the pleading are considered. If when those allegations are examined it is found that the alleged cause of action is certain to fail, the statement of claim should be struck out."[10] Hence though you may think that your opponent's pleading discloses no reasonable cause of action or defence to your claim, it by no means follows that you should at once apply to have it struck out or amended. So long as the statement of claim or the particulars served under it[11] disclose *some* cause of action, or raise some question fit to be decided by trial, the mere fact that a case is weak and not likely to succeed is no ground for striking it out.[12] It is custom and courtesy at the common law Bar before advising an application to be made under this rule

---

[7] R. 19(2); *Wenlock* v. *Moloney* [1965] 1 W.L.R. 1238.

[8] *Hubbuck & Sons* v. *Wilkinson* [1899] 1 Q.B. 86, 91.

[9] *Griffiths* v. *London and St. K. Docks Co.* (1884) 13 Q.B.D. at p. 261; *Steeds* v. *Steeds* (1889) 22 Q.B.D. at p. 542. See also *Dyson* v. *Att.-Gen.* [1911] 1 K.B. at p. 414; and the remarks of Selborne L.C. in *Burstall* v. *Beyfus* (1884) 13 Q.B.D. at p. 261; and of the Court of Appeal in *Worthington* v. *Belton* (1902) 18 T.L.R. 438; and *Lea* v. *Thursby* (1904) 90 L.T. 265. The court may strike out a defence even after substantial argument, both at first instance and on appeal: *Williams & Humbert Ltd.* v. *W. & H. Trade Marks (Jersey) Ltd.* [1986] 2 W.L.R. 24.

[10] Per Lord Pearson in *Drummond-Jackson* v. *British Medical Association* [1970] 1 W.L.R. 688 at p. 692.

[11] *Davey* v. *Bentinck* [1893] 1 Q.B. 185.

[12] *Moore* v. *Lawson* (1915) 31 T.L.R. 418; *Wenlock* v. *Moloney* [1965] 1 W.L.R. 1238, C.A.

to communicate with your opponent so that he may have an opportunity of amending his pleading.

Illustration

A defence alleging that the action by the plaintiff for declarations is based on foreign penal law which ought not to be recognised or enforced in England will be struck out when it appears that the plaintiff's action does not in fact amount to the indirect enforcement of the foreign law.

   Williams & Humbert Ltd. v. *W. & H. Trade Marks (Jersey) Ltd.* [1986] 2 W.L.R. 24. [1986] A.C. 368.

But a statement of claim alleging that the practice of the Jockey Club in refusing a trainer's licence to women is against public policy and claiming a declaration and injunction will not be struck out.

   Nagle v. *Feilden* [1966] 2 Q.B. 633, C.A.

In an action for malicious prosecution, where the facts disclosed show that it would be impossible for the judge at trial to rule that there was any want of reasonable or probable cause, particularly having regard to the fact that the prosecution had been instigated by the Director of Public Prosecutions, the statement of claim will be struck out as disclosing no reasonable cause of action.

   Riches v. *Director of Public Prosecutions* [1973] 1 W.L.R. 1019, C.A.[13]

(ii) *Where Action or Defence is Frivolous, Vexatious or an Abuse of Process*

As stated above, the court has power, both under the terms of the rule and under its inherent jurisdiction, to stay, strike out or dismiss proceedings in this category. But "it is a jurisdiction which ought to be very sparingly exercised and only in very exceptional cases."[14] It follows that an order will be made only in cases where it is obvious that the claim or defence is devoid of all merit or cannot possibly succeed.[15]

There appears to be no qualitative difference between a frivolous and a vexatious action, these terms being merely descriptive of a certain type of action or defence. In *Norman* v. *Matthews*[16] Lush J. propounded the test as follows: "In order to bring a case within the description it is not sufficient merely to say that the plaintiff has no cause of action. It must appear that his alleged cause of action is one which on the face of it is clearly one which no reasonable person could properly treat as bona fide, and contend that he had a grievance which he was entitled to bring before the Court."

---

[13] This case is also relevant on the question of when the court may strike out on the ground that the plaintiff's action may be barred by the Limitation Act 1980. See *ante*, Chap. 7. Many other illustrations of the exercise of this jurisdiction are to be found in R.S.C., paras. 18/19/3 *et seq.*

[14] *Per* Lord Herschell in *Lawrence* v. *Lord Norreys* (1890) 15 App.Cas. 210 at p. 219.

[15] *Willis* v. *Earl Beauchamp* (1886) 11 P.D. 59.

[16] (1916) 85 L.J.K.B. 857, 859. *Ashmore* v. *British Coal Corporation* [1990] 2 W.L.R. 1437, C.A.

Illustrations

Where a plaintiff brought a second action upon other defamatory statements in a publication which had already been decided to be a fair and accurate report of a judgment, it was held to be frivolous and vexatious and that a plea of *res judicata* must succeed.

MacDougall v. *Knight* (1890) 25 Q.B.D. 1.

The function of the courts is to consider and apply the enactments of Parliament, and there is no power to examine proceedings in Parliament to determine whether the passing of an Act had been obtained by fraud or other irregularity. Therefore a pleading alleging that a private Act of Parliament had been improperly obtained by misleading Parliament should be struck out.

British Railways Board v. *Pickin* [1974] A.C. 765.

The term "abuse of the process of the court" is similarly descriptive. It connotes that the powers of the court must be used bona fide and properly, and must not be abused. The court will prevent the improper use of its machinery and will not allow it to be used as a means of vexatious and oppressive behaviour in the process of litigation. In particular it is an abuse of the process for a plaintiff to litigate again an identical issue which has already been decided against him in earlier proceedings, even though the matter may not be strictly *res judicata*.[17] The operation of this principle may be avoided if the plaintiff can show that the earlier decision was obtained by perjury,[18] or if he can adduce fresh evidence; but such evidence must not have been obtainable by reasonable diligence at the time of the earlier proceedings and must show conclusively that the earlier decision was wrong.[19]

Illustrations

Where a defendant denied or refused to admit every allegation in a statement of claim and set up no case of his own and it was shown that in a previous action he had admitted on oath several of the more material allegations and not denied many of the others it was held that the defence was not honest and bona fide but a sham put in for the purpose of gaining time and must be struck out as an abuse of the process.

Remmington v. *Scoles* [1897] 2 Ch. 1.

Where the plaintiffs appealed against a decision of a district auditor without challenging the validity of the decision and lost, the Court of Appeal held that they would not be allowed to raise the issue of validity in fresh proceedings involving further parties. "Strictly the matter is not *res judicata* but these courts have ample power to prevent any abuse of their process. These proceedings are in my opinion an abuse. These [plaintiffs] are seeking by one shift or another, to escape the consequences of their own wrongdoing."

Asher v. *Secretary of State* [1974] Ch. 208, *per* Lord Denning M.R. at p. 222.

---

[17] *Stephenson* v. *Garrett* [1898] 1 Q.B. 677; *McIlkenny* v. *Chief Constable of West Midlands* [1980] 2 W.L.R. 689; affirmed in *Hunter* v. *Chief Constable of West Midlands Police* [1982] A.C. 529. Cf. *Gleeson* v. *J. Wippell & Co. Ltd.* [1977] 1 W.L.R. 510.

[18] See *D.P.P.* v. *Humphrys* [1977] A.C. 1, and cases there cited.

[19] *Phosphate Sewage Co.* v. *Molleson* (1879) 4 App.Cas. 801; *McIlkenny* v. *Chief Constable*, *supra*.

Normally it is an abuse of the process to ask the court to decide hypothetical questions, but the jurisdiction to strike out is discretionary. Therefore an action for a declaration that a right of way still existed and was exercisable would not be struck out on the grounds that if the question were tried as a preliminary issue a decision in favour of the defendants would be decisive of the dispute between the parties.

> *Hampshire C.C.* v. *Shonleigh Nominees Ltd.* [1970] 1 W.L.R. 865.

Finally, quite apart from this rule, the court has inherent power, where either party to an action has made repeated frivolous applications to the judge or master, to make an order prohibiting any further applications by him without leave.[20] Such an order is, however, rarely made.

(iii) *Where Objectionable Matter is Included*

Under the same rule a master may order to be struck out or amended any matter in any pleading which may be scandalous, frivolous or vexatious, or which may tend to prejudice, embarrass or delay the fair trial of the action. But such orders are not lightly made. One party cannot dictate how the other shall plead. The primary test of whether a pleading contains "scandalous" matter is whether that matter is relevant to an issue raised by the pleading. The test of relevance in this context is admissibility in evidence: "The sole question is whether the matter alleged to be scandalous would be admissible in evidence to show the truth of any allegation in the pleading which is material with reference to the relief prayed."[21] Where unnecessary matter in a pleading contains any imputation on the opponent or makes any degrading charges or allegations of misconduct or bad faith against him or anyone else then it becomes scandalous and will be struck out.

The mere fact that an allegation is unnecessary is no ground for striking it out; nor is a pleading embarrassing merely because it contains allegations which are inconsistent or stated in the alternative.[22] "I take 'embarrassing' to mean that the allegations are so irrelevant that to allow them to stand would involve useless expense, and would also prejudice the trial of the action by involving the parties in a dispute that is wholly apart from the issues."[23]

---

[20] *Grepe* v. *Loam* (1887) 37 Ch.D. 168; *Kinnaird* v. *Field* [1905] 2 Ch. 306. And see the Supreme Court Act 1981, s.42; *Re Chaffers* (1897) 13 T.L.R. 363; *Re Jones* (1902) 18 T.L.R. 476; *Re Boaler* [1915] 1 K.B. 21. *Re C., The Times,* November 14, 1989.

[21] *Per* Lord Selborne L.C. in *Christie* v. *Christie* (1873) L.R. 8 Ch. 499 at p. 503. The proposition is circular, since the test of admissibility in the law of evidence is relevance to a fact in issue. See Cross on Evidence (6th ed.), pp. 49 *et seq.*

[22] *Child* v. *Stenning* (1877) 5 Ch.D. 695; *Re Morgan* (1887) 35 Ch.D. 492.

[23] *Per* Pickford L.J. in *Mayor, etc. of London* v. *Horner* (1914) 111 L.T. at p. 514; and see *Willoughby* v. *Eckstein* [1936] 1 All E.R. 650.

Unless the pleading as it stands is really and seriously embarrassing, it is often better policy not to attack it; you only strengthen your opponent's position by compelling him to reform and thus to improve his pleading. But be careful in drawing a defence not to aid a defect in the claim in any way; the less said about that part of the pleading the better. Do not admit it; if need be, traverse it in so many words; but, after such denial, avoid the whole topic, if possible, leaving the plaintiff's counsel to explain it to the judge at the trial, if he can.

Illustrations

"A defendant may claim *ex debito justitiae* to have the plaintiff's case presented in an intelligble form, so that he may not be embarrassed in meeting it."
Per James L.J. in *Davy* v. *Garrett* (1878) 7 Ch.D. at p. 486.

In an action to enforce the compromise of a former action, it is unnecessary and embarrassing for the plaintiff to set out in his new pleading all the facts on which he relied before; for he will not be allowed to try the former action over again.
Knowles v. *Roberts* (1888) 38 Ch.D. 263.

(2) Particulars

The most usual way of attacking your opponent's pleading is by applying for particulars.

"The court may order a party to serve on any other party particulars of any claim, defence or other matter stated in his pleading, or in any affidavit of his ordered to stand as a pleading, or a statement of the nature of the case on which he relies, and the order may be made on such terms as the court thinks just" (Order 18, r. 12(3)). If either party considers that his opponent's pleading does not give him the information to which he is entitled, he should first apply for further particulars by letter, otherwise he may not get an order (r. 12(6)); the costs of such a letter are allowable.[24] If the particulars are refused, he should then apply to the master for an order, preferably upon the first hearing of the Summons for Directions. Care should be taken not to make the application prematurely, for under rule 12(5) particulars will not be ordered before defence unless the master deems them necessary or desirable to enable the defendant to plead or there are other special reasons.

---

[24] For a form of request for particulars see Precedent No. 60, and for an example of Further and Better Particulars see Precedent No. 61. Ord. 18, r. 12(7) requires that the request or order shall be incorporated with the particulars supplied pursuant to the request or order.

"The object of particulars is to enable the party asking for them to know what case he has to meet at the trial, and so to save unnecessary expense, and avoid allowing parties to be taken by surprise."[25] If your opponent has worded his pleading so vaguely that you cannot be sure what his line of attack or defence will be at the trial, it is worthwhile to apply for particulars, even though you think you can make a shrewd guess at his meaning. It is safer to pin him down to a definite story, otherwise it will be open to him at the trial to give evidence as to any fact which tends to support his vague allegation.[26] It is also most desirable to ascertain whether the plaintiff is relying on parol conversations or written documents as amounting to a misrepresentation or as establishing a contract. Always ask for particulars of losses, expenses and other special damage. For special damages in personal injury cases see Order 18, r. 12(1A)(b) which requires a statement of the special damages claimed to be served with the Statement of Claim.

Particulars are now ordered much more freely than in former days.[27] As Cotton L.J. remarked in *Spedding* v. *Fitzpatrick*[28]: "The old system of pleading at common law was to conceal as much as possible what was going to be proved at the trial." In modern times the courts are emphatic that pleadings should define with clarity and precision the issues to be tried, and in many cases particulars will be necessary of a general allegation (for example, the scuttling of a ship[29]) so that the party against whom the allegation is made will be informed of the case he has to meet and will be able to prepare his case properly to meet the allegation. In this way the furnishing of particulars will carry into operation the overriding principle that the litigation between the parties, and particularly the trial, should be conducted fairly, openly and without surprises and incidentally to reduce costs.[30]

Under the rules of 1883 it was sufficient to allege knowledge simply as a fact, without giving particulars of the circumstances relied on as showing or raising an inference of knowledge.[31]

---

[25] *Spedding* v. *Fitzpatrick* (1888) 38 Ch.D. at p. 413.

[26] *Chester (Dean and Chapter of)* v. *Smelting Corporation Ltd.* [1902] W.N. 5; *Hewson* v. *Cleeve* [1904] 2 Ir.R. 536.

[27] See, *e.g. Gale* v. *Reed* (1806) 8 Ea. 80; *Shum* v. *Farrington* (1797) 1 B. & P. 640; *Burton* v. *Webb* (1800) 8 T.R. 459; *Cornwallis* v. *Savery* (1759) 2 Burr. 772; *Forsyth* v. *Bristowe* (1853) 8 Ex. 350. In each of these cases the particulars asked for would now be ordered.

[28] (1888) 38 Ch.D. 414.

[29] *Astrovlanis Compania Naviera S.A.* v. *Linard* [1972] 2 Q.B. 611.

[30] R.S.C., para. 18/12/2, cited with approval by Edmund Davies L.J. in the *Astrovlanis* case, *supra*, at p. 620.

[31] See *Burgess* v. *Beethoven Electric Equipment Ltd.* [1943] K.B. 96.

Nor were particulars ordered of an allegation that a party had "notice" of a fact, unless the circumstances were material. Now, however, particulars may in either case be ordered at the master's discretion on such terms as may be just (Order 18, r. 12(4)). But if a party serves particulars he is bound by them at the trial and there are many cases where knowledge can only be established by cross-examination or after discovery of documents or interrogatories. Accordingly a convenient form of order may often be to the effect that if a party intends to adduce at the trial affirmative evidence showing that the other party knew the thing alleged, he do serve particulars of the facts relied on within so many days after inspection (or not less than so many days before trial, as the case may be). If it is practicable to give the necessary particulars in the pleading the costs of an application will be saved. Again, a plaintiff sometimes pleads "as the defendant ought to have known." In some cases this amounts to no more than an allegation that the defendant had notice of a particular fact, in which case particulars may be ordered at the master's discretion if the circumstances are material.[32] But if the intended effect of the allegation is that the other party was negligent in failing to observe or to infer the existence of a particular thing, particulars of the facts and circumstances relied on as constituting such negligence ought always to be given.[33]

Several examples of cases where particulars are necessary have already been referred to in Chapter 8. Some of these cases concern allegations such as fraud, breach of trust, etc., of which a party is expressly required by Order 18, r. 12(1) to give particulars. Other enactments may also expressly direct that particulars be given in certain cases; for example, in an action under the Fatal Accidents Act 1976 (as amended by the Administration of Justice Act 1982), the plaintiff must deliver "full particulars of the dependants for whom and on whose behalf the action is brought, and of the nature of the claim in respect of which damages are sought to be recovered" (s.2(4)). Similarly, Order 76, r. 9 makes detailed provision for the contents of pleadings in contentious probate proceedings.

There is another advantage in obtaining particulars from your opponent. It limits the issue. He is bound by his particulars, and cannot at the trial (without special leave, which will only be granted on terms) go into any matters not fairly

---

[32] Ord. 18, r. 12(4); and see *Cresta Holdings Ltd.* v. *Karlin* [1959] 1 W.L.R. 1055, decided under the former rule.
[33] *Fox* v. *H. Wood (Harrow) Ltd.* [1963] 2 Q.B. 601.

included therein.[34] Particulars thus "prevent surprise at the trial, and limit inquiry at the trial to matters set out in particulars. They tend to narrow issues, and ought to be encouraged."[35]

Illustrations

Particulars of general damage will very rarely be ordered. But when any special damage is claimed, without sufficient detail, particulars will be ordered of the alleged damage, *e.g.* if the plaintiff alleges that certain customers have ceased to deal with him, he will be ordered to state their names. This is a very useful order, for if the plaintiff cannot give the names, he will be compelled to strike out the allegation of special damage; and the summons should ask that it be struck out if such particulars be not delivered. If he gives the necessary particulars, he will be bound by them; he will not be allowed at the trial to give evidence of any special damage which is not claimed explicitly, either in his pleading or particulars. If ambiguous expressions be used in the statement of claim which may or may not amount to an allegation of special damage, the master will order "particulars of special damage, if any claimed."

In personal injury actions see Order 18, r. 12(1A) and Practice Note [1984] 1 W.L.R. 1127. Failure to comply with those requirements may be taken into account in deciding questions of costs. See also Order 18, r. 12(1B) which illustrates the Court's power to stay the proceedings for non-compliance with Order 18, r. 12(1A).

Hayward v. *Pullinger & Partners Ltd.* [1950] 1 All E.R. 581.

A plaintiff claiming damages for wrongful dismissal may be ordered to give as part of his particulars of special damage in respect of loss of salary an estimate of the amount of tax which he would have had to pay if he had remained in employment and the broad facts relied on in arriving at that estimate.

Phipps v. *Orthodox Unit Trusts Ltd.* [1958] 1 Q.B. 314.

Parsons v. *B.N.M. Laboratories Ltd.* [1964] 1 Q.B. 95.

It is no objection to an application for particulars that the applicant must know the true facts of the case better than his opponent. He is entitled to know the outline of the case that his adversary will try to make against him, which may be something very different from the true facts of the case. His opponent may know more than he does; in any event it is well to bind him down to a definite story. Particulars will be ordered whenever the master is satisfied that without them the applicant cannot tell *what* is going to be proved against him at the trial. But *how* his opponent will prove it is a matter of evidence of which particulars will not be ordered.

Again, where the party applying is in other respects entitled to the particulars for which he asks, it is not a valid objection to his application that if the order be made it will compel the party giving them to name his witnesses, or otherwise to disclose or

---

[34] *Woolley* v. *Broad* [1892] 2 Q.B. 317.
[35] *Per* Watkin Williams J. in *Thomson* v. *Birkley* (1882) 47 L.T. 700.

give some clue to his evidence. If the only object of the summons is to obtain particulars of the evidence on the other side, it should, of course, be dismissed as an improper application.[36] But where the information asked for is clearly necessary to enable the applicant properly to prepare for trial, or where in other respects the application is a proper one, the information must be given, even though it discloses some portion of the evidence on which the other party proposes to rely at the trial,[37] and even where the plaintiff is privileged from producing documents which would disclose such evidence.[38]

In certain cases, a party who is ordered to give particulars is allowed, before giving them, to interrogate his opponent or to obtain discovery of documents.[39] "It is good practice and good sense that where the defendant knows the facts and the plaintiffs do not, the defendant should give discovery before the plaintiffs deliver particulars."[40] But no hard and fast rule can be laid down to determine when particulars should precede discovery or discovery should precede particulars. Each case will depend on its own circumstances.[41]

Illustrations

So in an action for libel contained in a letter or other private document, the name of the person to whom each publication was made, and the date of such publication, must be stated in the pleading. This, however, is unnecessary in the case of a newspaper, prospectus, handbill or other document widely disseminated. A person libelled in a newspaper cannot be expected to tell the proprietor the names of all who take his paper; that would be oppressive.

Davey v. *Bentinck* [1893] 1 Q.B. 185.

And see Precedent No. 29.

Similarly, in an action for slander, the defendant is entitled to particulars of the times when, and the persons to whom (and in some cases, of the places where) the alleged slanders were published, if such details are not given in the statement of claim.

Roselle v. *Buchanan* (1886) 16 Q.B.D. 656.

If no facts be stated in a plea of justification, particulars will be ordered of the facts upon which the defendant intends to rely at the trial in support of that plea, unless the charge is specific and precise. The defendant will not be entitled to wait until discovery before giving the necessary particulars.

Wootton v. *Sievier* [1913] 3 K.B. 499.

Goldschmidt v. *Constable & Co.* [1937] 4 All E.R. 293.

---

[36] *Temperton* v. *Russell* (1893) 9 T.L.R. at p. 320.

[37] *Marriott* v. *Chamberlain* (1886) 17 Q.B.D. 154, 161; *Zierenberg* v. *Labouchere* [1893] 2 Q.B. at pp. 187, 188; *Bishop* v. *Bishop* [1901] P. 325.

[38] *Milbank* v. *Milbank* [1900] 1 Ch. 376.

[39] *Whyte* v. *Ahrens* (1884) 20 Ch.D. 717; *Leitch* v. *Abbott* (1886) 31 Ch.D. 374.

[40] Per Bowen L.J. in *Millar* v. *Harper* (1888) 38 Ch.D. 112. See also *Edelston* v. *Russell* (1888) 57 L.T. 927.

[41] *Waynes Merthyr Co.* v. *Radford* [1896] 1 Ch. 29; *Cyril Leonard & Co.* v. *Simo Securities Trust* [1972] 1 W.L.R. 80.

The mere fact that the defendant has already served his defence is no waiver of his right to particulars of the allegations in the statement of claim.[42] And where the pleadings contain sufficient particulars to raise issues which ought to be investigated by the court, neither further particulars nor discovery will be ordered before defence.[43] Accordingly, unless such particulars are necessary in order to enable him to plead, the proper time for his application is upon the first hearing of the Summons for Directions. If he makes a separate application earlier or later, as he may so long as he is not guilty of unreasonable delay, he will probably have to bear the costs, unless there was some very good reason for taking this course.

It is no hardship on a party who has a good case to be ordered to give particulars. It is often a benefit to him, for it compels him to get his case up carefully in good time before the trial. It is also sometimes an advantage to have full particulars of his grievance, loss, expenses, etc., clearly stated in black and white, and laid before the judge with the pleadings.

At the same time, particulars will not be exacted where it would be oppressive or unreasonable to make such an order; as where the information is not in the possession of either party, or could only be obtained with great difficulty, or where the particulars are not applied for till the last moment. An order is often made for "the best particulars the plaintiff can give."

Illustrations

Where the defendant on the face of his pleading disputes all the items of the plaintiff's claim, he cannot be made to give particulars stating which of them he really disputes. Where he alleges that all the prices charged by the plaintiff are unreasonable and excessive, he cannot be ordered to state to which items he objects.

> *James* v. *Radnor County Council* (1890) 6 T.L.R. 240. (Note, however, the use of a "Scott Schedule" in this type of case: (Supreme Court Practice 1991, para. 18/12/29).

Particulars of an immaterial allegation will not be ordered; particulars of an allegation which is not necessary may be ordered, if the master in his discretion thinks it right.

> *Gaston* v. *United Newspapers Ltd.* (1915) 32 T.L.R. 143.

As a rule, particulars will only be ordered of an affirmative allegation—not of a mere traverse or of a joinder of issue.[44] But this simple rule is not quite so easy to apply as might at first

---

[42] *Sachs* v. *Speilman* (1887) 37 Ch.D. 295.
[43] *Commission for Racial Equality* v. *Ealing London Borough Council* [1978] 1 W.L.R. 112.
[44] *Weinberger* v. *Inglis* [1918] 1 Ch. 133; *La Radiotechnique* v. *Weinbaum* [1928] Ch. 1.

appear. Where a negative allegation is traversed, this implies in some sense an affirmative. The question whether particulars will be ordered seems to depend on whether the traverse imports an affirmative allegation beyond that which is in any event to be implied (*i.e.* whether the traverse is what is called a pregnant negative, in which case particulars ought to be given[45]), or whether it is a mere traverse. It is not always easy to decide on which side of the line a given case falls. The relevant considerations are discussed at length in *Pinson* v. *Lloyds, etc., Bank Ltd.*[46]

Illustrations

A wife alleged that her husband had withdrawn from cohabitation and had kept and continued away without just cause. The husband denied that he withdrew or remained away without just cause—an undesirable way to plead on any showing (see *ante*, Chapter 9). *Held*, the plea amounted to an affirmative allegation of which particulars should be given.

MacLulich v. *MacLulich* [1920] P. 439.

The plaintiff alleged that he and his mistress contributed to the purchase of a house in equal shares and that he never intended that any contribution by him should be a gift to her. *Held*, that the negative allegation was of doubtful necessity (there being no matrimonial relationship) but having been pleaded it amounted to a positive averment warranting particulars of the overt acts of the plaintiff (if any) and the facts relied on to show that the contributions were made without such intention.

Feeney v. *Rix* [1968] Ch. 693.

An order for particulars does not automatically stay proceedings until the particulars are given or extend a party's time for pleading. Hence it is wise, and usual, if such further order is required, to ask for it in the summons. An order for particulars made against a plaintiff may contain a term that the action shall be dismissed if he fails to comply.[47] A defendant is, on the same principle, often subjected to a condition that any allegations, of which he fails to give particulars, shall be struck out.

It sometimes happens that a party, who in compliance with an order has given all particulars then within his knowledge, subsequently discovers new matter which he desires to add to the particulars already served. In such a case the proper course is to apply for leave to serve further particulars, unless a right to do so has already been reserved to him. For without such leave he has strictly no right to add anything to those already served and by which he is bound.[48] However, service of so-

---

[45] *Chapple* v. *Electrical Trades Union* [1961] 1 W.L.R. 1290; *Howard* v. *Borneman* [1972] 1 W.L.R. 863.
[46] [1941] 2 K.B. 72.
[47] *Davey* v. *Bentinck* [1893] 1 Q.B. 185.
[48] *Yorkshire Provident Co.* v. *Gilbert* [1895] 2 Q.B. at p. 152; *Emden* v. *Burns* (1894) 10 T.L.R. 400.

called "voluntary particulars" (without such leave) is becoming increasingly common in practice, by which a party ought to be equally bound. Objection to this course is rarely, if ever, taken though there is no provision for it in the rules.

CHAPTER 11

AMENDMENT

Now look at home. Your opponent may have raised some well-founded objection to your pleading; or new facts may have come to light, independently of your opponent's pleading; or it may even happen (though you should not lightly be moved to alter what you first drafted) that you have regretfully come to the conclusion that your own first thoughts, as expressed in your original pleading, are not the best or only way of framing your client's case. In such event you had best seek to amend before the costs increase. Many amendments can be made without leave. But remember that, if application to the court is necessary, the master can make the order upon the Summons for Directions and do not make a separate application unless it is essential. Again, further instructions may make it necessary to add another part or another cause of action or some technical defect may come to light, so that you must include the writ as well as the pleadings in the ambit of your review. The relevant rules are mainly to be found in Order 20.

Amending without Leave

After service the writ may be amended once without leave at any time before pleadings are closed. But this facility does not extend to an amendment consisting of the addition, omission or substitution of a party to the action, or an alteration of the capacity in which a party sues or is sued, or the addition or substitution of a new cause of action unless such amendment is made before the writ has been served (rule 1); normally, therefore, leave to make such an amendment will be necessary. Amendments to a statement of claim indorsed on the writ cannot be made under this rule but are dealt with as amendments to a pleading (see *infra*). Instances of the type of amendment which is permissible under this rule are where there has been a mistake in the spelling of a party's name or other misnomer not amounting to a change of identity[1]; a wrong address of the registered office of a limited company; an error in a general indorsement or in the formal parts of the writ; and there are many other possibilities. If the writ has already been served before amendment it must be re-served

---

[1] A mere misnomer on the writ is often corrected in the statement of claim without formal amendment.

197

unless a master dispenses with re-service; the application is made *ex parte*, ordinarily to the Practice Master.[2] The costs of and occasioned by any such amendment fall upon the plaintiff, unless a master on a summons for the purpose orders otherwise (Order 62, r. 6(5)). To make the amendment the plaintiff or his solicitor takes to the writ room in the Central Office the original writ and a copy marked (usually in red ink) with the amendment which he wishes to make and headed "Amended the——day of——19—under Order 20, rule 1" and stamped with the requisite fee; the copy is filed and the original is altered and sealed. If the alterations are so long or elaborate that the altered document would be difficult to read, a fresh document in the amended form must be prepared and reissued (rule 10).

In general an acknowledgment of service may not be amended without leave (rule 2(1)). However, if the acknowledgment of service contains a statement of intention to contest the proceedings, it may be amended without leave to substitute a statement to the opposite effect. This power extends to the converse situation also; that is, the party acknowledging service may amend his statement that he does not intend to contest the proceedings to the opposite effect, provided that he makes his substituted statement of intention to contest before judgment has been obtained in the proceedings (rule 2(2)).

Any pleading may be amended once without leave at any time before pleadings are closed (rule 3).[3] The amended pleading must be served on the opposite party, and subsequent pleadings, if already served, may if necessary be amended consequentially within the time limited by the rule.[4] The costs of and occasioned by an amendment of the writ or any pleading without leave fall on the amending party unless a master orders otherwise (Order 62, r. 6(5)). A party served with a writ or pleading amended without leave may within 14 days apply by summons to a master to disallow the amendment, and it may be disallowed or allowed to stand on terms as may be just (Order 20, r. 4).

Amending with Leave

(1) A writ[5] or any pleading may, with leave, be amended at any stage of the proceedings on such terms as may be just (rule

---

[2] See Chapter 1.

[3] Before 1964 amendment of pleadings subsequent to the statement of claim could only be made by leave.

[4] This implied right to make consequential amendments without leave relates only to those parts of the pleading concerned with the amended allegations: *Squire* v. *Squire* [1971] 2 W.L.R. 363.

[5] And an originating summons, a petition and an originating notice of motion (r. 7).

5). Certain special rules apply where the amendment involves a change of parties (see Chapter 2); but in general the master, the trial judge and the Court of Appeal have power to allow all such amendments as are necessary to enable justice to be done.[6]

Either party is ordinarily given leave to make such amendment as is reasonably necessary for the due presentation of his case on payment of the costs of and occasioned by the amendment, provided that there has been no undue delay on his part, and provided also that the amendment will not injure his opponent or affect his vested rights. Where the amendment is necessary to enable justice to be done between the parties, it will be allowed on terms even at a late stage.[7] "However negligent or careless may have been the first omission and however late the proposed amendment, the amendment should be allowed if it can be made without injustice to the other side. There is no injustice if the other side can be compensated by costs; but if the amendment will put them into such a position that they must be injured, it ought not to be made."[8] "Sometimes to correct the error will lead to injustice which cannot be cured, as when a witness who could give evidence cannot be got at, or the solvency of one party is doubtful."[9] If the application is made mala fide, or if the proposed amendment will cause undue delay, or will in any other way unfairly prejudice the other party, or is irrelevant or useless, or would raise merely a technical point, leave to amend will be refused.

Whereas formerly a plaintiff would not be allowed to amend by setting up fresh claims in respect of causes of action which since the issue of the writ had become barred by the expiry of any relevant period of limitation,[10] the court may now grant leave to amend under Order 20, r. 5(1) subject to section 35 of the Limitation Act 1980, even though it may deprive the

---

[6] See *Chatsworth Investments Ltd.* v. *Cussins (Contractors) Ltd.* [1969] 1 W.L.R. 1; *Sterman* v. *E.W. & W.J. Moore* [1970] 1 Q.B. 596.

[7] *Hunt* v. *Rice & Son Ltd.* (1937) 53 T.L.R. 931.

[8] *Clarapede & Co.* v. *Commercial Union Association* (1883) 32 W.R. 262, *per* Brett M.R.

[9] *Ibid.* at p. 263, *per* Bowen L.J.

[10] *Weldon* v. *Neal* (1887) 19 Q.B.D. 394; *Hall* v. *Meyrick* [1957] 2 Q.B. 455; and compare the cases on renewal of a writ (*ante*, Chap. 4). Note that "any relevant period of limitation" includes the application of a time limit by virtue of the Foreign Limitation Periods Act 1984.

defendant of a defence under that Act.[11] Specific power to do so is granted in three cases if justice so requires. (i) The name of a party may be corrected even if the effect is to substitute a new party, provided that the wrong name was given through a genuine mistake which was not misleading or such as to cause any reasonable doubt as to the identity of the intended plaintiff or defendant.[12] (ii) The capacity in which a party sues may be altered if the new capacity is one which he had at the date of the writ or has since acquired. (iii) A new cause of action may be added or substituted if it arises out of the same facts, or substantially the same facts, as give rise to a cause of action already pleaded (Order 20, r. 5(2)–(5)) (to be read with section 35 of the Limitation Act 1980).[13]

Where the action has been brought on a substantial cause of action, to which a good defence has been pleaded, the plaintiff will not be allowed to amend his claim by including in it, for the first time, a trivial and merely technical cause of action, which such defence may not cover.[14] In some cases the plaintiff may amend by adding a new defendant.[15] But a defendant cannot, as a rule, make a third person a defendant without the plaintiff's consent.[16] No person may be added as a plaintiff without his consent signified in writing or in such other manner as may be authorised (Order 15, r. 6). In some cases, if not all, the consent of the plaintiff already on the record will also be required.[17]

The court will refuse an amendment where the plaintiff seeks to introduce a cause of action which has accrued to him

[11] See the cases cited in note 6 (*supra*), and see also *Brickfield Properties Ltd.* v. *Newton* [1971] 1 W.L.R. 862; *Beck* v. *Valve Capital Ltd. (No. 2)* [1976] 1 W.L.R. 572; *Circle 33 Housing Trust Ltd.* v. *Fairview Estates (Housing) Ltd.* (1985) 4 Const.L.J. 282, C.A.; *Idyll* v. *Dineman Davison and Hillman* (1985) 4 Const.L.J. 294, C.A. But see *Ketteman* v. *Hansel Properties Ltd.* [1987] 2 W.L.R. 312: when a person is joined unconditionally as a defendant in an action to which the Limitation Act 1939 applies, the action is deemed to have begun as against him not on the date of the original writ but on the date on which the amended writ is served on him or the date on which he waives such service.

[12] See for example *Rodriguez* v. *Parker* [1967] 1 Q.B. 116; *Mitchell* v. *Harris Engineering Co. Ltd.* [1967] 2 Q.B. 703: *Evans Constructions Co. Ltd.* v. *Charrington & Co. Ltd. and Bass Holdings Ltd.* [1983] Q.B. 810, but see *Beardman Motors Ltd.* v. *Birch Brothers (Properties) Ltd.* (1959) Ch. 298.

[13] The effect, not the precise wording of the rule is here given.

[14] *Dillon* v. *Balfour* (1887) 20 L.R.Ir. 600.

[15] *Edward* v. *Lowther* (1876) 45 L.J.C.P. 417. However, an amendment adding a new defendant takes effect from the date of the amendment and does not "relate back" to the date of the original writ. Thus where a new defendant is joined against whom the relevant period of limitation has expired, the action against him will be summarily dismissed on the ground that it s time-barred: *Liff* v. *Peasley* [1980] 1 W.L.R. 781 and *Ketteman* v. *Hansel Properties Ltd.* (*ante*). But see now section 35 of the Limitation Act 1980.

[16] *McCheane* v. *Gyles* [1902] 1 Ch. 911.

[17] See *Pennington* v. *Caley* (1912) 106 L.T. 591; *Emden* v. *Carte* (1881) 17 Ch.D. 169, (joinder of plaintiff's trustee in bankruptcy).

only after the date of the issue of the writ.[18] But where the plaintiff is claiming an injunction, a defendant may be allowed to amend his defence to take advantage of subsequent legislation, since the question whether an injunction ought to be granted has to be determined by reference to the circumstances and the state of law existing at the date of the trial of the action and not at the date of the issue of the writ.[19]

(2) Any document in the proceedings (other than a judgment or order) may be amended under Order 20, r. 8 for the purpose of determining the real question in controversy between the parties or of correcting any defect or error in any proceedings. This may be done on the application of any party or by a master or judge on his own initiative at any stage of the proceedings. Terms may be imposed. Under this rule an issue might be ordered to be amended; answers to interrogatories or other affidavits might be allowed to be altered and resworn; a notice might be amended; and there are many other possible examples. Further, under Order 2, r. 1 irregular proceedings may be set aside or amended or otherwise dealt with at discretion.

(3) Clerical mistakes in judgments or orders, or errors arising from any accidental slip or omission, may at any time be corrected on motion or summons without the necessity for an appeal (r. 11). This is known as the "slip rule." It applies to clerical mistakes and accidental slips or omissions both by the officers of the court and by the parties, and has even been held to cover neglect to apply for certain special costs which a party would ordinarily have been given if he had asked for them[20]; but it does not apply where the judgment or order correctly represents what the court in fact, albeit wrongly, intended. Amendments cannot be made under the rule upon an *ex parte* application.

Except where this rule applies, when once a judgment has been entered or an order drawn up, a party who thinks that it is wrong and wishes to have it altered must, in the ordinary way, appeal against it.[21] A judgment or order pronounced or

---

· [18] *Eshelby* v. *Federated European Bank* [1932] 1 K.B. 254; *Halliard Property Co. Ltd.* v. *Jock Segal Ltd.* [1978] 1 W.L.R. 377.

[19] *Application des Gaz SA* v. *Falks Veritas Ltd.* [1974] Ch. 381.

[20] *Re Inchcape (Earl of)* [1942] Ch. 394. See also *Re H. (Infants) (No. 2)* [1970] 1 W.L.R. 69.

[21] But in *Thynne* v. *Thynne* [1955] P. 272 the court allowed in a decree absolute of divorce an amendment affecting the date and place of the marriage, these not being regarded as essential parts of the decree. Even after judgment the court retains the power under Ord. 20, r. 5 to give leave to amend the pleadings, but it is not appropriate to exercise the power in a case where the pleading sought to be amended has already been struck out: *Midland Bank Trust Co. Ltd.* v. *Green (No. 2)* [1979] 1 W.L.R. 460.

made either in court or chambers may be reviewed or recalled on the application of a party or on the judge's own initiative until it has been entered or drawn up, as the case may be. Meanwhile it is provisionally effective.[22] Even thereafter the court has an inherent power to vary the wording so as to give effect to its original intention if it has been wrongly expressed, but not to correct a mistake of law subsequently discovered.

[22] *Re Harrison's Share* [1955] Ch. 260; *Hall* v. *Meyrick* [1957] 2 Q.B. 455.

CHAPTER 12

STATEMENT OF CLAIM

A statement of claim should state the material facts upon which the plaintiff relies and then claim the relief he desires. As "pleadings now are to be merely concise statements of the facts which the party pleading deems material to his case," it is unnecessary to particularise the form of action in which the relief would in former days have had to be sought. To state what form the plaintiff's right takes is to state a conclusion of law; and it is always unnecessary now for either party to state conclusions of law in his pleading—the court will draw the proper inference from the facts alleged.[1]

"Forms of action" are in fact abolished: it is now no longer necessary to state either on the writ or on the pleadings whether the plaintiff is suing in trespass or on the case, in detinue or in trover. This is a most important alteration. Formerly, everything turned on the form of action in which the plaintiff elected to sue. If he selected the wrong one, he would in the end be non-suited, even though an action would have lain if the declaration had been differently drawn. If he sued on a money count and it turned out that there was a special contract, he was non-suited and had to pay the costs of the first action before he could bring another on the special contract.[2] Again, if he sued in trespass and trespass did not lie, he was non-suited, although trover or detinue would have lain. In all the old reports the form of action is usually stated first in capitals. And the court never decided that *no* action lay on such a set of facts; but only that the action did not lie in that form. Hence in some cases it was only by a costly process of elimination that a plaintiff could ascertain for certain which was his proper legal remedy. In 1875 there were seven different forms of *personal* actions: debt, covenant, assumpsit, detinue, trespass, trespass on the case, and replevin; there were three *real* actions[3]: dower, writ of right of dower, and *quare impedit*; and one *mixed* action: ejectment. And each form of action (except that last mentioned[4]) had its appropriate form of declaration; one of these forms, and only one, had to be pleaded.

---

[1] *Hanmer* v. *Flight* (1876) 35 L.T. 127; *Shaw* v. *Shaw* [1954] 2 Q.B. 429, 441.
[2] See *White* v. *G.W. Ry.* (1857) 2 C.B.(N.S.) 7.
[3] The other real actions had been abolished by the Real Property Limitation Act 1833.
[4] From 1852 to 1875 there were no pleadings in ejectment; but the plaintiff often had to deliver particulars.

This strictness had undoubted advantages; it taught barristers to be precise. But it was often disastrous for the suitors and has accordingly been abolished. Each party now states the facts on which he relies; and the court will declare the law arising upon the facts pleaded. If on those facts the plaintiff would have been entitled to recover in any form of action, he will now recover in the action which he has brought.[5]

Parties

Before drafting a statement of claim, counsel must carefully consider whether all necessary parties have been brought before the court, and also whether it was necessary to bring before the court all the parties named on the writ. He has to show in his pleading a right of action in every plaintiff, and a liability on the part of each defendant and he should consider whether an application to amend the writ will be necessary (see Chapter 11). The plaintiff can, at this early stage, discontinue the action against any of the defendants or withdraw any part of his complaint without any summons, merely by giving a notice in writing under Order 21, r. 2(1). He must, of course, pay the costs occasioned by the matter so withdrawn (see Chapter 17). The statements of claim served on all defendants who are kept as parties to the action must be identical, although they may show that different relief is claimed against different defendants. If any party sues, or is sued, in a representative character (*e.g.* as trustee in a bankruptcy or as executor of a will), this fact ought to be stated in the title or heading of the statement of claim, as well as on the writ.[6]

Illustrations
If any party to the action is improperly or imperfectly named on the writ and no change of identity is involved, the misnomer may be corrected in the statement of claim by inserting the right name with a statement that the party misnamed had sued or had been sued by the name on the writ, *e.g.* "John William Smythe (sued as 'J. M. Smith')." The defendant can take no advantage of such an alteration, but difficulty may arise in executing a judgment unless the plaintiff amends the writ.

Joinder of Causes of Action

The plaintiff may unite in one action several causes of action without leave, provided that such joinder does not contravene

5 See *Kelly* v. *Metropolitan Ry.* [1895] 1 Q.B. at p. 946.
6 *Re Tottenham* [1896] 1 Ch. 628.

the rules of Order 15 (see Chapter 2). And he ought to join in the one action all causes of action which can conveniently be tried together, and so save costs.

"A statement of claim must not contain any allegation or claim in respect of a cause of action unless that cause of action is mentioned in the writ or arises from facts which are the same as, or include or form part of, facts giving rise to a cause of action so mentioned; but subject to that, a plaintiff may in his statement of claim alter, modify or extend any claim made by him in the indorsement of the writ without amending the indorsement," *e.g.* by claiming further relief or stating the same claim in a different way.[7] Otherwise, matters which have arisen at any time, whether before or since the issue of the writ, may be included in any pleading.[8] But this rule does not entitle the plaintiff to add a new and totally different claim. On the other hand, if a plaintiff in his statement of claim omits all mention of a cause of action or a claim for relief which is stated on his writ, he will be deemed to have abandoned it.[9]

The result of Order 18, r. 15(2) is that a plaintiff may only include in his statement of claim causes of action which existed at the date of the writ. He can nevertheless recover damages accruing since that date from a cause of action vested in him before it or from a continuing cause of action. But he cannot claim damages in respect of a cause of action against the same defendant, which has vested in him since the date of the writ. If he wishes to do that, he must issue a second writ, and then apply to have the two actions consolidated, if they can conveniently be tried together. Freer use is made of the power to consolidate actions than was formerly possible.[10]

A plaintiff should as a rule avail himself of all his causes of action, and join as many of them as he can in one action. *e.g.* he should set out every covenant that there is any ground for believing broken, and allege every available breach of such covenant. But the facts upon which each claim is founded should, so far as possible, be stated separately and distinctly.

Illustrations

A repairing lease generally contains three concurrent covenants as to repairs:
  (a) A general covenant to repair.

---

[7] Order 18, r. 15(2); *Large* v. *Large* [1877] W.N. 198; *Graff Brothers Estates Ltd.* v. *Rimrose Brook Joint Sewerage Bd.* [1953] 2 Q.B. 318.

[8] Ord. 18, r. 9.

[9] *Harries* v. *Ashford* [1950] 1 All E.R. 427. And see *Sterman* v. *E.W. & W.J. Moore* [1970] 1 Q.B. 596.

[10] See *Horwood* v. *Statesman Publishing Co.* (1929) 98 L.J.K.B. 450; *Bailey* v. *Marchioness Curzon* [1932] 2 K.B. 392.

(b) A covenant to repair on three months' notice.

(c) A covenant to paint the outside once in every three years, and the inside once in every seven years.

Each of these is distinct and severable from the others, and every breach of any one of them is a separate cause of action; therefore set out all three and allege that each is broken, as you may win on one, though you fail on the others. See Precedent No. 32.

If the plaintiff sues the defendant for fraud and proves negligence, he cannot recover; hence it may be advisable, in such a case, to plead negligence in the alternative.

Connecticut Fire Insurance Co. v. *Kavanagh* [1892] A.C. 473.

It is often desirable to commence a statement of claim with some introductory averments stating who the parties are, what business they carry on, how they are related or connected, and other surrounding circumstances leading up to the dispute. These are called *matters of inducement*, because they explain what follows, though they may not be essential to the cause of action.[11] A good pleader always reduces such prefatory statements to a minimum, and states them as concisely as possible, though the temptation to "tell the story" may be great! Next should come the essential portions of the claim, *i.e.* the statement of the plaintiff's right which he alleges has been violated; and then the statement of the breach or wrong complained of. Then comes the allegation of damage, and last the claim for relief. This order should always be followed.

Tort

In an action of tort it is unnecessary to set out the right which has been violated in cases where that right is not peculiar to the plaintiff in any way, but is one possessed by every subject of the Crown. Thus, in actions of libel, slander, false imprisonment or assault, the claim is merely a statement of a wrong. In other cases where the plaintiff claims a special right in himself (*e.g.* an easement, or copyright), the right must be stated with all due particularity. This is specially so in actions for the recovery of land. And remember that it is not sufficient to allege in a pleading that a right or a duty or a liability exists; but the facts must be stated which give rise to such right or create such duty or liability.

Illustrations

In an action of libel or slander the precise words complained of are material, and they must be set out verbatim in the statement of claim.

---

[11] For typical examples see Precedents Nos. 16 and 29. (*cf.* Precedent No. 19 where it is material to allege that the defendants sell fertilisers in the course of a business.)

Harris v. *Warre* (1879) 4 C.P.D. 125, 48 L.J.C.P. 310.
Collins v. *Jones* [1955] 1 Q.B. 564.
And see Precedent No. 29.

For examples of forms setting out facts giving rise to rights or duties in common types of case see Precedent No. 25 (paras. 1 and 2: duty under the Occupiers' Liability Act 1957) and Precedent No. 26 (paras. 1, 2 and 3: right of the plaintiff to sue as widow of deceased employee for breach of employer's duty).

Contract

Where the action is brought on a contract, the contract must first be alleged, and then its breach. It should clearly appear whether the contract on which the plaintiff relies is express or implied; in the latter case the facts should be briefly stated from which the plaintiff contends a contract is to be implied. If the contract is by deed, it should be so stated; if it is not by deed, then a consideration should be shown, which must not be a past consideration.

Wherever the contract sued on is contained in a written instrument, the pleader should shortly state what he conceives to be its legal effect; he should not set out the document itself verbatim unless the precise words of the document, or some of them, are material (Order 18, r. 7(2)). It will be for the defendant, if he disputes the legal effect attributed to it by the plaintiff, to state his own version of the document, or, if he thinks fit, to set it out verbatim in the defence, with an allegation that this is the contract referred to in the statement of claim.

The actual contract which was in force between the parties at the date of breach should be the one alleged. There is no need to go into ancient history. If there have at different times been different agreements between the parties, it is unnecessary to set out the original terms which have been dispensed with. It is sufficient to state the contract as it stood when the plaintiff's right of action accrued.[12] And contingencies need not be stated, if the events upon which they were contingent never happened; they do not affect the plaintiff's right or title.

It is no longer necessary for a plaintiff to allege generally the performance of all conditions precedent, as was customary before the Judicature Act. Such an allegation is now implied in his pleading by Order 18, r. 7(4). Where, however, the plaintiff is conscious that he has not performed a condition precedent, and has a good excuse for such non-performance, he should in

[12] *Boone* v. *Mitchell* (1822) 1 B. & C. 18.

his statement of claim state the condition, the non-performance and the facts which afford him his excuse, *e.g.* that the defendant prevented or discharged him from performing it. At first sight this might appear to constitute an exception to the principle already stated "do not leap before you come to the stile." But this is not really so, even though to a certain extent the plaintiff may be anticipating the defence. For had he failed to mention the circumstances of his non-performance, due performance would have been impliedly alleged by virtue of Order 18, r. 7(4) and a false issue raised.

If either the consideration or the promise is in the alternative, this should be stated according to the fact. If the promise or covenant sued on contains an exception or proviso qualifying the defendant's liability, such exception or proviso should be stated; for it would be incorrect to state the contract as an absolute one. But if the promise or covenant sued on is absolute in itself and contains no exception or proviso, and no reference to any exception or proviso, it may be stated as an absolute contract, although there may be in a distinct part of the deed or instrument a proviso defeating or qualifying it in certain events. For such proviso is in the nature of a defeasance, and must be set up by the defendant if the facts permit. If, however, the subsequent clause is referred to by some such words as "save as hereinafter excepted," then strictly the exception or proviso ought to be set out in the statement of claim.

Illustrations

When the action is brought on a written contract, the pleader should describe it as a contract in writing, and give its date, and name the parties to it, so as to identify the document. If he merely states, "It was agreed between the plaintiff and the defendant," the defendant will apply for particulars.

Turquand v. *Fearon* (1879) L.J.Q.B. 703.

Where there are several covenants in the same deed, some of which are broken and some not, the plaintiff should, of course, omit all allusion to the covenants which he does not allege to have been broken. There is no need for him to set out the whole document. He should first of all set out all the covenants which he alleges have been broken in their order as they occur in the deed, and then allege separately the breach of each covenant in the same order.

Breach

The breach of contract, of which the plaintiff complains, must be alleged in the terms of the contract, or in words co-extensive with the effect or meaning of it. If, however, to allege a breach in the very words of the covenant would be too general an averment, particulars of the breaches should be set out in the pleading. But be careful in so doing not to narrow unduly the general averment that the covenant has been broken.

In averring a breach, "and" must always be turned into "or," and "all" into "any." If the contract is to do more things than one, the plaintiff must either state expressly that the defendant has done none of them, or else set out precisely what and how much he has in fact done. And generally the rules as to traversing apply to pleading a breach.

Illustrations

If the contract is to pay a sum of money, *e.g.* £9,000, the breach alleged must be not merely that the defendant did not pay £9,000; the plaintiff must add the words "or any part thereof," or else state how much has been paid and give the defendant credit for that amount, claiming only the balance.

So, again, if the promise be to pay on a particular day, the plaintiff must not merely allege that the defendant has not paid the money on that day; he must add the words "or at all."

For examples of forms setting out types of breach see Precedents Nos. 16 (para. 4); 17 (para. 3); 18 (para. 6); and 19 (para. 4).

The Claim for Damages

As to the allegation of damage, the distinction between special and general damage must be carefully observed. General damage such as the law will presume to be the natural or probable consequence of the defendant's act need not be specifically pleaded (subject to the provisions of Order 18, r. 12(1A)). It arises by inference of law, and need not, therefore, be proved by evidence, and may be averred generally. In some cases however, part of the general damages which it is sought to recover may have resulted from the wrong complained of in an unexpected though foreseeable way, in which case particulars should be given so as to avoid surprise at the trial and to enable your opponent to consider making a payment into court.[13] Where a claim for aggravated damages is made, the facts relied on to support the claim should be pleaded[14]; and where the claim is for exemplary damages, or provisional damages[15], it must be specifically pleaded together with the facts on which the party pleading relies. In an action for damages for personal injuries, it is good practice to plead specifically any claim for loss of future earning capacity to give fair notice to the defendant of that claim.[16]

---

[13] *Perestrello e Companhia Limitada* v. *United Paint Co. Ltd.* [1969] 1 W.L.R. 570; *Domsalla* v. *Barr* [1969] 1 W.L.R. 630.

[14] *Rookes* v. *Barnard* [1964] A.C. 1129.

[15] Ord. 18, r. 8(3).

[16] Per Lord Fraser in *Chan Wai Tong* v. *Li Ping Sum* [1985] 2 W.L.R. 396 at p. 404, P.C.

A claim for Provisional Damages under section 32A of the Supreme Court Act 1981 must be specifically pleaded in the body of the statement of claim as a condition precedent to the making of an award (Order 37, r. 8). Since the requirement of Order 37, r. 8 is also that the court is satisfied that the action is one to which section 32A applies, the facts relied on should include those set out in section 32A of the Supreme Court Act 1981 and must be pleaded. The facts are that there is a chance that at some definite or indefinite time in the future the plaintiff will develop some serious disease or suffer some serious deterioration in his physical or mental condition.[17] The precise disease or deterioration alleged must be pleaded. The prayer in the Statement of Claim should include: "an order for an award of provisional damages pursuant to section 32A of the Supreme Court Act 1981."[18]

Special damage, on the other hand, is such a loss as the law will not *presume* to be the consequence of the defendant's act, but which depends in part, at least, on the special circumstances of the case. It must therefore always be explicitly claimed on the pleadings, and at the trial it must be proved by evidence both that the loss was incurred and that it was the direct result of the defendant's conduct. A mere expectation or apprehension of loss is not sufficient. And no damages can be recovered for a loss actually sustained, unless it is either the natural or probable consequence of the defendant's act, or such a consequence as he in fact contemplated or could reasonably have foreseen when he so acted. All other damage is held "remote."[19] Loss of a kind which is foreseeable yet unexpected, and any damage (*e.g.* loss of profits) which, although the direct result of the wrongful act, may not have been the immediate consequence of it, should be pleaded in enough detail to inform your opponent of the case he will have to meet and, if possible, enable him to make his own calculation of their amount. In many cases, proof of special damage is essential to the right of action; in these the writ must not be issued till the special damage has accrued, and then it must be alleged with special care.

No general rule can be laid down as to the precise degree of exactness necessary in a claim of special damage. "The charac-

---

[17] See Practice Direction (Provisional Damages Procedure) [1985] 1 W.L.R. 961 relating to the orders made at trial, and after-trial practice.
[18] See Precedent No. 24.
[19] *The Wagon Mound* [1961] A.C. 388; *Smith* v. *Leech Brain & Co. Ltd.* [1962] 2 Q.B. 405; *Warren* v. *Scruttons Ltd.* [1962] 1 Lloyd's Rep. 497; *Hadley* v. *Baxendale* (1854) 9 Ex. 341; *The Heron II* [1969] 1 A.C. 350; *H. Parsons (Livestock) Ltd.* v. *Uttley Ingham & Co. Ltd.* [1978] Q.B. 791.

ter of the acts themselves which produce the damage, and the circumstances under which these acts are done, must regulate the degree of certainty and particularity with which the damage done ought to be stated and proved. As much certainty and particularity must be insisted on, both in pleading and proof of damage, as is reasonable, having regard to the circumstances and to the nature of the acts themselves by which the damage is done. To insist upon less would be to relax old and intelligible principles. To insist upon more would be the vainest pedantry."[20] And remember that a plaintiff who succeeds in recovering general damages may yet be ordered to pay the costs occasioned by a claim for special damage which he has failed to substantiate.[21]

So far as special damage in personal injury cases is concerned, see Order 18, r. 12(1A)(b) and Practice Note [1984] 1 W.L.R. 1127. With the object of minimising time wasted at trial over special damages which have never been pleaded or mentioned in correspondence, the note sets out which particulars must be given, and when. A schedule of particulars of any loss of earnings; loss of future earning capacity; medical and related expenses, and loss of pension rights claimed should be served upon all other parties not later than seven days after the case appears in the Warned List. Within seven days the other parties must reply indicating which items are agreed, and if not agreed, the reason why not, and any counter proposal. If there is a fixed date for the hearing then the plaintiff's particulars should be served not less than 28 days before that date, and the answer not later than 14 days thereafter. Order 18, r. 12(1A)(b) now requires a "statement of the special damages claimed" to be served with the Statement of Claim or as soon thereafter as the court specifies (rule 1B). It remains to be seen how this will affect the implementation of Practice Note (1984) 1 W.L.R. 1127. It seems, however, that the intention behind Order 18, r. 12(1A) is that the Defendant should be aware, at any stage of the action, what special damages are being claimed and this should render the Practice Note otiose.

Matters in aggravation of damages may be pleaded in the statement of claim.

Illustrations

In an action for wrongful dismissal, the loss of salary and commission, which the plaintiff would have earned, is special damage which must be specifically pleaded.

---

[20] *Per* Bowen L.J. in *Ratcliffe* v. *Evans* [1892] 2 Q.B. 532–533.
[21] *Forster* v. *Farquhar* [1893] 1 Q.B. 564.

Hayward v. *Pullinger & Partners Ltd.* [1950] 1 All E.R. 581.
For the recovery of damage not the natural and probable consequence of a breach of contract, *e.g.* loss of profit on particular subsequent agreements, see *Victoria Laundry (Windsor) Ltd.* v. *Newman Industries Ltd.* [1949] 2 K.B. 528.
And for a form of pleading such a loss, see Precedent No. 39.

The Claim for Relief

Every statement of claim must state specifically the relief which the plaintiff claims, either simply or in the alternative; but costs need not be specifically claimed (Order 18, r. 15). The same cause of action may entitle the plaintiff to relief of different kinds. In addition to claiming the payment of a debt (with interest, if appropriate) or damages, he may ask for one or more of the following kinds of relief:

(i) An injunction (either prohibitory or mandatory).
(ii) Possession of land.
(iii) Delivery up of a chattel.
(iv) A declaration of right or title.
(v) The appointment of a receiver.
(vi) An account.
(vii) Specific performance of a contract.

But remember that a statement of claim supersedes the writ; hence if some special form of relief be claimed on the writ, and not in the statement of claim, it will be taken that so much of the claim is abandoned.[22] It should be noted also that Order 18, r. 15(1) requires the statement of claim to specify at least one form of relief which the plaintiff claims; however, on proof of the necessary facts the court is not confined to granting that particular form of relief, but has jurisdiction to grant any relief it thinks appropriate to the facts as proved. But if in the course of the trial a party seeks to raise a new claim for relief not adumbrated in his pleading, the court should not give such relief without first offering the opposite party, if taken by surprise, an opportunity for an adjournment.[23]

Damages.—In an action for unliquidated damages, it is not necessary to insert any specific figure as the precise amount of damages claimed.[24] But where the plaintiff's claim is liquidated and can be ascertained exactly, the pleader should, of course, claim only the precise amount. Where he cannot be exact, it is wiser to claim too much rather than too little.

---

[22] *Harries* v. *Ashford* [1950] 1 All E.R. 427.
[23] *Belmont Finance Corporation Ltd.* v. *Williams Furniture Ltd.* [1979] 1 All E.R. 118.
[24] See *London and Northern Bank Ltd.* v. *George Newnes Ltd.* (1900) 16 T.L.R. 433 at p. 434; *cf.* *Thompson* v. *Goold & Co.* [1910] A.C. 409. But in the county court, where the scales of costs vary with the sum claimed, it is often expedient to do so.

Interest.—Order 18, r. 8(4) provides that a party must plead specifically any claim for interest under section 35A of the Supreme Court Act 1981. This alerts the other party to the addition of interest to the value of the claim and enables that party to calculate a payment into court under Order 22, r. 1(8) or a fair offer to settle the claim out of court.

Although it is sufficient to plead a claim for interest in the prayer only,[25] it is better practice to plead the claim in the body of the pleading as well as in the prayer.

The sanction is that if a claim for interest is not pleaded, the Court will not award the plaintiff any interest.[26]

If, however, the plaintiff recovers on a generally indorsed writ he can still be awarded interest even if not pleaded because there is nothing in Order 18, r. 8 that specifically requires a generally indorsed writ to contain a claim for interest, and in particular Order 18, r. 8(4) is not applicable to general indorsements on a writ.[27]

Equitable relief.—But while the common law courts could only compensate an injured plaintiff by awarding him damages or ordering his goods or land to be restored to him, courts of equity, even where recognising and enforcing exactly the same primary rights and liabilities as the common law courts, applied different remedies to protect and enforce them. And much of the value of the Chancery system depended upon the efficiency of these remedies. Where the common law could only award damages for a wrong when committed, equity could prevent its commission by injunction. Where law could only give damages for a breach of contract, equity could enforce its specific performance. Where law could give damages for fraud or breach of faith, equity could declare the property affected by it to be held in trust for the injured party—in fact, to be his property; or insist on an account being delivered of all moneys received. But now, by virtue of section 49 of the Supreme Court Act 1981, every kind of equitable relief can be claimed and given in an action in the Queen's Bench Division. And even where it is not claimed, yet if the right to it appears incidentally in the course of the proceedings, a party may, if necessary, be allowed to amend his claim and the appropriate relief will be granted.

Receiver.—The court has jurisdiction to appoint a receiver in all cases in which it appears to be just or convenient to make

[25] *McDonald's Hamburgers Ltd.* v. *Burgerking (UK) Ltd.* [1987] F.S.R. 112.
[26] *Ward* v. *Chief Constable for Avon and Somerset* (*The Times*, July 17, 1985, C.A.) 129 S.J. 537.
[27] *Edward Butler Vintners Ltd.* v. *Grange Seymour Internationale Ltd. and ors.* (*The Times*, June 9, 1987 C.A.) 131 S.J. 1188.

such an order, although the defendant may be in possession of the property[28]; and it will give the receiver possession of the property so far as is necessary for the preservation of the plaintiff's rights.[29] A receiver is an officer of the court, not the agent of or trustee for the parties.[30] He must ordinarily give security duly to account for what he shall receive as such receiver and to pay the same as the court shall direct (Order 30, r. 2(2)).

Injunction.—An injunction should be claimed whenever there is any reason to apprehend any repetition of the defendant's unlawful act. In such a case it must be averred that the defendant threatens and intends to repeat the unlawful act, unless such an intention is already apparent from the nature of the case or the facts pleaded.[31] Particulars of the alleged threats could always be ordered; now particulars of any facts relied on as showing intention must also be pleaded (Order 18, r. 12(1)(*b*)).

Under the Supreme Court Act 1981, s.37, the court may grant an injunction by interlocutory order in all cases in which it appears to be just or convenient so to do.[32] Application for such an order may, in cases of extreme urgency, be made *ex parte* (Order 29, r. 1(2)), and even, if necessary, before the writ is issued. If an *ex parte* injunction is granted it will normally be limited to the period necessary for the return to a summons or motion for an interim injunction pending the trial of the action; but the usual course is to apply after notice to the other side, in which case an interlocutory injunction until the trial of the action may be granted, or the defendant may prefer to give an undertaking. The application will normally be made to a judge in chambers in the Queen's Bench Division (in the Chancery Division by motion in open court) unless the terms of the injunction are agreed upon by the parties, in which case a master or district registrar has jurisdiction to grant it.[33] The evidence is given on affidavit. Notice of motion for an injunction may be served with the writ without leave (Order 8, r. 4) and this rule is in practice deemed to cover a summons for an injunction. If it is desired to serve short notice of motion (less

---

[28] Supreme Court Act 1981, s.37; *Gwatkin* v. *Bird* (1882) 52 L.J.Q.B. 263; *Leney & Sons* v. *Callingham* [1908] 1 K.B. 79.

[29] *Charrington & Co., Ltd.* v. *Camp* [1902] 1 Ch. 386.

[30] *Boehm* v. *Goodall* [1911] 1 Ch. 155.

[31] *Stannard* v. *Vestry of St. Giles* (1882) 20 Ch.D. at p. 195; and see *Att.-Gen.* v. *Dorin* [1912] 1 Ch. at p. 378.

[32] For *Mareva* injunctions, see Chap. 4.

[33] Ord. 32, r. 11(2).

than two clear days) special leave must be applied for (rule 2(2)). The plaintiff is usually required to give an undertaking to pay all damages caused to the defendant by the granting of an interlocutory injunction if the order ought not to have been made.

Specific Performance.—Formerly the courts of common law could only award damages for a breach of contract. The courts of equity, on the other hand, while they could not award damages, could compel each party to a contract to execute it precisely according to its terms. This was effected by a "decree for specific performance." But now by section 49 of the Supreme Court Act 1981 any division of the High Court may give judgment either for damages or for specific performance, or both. Nevertheless actions for specific performance of contracts for the sale of *real estates* and contracts for *leases* are, for the sake of convenience, assigned to the Chancery Division and should properly be commenced therein (Sched. 1, s.1). On the other hand, in any action for breach of contract to deliver specific or ascertained *goods*, any division of the High Court may direct that the contract shall be performed specifically, without giving the defendant the option of retaining the goods on payment of damages, or upon such other terms and conditions as to the court may seem just (Sale of Goods Act 1979, s.52; and *cf.* Order 14, r. 9). But no such order will be made where the plaintiff has been guilty of unreasonable delay in making his application, or has otherwise acted in a harsh or inequitable manner, or where damages would afford the plaintiff adequate compensation for the breach of contract.

Declaration of Right or Title.—In former days, questions of ownership were decided in *real* actions, questions as to possession in *mixed* actions. But real actions fell into disuse owing to the extreme technicality of their procedure, and the mixed action of ejectment was used to determine indirectly questions of title under the guise of a decision merely as to the right to possession of the property. Thus, if both A and B claimed to be seised in fee of Blackacre, and B was in possession of the land, A would not sue in his own name; for, if he did, he would have to bring a *real* action. He pretended that he had demised Blackacre a few days previously to John Doe or Richard Roe; and this fictitious lessee would obligingly lend his name as plaintiff; and as he claimed no title in himself, but only a right to possession derived from the lease, he could sue in ejectment, and the action would be called *Doe d. A* v. *B.* The plaintiff would plead A's seisin, and the demise to himself: the defendant was not allowed to traverse the fictitious demise, but he would deny A's seisin; and so A's title to the land would become an issue in the action, and be judicially decided. But it was not always possible to resort to this manoeuvre; moreover the Court of Chancery would not make a binding declaration of title, unless a right to "some consequential relief" was shown,[34] and this practice was followed—with some hesitation—in the High Court after the passing of the Judicature Act until 1883.[35] But by the Rules of 1883 and now by Order 15, r. 16 it has been clearly provided that "no action or other proceeding shall be open to objection on the ground that a merely declaratory judgment or order is sought thereby, and the court may make binding declarations of right, whether or not any consequential relief is or could be claimed." And this is now the practice. But the power is discretionary and to be used sparingly.[36] The declaration must be of some legal right, not merely in respect of professional ethics.[37] A plaintiff cannot avoid a prospective defendant's immunity from liability in tort by the device of framing the proceedings as a claim for a declaration of the plaintiff's rights instead of a direct claim in tort.[38] The High Court may make a declaration, even where it refuses to grant an injunction or to give any other relief, provided there has in fact been a disturbance of the right which the court is asked to declare.[39] (The jurisdiction of the county court in respect of declarations is more limited.) And see Precedent 34.

Account Stated

The law as to account stated is discussed in the judgment of Scrutton L.J. in *Joseph Evans & Co.* v. *Heathcote*[40] and in the subsequent cases of *Camillo Tank SS. Co.* v. *Alexandria Engineering Works*[41] and *Siqueira* v. *Noronha*.[42] From these authorities it appears that there are two kinds of account stated:

---

[34] *Rooke* v. *Lord Kensington* (1856) 2 K. & J. 753.
[35] *Cox* v. *Barker* (1876) 3 Ch.D. at pp. 370–372.
[36] *Guaranty Trust Company* v. *Hannay & Co.* [1915] 2 K.B. 536; *Russian Commercial, etc., Bank* v. *British Bank for Foreign Trade* [1921] 2 A.C. 438, 445; *Vine* v. *National Dock Labour Board* [1957] A.C. 488, 500. See also *Thorne R.D.C.* v. *Bunting* [1972] Ch. 470; *Wallersteiner* v. *Moir* [1974] 1 W.L.R. 921; *Imperial Tobacco Ltd.* v. *Attorney-General* [1980] 2 W.L.R. 466; *Amstrad Consumer Electronics plc* v. *The British Phonographic Industry Ltd.* [1986] F.S.R. 159.
[37] *Cox* v. *Green* [1966] 2 W.L.R. 369. See also *Malone* v. *Metropolitan Police Commissioner* [1979] 2 W.L.R. 700.
[38] *Trawnik* v. *Ministry of Defence* [1984] 2 All E.R. 791 at p. 797, *per* Sir Robert Megarry V.-C.
[39] *Llandudno Urban District Council* v. *Woods* [1899] 2 Ch. 705; *Dysart (Earl)* v. *Hammerton* [1914] 1 Ch. 822; [1916] A.C. 57.
[40] [1918] 1 K.B. at pp. 434–437.
[41] (1921) 38 T.L.R. 134.
[42] [1934] A.C. 332.

(i) Where there are cross-demands, *i.e.* where A owes B certain moneys and B also owes A money. In such a case, if A and B, either orally or in writing, state an account with items on both sides, and strike a balance, and agree on it, then if the balance be in favour of B, he can sue for that balance on an account stated. And, prima facie, he can sue for nothing else except that balance: all his other demands are now extinguished, are in fact paid; and the satisfaction of these is the consideration for A's implied promise to pay the balance. An account stated of this kind is usually conclusive, even though it contains items for which B could not have sued; but it may be reopened on the ground of fraud, or if it is shown that there are substantial errors in it, or if any of the items are such as, if actually paid, could have been recovered back. But the fact that some of the earlier items were barred by the Limitation Act is no reason why A should not pay the balance agreed on, for such earlier items are now considered paid. Similar principles apply to the case where there is an express promise for good consideration to pay a balance arrived at, whether as a result of items on both sides or on one only; but in this case it would seem that the account can only be reopened on the ground of fraud or some other ground which would vitiate the fresh contract, or in the exercise of the court's equitable jurisdiction.

(ii) Where the debt is all on one side, so that there are no cross-items which can be set off one against the other, and no balance to be struck, and there is an acknowledgment of the total amount due, but no fresh consideration to support an express or implied promise to pay it. This kind of account stated is not conclusive, and the debtor, even in the absence of fraud, may go behind it and dispute the validity or the original debt. One might have thought such an acknowledgment would be, at most, a mere admission by A of the pre-existing causes of action against himself—a useful piece of evidence in any action for the former debt, but not in itself a cause of action. It has been decided, however, that such an acknowledgment or admission of liability is in itself a new cause of action; and, for want of a better name, it also is called "an account stated."[43]

Examination into the original debts may show one of two things:

(a) that they were good and valid debts, in which case they would be a past executed consideration which would

---

[43] *Knowles* v. *Michel* (1811) 13 Ea. 249, 250; *Brown* v. *Tapscott* (1840) 6 M. & W. 123, 124.

support the fresh promise.[44] They will support it even though they could not have been enforced owing to some procedural bar, such as the Statute of Frauds or the Limitation Act—though in this case the account stated would have to be in writing owing to Lord Tenterden's Act,[45] or

(b) that the original debt was altogether non-existent, or void owing to the operation of a statute such as the Gaming Act—in which case the account stated would not assist the plaintiff—or that the antecedent obligation was executory in its nature, in which case the account stated is merely a piece of evidence like an I.O.U.[46]

An action on an account stated must be carefully distinguished from a claim for an account.

---

[44] *Lampleigh* v. *Brathwait* (1615) Hob. 105.
[45] *Jones* v. *Ryder* (1838) 4 M. & W. 32.
[46] *Lemere* v. *Elliott* (1861) 30 L.J.Ex. 350.

CHAPTER 13

DEFENCE

The defendant's counsel, before drafting the defence, should carefully consider the statement of claim, and the way in which the action is shaped against his client. Is any cause of action shown at all? Is the action frivolous or vexatious? If so, he may think it right to apply to strike out the statement of claim. Such an application should be made promptly—as a rule, before any defence is served. Then is the claim properly pleaded? Is any portion of it embarrassing? Or are particulars necessary? Have claims been joined which cannot conveniently be tried together? If so, the defendant should apply to sever them under Order 15, r. 5. Should the defendant interplead? (see post). Should the action be transferred to a county court, under section 40 of the County Courts Act 1984. Or is it from its nature one that ought to be referred, and has the plaintiff ever agreed in writing to submit the dispute to arbitration? If so, the defendant must at once, before serving any pleading to taking any other step in the action, except acknowledging service, apply to a master to stay the proceedings under section 4 of the Arbitration Act 1950.

The defendant must also consider whether the proper parties have been placed on the record. He can no longer plead in abatement. If he considers that the proper parties are not before the court, his remedy is to take out a summons under Order 15, rr. 6 and 7 to add or strike out or substitute a plaintiff or a defendant.

Formerly a defendant sued alone for a debt for which he was jointly liable with others, for example, a partnership debt,[1] could apply to have the other joint debtors joined as co-defendants and for proceedings in the action to be stayed until they were added as parties.[2] As a result of the Civil Liability (Contribution) Act 1978, s.3, the plaintiff may now choose which of a number of persons jointly liable to him he wishes to sue, and he need not, nor can he be compelled to, sue all. Accordingly, a defendant who wishes to recover contribution or indemnity from persons jointly liable with him should now consider third party proceedings (*infra*) and should not seek to have those persons added as defendants. In other cases the

[1] See *Pilley* v. *Robinson* (1887) 20 Q.B.D. 155.
[2] Under Ord. 15, r. 4(3) now revoked in consequence of the Civil Liability (Contribution) Act 1978.

defendant may still seek to alter or add parties on the grounds indicated in Order 15, rr. 6 and 7. A fresh plaintiff can only be added with his consent signified in writing or in such other manner as may be authorised (Order 15, r. 6). In some cases, if not all, the consent of a plaintiff already on the record will also be required.[3]

Order 15, r. 6 also permits intervention by persons not parties to the action as originally framed. Under sub-rule (2)(*b*)(i) the court can order the addition of a person whose legal rights will be directly affected by the granting of the relief claimed in the action, and who can therefore show that his presence is necessary to enable the court effectually and completely to adjudicate on the matters in dispute.[4] A wider power to add parties was subsequently[5] inserted into the Rules whereby the court may join "any person between whom and any party to the cause or matter there may exist a question or issue arising out of or relating to or connected with any relief or remedy claimed in the cause or matter which in the opinion of the court it would be just and convenient to determine as between him and that party as well as between the parties to the cause or matter."[6] The court also has an inherent jurisdiction to permit intervention by a non-party who is likely to be caused serious hardship or damage by the effect of particular proceedings.[7]

After considering the parties to the action, counsel for the defendant should then ask himself whether he has all the documents he needs to draft the defence. If any are referred to in the statement of claim, he may immediately give notice to the plaintiff to produce them for his inspection (Order 24, r. 10(1)); otherwise he will not usually see them until the stage of discovery. In exceptional cases the master may order discovery of documents before service of defence or even of the statement of claim; but this power is seldom exercised and never for the purpose of enabling a party to fish out a case.

As soon as these preliminary questions are disposed of, the defendant's counsel must proceed to draft the defence. The defendant must state in his defence every material fact on

---

[3] See *Pennington* v. *Caley* (1912) 106 L.T. 591; *Emden* v. *Carte* (1881) 17 Ch.D. 169 (joinder of plaintiff's trustee in bankruptcy).

[4] *Dollfus Mieg* v. *Bank of England* [1951] 1 Ch. 33; *Gurtner* v. *Circuit* [1968] 2 Q.B. 587. *Sanderstead Co. Inc.* v. *Entores Metal Brokers Ltd.* [1984] 1 W.L.R. 452.

[5] In 1971, by sub-rule 2(*b*)(ii), negativing the effect of *Vandervell's Trustees Ltd.* v. *White* [1971] A.C. 912.

[6] See *Tetra Molectric Ltd.* v. *Japan Imports Ltd.* [1976] R.P.C. 541.

[7] See *The Mardina Merchant* [1975] 1 W.L.R. 147 and *Gurtner* v. *Circuit* [1968] 1 All E.R. 328.

which he proposes to rely at the trial. He must deal specifically with every fact alleged in the statement of claim, either admitting or denying it; he may plead further facts in answer to those he admits; he may object to the whole pleading as insufficient in law; or he may rely on a set-off or counterclaim. (See Chapter 14.) All these separate grounds of defence must be stated, as far as may be, separately and distinctly, especially where they are founded upon separate and distinct facts.

Any number of defences may be pleaded together in the same action, although they are obviously inconsistent. A defendant may "raise by his statement of defence, without leave, as many distinct and separate, and therefore inconsistent, defences as he may think proper, subject only to the provision" contained in Order 18, r. 19 for striking out embarrassing matter.[8] And a defence is not embarrassing merely because it contains inconsistent averments,[9] provided such averments are not fictitious.[10]

As to traverses, do not deny everything. It causes useless expense. Admit all you can. But when you traverse, traverse well and boldly.

Denials Must be Specific

"Any allegation of fact made by a party in his pleading is deemed to be admitted by the opposite party unless it is traversed by that party in his pleading or a joinder of issue under rule 14 operates as a denial of it" (Order 18, r. 13(1)).

"A traverse may be made either by a denial or by a statement of non-admission and either expressly or by necessary implication" (Order 18, r. 13(2)).

"Every allegation of fact made in a statement of claim or counterclaim which the party on whom it is served does not intend to admit must be specifically traversed by him in his defence or defence to counterclaim, as the case may be; and a general denial of such allegations, or a general statement of non-admission of them, is not a sufficient traverse of them" (Order 18, r. 13(3)).

The rules of 1883 dealt with these matters in greater detail and with instances. The effect of the rules is to prevent a defendant pleading the general issue, as it was called, and to make him "take matter by matter, and traverse each of them

---

[8] *Per* Thesiger L.J. in *Berdan* v. *Greenwood* (1878) 3 Ex.D. at p. 255.
[9] *Child* v. *Stenning* (1877) 5 Ch.D. 695.
[10] *Re Morgan* (1887) 35 Ch.D. at p. 496.

separately."[11] Hence a defendant should not plead merely that "he denies specifically every allegation contained in the statement of claim," or he may find that he has broken Order 18, r. 13(3) and his pleading may be struck out under rule 19(1). On the other hand he cannot be expected to write out and traverse every sentence in the statement of claim.[12] It is usually considered sufficient, when dealing with matters of inducement or other allegations which do not go to the gist of the action, to plead that "the defendant denies each of the allegations contained in paragraph 3." But when the pleader comes to those allegations which are the gist of the action, he should be more precise and should plead, *e.g.* "The Defendants deny that they dismissed the Plaintiff in breach of contract as alleged or at all," or "The Defendants deny that they were negligent and/or in breach of statutory duty as alleged or at all."

There are two important exceptions to the rule that a defendant must specifically traverse every allegation of fact in the statement of claim which he does not admit. Both are legacies from the old procedure and are very sensible and proper provisions.

(i) *Pleading to Particulars*

Before the Judicature Act it was not the practice for the plaintiff to set out in his declaration any details which were not a necessary part of the cause of action; such matters were stated, if at all, in a separate document, subsequently delivered, which was called "Particulars." And it was then a clear rule that the defendant must not plead to anything stated in the "Particulars," but only to the matters alleged in the declaration. The rules of pleading at present in force require a plaintiff to insert all necessary details in his statement of claim, except that particulars of debt, expenses or damages exceeding three folios in length must be served separately[13]; but it still remains the practice that the defendant does not plead specifically to matter alleged under the head of "Particulars," as in answering the body of the pleading he will have dealt with the substantive allegation to which the particulars refer and the particulars will ordinarily be covered by implication. Unfortunately, it sometimes happens that a plaintiff inserts in his particulars allegations of fact which go beyond what is alleged in the body of the

---

[11] *Per* Thesiger L.J. in *Byrd* v. *Nunn* (1877) 7 Ch.D. at p. 287.
[12] *John Lancaster Radiators Ltd.* v. *General Motor Radiator Co. Ltd.* [1946] 2 All E.R. 685.
[13] Ord. 18, r. 12(2).

pleading. This puts the defendant in a difficulty. It would hardly be appropriate to take out a summons attacking the statement of claim as embarrassing, but at the same time it will not be wise for him to allow the action to go for trial without denying the matters in question or pleading the facts which answer them. Hence he usually pleads to them as though they had been stated in their proper place.

(ii) *Pleading to Damages*

"Any allegation that a party has suffered damage is deemed to be traversed unless specifically admitted" (Order 18, r. 13(4)). This rule applies to damage of all kinds, whether special or general, and whether the alleged damage is part of the cause of action or not.[14]. Order 18, r. 12(1)(c) provides that "where a claim for damages is made against a party pleading, particulars of any facts on which the party relies in mitigation of, or otherwise in relation to, the amount of damages" must be included in such a pleading. Thus, since the *amount* of damages will no longer be deemed to be traversed, the Defendant, if so advised, must specifically traverse the allegations as to the amount of the damages claimed, either by denial or a non-admission. Moreover, the Defendant must plead any specific facts upon which he intends to rely in support of any claim for a reduction in the damages. Where special damage is necessary in law to support the action, the other party may object that the special damage stated is too remote, or is not sufficient in point of law.

Special Defences

"A party must in any pleading subsequent to a statement of claim plead specifically any matter, for example, performance, release, the expiry of a relevant period of limitation, fraud or any fact showing illegality—(a) which he alleges makes any claim or defence of the opposite party not maintainable; or (b) which, if not specifically pleaded, might take the opposite party by surprise; or (c) which raises issues of fact not arising out of the preceding pleading" (Order 18, r. 8(1)). In all such cases the fresh facts on which the defence is based must be specifically pleaded.

Such special defences should not be mixed up with traverses or incorporated into pleas denying facts alleged by the plaintiff.

---

[14] See the remarks of Smith L.J. in *Greenwell* v. *Howell* [1900] 1 Q.B. at p. 538.

"The office of a traverse is to contradict, not to excuse or justify, the act complained of; its object is to compel the plaintiff to prove the truth of the allegations traversed, not to dispute its sufficiency in point of law. All matters justifying or excusing the act complained of must be specifically pleaded (*Att.-Gen.* v. *Lord Mayor of Sheffield* (1912) 106 L.T. 367); so must all matters which go to show that the contract sued on is illegal or invalid, or which if not expressly stated, might take the opposite party by surprise, or would raise issues of fact not arising out of the preceeding pleading. And no evidence of such matters can, as a rule, be given at the trial if they be not expressly pleaded."[15]

Illegality

The defence that a contract is a wager within the Gaming Acts should be specially pleaded; and the facts which are relied on to bring the transactions within those Acts should be stated.[16] However, the court itself will take notice of any illegality of the contract on which the plaintiff is suing, if it appears on the face of the contract or from the evidence brought before it by either party, and even though the defendant has not pleaded the illegality.[17] Illegality, once brought to the attention of the court, overrides all questions of pleadings, including any admissions made therein.[18] Otherwise, where the contract is not *ex facie* illegal, as a general rule the court will not entertain the question of illegality unless it is specifically pleaded and the court is satisfied that it has before it all the necessary facts concerning the contract and its setting.[19]

Plea of the Statute of Frauds

The operation of the Statute of Frauds was greatly curtailed by the Law Reform (Enforcement of Contracts) Act 1954. The appropriate plea of the Statute was: "There is no memorandum

[15] R.S.C. para. 18/8/1, cited with approval by Havers J. in *Davie* v. *New Merton Board Mills Ltd.* [1956] 1 All E.R. 379.
[16] *Colborne* v. *Stockdale* (1722) 1 Str. 493; *Grizewood* v. *Blane* (1851) 11 C.B. 526; *Willis* v. *Lovick* [1901] 2 K.B. 195; and see *Ladup Ltd.* v. *Shaikh* [1983] Q.B. 225 (Illegality under Gaming Act 1968 s.16(1)).
[17] *Gedge* v. *Royal Exchange Assurance* [1900] 2 Q.B. 214; *Edler* v. *Auerbach* [1950] 1 K.B. 359; *Snell* v. *Unity Finance Ltd.* [1964] 2 Q.B. 203.
[18] Per Donaldson J. in *Belvoir Finance Co. Ltd.* v. *Harold G. Cole and Co.* [1969] 2 All E.R. 904, 908. Cf. *Shelley* v. *Paddock* [1978] 2 W.L.R. 877.
[19] *Re Robinson's Settlement* [1912] 1 Ch. 717; *North Western Salt Co.* v. *Electrolytic Alkali Co.* [1914] A.C. 461.

in writing of the alleged contract sufficient to satisfy the Statute of Frauds." It was not necessary to plead any particular section and was wiser not to do so. For if the defendant specified a particular section, he could not avail himself of another without leave.[20] If the plaintiff sued on a written contract, and then at the trial sought to rely on a parol agreement, the judge should either exclude all evidence of the parol agreement, or else allow the defendant to amend by pleading the Statute of Frauds if applicable.[21]

Plea of the Statute of Limitations

"The plaintiff's cause of action, if any, did not accrue within six[22] years before this suit, and the defendant will rely on the Limitation Act 1980." The objection that the action is brought too late must be raised by a special plea, even though it appears on the face of the statement of claim.[23] The date at which an action commenced is the date on which the writ was issued and not the date of service.[24]

It is now the same in an action for the recovery of land. The defendant must specially plead the Limitation Act and should do so in this form: "The plaintiff's claim is barred by the Limitation Act 1980 and his right and title (if any) to the said land were extinguished by virtue of that Act."[25]

Important changes in the law of limitation of actions for personal injuries are set forth in the Limitation Act 1980. A new time limit of "date of knowledge" (if later than the date on which the cause of action accrued) is contained in section 11 and defined in section 14, and there is also a power to override the time limits in certain circumstances (section 33). From the point of view of pleading, the defendant should follow the usual rule of pleading expressly any facts and matters in support of a positive case that, for example, the plaintiff had "knowledge" before the date alleged by him; otherwise, if the

---

[20] *James* v. *Smith* [1891] 1 Ch. 384; *Hills and Grant Ltd.* v. *Hodson* [1934] Ch. 53.

[21] *Brunning* v. *Odhams* (1897) 75 L.T. 602.

[22] In the case of actions for damages for personal injuries caused by negligence, nuisance or breach of duty the period is three years (Limitation Act 1980, s.11, but see also s.33). The day on which the accident occurred is excluded from the reckoning in personal injury cases generally, so that the action may validly be commenced on the anniversary of that day (*Marren* v. *Dawson Bentley & Co. Ltd.* [1961] 2 Q.B. 135). But see now *Dodds* v. *Walker* [1981] 1 W.L.R. 1027 (H.L.).

[23] *Hawkings* v. *Billhead* (1636) Cro. Car. (3) 404.

[24] See, however, *Ketteman* v. *Hansel Properties Ltd.* [1987] 2 W.L.R. 312 (H.L.) and *Leicester Wholesale Fruit Market Ltd.* v. *Grundy* [1990] 1 W.L.R. C.A.

[25] See *Dawkins* v. *Lord Penrhyn* (1878) 6 Ch.D. at p. 323; 4 App.Cas. at pp. 59, 64; and *Tichborne* v. *Weir* (1892) 67 L.T. 735.

defendant raises the defence of limitation and denies the facts alleged by the plaintiff as to the date of "knowledge," he will merely put these facts in issue. Similarly, where the defendant wishes to contend that the court should not exercise its overriding powers under section 33 of the Act, a simple denial of the facts alleged by the plaintiff will put them in issue, but additional facts intended to be relied on should be expressly pleaded. In *Ogunsanya* v. *Lambeth Area Health Authority*, July 3, 1985 (unreported) Bristow J. stated that the proper pattern of pleading is that the plaintiff should make no mention of the limitation point in his statement of claim, but should leave this to be raised in the defence to which the plaintiff should then serve his reply to raise the facts and contentions relied on as to date and knowledge and the power of the court to override the defence of limitation.

Former Proceedings

That the plaintiff brought a previous action and recovered damages[26] against the *same* defendant for the same cause of action is a bar to any subsequent action, even though fresh damage has since arisen from the defendant's unlawful act; for the judge or jury in the former action must be taken to have assessed the damages once for all, and the probability or possibility that this subsequent damage would follow should have been submitted to their consideration then. An exception to this rule arises when provisional damages are awarded in personal injury cases. Nor does this rule apply to cases where special damage is essential to the cause of action; in such cases a second action can be brought if fresh special damage accrues from the same cause of action.

The Civil Liability (Contribution) Act 1978 provides that where more than one person is involved, judgment recovered against any person liable in respect of any debt or damage is no bar to an action, or the continuance of an action, against any other person who is jointly liable in respect of the same debt or damage.[27] This provision, which extends and replaces section 6 of the Law Reform (Married Women and Tortfeasors) Act 1935, means that neither a joint tortfeasor nor a joint contractor may now plead in defence a judgment previously obtained against any other person jointly liable with him.

A plaintiff who brings successive actions in respect of the same damage will be at risk as to costs, in that he will not be

---

[26] Or accepted money paid into court (*Derrick* v. *Williams* [1939] 2 All E.R. 559).
[27] Civil Liability (Contribution) Act 1978, s.3.

entitled to costs in any of the actions, other than the one in which judgment is first given, unless the court is of the opinion that there was reasonable ground for bringing the action.[28] However, he is not now limited to execution for no more than the amount of the judgment in the first action.[29]

If the former action was unsuccessful, this will be a bar to a second action against the same defendant; unless, indeed, the plaintiff lost the former action only on some technical ground, and the judge, instead of giving judgment against him, gave him leave to discontinue. So also, if A and B are jointly liable and the plaintiff sues A and fails, the judgment in the action against A will afford B a good defence to a subsequent action against him, provided that A succeeded on a ground which is also open to B.[30]

The defence of *res judicata* cannot be raised, unless it is specially pleaded in the defence. The cause of action must be the same in both actions,[31] and both actions must be brought against the same defendant,[32] or against persons jointly liable on the same cause of action. A long series of cases, many of them difficult to reconcile, has left the law in a rather confused state.

Where, for any reason, the strict defence of *res judicata* is not applicable (*e.g.* where the actions are not between precisely the same parties or persons suing in the same capacity), still, if the plaintiff is "suing substantially by virtue of the same alleged title," or if the issues raised in the second action are identical with those decided in the first, the court will stay the second action,[33] at all events until the costs of the first action are paid[34]; but not where the former action, though similar in its nature, was brought against a different defendant.[35]

There is machinery for registering in this country judgments of the superior courts of many of the Commonwealth countries, colonies and other territories, of such foreign countries as give reciprocal facilities and of European Community institutions, so that execution may be had thereon unless application

---

[28] *Ibid.* s.4.

[29] s.4. does not re-enact this limitation which was formerly set out in s.6(1)(*b*) of the Law Reform (Married Women and Tortfeasors) Act 1935. See further, Law Commission, *Report on Contribution* (Law Com. No. 79), para. 41.

[30] *Phillips* v. *Ward and Others* (1863) 2 H. & C. 717.

[31] *Serrao* v. *Noel* (1885) 15 Q.B.D. 549; *Ord* v. *Ord* [1923] 2 K.B. 432.

[32] *Isaacs & Sons* v. *Salbstein* [1916] 2 K.B. 139.

[33] *Arnold* v. *National Westminster Bank plc* [1990] 1 All E.R. 529, C.A.

[34] *Martin* v. *Earl Beauchamp* (1883) 25 Ch.D. 12; *MacDougall* v. *Knight* (1890) 25 Q.B.D. 1; *M'Cabe* v. *Bank of Ireland* (1889) 14 App.Cas. 413. Except where the plaintiff is a minor: *Re Payne* (1883) 23 Ch.D. 288.

[35] *Le Mesurier* v. *Ferguson* (1903) 20 T.L.R. 32.

is made to set the registration aside. Whether registered or not, they are in some circumstances regarded as conclusive between the parties. (See Administration of Justice Act 1920; Foreign Judgments (Reciprocal Enforcement) Act 1933. Civil Jurisdiction and Judgments Act 1982; and Order 71).

Estoppel

In some cases the law will not allow a litigant to attempt to prove allegations which are directly contrary to that which has already been decided against him, or to that which he has himself deliberately represented to be the fact. He is said to be "estopped" from proving such matters. An estoppel debars a party from raising a particular contention in an action, when to raise it would be inequitable or contrary to the policy of the law. It binds not only the original parties but also all who claim under them. It is not a cause of action but a rule of evidence.

Estoppels are of three kinds:
  (i) By record.
  (ii) By deed.
  (iii) By conduct.

(i) *Estoppel by record, e.g.* by a judgment of a court of competent jurisdiction.[36] The matter becomes *res judicata* even though judgment is delivered after the commencement of fresh proceedings.[37] So long as that judgment stands, no one who was a party to it can reopen that litigation.[38] The judgment binds the plaintiff, the defendant and the executor, administrator or assign to each of them, and all claiming under them.[39] Where in a first action the defendant does not traverse an allegation which he might have traversed, he will be estopped from traversing a similar allegation in a second action by the same plaintiff.[40] A record will not create an estoppel if the judgment was obtained by fraud or collusion.

(ii) *Estoppel by deed.*—If under his hand and seal a man asserts a thing to be, he cannot set up the contrary in any

---

[36] See *Nokes* v. *Nokes* [1957] P. 213.
[37] *Bell* v. *Holmes* [1956] 1 W.L.R 1359.
[38] See, for example, *Hill* v. *Hill* [1954] P. 291 and *Wood* v. *Luscombe* [1966] 1 Q.B. 169. But the principle will not operate in matrimonial cases where the court, exercising its statutory duty to inquire into the truth of the petition, decides to reopen the issue. (*Thompson* v. *Thompson* [1957] P. 19.)
[39] *Marchioness of Huntly* v. *Gaskell* [1905] 2 Ch. 656.
[40] See p. 227, *ante*.

litigation between him and the other party to that deed. Both parties are bound by the language of the deed; and so are all claiming under them.[41] But there will be no estoppel if the deed was obtained by fraud or duress, or is tainted with illegality.

(iii) *Estoppel by conduct*.[42]—If A by word or conduct induces B to believe that a certain state of things exists, and B in that belief acts in a way in which he would not have acted unless he so believed and is thereby prejudiced, then A cannot in any subsequent proceeding between himself and B or any one claiming under B be heard to deny that that state of things existed.[43] But A will not be estopped from averring the truth in any other proceeding. The estoppel only arises in favour of some person whom A has induced by word or conduct to do or abstain from doing some particular thing. The words may be written or spoken; the conduct may be any act, omission or neglect, provided it be an omission to do something which A ought to do—the neglect of some legal duty which A owes B; provided also that such omission or neglect misleads B and misleads him to his prejudice.[44] Even silence may be sufficient where there is a duty to speak, and where silence will create an erroneous impression which causes B to alter his position for the worse; as in *Pickard* v. *Sears*,[45] where a man stood by and saw his goods sold to a bona fide purchaser.

An estoppel must always be specially pleaded[46]; unless it appears on the face of the adverse pleading, when it is ground for an object in point of law; or unless there was no opportunity to plead it, as there was not in *Coppinger* v. *Norton*.[47] It cannot be pleaded by a stranger to the estoppel. A plea of estoppel must always be drafted with great care and particularity. It must state in full detail the facts on which the party pleading relies as constituting the estoppel, and should also specify the allegations which it is contended the other party is precluded from proving.

---

[41] *Bateman* v. *Hunt* [1904] 2 K.B. 530.

[42] The third kind of estoppel was formerly called estoppel *in pais* (*i.e.* in the country), because it depended on matters outside the four corners of any record or deed. Estoppel by conduct is a clearer phrase.

[43] See *Square* v. *Square* [1935] P. 120; 104 L.J.P. 46.

[44] *Lewis* v. *Lewis* [1904] 2 Ch. 656.

[45] (1837) 6 A. & E. 469; and see *Nana Ofori Atta II* v. *Nana Abu Bonsra II* [1958] A.C. 95.

[46] It has been held that an estoppel by *record* or *deed* must be specially pleaded (*Bowman* v. *Rostron* (1835) 2 A. & E. 295n.) but that an estoppel by conduct might in some cases be given in evidence without being specially pleaded. (*Freeman* v. *Cooke* (1848) 2 Ex. 654; *Phillips* v. *Im-Thurm* (1865) 18 C.B., N.S. 400.) Under the present rules the proper course is to plead an estoppel of any kind, if it be practicable to do so (Ord. 18, r. 8(1)).

[47] [1902] 2 Ir.R. 241.

Release

This defence must be specially pleaded (Order 18, r. 8(1)). If one of several joint creditors releases the debtor, the other joint creditors are barred, unless the release was obtained fraudulently. So the release of one joint debtor releases all who are jointly liable with him, unless the right to release one without discharging the others was expressly or impliedly[48] reserved; but where the liability is several, the release of one debtor does not affect the others, except possibly in the case of co-sureties. If the right of one co-surety to contribution be taken away by a release given to another co-surety, both are discharged.[49]

Rescission

This must be specially pleaded; similarly, any bar to a claim for rescission should be pleaded together with the facts relied on. (See Precedent No. 37).

Lien

This defence must be specially pleaded, for it admits the plaintiff's property in the goods he seeks to recover, but states a good reason why he should, for the time, be deprived of the possession of them. It is thus a plea of confession and avoidance. Where it is pleaded, the master may order the goods to be given up to the plaintiff on his paying into court, to abide the event of the action, the full sum claimed by the defendant as the amount of his lien, together with a further sum for interest and costs.[50]

Accord and Satisfaction

These are both technical terms, and the plea must allege both. Suppose that B has broken his contract with A; then A and B agree[51] together that B shall give or do something to or for A, and that A shall accept this in discharge of his cause of action against B. This is an "accord"; and if the matter rests there, there is no defence to an action brought by A on the original

---

[48] *Gardiner* v. *Moore* [1969] 1 Q.B. 55.
[49] *Ward* v. *National Bank of New Zealand* (1883) 8 App. Cas. 755.
[50] Ord. 29, r. 6; and see *Gebrüder Naf* v. *Ploton* (1890) 25 Q.B.D. 13.
[51] Such agreement must be complete and either under seal or supported by consideration. (*D. & C. Builders Ltd.* v. *Rees* [1966] 2 Q.B. 617).

contract. But if B in pursuance of the "accord" gives to A or does for him what was agreed, this is a "satisfaction," and the two together afford B a good defence to any action on the original contract. If, for example, X agrees to sell and deliver to Y a Broadwood piano for £2000, but is unable to obtain a Broadwood piano. He asks Y to accept an Erard piano of at least equal value, and Y agrees to do so. This agreement alone affords X no defence to an action by Y, unless and until X delivers the Erard piano to Y. An accord and satisfaction made by a third party on the defendant's behalf, and accepted by the plaintiff in discharge, will be a bar to the action.[52] This defence could not formerly be pleaded to a claim on a bond or other specialty, because there was a maxim that a contract under seal could only be discharged by performance or some other contract under seal. But now an accord and satisfaction is an answer to an action on a specialty debt.[53]

Tender

"The defendant, before action, to wit, on March 23, 1990, tendered to the plaintiff the sum of £——, which the plaintiff claims in this action, but the plaintiff then refused to accept it. And the defendant now brings the sum of £——into court ready to be paid to the plaintiff." A plea of tender must show that the tender was made before action brought; and the sum alleged to have been tendered must be brought into court. (Order 18, r. 16.) This plea cannot strictly be pleaded to actions for unliquidated damages, whether sounding in contract or in tort,[54] unless there be some special statutory provision enabling a defendant to tender amends. But there is a difference between a payment into court *simpliciter* and a payment into court with a plea of tender. A tender is a defence proper[55]; hence the plaintiff cannot, without the leave of a master, take out money paid in with a plea of tender (Order 22, r. 4(1)). If he gets leave and takes the money out in satisfaction, the order of the master must deal with the whole costs of the action or of the cause of action to which the payment relates (*ibid.*); and he would ordinarily award them to the defendant, since the plaintiff should have accepted the money tendered and not have sued for it.[56]

---

[52] *Jones* v. *Broadhurst* (1850) 9 C.B. 173.
[53] *Steeds* v. *Steeds* (1889) 22 Q.B.D. 537.
[54] *Dearle* v. *Barrett* (1834) 2 A. & E. 82; *Davys* v. *Richardson* (1888) 21 Q.B.D. 202.
[55] But as to the position in Admiralty proceedings see *The Mona* [1894] P. at p. 286.
[56] *Griffiths* v. *Ystradyfodwg School Board* (1890) 24 Q.B.D. 307.

As a plea of tender must necessarily disclose the fact that money has been paid into court, it is one of the exceptions to the general rule that that fact should not be known to the judge at the trial (Order 22, r. 7); the issue is simply, was a good tender made before action brought?

Payment

Payment before action is a matter of defence which must be pleaded and proved by the defendant. A plea of payment should state that the payment relied on was made before the issue of the writ, giving dates and amounts of payments and also any facts showing an appropriation of such payments to the debt sued for in the action. But there is no need for the defendant to plead that he paid any sums for which he is expressly given credit in the statement of claim. The plaintiff is taken to be suing for the balance due after crediting payments he admits.

The fact that money has been paid into court no longer appears, as it used to do, on the face of the defence except where tender before action or a defence under the Libel Act 1843, s.2, is pleaded (Order 22, r. 7; Order 82, r. 4(2)).

Fraud

Where fraud is intended to be charged, it must be distinctly charged, and its details specified. General allegations, however strong, are insufficient to amount to an averment of fraud of which any court ought to take notice.[57] Counsel must insist on being fully instructed before placing a plea of fraud on the record. Such a plea should never be drafted on insufficient material, nor without warning to the client, if appropriate, that by adopting such an aggressive line of defence he may double or treble the amount of damages which he may ultimately have to pay.

Justification in Libel and Slander

This also is a most dangerous plea, and should never be placed on the record without careful consideration of the sufficiency of the evidence by which it is to be supported. "Like a charge of fraud, counsel must not put a plea of justification on the record

---

[57] *Wallingford* v. *Mutual Society* (1880) 5 App. Cas. at p. 697; *Lawrence* v. *Lord Norreys* (1890) 15 App. Cas. at p. 221.

unless he has clear and sufficient evidence to support it."[58] Full particulars will almost certainly be ordered and at the trial the strictest proof will be required.[59] And if the plea is not proved, the defendant's persistence in the charge is some evidence of malice, and will always tend to aggravate the damages given against him. The defence cannot be raised without a special plea; and counsel should never draw such a plea without express instructions, and even then should always caution the defendant as to the risk he runs. The plea must justify the precise charge which the defendant has made, and, as a rule, the whole of that charge.[60]

Where the defendant did not make a direct charge himself, but only repeated what A said, a general plea that the words are true will be insufficient; he must plead and prove not only that A said so, but in addition that what A said was true.[61] The defendant cannot in any case plead that other words not set out in the statement of claim are true.[62]

Privilege

Formerly, it was unnecessary specially to plead privilege; this defence was available under the plea of Not Guilty, as it still is in criminal cases. But since the Judicature Act privilege must be specially pleaded, and the facts and circumstances on which the defendant will rely as rendering the occasion privileged must be set out either in the plea or in the particulars.[63] Any plea which wears a doubtful aspect, which may be either a plea of privilege, or a mere traverse, or a justification, will be struck out as embarassing.

Equitable Defences

Equitable defences may be pleaded in the Queen's Bench Division. And so may equitable counterclaims, *e.g.* for specific performance or rescission or rectification of an agreement. The Supreme Court Act 1981, s.49(2), provides that every court exercising jurisdiction in a civil case shall continue to give effect

---

[58] *Associated Leisure Ltd.* v. *Associated Newspapers Ltd.* [1970] 2 Q.B. 450 at p. 456, *per* Lord Denning M.R.

[59] See *Leyman* v. *Latimer* (1877) 3 Ex. D. 15, 352.

[60] Subject to the defence under s.5 of the Defamation Act 1952 (intention to rely on this defence must also be expressly pleaded: *Moore* v. *News of the World Ltd.* [1972] 1 Q.B. 441). Justification of some of the words used may go in mitigation of damages.

[61] *Duncan* v. *Thwaites* (1824) 3 B. & C. 556; *M'Pherson* v. *Daniels* (1829) 10 B. & C. 263.

[62] *Rassam* v. *Budge* [1893] 1 Q.B. 571.

[63] *Elkington* v. *London Association for the Protection of Trade* (1911) 27 T.L.R. 329.

"to all equitable estates, titles, rights, reliefs, defences and counterclaims, and to all equitable duties and liabilities." Equitable defences must be pleaded fully,[64] even in actions for the recovery of land.

Settled Account

A settled account is a statement of the accounts between two parties which is agreed to and accepted by both as correct. It must be final, that is, it must show clearly what balance is due, or that no balance is due. An informal release of all demands may be a settled account. The fact that it is stated with the qualification "errors excepted" will not prevent its being a good settled account. It is not enough for the accounting party merely to deliver his account; there must be some evidence that the other party has accepted it as correct. But such acceptance need not be express; contemporaneous or subsequent conduct may amount to a sufficient acquiescence.[65] The fact that the accounting party delivered up his vouchers to the other party is evidence that both regarded the settlement as final.

The plea of a settled account is a good defence to a claim for an account; and if coupled with an allegation that the balance shown by such account had before action been paid to the plaintiff, it is also a good defence to an action for money received by the defendant to the use of the plaintiff. In reply to such a plea, however, the plaintiff may allege that the settlement ought to be set aside, because the account contains errors of such a kind, or to such an extent, that it would be inequitable to hold him bound by it. He must, in his reply or other pleading, specify the errors upon which he relies[66]; and if he contends that such errors were made fraudulently, this must also be clearly stated. If he succeeds in proving fraud, the account will be wholly set aside, and the defendant must account *de novo* for every penny which he has received. The same result will follow where there is no fraud, if a considerable number of errors is shown in the account. Indeed, if the parties stand to each other in a fiduciary relation (*e.g.* as solicitor and client, trustee and *cestui que trust*, guardian and ward), the plaintiff need only prove one "grave or substantial error," and the account will be taken as though there had been

[64] *Sutcliffe* v. *James* (1879) 40 L.T. 875.
[65] *Clark* v. *Glennie* (1820) 3 Star. 10; *Irvine* v. *Young* (1823) 1 Sim. & St. 333.
[66] *Parkinson* v. *Hanbury* (1866) L.R. 2 H.L. 1, 19.

no settlement.[67] Where there is no such relation, and no fraud, and the plaintiff cannot prove any large number of errors he will probably only obtain leave to "surcharge and falsify," as it is called. Proof of one "definite and important error" will entitle him to this.[68] It means that the account stands for what it is worth; but that either party may try to amend it, either by adding items in his favour which were wrongly omitted (that is, surcharging), or by striking out items against himself which were wrongly inserted (that is, falsifying). Whether an account shall be opened, or leave only given to surcharge and falsify, is a matter entirely in the discretion of the court; and whenever one party is allowed to surcharge and falsify, the other may do so too.[69]

Matter Arising Since Writ

A ground of defence which arose after action brought may nevertheless be pleaded (Order 18, r. 9) or raised subsequently by amendment of the defence.[70] Faced with this, the plaintiff may consider it useless to continue the action; yet up to this point he may have been fully justified in bringing it. What is he then to do? If he cannot effect a settlement, he may apply to a master to stay the proceedings or for leave to discontinue them under Order 21, r. 3 (see Chapter 17), on such terms as may be just, including the payment of his costs to date. A difficult question may then arise if the defendant contends that the action would in any event have failed by reason of some other defence which he has. Since it would be ridiculous to carry the issues to trial merely for the sake of costs, an order which does substantial justice can usually be devised.[71]

Set-off and Counterclaim

Any defendant to an action may now plead a set-off or a counterclaim. A set-off is a statutory defence to a plaintiff's action: a counterclaim is substantially a cross-action. In certain cases the defendant may join a third person and make him a

---

[67] *Per* Davey L.J. in *Re Webb* [1894] 1 Ch. at pp. 83–86.
[68] *Parkinson* v. *Hanbury, supra.*
[69] See *Williamson* v. *Barbour* (1877) 9 Ch.D. 529, 532; *Gething* v. *Keighley, ibid.* 547.
[70] For the converse case where the defendant satisfies the plaintiff's claim and therefore serves no defence, see Ord. 13, r. 6(2).
[71] The Rules of 1883 contained somewhat elaborate provisions enabling a defendant to deliver a "further defence" and the plaintiff to deliver a "confession" of such defence. These are now abolished.

party to the counterclaim along with the plaintiff. These matters are fully dealt with in the next chapter.

Third Parties

Again, there may be someone from whom the defendant, if himself found liable in the action, will be entitled to recover some portion of the amount which he will have to pay the plaintiff—in other words, from whom he is entitled to "contribution." Or there may be someone by whom the defendant, if found liable, will be entitled to be wholly reimbursed—that is, he is entitled to an "indemnity." Thus, the defendant may be sued as a surety, and, if found liable, may be entitled to contribution from a co-surety. He may be sued upon a contract which he made as agent for an undisclosed principal and may be entitled to be indemnified by his principal. Or he may be sued for negligent driving and wish to claim contribution from some other driver whom the plaintiff has not elected to sue. In such cases it is obviously desirable to bring in the third person against whom the defendant claims to have a remedy, so that the decision as to the liability of the defendant and of this third person shall be finally settled in one and the same action. The latter can therefore be served with a third-party notice calling upon him to acknowledge service, stating whether he intends to contest the proceedings, within 14 days. Cases of contribution and indemnity were formerly the only ones in which the defendant could do this. Since 1929, however, third-party procedure is also available where the defendant claims that he is entitled to any relief or remedy relating to or connected with the original subject-matter of the action and substantially the same as some relief or remedy claimed by the plaintiff; and also where the defendant requires that any question between the defendant and the third party relating to the original subject-matter should be determined not only as between the plaintiff and the defendant but also as between either or both of them and a person not already a party to the action.[72]

The notice to the third party can be issued without leave at any time after notice of intention to defend and before the defence is served, or later with the leave of a master (Order 16, rr. 1 and 2). It must state the nature and grounds of the claim or the nature of the question to be determined, and the relief sought. The third party, on being served, becomes a party to

---

[72] Order 16, r. 1; *Re Burford, Burford* v. *Clifford* [1932] 2 Ch. 122; *Myers* v. *N. & J. Sherick Ltd.* [1974] 1 W.L.R. 31.

the action *quoad* the defendant as though he had been sued by him; he may give notice of intention to defend, defend, and even counterclaim against the defendant.[73] If he does give notice of intention to defend pursuant to such notice, the master, if satisfied that there is a question proper to be determined as to his liability, may order this question to be tried in such manner as he may direct, or allow him to appear at the trial between the plaintiff and the defendant and take such part in it as may be just. (Order 16, r. 4.) Or, again, he may refuse to make any order, in which case the third-party proceedings fall to the ground. If, on the other hand, the third party does not acknowledge service of the notice, giving notice of intention to defend the proceedings, he will be taken to admit the validity of any judgment which the plaintiff may obtain and his own liability to the defendant to the extent claimed (rule 5). Moreover, a third party may in his turn bring in a fourth party, the fourth a fifth, and so on (rule 9) or he may bring a counterclaim against the defendant.[74] A defendant who has given notice of intention to defend may without leave issue a similar notice to a person who is already a party to the action, *e.g.* a co-defendant (rule 8). Where the defendant in an action counterclaims, the plaintiff can serve a third party notice on a person from whom he claims contribution, indemnity or similar relief in respect of the counterclaim (rule 11). The court will endeavour as far as possible to prevent the plaintiff from being embarrassed in his claim against the defendant by the latter's use of third-party procedure.

Severing Defences

If counsel is instructed on behalf of more than one defendant, the question will arise, should he draw one defence for all, or should they put in separate defences? This depends on what their case will be at the trial. If for any reason they ought to be separately represented then, they must sever now; if they join in one defence, they cannot appear by different counsel at the hearing. If their interests are practically identical, this does not matter; but if they occupy different positions, hold different offices, or took different shares in the transaction, they had better sever; otherwise a special defence peculiar to one of

---

[73] *Barclays Bank* v. *Tom* [1923] 1 K.B. 221. It follows that third party proceedings may thus continue independently of the main action (see, *e.g. Stott* v. *West Yorkshire Road Car Co. Ltd.* [1971] 3 W.L.R. 282), and for the purposes of costs may be regarded as a separate action brought by the defendant (*Johnson* v. *Ribbins* [1977] 1 W.L.R. 1458).

[74] *The Normar* [1968] P. 362. And see *Harper* v. *Gray & Walker* [1985] 1 W.L.R. 1126.

them may be lost.[75] But a special order as to costs may be
made, if defendants improperly sever.[76]

Interpleader

An action is sometimes brought or threatened against a person
(such as a banker, warehouseman or stakeholder) in possession of money or goods in which he himself has no interest but
which are the subject of rival claims. It is obviously unjust that
he should be put to the expense of defending an action in
which he has no interest and he may have no means of
knowing who is really entitled; yet if he hands over the
property to one claimant he may expose himself to an action by
the other. In such circumstances he may bring the claimants
before the master and obtain protection by issuing an interpleader summons under Order 17. (This is known as a
"stakeholder's interpleader" as distinguished from a "sheriff's
interpleader," see Chapter 24). He must swear an affidavit
showing that he claims no interest in the subject-matter other
than for charges or costs; that he does not collude with any
claimant; and that he is willing to deal with the subject-matter
of the dispute as the master may direct. The master may then,
if it seems just, stay proceedings against the applicant and
order an issue to be tried between the claimants and give such
other directions with regard to the property and generally as
may be appropriate.

[75] *Born* v. *Turner* [1900] 2 Ch. 211.
[76] *Re Isaac* [1897] 1 Ch. 251; *Bagshaw* v. *Pimm* [1900] P. 148.

CHAPTER 14

SET-OFF AND COUNTERCLAIM

Even though the plaintiff was the first to commence litigation it may happen that the defendant has a claim of some kind against the plaintiff. If so, the question at once arises, must the defendant issue a separate writ for this, or can he set up his claim in the plaintiff's action?

If the defendant's claim can be tried without inconvenience at the same time and by the same tribunal as the plaintiff's, the defendant will be allowed to plead in the plaintiff's action (a) in some cases a "set-off," (b) in all cases a "counterclaim." The distinction between set-off and counterclaim should be carefully noted, though it must be said that the modern tendency is rather to slur over the differences and emphasise the similarities.

Speaking generally, a set-off may be described as a shield which operates only as a defence to the plaintiff's action, and a counterclaim as a sword with which the plaintiff may be attacked, but which does not afford the defendant any protection unless it is of such a nature that it can also be pleaded as a set-off. The distinction is important; for if A is both a creditor of, and a debtor to, B in respect of different transactions, and B's solvency is doubtful, it is obviously to A's advantage to set off one amount against the other if he can. On the other hand, if the plaintiff's action is discontinued, it would seen to follow that the defendant's set-off would fall to the ground; but if he had pleaded a counterclaim, he could obtain judgment upon it.[1]

Both are to a large extent the creatures of statute-law. Under the old common law a defendant who had any cross-claim against the plaintiff could not raise it in the plaintiff's action: he had to bring a cross-action. But two statutes (now repealed) were passed in the reign of George II, which enabled *mutual debts* to be set off; the scope of these statutes was, however, somewhat limited. Courts of equity would also give effect to a set-off independently of the statute, in cases where it appeared that the defendant ought thus to be protected against the plaintiff's demand.[2] By the Judicature Act 1873, s.24(3),[3] the court was given power to give a defendant in the plaintiff's

[1] *McGowan* v. *Middleton* (1883) 11 Q.B.D. 464, 470; Order 15, r. 2(3).
[2] *Rawson* v. *Samuel* (1839) 1 Cr. & Ph. 161.
[3] See now the Supreme Court Act 1981, s.49(2).

action such relief, both in respect of legal and equitable rights, as was properly claimed by his pleading and could have been given in a separate action. Now by Order 18, r. 17, "where a claim by a defendant to a sum of money (whether of an ascertained amount or not) is relied on as a defence to the whole or part of a claim made by the plaintiff, it may be included in the defence and set off against the plaintiff's claim, whether or not it is also added as a counterclaim." And by Order 15, r. 2(1) a defendant in any action "who alleges that he has any claim or is entitled to any relief or remedy against a plaintiff in the action in respect of any matter (whenever and however arising) may, instead of bringing a separate action, make a counterclaim in respect of that matter; and where he does so he must add the counterclaim to his defence." The court may then pronounce a final judgment in the action, both on the original claim and on the cross-claim. This is subject to the power of the court under Order 15, r. 5 to exclude a counterclaim, if satisfied that the defendant's claim ought not to be disposed of by way of counterclaim but in an independent action.

A counterclaim or set-off in an action by or against the Crown is now permissible, subject to the general law and to the limitations imposed by Order 77, r. 6. No set-off or counterclaim can be raised against the Crown in proceedings for the recovery of taxes, duties or penalties, nor can a claim for repayment of taxes, duties or penalties be pleaded by way of set-off or counterclaim in any proceedings by the Crown (rule 6(1)). Leave must be obtained to raise a counterclaim or set-off in proceedings by or against the Crown in two cases— (a) if the Crown sues or is sued in the name of a government department to which the counterclaim or set-off does not relate; and (b) if the Crown sues or is sued in the name of the Attorney-General (rule 6(2)).

Under Order 15, r. 2(4) where a counterclaim is established against the plaintiff's claim, the court may, if the balance is in favour of one of the parties, give him judgment for such balance without prejudice to the court's discretion as to costs.

The correct interpretation of the Judicature Act and the rules has been a matter of some doubt. It was at one time thought that their effect was to enlarge the right of set-off, so that any cross-claim by the defendant raised in the plaintiff's action would operate as a defence to the action. This view did not prevail, and it has been held that the alteration has been one of procedure only, and that the rights of the parties are unchanged.[4] The result appears to be that whatever was a good

---

[4] *Stooke* v. *Taylor* (1880) 5 Q.B.D. 569; *Stumore* v. *Campbell & Co.* [1892] 1 Q.B. 314.

set-off, either at law or in equity, in 1875 is a good set-off still: and nothing else is admissible as a set-off, though it may be an excellent counterclaim. We must therefore approach the subject historically.

Set-off

A set-off is a defence to the whole or to a portion of the plaintiff's claim. Under Order 15, r. 2(4) the court appears to have no power to give the defendant judgment for the balance of a *set-off* over-topping the plaintiff's claim. In any event the court would not do so unless such balance was "properly claimed by his pleading" (Judicature Act 1925, s.39), and the proper way of doing so would seem to be by pleading a counterclaim.[5] It is thought that the position remains the same under the Supreme Court Act 1981, s.49(2), which provides that the court "shall give the same effect as hitherto—(a) to all equitable estates, titles, rights, reliefs, defences and counterclaims . . . and (b) subject thereto, to all legal claims and demands and all estates, titles, rights, duties, obligations and liabilities existing by the common law or by any custom or created by any statute. . . . " At common law a set-off could only be raised by a cross-action, although a defendant sued for the price of goods could give evidence of a breach of warranty in reduction of the price.[6] Under the Insolvent Debtors Relief Act 1729, s.13, and the Debtors Relief Amendment Act 1735, s.4, mutual debts between plaintiff and defendant (or if either party sued or was sued as executor or administrator, between the deceased and the other party) could be set off. This was so although the debts might be of a different nature (*e.g.* speciality or simple contract debts); but if either had accrued by reason of a penalty contained in a bond or specialty, judgment would only be entered for the amount justly due. It was held under these statutes that there could only be a set-off where both debts were legal debts, such as would support an action of debt, covenant, or assumpsit for the non-payment of money; it was not allowed in actions of trespass or upon the case or for general damages; and the demand intended to be set off must have been liquidated and not in the nature of a penalty. The debts must have been due from and to the same parties in the same right[6a]; thus, a joint debt could not be set off against a

---

[5] *Stooke* v. *Taylor* and *Stumore* v. *Campbell & Co., supra;* but see *Gathercole* v. *Smith* (1881) 7 Q.B.D. 626, 629.
[6] See Sale of Goods Act 1979, s.53.
[6a] See *Reeves* v. *Pope* [1914] 2 K.B. 284.

separate one, nor could a defendant, sued as executor, set off a debt due to him personally; a defendant trustee could, however, set off money due to the *cestui que trust*. The debt sought to be set off must have been in existence at the time of the issue of the writ; now, however, a set-off arising after action brought may be relied on by the defendant, if pleaded as such.[7]

Although in the main equity followed the law, the rigidity of these rules was, to a limited extent, mitigated by the Court of Chancery. Even where there was no legal debt, if either of the cross-demands was a matter of equitable jurisdiction and there was some special reason why equity should intervene, an equitable set-off might be allowed. Thus, in the case of the equitable assignment of a debt the debtor could set off another debt due to him from the assignee.[8] Again, a principal indebted jointly with his surety was allowed to set off a separate debt due from the creditor to himself.[9] Matters of complaint connected with the plaintiff's claim may often be set up to reduce or extinguish it; and it may be inequitable for the plaintiff's claims to be insisted on without taking those of the defendant into account, even though they are unliquidated.[10] But nothing which is not a money claim (whether of an ascertained amount or not) can be set off (Order 18, r. 17). Since the Judicature Act equitable set-offs are recognised in every division of the High Court. As a result of the fusion of law and equity there may be pleaded by way of set-off (i) mutual debts; (ii) such matters of complaint as are allowable to reduce or extinguish the claim; or (iii) other matters of equity which formerly might have called for injunction or protection.

Illustrations

The defendant owed the plaintiff £45. The defendant was executor of the estate of John Grimes, deceased. The plaintiff owed that estate more than £45. *Held*, that the defendant, when sued for his personal debt of £45, could not set off the debt due from the plaintiff to John Grimes' estate.

Nelson v. *Roberts* (1893) 69 L.T. 352.

A's solicitor had in hand £15 belonging to A. A became bankrupt. The solicitor then rendered certain professional services to A, the fair remuneration for which was £12 13s 4d. A's trustee in bankruptcy sued for £15: *Held*, that the solicitor could not set off the £12 13s 4d. against the trustee's claim; for that was money earned since the bankruptcy.

Stumore v. *Campbell & Co.* [1892] 1 Q.B. 314; 61 L.J.Q.B. 463.

A claim for damages for negligence by a bailee may be set off against an admitted claim for storage charges; but not, it would seem, a totally unconnected claim such as damages for libel.

---

[7] Ord. 18, r. 9: *Ellis* v. *Munson* (1876) 35 L.T. 585.
[8] *Cavendish* v. *Geaves* (1857) 24 Beav. 163.
[9] *Ex p. Hanson* (1806) 12 Ves. Jr. 346.
[10] *Hanak* v. *Green* [1958] 2 Q.B. 9 (C.A.).

Morgan & Son, Ltd. v. *S. Martin Johnson & Co., Ltd.* [1949] 1 K.B. 107. And see *Hale* v. *Victoria Plumbing Co. Ltd.* [1966] 3 W.L.R. 47.

Against a claim for damages for failure to complete certain work and for bad workmanship there may be set off claims (i) for extras; (ii) for loss through failure to admit the defendant's workman; and (iii) for damages for trespass to the defendant's tools.

Hanak v. *Green* [1958] 2 Q.B. 9.

In an action for damages for negligence by solicitors, the defendants were allowed to set off the value of a benefit accruing to the plaintiffs as a result of the negligent act, since the benefit was sufficiently closely related to a particular head of damage claimed.

Nadreph Ltd. v. *Willmett & Co.* [1978] 1 W.L.R. 1537.

The plaintiff is entitled to plead in reply to a set-off that it was barred by the Limitation Act, or was for any other reason not an actionable debt at date of writ.

Smith v. *Betty* [1903] 2 K.B. 317.

Counterclaim

As we have seen, the modern counterclaim was entirely the creation of the Judicature Act 1873. It need not relate to or be in any way connected with the plaintiff's claim, or arise out of the same transaction.[11] It need not be "an action of the same nature as the original action"[12] or even analogous thereto. If the defendant has any valid cause of action, legal or equitable, against the plaintiff, there is no necessity for him now to bring a cross-action, unless his counterclaim is of such a nature that it cannot conveniently be tried by the same tribunal or at the same time as the plaintiff's claim.

Every cross-claim of whatever kind can now be pleaded as a counterclaim. It does not matter what the amount of it may be. It may be for either liquidated or unliquidated damages (Order 15, r. 2(1)). It may exceed in amount the plaintiff's claim[13]; or it may be less than the plaintiff's claim.[14] If the amount which is found due to the plaintiff on his claim exceeds the amount established by the defendant on his counterclaim, the plaintiff will recover the difference; if, on the other hand, the balance is in favour of the defendant, judgment may be given for the defendant for such balance (Order 15, r. 2(4)). Or he may be granted such other relief as he may be entitled to on the merits of the case. It is more usual nowadays to give separate judgments upon the claim and counterclaim with the appropriate costs of each instead of one judgment for the balance, but this is entirely a matter of discretion.

---

[11] Ord. 15, r. 2(1).
[12] *Per* Fry J. in *Beddall* v. *Maitland* (1881) 17 Ch.D. at p. 181.
[13] *Winterfield* v. *Bradnum* (1878) 3 Q.B.D. 324.
[14] *Mostyn* v. *West Mostyn, etc., Co.* (1876) 1 C.P.D. 145.

In one respect a defendant who is pleading a counterclaim is in a better position than if he were seeking to enforce the same claim as a plaintiff in a separate action. An action may be brought in our courts against a foreigner resident out of the jurisdiction, only in the cases specified in Order 11 unless he can be found temporarily within the jurisdiction and served. But if that foreigner commences an action here, and so brings himself within the jurisdiction of our courts, he is liable to any counterclaim that can conveniently be tried with his claim. And if that counterclaim overtops his claim, judgment may be recovered and enforced against him for the balance, unless he is a foreign sovereign or state.[15]

Illustrations

"A claim founded on tort may be opposed to one founded on contract, or vice versa." *Per* Cockburn C.J. in

Stooke v. *Taylor* (1880) 5 Q.B.D. at p. 576.

In an Admiralty action *in rem* for salvage services the defendant may counterclaim *in personam* for damages for breach of a charterparty.

The Cheapside [1904] P. 339; 73 L.J.P. 117.

If the defendant seeks to bring in some person who is not already a party to the action, and make him defendant to the counterclaim, either that person must be liable to him along with the plaintiff in respect of the subject-matter of the counterclaim, or the relief for which the defendant asks against him must relate to or be connected with the original subject-matter of the action.

Order 15, r. 3(1).

Barber v. *Blaiberg* (1882) 19 Ch.D. 473; 51 L.J. Ch. 509.

Smith v. *Buskell* [1919] 2 K.B. 362; 88 L.J.K.B. 985.

Even a cause of action which has accrued to the defendant since the plaintiff issued his writ can be pleaded as a counterclaim. The words of the rule are "whenever and however arising." (But it should either be stated expressly, or appear clearly from the dates mentioned in the counterclaim, that the defendant's claim arose after action brought, so that the plaintiff may have an opportunity of discontinuing or taking other appropriate action.)

Order 15, r. 2(1); Order 18, r. 9.

A counterclaiming defendant is in no way limited to a claim for damages. The court will give him judgment for such relief as he may be entitled to upon the merits of the case. (Supreme Court Act 1981, s.49(2) and see Precedents Nos. 40, 46 and 47.)

Illustrations

A defendant may by his counterclaim ask for a declaration of his rights, or for relief against forfeiture, or for a vesting order under section 146(4) of the Law of Property Act 1925.

Adams v. *Adams* 45 Ch.D. 426; [1892] 1 Ch. 369.

In certain cases, a defendant may, even before serving his counterclaim, apply for an *interim* injunction or for the appointment of a receiver to protect his interests.

Collison v. *Warren* [1901] 1 Ch. 812; 70 L.J. Ch. 382.

---

[15] *South African Republic* v. *La Compagnie Franco-Belge* [18897] 2 Ch. 487; [1898] 1 Ch. 190. State Immunity Act 1978, s.2(6).

A counterclaim is governed by the same rules of pleading as a statement of claim, and the reply to it by the same rules as a defence. All the facts relied on by way of counterclaim must be stated in numbered paragraphs (following on in the same serial from those of the defence, not starting a fresh series) under the heading "Counterclaim," so as to distinguish them from facts alleged by way of defence. If any of the facts on which the counterclaim is founded have been already stated in the defence, they need not be restated in the counterclaim, but may be incorporated by reference under the heading "counterclaim," thus: "The defendant repeats paragraphs 1–6 inclusive of the defence." It is, however, undesirable thus to repeat paragraphs containing matter which is irrelevant to the counterclaim. A counterclaim may comprise several distinct causes of action; but the facts on which each cause of action is founded must be stated, as far as may be, separately and distinctly, and the relief claimed be stated specifically, either simply or in the alternative. And the several causes of action must be such as could properly be joined in one independent action.[16] The provisions of Order 15 apply to the joinder of various claims in a counterclaim.

Ample provision is made to protect the plaintiff from inconvenient and improper counterclaims. If he can show that the counterclaim is one which cannot conveniently be disposed of in the pending action, or ought not to be allowed, the master may strike it out or exclude it under Order 15, r. 5 leaving the defendant to bring a cross-action. If the counterclaim is frivolous or vexatious, or if it discloses no valid cause of action, or if it may prejudice, embarrass or delay the fair trial of the action or is otherwise an abuse of the process of the court, the master may order that it be struck out or amended under Order 18, r. 19(1). Or objection may be taken to it in point of law under Order 18, r. 11. It must be properly pleaded or further particulars may be demanded under Order 18, r. 12.

A counterclaim must always claim relief against the plaintiff. "A pleading which asks no cross-relief against a plaintiff either alone or with some other person is not a counterclaim."[17] It has been held that it need not be a claim against the plaintiff in the same capacity as that in which he sues.[18]

Illustrations
To a joint claim by two plaintiffs a separate counterclaim against each of them will be allowed.

Manchester, etc., Ry. v. *Brooks* (1877) 2 Ex.D. 243.

---

[16] *Compton* v. *Preston* (1882) 21 Ch.D. 138.
[17] *Per* Jessel M.R. in *Furness* v. *Booth* (1876) 4 Ch.D. at p. 587.
[18] *Re Richardson* [1933] W.N. 90.

And on a counterclaim against two plaintiffs, the defendant may recover judgment against one.

    Hall v. *Fairweather* (1901) 18 T.L.R. 58.

If one member of a firm sues for a debt due to him personally, the defendant may counterclaim for a debt due to him from the firm and can make the plaintiff's partner a party to the counterclaim or not, as he pleases. If the defendant does not join the partner, the plaintiff can subsequently apply to add him.

    Eyre v. *Moreing* [1884] W.N. 58.

Where a plaintiff sues in his own right, the defendant can counterclaim against him as trustee or executor or administrator, provided that no practical inconvenience will result. It would seem to follow that if the plaintiff sues as trustee or executor or administrator, the defendant could counterclaim against him in his own right.

    Re Richardson [1933] W.N. 90.

The defendant can also plead a counterclaim against the plaintiff along with some other person, not already a party to the action, described as a "defendant to counterclaim" in the title of the action, provided that it either (a) alleges that such other person is liable to the defendant along with the plaintiff in respect of the subject-matter of the counterclaim, or (b) relates to or is connected with the subject-matter of the plaintiff's claim.[19] And his counterclaim may seek relief jointly, severally, or in the alternative. Or he can plead such a counterclaim against a co-defendant along with the plaintiff. But he cannot counterclaim against any co-defendant or third person alone without the plaintiff, though he can claim contribution, indemnity or other similar relief from such a person as a "third party" under Order 16.

Whenever such a counterclaim is pleaded, the defendant must place at the head of his defence an additional title, stating the names of all persons whom he has thus made defendants to his counterclaim and serve the counterclaim and pleadings upon them. (Order 15, r. 3(2)). Thereafter each defendant to the counterclaim becomes a party in the action "with the same rights in respect of his defence to the counterclaim and otherwise as if he had been duly sued in the ordinary way by the party making the counterclaim" (*ibid.*). Each new defendant must acknowledge service of the counterclaim as though he had been served with a writ and plead to it (rule 3(5)). Any person thus made defendant to a counterclaim, whether plaintiff, co-defendant or new party, may, before replying, apply to the master to exclude the counterclaim on the ground that it ought to be disposed of in an independent action, and not by way of counterclaim (rule 5). A plaintiff against whom a

---

19 Order 15, r. 3(1); *Smith* v. *Buskell* [1919] 2 K.B. 362; *Barber* v. *Blaiberg* (1882) 19 Ch.D. 473.

counterclaim is pleaded can in certain cases counterclaim against the defendant's counterclaim. He may also issue a third-party notice against a person not a party to the action from whom he claims contribution, indemnity or such other relief as is permitted under Order 16.[20] Similarly, a new party brought in as defendant to a counterclaim may counterclaim against the defendant who brought him in, and he may also utilise third-party procedure against the plaintiff (whose co-defendant he has become).

Where a plaintiff fails to serve a defence to counterclaim, the defendant may sign judgment in default of pleading in any of the ways provided in Order 19, rr. 2 to 7 inclusive (Order 19, r. 8). A counterclaim having been made against the plaintiff and a co-defendant or other person not already a party to the action, the defendant is then entitled to apply for summary judgment under Order 14 on his counterclaim against that defendant or added party (Order 15, r. 3(5A)).

Illustrations

A counterclaim is admissible against the plaintiff and a new party along with the plaintiff if its matter be connected with that of the plaintiff's claim, even though such new party could not possibly have been made a party in the plaintiff's original action.

Turner v. Hednesford Gas Co. (1878) 3 Ex.D. 145.

A defendant cannot join a new party to be a joint plaintiff with himself in a counterclaim against the original plaintiff.

Pender v. Taddei [1898] 1 Q.B. 798; 67 L.J.Q.B. 703.

How Far a Counterclaim is an Independent Action

For many purposes a counterclaim is substantially a cross-action. "A counterclaim is to be treated, for all purposes for which justice requires it to be treated, as an independent action."[21] If, after the defendant has pleaded a counterclaim, the plaintiff's action is for any reason stayed, discontinued or dismissed, the counterclaim may nevertheless be proceeded with (Order 15, r. 2(3)). The court may order a counterclaiming defendant to give security for costs[22]; but not where the counterclaim is in substance a defence to the action.[23]

---

[20] Order 16, r. 11.

[21] *Per* Bowen L.J. in *Amon v. Bobbett* (1889) 22 Q.B.D. at p. 548. However, a counterclaim is dependent on the plaintiff's action to the extent that the counterclaim cannot properly be pleaded after the plaintiff has obtained a judgment which has been satisfied, since there is then no cause or matter extant for the purposes of Order 15, r. 2: *CSI International Co. Ltd. v. Archway Personnel (Middle East) Ltd.* [1980] 3 All E.R. 215.

[22] Order 23, r. 1; *Sykes v. Sacerdoti* (1885) 15 Q.B.D. 423; *Lake v. Haseltine* (1885) 55 L.J.Q.B. 205.

[23] *Neck v. Taylor* [1893] 1 Q.B. 560; and see *New Fenix Compagnie v. General Accident, etc., Corporation* [1911] 1 K.B. 619.

Yet a counterclaim differs in some respects from a cross-action. The issues of fact raised by claim and counterclaim, respectively, must, as a rule, be tried together. But if both parties succeed, there may be two judgments—one for the plaintiff on his claim, with costs, and the other for the defendant on his counterclaim, with costs—though execution will issue only for the balance.[24] A former difference was that trial of an action, but not a counterclaim,[25] could be transferred to a County Court on the ground of the plaintiff's lack of means. This power has now been abolished.[26] If foreign plaintiffs bring an action here against a British subject who counterclaims, the court has no jurisdiction to make an order staying proceedings in the action until the foreign plaintiffs give security for damages under the counterclaim.[27]

And, although as a rule a counterclaim may be of any amount, overtopping the plaintiff's claim and entitling the defendant to a judgment, still there are two exceptions to this rule, two cases in which a counterclaim, like a set-off, serves only as a defence, and is not a cross-action—or, to employ the time-honoured metaphor, can be used only "as a shield, not as a sword."[28]

(i) If a debt is assigned the debtor may in certain cases set off or counterclaim against the assignee a debt due from the assignor to himself; but if the amount of such set-off or counterclaim exceeds the amount of the debt assigned, the defendant can recover nothing from the assignee; he must sue the assignor for the balance.[29] In general, any cross-claim arising out of a contract may be set off against an assignee of that contract; but a different rule applies in the case of an assignment of a reversion on a lease.[30]

(ii) A similar rule applies when a sovereign prince or state over whom our courts have no jurisdiction brings an action in this country. The defendant is allowed to plead any set-off or counterclaim against him which is an

---

[24] It is otherwise in the case of a set-off, which is a defence proper. There can be only one judgment—either judgment for the plaintiff for the balance found due; or, if the defendant establishes a set-off equal to or exceeding the amount to which the plaintiff is entitled, judgment for the defendant. *Provincial Bill Posting Co.* v. *Low Moor Iron Co.* [1909] 2 K.B. 344; *Sharpe* v. *Haggith* (1912) 106 L.T. 13.

[25] *Delobbel-Flipo* v. *Varty* [1893] 1 Q.B. 663.

[26] Administration of Justice Act 1969, s.11(2).

[27] *The James Westoll* [1905] P. 47.

[28] Per Cockburn C.J. in *Stooke* v. *Taylor* (1880) 5 Q.B.D. at p. 575.

[29] *Young* v. *Kitchin* (1873) 3 Ex.D. 127; *Government of Newfoundland* v. *Newfoundland Ry.* (1888) 13 App. Cas. 199.

[30] *Reeves* v. *Pope* [1914] 2 K.B. 284.

answer to his demand, but not to recover any judgment against him for the excess, or to raise any counterclaim which is outside and independent of the subject-matter of the claim.[31]

Costs of Set-off and Counterclaim

In the matter of costs, however, a counterclaim which is not a set-off is treated as a cross-action, whereas a set-off remains what it was in the days of George II—a defence to the plaintiff's action. Therefore, a plaintiff, who brings an action and is met by a set-off equal in amount to his claim, must ordinarily pay the defendant his costs of the whole action; for he has failed in the whole action.[32] Whereas, if the defendant can plead only a counterclaim and recovers an amount equal to or greater than the plaintiff's claim, the plaintiff will (subject to the court's discretion) recover his costs of the claim, and the defendant only his costs of the counterclaim. The proper principles on which in such a case taxation should be conducted, in the absence of any special order, are laid down in *Atlas Metal Co.* v. *Miller*[33] and *Medway Oil Co.* v. *Continental Contractors.*[34] The costs of the plaintiff's claim should first be taxed as if it were a separate action with no counterclaim. Then the costs occasioned by the counterclaim must be taxed, as though they were part of the costs of a separate action. The taxing master must ascertain what items are really costs of claim and counterclaim, respectively, dealing with the matter as one of substance and not of form; and any items which have been incurred partly on account of each, such as brief fees to counsel, must be divided. But in the absence of a special order, there should be no apportionment of general costs. Then whichever be the smaller amount—the costs of the claim or the costs of the counterclaim—must be deducted from the larger; and the successful party will be entitled to recover the balance. Similar principles apply where both claim and counterclaim fail: the proper method is to tax the costs of the defendant except so far as they have been increased by the counterclaim, and to tax the costs of the plaintiff only so far as they have

---

[31] *Duke of Brunswick* v. *King of Hanover* (1844) 6 Beav. 1, 38; *High Commissioner for India* v. *Ghosh* [1960] 1 Q.B. 134. State Immunity Act 1978, s.2.
[32] *Hanak* v. *Green* [1958] 2 Q.B. 9.
[33] [1898] 2 Q.B. 500.
[34] [1929] A.C. 88. But see *Millican and Another* v. *Tucker and Others* [1980] 1 W.L.R. 640, where the C.A. held it was well within the judge's discretion *inter partes* to order the apportionment of the costs of claim and counterclaim equally.

been increased by the counterclaim, with a set-off of the one against the other.[35]

The court, however, has power and is encouraged to make a special order as to costs (*e.g.* that a proportion only of his total costs shall be paid to the successful party), thus avoiding the complications set out above.[36]

Where a defendant, who has been sued in the High Court, counterclaims for an amount within the county court jurisdiction, the party succeeding on the counterclaim is entitled to High Court costs; section 20 of the County Courts Act 1984 does not apply to a counterclaim.[37]

---

[35] *James* v. *Jackson* [1910] 2 Ch. 92; *Medway Oil Co.* v. *Continental Contractors, supra.*
[36] Ord. 62. *Chell Engineering Ltd.* v. *Unit Tool and Engineering Co. Ltd.* [1950] 1 All E.R. 378 (especially the remarks of Denning L.J.); *Childs* v. *Gibson* [1954] 1 W.L.R. 809.
[37] See *Blake* v. *Appleyard* (1878) 3 Ex.D. 195; *Amon* v. *Bobbett* (1889) 22 Q.B.D. 543.

CHAPTER 15

REPLY AND SUBSEQUENT PLEADINGS

If no defence is served, the plaintiff may enter judgment in default under Order 19.[1] (As to service of defence out of time, see Chapter 6). The procedure for obtaining final or interlocutory judgment appropriate to the various causes of action described in Chapter 4 is followed, but no affidavit of service of the writ is required as the defendant has now acknowledged service.

If the defendant has paid money into court and the plaintiff is content to accept it in satisfaction of his claim, or of those causes of action only in respect of which it was paid in, he may take the money out within 21 days of the receipt of the notice of payment in (see Chapter 17).

If a defence is served containing express or implied admissions of fact, so that it purports to offer an answer to part only of the plaintiff's alleged cause of action, the plaintiff may in most cases, by leave of a master, obtain final or interlocutory judgment for the part admitted, if that part is severable from the rest (Order 27, r. 3).[2] Or the plaintiff may apply for an order that the defendant pay into court any money which he admits is in his hands.[3] He may do this even though he has already served a reply and set the action down for trial[4]; but in that case the defendant should be indemnified against any costs incurred by him through the plaintiff's delay.[5]

Reply

The student should distinguish carefully a "reply" from a "defence to counterclaim," although if both are pleaded they must appear in one document (Order 18, r. 3(3)). A reply, if required must be served within 14 days after the defence to which it relates has been served, unless the time is extended by consent or by order (rule 3(4)). A reply is not necessary if its sole object is to deny what the defendant has stated in his defence, for in its absence there is an implied joinder of issue

---

[1] Leave is necessary in certain claims for possession of land, and in actions in tort between husband and wife.
[2] See *Ellis* v. *Allen* [1914] 1 Ch. 904; *Lancashire Welders Ltd.* v. *Harland & Wolff Ltd.* [1950] 2 All E.R. 1096; *Murphy* v. *Culhane* [1977] Q.B. 94.
[3] *Crompton* v. *Burton* [1895] 2 Ch. 711.
[4] *Brown* v. *Pearson* (1882) 21 Ch.D. 716.
[5] *Tottenham* v. *Foley* [1909] 2 Ir.R. 500.

(rule 14(1)). Its main function is to raise in answer to the defence any matters which must be pleaded by way of confession and avoidance under rule 8, or to make any admissions which you may be disposed to make. And in actions of libel or slander, where the defendant pleads that the words were published on a privileged occasion or as fair comment on a matter of public interest and were so published without malice, the plaintiff, if he intends to set up express malice in answer to such plea of privilege or fair comment, must serve a reply setting out the facts on which he relies (Order 82, r. 3(3)). If no reply be served within 14 days, all material statements of fact in the defence will be deemed to have been denied and put in issue. But where a counterclaim is pleaded, the plaintiff must within 14 days serve a defence to counterclaim, which is subject to the rules applicable to defences (Order 18, r. 18(b)).

It has hitherto been common practice, when a defence to counterclaim was pleaded, to preface it with a reply stating: "The plaintiff joins issue with the defendant on his defence (save so far as the same consists of admissions)."[6] This is no longer necessary where no special reply is to be pleaded. But it is permissible under rule 14 to say, "The plaintiff admits the facts alleged in paragraph 1 of the defence, but save as aforesaid he joins issue on the defence." There cannot be a mere joinder of issue upon a counterclaim: the plaintiff must plead to it with a "defence to counterclaim" as though he were pleading a defence to a statement of claim (rules 14(3) and 18). The effect of joining issue is merely to *deny*; it does not confess and avoid. It is simply a comprehensive and compendious *traverse*. "The reply is the proper place for meeting the defence by confession and avoidance."[7]

The plaintiff must therefore be careful not to join issue merely, where he ought to allege new facts in his reply; for a joinder of issue only contradicts the facts alleged by the defendant.

Illustrations

A reply must not set up new claims. A reply should not plead mere evidence or argument, or state conclusions of law to be drawn or inferred from the facts pleaded.

    Williamson v. *L. & N.W. Ry.* (1879) 12 Ch.D. 787.

However, the plaintiff must serve a reply and plead specifically any matter, for example, performance, release, the expiry of a relevant period of limitation, fraud or any fact showing illegality which he alleges makes the defence not

---

6 The words in brackets were always unnecessary, for an admission is not an allegation of fact to which it is necessary to plead.

7 *Per* James L.J. in *Hall* v. *Eve* (1876) 4 Ch.D. at p. 345.

available or which might otherwise take the defendant by surprise or raise issues of fact not arising out of the defence.

Order 18, r. 8(1).

In an action for specific performance of an agreement to grant a lease, the defendant pleaded breaches of contract entitling him to put an end to the agreement and to refuse to grant a lease. In his reply the plaintiff denied all such breaches, but pleaded also that if any were committed, they were waived and this reply was held good. A plaintiff may confess and avoid by his reply; for it is no part of the statement of claim to anticipate the defence, and the old rule of pleading still holds, "that you should not leap before you come to the stile."

Hall v. *Eve* (1876) 4 Ch.D. 341.

Departure

It is at the stage of reply that the rule against what is called "a departure in pleading" applies for the first time. "A party shall not in any pleading make any allegation of fact, or raise any new ground of claim, inconsistent with a previous pleading of his."[8]

A departure takes place when in any pleading the party deserts the ground that he took up in his preceding pleading, and resorts to another and a different ground; or, to give Sir Edward Coke's definition, "A departure in pleading is said to be when the second plea containeth matter not pursuant to his former, and which fortifieth not the same; and therefore it is called *decessus*, because he departeth from his former plea" (Co.Litt. 304a). This is clearly embarrassing; a reply is not the proper place in which to raise new claims; to permit this would tend to spin out the pleadings to an intolerable length. The plaintiff must amend his statement of claim by adding the new matter as a further or alternative allegation.

Defence to Counterclaim

"There can be no joinder of issue, implied or express, on a statement of claim or counterclaim" (Order 18, r. 14(3)). Thus the plaintiff *must* plead to a counterclaim if only for the purpose of denying specifically those allegations of fact in it which he does not admit. The correct pleading for this purpose is a defence to counterclaim and not a reply (rule 3(2)). If he does not serve a defence to counterclaim, the allegations of fact in the counterclaim are deemed to be admitted (rule 13). As we have seen, the plaintiff may go further and serve a reply if it is needed for compliance with rule 8. If so, it must be included in

---

[8] See Ord. 18, r. 10; *Herbert* v. *Vaughan* [1972] 1 W.L.R. 1128.

the same document (rule 3(3)). He may pay money into court in satisfaction of a counterclaim in accordance with the rules applicable to a defendant paying in, with the necessary modifications. (Order 22, r. 6). He may even in rare cases counterclaim to it.[9]

Rejoinder, etc.

The defendant's answer, if any, to a reply, is called a Rejoinder; but it is now very seldom pleaded, except where there has been a counterclaim and the defendant desires to confess and avoid some allegation in the defence to counterclaim. The rejoinder is then, in effect, a reply to the defence to counterclaim. Further pleadings are possible; there can be a Surrejoinder, a Rebutter, and a Surrebutter; but they are very seldom met with.

None of these pleadings can be served without leave (Order 18, r. 4) and the time for serving them will be stated in the master's order. He must be satisfied that such a pleading is necessary. If to any such pleading no answer is delivered, every material statement in it will be deemed to be denied, not admitted (rule 14). The principle of rule 8 of Order 18 applies to all these subsequent pleadings. Hence, if the defendant desires to give evidence at the trial of any fresh facts by way of confession and avoidance in answer to the plaintiff's reply, he must allege them specially in his rejoinder, and not merely join issue.

Unless a pleading subsequent to a reply is ordered the pleadings are deemed to be closed at the expiration of 14 days after service of the reply or defence to counterclaim; or, if there is no reply or defence to counterclaim, 14 days after service of the defence (rule 20). There is then (except in the case of a counterclaim to which no defence has been pleaded) an implied joinder of issue and every material allegation of fact in the pleading last served is deemed to have been denied (rule 14). The issues are now clear and the parties can take stock of the position and proceed to discovery.

---

[9] *e.g.* if any cross-claim has accrued to him either before or after the issue of the writ, which arose at the same time and out of the same transaction as the counterclaim and is not strictly pleadable as a set-off, provided that the plaintiff desires to use such cross-claim merely as a shield against the defendant's counterclaim; otherwise he must amend his statement of claim or issue a fresh writ. See *Toke* v. *Andrews* (1882) 8 Q.B.D. 428; *Renton Gibbs & Co. Ltd.* v. *Neville & Co.* [1900] 2 Q.B. 818.

CHAPTER 16

DISCOVERY OF DOCUMENTS

The issues in the action being now clearly stated in the pleadings, each party naturally proceeds to consider how he shall prove his case. What evidence is available? Some letters have, as a rule, passed between the parties before the action was commenced, and these may contain important admissions, or be evidence of some material fact; but the plaintiff has the defendant's letters, and the defendant has the plaintiff's; and, in the absence of copies, neither set is properly intelligible without the other. It is most desirable that anyone who intends to give evidence should, if possible, read over his own letters before he enters the witness-box. For his recollection of an interview which took place many months ago is probably somewhat hazy now, and far less reliable than his account of it, given in a letter written at the time, which remains in black and white as clear and intelligible now as it ever was. Moreover, there is no better material for cross-examining an opponent than his letters written before the dispute arose. Hence it is generally desirable for each party to see all material documents in the possession of his opponent, and to take copies of the more important ones. Such disclosure is obtained by the process—formerly only available in equity, but now freely used in all divisions of the High Court—called "Discovery of Documents." Two stages are involved: the disclosure of what documents exist (coupled with any claim that any of them are privileged from production) and the inspection of such of those documents as the opposite party is entitled to see.

Discovery of Documents

It may be that one party has, in his pleadings or particulars, or in an affidavit, whether filed or not, referred to some document; and he cannot say that it is not material as he relies on it himself. His opponent is entitled at any time to give notice under Order 24, r. 10, that he desires to see that document and take a copy of it, if he deems it sufficiently material.[1] The party

---

[1] *Quilter* v. *Heatly* (1883) 23 Ch.D. 42; *Smith* v. *Harris* (1883) 48 L.T. 869. In *Dubai Bank Ltd.* v. *Galadari (No. 2)* [1990] 1 W.L.R. 731 the Court of Appeal held that for the purposes of this rule the reference had to be made to a document or documents and that the court would not enter into a process of inference. Simply because on the balance of probabilities a transaction referred to in a pleading or affidavit must have been effected by a particular document does not give the court jurisdiction to make an order under this rule for the disclosure of that document. Therefore if it is asserted in an affidavit that "Blackacre was conveyed by A to B" there is no "reference to" the document effecting the conveyance for the purposes of rule 10.

255

who has referred to the document must then name a time within seven days when, and a place where, the document can be inspected, and state any grounds he has for objecting to the production of it. The power of the court to order production can then, if necessary, be invoked.[2] Or it may be that one party knows or suspects that the other has certain material documents, or a class of documents, in his possession though they are not referred to in any pleading or affidavit. In such a case he may be able to obtain an order for specific discovery of them. But in most cases neither party has any clear idea as to the documents in his opponent's possession. He may be able to guess at some of them; but he would like a detailed list of all that are material—and this he can generally obtain.

Under the former rules discovery of documents took place as the result of an application which was usually made at the first or at an adjourned hearing of the "summons for directions." Now, the plaintiff and defendant in an action begun by writ will normally exchange lists of documents[3] between themselves in accordance with Order 24, rr. 1 and 2, without the necessity of attending before a master. Unless dispensed with by order or by agreement this must be done within 14 days of the close of pleadings. To allow time for this and for the inspection of the documents disclosed, the summons for directions need not be issued until one month from the close of pleadings.

The list of each party must set out all the documents "which are or have been in his possession, custody or power relating to any matter in question between them in the action" (Order 24, r. 2(1)). Detailed interpretation of this rule is discussed later in this chapter. Either party is at liberty to serve a notice on the other requiring him to verify his list by affidavit, and this may be done at any time before the summons for directions is taken out (rule 2(7)). If, however, the parties agree that discovery is not necessary at all, or that only limited discovery is necessary, they may dispense with or limit it accordingly, without the intervention of the court. If one party is willing to dispense with or limit it, but the other will not agree, or if either party thinks that is should be postponed, he may apply by summons to a master under rule 2(5); and if the master thinks that immediate and full discovery is not necessary either for disposing fairly of the action or for saving costs he will make an appropriate order.

---

[2] Ord. 24, rr. 11 and 13. See *Rafidain Bank* v. *Agom Universal Sugar Trading Co. Ltd.* [1987] 1 W.L.R. 1606, and see p. 282. See also *R.* v. *I.R.C., ex p. Taylor* [1989] 1 All E.R. 906.

[3] The term "documents" has a wide meaning and includes, for instance, a tape recording of a conversation since this could properly be described as documentary evidence of the conversation: *Grant* v. *Southwestern and County Properties Ltd.* [1975] Ch. 185.

In "collision cases" (*i.e.* all cases arising out of an accident on land due to a collision or apprehended collision involving a vehicle) discovery should not be made *by a defendant* unless the master so orders.[4] And in actions for the recovery of any penalty under a statute the defendant need not make discovery.[5]

There are many cases in which the foregoing provision for "automatic" discovery does not apply—*e.g.* in actions begun by originating summons and in civil proceedings to which the Crown is a party.[6] Or your opponent may fail to give the discovery which he is required to give. Accordingly, rule 3 gives power to the master to order a party to furnish a list of all the relevant documents which are or have been in his possession, custody or power, and if necessary to verify it by affidavit. This is sometimes referred to as an order for "general discovery." The order may be limited to certain classes of documents or to certain issues in the action; or its operation may be postponed until certain issues have been tried. And discovery is sometimes ordered as to special damage only (including documents relating to the plaintiff's industrial injury, industrial disablement or sickness benefit rights); or discovery on the issue of damage may be postponed until the questions of liability have been tried. The power is subject to this overriding limitation, that discovery will not be ordered except where it is necessary either for disposing fairly of the action or for saving costs (rule 8).[7] The party seeking discovery should see that the master's order is drawn up and should, if necessary, serve it on his opponent.

Subject to the same limitation the master has power under rule 7 to order discovery of particular documents or classes of documents. This he may do at any stage of the action. He may be asked to do so before general discovery takes place because a party has reason to believe that the other has relevant documents in his possession which it is necessary in the interests of justice that the applicant should see at once. There is no power to order discovery of documents before the issue of a writ (apart from under section 33(2) of the Supreme Court Act 1981, and it is only seldom ordered before the close of pleadings. In exceptional circumstances discovery can be

---

[4] Rule 2(2). The master might do so, for example, where improper maintenance of the brakes or light of the defendant's vehicle is alleged.
[5] Rule 2(3).
[6] Ord. 77, r. 12(1).
[7] Discovery solely for impeaching the credit of the other party will be refused under this rule: *George Ballantine & Son Ltd.* v. *F.E.R. Dixon & Son Ltd.* [1974] 1 W.L.R. 1125.

ordered before the delivery of a statement of claim.[8] In *Bankers Trust Co. v. Shapira*[9] the plaintiffs claimed to have been defrauded of a large sum of money by customers of the defendant bank, and they sought to trace the money into the customers' accounts. Contemporaneously with the issue of the writ in the action the plaintiffs applied for an order against the defendant bank for immediate disclosure of the state of the accounts and of all documents and correspondence with the customers relating to these accounts from the time of the alleged fraud. The Court of Appeal took the view that the equitable remedy of tracing depended for its effectiveness in this case on the plaintiffs being able to follow their money as soon as possible, and, in view of the strong prima facie case of fraud, granted the order for immediate discovery.

You may also have grounds for believing that material documents have been omitted from the list which your opponent has furnished under rule 2 or in pursuance of an order under rule 3. In such cases you may take out a summons, or apply under the summons for directions, specifying the document or class of document of which discovery is sought and asking for an order requiring your opponent to state whether he has or ever has had it in his possession, custody or power, and, if he has parted with it, what has become of it (rule 7).[10] The application must be supported by an affidavit stating that the deponent believes, with the grounds of his belief, that the other party has, or has had, the document or class of document and that it is relevant. If the other party has already made an affidavit verifying his list of documents so as to show that he has not, and has not had, any relevant documents other than those which he has disclosed, his oath must in some way be displaced. In an application under rule 7 this can be done by an affidavit disclosing prima facie grounds for supposing that specific documents or classes of documents are relevant and that they exist. If the existence of further documents is then disclosed, but they are shown not to be material, the matter

---

[8] *Gale* v. *Denman Picture Houses Ltd.* [1930] 1 K.B. 588. See also *Huddleston* v. *Control Risks Information Services Ltd.* [1987] 1 W.L.R. 701. See *R.H.M. Foods Ltd.* v. *Bovril Ltd.* [1982] 1 W.L.R. 661 where an order for specific discovery under rule 7 was denied before the service of the statement of claim and before the motion for an interlocutory injunction even where the outcome of this application was likely in practice to dispose of the action.

[9] [1980] 1 W.L.R. 1274. The defendant bank, although innocent of any wrongdoing itself, was liable under the rule in *Norwich Pharmacal Co.* v. *Commissioners of Customs and Excise* [1974] A.C. 133 (see *infra*), to give information relating to the wrongdoers with whose activities it had become "mixed up." A similar order for early discovery was made by Robert Goff J. in *A.* v. *C.* [1980] 2 All E.R. 347.

[10] And see *White* v. *Spafford* [1901] 2 K.B. 241; *Astra-National Productions Ltd.* v. *Neo-Art Productions Ltd.* [1928] W.N. 218.

can be tested upon an application for production; but such further oath is usually regarded as conclusive.[11] The master may, however, inspect the document in order to arrive at a decision (rule 13(2)).

Apart from rule 7, further discovery can only be obtained in special circumstances. A list which, for example, omits all reference to the documents which the deponent once had but has not now in his possession will be deemed an insufficient compliance with the rules and a proper list may be ordered under rule 3. But if a list of documents is drawn up in proper form and verified by affidavit, it is as a rule conclusive. No counter-affidavit will be permitted except on an application under rule 7.[12] But if it can be shown from the list itself, or from the documents disclosed in it, or from any admission made by the party, or from correspondence or other documents, that he has in his possession other material documents which he has not disclosed, a further and better list may be ordered under rule 3,[13] so also where it is clear that a party has compiled his list under a misconception of the real issues and that he almost certainly must have documents which ought to have been disclosed and which he would have disclosed if he had rightly conceived his case.[14]

There is an implied undertaking given by a party and his legal advisers that documents disclosed on discovery will not be used for any purpose other than the proper conduct of that action.[15] A party can also be required to give an express undertaking not to divulge the contents of such documents to any person otherwise than for the purposes of the litigation.[16] The court can, however, in appropriate circumstances and on the application of a party, release or modify the undertaking so as, for instance, to allow a party to use documents disclosed in one action to be used in another action against the same

---

[11] *Chowood Ltd.* v. *Lyall* [1929] 2 Ch. 406.

[12] *Edmiston* v. *British Transport Commission* [1956] 1 Q.B. 191.

[13] *Compagnie Financière du Pacifique* v. *Peruvian Guano Co.* (1882) 11 Q.B.D. 55; *Kent Coal Concessions Ltd.* v. *Duguid* [1910] 1 K.B. 904, [1910] A.C. 452.

[14] *British Assn. of Glass Bottle Mfrs. Ltd.* v. *Nettlefold* [1912] 1 K.B. 369, [1912] A.C. 709; *Chowood Ltd.* v. *Lyall* [1929] 2 Ch. 406.

[15] *Home Office* v. *Harman* [1983] 1 A.C. 280.

[16] *Alterskye* v. *Scott* [1948] 1 All E.R. 469; *Distillers Co. (Biochemicals) Ltd.* v. *Times Newspapers Ltd.* [1975] Q.B. 613; *Church of Scientology* v. *D.H.S.S.* [1979] 1 W.L.R. 723; *Davies* v. *Eli Lilly & Co.* [1987] 1 W.L.R. 428. See p. 285.

defendant.[17] In addition, rule 14A provides that any undertaking, whether express or implied, not to use a document for any purposes other than those of the proceedings in which it is disclosed, shall cease to apply to that document after it has been read to or by the court, or referred to in open court unless the court has made some special order following the application of a party or of the person to whom the document belongs.

The List of Documents

The documents contained in the list must be described with particularity sufficient to identify them, should the court think fit to order any of them to be produced.[18] If objection is to be made to their production, the grounds must be set out.[19] All material documents (including tape recordings) must be specified—immaterial documents should be altogether omitted. Any document set out is admitted to be material.

There is thus placed on the practitioner the somewhat invidious burden of deciding whether a document is material or not. If he decides it is not, the correct course is to omit all mention of it; it follows that the correctness of his decision on materiality is not capable of challenge in the same way as it would be on, say, a doubtful claim to privilege. If his opponent has good ground for supposing that a document exists and that it is material, his only remedy is to apply for further discovery in the manner already described.

If, however, a document is material, the fact that a party intends to object to its production or does not propose himself to put the document in evidence is no ground for not disclosing it; still less if it may assist his opponent. If it throws light on any part of the case, it is material. If parts only are relevant and he does not wish to disclose the whole, he should specify the relevant parts; it is in his possession and he must take the responsibility.[20] Both discovery and inspection are strictly limited to the "matters in question" in the action.

---

[17] *Crest Homes plc* v. *Marks* [1987] A.C. 829 where at 859 Lord Oliver stated that in order to secure a release from the undertaking it was necessary for the applicant to demonstrate "cogent and persuasive reasons why it should be released." See also *Sybron Corp.* v. *Barclays Bank plc* [1985] Ch. 299 and *Bibby Bulk Carriers* v. *Cansulex Ltd.* [1988] 2 All E.R. 820, where it was held that r. 14A did not have restrospective effect but that the fact that a document had been read to the court before the new rule came into force was one factor to be taken into account by the judge in the exercise of his discretion whether to release a party from his undertaking.

[18] Rule 5(1); *Taylor* v. *Batten* (1878) 4 Q.B.D. 85.

[19] Rule 5(2); see below.

[20] *Yorkshire Provident Co.* v. *Gilbert* [1895] 2 Q.B. 148, 153.

Materiality for the purpose of disclosure is a concept not restricted to documents which would be evidence on any issue in the case. Documents will also be material if it is reasonable to suppose they contain information which may either directly or indirectly enable the party seeking discovery either to advance his own case or to damage the case of his adversary, or which may fairly lead him to a train of inquiry which may have either of those consequences.[21]

The list of documents and the affidavit by which it is verified must be in Forms Nos. 26 and 27 in Appendix A of R.S.C. (rule 5). The list itself has two schedules and the first schedule has two parts. In Schedule 1, Part 1, the plaintiff or defendant sets out the documents relating to the matters in question in the action which he has in his possession, custody or power, and is willing to produce; in Part 2, he sets out all documents which, although relevant, he objects to producing, either on the grounds of privilege, or for some other reason.[22] The claim of privilege with "a sufficient statement of the grounds" must be set out in paragraph 2 of the body of the list. In Schedule 2 he sets out documents which he once had in his possession, custody or power, but which, at the date of service of his list, he no longer has. He must state in paragraph 4 of the body of the list what has become of them and in whose possession they now are. In each schedule he must "enumerate the documents in a convenient order and as shortly as possible" but describe each of them, or, in the case of bundles of documents of the same nature, each bundle, sufficiently to enable it to be identified (rule 5(1)).

At the end of the list is appended a "notice to inspect" which sets out the place at which and the date and time when the documents which a party is willing to produce may be inspected by his opponent.

Objections to Production

Under this heading are considered a number of grounds on which a party may object to producing certain documents for inspection. A party may refuse as of right to produce for inspection documents protected by privilege; he may also argue that disclosure of certain documents would be injurious to the public interest, and he may claim that there are other

---

[21] *Compagnie Financière du Pacifique* v. *Peruvian Guano Co.* (1882) 11 Q.B.D. 55.
[22] *e.g.* that he has a lien over the documents which would be defeated by inspection: *Woodworth* v. *Conroy* [1976] Q.B. 884.

reasons why production should not be ordered or why inspection should be limited on terms laid down by the court. There is no general principle allowing a party to protection from discovery of confidential communications.[23] Discovery is a process of involuntary disclosure and is always to greater or lesser extent, an invasion of privacy.[24] Where objection is made to production the court has power to inspect the document itself for the purpose of deciding whether the objection is valid,[25] and Order 24, r. 13(1) declares that no order for the production of any documents for inspection shall be made unless the court is of opinion that the order is necessary either for disposing fairly of the cause or matter or for saving costs. The various grounds of objection will now be considered.

1. *Legal Professional Privilege*

This privilege concerns confidential communications passing between a lawyer and his client, and extends in some cases to protect confidential communications between the lawyer or client and third parties. The privilege is that of the client, who cannot be compelled to produce for inspection documents protected by the privilege, nor can he be compelled to produce privileged documents or give evidence of such communications at the trial of the action. However, the privilege may be waived by the client, either wholly or in part. It is clear that before trial the client can waive privilege in relation to some documents while retaining privilege for others.[26]

However, care is needed where waiver of privilege for *part* of a document is contemplated since the waiver will apply to the whole unless it can be divided into separate parts dealing with entirely different subject-matters.[27]

A further point to consider is the possibility of "referential" or "associative" waiver. If privilege is waived for certain evidence of a particular transaction the extent of the waiver can

---

[23] *D.* v. *N.S.P.C.C.* [1978] A.C. 171.

[24] *Shearson Lehman Hutton Inc.* v. *Maclaine Watson & Co. Ltd.* [1989] 1 All E.R. 1056.

[25] Ord. 24, r. 13(2).

[26] *Lyell* v. *Kennedy (No. 3)* (1884) 27 Ch.D. 1 at 24. It has been held that where a plaintiff makes privileged documents available to the police in accordance with the public duty to assist in the conduct of criminal investigation and proceedings such disclosure does not amount to an express or implied waiver of the privilege which the plaintiff may wish to claim in the civil proceedings for which the documents had been created: *British Coal Corporation* v. *Dennis Rye Ltd.* [1988] 3 All E.R. 816.

[27] *Burnell* v. *British Transport Commission* [1955] 1 Q.B. 187; *Great Atlantic Insurance Co.* v. *Home Insurance Co.* [1981] 1 W.L.R. 529; *Pozzi* v. *Eli Lilly & Co., The Times,* December 3, 1986. This is especially so where one party waives privilege for a document by cross-examining his opponent on part of that document.

go beyond the particular document or evidence for which privilege was waived. This is because the opposite party is then entitled to ask for and see all the other documents which are relevant to the transaction.[28] The underlying principle is that of fairness in the conduct of the action and that

> "where a party is deploying in court material which would otherwise be privileged, the opposite party and the court must have an opportunity of satisfying themselves that what the party has chosen to release from privilege represents the whole of the material relevant to the issue in question. To allow an individual item to be plucked out of context would be to risk injustice through its real weight or meaning being misunderstood."[29]

Therefore if one party puts in evidence a conversation between him and his solicitor his opponent would be entitled to ask for other privileged communications regarding the contents or what was said in the course of the conversation.[30]

Documents protected by this privilege may be divided into two classes.[31] The first class concerns letters and other communications passing between a client and his solicitor. The general rule is that if these communications are made in confidence, to or by the solicitor in his professional capacity, and for the purpose of obtaining or giving legal advice, then they are privileged, even though there may be no litigation pending or contemplated at the time.[32] Some of the older cases which have *dicta* to the effect that this privilege extends to *all* communications between solicitor and client within the ordinary business of a solicitor are too wide.[33]

---

[28] *Doland (George) Ltd.* v. *Blackburn & Co. Ltd.* [1972] 1 W.L.R. 1338; *Great Atlantic Insurance Co.* v. *Home Insurance Co.* [1981] 2 All E.R. 485.

[29] Per Mustill J. in *Nea Karteria Maritime Co. Ltd.* v. *Atlantic and Great Lakes Steamship Corp. (No. 2)* [1981] Com.L.R. 138 at 139.

[30] *Doland (George) Ltd.* v. *Blackburn & Co. Ltd. supra.* See also *General Accident Fire and Life Assurance Corp. Ltd.* v. *Tanter* [1984] 1 W.L.R. 100 where Hobhouse J. was concerned about the width of the waiver that might result under this principle and therefore limited waiver to documents relating to the contents of a conversation about a transaction rather than to all privileged communications concerning the same subject matter of the transaction. See the discussion of this case in *Re Konigsberg (a bankrupt)* [1989] 3 All E.R. 289 at 295 and the criticism of it in *Phipson on Evidence* (ed. 13, 1982) para. 15–20.

[31] For a recognition of the distinction see Mellish L.J. in *Anderson* v. *Bank of British Columbia* (1876) 2 Ch.D. 644 at 658 and Sir George Jessel M.R. in *Wheeler* v. *Le Marchant* (1881) 17 Ch.D. 675 at 681, 682.

[32] *Greenough* v. *Gaskell* (1833) 1 My. & K. 98; *Minet* v. *Morgan* (1873) 8 Ch.App. 361. See also *Lawrence* v. *Campbell* (1859) 4 Drew 485.

[33] *Carpmael* v. *Powis* (1846) 1 Ph. 687. For examples of communications between client and solicitor which are not privileged, see *Smith-Bird* v. *Blower* [1939] 2 All E.R. 406 and *Conlon* v. *Conlons Ltd.* [1952] 2 All E.R. 462.

On the other hand, a communication need not specifically seek or convey advice in order to enjoy privilege. Further, "legal advice is not confined to telling the client the law"; it also includes "advice as to what should prudently and sensibly be done in the relevant legal context."[34] Therefore, if there is a series of communications between solicitor and client relating to, for instance, a protracted conveyancing transaction, all communications which had as their aim the obtaining of appropriate legal advice in the above wide sense of the term, even if the advice was not specifically requested, would be privileged.[35] The operation of this rule is not restricted to communications with solicitors in private practice. It extends to documents prepared for and by counsel,[36] to communications with full-time salaried legal advisers[37] ("in-house" lawyers) and to communications with foreign legal advisers.[38] These communications are protected whether made by the client personally or by his agent, and whether made by the solicitor or by an agent or clerk employed by him.[39] Documents privileged in the hands of a predecessor in title to a party remain privileged,[40] and the successor in title can object successfully to their production in the same or any other litigation.[41]

The second class of protected documents concerns confidential communications with third parties, and the rule for this class is narrower. Such communications between the lawyer or client and a third party are privileged only if they are brought into existence after litigation has commenced or is a reasonable prospect and they are made for the purpose of giving or obtaining legal advice in the litigation or for the

---

[34] *Per* Taylor L.J. in *Balabel* v. *Air India* [1988] 2 W.L.R. 1036 at 1046.
[35] *Balabel* v. *Air India, supra.* See *Ventouris* v. *Mountain* [1990] 3 All E.R. 157.
[36] *Bristol Corporation* v. *Cox* (1884) 26 Ch.D. 678; *R.* v. *Godstone R.D.C.* [1911] 2 K.B. 465; *R.* v. *Inland Revenue Board, ex p. Goldberg* (1988) 132 Sol.Jo. 1035.
[37] *Alfred Crompton Amusement Machines Ltd.* v. *Commissioners of Customs and Excise (No. 2)* [1974] A.C. 405. For privilege to attach, the communication must relate to legal as distinct from administrative matters.
[38] *Re Duncan, Garfield* v. *Fay* [1968] P. 306; *Macfarlan* v. *Rolt* (1872) L.R. 14 Eq. 850.
[39] *Wheeler* v. *Le Marchant* (1881) 17 Ch.D. 675; *Anderson* v. *Bank of British Columbia* (1876) 2 Ch.D. 644. Also if a solicitor receives information from a third party in a professional capacity and conveys this to his client this information is privileged: *Re Sarah C. Getty Trust* [1985] Q.B. 956.
[40] *Minet* v. *Morgan (supra); Calcraft* v. *Guest* [1898] 1 Q.B. 759.
[41] *Crescent Farm (Sidcup) Sports Ltd.* v. *Sterling Offices Ltd.* [1972] Ch. 553.

obtaining of information and evidence for use in the litigation.[42] Two aspects of this rule require further comment. First, the application of the rule presents no difficulty when the third party supplies information in response to a request from a solicitor who has actually been instructed in connection with existing or pending litigation.[43]

The position has not been so clear, however, where information was supplied by the third party to the client at a time when the client may have been contemplating litigation but had not at that stage instructed his solicitor in connection with it. A second and closely related aspect of the rule concerns documents which are brought into existence for more than one purpose.[44]

It now appears that documents will be privileged if, at the time they were brought into existence, there was a reasonable prospect of litigation *and* if the dominant purpose of the author or composer "or of the person or authority under whose direction . . . it was produced or brought into existence"[45] was to use it or its contents in order to obtain legal advice or to conduct or aid in the conduct of litigation.[46] Therefore, there does not have to have been a decision taken to bring proceedings or defend a claim, but simply that there is a reasonable prospect of this happening.

The dominant purpose test was approved by the House of Lords in *Waugh* v. *British Railways Board*[47] to determine whether a document which is brought into existence for more than one reason or purpose is privileged or not. In this case the

---

[42] *Wheeler* v. *Le Marchant* (1881) 17 Ch.D. 675. See also *Buttes Gas and Oil Co.* v. *Hammer (No. 3)* [1980] 3 W.L.R. 668 where the Court of Appeal took the view that legal professional privilege extends to the exchange of confidential communications between a party to litigation and third persons where there is a common interest and legal advisers in common, and the communications relate to pending litigation. On appeal, the proceedings in this case were stayed on other grounds: [1982] A.C. 888.

Note also that if a document is privileged by reason of the fact that it is a communication *between solicitor and client* the whole of the document can be privileged despite the fact that part of it records a conversation between the solicitor and a third party at a time when no litigation was in prospect: see Templeman L.J. in *Great Atlantic Insurance Co.* v. *Home Insurance Co.* [1981] 1 W.L.R. 529 at 534.

[43] *Seabrook* v. *British Transport Commission* [1959] 1 W.L.R. 509.

[44] The fact that they can be so closely related is shown in *Guinness Peat Ltd.* v. *Fitzroy Robinson* [1987] 1 W.L.R. 1027 where at first instance concern mainly centred around the first aspect of the rule, whereas in the Court of Appeal emphasis was placed on the second aspect.

[45] Barwick C.J. in *Grant* v. *Downs* (1976) 135 C.L.R. 674 at 677. See also Slade L.J. in *Guinness Peat Ltd.* v. *Fitzroy Robinson* at 1036E-F.

[46] Lord Edmund-Davies in *Waugh* v. *British Railways Board* [1980] A.C. 521 at 544 and Oliver L.J. in *Re Highgrade Traders Ltd.* [1984] B.C.L.C. 151 at 173 approving the test propounded by Barwick C.J. in *Grant* v. *Downs* (1976) 135 C.L.R. 674.

[47] [1980] A.C. 521.

defendants claimed privilege for an "internal inquiry" report made by two of their employees shortly after an accident in which the plaintiff was injured. It was argued that the report had been prepared for two equally important purposes: one being the investigation of the cause of the accident for the purpose of railway operation and safety, the other being the submission of information to the defendants' solicitor for use in the litigation which the defendants claimed they anticipated would follow from the fact of the accident. The House of Lords held that for the report to be privileged the submission to the defendants' legal advisers for advice on and use in litigation must be at least the *dominant* purpose for which it had been prepared. Accordingly the claim for privilege failed and production of the report was ordered.[48]

The point is one of general practical importance since such reports are often compiled very soon after the events they record and so may well contain detailed accounts of accidents, statements of witnesses and conclusions as to cause and therefore may well be the best evidence available.

The *Waugh* decision overruled earlier authorities which stated that if only one of the reasons why a document was brought into existence was to supply information to a solicitor with a view to litigation then it would be privileged.[49] This position is however too generous to a party to litigation since there is an important public interest in the due administration of justice in the disclosure of this type of document which has to be weighed against the party's interest in keeping certain information confidential.[50]

In *Guinness Peat* v. *Fitzroy Robinson*[51] it was held by the Court of Appeal that a letter written to the defendants' insurers at a time before proceedings had been instituted in order to comply with the terms of their insurance policy could be subject to privilege since on the facts the dominant reason why the

---

[48] The "dominant purpose" test was applied shortly afterwards by the Court of Appeal in *Neilson* v. *Laugharne* [1981] 1 Q.B. 736, where legal privilege was unsuccessfully claimed in respect of statements made to a police officer investigating a complaint under s.49 of the Police Act 1964. However, it was held further that the statements should not be disclosed on the ground of public interest immunity (see p. 279).

[49] *Birmingham and Midland Motor Omnibus Co. Ltd.* v. *London and North Western Railway Co.* [1913] 3 K.B. 850; *Ankin* v. *London and North Eastern Railway Co.* [1930] 1 K.B. 527; *Ogden* v. *London Electric Railway Co.* (1933) 49 T.L.R. 542; *Westminster Airways Ltd.* v. *Kuwait Oil Co. Ltd.* [1951] 1 K.B. 134; *Seabrook* v. *British Transport Commission* [1959] 1 W.L.R. 509, where the earlier cases are fully reviewed. See also *Longthorn* v. *British Transport Commission* [1959] 1 W.L.R. 530.

[50] Lord Wilberforce and Lord Simon in *Waugh* v. *British Railways Board* [1980] A.C. 521 at 531, 535.

[51] [1987] 1 W.L.R. 1027.

insurers required letters of this sort was in order to obtain legal advice and to assist them in any ensuing litigation.[52]

So the dominant purpose of bringing a document into existence is not necessarily ascertained by reference simply to the intention of its author or composer. The court should look objectively at the reason for its coming into existence. In *Guinness Peat* the intention of the actual author was simply to comply with the terms of the insurance policy, but the reason why the insurers required the notice in writing ("the person under whose direction the letter was brought into existence") was that in most cases they would use it to seek legal advice on whether a claim should be paid or resisted.[53] Even where both the author and the solicitor depose that a document was only prepared or the dominant purpose of its preparation was in anticipation of litigation and the document itself only refers to that purpose the court can still hold that a document does not enjoy legal professional privilege.[54]

The time at which the document is brought into existence is the relevant time for determining whether or not the dominant reason for its being brought into existence is the obtaining of legal advice as to whether a claim should be made or resisted. The subsequent use of a document in connection with litigation or subsequent events is of no relevance in determining the dominant reason for its existence. For example, in *Alfred Crompton Amusement Machines Ltd.* v. *Customs and Excise Commissioners (No. 2)*[55] the Commissioners sought unsuccessfully to claim privilege for internal communications and memoranda which contained information which assisted them in the com-

---

[52] In this situation both the defendants and their insurers could claim privilege for this document since, as was stated by Brightman L.J. in *Buttes Gas and Oil Co.* v. *Hammer (No. 3)* [1981] Q.B. 223 at 267: "if two parties with a common interest and a common solicitor exchange information for the dominant purpose of informing each other of the facts, or the issues, or advice received, or of obtaining legal advice in respect of contemplated or pending litigation, the documents or copies containing that information are privileged from production in the hands of each."

[53] Contrast this situation with that in *Jones* v. *Great Central Railway Co.* [1910] A.C. 4. There the information supplied to a trade union by a dismissed employee as required by the rules of the union to determine whether an action could be brought by the employee at the union's expense was held not to be privileged by the House of Lords because the information here had to be delivered to a person who had himself to consider and then possibly act upon it. However, in the light of the consideration given to this case and *Crompton* by the Court of Appeal in *Re Highgrade Traders Ltd.*, *Jones* is probably better distinguished by the fact that the relationship between trade union and member is very unlike that between insurer and insured where in the event of litigation the insurers will be the effective defendants.

[54] *Lask* v. *Gloucester Health Authority, The Times*, December 13, 1985, where the dominant reason for the preparation of a confidential accident report was to enable measures to be taken to avoid a repetition of the accident.

[55] [1974] A.C. 405.

putation of purchase tax. The purpose for which the documents were composed by the Commissioners was to comply with their statutory duties and the fact that the documents were subsequently used to obtain legal advice in connection with arbitration proceedings did not alter the court's view on whether they should be privileged or not. This was so even though at the time they were prepared it was expected that the Commissioners' assessment and opinion would be challenged.[56]

As indicated above, documents will not be protected where the client has waived the privilege, and there are a number of other cases in which a claim of privilege may be defeated. For instance, where it is alleged, and a prima facie case is made out, that a communication between a client and his legal adviser was intended to facilitate or to guide the client in the commission of a crime or fraud or that the legal adviser's advice was obtained for a fraudulent purpose, then privilege will not attach to that communication or advice and the judge has a discretion to order disclosure.[57] The principle applies not only when the legal adviser is a knowing party to the crime or fraud but also when he is ignorant of the purpose for which his advice is sought.

This principle should not, however, be taken too far. For instance, privilege will not be lost and documents will not be ordered to be disclosed where a client uses his solicitor to put forward a wholly bogus defence to a charge of fraud and supplies the solicitor with documents designed to assist in the maintenance of this defence.[58] To hold otherwise and to order production of these documents at an interlocutory stage based upon prima facie evidence of fraud put forward by the plaintiff would make a serious inroad into legal professional privilege. It would run a greater risk of injustice to the defendant to order disclosure than if he were allowed to keep this material confidential.[59]

Secondly, privilege will not protect documents concerned with the seeking or giving of legal advice, if the nature of that

---

[56] It was largely for this reason that Viscount Dilhorne dissented on this point.

[57] *R.* v. *Cox and Railton* (1884) 14 Q.B.D. 153; *Williams* v. *Quebrada Railway Land and Cropper Co.* [1895] 2 Ch. 751; *O'Rourke* v. *Darbishire* [1920] A.C. 581; *Butler* v. *Board of Trade* [1971] Ch. 680. "Fraud" in this context is not limited to the tort of deceit and includes all forms of fraud and dishonesty such as fraudulent breach of trust, fraudulent conspiracy, trickery and sham contrivances, but does not extend to such torts as inducing breach of contract: *Crescent Farm (Sidcup) Sports Ltd.* v. *Sterling Offices Ltd.* [1972] Ch. 553, 565, *per* Goff J. See also *Francis & Francis (a firm)* v. *Central Criminal Court* [1988] 3 All E.R. 775.

[58] Of course, if the solicitor is aware of the bogus nature of the defence or that an affidavit sworn by his client is untrue he is under a duty to the court either to inform the opposing party or to cease to act for that client: *Myers* v. *Elman* [1940] A.C. 282.

[59] *Chandler* v. *Church* (1987) 137 N.L.J. 451.

advice and the circumstances in which it was sought and given are themselves material facts. This may be the case, for example, where a party requests relief under section 33 of the Limitation Act 1980 (a consolidation of earlier statutes).[60] The court in such a case is directed by the statute to have regard to the steps taken by the plaintiff to obtain legal advice and the nature of any advice received.

Lastly, privilege cannot be asserted for documents or communications where the parties to the proceedings previously employed the same solicitor and the documents or communications in question were made by one party to the solicitor in his capacity as solicitor for both parties.[61]

Where one party, as a result of inadvertence or a mistake, allows the other to see and make copies of documents for which privilege could have been claimed,[62] then the general rule is that it is too late for that party to claim privilege and the other party will be able to rely on those documents.[63] However, this is not the inevitable result since the court does have a discretion to intervene under its equitable jurisdiction and grant an injunction to prevent the use of documents or information obtained as a result of a mistake. The factors which the court will take into account in deciding whether or not to exercise its discretion to grant relief are the circumstances in which the document came into the hands of the other party (*e.g.* was it procured by fraud or trickery of the other party)[64] where on inspection the other party realised that he has been permitted to see the document only by reason of an obvious

---

[60] *Jones* v. *G.D. Searle & Co. Ltd.* [1979] 1 W.L.R. 101.

[61] *Shore* v. *Bedford* (1843) 5 Man. & G. 271. See also *Re Konigsberg (a bankrupt)* [1989] 3 All E.R. 289 where a wife could not assert legal professional privilege against the trustee in bankruptcy of her husband in respect of communications from the solicitor acting for both the husband and the wife in a previous transaction.

[62] For instance by including the documents in Schedule 1, Part 1 of the list of documents. If one party has done this, then, at any time before inspection the court will normally allow this party to amend the list under Order 20, r. 8.

[63] *Re Briamore Manufacturing Ltd.* [1986] 1 W.L.R. 1429. Especially if the mistake is made during a stage of litigation: see Slade L.J. in *Guinness Peat Ltd.* v. *Fitzroy Robinson* [1987] 1 W.L.R. 1027. In *Calcraft* v. *Guest* [1898] 1 Q.B. 759 it was held that one party was entitled to adduce secondary evidence of privileged documents and to use *copies* those documents which had come into its hands for that purpose although the original documents remained privileged and were held by the other party.

[64] But see Nourse L.J. in *Goddard* v. *Nationwide Building Society* [1987] Q.B. 670 at 685.

mistake, the issues in the action and any delay on the part of the party seeking the relief.[65]

Professional privilege is restricted to the legal profession,[66] and does not extend to protect communications with other professional advisers, such as accountants[67] and doctors.[68]

2. *Privilege Against Self-incrimination*

Privilege may be claimed for documents which, if produced, would tend to expose the party producing them, or his spouse, to proceedings for a criminal offence or for the recovery of a penalty under the law of any part of the United Kingdom.[69] At common law this privilege extended also to documents tending to expose the party to proceedings for a forfeiture of a lease,[70] but this extension was abolished for civil cases by section 16(1)(a) of the Civil Evidence Act 1968. Section 14(1)(a) of this Act makes clear that the privilege does not extend to incrimination under foreign law, but, for the purposes of the section, the word "penalties" has been held to include fines imposed by administrative action of the European Economic Commission under the EEC legislation relating to cartels and recoverable under English law by virtue of the European Communities Act 1972.[71]

This privilege relates to production of documents for inspection. Except where the action is for the recovery of a penalty under a statute[72] a party cannot refuse to make a list of documents on the ground that he might thereby criminate

---

[65] *Lord Ashburton* v. *Pape* [1913] 2 Ch. 469; *Goddard* v. *Nationwide Building Society* [1986] 3 W.L.R. 734; *English and American Insurance Co. Ltd.* v. *Herbert Smith & Co.* (1987) 137 N.L.J. 148; *Guinness Peat Ltd.* v. *Fitzroy Robinson* [1987] 1 W.L.R. 1027. On Scott J.'s analysis in *Webster* v. *James Chapman & Co.* [1989] 3 All E.R. 939 the power to grant relief to a party whose documents have been inadvertently disclosed arises from its jurisdiction to protect confidential information or confidential documents. Since it will almost invariably be the case that a privileged document is also a confidential document it may well be eligible for protection against unauthorised use or further disclosure. Where a party seeks an order protecting confidential information the court is required to exercise its discretion by balancing the legitimate interests of that party in seeking to keep the confidential information suppressed and the legitimate interests of the other party in seeking to make use of it.

[66] *Slade* v. *Tucker* (1880) 14 Ch.D. 824.

[67] *Chantrey Martin* v. *Martin* [1953] 2 Q.B. 286.

[68] *Wheeler* v. *Le Marchant* (1881) 17 Ch.D. 675, 681; *Hunter* v. *Mann* [1974] Q.B. 767.

[69] Civil Evidence Act 1968, s.14(1); *Rank Film Distributors Ltd.* v. *Video Information Centre* [1980] 3 W.L.R. 487.

[70] *Blunt* v. *Park Lane Hotel Ltd.* [1942] 2 K.B. 253, 257, *per* Goddard L.J.; *Seddon* v. *Commercial Salt Co. Ltd.* [1925] Ch. 187.

[71] *Rio Tinto Zinc Corporation* v. *Westinghouse Electric Corporation* [1978] A.C. 547; *British Leyland Motor Corporation* v. *T.I. Silencers* [1979] F.S.R. 591.

[72] In this case or in relation to this issue a defendant does not have to make discovery by exchanging lists at all: Order 24, r. 2(3).

himself. Instead the proper practice is that he must take this ground of objection to production in clear terms in his list,[73] although it will be sufficient to state: "the production will to the best of my information and belief, tend to criminate me."[74]

One important exception to the privilege must be noted. Following the suggestions made by the House of Lords in *Rank Film Distributors Ltd.* v. *Video Information Centre*[75] the legislature moved swiftly to introduce a provision in the Supreme Court Bill restricting a defendant's privilege where the action is brought by a plaintiff alleging infringements of his patents or copyright. Although the provision was primarily aimed at restoring the full availability of the Anton Piller order in these circumstances it withdraws the privilege generally.

So now, where civil proceedings are brought in the High Court relating to infringement of intellectual property rights or for passing off then by s.72 of the Supreme Court Act 1981 a party cannot enjoy privilege on the grounds that to disclose information or documents would expose that party or his or her spouse to criminal proceedings or for the recovery of a penalty. This section should be read widely and therefore applies whether or not the criminal proceedings have already been commenced.[76]

Section 72(3) enables discovery or interrogatory orders to be made in intellectual property cases against a party without the answers being admissible in criminal proceedings brought against that party for related offences.[77]

3. *Privilege Relating to "Without Prejudice" Documents*

A joint privilege attaches to communications between parties which are made during negotiations to resolve a dispute. Documents brought into existence for this purpose containing concessions as part of an attempt to settle a dispute, may not be used subsequently to the prejudice of either party, and accordingly, an order for production in an action between the same or different parties on the same dispute will not be made.[78]

---

[73] *Spokes* v. *Grosvenor Hotel Co.* [1897] 2 Q.B. 124, 130; *National Association of Operative Plasterers* v. *Smithies* [1906] A.C. 434.

[74] *Lamb* v. *Munster* (1882) 10 Q.B.D. 10. See also *Triplex Safety Glass Co. Ltd.* v. *Lancegaye Safety Glass (1934) Ltd.* [1939] 2 K.B. 395 which concerns the same privilege in relation to interrogatories.

[75] [1982] A.C. 380, see especially Lord Russell of Killowen at 448.

[76] *Charles of the Ritz Group Ltd.* v. *Jory* [1986] F.S.R. 14.

[77] Except where the criminal proceedings against that party are for perjury or contempt of court: s.72(4).

[78] *Rush and Tompkins Ltd.* v. *Greater London Council* [1988] 3 All E.R. 737, H.L.; *Walker* v. *Wilsher* (1889) 23 Q.B.D. 335; *Rabin* v. *Mendoza & Co.* [1954] 1 W.L.R. 271.

The rule is based partly on public policy grounds since it is better for the parties to agree a compromise than to go ahead with a full-blown litigation and the existence of this privilege encourages moves towards a compromise. The rule is also partly based on an implied agreement between the parties.[79]

The existence of the privilege does not depend on the use of the actual phrase "without prejudice." The courts will readily draw the inference that attempts to settle a dispute are made on the basis that any negotiations are subject to this privilege.[80]

Conversely, the use of the words "without prejudice" does not necessarily or inevitably mean that the document will be privileged. The court will look at the document to determine its nature since only documents which are produced in circumstances where there is a dispute or there are negotiations on foot to settle a dispute will be protected by this privilege.[81] This does not mean that to be privileged the document must itself contain an offer but it must form part of negotiations.[82]

The privilege determines once agreement on a settlement has been reached, and the "without prejudice" documents may then be used to prove the terms of the agreement.[83]

4. *Former Privileges*

A word may be briefly said here about certain former privileges abolished for civil cases by the Civil Evidence Act 1968. There was an old common law rule that a party could not be compelled to produce his title deeds or other documents relating to his title to any real property. This rule was abrogated by section 16(1)(*b*) of the Act. The privilege whereby a party could not be compelled to produce any document relating solely to his own case and in no way tending to impeach that case or support the case of any opposing party was abrogated by section 16(2), and subsections (3) and (4) of section 16 removed privileges concerning evidence of marital communications and marital intercourse respectively.

5. *Public Interest Immunity (Crown Privilege)*

Production of documents may sometimes be refused on the ground of what used to be called Crown privilege, but which is

---

[79] *Per* Fox L.J. in *Cutts* v. *Head* [1984] Ch. 290 at 313.

[80] *Per* Megarry V.-C. in *Chocoladefabriken Lindt & Sprungli AG* v. *The Nestlé Co. Ltd.* [1978] R.P.C. 287. See the speech of Lord Griffiths in *Rush & Tompkins Ltd.* v. *Greater London Council and another* [1988] 3 All E.R. 737, (H.L.).

[81] *In re Daintrey, ex p. Holt* [1893] 2 Q.B. 116. However, once the court finds that the documents do enjoy this privilege it has no general discretion to admit them: *per* Megarry V.-C in *Chocoladefabriken Lindt, supra* at 289.

[82] *South Shropshire District Council* v. *Amos* [1986] 1 W.L.R. 1271, disapproving *Norwich Union Life Insurance Society* v. *Tony Waller Ltd.* (1984) 270 E.G. 42.

[83] *Tomlin* v. *Standard Telephones & Cables Ltd.* [1969] 1 W.L.R. 1378.

now more commonly and more accurately referred to as public interest immunity.[84] The objection that disclosure would be injurious to the public interest may be taken by the Crown directly if it is a party to the action. In other cases a party may take the objection acting on instructions from the appropriate government department,[85] or the Attorney-General may intervene directly where a party is otherwise willing to produce the relevant documents.[86] In any event, the matter is one of public interest and one that the judge himself can raise even if no objection to production has been taken formally.[87]

As will appear below, important state documents are obvious examples of communications which can enjoy immunity from production, but the immunity is not restricted to public official documents of a political or administrative character. The general principle is to be found in the speech of Lord Simon in *Duncan* v. *Cammell Laird & Co.*[88]

"The principle to be applied in every case is that documents otherwise relevant and liable to production must not be produced if the public interest requires that they should be withheld. This test may be found to be satisfied either (a) by having regard to the contents of the particular document, or (b) by the fact that the document belongs to a class which, on grounds of public interest, must as a class be withheld from production."

Generally speaking, if the matter comes within the scope of a particular government department or other public body, it will be appropriate for the objection to production to be taken by the minister or other political head of the department.[89] The objection will be in the form of an affidavit setting out the minister's contention that disclosure of the relevant documents would be injurious to the public interest, and if it is a "class" claim, the class to which the documents belong should be specified.[90] Before *Conway* v. *Rimmer*[91] it was thought that such a ministerial certificate in proper form was conclusive and

---

[84] For discussion of the terminology, see *Duncan* v. *Cammell Laird & Co. Ltd.* [1942] A.C. 624; *Rogers* v. *Secretary of State for the Home Department* [1973] A.C. 388; *Science Research Council* v. *Nasse* [1980] A.C. 1028.

[85] As in *Duncan* v. *Cammell Laird, supra.*

[86] As in *Burmah Oil Co. Ltd.* v. *Bank of England* [1980] A.C. 1090.

[87] *Duncan* v. *Cammell Laird, supra.*

[88] See [1942] A.C. 624, 636.

[89] *Alfred Crompton Amusement Machines Ltd.* v. *Commissioners of Customs and Excise* [1971] 2 All E.R. 843 (Eveleigh J.).

[90] *Re Grosvenor Hotel, London* [1964] Ch. 464; *Merricks* v. *Nott-Bower* [1965] 1 Q.B. 57.

[91] [1968] A.C. 910.

binding on the court,[92] but in that case the House of Lords declared that the question whether the public interest required the withholding of the relevant documents was ultimately for the court to decide. While full weight should be given to the minister's view, particularly where his reasons for objecting to production are of a character outside the scope of judicial experience,[93] the court is not necessarily obliged to accept his view of the public interest. In an appropriate case therefore, the court may review the objection.[94] When undertaking such a review, the court has to balance the competing interests of preventing harm to the state or the public service by disclosure and preventing frustration of the administration of justice by withholding disclosure, and it may inspect the documents concerned privately in order to determine where the balance of public interest lies.[95]

The application of the principles set out in *Duncan* v. *Cammell Laird* has led to a considerable body of case-law and some difference of opinion among the judges. In one case,[96] for example, Lord Hailsham indicated his disapproval of an attempt to define rigidly the nature of the public interest sufficient for the privilege to apply, and declared that "the categories of public interest are not closed, and must alter from time to time whether by restriction or extension as social conditions and social legislation develop." However, in *Science Research Council* v. *Nasse*[97] Lord Scarman deprecated efforts to extend the immunity beyond the protection of "information the secrecy of which is essential to the proper working of the government of the state," and proceeded to list specific types of public interest sufficient for immunity. There is then some lack of judicial agreement on the general approach to public interest immunity, but certain points do emerge clearly from the authorities.

Documents containing important state secrets will generally be protected under Lord Simon's first principle. Where the

---

[92] For discussion, see *Cross on Evidence* (6th ed., 1985), p. 411.

[93] *Conway* v. *Rimmer, supra.*

[94] See also *Sethia* v. *Stern, The Times,* November 4, 1987, showing that the contents of a certificate (*i.e.* the facts and opinions put forward in it) can be challenged by the parties.

[95] *Burmah Oil Co. Ltd.* v. *Bank of England, supra,* restating the principle set out in *Conway* v. *Rimmer*; *Campbell* v. *Tameside M.B.C.* [1982] Q.B. 1065.

[96] *D.* v. *N.S.P.C.C.* [1978] A.C. 171, 230.

[97] [1980] A.C. 1028 at p. 1087. Lord Scarman also rejected the suggested power in the court to refuse disclosure where a confidential relationship exists and disclosure would be in breach of some ethical or social value involving the public interest: see Lord Edmund-Davies in *D.* v. *N.S.P.C.C., supra,* at p. 245. Such a power would have far-reaching effects, and seems difficult to reconcile with the repeated judicial denials that confidentiality is not a ground of privilege: see below.

claim is that disclosure of the *contents* of particular documents would be injurious to the interests of national security[98] or of good diplomatic relations,[99] the claim will almost certainly be accepted. In *Conway* v. *Rimmer* Lord Reid commented that "cases would be very rare in which it could be proper to question the view of the responsible minister that it would be contrary to the public interest to make public the contents of a particular document."[1] In relation to claims for immunity for *classes* of documents, the test is whether secrecy for such classes is necessary for the proper functioning of the public service.[2] At one time protection under this heading was given extensively to government departments in respect of a number of their functions, including cases in which the documents in question were of a quite routine nature. For example, immunity from production was successfully claimed by the Home Office for reports by doctors and police officers concerning the mental state of a prisoner awaiting trial,[3] by the Inland Revenue for a company's balance-sheets,[4] and by the Minister of War for a soldier's medical sheet[5] and the reports of a Ministry-appointed body trying to effect reconciliations between servicemen and their estranged spouses.[6]

However, these claims were made and succeeded at a time when the courts regarded ministerial certificates as conclusive on the question of whether the public interest required non-disclosure. As indicated above, *Conway* v. *Rimmer* marked a change of judicial attitude on this question. Subsequent cases have shown that the courts are now much more willing to evaluate a "class" claim for themselves, even where the documents are concerned with matters of policy rather than routine administration. For example, communications between ministers or between senior civil servants on important matters of government policy have often been cited as examples of a class of documents requiring immunity from production. In *Conway*

---

[98] *Asiatic Petroleum Co. Ltd.* v. *Anglo-Persian Oil Co. Ltd.* [1916] 1 K.B. 822; *Duncan* v. *Cammell Laird, supra.*

[99] *Chatterton* v. *Secretary of State for India* [1895] 2 Q.B. 189; *M. Isaacs & Sons Ltd.* v. *Cook* [1925] 2 K.B. 391. And by analogy the court will recognise a public interest of the United Kingdom in refusing to order disclosure of documents addressed to or emanating from a foreign sovereign state, where the documents concern an international dispute and the rights of the foreign sovereign: *Buttes Gas and Oil Co.* v. *Hammer (No. 3)* [1980] 3 W.L.R. 668.

[1] [1968] A.C. 910 at p. 943.

[2] *Duncan* v. *Cammell Laird, supra,* at p. 642.

[3] *Ellis* v. *Home Office* [1953] 2 Q.B. 135.

[4] *Re Joseph Hargreaves Ltd.* [1900] 1 Ch. 347.

[5] *Anthony* v. *Anthony* (1919) 35 T.L.R. 559.

[6] *Broome* v. *Broome* [1955] P. 190.

v. *Rimmer* itself (a case concerned with routine reports, production of which was ordered by the House of Lords after a private inspection), Lord Reid stated that Cabinet papers and similar documents should not be disclosed because of the need to prevent the growth of "ill-informed or captious public or political criticism" and the need to ensure candour of communication in the public service and this would "also apply to all documents concerned with policy making within departments."[7] Now, however, the courts have demonstrated their willingness to scrutinise even claims for documents in this class[8] where the documents are very likely to give substantial support to the plaintiff and their absence might deprive him of the means to present his case properly.[9]

In *Burmah Oil Co.* v. *Bank of England*[10] the plaintiff company were seeking to avoid a contract made with the defendant bank for the sale and purchase of the plaintiffs' large and valuable shareholding in the British Petroleum Co. In the course of the litigation the defendants objected to producing a number of documents, some of which were described as a class consisting of ministerial communications on matters of government policy relating to the difficulties of the plaintiff company, while a second class consisted of communications between senior civil servants on the same matters of policy. The House of Lords refused to order production of the documents in either class, but did so only after inspecting the documents privately[11] and deciding that they did not contain material necessary for disposing fairly of the case. The speeches in this case emphasise that there is no rule of law that a claim by the Crown to withhold from production a class of documents of a high level of public importance is conclusive. The inspection by the court in this case of the documents revealed that their significance was not such as to override the public service objections to their production. In some cases where the nature of the information to be kept confidential is reasonably clear, a judicial inspection will presumably serve no useful purpose.

---

[7] [1968] A.C. 910, 952.

[8] See *Air Canada* v. *Secretary of State for Trade* [1983] 2 A.C. 394, where Lord Fraser was of the opinion that even Cabinet minutes might, in an appropriate case, be disclosed. See also *Re HIV Haemophiliac Litigation* (1990) 140 N.L.J. 1349.

[9] For a recent example of a successful "class claim" see *Evans* v. *Chief Constable of Surrey* [1989] 2 All E.R. 594 where it was held that it would be contrary to the public interest for reports which were sent by the police to the Director of Public Prosecutions to be disclosed in civil proceedings.

[10] [1980] A.C. 1090.

[11] See Order 24, r. 13(2) which gives the court power to inspect documents for which privilege is claimed.

The court's decision will be limited to balancing the two types of public interest, as indicated above.

In *Air Canada* v. *Secretary of State for Trade*[11a] clearer guidelines were laid down by the House of Lords as to when the court should exercise its discretion to inspect. The plaintiff, an international airline, brought an action against the Secretary of State alleging that he had acted unlawfully and *ultra vires* in directing the British Airports Authority to increase their landing charges at Heathrow airport. The plaintiff requested production of certain ministerial documents which included communications between government Ministers and minutes of ministerial meetings relating to the formation of government policy and for which the Secretary of State claimed privilege on the grounds of public interest immunity. The plaintiff requested the court to inspect the documents stating that they were necessary for fairly disposing of the case. The House of Lords rejected the plaintiff's claim, holding that before the court will embark on an inspection of documents for which public interest immunity is claimed the party seeking disclosure has to show that the information sought was likely to support his case or damage his adversary's. There must be some concrete grounds giving rise to a belief that the information will materially assist the party's case which takes the matter "beyond a mere fishing expedition." This should be the approach taken by the court both at the inspection stage and at the later production stage. The House of Lords, in emphasising the adversarial nature of civil proceedings, rejected the approach (taken by Bingham J. at first instance) that the court should inspect if the documents would assist the court in eliciting the true facts of the case regardless of whether they would assist one party or the other.[12]

One class of documents for which protection is still readily given concerns sources of information. In some cases government departments, or non-governmental agencies exercising public functions, depend for the efficient discharge of their functions on information requested from or volunteered by outside bodies or members of the public. Where the court takes the view that such information would cease to be forthcoming if it were not protected from disclosure, production of it will not be compelled on the ground that immunity is necessary for the proper functioning of the public service. Applying this

---

11a [1983] 2 A.C. 394.
12 See also *Continental Reinsurance Corporation (U.K.) Ltd.* v. *Pine Top Insurance Ltd.* [1986] 1 Lloyd's Law Reports 8.

principle, protection has been afforded to the statements and identity of police informers,[13] to information supplied to the Gaming Board concerning the suitability of an applicant for a gaming licence,[14] to material supplied by businessmen to the customs and excise authorities concerning the value of certain machines for purchase tax,[15] and to a complaint by a member of the public to the N.S.P.C.C. concerning alleged child abuse.[16] However, not all claims to protect confidential sources of information succeed. The House of Lords has reiterated several times in recent years that confidentiality by itself is not a ground of privilege,[17] although it is material in considering whether production should be ordered where some other ground of objection is put forward. In *Norwich Pharmacal* v. *Commissioners of Customs and Excise*[18] immunity was refused to documents disclosing the names of persons wrongfully importing drugs in breach of the plaintiffs' patent, on the ground that dishonest traders did not deserve protection, and that honest traders would not be deterred from giving information to the customs authorities by the thought that the identity of wrongdoers might be disclosed. In *Science Research Council* v. *Nasse*[19] the House of Lords refused public interest immunity to confidential reports on employees applying for promotion or transfer and who subsequently alleged discrimination against themselves, on the ground that the matter was essentially one of private right, and not concerned with information necessary to the proper working of the government of the state.

In *British Steel Corporation* v. *Granada Television Ltd*[20] the rule was reaffirmed that journalists have no immunity based on public interest against disclosure of their sources of information. The House of Lords was emphatic in this case that *at common law* journalists are in no better positions than priests, doctors, bankers and other recipients of confidential information, none of whom has a privilege to refuse to answer questions where the interests of justice require those questions to be answered. Shortly after this decision, section 10 of the

---

[13] *Marks* v. *Beyfus* (1890) 25 Q.B.D. 494.

[14] *Rogers* v. *Secretary of State* [1973] A.C. 388. See also *Neilson* v. *Laugharne* [1981] 2 W.L.R. 537.

[15] *Alfred Crompton Amusement Machines Ltd.* v. *Commissioners of Customs and Excise* [1974] A.C. 405. See also *Lonrho Ltd.* v. *Shell Petroleum Co. Ltd.* [1980] 1 W.L.R. 627.

[16] *D.* v. *N.S.P.C.C.* [1978] A.C. 171. See also *Gaskin* v. *Liverpool City Council* [1980] 1 W.L.R. 1549.

[17] The leading pronouncement is that of Lord Cross in the *Alfred Crompton* case: [1974] A.C. 405, 429–430.

[18] [1974] A.C. 133.

[19] [1980] A.C. 1028.

[20] [1980] 3 W.L.R. 774.

Contempt of Court Act 1981 was enacted which provides as follows:

> "No court may require a person to disclose, nor is any person guilty of contempt of court for refusing to disclose, the source of information contained in a publication for which he is responsible, unless it be established to the satisfaction of the court that disclosure is necessary in the interests of justice or national security or for the prevention of disorder or crime."

In *X Ltd.* v. *Morgan-Grampian Ltd.*[21] the House of Lords held that a journalist and his publisher could be ordered to disclose the notes of a telephone conversation in which an unidentified source gave confidential information to the journalist because the court was satisfied that disclosure was "necessary in the interests of justice" in order to help identify the source. The House of Lords held that the phrase "the interests of justice" is not to be construed narrowly to mean "necessary for the administration of justice in the course of legal proceedings in a court of law. It will be in "the interests of justice" within the meaning of section 10 "that persons should be enabled to exercise important legal rights and to protect themselves from serious legal wrongs whether or not resort to legal proceedings in a court of law will be necessary to attain these objectives."[22]

In order to determine whether disclosure is necessary in these cases a balancing exercise is to be carried out by the court between the public importance on the one hand attached to the preservation of the confidentiality of sources which is enshrined in the statutory prohibition against ordering disclosure and, on the other hand, the relative public importance of the four interests listed in the section. So, in any particular case the court is not permitted to order the disclosure of a source unless it is satisfied that one of the four interests is of "such preponderating importance" that the ban on disclosure "really needs to be overridden."[23]

It has been held that statements made during the course of a private investigation by the police into alleged police misconduct pursuant to section 49 of the Police Act 1964 are covered by public interest immunity.[24] However, where statements are

---

[21] [1990] 1 All E.R. 1.

[22] *Ibid. per* Lord Bridge at 9. *Cf. Handmade Films (Productions) Ltd.* v. *Express Newspapers plc* [1986] F.S.R. 463.

[23] *Ibid. per* Lord Oliver at 16.

[24] *Neilson* v. *Laugharne* [1981] Q.B. 736; *Hehir* v. *Commissioner of Police for the Metropolis* [1982] 1 W.L.R. 715.

made to the police in circumstances where there is both a section 49 inquiry and a general investigation by the police into, for instance, a violent death, it is the dominant purpose for which the statements were taken which determines whether or not the statements can be ordered for production. If the dominant purpose is a general investigation then there are no public interest considerations in withholding the statements since the persons giving them will have expected that they might well be disclosed in the future.[25]

Since public interest immunity exists for the protection of the public it cannot be waived by the parties to the proceedings.[26] However, it is possible that in certain circumstances the immunity may evaporate if the persons involved in giving and receiving the information have given the relevant consents to its disclosure.[27] It is, of course, for the court in any particular case to decide whether public interest immunity should attach weighing the competing public interests in the balance, but one factor which it can take into account is whether the immunity has already been eroded by partial disclosure.[28]

Finally, it should be noted that the provisions of Order 24 are stated (in rule 15) to be without prejudice to any rule of law which authorises or requires documents to be withheld on the ground that their disclosure would be injurious to the public interest. Accordingly, if the claim to immunity is made out, production of the relevant documents will not be ordered and oral evidence of them at the trial will also be excluded.

6. *Documents which are the Property of a Third Person*

As stated earlier, a party is obliged by Order 24, r. 2(1) to make discovery of all documents which are or have been in his "possession, custody or power." Possession here means legal possession, as distinct from mere corporeal holding,[29] and power means "a presently enforceable legal right to obtain from whoever actually holds the document inspection of it without the need to obtain the consent of anyone else."[30]

---

[25] *Peach* v. *Commissioner for Police of the Metropolis* [1986] Q.B. 1064.

[26] *Per* Lord Simon in *R.* v. *Lewes Justices, ex p. the Gaming Board of Great Britain* [1973] A.C. 388 at 407.

[27] See *Hehir* v. *Commissioner of Police for the Metropolis* [1982] 1 W.L.R. 715 at 722 (Lawton L.J.) and 723 (Brightman L.J.); *Multi Guarantee Co. Ltd.* v. *Cavalier Insurance Co. Ltd., The Times,* June 24, 1986.

[28] *Multi Guarantee Co. Ltd.* v. *Cavalier Insurance Co. Ltd.* (*supra*).

[29] Supreme Court Practice 1982, para. 24/2/3.

[30] *Lonrho Ltd.* v. *Shell Petroleum Co. Ltd.* [1980] 1 W.L.R. 627, 635, *per* Lord Diplock. See also *B.* v. *B. (Matrimonial Proceedings: Discovery)* [1978] Fam. 181, 186 (Dunn J.).

Therefore, it has been held that documents in the possession of subsidiary companies were not in the "power" of the parent company where the subsidiary companies had independent boards of directors who refused to disclose the documents after considering what was in the best interests of their companies.[31] It has also been held that company documents are not necessarily in the power of its majority shareholder. For this to be the case it would have to be shown that the company was under the unfettered control of the majority shareholder and not that this person was simply the dominant figure in the running of the company's business.[32]

The word "custody" was added to the terms of the rule in 1964, with the effect that a party must also disclose documents which he holds or has held physically even though he is not the owner or sole owner of them. According to the rules of Order 24 the party making discovery is obliged to produce for inspection all the documents disclosed in his list unless he can claim one of the privileges or immunities which are discussed above. However, the court still has a discretion whether to order inspection, and, in the exercise of such discretion, it will have regard to any prejudice to persons having a right to the documents in question and objecting to their production. Moreover, the court will not make an order either for discovery or inspection which is premature or not necessary for disposing fairly of the cause or matter or for saving costs.[33]

Thus it is open to a party who discloses a document in his physical control to object to produce it on the grounds that it does not belong to him, and that the owner does not consent to its production. Where such an objection is made it is thought that the authorities, decided under the former rule, dealing with documents not belonging to the party making discovery, may be relevant and helpful in assisting the court in the exercise of its discretion. Thus discovery would not formerly be ordered against a person holding documents merely as agent or trustee for another person not a party to the action and who objected to their production.[34] A person holding documents in the joint possession of himself and another would not generally be ordered to produce them unless the co-

---

[31] *Lonrho* v. *Shell Petroleum* (*supra*).
[32] *Re Tecnion Investments Ltd.* [1985] B.C.L.C. 434.
[33] Supreme Court Practice, para. 24/2/4, approved in *Alfred Crompton Amusement Machines Ltd.* v. *Commissioners of Customs and Excise (No. 2)* [1974] A.C. 405, 429 (Lord Cross of Chelsea).
[34] See, for example, *Procter* v. *Smiles* (1886) 2 T.L.R. 474; *Chantrey Martin* v. *Martin* [1953] 2 Q.B. 286.

owner consented.[35] A clerk or servant could not be compelled to make and exhibit copies of documents which were the property of his employer in answer to interrogatories as to their contents.[36]

Production and Inspection

A party who has served a list of documents on any other party, whether he has done so as part of the process of "automatic" discovery under rule 2 or because he has been ordered to do so under rule 3, must allow the other party to inspect[37] and take copies of all the documents other than those which he objects to producing. To this end he must, together with the list, serve a notice stating a time within seven days when and a place where the documents may be inspected (rule 9). Again, as we have seen, a party may be bound to produce a document because he has referred to it in his pleading, particulars or an affidavit and therefore have been required to serve a similar notice under rule 10. The court can make an order for discovery of documents referred to in pleadings or affidavits notwithstanding that those documents are not in the "possession, custody or power" of the party against whom the order is sought. The court has a discretion whether or not to make an order for production and inspection under rule 11(1) and the absence of possession, custody or power in some cases will be a good reason for the court not to exercise its discretion.[38] Failure in either case to serve the requisite notice offering inspection, or an offer of inspection at an unreasonable time or place, entitles the other side to apply to a master for an order to produce the documents for inspection (rule 11). And a flagrant defiance of these rules may be dealt with under the wide, and if necessary penal, provisions of rule 16, *infra*. Also under rule 11 an application may be made for the production of documents which a party objects to producing and the master will rule on the grounds of objection; furthermore the master has a discretionary power to order inspection to be given to a party who would not otherwise be entitled to ask for it—*e.g.* to a plaintiff by a third party and vice versa—provided that the application be supported by an affidavit specifying or describ-

---

[35] *Hadley* v. *McDougall* (1872) L.R. 7 Ch. 312; *Kearsley* v. *Philips* (1882) 10 Q.B.D. 36, 40, 43 (C.A.); but see *Rattenberry* v. *Monro* (1910) 103 L.T. 560.

[36] *Balfour* v. *Tillett* [1913] W.N. 70.

[37] This includes examining tape recordings with suitable equipment. *Grant* v. *South Western and County Properties, supra.*

[38] *Rafidian Bank* v. *Agom Universal Sugar Trading Co. Ltd.* [1987] 1 W.L.R. 1606.

ing the documents which the applicant wishes to inspect and stating his belief that the other party has them and that they are relevant. If a party has disclosed the existence of a document as a result of an order for specific discovery under rule 7, he becomes liable to produce it under rule 10 as a document referred to in an affidavit. Moreover, at any stage of the proceedings the master may order any party to produce any relevant document to him, and may deal with it when produced as he thinks right (rule 12). If objection is taken to the production of a document, either to another party or to the master, on the ground of privilege, irrelevance or any other ground, the master may look at the document, before formally ordering its "production," for the purpose of deciding whether the objection is valid (rule 13(2)). All the before-mentioned powers of the master are subject to two overriding limitations: he must only exercise them in so far as he is of opinion that his order is necessary either for disposing fairly of the cause or matter or for saving costs (rule 13(1)); and he must not order production of, or even look at, a document if a rule of law authorises or requires it to be withheld on the ground that its disclosure would be injurious to the public interest (rule 15).[39]

The court also has an inherent jurisdiction to prevent the abuse of its own process and as Lord Denning M.R. said in *Riddick* v. *Thames Board Mills Ltd.*[40]

"[a] party who seeks discovery of documents gets it on condition that he will make use of them only for the purposes of that action, and no other purpose."

Therefore, if the court apprehends that there is a real risk of a party using his right to discovery for a collateral purpose, the court has power to impose restrictions on inspection in order to prevent or discourage him from doing so.[41] For instance, it can refuse an order for inspection except on an undertaking given by the party seeking the order.[42] In addition, any action which is based on the misuse of a document is liable to be struck out as an abuse of the process of the court.

The party producing any book or document may seal or cover up any part which he can truthfully say is not material to any issue in the action.[43] No order will be made for inspection

---

[39] See the discussion of public interest immunity, *supra.*
[40] [1977] Q.B. 881 at 896.
[41] *Church of Scientology* v. *D.H.S.S.* [1979] 1 W.L.R. 723.
[42] See p. 259.
[43] *Blanc* v. *Burrows* (1896) 12 T.L.R. 521; *Pardy's Mozambique Syndicate Ltd.* v. *Alexander* [1903] 1 Ch. 91.

of a document which is not relevant to any question in the action, even though it has been disclosed in the list.[44] It is not an answer to an application for production of documents that they are in the hands of a party's former solicitors, who claim a lien over them for costs, and that he disputes the bill; but the order for production will contain liberty to apply in case he really cannot obtain the documents.[45]

An inspecting party has always been entitled to make a copy of any document produced to him.[46] Now, by rule 11A any party who is entitled to inspect any documents may, at or before the time when inspection takes place, serve on a party who is required to produce such documents for inspection a notice requiring him to supply a true copy of any such document. The notice shall contain an undertaking by the inspecting party to pay any reasonable charges. Then, the party on whom such a notice is served must, within seven days of receiving the notice, supply the copy requested together with an account of reasonable charges.[47] If one party fails to supply another party with a copy of a document under this rule then the court may, on the application of either party, make such order as to the supply of that document as it thinks fit.[48] A party, once inspection has taken place, cannot correct a mistake in the list so as to belatedly claim privilege for a document mistakenly disclosed and prevent copies being taken. It is clear from Order 24, r. 9 that taking copies is an ancillary and incidental right to inspection and once inspection has been made it would be illogical to prevent copies being taken.[49]

It is on an application under rule 11 that the validity of any claim of privilege from inspection will be generally tested. The master may in every case inspect the document himself, if he thinks fit.[50] Otherwise the only question is whether the party has in his list said enough about the document to entitle him to refuse production on the ground of privilege—unless the master is satisfied that the party has misrepresented or misconceived its effect.[51]

---

[44] *Hope* v. *Brash* [1897] 2 Q.B. 188; *Angell* v. *John Bull Ltd.* (1915) 31 T.L.R. 175.

[45] *Lewis* v. *Powell* [1897] 1 Ch. 678.

[46] *Ormerod, Grierson & Co.* v. *St. George's Ironworks* [1905] 1 Ch. 505.

[47] Rule 11A(2).

[48] Rule 11A(3).

[49] *Re Briamore Manufacturing Ltd.* [1986] 1 W.L.R. 1429, where Hoffman J. expressed the opinion that it might be possible in certain circumstances to amend the list *before* inspection. But see p. 269. See also *Mutter* v. *Eastern and Midlands Railway Co.* (1888) 38 Ch.D. 92.

[50] Rule 13(2); *Ehrmann* v. *Ehrmann* [1896] 2 Ch. 826.

[51] *Roberts* v. *Oppenheim* (1884) 26 Ch.D. 724.

Any party to the action may be ordered to attend at any stage of the proceedings for the purpose of producing—subject to a claim of privilege—any document named in the order.[52] A person not a party to the action may also be ordered to attend and produce specified documents for the purpose of a proceeding,[53] and such an order has the effect of a *subpoena duces tecum*, but the rule does not confer a right of discovery against persons not parties to the action.[54]

In a case where the documents to be inspected are highly technical, specialist documents and especially where there is a great volume of them, the court will allow a party to appoint someone to carry out the inspection who is not a lawyer acting on behalf of that party in the litigation. The discovering party has to show that there is a need to appoint this person, because, for example, he has some expertise in the matters in dispute. However, the opposing party can object by showing that there is a real risk that the proposed person would use the material obtained on inspection for a collateral purpose and in breach of the implied obligation of confidentiality.[55]

Where there are several defendants each one is entitled, after he has pleaded, to have free, on request, a copy of the list of documents, and any affidavit in support of it, served on the plaintiff by each of the others.[56] A similar rule applies in favour of a plaintiff against whom, together with others, a counterclaim is made.

A party who serves a list of documents is himself deemed to have been served with a notice to produce at the trial all the documents in his list which he states are in his possession, custody or power.[57] And a party upon whom a list is served is, unless he gives notice or has already pleaded to the contrary, deemed to admit the authenticity of all the documents set out in the list.[58] In consequence of this rule notices to admit and produce documents are now rarely needed.

---

[52] Ord. 38, r. 13; *Straker* v. *Reynolds* (1889) 22 Q.B.D. 262; *Elder* v. *Carter* (1890) 25 Q.B.D. 194.

[53] Ord. 38, r. 13.

[54] See cases in note 52, *supra*.

[55] *Davies* v. *Eli Lilly & Co.* [1987] 1 W.L.R. 428 where a medical writer and journalist was allowed to inspect the documents of the defendant pharmaceutical companies, which were very numerous and were of a scientific and medical nature. Here though, because of the exceptional circumstances of the case, the person appointed by the plaintiff to inspect should give an express undertaking to the court to preserve the confidentiality of the defendants' documents and which restricted his ability to use any of the material disclosed. See also Ord. 24, r. 14A. See also *Church of Scientology* v. *D.H.S.S.* [1979] 1 W.L.R. 723.

[56] Ord. 24, r. 6(1), (2).

[57] Ord. 27, r. 4(3).

[58] *Ibid*. r. 4(1), (2).

Copies of business books properly verified by affidavit may be ordered to be produced for inspection if production of the originals is, in the opinion of the master, unnecessary.[59]

Discovery before Action in Personal Injury Cases

Section 31 of the Administration of Justice Act 1970 gave a new power to the courts. This power, which is now contained in section 33(2) of the Supreme Court Act 1981, enables a person, before he brings an action, to apply to the court for discovery of documents. A person who appears to be likely to be a party to subsequent proceedings in which a claim in respect of personal injuries to a person or in respect of a person's death is likely to be made, may apply for an order that a person who appears to the court to be likely to be a party to the proceedings should disclose whether he has in his possession, custody or power any documents relevant to an issue arising out of the claim and should produce those documents.

The application must be made by originating summons supported by an affidavit stating the grounds on which it is alleged that the applicant and the defendant to the summons are likely to be parties to subsequent proceedings and specifying or describing the documents and showing, if practicable by reference to any pleading intended to be served in the proceedings, that the documents are relevant to an issue arising or likely to arise out of a claim for personal injuries. A copy of the affidavit must be served with the summons. No person may be compelled to produce any document which he could not be compelled to produce if the subsequent proceedings had already been begun (Order 24, r. 7A).

It is important to note that this power is applicable only to cases in respect of personal injuries or death. Lord Denning M.R. in *Dunning* v. *United Liverpool Hospitals Board of Governors* stated that one of the objects of the section is to enable the plaintiff to find out before he starts proceedings whether he has a good cause of action or not. That object would be defeated if he had to show in advance that he already had a good cause of action before he saw the documents. This will, therefore, necessarily entail a more liberal construction of the phrase "likely to be a party to subsequent proceedings" in section 31(2) since the potential plaintiff will often be in the position, as in *Dunning* itself, where the decision whether or not to commence proceedings at all will be dependent on the

---

[59] Ord. 24, r. 14.

outcome of the discovery. Lord Denning was in favour of construing "likely" as "may" or "may well be made" whereas James L.J. preferred the stricter approach of asking whether there was a reasonable prospect of the party being made a party to subsequent proceedings.[60]

Disclosure will be ordered if the prospective plaintiff has stated in an affidavit his own knowledge of how the accident occurred and shows that production of the documents is likely to determine whether litigation will be commenced. In *Shaw v. Vauxhall Motors Ltd.*[61] the Court of Appeal ordered discovery of the maintenance records of a fork-lift truck which the applicant had been driving and which he alleged had defective brakes, it being conceded that if the records showed the machine not to be defective, a claim for damages would not be brought. The Court of Appeal made it clear that it would be preferable for the plaintiff to put his account of the accident in an affidavit or other written form which could subsequently be used at the trial.

Where the plaintiff is legally aided there are special grounds for saying that it is desirable and in the public interest that early disclosure should take place where the material to be disclosed would almost certainly decide whether the action be abandoned or commenced.

The power to order production of documents before action is discretionary in the sense that the court can decline to make the order if it thinks that the order is unnecessary or oppressive, and section 35(1) of the Supreme Court Act 1981 provides that the court shall not make an order under section 33 if it considers that compliance with the order, if made, would be likely to be injurious to the public interest.[62] Where an order is made under section 33(2), the court has a further discretion to order disclosure to the applicant himself, or, on conditions, to any medical, legal or other professional adviser of the applicant.[63]

Discovery against Non-Parties: Action for Discovery

Discovery as a general rule is only available against a person who is a party to the proceedings, and it is improper to join a

---

[60] Stamp L.J., dissenting, was concerned that the section would be used for fishing expeditions and was not in favour of ordering discovery unless the grounds for bringing proceedings had already been made by the applicant or failing that the "fishing expedition [should] only . . . have the approval of the court if the court is persuaded on the facts before it that the fisherman is likely to find a worthwhile and catchable fish."

[61] [1974] 1 W.L.R. 1035.

[62] *Taylor v. Anderton, The Times*, October 21, 1986.

[63] Reversing *McIvor v. Southern Health and Social Services Board* [1978] 1 W.L.R. 757.

person as a party merely for the purpose of obtaining discovery against him.[64] If information or documents in the possession of a person are required, the proper procedure is to call him as a witness to give oral testimony or to serve a *subpoena duces tecum*. To this rule there are, however, three exceptions.

First, in *Norwich Pharmacal Co.* v. *Customs and Excise Commissioners* an action was allowed to be brought specifically for discovery.[65] The House of Lords held that where a person through no fault of his own, and voluntarily or as a matter of duty "gets mixed up in the tortious acts of others *so as to facilitate* their wrongdoing he may incur no personal liability but he comes under a duty to assist the person who has been wronged by giving him full information and disclosing the identity of the wrongdoers . . . justice requires that he should co-operate in righting the wrong if he unwittingly facilitates its perpetration."[66] Applying this principle, the House of Lords ordered the disclosure of documents identifying the importers of a chemical compound in respect of which the appellants held a patent which they alleged was being infringed by illicit imports of the compound from abroad.

A limitation on the principle laid down in *Norwich Pharmacal* itself is that an action for discovery will not lie against a stranger who is uninvolved with the wrongdoing and did not facilitate its commission, merely because he can give information as to the identity of the wrongdoer without which the plaintiff is unable to proceed.[67] "A person injured in a road accident might know that a bystander had taken the number of the car which ran him down and have no other means of tracing the driver. Or a person might know that a particular person is in possession of a libellous letter which he has good reason to believe defames him but the author of which he cannot discover . . . it would not be proper in either case to order discovery in order that the person who has suffered damage might be able to find and sue the wrongdoer."[68]

In *X Ltd.* v. *Morgan-Grampian Ltd.*[69] the plaintiffs obtained an *ex parte* injunction preventing a magazine publishing an article which contained confidential information given to a journalist by an unidentified person during a telephone conversation.

---

[64] *Douihech* v. *Findlay* [1990] 1 W.L.R. 269.
[65] [1974] A.C. 133. See also *RCA Corporation* v. *Reddingtons Rare Records* [1974] 1 W.L.R. 1445 and *Loose* v. *Williamson* [1978] 1 W.L.R. 639.
[66] *Ibid.* p. 175.
[67] *Ricci* v. *Chow* [1987] 3 W.L.R. 293.
[68] [1974] A.C. 133, 174.
[69] [1990] 1 All E.R. 1.

There was a strong inference that the information given to the journalist had been obtained from a stolen draft plan belonging to the plaintiffs, and the publication of this information would have resulted in serious harm to the plaintiffs. Therefore, the plaintiffs in addition sought disclosure of the journalist's notes since these would probably identify the informant and the plaintiffs could then take action to prevent any recurrence. The House of Lords was of the opinion that the journalist and the publishers were within the *Norwich Pharmacal* principle since the plaintiffs were here seeking the identity of the informant to enable them to take the necessary steps to protect themselves from other tortious dissemination of confidential information.[70] Lord Bridge said:

> "Just as the commissioners in the *Norwich* case were, in Lord Reid's phrase, 'mixed up' in the tortious acts of others from the moment they received the infringing goods tortiously imported, so the defendants here were 'mixed up' in the tortious acts of the source from the moment [the journalist] in the course of his employment by the publishers received the confidential information tortiously disclosed."[71]

Secondly, where a corporation is a party to proceedings and has an order for discovery made against it the court does have jurisdiction to require its servants and agents to make discovery on its behalf.[72]

Thirdly, in any proceedings in which there is a claim for damages in respect of personal injuries or death, the Supreme Court Act 1981, section 34, gives the court power to order a person who is not a party to the proceedings to give discovery of documents in his possession, custody or power which are relevant to an issue arising out of the claim for damages.[73] Any party to the proceedings may apply for such an order by

---

[70] In fact this was strictly unnecessary since their Lordships held that the journalist and the magazine publishers were not in the position of mere witnesses since they had already been properly impleaded as defendants in the claims for interlocutory injunctions to restrain the publication of material imparted to them in breach of confidence: [1990] 1 All E.R. 1 at 5, *per* Lord Bridge.

[71] It is to be noted that there is no discussion of whether the defendants *facilitated* the wrongdoing though by their original intention of publishing the confidential information the defendants may have been assisting and furthering the breach of confidence.

[72] *Harrington* v. *Polytechnic of North London* [1984] 1 W.L.R. 1293, applying *Dummer* v. *Chippenham Corporation* (1807) 14 Ves.Jun. 245.

[73] See, *e.g. Walker* v. *Eli Lilly & Co., The Times*, May 1, 1986 where Hirst J. expressed the hope that health authorities and medical practitioners would respond readily and promptly to any requests for disclosure so that unnecessary expense and delay could be avoided.

summons in the action, directed to the person against whom the order is sought and supported by affidavit. The summons must be served on such person and on every other party to the proceedings. The order for disclosure may be made conditional on the applicant giving security for costs or on other terms, but cannot require the disclosure of privileged documents (Order 24, r. 7A).

The principal value of this procedure is that it permits a plaintiff in a personal injuries claim to obtain discovery before trial of hospital records relating to his treatment. However, it is not restricted to those circumstances, and an order may be made in any proceedings in which a claim "in respect of" personal injuries is made. These words are broadly construed to cover a case in which the nature and extent of personal injuries are an essential element in the plaintiff's claim, even if the cause of action is not in fact for damages for personal injuries. In *Paterson* v. *Chadwick*,[74] Boreham J. ordered discovery of hospital records relating to the plaintiff's treatment in an action by the plaintiff against her former solicitor for negligence in prosecuting a claim on her behalf against the hospital concerned. The claim against the solicitor was connected with and related to her personal injuries and was therefore a claim "in respect of" personal injuries.

It is no answer to an application for an order under section 34(2) that the documents could be obtained from a non-party by the issue of a writ of *subpoena duces tecum* at trial. This is because the power is to be exercised by the court so as to achieve the proper administration of justice and the interests of justice are not served by forcing one party to delay the full preparation of his case until after the trial has begun. Also the disclosure of relevant documents at an early stage may lead the parties to consider a settlement of the action.[75]

The power to order discovery against a non-party, like the power to order discovery before action, originated in the Administration of Justice Act 1970. Similar principles govern the exercise of both powers so that, for example, discovery by a non-party may be ordered to be made to the applicant himself, or, on conditions, to his professional advisers[76] and section 35(1) of the Supreme Court Act 1981 prevents an order under section 34, as in the case of section 33, if the court considers

---

[74] [1974] 1 W.L.R. 890; *cf. Ackbar* v. *C.F. Green & Co. Ltd.* [1975] Q.B. 582.

[75] *O'Sullivan* v. *Herdmans Ltd.* [1987] 3 All E.R. 129.

[76] Supreme Court Act 1981, s.34(2)(*b*). Note also that *Church of Scientology* v. *D.H.S.S.* [1979] 1 W.L.R. 723 would appear to suggest that the court has an *inherent* jurisdiction to restrict inspection in special cases to prevent an abuse of process.

that compliance with such an order would be injurious to the public interest.[77] Note also that rule 8 (giving the court the power to refuse to make an order for discovery where it is of the opinion that it is not necessary either for fairly disposing of the case or for saving costs) also applies to applications under rule 7A.[78]

Default in Making Discovery

If any party fails to discover or produce or allow inspection of documents as provided by any of the foregoing rules, or as ordered, the court has power under rule 16(1) to make any order it thinks just. This includes, in particular, the power to order that an action be dismissed, or that a defence be struck out with judgment to be entered accordingly.[79] Normally, however, the court is reluctant to exercise such power and will only do so when a party has at least once disobeyed a peremptory order insisting, for example, that he make discovery within a time specified in the order. A party who fails to comply with an order for discovery or production is also liable to committal (rule 16(2)). These are highly penal provisions and will only be enforced in the last resort, where it seems clear that the party in default really intends not to comply with an order of the court.

---

[77] *Taylor* v. *Anderton, The Times,* October 21, 1986.

[78] *Cf. O'Sullivan* v. *Herdmans Ltd.* [1987] 1 W.L.R. 1027 where the House of Lords held that this restriction in relation to orders for production did not apply in Northern Ireland because of differently worded rules of court.

[79] And see *Salomon* v. *Hole* (1905) 53 W.R. 588; *Chipchase* v. *Rosemond* [1965] 1 W.L.R. 153; *Husband's of Marchwood Ltd.* v. *Drummond Walker Developments Ltd.* [1975] 1 W.L.R. 603.

CHAPTER 17

SETTLING OR WITHDRAWING AN ACTION

The possibility of settling the action is probably in the minds of the parties at all stages of the proceedings, but assumes special prominence after discovery, when each party has a clearer picture of the strength or weakness of his case. An action is often settled by agreement before or at the trial, or is allowed to go to sleep without any definite settlement being arranged. If the plaintiff does not proceed, the defendant can apply for it to be dismissed with costs for want of prosecution; but this is not always wise. If an action lies dormant and no proceeding is taken for a whole year, any party desiring to proceed must give a month's notice of his intention (Order 3, r. 6).

If no order of the court is required and all parties have given their written consent, an action may be withdrawn before trial without any leave by producing the consents to the appropriate officer of the court (Order 21, r. 2(4)). If an order staying proceedings on terms agreed is required, it may be made by a master. The applicant issues a summons setting out the order required, and the signed consent of the solicitors for the other parties is indorsed upon it, unless for any special reason they wish to see the master. The applicant may then take the summons so indorsed to the Practice Master[1] to make the order. It is unnecessary to put the summons in the list or to obtain a special appointment from the master to whom the action is assigned unless it is one in which the approval of the court or an order for investment of funds is required, as where a minor or patient is a party.[2] In such cases an appointment is obtained and both sides usually attend. And if a claim by a minor or a patient is settled before proceedings are begun, Order 80, r. 11, makes it possible to apply for the approval of the court and any necessary directions by originating summons.

It is wise to ask that the stay of proceedings should take effect after the terms have been complied with, or "except for the purpose of carrying out this order," and for liberty to apply[3]; otherwise, in case of default, the party aggrieved may

---

[1] See Chap. 1.

[2] See Ord. 80, rr. 10–12. Apart from these rules, which deal with money claims on behalf of such persons, a minor or a patient may repudiate a contract if it is not for his benefit; therefore it is wise to obtain the court's approval of a settlement in all cases where they are parties.

[3] This is known as a "Tomlin order."

have no remedy except to commence fresh proceedings to enforce the terms.[4] If the action has been set down for trial, the solicitors *must* inform the Clerk of the Lists or, in cases set down for trial outside London, the district registrar that it has been settled and the summons should ask "that the record be withdrawn." This means that the copies of pleadings which are required to be lodged with the court when the action is set down are returned to the solicitors and the action is withdrawn from the list. It does not mean that all records of the proceedings which the court is required to keep—*e.g.* the cause book,[5] or the filed copy of the writ[6] or other documents—are erased; although, no doubt, if any scandalous matter which constituted an abuse of the process of the court appeared therein, the court might order it to be struck out or expunged, as is occasionally done in the case of an affidavit.[7]

A defendant may acknowledge that the claim against him is well founded, though he may think that the damages claimed are excessive; he may therefore desire to insure himself, as it were, against the plaintiff's probable success; this he can do by making a payment of money into court as discussed later in this chapter. Or it may be that the plaintiff is now satisfied that he cannot succeed. If so, he may at any time consent to judgment against himself; and from that two results will follow: (a) he must pay the defendant his costs; (b) he can never take any subsequent proceeding upon the same cause of action against the defendant. But there is a less drastic course open to him, namely, discontinuance.

Discontinuance

A plaintiff, who is compelled through lack of some necessary piece of evidence or for some other adequate reason to abandon his present proceedings, may yet desire to preserve his right to bring a fresh action under more favourable circumstances. At common law, before the Judicature Act, he was allowed to discontinue his action at any time before judgment, or to withdraw the record before the jury were sworn, or to elect to be non-suited,[8] and was yet at liberty to re-enter the cause, or bring a second action. But now this liberty has been

---

[4] See *Green* v. *Rozen* [1955] 1 W.L.R. 741; in special circumstances such a stay may be removed: *Cooper* v. *Williams* [1963] 2 Q.B. 567.
[5] See Ord. 1, r. 4.
[6] See Ord. 6, r. 7(5).
[7] Ord. 41, r. 6.
[8] *Clack* v. *Arthur's Engineering Ltd.* [1959] 2 Q.B. 211.

greatly curtailed; there is no longer such a thing as a non-suit in the High Court.[9] The plaintiff in any action begun by writ may now discontinue the action, or withdraw any part of it, by giving notice in writing to the defendant. If he does so before the defence is served, or within 14 days after its service, he may discontinue without leave (Order 21, r. 2) and may yet bring a second action. He must, however, pay the other party's costs (Order 62, r. 5) and any further action may be stayed until he does so.[10] But Order 21, r. 2A provides that a party in whose favour an interim payment has been ordered may not discontinue any action or counterclaim or withdraw any particular claim therein, except with the leave of the court or the consent of all the other parties.[11]

At any later stage of the action the plaintiff can only discontinue by leave, and the master or the trial judge can make it a condition of giving such leave that no subsequent action shall be brought (Order 21, r. 3).

A defendant who wishes to discontinue his counterclaim, or withdraw any part of it, is subject to similar rules.[12]

Withdrawal of Defence

In some cases it may be better and cheaper for a defendant who has no real answer on liability to put in no defence and let judgment go by default. Damages are then assessed by a master, unless he orders some other mode of assessment (see Chapter 4). A defendant who has put in a defence, but is minded to withdraw it, or any part of it, may do so at any time without leave by giving notice to the plaintiff in writing (Order 21, r. 2(2)(a)). If the whole defence is withdrawn, the plaintiff can enter judgment in default with costs under Order 19. If only part is withdrawn it may be possible for the plaintiff to enter judgment for any part of his claim which stands admitted. But where only one of several defences to the same claim is withdrawn—*e.g.* a plea of justification in a libel action, while a plea of privilege remains—he will have to make a special application for any costs to which he has been put by the matter withdrawn.

---

[9] *Fox* v. *The Star Newspaper Co. Ltd.* [1898] 1 Q.B. 636; [1900] A.C. 19; *aliter* at present in the county court (see *Clack* v. *Arthur's Engineering Ltd., supra*).

[10] Ord. 21, r. 5.

[11] See *Castanho* v. *Brown & Root (U.K.) Ltd.* [1981] A.C. 557, H.L., where the discontinuance took place before rule 2A was introduced.

[12] But see *Chapman* v. *Chief Constable of South Yorkshire and Others, The Times*, March 20, 1990 as regards third party and contribution proceedings.

Payment into Court

A defendant who has no defence should pay money into court. This he can do at any stage of the action after service of the writ, and before the judgment or summing-up begins, but the earlier the better. Similarly, if he admits part of the claim, he should at once pay in what he admits. The defendant may pay into court whether the claim is liquidated or unliquidated and he may pay in without specifying whether he admits or denies liability. The right is a valuable one for the protection of defendants and effectively ensures that a plaintiff cannot continue litigation oppressively against a defendant who submits and is willing to give the plaintiff his rights. For the court in its discretion over costs may, and ordinarily will, order that a plaintiff, who insists on continuing his action and does not recover more than the amount paid in, shall pay the costs of both sides incurred after payment in.

Not only is a defendant thus protected when faced with a claim for a liquidated amount which he admits to be due. He also has a powerful weapon to curb the zeal of a plaintiff where the claim is unliquidated, *e.g.* in an accident case. The plaintiff, faced with a substantial payment in, whereas damages are at large, will hesitate long before incurring the risk of going on and perhaps having to pay the costs of both sides.

Payment into court is thus not strictly a defence; it is rather an attempt to force a compromise.[13] No such plea was known to the common law; it is entirely the creature of statute. In 1834 payment into court was permitted in actions of contract; in 1843 in actions of newspaper libel; in 1852 in some actions of tort. But in 1875 payment into court was for the first time permitted in all actions for debt or damages. In such cases a defendant is allowed at any time after service of the writ to pay money into court whether he admits or denies liability.

If the statement of claim contains two or more independent causes of action, the defendant has two courses open to him: he may make separate payments of specified amounts in respect of each or of any two or more of the causes of action, identifying them; or he may make a single payment stated to cover either all the causes of action or any one or more of them. Leave is not required to make a "general" payment in covering more than one cause of action without allocating a

---

[13] The procedure was described as a "blunt instrument" by the (Winn) Committee on Personal Injuries Litigation 1968 (Cm. 3691) which recommended its abolition. Reform has been widely advocated. See 140 N.L.J. 400 (Witcomb).

sum to each; but if the result is to embarrass the plaintiff, the defendant may be ordered to make such an allocation (Order 22, r. 1(5)). He may also pay in a sum of money which takes into account both the plaintiff's claim and the whole or part of any counterclaim of his own, expressing his intention to satisfy at one and the same time all such causes of action (rule 2). Where a defendant, after complying with an order to make an interim payment, pays money into court he must state in his notice of payment (*infra*) that he has taken the award into account (Order 29, r. 16).

The payment in is made at the Court Funds Office or a District Registry[14] and a notice[15] is sent to the plaintiff and to the co-defendants (if any). The plaintiff must acknowledge its receipt within three days. If the payment in is made *before* the hearing, the plaintiff may, within 21 days from receipt of the notice (but in any event before the trial begins), accept the money in satisfaction of his claim, or of the causes of action in respect of which it was paid in, by giving a notice of acceptance[16] to all defendants. But where the payment in is made, or increased, *after* the hearing has begun, the plaintiff must make up his mind before the judge begins his judgment (or summing-up to a jury), and in any case within two days, whether or not to accept the money (Order 22, r. 3). Only if the plaintiff decides to accept may he or his counsel mention the payment to the judge.[17]

On the plaintiff accepting money paid into court, further proceedings in the action, or upon a particular cause of action, are stayed both against the defendant making the payment and any other defendant sued jointly with or in the alternative to him (Order 22, r. 3(4)) except (a) where the plaintiff is a minor or a patient, in which case the approval of the court is required (Order 80, r. 12); and (b) in defamation and certain other actions, which are discussed below. No fresh action can be brought upon the same cause of action; but exceptionally (*e.g.* in a case of fraud) a plaintiff might be allowed to resile from his acceptance and have the stay removed.

If notice of acceptance is given, the plaintiff can usually get the money out of court without leave, tax his costs to the time of receipt of the notice of payment in and sign judgment for them if not paid (see Chapter 25). But in some cases an order of

---

14 Court Funds Rules 1987, r. 16.
15 In Form 23.
16 In Form 24.
17 See rule 7.

the court is required and this must further deal with the costs
(Order 22, r. 4). This is so (a) in the case of a minor or a
patient; (b) where the money was paid in by some only of
defendants sued jointly or in the alternative, unless the plaintiff discontinues against the others and they consent in writing
to the payment out; (c) where the money was paid in with a
defence of tender before action; (d) where the money was paid
in in satisfaction of causes of action arising both under the Fatal
Accidents Act 1976 and the Law Reform (Miscellaneous Provisions) Act 1934; or under the Fatal Accidents Act 1976 only,
where more than one person is entitled to the money.

After 21 days the plaintiff needs leave to take the money out
of court, and this will not necessarily be granted.[18] Or he may
continue the action in the hope that he will obtain a larger
amount, but in that case he cannot take the money out of
court—he can only do this in satisfaction of his claim. If he
goes on with the action, claiming more, the money must
remain in court (r. 5), and the plaintiff may have to pay the
defendant a substantial sum for costs, if he is not awarded
more than the sum paid into court.[19]

Hence, if the defendant pays money into court at all, he will
be wise to pay in a good round sum. The court will give
judgment without reference to the amount paid in; indeed,
neither the fact that money has been paid into court, nor the
amount paid in, may ordinarily be mentioned to the judge or
jury until all questions as to liability and the amount of debt or
damages to be awarded have been decided (r. 7). If it is, the
judge must in his discretion decide whether the case should
continue or be retried elsewhere.[20]

A third party, or a co-defendant against whom a claim for
contribution is made as a joint tortfeasor pursuant to the Civil
Liability (Contribution) Act 1978 may make a written offer to
contribute to a specified extent to such debt or damages as may
be recovered by the plaintiff and obtain advantages similar to
those accruing from a payment into court.[21] And a plaintiff or
other defendant to a counterclaim may pay in (see Order 22,
r. 6).

---

[18] Rule 5; *Cumper* v. *Pothecary* [1941] 2 K.B. 58; *Practice Note (Millar* v. *Building Contractors
(Luton) Ltd.)* [1953] 1 W.L.R. 780; [1953] 2 All E.R. 339.
[19] If the defendant makes a payment in less than 21 days before the trial, both the fact and
the amount of the payment in must be taken into account when costs are awarded, since
there is nothing in Order 22 which renders ineffective a payment in made less than 21
days before trial: see *King* v. *Weston Howell* [1989] 2 All E.R. 375 (C.A.), doubting *Bowen*
v. *Mills & Knight Ltd.* [1973] 1 Lloyd's Rep. 580.
[20] *Millensted* v. *Grosvenor House Ltd.* [1937] 1 K.B. 717.
[21] See Ord. 16, r. 10; Ord. 62, r. 9(1)(a).

Rule 1(8) provides that the plaintiff's cause of action in respect of a debt or damages shall be construed as a cause of action in respect, also, of such interest as might be included in the judgment, whether under section 35A of the Supreme Court Act 1981 or otherwise, if judgment were given at the date of the payment into court. This rule was introduced to overcome the ruling in *Jefford* v. *Gee*[22] that a claim for interest under that 1934 Act was not a cause of action in itself, so that a sum in respect of interest need not be included when a defendant makes a payment into court. As a result of rule 1(8) a defendant who fails to include a sum in respect of interest when making a payment into court may put himself at risk in respect of costs if the plaintiff is awarded damages with interest.

In actions for libel or slander, malicious prosecution or false imprisonment, there are two peculiarities. Formerly in a defamation action a defendant could only pay in if he admitted liability. Now that it is no longer necessary to state, when paying in, whether liability is admitted or denied, a plaintiff who thinks the sum paid in is sufficient but wishes to clear his name may, before or after accepting the payment, apply to a judge in chambers for leave to make in open court a statement in terms approved by the judge (Order 82, r. 5(1)).[23] If such an action is settled without a payment having been made into court, it can nevertheless be ordered to be set down in the list so that an approved statement may be made (see r. 5(2)). Secondly, if one of two or more defendants sued jointly in a defamation action pays money into court in satisfaction of the cause of action against him, and the plaintiff accepts it, the action is not stayed against the others; but the plaintiff, if he gets judgment against them, can only execute for any excess which may be awarded to him against any defendant over and above the sum paid into court; and he will get no costs against a defendant after the date of payment in, unless either he is awarded some excess against him or the judge considers that he had reasonable ground for proceeding with the action against him (rule 4).

A defendant may at any time without leave increase the amount which he has paid into court, in which case the time for acceptance runs from the receipt of the last notice of increase. But if he wishes to withdraw or amend the notice, he

22 [1970] 2 Q.B. 130, C.A.
23 See Listing Statement, *The Times*, August 15, 1989. *Smith* v. *Commissioner of Police, The Times*, May 4, 1990.

must obtain leave (Order 22, r. 1(3)). Thus in special circumstances a defendant who has paid money into court may apply to take some or all of it out again, and the master or trial judge may grant or refuse leave at his discretion.[24]

Consent Judgments and Orders in the Queen's Bench Division

Order 42, r. 5A introduced in 1980 a radical change in practice with regard to the settlement of actions in the Queen's Bench Division. The rule makes it possible for the parties to an action, provided they are legally represented and not under a disability, to consent to the settlement of their dispute and to a judgment being entered embodying the terms of the settlement without the necessity of the settlement being approved by a judge, master or other judicial officer. The procedure is intended to save time—of the parties and of the court—as well as costs.

The procedure applies to any cause or matter in the Queen's Bench Division only, except any proceedings pending in the Admiralty Court or the Commercial Court or before an official referee or any proceedings in which any of the parties is a litigant in person or a person under a disability (rule 5A(4) and (5)). Subject to those exceptions, where all the parties to a cause or matter in the Queen's Bench Division are agreed upon the terms in which a judgment should be given, or an order should be made, a judgment or order in such terms may be given effect as a judgment or order of the court (rule 5A(1)). The procedure is applicable to any judgment or order which consists of one or more of the following (rule 5A(2)):

   (a) any judgment or order for—
      (i) the payment of a liquidated sum, or damages to be assessed, or the value of goods to be assessed;
     (ii) the delivery up of goods, with or without the option of paying the value of the goods to be assessed, or the agreed value;
    (iii) the possession of land where the claim does not relate to a dwelling-house;

   (b) any order for—
      (i) the dismissal, discontinuance or withdrawal of any proceedings, wholly or in part;

---

[24] *Cumper* v. *Pothecary* [1941] 2 K.B. 58.

 (ii) the stay of proceedings, either unconditionally or upon conditions as to the payment of money;

 (iii) The stay of proceedings upon terms which are scheduled to the order but which are not otherwise part of it (a "Tomlin order");

 (iv) the stay of enforcement of a judgment, either unconditionally or upon condition that the money due under judgment is paid by instalments specified in the order;

 (v) the setting aside of a judgment in default;

 (vi) the transfer of any proceedings to a county court, under section 40 of the County Courts Act 1984;

 (vii) the payment out of money in court;

(viii) the discharge from liability of any party;

 (ix) the payment, taxation or waiver of costs, or such other provision for costs as may be agreed;

 (c) any order, to be included in a judgment or order to which the preceding sub-paragraphs apply, for—

 (i) the extension of the period required for the service or filing of any pleading or other document;

 (ii) the withdrawal of the record;

 (iii) liberty to apply, or to restore.

Before any judgment or order to which the rule applies may be entered, or sealed, it must be drawn up in the terms agreed and expressed as being "By Consent" and it must be indorsed by solicitors acting for both parties (rule 5A(3)). Upon indorsement it should be presented to the court office to be given effect as a judgment or order of the court by the procedure provided by Order 42, r. 5. A consent judgment or order under rule 5A has the same effect and all the consequences of a court judgment or order despite the absence of approval or even scrutiny by any judicial officer.[25]

Dismissal of Action for Want of Prosecution

A defendant may apply for an order to dismiss the action for want of prosecution on breach by the plaintiff on any of several

---

[25] A court has no power to vary a consent judgment or order previously made in that court. The only means open to a party to set aside a consent judgment or order on the ground of fraud or mistake is to bring a new action for that purpose: *de Lasala* v. *de Lasala* [1980] A.C. 546 (P.C.). And see *Chanel Ltd.* v. *F.W. Woolworth & Co. Ltd.* [1981] 1 W.L.R. 485, C.A.

specific rules of court. The more important examples are failure by the plaintiff to issue a summons for directions within the specified time (Order 25, r. 1(4)); failure to serve a statement of claim[26] (Order 19, r. 1); default in discovery of documents[27] (Order 24, r. 16(1)); default in answer to interrogatories (Order 26, r. 6(1)); failure to set the action down for hearing (Order 34, r. 2). But the courts have in recent years made it clear that in addition to these specific instances the court has an inherent jurisdiction to dismiss an action for want of prosecution where there is failure to comply with an order of the court or where the plaintiff is guilty of excessive delay in the prosecution of the action.

In a speech described by Lord Edmund-Davies as "seminal," Lord Diplock offered, in *Bremer* v. *South Indian Shipping Corporation Ltd.*,[28] an analysis of the source of the jurisdiction to dismiss an action for want of prosecution. Lord Diplock said[29]:

> "The High Court's power to dismiss a pending action for want of prosecution is but an instance of a general power to control its own procedure so as to prevent its being used to achieve injustice. Such a power is inherent in its constitutional function as a court of justice. Every civilised system of government requires that the state should make available to all its citizens a means for the just and peaceful settlement of disputes between them as to their respective legal rights. The means provided are courts of justice to which every citizen has a constitutional right of access in the role of plaintiff to obtain the remedy to which he claims to be entitled in consequence of an alleged breach of his legal or equitable rights by some other citizen, the defendant. Whether or not to avail himself of this right of access to the court lies exclusively within the plaintiff's choice; if he chooses to do so, the defendant has no option in the matter; his subjection to the jurisdiction of the court is compulsory. So, it would stultify the constitutional role of the High Court as a court of justice if it were not armed with power to prevent its process being misused in such a way as to diminish its capability of arriving at a just decision of the dispute.
>
> The power to dismiss a pending action for want of prosecution in cases where to allow the action to continue

---

[26] *Clough* v. *Clough* [1968] 1 W.L.R. 525.
[27] See *Chipchase* v. *Rosemond* [1965] 1 W.L.R. 153.
[28] [1981] A.C. 909, H.L.
[29] *Ibid.* at p. 917. See also Jacob in *The Reform of Civil Procedural Law*, p. 221.

would involve a substantial risk that justice could not be done is thus properly described as an 'inherent power' the exercise of which is in the 'inherent jurisdiction' of the High Court. It would I think be conducive to legal clarity if the use of these two expressions were confined to the doing by the court of acts which it needs must have power to do in order to maintain its character as a court of justice."

Despite this cogent justification of the inherent jurisdiction, the modern practice emerged only in 1967. Before then applications to dismiss an action were not made except upon disobedience to a previous peremptory order (an "unless" order) that the action should be dismissed unless the plaintiff took within a specified additional time the step on which he had defaulted. But by 1967 "the dilatory conduct of proceedings in the High Court by solicitors to plaintiffs whose causes of action would turn upon the reliability of witnesses' recollections of past events had become a scandal, particularly in the case of those who litigated with the help of legal aid. Postponement of a trial until memories had faded and witnesses had vanished created a substantial risk that justice would not be done. True it is that at the trial the evils of delay would be likely to bear more heavily on the plaintiff on whom the onus would lie of proving that things had happened as he alleged, but the risk that justice would not be done to him extended also to the defendant and, even if successful at the trial, the defendant was likely to be out of pocket for his costs, which in legally aided cases he had little prospect of recovering."[30]

The modern basis of the remedy of dismissal was established by the decision of the Court of Appeal in the three cases heard together as *Allen* v. *Sir Alfred McAlpine & Sons Ltd.*[31] in which "the law's delays have been intolerable. They have lasted so long as to turn justice sour."[32] The Court of Appeal held that the power to dismiss should be exercised only where the court is satisfied either (i) that the default has been intentional and contumelious, *e.g.* disobedience to a peremptory order of the court or conduct amounting to an abuse of the process of the court; *or* (ii) (a) that there has been inordinate and inexcusable delay on the part of the plaintiff or his lawyers, *and* (b) that such delay will give rise to a substantial risk that it is not

---

[30] *Per* Lord Diplock in *Birkett* v. *James* [1978] A.C. 297.
[31] [1968] 2 Q.B. 229.
[32] *Ibid.* at p. 243, *per* Lord Denning M.R.

possible to have a fair trial of the issues in the action or is such as is likely to cause or to have caused serious prejudice to the defendants either as between themselves and the plaintiff or between each other or between them and a third party.

These principles were approved by the House of Lords in *Birkett* v. *James*[33] where the plaintiff sued the defendant for £1,000,000 alleged to be due under oral agreements. The writ was issued two and a half years after the date of the alleged agreements and the action had still not been set down for trial, despite an order to that effect, when the defendant applied to dismiss the action for want of prosecution some six months before the limitation period for the plaintiff's cause of action would expire. Before judgment on the application was given by the judge, the plaintiff took the precaution of issuing a fresh writ in respect of the same cause of action and later served it on the defendant. The House of Lords refused to dismiss the first action for want of prosecution and held that as a plaintiff whose action was dismissed for want of prosecution before the limitation period has expired is, save in an exceptional case, entitled to issue a fresh writ for the same cause of action, the power to dismiss an action for want of prosecution, other than in a case of contumelious conduct on the plaintiff's part, should not normally be exercised within the currency of the limitation period. To do so would only aggravate the prejudice to the defendant from delay and add to costs. In this case the fact that the plaintiff was not only likely to issue a fresh writ but had in fact done so and served it within the time limited by rules of court, was a conclusive reason against dismissing the first action.

The House of Lords considered two further problems; first the relevance of delay by the plaintiff before issuing his writ. The members of the House were agreed that such delay cannot of itself constitute inordinate delay however much the defendant may already have been prejudiced. To justify dismissal of the action the delay relied upon must relate to the time which the plaintiff allows to lapse unnecessarily after the writ has been issued. "A late start makes it the more encumbent upon the plaintiff to proceed with all due speed and a pace which might have been excusable if the action had been started sooner may be inexcusable in the light of the time that has already passed before the writ was issued . . . once it is accepted that Limitation Acts confer upon a person who claims to have a cause of action a legal right to start his action at any

[33] [1978] A.C. 297.

time up to the expiration of the statutory limitation period it must follow that he has a corresponding right to continue to prosecute it to trial and judgment so long as he does so with reasonable diligence . . . the contrary view would lead to the conclusion that even though the plaintiff had acted well within the timetable laid down in the rules for taking each successive step his action could be dismissed for want of prosecution simply because of prejudice to the defendant which had been wholly caused by the delay before the action started."[34]

The second problem considered in *Birkett* v. *James*[35] was whether the court should estimate the plaintiff's prospects of success in any claim for negligence he might have against his solicitor if the action were dismissed for want of prosecution and, if so, how the estimate should affect the decision of the court. The majority of the House of Lords were agreed that the fact that the plaintiff may or may not have an alternative remedy against his solicitor is not a relevant consideration in considering whether to dismiss an action for want of prosecution. Lord Salmon, however, took the view that in a case where inordinate delay was the fault solely of the plaintiff's solicitor who might be insolvent and uninsured, the plaintiff's inability to recover damages from him might be decisive in the plaintiff's favour, though not weighty in itself, when the other relevant factors were evenly balanced.

The (Cantley) Working Party on Personal Injuries Litigation in 1979[36] took the view that the law as stated in *Birkett* v. *James* may in fact cause delay by encouraging defendants to allow cases to go to sleep with the hope of applying later to have the action dismissed for want of prosecution. In *Tolley* v. *Morris*[37] differing opinions were expressed in the House of Lords as to the effectiveness of a more activist attitude by a defendant. Lord Diplock and Lord Keith of Kinkel were of opinion that where a plaintiff delays excessively in taking a procedural step the defendant may obtain a peremptory order which unless it is obeyed attracts the sanction that the action is dismissed; and that disobedience to a peremptory order would generally amount to contumelious conduct which would justify striking out a fresh action for the same cause of action as an abuse of

---

[34] *Ibid. per* Lord Diplock at pp. 322–323. In *Department of Transport* v. *Chris Smaller (Transport) Ltd.* [1989] 1 All E.R. 897 the House of Lords declined to depart from the principles laid down in *Birkett* v. *James*. But see *Barclays Bank plc* v. *Miller and another* [1990] 1 All E.R. 1040 (C.A.).

[35] *Ante*, note 33.

[36] 1979 Cmnd. 1476.

[37] [1979] 1 W.L.R. 592. *Simpson* v. *Smith, The Times,* January 19, 1989, C.A.

the process of the courts. Lord Edmund-Davies was however unwilling to express a final conclusion on the question whether a second action brought in such circumstances within the limitation period could be struck out as an abuse of the process of the court. The majority of the House of Lords held that the provision now contained in the Limitation Act 1980, section 28[38] conferred on a plaintiff under a disability a right to bring more than one action within the extended limitation period conferred by the section; and that although there had been inordinate and inexcusable delay in prosecuting the plaintiff's claim, it should not be dismissed since the plaintiff could issue a fresh writ for the same cause of action.[39]

The question whether disobedience to a peremptory order of the court would amount to such contumelious conduct as would justify striking out a second action for the same cause of action, brought within the limitation period, arose directly for determination by the Court of Appeal in *Janov* v. *Morris*,[40] where in an action for damages for breach of contract the plaintiff failed to take any steps for a period of 10 months after the defendant delivered particulars of the defence. On the defendant's application, the master ordered that the action be struck out unless the summons for directions be served by a specified date. The plaintiff failed to comply with the order or to offer any explanation for his delay. Judgment was given for the defendant and shortly thereafter the plaintiff issued a second writ, within the limitation period, pleading the same cause of action. The Court of Appeal held that Order 18, r. 19 conferred on the court a discretion to strike out any pleading as an abuse of the process of the court. In the absence of clear guidance from the House of Lords, the court should have due regard to the necessity of maintaining the principle that orders are made to be complied with and not ignored, and the second action should be struck out.

---

[38] The provision then in force was s.22(1) of the Limitation Act 1939 as amended.
[39] In *Bremer* v. *South India Shipping Corporation Ltd.* [1981] A.C. 909 the House of Lords held that the court has no jurisdiction to restrain a claimant in an arbitration from pursuing his claim on the ground of inordinate delay. But see now s.13A, Arbitration Act 1950, added by Courts and Legal Services Act 1990.
[40] [1981] 1 W.L.R. 1389.

CHAPTER 18

SUMMONS FOR DIRECTIONS

As we have seen, under Order 18, r. 20, unless a subsequent pleading has been ordered, the pleadings are deemed to be closed at the expiration of 14 days after service of the defence, or of the reply or defence to counterclaim (if any). It then becomes the duty of the plaintiff within one month to take out a "summons for directions" returnable in not less than 14 days (Order 25, r. 1(1)).[1] These periods are designed to enable discovery to take place before the summons is heard and to give all parties an opportunity to consider what directions they should ask for. If the plaintiff fails to issue the summons, any defendant may do so or may apply for an order to dismiss the action, whereupon the master may either dismiss the action on such terms as may be just, or deal with the application as though it were a summons for directions (rule 1(4) and (5)).

This rule applies to all actions begun by writ with the exceptions listed in rule 1(2). Of these by far the most important are actions for personal injuries, which are now subject to automatic directions and are discussed later in this chapter. The other exceptions most commonly met with (apart from patent actions) are actions where directions have been given upon an application for summary judgment or for trial without pleadings, actions which have been referred for trial to a referee and actions in which an application for transfer to the commercial list is pending or such transfer has been ordered. In such cases the referee or the judge, as the case may be, will give the directions.

The object of the summons for directions is to provide an occasion for the consideration by the master of the preparations for the trial of the action, so that—

  (a) all matters which must or can be dealt with on interlocutory applications and have not already been dealt with may so far as possible be dealt with: and

  (b) such directions may be given as to the future course of the action as appear best adapted to secure the just, expeditious and economical disposal thereof (Order 25, r. 1(1)).

---

[1] This does not mean that he cannot in any circumstances take out a summons for directions unless and until the pleadings are closed (see *Nagy* v. *Co-operative Press* [1949] 2 K.B. 188). If a party has to make any interlocutory application at an earlier stage, he may include therein all matters upon which he then desires the master's directions; but it is not ordinarily convenient to give extensive directions before the issues have been defined, and a summons under Ord. 25 would still be necessary at the appropriate time.

This tends to cheapen the cost of litigation in two ways: first, by reducing the number of interlocutory applications; and, secondly, by providing a stock-taking process before the action comes to trial, so that the parties shall not incur unnecessary expense at the trial, *e.g.* by calling witnesses to prove facts which could be proved by production of a document or which, although formally in issue upon the pleadings, are not seriously contested and might, with a little encouragement, be admitted. It is not always possible when the summons first comes to be heard to give all the directions which may eventually be found necessary; but rule 2 requires the master to deal forthwith with all the matters which it is possible then to deal with; if he thinks it expedient to adjourn the summons for consideration of any matters at a later stage, he will do so.

The summons must be issued in the form provided (see Precedent No. 55) and served on all parties to the action who may be affected by it. It is returnable in not less than 14 days. Each party served must, seven days before the hearing, give to the plaintiff and to any other parties written notice of any further or other directions which he may wish the master to make, including so far as possible all matters capable of being dealt with on interlocutory application (rule 7). If the summons is adjourned, any party desiring directions not already asked for must give written notice not less than seven days before the resumed hearing. The master has power to give such directions as he thinks proper, whether the parties have asked for them or not; indeed, as we shall see, there are certain matters which he is specifically required by rules 3 and 4 to consider of his own motion if necessary; and it is his duty under rule 2(3) to endeavour to secure that all outstanding matters which must or can be dealt with by interlocutory application are dealt with either upon the first or any resumed hearing of the summons for directions.

Any interlocutory application after the hearing of the summons for directions has been completed should be made by issuing a notice for further directions under the summons; two clear days' notice to the other parties is necessary stating the grounds of the application. On issuing a notice for further directions, as contrasted with an adjournment of the summons, a fee is payable as on the issue of a summons. If the order asked for is one which could have been granted at the hearing of the original summons, the applicant may have to bear the cost unless the master thinks that there was sufficient reason for the separate application (Order 62, r. 10).

In these ways the object of reducing the number of interlocutory applications is in many cases achieved.

Since discovery now takes place before the summons is heard, an adjournment will less often be necessary. Nevertheless there may be cases where it will be preferable for the plaintiff to ask the master to postpone certain questions until an adjourned hearing, either to save expense or because they are not yet ripe for decision. For example, you may need to ask for leave to make an amendment to the writ or pleadings which will give a completely new turn to the action, or to ask for an order for further discovery. Again, it may seem likely that an important witness will be unable to attend the trial; but this may be ascertainable with greater certainty at a later date, so that it would be premature to ask for him to be examined now or for his statement to be admitted under the provisions of the Civil Evidence Act 1968.

To secure that the pre-trial stocktaking shall in fact take place in all cases to which Order 25 applies it is provided by rule 2(4) that, unless all parties agree, no order as to the place or mode of trial shall be made until all the matters required by the Order to be considered have been dealt with. This does not apply where the master orders the action to be transferred to a county court or to an official referee; in the latter case an application for directions must be made to the referee.

Some of the problems likely to arise upon the stocktaking are dealt with in Appendix 2 on Advice on Evidence; and thought should have been given to them on those lines before the parties come before the master. It is the duty of the parties and their advisers under rule 6 to give (subject to any claim to privilege) all such information and produce all such documents to the master as he may reasonably require in order to deal properly with the summons. If they are not ready with it upon the hearing or refuse to give it they are likely at the least to be penalised in costs and in flagrant cases may have their pleadings struck out.

No affidavit is to be used on the hearing of the summons without the leave or direction of the master except where it is specifically required by some other rule, *e.g.* in support of an application to take evidence before an examiner, or an application for discovery of specific documents.

Power to Give Directions

It follows from rule 1(1) that the master may give all such directions as he may think proper with a view to the just, expeditious and economical disposal of the action. Further, the court has inherent jurisdiction to give directions for the conduct of an action[2]; but how far this power will be exercised in any particular case in the absence of a specific rule is doubtful.[3] In many cases the parties are before the master upon an earlier application in the action and he is empowered by rule to give directions at that stage as to all matters capable of being dealt with on interlocutory application. Thus if leave to defend is given on an application for summary judgment, all appropriate directions will be given then (Order 14, r. 6). There are many other instances.[4] In actions transferred to the Commercial List or to a referee, the judge or referee will give the necessary directions.

Matters Dealt With on the Summons

The wide scope of the summons can be seen from the form provided (Precedent No. 55). This form refers to numerous orders which may be made, not all of which are applicable in any particular action. This is done partly in order to help in the speedy disposal of the summons by saving the master from much writing and partly to ensure that nothing of importance which ought to be dealt with on the hearing shall be overlooked; but the list is not exhaustive. It will be convenient to describe the items which appear on the form, as well as other matters which may arise.

Consolidation of actions.—The master has power to consolidate actions pending in the same Division of the High Court (Order 4, r. 9). It is exercisable where some common question of law or fact arises in all the actions to be consolidated; or where the rights to relief arise out of the same transaction or series of transactions; and generally where in the master's discretion it seems desirable. Thus actions brought by the same persons against different defendants in respect of the same libel[5] or other connected cause of action[6] can be consolidated; and generally when the plaintiffs could have joined in one action under the provisions of Order 15, r. 4,[7] consolidation may often appropriately be ordered. The master may in his discretion order consolidation, subject to any special directions

---

[2] *Nagy* v. *Co-operative Press* [1949] 2 K.B. 188 (C.A.).
[3] See *Sigley* v. *Hale* [1938] 2 K.B. 630.
[4] See, *e.g.* Ord. 18, r. 21 (trial without pleadings); Ord. 24, r. 4 (preliminary issue); Ord. 29, rr. 7, 13 (preservation orders, interim payments, etc.); Ord. 86, r. 6 (specific performance).
[5] Law of Libel Amendment Act 1888, s.5; Defamation Act 1952, s.13.
[6] *Bailey* v. *Marchioness Curzon; Same* v. *Duggan* [1932] 2 K.B. 392.
[7] See Chap. 2.

which he may think fit to give,[8] or refuse it. If consolidated, the several actions concerned proceed thenceforth in chambers and at the trial as a single action. As an alternative to consolidation, the master may order that the actions be tried at the same time or one immediately after another, or he may order one or more actions to be stayed to await the determination of the other action.

Sometimes when the same point arises for decision in several actions proceeding simultaneously, all parties agree that one shall be tried first as a test action and to be bound by that decision. Any such agreement may be recorded in the orders for directions and the other proceedings may be stayed temporarily or ordered to be set down later.

Transfer to an Official Referee.—Circuit judges, deputy circuit judges or recorders may be nominated by the Lord Chancellor to discharge the functions of official referees. They sit in London and in each of the five circuits other than the South Eastern Circuit. Business may be referred to them for inquiry and report or for trial,[9] or for arbitration.[10] Official referees' business is defined by Order 36 as including any cause or matter (a) which involves a prolonged examination of documents or accounts, or a technical, scientific or local investigation such as could more conveniently be conducted by an official referee; or (b) for which trial by an official referee is desirable in the interests of one or more of the parties on grounds of expedition, economy or convenience or otherwise. Reference for trial may be made upon application by any party or by the master on his own motion. Both these powers are subject to any right to trial by jury. Disputes on building contracts and schedules of dilapidations are often so referred. Cases involving a charge of fraud, or of negligence against a professional man, may properly be referred for trial by an official referee[11] especially if one of the above-mentioned reasons makes this desirable.

Transfer to a county court.—Rule 3 provides that the court "shall in particular consider, if necessary of its own motion, whether any order should be made . . ." under section 40 of the County Courts Act 1984. This section permits the High Court to transfer the whole or any part of proceedings to a county court if—

---

[8] See *Healey* v. *A. Waddington & Sons Ltd.* [1954] 1 W.L.R. 688.
[9] Ord. 36; see also *Practice Direction* [1968] 1 W.L.R. 1425. Ord. 36 permits an action to be commenced as "official referees' business."
[10] Arbitration Act 1950, s.11.
[11] *Scarborough R.D.C.* v. *Moore* (1968) 112 S.J. 986.

(a) the parties consent to the transfer; or

(b) the High Court is satisfied—
    (i) that the amount remaining in dispute after any set-off, etc., is within the monetary limit of the jurisdiction of the county court or is likely to be so; *or*
    (ii) the High Court considers that "the proceedings are not likely to raise any important question of law or fact and are suitable for determination by a county court."

It is important to appreciate that the size of the claim is not of itself a bar to an order to transfer if the requirements of the section are satisfied. Order 107, r. 2(1) prohibits transfer unless the parties have had an opportunity of being heard on the issue or have consented, but section 40(10) provides that where proceedings are transferred, the county court shall have jurisdiction to award any relief, including any amount of damages, which could have been awarded by the High Court. The normal jurisdictional limit of the county court does not limit any possible award of damages or other remedy when a case has been transferred from the High Court.[12]

The Civil Justice Review recommended a very substantial increase in the powers of the county courts by the removal of their upper jurisdictional limit and by a restriction in the type of cases which should be considered appropriate for trial in the High Court. The Courts and Legal Services Act 1990 confers powers on the Lord Chancellor to make regulations which would implement these major jurisdictional changes and substitutes an amended section 40 of the County Courts Act.[13]

Amendments of the writ or pleadings.—See Chapter 11. Now is the time when you can make any necessary application to amend without incurring the costs of a special summons, although you may have to bear the costs of actually making the amendment and any costs thrown away as a result of it; and now is the time when such application should be made unless it was desirable to apply earlier. Before the summons look carefully through the pleadings to see whether any amendment is necessary or desirable and draft it; for although this is one of the matters which by Order 25, r. 3, the master is specifically required to consider on the hearing of the sum-

[12] A series of practice directions governs the procedure for transfer.
[13] See App. 3, pp. 538 *et seq.*

mons, if necessary of his own motion, the initiative should come from the parties and not from the master, who may be seeing the case for the first time and will be reluctant to interfere with counsel's pleadings unless application is made. Consider also whether any further pleading (Chapter 15) is necessary, and save the costs of a separate application by asking on this summons for leave to serve it.

Particulars.—See Chapter 10. The first hearing of the summons for directions is the time when an application to the court for an order for particulars can and should be made, unless an earlier application was essential. In the first instance you should normally apply by letter, otherwise an order—or at least the costs of the application—may be refused (Order 18, r. 12(6)). Much time and trouble may be saved if your opponent gives all or some of the particulars beforehand.

Security for costs.—The defendant may in certain cases ask for an order to compel the plaintiff to give security for the costs of the action (Order 23, r. 1), *e.g.* where the plaintiff is ordinarily resident abroad, and has no substantial property, real or personal, in England[14]; or is a merely nominal and impecunious plaintiff suing for the benefit of some other person; or is an insolvent company[15]; or has deliberately omitted or misstated his address in the writ; or has changed his address with a view to evading the consequences of litigation. The fact that an individual is impecunious or of foreign nationality may be a relevant but is not a decisive factor in the exercise of the court's discretion to order security to be given.[16] And since the Civil Jurisdiction and Judgments Act 1982, section 18, permits a High Court judgment to be enforced in any part of the United Kingdom, the fact that the plaintiff is an individual resident in Scotland or Northern Ireland does not justify an order for security for costs.

Before exercising its discretion to order any plaintiff to give security for costs, the court will have regard to all the circumstances of the case and will make the order if it thinks it just to do so. The circumstances which the court may take into account include: the plaintiff's bona fides and his prospects of

---

14 See *Kevorkian v. Burney (No. 2)* [1937] 4 All E.R. 468. The court will normally order a plaintiff who is ordinarily resident abroad to give security for costs, but the power so to order is discretionary. *Aeronave S.P.A. v. Westland Charters Ltd.* [1971] 1 W.L.R. 1445. See also *R. v. London Borough of Barnet, ex p. Shah* [1983] 1 All E.R. 226, H.L. Ord. 23 does not conflict with the prohibition against discrimination on grounds of nationality contained in Art. 7 of the Treaty of Rome: *Berkeley Administration Inc. v. McClelland and ors.* [1990] 1 All E.R. 958, C.A.

15 See Companies Act 1985, s.726(1).

16 *Thune and Another v. London Properties Ltd.*, [1990] 1 All E.R. 972, C.A.

success; whether the defendants have admitted on the pleadings or elsewhere that money is due; whether there is a substantial payment into court or an "open offer" of a substantial amount; whether the application for security is being used oppressively, *e.g.* so as to stifle a genuine claim; whether the plaintiff's want of means has been brought about by any conduct of the defendants such as delay in payment or in doing their part of the work; the substantial rights of enforcement of judgments within the member states of the EEC available to a defendant under the Civil Jurisdiction and Judgments Act 1982[17]; and the stage of the proceedings at which the application is made.[18]

Discovery and inspection of documents.—See Chapter 16. In so far as an order for discovery or further discovery or for inspection may be required it will usually be appropriate to be dealt with when the summons for directions first comes to be heard.

Interrogatories.—See Chapter 19. Since 1990, Order 26 has permitted interrogatories to be served without leave, but Order 26, r. 1(2) preserves the right of any party to apply to the court for an order giving leave to serve interrogatories relating to any matter in question between the applicant and the party to be served. Such "ordered interrogatories" may sometimes be desirable and the summons for directions may provide an appropriate opportunity to seek leave to serve them.

Inspection or preservation of real or personal property.—The master may under Order 29, r. 2, provide for the preservation or inspection of any property or thing to which the action relates. This rule, however, applies only to physical things and not, for instance, to a process of manufacture.[19] Inspection should first be requested in writing.[20] If it is not given and the master makes an order, he may take the refusal into consideration when dealing with the costs of the application. Rule 3 empowers him to order samples to be taken or experiments to be made. Under rule 4 he may order the sale of perishable property, but it is at an earlier stage of the action that occasion for this would be likely to arise. Rule 2A enables the master, on the application of any party, to make an order under section 4 of the Torts (Interference with Goods) Act 1977 for the delivery

---

[17] See *Porzelack K.G.* v. *Porzelack (UK) Ltd.* [1987] 1 All E.R. 1074.
[18] *Sir Lindsay Parkinson & Co. Ltd.* v. *Triplan Ltd.* [1973] Q.B. 609, *per* Lord Denning M.R.
[19] *Tudor Accumulator Co.* v. *China Navigation Co.* [1930] W.N. 200; though, exceptionally, such an inspection may be ordered in a patent action.
[20] Exceptionally, an order for inspection may be made *ex parte* and without notice under the *Anton Piller* jurisdiction: see Chap. 4.

up of any goods which are the subject-matter of a cause or matter or as to which any question may arise therein.

The Supreme Court Act 1981, section 33(1), enables the court to order the inspection, photographing, preservation, custody, detention, sampling or testing of any property which may become the subject-matter of subsequent proceedings or as to which any question may arise in any subsequent proceedings. An application for such an order must be made by originating summons supported by affidavit, and the person against whom the order is sought must be made defendant to the summons (Order 29, r. 7A(1)).

In personal injuries cases, section 34 of the Supreme Court Act 1981 enables the court to make similar orders in respect of property which is not the property of or in the possession of any party to proceedings but which is the subject-matter of the proceedings or as to which any question arises in them. An application for an order under this section must be made by summons in the action, supported by affidavit, and directed to the person against whom the order is sought. The summons must be served on him and on every other party to the action (Order 29, r. 7A(2)).

In both of the above cases an order may be made conditional on an applicant giving security for costs or on other terms, and in neither case will an order be made which would result in the disclosure of information relating to a secret process, discovery or invention which is not in issue in the proceedings (Order 29, r. 7A(5), (6)).

Evidence.—Subject to the Rules of the Supreme Court, to the Civil Evidence Acts 1968 and 1972, and to any other enactment relating to evidence, any fact required to be proved by the evidence of witnesses at the trial of any action begun by writ is to be proved by the examination of the witnesses orally and in open court (Order 38, r. 1). The expense of calling witnesses bulks largely in a bill of costs, but it may be significantly reduced if thought is given to the numerous provisions by which other methods of proof may be substituted. Before the summons for directions or the adjourned hearing, as the case may be, each party should carefully consider what are the facts which it will be incumbent on him to prove and how he can most satisfactorily prove them, with due regard to the expense involved; and the observations in Appendix 2 on "Advice on Evidence" should be borne in mind. Upon the hearing of the summons the master should be asked to make all such orders as it is then possible to make with regard to method of proof so as to achieve the maximum saving of costs. This is a matter which he is required to consider, if necessary of his own motion; but it is more difficult for the master to achieve the object in view if the parties do not exercise forethought and initiative.

A very brief summary of the effect of the Civil Evidence Acts 1968 and 1972 is set out in Appendix 2. This is supplemented by the following provisions.

An order may be made that *all or any of the evidence* shall be given by affidavit (Order 38, r. 2). Unless the order, or some subsequent order, otherwise directs, the deponent will not be subject to cross-examination and need not attend the trial. As to affidavit evidence generally, see Order 41. If an affidavit contains statements of information or belief—as it may on interlocutory proceedings or, if the master or judge so orders, when used as evidence at the trial—the sources and grounds of the belief must be stated. An affidavit in the form "I am informed and verily believe that . . ." will not be accepted unless the deponent states by whom he was informed.

A significant development in procedure was introduced by Order 38, r. 2A which since 1988 has applied to all divisions of the High Court. Rule 2A provides that at any stage in any cause or matter the Court may, if it thinks fit for the purpose of disposing fairly and expeditiously of the cause or matter and saving costs, direct any party to serve on the other parties, on such terms as the court thinks just, written statements of the oral evidence which the party intends to lead on any issues of fact to be decided at the trial. The power to order exchange of witness statements conferred by this rule is widely used and it is now "normal" for an order to be made for the exchange of proofs of oral evidence of witnesses of fact.[21]

Under Order 38, r. 3, the master may order that evidence of any particular *fact* shall be given at the trial in such manner as may be specified by the order. In particular, he may order it to be given by statement on oath of information and belief; by the production of documents or entries in books; by copies of documents or entries in books; or, in the case of a fact which is or was a matter of common knowledge either generally or in a particular district, by the production of a specified newspaper which contains a statement of that fact.

Now, therefore, is the time when the master should be asked to order, for example, that a statement or measurements in a police report should be admissible without calling the const-

---

[21] See *Richard Saunders and Partners (a firm)* v. *Eastglen Ltd.*, *The Times* July 28, 1989. Courts and Legal Services Act 1990, s.5.

able; or that the date when the Derby was run and the winner—for the court does not take judicial notice of this— should be proved by production of a newspaper; or that the price at which shares were dealt with on a particular day on the Stock Exchange, or goods upon the market, should be proved by an official or trade publication, and so forth.

It may also be necessary to have the evidence of some person abroad taken under letters of request or before a British consul or a special examiner (see Appendix 2), or to have a witness who is dangerously ill or about to go abroad examined here before the trial; or to obtain a copy of an entry in a banker's book under the Bankers' Books Evidence Act 1879; or of entries in other business books under Order 24, r. 14.

The master may order that the number of medical or expert witnesses who may be called at the trial shall be limited (Order 38, r. 4). Important changes imposing restrictions on adducing expert evidence and directing that reports of experts be disclosed in all cases have been introduced by Order 38, rr. 36 and 37. Rule 36 provides that in the absence of agreement or leave, no expert evidence may be adduced at the trial without an application for a direction under rule 37. That rule provides that on any such application the court shall, in the absence of special reasons for not doing so, direct that the substance of the evidence be disclosed in the form of a written report to the other parties. By rule 37(2), where a party claiming damages for personal injuries discloses a further medical report, in addition to the report which is now required to be served with the statement of claim in such cases pursuant to Order 18, r. 12, the further report must be accompanied by a statement of the special damages claimed.

Order 38, r. 38 provides for meetings of experts to be ordered. In any cause or matter the Court may direct that there be a meeting "without prejudice" of such experts for the purpose of identifying those parts of their evidence which are in issue. At such a meeting, the experts may prepare a joint statement indicating the parts of their evidence upon which they are in agreement. The procedure to be followed at the Summons for Directions in relation to medical and other expert evidence is discussed in Appendix 2.

The use of plans, photographs and models at the trial is restricted by Order 38, r. 5. Unless for special reasons the master or the judge gives leave, no plan, photograph or model is receivable in evidence in any case unless at least 10 days before the trial the other parties have been given an opportunity of inspecting it and agreeing to its admission without further proof.

Admissions.—The parties should make all admissions and all agreements as to the conduct of the proceedings which ought reasonably to be made, and the master is to do his best to secure that they do so (Order 25, r. 4). Here again forethought by the parties will lighten the master's task and speed the hearing of the summons. If they do not co-operate, the master may specially note the refusal to admit or to agree, so that the trial judge may deal appropriately with the costs thereby occasioned; or if the refusal to admit is clearly unreasonable, the master himself may make an appropriate order as to the costs of proving the relevant facts, subject to the discretion of the trial judge. A stronger weapon is the service of a notice under Order 27, r. 2(1) requiring a party to admit "such facts, or such part of his case, as may be specified in the notice"[22]; for under Order 62, r.6(7), unless the facts in the notice are admitted within 14 days or any extended time, the cost of proving them falls automatically upon the other side, whatever the result of the action, unless an order to the contrary is obtained. The process should not be abused by calling on the other side to admit matters which, from the nature of the action, must obviously be seriously in issue. The admissions are for the purposes of the action only and may by leave be amended or withdrawn on terms. The notice must be given not later than 21 days after the action has been set down for trial. It may be done much earlier, even at the time when the statement of claim is delivered. The expense of interrogatories may sometimes by avoided by judicious use of the procedure; or, if interrogatories have subsequently to be resorted to, your opponent may have to pay the costs of them. (As to admissions of documents, see Appendix 2).

Right of appeal.——Costs can be saved if the parties agree, as they may, that there shall be no appeal from the decision of the trial judge, or that any appeal shall be limited to the Court of Appeal or to questions of law only. It is not for the court to try to force the parties into an agreement of this kind, but the order for directions may record any such agreement which, it seems, would not be enforceable unless embodied in an order[23] (Order 25, r. 5).

Other matters.—All matters capable of being dealt with by interlocutory application ought, so far as possible, to be dealt

---

[22] The scope of rule 2 was broadened in 1981 (R.S.C. (Amendment No. 3) 1980). Previously the scope of the rule was limited to a notice to admit facts.
[23] *Re Hull and County Bank* (1879) 13 Ch.D. 261. *Aliter* in the county court (County Courts Act 1984, s.79).

with on the summons for directions. It is impossible to enumerate them all, but the following should also be mentioned—

Court expert.—In non-jury cases involving any question for an expert witness either party may apply under Order 40 for the appointment of an independent expert, called the court expert, to inquire and report upon any question of fact or of opinion not involving questions of law or construction. Leave may be obtained to cross-examine the court expert upon his report and provision is made for the calling of one (or in exceptional cases more than one) expert witness by each party.[24] Unexpected difficulties are sometimes encountered in the practical application of this procedure, though it has been found of use particularly in probate actions. Reference to a skilled arbitrator or special referee may be preferred by the parties, notwithstanding that they may then be at the expense of calling their own expert witnesses.

Place of trial.—The place of trial is fixed by the master on the summons for directions (Order 33, r. 4); but except where the action is transferred to a county court or to an official referee no order as to the place or mode of trial is to be made (unless by consent) until all matters required to be dealt with on the summons have been dealt with.[25] The place of trial will be determined, as a rule, by considerations of economy and convenience; the master will fix it in the place which he deems least expensive and most convenient for both parties and the majority of the witnesses on both sides, and will have regard to the date when the trial can take place according to the state of the lists and the facilities for trial at any particular centre. Neither party has any prima facie right of preference, except that the Crown can insist on trial in London.[26] Where the cause of action arose has but little to do with the question. But if for any reason it appears that a fair trial could not be had at the place which would otherwise be most convenient, the master will fix it elsewhere. He will, however, have regard to the burden imposed on jurors, if any.

Mode of trial.—The master must also direct the mode of trial. Shall it be with or without a jury, by a judge or by an official or special referee? The order must ordinarily contain an estimate of the length of the trial and in London cases must specify the

---

[24] But the costs will not be allowed on taxation unless the judge certifies that the calling of the witness was reasonable (Ord. 62, App. 2, para. 3(2)).

[25] Ord. 25, r. 2(4).

[26] Ord. 77, r. 13(1).

list into which it is to be put[27] (Order 34, r. 2(3)). If it is to be tried without a jury, it will usually be entered in the Short Cause List or the Non-jury List, according to the master's estimate of the length of the trial, those up to four hours being appropriate for the Short Cause List in the Queen's Bench Division.[28] The action must also be placed in the appropriate Listing Category, A, B, or C according to its substance, difficulty or importance. Few cases fall into Category A but the others may be listed for trial by a deputy High Court judge when the business of the court is heavy.

The master is required by Order 25, r. 3(*d*) to consider whether certain issues in an action should be tried before others or by a different mode, as is permitted by Order 33, r. 4(2). An order to this effect is appropriate where, for example, it is desirable to allow a separate trial of a preliminary point of law which arises in a case. Order 33, r. 4(2A), introduced in 1990, deals with personal injuries actions, and permits the Court of its own motion to order the issue of liability to be tried before any question of the amount of damages. It remains to be seen whether this new rule will be widely implemented in view of the fact that personal injuries actions are normally subject to automatic directions, as described below.

The rights of the parties to a jury in a civil case are limited by section 69 of the Supreme Court Act 1981. It is a matter of discretion in most actions in the Queen's Bench Division whether there shall be trial by jury, but unless the case falls within one of the categories described below, it is rare for trial by jury to be ordered.[29] Matters to be taken into consideration include whether there is likely to be an acute conflict of evidence, and whether the issues either as to liability or damage are such as can better be decided by a consensus of ordinary lay opinion than by a single judge. But in a personal injury case trial by jury will now be ordered only in exceptional circumstances.[30] A party may, however, claim a jury as of right if a charge of fraud against him is in issue; so can either party where a claim in respect of libel, slander, malicious prosecution

---

[27] The following lists exist for the trial of Queen's Bench actions in London: the Crown Office List, the Jury List, the Non-Jury List, the Short Cause List, the Commercial List, the Arbitration Case List, the Admiralty List. See *Practice Direction* [1981] 1 W.L.R. 1296. Other Directions have been issued for trial out of London: see *Practice Direction* [1987] 1 W.L.R. 1322.

[28] *Practice Direction* [1981] 1 W.L.R. 1296.

[29] *Williams* v. *Beesley* [1973] 3 W.L.R. 669.

[30] See *Ward* v. *James* [1966] 1 Q.B. 273; *Hodges* v. *Harland & Wolff Ltd.* [1965] 1 W.L.R. 523.

or false imprisonment is in issue; provided always that the trial will not require prolonged examination of documents or accounts or any scientific or local investigation which cannot conveniently be made with a jury. Any other type of case "shall be tried without a jury unless the court in its discretion orders it to be tried with a jury" (section 69(3)).[31] The right to claim a jury by virtue of the Act of 1981 must be exercised before the master first fixes the place and mode of trial.[32] Afterwards, although there is always a discretion to vary the former order,[33] a party can no longer insist on it.

If the trial is without a jury, it may be either before a judge alone, or a judge sitting with assessors,[34] or before an official or special referee or a master. Assessors are professional or scientific persons who assist the judge with their special knowledge; they are most frequently seen in the Admiralty Court in cases of collision between two vessels; but they may also sit in the Queen's Bench Division if any issue requires scientific investigation,[35] or if questions of seamanship and navigation arise.[36]

Setting Down.—On the summons for directions the master must fix a period within which the plaintiff is to set the action down for trial, *e.g.* within so many days after the date of the order (Order 34, r. 2).

Commercial cases.—These are causes arising out of the ordinary transactions of merchants and traders—amongst others, those relating to the construction of mercantile documents, export or import of merchandise, affreightment, insurance, banking and mercantile agency and usages (Order 72, r. 1(2)).

The Supreme Court Act 1981, section 6, constitutes the Commercial Court as part of the Queen's Bench Division and provides that the judges of the Commercial Court shall be those judges nominated by the Lord Chancellor to be Commercial Judges. A separate list of cases, called "the commercial list" for trial in the Commercial Court, is kept in the charge of one of the Commercial Judges (Order 72, r. 2(1)).[37]

An action may be entered in the commercial list at the outset by marking the writ in the top left hand corner with the words

---

[31] See *Goldsmith* v. *Pressdram Ltd.* [1987] 3 All E.R. 485, C.A., *Viscount De L'Isle* v. *Times Newspapers Ltd.* [1987] 3 All E.R. 499, C.A., *Beta Construction Ltd.* v. *Channel Four Television Company Ltd.* [1990] 2 All E.R. 1012, C.A.

[32] Ord. 33, r. 5. *Cropper* v. *Chief Constable of the South Yorkshire Police* [1990] 2 All E.R. 1005, C.A.

[33] Ord. 33, r. 4(1).

[34] Supreme Court Act 1981, s.70; Ord. 33, rr. 2 and 6.

[35] See *Richardson* v. *Redpath* [1944] A.C. 62.

[36] *Esso Petroleum Co. Ltd.* v. *Southport Corporation* [1956] A.C. at pp. 222, 238.

[37] And see generally *Guide to Commercial Court Practice, 1990*; Ord. 72.

"Commercial Court" (Order 72, r. 4), or an application for the transfer to the commercial list of an action not so begun may be made on the summons for directions, which may be issued even before the defendant acknowledges service, and is heard by the judge in charge of that list. If on a summons for directions before a master it appears that the action may be suitable for trial in the commercial list, he may adjourn the summons to be heard by the judge and treated as an application to transfer. The judge will give directions in the action, if transferred. Either party may appeal against an order transferring an action to the commercial list on the ground that it is not a commercial cause at all (Rule 6).

The pleadings in an action in the commercial list must be in the form of points of claim or of defence and must be as brief as possible, or the judge may order that the case be tried without pleadings (Order 72, r. 7). Other departures from normal procedure may be ordered by consent in order to ensure the speedy and economical disposal of the case.

Costs

The master has power under Order 62 to deal at the summons for directions not only with the costs of the summons itself, but of any incidental proceedings in the action. Orders for further discovery of books, accounts and other documents often cause great expense and so may orders for interrogatories. Although such orders may appear necessary in the interests of justice at the time when they are made, only too often the practical result which is produced turns out to be negligible. Yet for lack of a special application the costs are allowed to be "costs in the cause" (see Chapter 25) and the general cost of the litigation is thereby unduly swollen. You should, therefore, when appropriate, ask the master to reserve the costs *occasioned by* such an order, even though the cost *of* the application may properly be costs in the cause.

Automatic Directions in Personal Injury Actions

In 1980 a radical departure from previous practice was made in respect of directions in personal injuries actions. Previously directions in such cases were made by the Master at a summons for directions in the way described above, but the practice was condemned as wasteful by the (Winn) Committee on Personal Injuries Litigation[38] in 1968 and by the (Cantley)

[38] Cmnd. 3691 (1968).

Working Party on Personal Injuries Litigation[39] in 1979. Both these committees recommended that the summons for directions should be automatic, in the sense that a standard form of order for directions should apply regulated by rules of court. Order 25, r. 8 implements these proposals.

The automatic directions apply to any action for personal injuries except any Admiralty action and any action where the pleadings contain an allegation of a negligent act or omission in the course of medical treatment.[40] An "action for personal injuries" is itself defined by Order 1, r. 4 as:

> "an action in which there is a claim for damages in respect of personal injuries to the plaintiff or any other person or in respect of a person's death; and 'personal injuries' includes any disease and any impairment of a person's physical or mental condition."

The definitions mean that the automatic directions do apply to fatal accident claims but not to medical negligence actions.

Rule 8 provides that the following directions shall take effect when the pleadings in the action are deemed to be closed:

1. There shall be discovery of documents within 14 days in accordance with Order 24, r. 2,[41] and inspection within seven days thereafter, save that where liability is admitted, or where the action arises out of a road accident, discovery shall be limited to disclosure by the plaintiff of any documents relating to special damages (including documents relating to industrial injury, disablement or sickness benefit rights, and, in fatal accident cases, documents relating to a claim for dependency).

2. Where a party intends to rely on expert evidence at the trial, he shall, within 10 weeks, disclose a written report of the evidence to the other parties; and the report shall be agreed if possible. Where both parties intend to rely on expert evidence, they shall exchange their reports, medical for medical and non-medical for non-medical within the 10 weeks or as soon as the reports are available thereafter. If the plaintiff discloses a further medical report in addition to the report which since 1990 is required to be served with the statement of claim in a personal injuries action pursuant to Order 18, r. 12(1A), the further report must be accompanied by a statement of the special damages claimed.

---

[39] Cmnd. 1476 (1979).
[40] Ord. 25, r. 8(5).
[41] See Chap. 16.

3. If the reports are not agreed, the parties may call the experts whose reports have been disclosed, but the number of expert witnesses in any case is limited to two medical experts and one other.

4. Photographs, a sketch plan and a police accident report shall be receivable in evidence at the trial, and shall be agreed if possible.

5. The action shall be tried in London if it is proceeding there; or at the designated trial centre if it is proceeding at a District Registry. But the trial shall be in London where the Crown is a party unless the Crown consents to trial elsewhere (Order 77, r. 13).

6. The action shall be tried by Judge alone as a case of substance or difficulty (category B) and shall be set down within six months.

7. On setting down the court shall be notified of the estimated length of the trial.

8. Notwithstanding the automatic directions, any party may apply for such further or different directions as may be appropriate and the case may be transferred to a county court.[42]

The abolition of the summons for directions and the substitution of automatic directions by rule in personal injuries cases was intended to save costs and time for the parties and the time of the court in dealing with routine summonses. The automatic directions reproduce as nearly as possible the directions which were ordered by the Master in the overwhelming majority of personal injuries cases before 1980, and the change in practice has been well received.

---

[42] See *Practice Direction* [1984] 1 W.L.R. 1023. The Civil Justice Review recommended that there should be a single point of entry in the County Court for personal injury cases (see App. 3, p. 539). Significant changes in procedure are expected to follow the Courts and Legal Services Act 1990.

CHAPTER 19

INTERROGATORIES

Besides discovery of documents the parties may also require discovery of facts.[1] Indeed, they will especially require this in those cases where there are no material documents to be disclosed. For it is in those very cases that there is likely to be a conflict of evidence; and that makes it all the more desirable for the parties to ascertain before the hearing what are the exact points on which the conflict will arise. An example would be an action for personal injuries caused by a collision on a railway; such documents as exist may not throw much light on the matter. Yet it is most important for the plaintiff to know before he comes into court whether at the trial the defendant will seriously contend that no such collision ever took place, or that the plaintiff was not a passenger in either train on the day of the collision, or that he was not injured thereby. Hence in a proper case rules of court allow one party to administer a series of questions to the other, and compel that other to answer them on oath before the trial. The object is that the answers given to these questions or "Interrogatories" should save trouble and expense in preparing for the trial.[2] Sometimes, however, both discovery of documents and interrogatories are necessary; and discovery of documents will generally come first; inspection of the documents disclosed may render the proposed interrogatories or some of them unnecessary.

For almost a century[3] interrogatories could only be administered with leave. But the Civil Justice Review recommended that there should be a right to administer interrogatories without leave, and the new Order 26 implements this proposal with effect from 1990. Rule 1(1) provides that a party to any cause or matter may serve on any other party interrogatories relating to any matter in question between the applicant and that other party which are necessary either—
(a) for disposing fairly of the cause or matter, or
(b) for saving costs.
Despite this major change in procedure, the right to seek leave to serve interrogatories is retained. Rule 1(2) provides that:

---

[1] See Tomlin J. in *Duke of Sutherland* v. *British Dominions Land Settlement Corporation* [1926] 1 Ch. 746 on the role and use of interrogatories. *Cf.* Sir John Donaldson M.R. in *Naylor* v. *Preston AHA* [1987] 2 All E.R. 353 where he describes the right to interrogate as a "clumsy and over-formal procedure."

[2] See, *e.g. A.-G.* v. *Gaskill* (1882) 20 Ch.D. 519 at 528.

[3] The requirement of leave to administer interrogatories was introduced in 1893.

"without prejudice to the provisions of paragraph (1) a
party may apply to the court for an order giving him leave
to serve on any other party interrogatories relating to any
matter in question between the applicant and that other
party in the cause or matter."

Interrogatories served under paragraph 1 are described as
"interrogatories without order," and those served under paragraph 2 are described as "ordered interrogatories." By rule 3,
interrogatories without order may be served on a party not
more than twice, but shall not be served on the Crown. A
party on whom interrogatories without order are served may,
within 14 days of service, apply to the Court for the interrogatories to be varied or withdrawn.

The interrogatories must in either case state the period (not
less than 28 days) within which they must be answered and
the answers must be on affidavit unless otherwise ordered.
(Rule 2).

Since 1990 it should rarely be necessary to seek leave for
ordered interrogatories, but it must be noted that the new right
to serve interrogatories without order is not unrestricted. In
every case the interrogatories must be necessary for the purposes stated in rule 1(1), *sc.* for disposing fairly of the cause or
matter, or for saving costs.

The pre-1990 cases may therefore be a guide to the per-
missibility of interrogatories without order and an indication
how the discretion will normally be exercised in the cases
where leave is sought to administer ordered interrogatories.

Save in exceptional circumstances, interrogatories will not be
in order before defence, as the defence may contain admissions
which will render them unnecessary.[4]

Either party may at the trial read in evidence any one or
more of the answers, or any part of an answer, which he has
obtained to the interrogatories served upon his opponent. He
need not put in the rest of them unless the judge directs him so
to do (Order 26, r. 7). In some cases the master, when ordering
interrogatories, may impose a condition as to the admissibility
of the answers.[5]

As a general rule, interrogatories may be allowed whenever
the answers to them will serve either to support or maintain

---

[4] *Mercier* v. *Cotton* (1876) 1 Q.B.D. 442; *cf. Beal* v. *Pilling, Pilling, Potter and Lowe* (1878) 38
L.T. 486.
[5] *Leeke* v. *Portsmouth Corporation* (1912) 106 L.T. 627.

the case of the party administering them or to impeach or destroy the case of his adversary.[6]

However, "ever since they were first invented, it has become recognised that they constitute a process which might become oppressive, and be used for improper purposes; and therefore that the allowance or disallowance of interrogatories is a matter of discretion, and they should be allowed or disallowed on the merits of the particular case."[7]

Order 26 allows "[a] party to any cause or matter" to apply for leave to serve interrogatories on "any other party." The interrogatories must concern a matter in question between the applicant and the other party. So, for example, a defendant can interrogate a co-defendant if there was some question of adjustment of rights between them. An interrogatory may not however be served where there is no issue between an applicant and the other party.[8]

Where for some reason a party seeks leave to serve ordered interrogatories under r. 1(2), he may apply by summons to the master for an order giving him leave to serve interrogatories on any other party and requiring him to answer them on oath within such period as may be allowed. The interrogatories must have a note at the foot stating which of them are to be answered by each of the other parties. The particular interrogatories sought to be served must be submitted to the master, who will then in all cases exercise a discretion and allow only those he considers necessary either for disposing fairly of the matter or for saving costs (Order 26, r. 1).

The master will "take into account any offer made by the party to be interrogated to give particulars or to make admissions or to produce documents relating to any matter in question (r. 4(2)) and whether or not interrogatories without order have been administered.

The master's discretion as to whether or not to allow an interrogatory is subject to an appeal to a judge in chambers (Order 58, r. 1) and then to the Court of Appeal. However, the Court of Appeal will not lightly interfere with the exercise of discretion[9] unless the judge or master has acted on a wrong principle.[10]

6 *Per* Esher M.R. in *Hennessey* v. *Wright* (No. 2) (1890) 24 Q.B.D. at 447n. and *per* Stirling L.J. in *Plymouth Mutual, etc., Society* v. *Traders' Publishing Association* [1906] 1 K.B. at 416; and see *Lyle-Samuel* v. *Odhams Ltd.* [1920] 1 K.B. 135.
7 *Per* Vaughan Williams L.J. in *Heaton* v. *Goldney* [1910] 1 K.B. at 758.
8 *Shaw* v. *Smith* (1887) 18 Q.B.D. 193; *Molloy* v. *Kilby* (1880) 15 Ch.D. 162.
9 *Maass* v. *Gas Light and Coke Co.* [1911] 2 K.B. 543; *Dawson* v. *Dover and County Chronicle Ltd.* (1913) 108 L.T. 481; *Ali* v. *St. Mary's Private Hospital* (unreported) October 21, 1981.
10 *Griebart* v. *Morris* [1920] 1 K.B. 659.

Where a party wishes to serve interrogatories on another party which happens to be a company or unincorporated association, a note at the end of the interrogatories must specify the officer or member of the body on whom the interrogatories are to be served.[11] Normally this will be the secretary, but if there is any doubt on the matter the order can state that the interrogatories are to be answered by "the Secretary or other proper officer of the company."[12]

The object of interrogating is twofold: first, to obtain admissions to facilitate the proof of your own case; secondly, to ascertain, so far as you may, the case of your opponent. There is therefore some art required in drawing interrogatories. Think rather of the answer the defendant will probably give you than the answer which you are instructed he ought to give. The defendant's version of the matter must differ from the plaintiff's version, and your object is to discover precisely where and to what extent they differ. Your questions then should be framed so as to elicit, if possible, the admission you desire; and at the same time, failing that admission, to get at all events some definite statement sworn to, from which the party interrogated cannot afterwards diverge. Leave him no loophole of escape. If he will not answer the question your way, still at least find out how far he is prepared to go in the opposite direction. To secure this, it is well to ask a series of short questions rather than one long question. Each additional detail should be put in a question by itself.

Illustrations

In an action for slander it will not help the plaintiff to ask the defendant this question: "Did you not on April 14, 1989, speak the words complained of in the presence and hearing of John Smith and Richard Robinson?" The defendant may simply answer "No," and the plaintiff will be none the wiser as to what the defendant admits or denies. The plaintiff should split up the question—"Did you not, on April 14, 1989, or on some other and what other date, speak the words complained of in paragraph 2 of the statement of claim, or some and which of them? Did you not speak the said words in the presence and hearing of John Smith and Richard Robinson or either and which of them or in the presence and hearing of some other and which persons?" In this way the plaintiff will be able to pin the defendant down, and may be able to obtain an admission which will render it unnecessary to call witnesses as to the uttering of the alleged slander.

Here is a bad interrogatory: "Do you deny that the delay occasioned in the signing of the contract for the sale of the brewery to the purchasers arose wholly or in part from the fact that the 'tied houses' alleged to be connected

---

[11] Ord. 26, r. 2(1)(*b*).
[12] *Chaddock* v. *British South Africa Co.* [1896] 2 Q.B. 153, *A.-G.* v. *North Metropolitan Tramways Co.* [1892] 3 Ch. 70.

with the brewery were in your possession or connected with the brewer?" This should be split up into eight or nine separate questions. As it stands, it assumes the existence of numerous facts, each of which may be in dispute. Possibly only one of them may be really in dispute, but an interrogatory in this shape will not help you to ascertain which one that is.

And see Precedent No. 62.

What Interrogatories are Admissible

There are certain rules which determine what interrogatories may be administered and which are inadmissible "for disposing fairly of the cause or matter, or for saving costs":

1. Interrogatories must be relevant to the matters in issue. If particulars have been delivered which restrict the issue, the interrogatories must be confined to the matters stated in such particulars.[13] Not every question which could be asked of a witness in the box may be put as an interrogatory. Thus, questions which are only put to test the credibility of the witness (questions "to credit," as they are called) will not be allowed, although of course they may be asked in cross-examination (Order 26, r. 1(3)). "We have never allowed interrogatories merely as to the credibility of a party as a witness."[14] "Scandalous" interrogatories will not be allowed. A scandalous interrogatory may be described as an insulting or degrading question which is irrelevant or impertinent to the matters in issue. "Certainly nothing can be scandalous which is relevant."[15]

Again, no question need be answered which is not put bona fide for the purposes of the present action, but with a view to future litigation.[16] Interrogatories will not be allowed if they are oppressive, that is, if they put an undue burden on the party interrogated[17]; nor if their object is only to establish certain facts which, if proved, would be no defence in law to the action.[18]

Illustrations

A defendant cannot be asked: "If you did not print the libel, did M'C & Co., or some other and what firm print it?"

Pankhurst v. *Wighton & Co.* (1886) 2 T.L.R. 745.

"If A's carriage is damaged by a collision in the street, and B is sued for damages as having caused the collision . . . A must establish that the vehicle

13 *Yorkshire Provident Co.* v. *Gilbert* [1895] 2 Q.B. 148; *Arnold & Butler* v. *Bottomley* [1908] 2 K.B. 151.

14 *Per* Cockburn C.J. in *Labonchere* v. *Shaw* (1877) 41 J.P. 788.

15 *Per* Cotton L.J. in *Fisher* v. *Owen* (1878) 8 Ch.D. 653; and see *Kemble* v. *Hope* (1894) 10 T.L.R. 254.

16 *Edmondson* v. *Birch & Co. Ltd.* [1905] 2 K.B. 523; *Chapman* v. *Leach* [1920] 1 K.B. 336.

17 *Heaton* v. *Goldney* [1910] 1 K.B. 754.

18 *Rogers & Co.* v. *Lambert & Co.* (1890) 24 Q.B.D. 573.

which ran into his carriage was B's vehicle, and he ought not to be allowed to interrogate B to say if it was not B's vehicle, whose vehicle it was."

Per Cozens-Hardy M.R. in *Hooton* v. *Dalby* [1907] 2 K.B. at p. 20.

There is a well established rule that in an action for libel against a newspaper in respect of material published by it, the court will not normally allow the plaintiff to interrogate the newspaper so as to discover the identity of the writer unless the identity of such a person is a fact material to some issue raised in that action.[19]

In relation to publications which are not newspapers it is a matter of discretion for the court.[20]

The plaintiff has, however, a statutory right to obtain discovery by interrogatories of the name of the printer, publisher or proprietor of a newspaper. See the Newspapers, Printers and Reading Rooms Repeal Act 1869, Sched. 2 and *Ricci* v. *Chow* [1987] 1 W.L.R. 1658. *Hillman's Airways Ltd.* v. *Soc. Anon. d'Editions Aéronautiques* [1934] 2 K.B. 356; 103 L.J.K.B. 670.

In an action for a declaration that a certain piece of land was purchased by the defendant and C as partners, interrogatories as to other prior and subsequent purchases by them in order to prove partnership in those transactions were held irrelevant and oppressive and were disallowed.

Kennedy v. *Dodson* [1895] 1 Ch. 334; 64 L.J. Ch. 257.

And see *Ramsey* v. *Ramsey* [1956] 1 W.L.R. 542.

Interrogatories asking the plaintiff whether similar charges had not been made against him previously in a newspaper, and whether he had contradicted them or taken any notice of them on that occasion, are clearly irrelevant.

Pankhurst v. *Hamilton* (1886) 2 T.L.R. 682.

However, interrogatories are not, like pleadings, confined to the material facts on which the parties intend to rely; they should be, and generally are, directed to obtaining admissions on matters which the party interrogating desires to establish as facts at the trial.[21] "Discovery is not limited to giving the plaintiff a knowledge of that which he does not already know, but includes the getting of an admission of anything which he has to prove on any issue which is raised between him and the defendant. The object of the pleadings is to ascertain what the issues are, the object of interrogatories is not to learn what the issues are, but to see whether the party who interrogates cannot obtain an admission from his opponent which will make the burden of proof easier than it otherwise would have been."[22] Either party may be allowed to interrogate as to any link in the chain of evidence necessary to substantiate his own case; the question is relevant as leading up to a matter in issue in the action.

---

[19] *Plymouth Mutual Society* v. *Trader's Association* [1906] 1 K.B. 403; *Hennessey* v. *Wright (No. 2)* (1890) 24 Q.B.D. 445 n; *Hope* v. *Brash* [1897] 2 Q.B. 188.

[20] See, *Georgius* v. *Oxford University Press* [1949] 1 K.B. 729 where Denning L.J. was of the opinion that the rule should be extended to all periodicals. See also *Plymouth Mutual Society* v. *Trader's Association* [1906] 1 K.B. 416.

[21] *A.-G.* v. *Gaskill* (1882) 20 Ch.D. 519.

[22] *Ibid. per* Cotton L.J. at pp. 528–529.

Illustrations

If the defendant denies that he wrote a material document, he may be asked whether other documents produced to him are not in his handwriting, though such other documents have nothing to do with the action, and will only be used for comparison of handwriting.

Jones v. *Richards* (1885) 15 Q.B.D. 439.

When a defendant has pleaded that his words are true, he may interrogate as to any fact material to his case on that issue,

Marriott v. *Chamberlain* (1886) 17 Q.B.D. 154; 55 L.J.Q.B. 448.
Peter Walker & Son Ltd. v. *Hodgson* [1909] 1 K.B. 239; 78 L.J.K.B. 193.

In an action for libel or slander where the defendant pleads that the words or matters complained of are fair comment on a matter of public interest or were published on a privileged occasion, no interrogatories as to the defendant's sources of information or grounds of belief shall be allowed.

Order 82, r. 6. *Adams* v. *Sunday Pictorial Newspapers (1920) Ltd.* [1951] 1 K.B. 354.

Similarly, in an action for malicious prosecution, special caution needs to be exercised by the court where the plaintiff interrogates as to the identity of persons supplying information to the prosecutor. It would be against the public interest to inhibit these persons supplying such information in future cases.

Maass v. *Gas Light and Coke Co.* [1911] 2 K.B. 543.

In some cases also interrogatories are admissible as to matters which are only relevant in aggravation or mitigation of damages; but as a rule such interrogatories are not encouraged.[23]

Illustrations

A plaintiff is entitled to obtain an approximate statement in round numbers of the circulation of any obscure newspaper in which a libel has appeared. But in the case of any well-known London or provincial newspaper such an interrogatory would be held unnecessary and vexatious.

Whittaker v. *"Scarborough Post"* [1896] 2 Q.B. 148; 65 L.J.Q.B. 564.
James v. *Carr* (1890) 7 T.L.R. 4.

2. The party interrogating may put his whole case to his opponent if he thinks fit, though it is not always wise to do so; he may also interrogate in full detail as to matters common to the case of both parties; but he is not entitled to obtain more than an outline of his opponent's case. A distinction has to be made between the facts which a party seeks to rely on at the trial and the evidence by which he will prove those facts. A party can compel his opponent to disclose the facts which he alleges[24] but he cannot compel disclosure of the evidence by which the opponent proposes to prove those facts.[25] Similarly, he is not entitled to know how the opponent intends to

---

[23] *Heaton* v. *Goldney* [1910] 1 K.B. 754.
[24] *Marriott* v. *Chamberlain* (1886) 17 Q.B.D. 154 at 163.
[25] *Knapp* v. *Harvey* [1911] 2 K.B. 725 at 731, 732; *A.-G.* v. *Gaskill* (1882) 20 Ch.D. 519 at 531.

conduct his case.[26] He cannot claim to "see his opponent's brief," or ask him (subject to Order 38, r. 2A and part IV, discussed in the previous chapter) to name the witnesses whom he means to call at the trial.[27] The party interrogating may ask anything to support his own case or answer his opponent's case; he is entitled to know precisely what is the charge made against him, and what is the case which he will have to meet. However, he is not entitled to discover in what way his opponent intends to prove his case.[28]

Illustrations

In an action for the recovery of land, the defendant is entitled to know the facts showing the nature of the plaintiff's title, and he may, therefore, administer to the plaintiff interrogatories as to the links through which he traces his pedigree, etc.; but he is not allowed to inquire into the evidence by which the plaintiff seeks to prove his title.

Flitcroft v. *Fletcher* (1856) 11 Ex. 543; 25 L.J. Ex. 94.

The plaintiff in such an action is entitled to interrogate the defendant on all matters relevant to his own case; and he will not be deprived of that right merely because such discovery may have the effect of disclosing the defendant's case. But he cannot compel the defendant to disclose any matter which relates exclusively to his own title.

Lyell v. *Kennedy* (1883) 8 App.Cas. 217; 52 L.J. Ch. 385.

Pye v. *Butterfield* (1864) 5 B. & S. 829; 34 L.J.Q.B. 17.

A party cannot be asked to give the names of those who were present when any material act was done. This would be asking him to name his witnesses.[29]

Eade v. *Jacobs* (1877) 3 Ex.D. 335; 47 L.J.Ex. 74.

But if the party interrogating is in other respects entitled to certain information, he will not be debarred from it merely because supplying it will necessarily disclose the names of persons whom the party interrogated may hereafter wish to call as his witnesses, or otherwise give some clue to his evidence.

Marriott v. *Chamberlain* (1886) 17 Q.B.D. 154; 55 L.J.Q.B. 448.

Thus, a plaintiff is entitled to interrogate the defendant as to whether he did not speak the words complained of in the presence of persons named in the plaintiff's particulars or any and which of them.

Dalgleish v. *Lowther* [1899] 2 Q.B. 590; 68 L.J.Q.B. 956.

3. But even in interrogating as to your own case, the questions asked must not be "fishing," that is, they must refer to some definite and existing state of circumstances, and not be put merely in the hope of discovering something which may help the party interrogating to make out *some* case. They must be confined to matters which there is ground for believing have actually occurred. Thus, if in an action of defamation the plaintiff relies in his statement of claim on publications only to

---

[26] *Lever Brothers* v. *Associated Newspapers* [1907] 2 K.B. 626 at 629.
[27] *Knapp* v. *Harvey* [1911] 2 K.B. 725.
[28] *Ridgway* v. *Smith & Son* (1890) 6 T.L.R. 275.
[29] Divorce practice differs: *Bishop* v. *Bishop* [1901] P. 325.

A, B and C, he cannot, as a rule, interrogate the defendant as to whether he did not also publish the words to X, Y or Z.[30] In *Rofe* v. *Kevorkian*[31] Greer L.J. described as "fishing" an interrogatory "by a man who is trying to make a case and has not already the evidence which would justify him in making the case."

Illustrations

Where the plaintiff was charged with having used certain blasphemous phrases, interrogatories were disallowed as "fishing," the object of which was to show that if the plaintiff had not said what he was charged with saying, he had on other occasions said something very much like it.
  Pankhurst v. *Hamilton* (1886) 2 T.L.R. 682.
But the defendant in an action of slander may be asked whether he did not speak "the words set out in paragraph 3 of the statement of claim, or some and which of them, or some other and what words *to the same effect.*"
  Dalgleish v. *Lowther* [1899] 2 Q.B. 590; 68 L.J.Q.B. 956.

The principle prohibiting "fishing" interrogatories has to be distinguished from a plaintiff's right to require a defendant to disclose the identity of persons involved in the commission of a wrong under the court's jurisdiction as stated in *Norwich Pharmacal Co.* v. *Customs and Excise Comrs.*[32] This right is independent of any right to serve interrogatories.[33]

Interrogatories can, however, be served to compel a defendant to disclose the names of tortfeasors under the *Norwich Pharmacal* principle but this is not the case where the defendant is a "mere witness" and in no way facilitated the wrong and did not take part in its commission.[34]

4. Interrogatories are not ordinarily allowed as to the contents of written documents, unless there is evidence that such documents, have been lost or destroyed. An interrogatory as to whether a party has or has had a document has been allowed in certain circumstances, but the appropriate remedy is now an application under Order 24, r. 7.[35] Nor will interrogatories be allowed, the object of which is to contradict a written document.[36] A party may be asked whether he wrote a certain letter, but, if the letter or a copy of it is not in his possession he may demand to see it before he answers.[37]

5. Questions which tend to criminate may be asked if they are relevant,[38] though the party interrogated is not bound to

---

30 See *Barham* v. *Lord Huntingfield* [1913] 2 K.B. 193; *Russell* v. *Stubbs, ibid.* p. 200n. (H.L.).
31 [1936] 2 All E.R. 1334 at pp. 1337–1338.
32 [1974] A.C. 133.
33 *Loose* v. *Williamson* [1978] 1 W.L.R. 639.
34 *Ricci* v. *Chow* [1987] 1 W.L.R. 1658.
35 *Supra*, Chap. 16.
36 *Moor* v. *Roberts* (1857) 2 C.B.(N.S.) 671.
37 See *Dalrymple* v. *Leslie* (1881) 8 Q.B.D. 5.
38 *Allhusen* v. *Labouchere* (1878) 3 Q.B. 654.

answer them.[39] Such questions are not scandalous, unless they are either irrelevant or "fishing," and will not, therefore, be disallowed; the party interrogated must take the objection on oath in his answer. That the interrogatories will tend to criminate others (except the spouse of the party interrogated) is no objection, if they are put bona fide for the purposes of the present action.[40] That to answer them would expose the party interrogated, or third persons, to civil actions was never an objection.[41]

6. Interrogatories may now be administered to the defendant in an action for the recovery of land even if the answers might subject him to a forfeiture.[42] Thus, a tenant may be interrogated as to whether he has not assigned or underlet the premises contrary to a covenant in his lease. And he may be interrogated as to whether his term or other interest has not expired or been duly determined by a notice to quit.[43] Again, leave will not be given to administer interrogatories in any action brought to recover penalties under a statute.[44] And a person may refuse to answer on the ground of privilege any interrogatory if to do so would tend to expose him or his spouse to proceedings for an offence or for the recovery of a penalty provided for by criminal law.[45]

7. A party will generally not be allowed to interrogate so as to obtain an admission of a fact which could be proved by a witness who *in any event* will be called at the trial since the interrogatory here will add to and not save costs. So, in running down cases, for example, the defendant may not normally be interrogated as to facts relating to the allegation of negligent driving (*e.g.* how fast was the defendant driving; what was the plaintiff's position when the defendant first saw him). However, this does not apply where there are special reasons, for instance where the plaintiff's injuries are such that he has no recollection of the accident and there are no witnesses he can call. Similarly where an action is brought by, for example, the widow of a man who has died in hospital:

"prima facie there may be a good many things which the plaintiff cannot possibly know but which must be within

---

[39] *Alabaster* v. *Harness* (1894) 70 L.T. 375.
[40] *McCorquodale* v. *Bell* [1876] W.N. 39; Civil Evidence Act 1968, s.14(1).
[41] *Tetley* v. *Easton* (1856) 18 C.B. 643.
[42] Civil Evidence Act 1968, s.16(1)(a).
[43] *Wigram on Discovery*, 81.
[44] *Martin* v. *Treacher* (1886) 16 Q.B.D. 507; *Saunders* v. *Weil* [1892] 2 Q.B. 321; *Derby Corporation* v. *Derbyshire* C.C. [1897] A.C. 550.
[45] Civil Evidence Act 1968, s.14(1).

the knowledge of the defendant hospital, and that is the kind of case, rather like an unwitnessed fatal accident or an accident in which a plaintiff is knocked unconscious, in which interrogatories as to the facts are ordered to enable the plaintiff to prove her case."[46]

8. A defendant who pleads the Limitation Act in an action for debt need not answer an interrogatory the answer to which could operate as an acknowledgment of the debt, for the plaintiff could then tear up the writ and start another action using the answer as an acknowledgement of the debt. That "would reduce the Limitation Act to a farce; it would make it a complete nullity, and obviously defeat the intention of Parliament."[47]

9. In exercising the discretion it is proper to have regard *inter alia* to the nature of the action and the probable consequences of allowing the particular interrogatory.

In an action for malicious prosecution, for example, there are special reasons for exercising caution where the plaintiff seeks the identity of those persons who provided the prosecutor with information since this would inhibit persons supplying such information in future cases.[48]

Answers to Interrogatories

The interrogatories allowed by the master must be answered in full detail and on oath within the time specified pursuant to rule 2 unless some valid objection can be raised to any of them.[49] If a person objects to answering an interrogatory on the ground of privilege, he may take the objection in his affidavit in answer (Order 26, r. 5(1)).[50] Privilege for this purpose includes an objection that the answer may tend to criminate.[51]

The answers must be carefully drawn. The party interrogated may answer guardedly, and make qualified admissions

---

[46] *Griebart* v. *Morris* [1920] 1 K.B. 659. *Ali* v. *St. Mary's Private Hospital* (unreported) October 21, 1981, *per* Stephenson L.J.

[47] *Lovell* v. *Lovell* [1970] 1 W.L.R. 1451 at p. 1454, *per* Salmon L.J.

[48] *Maass* v. *Gas Light & Coke Co.* [1911] 2 K.B. 543.

[49] The affidavit must be filed and the party interrogating can obtain an "office copy," which will be admissible at the trial as evidence of the answers. In practice it is not uncommon to allow interrogatories to be answered by letter and not on oath.

[50] The rules formerly permitted objection to be taken in the answer on the ground that the interrogatory was scandalous or irrelevant or on other grounds, notwithstanding that the interrogatory had previously been allowed by the master. This is no longer permissible.

[51] *Lamb* v. *Munster* (1882) 10 Q.B.D. 110; *Ex p. Reynolds* (1882) 20 Ch.D. 294, 299. See privilege in relation to Discovery generally.

only, so long as both the admission and the qualification are clear and definite. He may answer "Yes" or "No" simply, so long as it is clear how much is thus admitted or denied. The following answer was held sufficient[52]: "I kept no copy and have no copy of the said letter, and I am unable to recollect with exactness what the statements contained therein were." It is quite admissible to say "I do not know" where the matter is clearly not within the deponent's own knowledge. He is not bound to procure information from others for the purpose of answering.[53] If, however, he "is interrogated about acts which are done in the presence of persons employed by him, their knowledge is his knowledge, and he is bound to answer in respect of that."[54] A party to a cause is not excused from answering relevant interrogatories if such matters are within the knowledge of his agents or servants, and such knowledge was acquired by them in the ordinary course of their employment. A banker or solicitor may be such an agent.[55] In such a case the party interrogated is bound to obtain the information from his agents or servants or former servants and agents unless he can show that it would be oppressive to require him to elicit such information from these persons.

Where the party being interrogated is a company the interrogatories must be answered by the person specified at the end of the interrogatories (rule 2). In answering the interrogatories that person is bound to make all reasonable inquiries from company officers, servants and agents to determine what is known or was known by the company. This may include making inquiries from former servants of the company.[56] The officer of a company, answering interrogatories on its behalf, is only bound to answer as to his knowledge acquired in the course of his employment by the company; he is not bound to

---

[52] *Dalrymple* v. *Leslie* (1881) 8 Q.B.D. 5.

[53] *Per* Brett J. in *Phillips* v. *Routh* (1872) L.R. 7 C.P. 287; and see *Rofe* v. *Kevorkian* [1936] 2 All E.R. 1334.

[54] *Per* North J. in *Rasbotham* v. *Shropshire Union Ry. and Canal Co.* (1883) 24 Ch.D. at p. 113.

[55] *Alliott* v. *Smith* [1895] 2 Ch. 111.

[56] *Bibby Bulk Carriers Ltd.* v. *Cobelfret N.V.* (unreported) September 3, 1984 C.A. *Stanfield Properties Ltd.* v. *National Westminster Bank plc* [1983] 1 W.L.R. 568. It is desirable that the person answering on behalf of the company make some statement that he has addressed his mind to this duty imposed upon him and has attempted to discharge it.

With regard to former servants of the company Megarry V.-C. held that the test is one of reasonableness whereas the Court of Appeal in *Bibby Bulk Carriers Ltd.* v. *Cobelfret N.V.* was of the opinion that circumstances would have to make it oppressive to relieve a party from being required to find out information from a former servant. *Stanfield* was not cited in the Court of Appeal judgments in *Bibby*, but both cases clearly show that the *dicta* of Brett L.J. in *Bolckow* (*post*) regarding *former* servants and agents do not represent the law.

disclose information which has come to him accidentally or in some other capacity.[57]

Illustrations

Action by the owners of a cargo against the owners of a ship for a loss alleged to have arisen from negligence in the navigation which caused the ship to run ashore and be stranded. Interrogatories as to what was done by those on board with regard to such navigation at the time of the accident. The defendants answered that they were not on board at the time, and had no knowledge or information respecting the matters inquired into, except as appeared by the protest, of which the plaintiffs had had inspection. This answer was held insufficient, as it did not appear that there was any difficulty in the defendants obtaining the required information from those who were in charge of the ship at the time of the accident and who were still employed by the defendants.

Bolckow, Vaughan & Co. v. *Fisher and others* (1883) 10 Q.B.D. 161; 52 L.J.Q.B. 12.

Action for the value of certain missing casks, of which full particulars were given. Interrogatories by the plaintiffs asking whether the defendant company had not received the casks, whether they had lost them, or what had become of them. The information asked for was admittedly contained in the books of the defendant company, or of their agents. The defendant company refused the information, on the ground that it would be a great trouble to search through all these books for many years back, and that such an inquiry would be attended with great expense:—*Held* by Lord Coleridge C.J. and Denman J. (Grove J. *dissentiente*) that the defendant company must answer the interrogatories.

Hall v. *L.N.W. Ry.* (1877) 35 L.T. 848.

But it is not reasonable to require a party to make admissions as to matters which are not within his own knowledge, and as to which he can only obtain information by writing to his rivals in the trade, or by asking his own servants for information which they have acquired accidentally and not in the course of their employment by him.

Ehrmann v. *Ehrmann* [1896] 2 Ch. 611; 65 L.J. Ch. 745.

Welsbach, etc., Co. v. *New Sunlight Co.* [1900] 2 Ch. 1.

An objection to answering any one or more of several interrogatories should be taken in the affidavit in answer. It is usually in the following or some similar form:

1. "I object to answer on the ground that the question constitutes an inquiry as to communications passing between me and my solicitor confidentially and in his professional capacity." But it has been held that the privilege does not extend to communications which the client had instructed the solicitor to repeat to the other party.[58] On this ground a client may, for example, refuse to disclose information which he only obtained from his solicitor since the action was commenced, and which was the result of inquiries instituted by the solicitor for the purposes of the litigation.[59] If the person interrogated is a solicitor, it is a sufficient answer to state, "I have no real personal

[57] *Welsbach, etc., Co.* v. *New Sunlight Co.* [1900] 2 Ch. 1.
[58] See *Conlon* v. *Conlons Ltd.* [1952] 2 All E.R. 462.
[59] *Proctor* v. *Raikes* (1886) 3 T.L.R. 229.

knowledge of the matter referred to in this interrogatory, and the only information and belief that I have received or have respecting any of such matters has been derived from and is founded on information of a confidential character procured by me as solicitor of the said C, and not otherwise, for the purpose of litigation between the plaintiff and C, either pending or threatened by the plaintiff. I claim to be privileged from answering this interrogatory further."[60]

2. "In answer to the fifth interrogatory, I say that to answer it would tend to criminate me, and I therefore submit that I am not bound to make any further or other answer to it." This objection must be stated in clear and unequivocal language. In *Lamb* v. *Munster*[61] it was held sufficient for the defendant to state on oath, "I decline to answer all the interrogatories upon the ground that my answer to them might tend to criminate me."[62]

Insufficient Answers

If insufficient answers are given to interrogatories without order the party serving the interrogatories may ask for further and better particulars of the answer given. (Rule 5). Such a request is not treated as the service of further interrogatories for the purposes of rule 3(1) (which prohibits service of interrogatories without order on a party more than twice).

In the case of insufficient answers to ordered interrogatories, rule 5(2) permits the court to order a further answer, either by affidavit or on oral examination. In practice, orders for oral examination are not normally made.[63]

Default in Answering Interrogatories

Any party failing to answer interrogatories is liable to the same penalties by way of committal and having his action dismissed or defence struck out, as in the case of failure to give discovery of documents; and the power of the court so to order is exercised upon the like principles (see Order 26, r. 6). The power will, however, only be exercised where no answer at all is forthcoming or where the answer given is "so palpably insufficient as to show want of bona fides."[64]

---

[60] *Procter* v. *Smiles* (1886) 55 L.J.Q.B. 467, 527.
[61] (1882) 10 Q.B.D. 110.
[62] And see *Jones* v. *Richards* (1885) 15 Q.B.D. 439.
[63] For an example of an unsuccessful application for an order under this rule, see *Stanfield Properties Ltd.* v. *National Westminster Bank plc* [1983] 1 W.L.R. 568.
[64] *Kennedy* v. *Lyell* [1882] W.N. 137.

CHAPTER 20

TRIAL

Before dealing with the proceedings at the trial let us see how the action comes into a list for trial so that the parties know when to attend.

Setting Down, Fixtures and Postponements

As we have seen, the master will have given directions for the action to be set down for trial or automatic directions will apply in personal injuries actions.[1] If the plaintiff fails to do so, the defendant may set it down himself or may apply to the master to dismiss it for want of prosecution[2] (Order 34, r. 2(2)).

Since 1979 the plaintiff need no longer obtain the leave of the court or the consent of the defendant before setting an action down for trial out of time, but default may entail the dismissal of the action for want of prosecution, and by Order 3, r. 6, a month's notice of intention to proceed must be served on all other parties where a year or more has elapsed since the last proceeding in the matter.[3] To set down for trial, the plaintiff must take or send to the "proper officer"[4] a request to set the action down at the place directed, together with two bundles of the pleadings and other documents specified in Order 34, r. 3[5]; and within 24 hours after doing so he must notify the other parties (r. 8).

In trial centres out of London the district registrar keeps a list of the actions set down for trial before a judge (Order 34, r. 5). In a Queen's Bench action, the plaintiff must give notice of setting down within seven days to all other parties and must lodge with the pleadings a statement which states whether the Order made on the summons for directions has been complied with, in particular with regard to agreement of medical and other expert reports, plans and photographs; it must give an up-to-date estimate of the length of trial; and it must give

---

[1] See Chap. 18.
[2] See Chap. 17.
[3] See *Suedeclub Ltd.* v..*Occasions Textiles Ltd.* [1981] 1 W.L.R. 1245.
[4] In Q.B. actions for trial in London, the head clerk of the Crown Office or the chief clerk of the Admiralty and Commercial Registry; in Chancery actions for trial in London, the cause clerk in Chancery Chambers (Order 34, r. 3); in an action in any Division for trial outside London, the appropriate district registrar.
[5] Agreed expert reports in personal injury actions should also be lodged as soon as practicable after setting down. Practice Direction [1979] 1 W.L.R. 290 and Practice Direction by the Senior Master, with effect from January 1, 1990.

particulars of the parties' solicitors and counsel. The district registrar will then notify the parties when it may be expected to be heard.[6]

Actions for trial in the Queen's Bench Division in London must be set down in the appropriate list. Those in the Non-Jury List are in the first instance set down in a Non-Jury General List. Thence, if a fixed date of trial is desired, they may be transferred to a "Fixture List" on application within four weeks to the Clerk of the Lists.[7] He will either fix a date or, if it is objected that the date proposed is too far ahead, he may leave the action in the General List, if necessary marking it not to come on before a certain date so as to give the parties time to prepare for trial. A party who is dissatisfied may within seven days apply to the judge in charge of the Non-Jury List; otherwise no alteration of a fixed date (except to allot an earlier vacated date) will be permitted without the judge's leave. A postponement will only be allowed for good cause and the action may be sent back to the General List.

For each week of each sittings a "Weekly List" of non-jury actions is published on the Monday containing (a) the "Week's List" comprising actions both in the Fixture and General Lists expected to be tried that week; (b) other actions in the General List except those which have by order or by consent been stood out; and (c) other actions in the Fixture List fixed for trial during the current sittings. Each day there is published a "Daily Cause List" showing the actions to be tried on the following day; and this is also described as the "Warned List."

As the trial draws near, one or other of the parties often desires to postpone the hearing of the case owing, perhaps, to the illness of himself or of an important witness, or because a late amendment of the pleadings or further discovery has become necessary. If the other side agrees and the case is *not* in the Fixture or the Warned List, a consent for a postponement, signed by all parties, may on proper grounds be lodged with the Clerk of the Lists and the case may then be taken out of the list and restored when the parties are ready. If the action is in the Fixture or the Warned List, an application to the judge in charge of the list showing good cause will be necessary. But your opponent may object strongly to any postponement, or to any application which will have that result. A contested

---

[6] See directions for trial out of London given by the Lord Chief Justice [1987] 2 All E.R. 1039. See also Order 34, r. 5.

[7] The practice here set out is mainly governed by the L.C.J.'s Directions For London [1981] 3 All E.R. 61.

application involving an adjournment of a case in the General List but not yet in the Warned List must be made to the judge in charge of the List. A series of Practice Directions and Listing Statements has been issued with a view to reducing delay between setting down and trial. The judge will have regard to the wishes and interests of the parties, the state of the lists and all the circumstances of the case.

It is the duty of all parties at once to inform the officer who keeps the list, whether in London or the trial centre, if the case is or is likely to be settled or of a different length from that estimated.

Procedure at the Trial

If neither party appears when the case is called on for trial, the action may be struck out of the list; then if the plaintiff wishes to proceed, he must obtain a judge's direction that it be restored. If the plaintiff appears and the defendant does not, the plaintiff may be allowed to prove his claim and obtain judgment in the defendant's absence; if the defendant has a counterclaim the plaintiff will ordinarily ask to have it dismissed with costs. If the defendant appears, and not the plaintiff, the defendant may be given judgment at once, dismissing the plaintiff's claim in the action; if he has a counterclaim, he may prove it (Order 35, r. 1). But any verdict or judgment obtained in the absence of one party may be set aside upon terms, if application is made within seven days after the trial.[8]

The trial will take place in open court,[9] unless for some solid and special reason the judge orders trial *in camera, e.g.* on grounds of national security[10] or where a hearing in public would defeat the ends of justice.[11] An official shorthand note or recording of the oral evidence and of the judge's summing-up and judgment will normally be taken (Order 68).

If both parties appear, the jury (if any) is sworn. Formerly junior counsel for the plaintiff had to "open the pleadings" to a jury, briefly stating their effect. This ceremony has now been

---

[8] Order 35, r. 2; and see *Schafer* v. *Blyth* [1920] 3 K.B. 140; *Grimshaw* v. *Dunbar* [1953] 1 Q.B. 408. In *Re Barraclough, decd.* [1965] 3 W.L.R. 1023 such an application was refused where the defendant was purposely absent and there was no element of mistake or lack of opportunity.

[9] See *McPherson* v. *McPherson* [1936] A.C. 177; *Hawksley* v. *Fewtrell* [1954] 1 Q.B. 228; *Stevens* v. *Stevens* [1954] 1 W.L.R. 990; Supreme Court Act 1981, s.67.

[10] *Baker* v. *Borough of Bethnal Green* [1945] 1 All E.R. 134, 143.

[11] See *Badische, etc.* v. *Levinstein* (1883) 24 Ch.D. 156; but see *B. (orse P.)* v. *Attorney-General* [1967] P. 119.

abolished.[12] If the action is brought for unliquidated damages, counsel must not state the amount claimed.[13] And on no account must he mention the fact that money has been paid into court in satisfaction save in the excepted cases.[14]

First may arise the question as to which side begins. Normally the plaintiff will begin by "opening his case" (Order 35, r. 7(2)), but this depends to a large extent on the pleadings, for where the burden of proof of *all* the issues in the action lies on the defendant he will invariably begin (r. 7(6)). If the burden of proving one issue only lies on the plaintiff, it does not matter that there are others which lie on the defendant; the plaintiff will begin unless the judge otherwise directs. Thus, whenever damages (particularly unliquidated damages) are in issue, the plaintiff should begin, unless a precise sum is claimed which the defendant admits that the plaintiff is prima facie entitled to recover.[15] If the damages claimed are liquidated, still, if the defendant has traversed any material allegation which is essential to the plaintiff's case, the plaintiff should begin. But the defendant may have made admissions in his defence with a view to gaining the advantage of the first word. Moreover, unless no evidence is called on the opposite side, the first word means the last word too; and to have the last word is sometimes important. But in every case, the trial judge may give directions as to the party to begin and the order of speeches and it is only in the absence of such a direction that the plaintiff begins (r. 7(1)).

The leading counsel for the plaintiff (if the plaintiff is to begin) will now "open his case"; that is, he states in chronological order the facts on which the plaintiff relies. Modern practice encourages brevity in oral presentation, and it is common for a written précis of the opening to be required. Counsel must not open any fact which he is not prepared with evidence to prove. He should consider the likely reliability of his witnesses when deciding how confidently to pitch his opening speech; for witnesses often disappoint counsel who has opened his case strongly. Counsel for the plaintiff then calls the first witness, who is generally the plaintiff himself, and examines him "in chief," as it is called. The witness is cross-examined by the defendant's counsel, and re-examined by counsel for the plaintiff. The next witness is then called and

---

[12] Practice Direction [1960] 1 W.L.R. 658.
[13] *Per* Lord Halsbury in *Watt* v. *Watt* [1905] A.C. at p. 118.
[14] See Order 22, r. 7.
[15] *Carter* v. *Jones* (1833) 6 C. & P. 64; *Mercer* v. *Whall* (1845) 5 Q.B. 447, 462, 463.

examined by one or other of the plaintiff's counsel, and so the
case proceeds. When two counsel for a party are briefed they
can take the witnesses alternately or as may be convenient.[16]
When all the plaintiff's witnesses have been examined, and all
documents material to his case—including such of the defendant's answers to interrogatories as the plaintiff desires to
use—have been put in and read, the plaintiff's case is closed.

The defendant's counsel must now make up his mind
whether to call evidence or whether to submit that the plaintiff
has made out no case to answer in law. He will not ordinarily
be allowed to submit no case unless he tells the judge that he
intends to rely on the submission alone and call no evidence. If
counsel for the defendant adopts this course, counsel for the
plaintiff will be entitled to reply to his submission that there is
no case for the defendant to answer in law. If the judge
overrules the submission, judgment will then be entered for
the plaintiff. Another course which the defendant's counsel
may adopt at the close of the plaintiff's case is to state, if such
be the fact, that he does not intend to call any witnesses; and
in that event the plaintiff's counsel at once addresses the court
(Order 35, r. 7(3)),[17] summing up his own evidence, and
commenting on the defence, so far as it has been fore-
shadowed by the cross-examination, and also, no doubt, on
the fact that the defendant does not venture to go into the box.
The defendant's counsel then addresses the court, criticising
the evidence for the plaintiff. But if the defendant's counsel
intends to call witnesses, he is entitled to address the court at
the end of the plaintiff's case, opening the defence. He then
calls his witnesses, each of whom may be examined, cross-
examined and re-examined, and he usually makes a second
speech for the defendant, at the conclusion of which the
leading counsel for the plaintiff replies on the whole case. This
disadvantage necessarily attends calling witnesses for the
defendant; it gives the plaintiff the last word; and in a doubtful
case the reply of an able advocate can determine the result of
the action in his client's favour, especially in a jury case. But,
on the other hand, the judge and jury like to see the defendant
in the box, and to learn from his own lips his reasons for his
conduct. If there are two defendants who appear separately or
are separately represented, the order of speeches is governed
by rule 7(5).

---

[16] The leader in his discretion sometimes entrusts the examination of the client to his
junior, who has probably acquired some knowledge of the client's idiosyncrasies from
conferences in the interlocutory stages.

[17] Formerly, if the defendant's counsel put in a document in the course of the plaintiff's
case he lost the last word.

When counsel having the last word raises in his speech any fresh point of law or cites any authority not previously mentioned during the course of the trial, his opponent may reply to the point of law or deal with the authority cited (r. 7(7)).

In citing reported cases it is helpful to the court first to summarise the proposition of law in support of which the case is cited, then to give distinctly and accurately the name of the case and its reference in the law reports, giving the judge time to make a note of it, and then to read such passages as bear upon the point at issue. Counsel owe a duty to the court to bring to its notice all relevant authorities of which they are aware even though they may tell against their case. The *ratio decidendi*, or principle of law on which a case is decided, alone has binding force, as opposed to *obiter dicta* of the judges as to matters not necessary to their decision or not argued before them. Decisions of the House of Lords on questions of law bind all inferior courts, but since 1966, the House has been free to depart from its own previous decisions "when it appears right to do so"[18]; those of the Privy Council, though not technically binding, have almost equal authority. Decisions of the Court of Appeal must be followed by courts of first instance; they also bind the court itself unless (1) there is some conflicting decision of its own; (2) the decision is inconsistent with a decision of the House of Lords, or (3) the decision was given *per incuriam*.[19] Decisions of Divisional Courts bind courts of first instance and are usually followed by other Divisional Courts. A judge of the High Court, while he will allow great weight to the decision of another judge of that court, is not bound by it or relieved from considering the point for himself.[20]

When speeches by counsel are finished, the judge sums up the whole case to the jury, and then follow verdict and judgment; if there is no jury, the judge delivers (or reserves) judgment.

It is improper for counsel in a civil case to invite the jury to stop the case before the judge has summed up,[21] though the judge himself may do so subject to the right of the plaintiff's counsel to address them.

---

[18] See Practice Statement of July 26, 1966 (1 W.L.R. 1234). *Food Corp. of India* v. *Antclizo Shipping Corp., The Antclizo* [1888] 2 All E.R. 513, H.L.

[19] See *Young* v. *Bristol Aeroplane Co. Ltd.* [1944] 1 K.B. 718; *Davis* v. *Johnson* [1979] A.C. 264 (H.L.); *Rickards* v. *Rickards* [1989] 3 W.L.R. 748. *Rakhit* v. *Carty* [1990] 2 All E.R. 202, C.A.

[20] *Green* v. *Berliner* [1936] 2 K.B. 477, 493. *Colchester Estates* v. *Carlton Industries plc* [1986] Ch. 80.

[21] *Alexander* v. *H. Burgoine & Sons Ltd.* [1940] W.N. 8; *Beevis* v. *Dawson* [1957] 1 Q.B. 195.

Examination in Chief

The witnesses are always examined *viva voce* and in open court, unless a master or the trial judge has ordered that an affidavit or written statement shall be admissible[22] (Order 38, r. 1).

The success of a case depends largely on how the witnesses are handled. The timid witness must be encouraged; the talkative witness repressed; the witness who is too strong a partisan must be kept in check; and yet such management must not be obvious. Counsel has a discretion to call such witnesses as he thinks proper and in whatever order he considers most appropriate.[23] It is a great art to cross-examine well. It requires even greater skill to examine in chief with uniform success, the chief aim being to bring out clearly and in proper chronological order just so much as is wanted and no more. Nothing will induce some witnesses to swear up to their proofs; from forgetfulness or some other reason they omit the most material circumstance, and supply in its place a host of immaterial details. And yet counsel must not seem to suggest anything to the witness. In cases where an order has been made under Order 38, r. 2A for exchange of witnesses' statements, no evidence may be led, the substance of which is not included in the statement of the witness in question, except in relation to new matters which have arisen in the course of the trial; or the court may direct that the statement shall stand as the evidence in chief of that witness (rule 2A(5)).

Objections are frequently taken either to questions put by counsel or to something which the witness is endeavouring to say. An objection to the admissibility of any evidence must be taken as soon as it is tendered; no objection can be raised after the evidence has once been received. Such an objection is often stated in the compendious form, "That is not evidence." This may mean one or other of two very different things; either (a) that the fact sought to be proved is irrelevant to every issue in the action, or (b) that the proposed method is not the proper method of proving a relevant fact. Anything that goes to prove a material fact is relevant; everything else will be rigorously excluded. And relevant facts must be proved in a legitimate way; a fact may be most material, but that is no reason why

---

[22] At one time affidavit evidence could be admitted by written agreement of the parties. Order 38, r. 2, does not so provide; but if the parties are agreed, there should be no difficulty in obtaining the necessary order. A statement is also admissible by agreement of the parties under s.1, Civil Evidence Act 1968.

[23] *Briscoe* v. *Briscoe* [1966] P. 501. The judge may direct that an expert witness be called after other witnesses have been heard.

you should be allowed to prove it by inadmissible evidence. Counsel examining in chief must keep rigidly to what is relevant, and must properly prove all relevant facts by admissible evidence.

And he may not ask leading questions. A "leading question" is one which suggests to the witness the answer which it is desired he should give to it. Counsel may not, therefore, put such a question to his own witness, unless it is merely introductory, or relates to matters as to which there is no dispute. In most cases, however, it is necessary to prove a certain number of uncontested facts, in order that judge and jury may understand the position of the parties and the circumstances surrounding the case. As to these matters, leading questions are often put with the permission of counsel on the other side. Leading questions may also be proper to contradict evidence already given by a witness on the other side; *e.g.* if the plaintiff has sworn that the defendant said: "The goods need not all be equal to sample," the defendant can, and should, be asked in chief: "Did you ever say to the plaintiff that the goods need not all be equal to sample, or any words to that effect?"

In no circumstances may a party attack the character of a witness whom he has called himself, or call evidence to discredit him. If a party voluntarily places a witness before the court to give evidence, he represents that he is worthy of belief. Sometimes, however, the judge will allow a witness, who has given evidence adverse to the party who called him, to be treated as hostile, and then he may be cross-examined and contradicted. He may be asked leading questions. He can also be asked about any previous statement made by him orally or in writing, such as a signed proof of his evidence; and if he denies that he made the statement, proof that he did so may by leave of the judge be given, and the statement, if in writing, may be put in evidence to contradict him. (Criminal Procedure Act 1865, s.3). That statement then becomes admissible as evidence of any fact stated therein by virtue of section 3 of the Civil Evidence Act 1968. Counsel may not treat a witness as hostile merely because the evidence he is giving is unfavourable to the party who called him. Permission will only be given where the witness shows a decided bias against that party, and a reluctance to state anything that tells in his favour.

A witness should always state what happened according to his own personal recollection, and not according to what he has since been told. But he is allowed to refresh his memory, when in the box, by looking at an entry or memorandum which he himself wrote or dictated very shortly after the event which it records, or even at any entry made by someone else, which he saw, read and approved as correct very shortly after the event. It does not matter that the document is not evidence for either party, or even that it should be and is not stamped.[24] The witness should not read it aloud to the jury, unless the other side consents; he should merely refer to it to refresh his memory. Counsel on the other side is entitled to look at any document by which the witness has refreshed his memory and to cross-examine him on it; and he may, if he thinks fit, put it in evidence.

Cross-examination

Counsel, when cross-examining, has a much freer hand than when examining in chief. He may and often should ask leading questions, although answers which a witness is thus induced to give are not always so convincing. And he need not confine his questions to the fact in issue; he may branch out into many collateral matters; he may attack the character and impugn the credit of the witness to any extent which his instructions justify. But he should use this liberty guardedly. Moreover, the judge may disallow vexatious and irrelevant questions.

This much counsel is bound to do, when cross-examining: he must put to each of his opponent's witnesses so much of his own case, in substance, as concerns that particular witness or in which that witness had any share. Thus, if the plaintiff has deposed to a conversation with the defendant, it is the duty of the counsel for the defendant to indicate by his cross-examination how much of the plaintiff's version of the conversation he accepts, and how much he disputes, and to suggest what the defendant's version will be. If he asks no question about it, he will be taken to accept the plaintiff's account in its entirety.

But in all other matters it is often safer to ask too little than too much. It is quite unnecessary to take the witness through the whole of the story which he has already given in chief: the usual result of doing so is that the witness merely repeats his former evidence with greater emphasis and clearness and brings out many minor incidents and considerations which elaborate his tale and serve to make it sound all the more convincing.

Moreover, reckless cross-examination often lets in awkward pieces of evidence which hitherto were not admissible. Thus, if

[24] *Birchall* v. *Bullough* [1896] 1 Q.B. 325.

you ask a witness called by the other side whether he did not meet Mr. X at Ilminster Fair last September, and whether Mr. X did not then tell him so and so, your opponent, in reply, will be able to ask the witness what Mr. X really did say to him on that occasion, although this was not admissible in chief, because your client was not present at the conversation. In cases where witnesses' statements have been exchanged under Order 38, r. 2A any party may put the statement of a witness in cross-examination of that witness. (r. 2A(5)(c)).

Witnesses may be cross-examined not only as to the facts of the case but also "to credit," that is, as to matters not material to the issue, with the view of impugning their credit and thus shaking their whole testimony. But, in order to prevent the case from thus branching out into all manner of irrelevant issues, it is wisely provided that on such matters the answer of the witness must ordinarily be treated as final, no evidence being admissible to contradict it. There are important exceptions to this rule. Thus, a witness can always be asked whether he has been convicted of a crime, and if he either denies the fact, or refuses to answer, the opposite party may prove such conviction (other than a "spent" conviction under the Rehabilitation of Offenders Act 1974) however irrelevant to the issue the fact of the conviction may be. (Criminal Procedure Act 1865, s.6; and see Appendix 2). (See further the Civil Evidence Act 1968, s.11, as to the admissibility and effect of evidence that a person has been convicted of an offence which should have been properly pleaded in compliance with Order 18, r. 7a).

If the witness has previously made a statement material to the issue which is inconsistent with his present testimony, the previous statement may be proved. If it was oral, the circumstances under which it was made must first be put to him, and he must be asked if he admits having made it. If it was in writing, he may be cross-examined upon it without it being shown to him; but if it is intended to put it in evidence, the material parts must be shown to him so that he may have an opportunity of explaining the inconsistency. In any case the judge may insist on seeing the document and may put it in evidence if he thinks it right to do so (Criminal Procedure Act 1865, ss.4 and 5). The contents of the document then become admissible as provided by the Civil Evidence Act 1968, s.3.

There are some questions, moreover, which a witness will not be compelled to answer, either in cross-examination or in chief:

(i) He may refuse to answer any question which tends, directly or indirectly, to show that he or his spouse has committed a crime, and there is reasonable ground for apprehending that criminal proceedings may be taken against him; or which tends to expose him or his spouse to proceedings for the recovery of a penalty.[25]

(ii) No barrister or solicitor may, unless his client consents, disclose any fact which his client communicated to him in his professional capacity, or the professional advice he gave his client—nor can the client be compelled to make any such disclosure—so long as such communication was not made, nor such advice given, in furtherance of any criminal or fraudulent purpose.[26]

(iii) No juror is allowed to give evidence as to the discussions in the jury box or in the jury room.[27] No judge should be called to give evidence as to facts which can equally well be proved by someone else.[28] Apart from this, a judge of a superior court appears to be privileged from testifying as to proceedings before him, though he may give evidence as to extraneous matters, *e.g.* a riot in court.[29]

Re-examination

The object of re-examination is merely to give the witness an opportunity of explaining any seeming inconsistency in his answers, and of stating the whole truth as to any matter which was touched on, but not fully dealt with, in cross-examination. Counsel, when re-examining, can ask no question that does not arise out of the cross-examination, except by consent; he has no more right to ask his own witness leading questions at this stage than at any other; and it is a mere waste of time to ask over again questions already put in chief.

After re-examination, counsel will request the release of the witness, but the judge often asks him a few questions. Neither counsel has any right to re-examine the witness on the answers which he has given to the judge; but he may ask the judge to put another question to the witness to make those answers clear. After a witness has once left the box, he cannot be

[25] Civil Evidence Act 1968, s.14(1); Supreme Court Act 1981, s.72; and see Chap. 16.

[26] *Williams* v. *Quebrada* [1895] 2 Ch. 751; *Minter* v. *Priest* [1930] A.C. 558; *Butler* v. *Board of Trade* [1971] Ch. 680. *Balabel* v. *Air India* [1988] 2 All E.R. 246, C.A.

[27] *Ellis* v. *Deheer* [1922] 2 K.B. 113; *Boston* v. *Bagshaw* [1966] 1 W.L.R. 1135. And see *Nanan* v. *The State* [1986] 3 All E.R. 248, P.C.

[28] *Florence* v. *Lawson* (1851) 17 L.T.(O.S.) 260; *R.* v. *Gazard* (1838) 8 C. & P. 595.

[29] *R.* v. *Harvey* (1858) 8 Cox C.C. 99; *Duke of Buccleuch* v. *Metropolitan Board of Works* (1872) L.R. 5 H.L. 418, 433; *R.* v. *Earl of Thanet* (1799) 27 How.St.Tr. 845.

recalled, except by the leave of the judge; and counsel, when asking leave, is expected to indicate the matters on which he desires him to give further evidence. If the judge consents, and the witness is recalled, the counsel recalling him will be confined to the matters so indicated; but his opponent may, apparently, cross-examine him generally with a view to shaking his testimony. The judge has power to call and examine a witness who has not been called by either party, but only if neither party objects.[30] If he does so, neither party has a right to cross-examine that witness without leave; this, however, will always be granted if the evidence is adverse to either party.[31]

Documents

Subject to certain statutory exceptions (see Appendix 2) the original document itself must be produced at the trial, if it is possible to obtain it. And if the plaintiff puts it in, the defendant is entitled to have the whole of it read as part of the plaintiff's case. If the original is not produced, it should be satisfactorily accounted for, and its loss or destruction proved. In practice, it is now common for the parties to agree a bundle of copy documents in advance, and the process of agreement will include the resolution of any dispute as to the authenticity of a particular document. It is only if agreement cannot be reached that a document will be in issue.

If a person is only called to produce a document and is not sworn or asked any question in chief, the other side has no right to cross-examine him; sometimes he is called on to produce a document while some other witness is in the box, and is himself called as a witness at a later period of the case. A party who is under notice to produce is not bound to comply with it; when the other side calls for a document, his counsel may say, "I do not produce it." Counsel must not say more; for he is not entitled to give evidence; his witnesses may subsequently explain why it is not produced, *e.g.* that it has been lost or destroyed.

If the original is produced, a dispute may arise as to who wrote it; and it may be necessary to call witnesses to prove the handwriting. Anyone who has ever seen A write (even though only once) can be called to prove his handwriting. So can

---

[30] *Re Enoch and Zaretzky, Bock & Co.'s Arbitration* [1910] 1 K.B. 327; *Fallon* v. *Calvert* [1960] 2 Q.B. 201.
[31] *Coulson* v. *Disborough* [1894] 2 Q.B. 316.

anyone who has corresponded with A, or seen letters which
have arrived in answer to letters addressed to A. Thus, a clerk
in a merchant's office, who has corresponded with A on his
employer's behalf, may be called to prove his handwriting,
though he has never see A write.[32] The usual course is for the
counsel who tenders the document merely to ask the witness,
"Do you know Mr. A's handwriting?" leaving it to his opponent to cross-examine as to the extent of the witness's acquain-
tance. Such cross-examination will only weaken the force of his
evidence, not destroy its admissibility.

Every material document is prima facie admissible in evidence against the writer. It is, however, manifestly desirable
that the parties to a dispute should be free to enter into
negotiations with a view to compromise without running the
risk of having their letters given in evidence against them if the
negotiations fail and an action ensues. They are therefore
allowed after a dispute has arisen, whether proceedings have
been commenced or not, to mark any documents which form
part of such negotiation with the words "Without prejudice,"
and documents so marked cannot be read at the trial without
the consent of the writer.[33] The expression "without prejudice"
means that the document is not to be used to the prejudice of
either party in the dispute, if the negotiations fail. The application of the rule is not dependent on the use of the phrase
"without prejudice" if it is clear that the parties were seeking
to compromise the action.

Sometimes, too, when a document is tendered in evidence,
the officer of the court takes the objection that it ought to be,
and is not, stamped. It is considered unprofessional (except in
revenue cases) for counsel to object to a document on the
ground that it is not sufficiently stamped, unless such defect
goes to the validity of the document as opposed to its
admissibility. Before the Finance Act 1970 bills of exchange and
promissory notes were required to be stamped before issue;
and in such cases the objection was fatal; no copy could be put
in, even by consent, after it was known to the court that the
original was unstamped. If, however, the document is one
which can by law be stamped after its issue or execution, the
objection can be met by paying the proper officer the amount
of the stamp duty and a penalty; or, if the document is

---

[32] *cf. R.* v. *Turner* [1910] 1 K.B. at pp. 357, 358.
[33] *Rush and Tompkins Ltd.* v. *Greater London Council and Another* [1988] 3 W.L.R. 939. But see
Tomlin v. *Standard Telephones and Cables Ltd.* [1969] 1 W.L.R. 1378. See Chap. 16. A
written offer "without prejudice save as to costs" (a *Calderbank* letter) may not be
communicated to the court until the question of costs falls to be decided (Ord. 22, r. 14).

insufficiently stamped, the amount of the deficiency and a penalty. If there is any question as to the necessity for a stamp, or as to its proper amount, the judge decides it then and there; if he admits the document, his decision is final, and a new trial will not be granted nor will an appeal lie if he is subsequently proved to have been wrong (Order 59, r. 11(5)). If the judge holds that the stamp is insufficient, the party tendering the document must either dispense with it or pay the penalty.

All documents put in evidence at the trial are marked and listed as exhibits by the associate (Order 35, r. 11). At the conclusion of the trial each party by his solicitor applies for the return of the exhibits which he puts in; and he must carefully preserve them in case there should be an appeal (r. 12).

Secondary Evidence of Documents

If the original document has been lost or destroyed, secondary evidence may be given of its contents. But—subject to the provisions of the Civil Evidence Act 1968 and of Order 38, r. 3 (see Appendix 2)—its loss or destruction must first be proved. It is not necessarily enough for a witness to say it is lost; he must show that he has made a real search for it, before he will be allowed to produce a copy or state his recollection of its contents. If counsel seeks to put in a copy, he must usually, in the absence of agreement or special leave, prove that it is a correct copy by calling the man who made it or otherwise. But copies of correspondence are generally agreed and allowed to be read when it is common ground that such letters were in fact written and received.

Where, however, the document is still in existence and capable of being brought into court, the party desiring to give secondary evidence of its contents must ordinarily prove that he has done all in his power to obtain the original document. Thus, the plaintiff is entitled to give secondary evidence if the original is in the defendant's possession and is not produced when called for, provided it is among the documents set out in his list for discovery or due notice to produce it was served on the defendant's solicitor a reasonable time before the trial; and also if the document is in the possession of someone beyond the jurisdiction of the court, who refuses to produce it on request, although informed of the purpose for which it is required. If it is in the possession of a third person within the jurisdiction, but a stranger to the cause, who refuses to produce it, although duly served with a *subpoena duces tecum* for the purpose, then the right to give secondary evidence of its contents appears to depend on whether such refusal is rightful or wrongful. If it is a *wrongful* refusal, the remedy of the party is against the witness only.[34] If it is a *rightful* refusal, then secondary evidence is, as a rule, admitted, as the party has done all in his power to produce primary proof.

Verdict

In jury cases, as soon as all the evidence has been heard and the counsel on both sides have addressed the jury, the judge sums up the evidence. He may either leave the jury to return a general verdict for the plaintiff or for the defendant, or ask them to answer certain questions; in the latter case it will be for the judge to determine subsequently what is the legal result of their findings. Once the jury has given a general verdict, the judge is not entitled to ask them any further question.[35]

The jury now consider their verdict.[36] They must determine all issues of fact, and, if they are in favour of the plaintiff, they must also assess the damages. Where there are two or more distinct causes of action, they should assess the damages on each of them separately.[37] In arriving at the amount, the jury must not have regard to any questions of costs; that is a matter for the judge. And they must not be informed that any money has been paid into court. In some cases the amount to which the plaintiff is entitled can be ascertained by mere arithmetic, or calculated according to a scale of charges or some other accepted rate or percentage. The damages are then said to be *liquidated* or "made clear." When, however, the amount to be recovered depends on all the circumstances of the case, and on the conduct of the parties, or is fixed by opinion or by an estimate, the damages are said to be *unliquidated*. Thus, in an action on a bill of exchange or a promissory note, the amount of the verdict, if it is for the plaintiff at all, can be reckoned beforehand: so much for principal, so much for interest, so much for notarial expenses. But in an action of libel, for instance, it is open to the jury to award the plaintiff a penny, or a hundred pounds, or one hundred thousand pounds; and no one can say beforehand what the precise figure will be. Where the damages are unliquidated, the sum which the jury awards to a successful plaintiff may be:

[34] R. v. *Inhabitants of Llanfaethly* (1853) 2 E. & B. 940; *Rowell* v. *Pratt* [1938] A.C. at p. 116.
[35] *Arnold* v. *Jeffreys* [1914] 1 K.B. 512.
[36] As to taking a verdict in the judge's absence, see *Hawksley* v. *Fewtrell* [1954] 1 Q.B. 228.
[37] *Weber* v. *Birkett* [1925] 2 K.B. 152; but see *Barber* v. *Pigden* [1937] 1 K.B. 664.

(i) Contemptuous;
(ii) Nominal;
(iii) Substantial; or
(iv) Exemplary.

(i) Contemptuous damages are awarded when the jury consider that the action should never have been brought. The defendant may have just overstepped the line, but the plaintiff may also be to blame or have rushed into litigation unnecessarily; so he only recovers a penny.

(ii) Nominal damages are awarded where the action was a proper one to bring, but the plaintiff has not suffered any actual damage, and does not desire to put money into his pocket; he has established his right or cleared his character, and is content to accept a nominal sum and his costs.

(iii) Substantial damages are awarded where the jury endeavour to arrive at a figure which will fairly compensate the plaintiff for his actual loss or injury in all the circumstances of the case.

(iv) Exemplary damages are awarded where the jury desire to mark their disapproval of the defendant's conduct towards the plaintiff; they therefore punish him by awarding the plaintiff damages beyond the amount which would be adequate compensation for his actual loss or injury. They are only allowed to give such damages in actions where there has been oppressive, arbitrary or unconstitutional conduct by a government official, or where the defendant has sought to achieve some financial or material gain for himself unless such damages are expressly authorised by statute.[38] Everything which aggravates or mitigates the conduct of the defendant may be taken into consideration, including the means of the parties.[39] But a claim for exemplary damages must be specifically pleaded together with the facts relied on.

Judgment

In jury cases as soon as the verdict has been returned, counsel for the successful party formally asks for judgment and the judge will direct that judgment be entered as he thinks right. In non-jury cases he gives judgment at the conclusion of

---

[38] See, *e.g.* the Reserve and Auxiliary Forces (Protection of Civil Interests) Act 1953, s.13(2).
[39] For the rules of common law relating to exemplary damages, see *Rookes* v. *Barnard & Others* [1964] A.C. 1129, *per* Lord Devlin at pp. 1221 *et seq.*; *Broome* v. *Cassell & Co. Ltd.* [1972] A.C. 1027.

counsel's speeches, stating his reasons.[40] Sometimes, if difficult
questions are raised, the judge does not give judgment at once,
but takes time to consider it.[41] As a rule, however, he gives
judgment then and there, according to the findings of the jury
if there is one. A judgment debt carries interest (Judgments Act
1838, s.17). The rate of interest, originally 4 per cent. under
that Act, is now variable (see Administration of Justice Act
1970, s.44). In personal injuries actions, the judge may make an
award of provisional damages under Order 37, Pt. II provided
that the plaintiff has pleaded such a claim and the judge is
satisfied that the action is one to which section 32A of the
Supreme Court Act 1981 applies; such an action is one in which
there is proved or admitted to be a chance that at some definite
or indefinite time in the future the injured person will, as a
result of the act or omission which gave rise to the cause of
action, develop some serious disease or suffer some serious
deterioration in his physical or mental condition. An order for
an award of provisional damages must specify the disease or
type of deterioration in respect of which an application may be
made at a future date for an award of further damages, and
will normally specify the period within which such an application may be made.[42]

In the Chancery Division, where issues are apt to be more
complicated and parties more numerous, it is usual for the
judge to give an oral judgment indicating the general sense in
which he decides the action but not to direct the entry of
judgment there and then. Before this is done junior counsel on
each side must agree "minutes of judgment" which, upon
approval by the judge, will form the basis of the formal
judgment which is then drawn up (see Chapter 21).

But the duties of counsel are not yet over. Now is the time to
ask for any special costs, such as the costs of taking evidence
abroad, of photographic copies of any document, of transcripts
of recorded evidence or shorthand notes,[43] the costs of proving
particular documents or facts, and any costs reserved to be
disposed of at the trial, or specifically mentioned in the order
for directions. Counsel for the successful party must also ask

---

[40] The word "judgment" is used in two senses. Strictly it means the formal judgment
which is sealed and issued to the successful party and entered in the books of the court.
But it is also commonly used to mean the reasoned judgment which is delivered by a
judge sitting without a jury or by a Lord Justice in the Court of Appeal. In the House of
Lords "speech" rather than "judgment" is the correct word when it is used in this
sense.

[41] This is indicated in law reports by the abbreviation c.a.v. (*curia advisari vult*).

[42] See Ord. 37, r. 8. Practice Direction [1985] 2 All E.R. 895.

[43] See Order 68.

for the general costs of the action, which are in the discretion of the trial judge (Order 62, r. 3). This discretion must, of course, be exercised judicially and the judge will order that costs follow the event unless the circumstances justify some other order. If any money has been paid into court and is still in court, the judge should be asked to make some order with regard to it (Order 22, rr. 5 and 8). He may only be informed of a payment into court in satisfaction after all questions of liability and amount of debt or damages have been decided (rule 7). If the defendant is entitled to any costs, his counsel may ask the judge to direct that such money remain in court until after taxation with liberty to apply.[44] If the plaintiff's damages are assessed at a figure less than the amount paid into court, the judge will take that fact into consideration when exercising his discretion as to costs. If either party is an assisted person under the Legal Aid Act 1988, his counsel should ask for a direction that his costs be taxed in accordance with the Act, so that the proper amount payable out of the legal aid fund may be ascertained; otherwise extra expense may be caused by the necessity for a subsequent application.

Counsel for the unsuccessful party, if he desires a stay of execution because he thinks of appealing or on other grounds should now apply for it, although an application may be made later (Order 47, r. 1). To obtain a stay of execution from the court below is not to take a benefit under the judgment so as to preclude the appellant from seeking to set it aside.[45] As a rule a stay pending appeal will only be granted on terms. A usual condition is that the unsuccessful party shall bring a sum of money into court and give notice of appeal within so many days; and the costs of the trial may be ordered to be taxed and paid, subject to an undertaking by the respondent's solicitor to refund them if the appeal is successful. Interest will be allowed for the period during which execution has been delayed by the appeal, unless an express order to the contrary is made (Order 59, r. 13). The lodging of a notice of appeal does not itself operate as a stay of execution, but the Court of Appeal can order a stay (*ibid.*). The application should, however, be made in the first instance to the court below (rule 14(4)).

A judgment finally disposes of all controversy as to any of the matters in issue in the action. The rights of the parties as to any such matter depend in future wholly on the judgment. As

---

[44] Under Order 22, r. 5, an order may be made *after trial* to pay money out otherwise than in satisfaction of the causes of action in respect of which it was paid in.

[45] *Evans* v. *Bartlam* [1937] A.C. at p. 479.

long as that judgment stands, none of the issues raised in the
action can be retried.[46] The original cause of action is gone—
transit in rem judicatam—it is merged in the judgment. This
result is peculiar to a judgment: a mere stay of proceedings, or
the acceptance of money paid into court, has not the same
effect.[47] Clerical mistakes in a judgment or order, or errors
arising from any accidental slip or omission, may be corrected
on motion or summons (Order 20, r. 11); but a judge has no
power under this rule to alter the substance of his judgment,
once it has been formally drawn up.

[46] *Ralli* v. *Moor Line* (1925) 22 Ll.L.R. 530.
[47] *Coote* v. *Ford* [1899] 2 Ch. 93.

CHAPTER 21

THE CHANCERY DIVISION: GENERAL PROCEDURE AND ACTIONS BEGUN BY WRIT

All divisions of the High Court have concurrent jurisdiction,[1] so that in theory any action may be brought in any Division unless by statute required to be brought in some other Division or in the County Court.[2]

However, the present Chancery Division is the historic successor to the old Equity Courts, and has inherited a large part of their jurisdiction. From early times, the Courts of Chancery had a large staff of officials to whom complicated accounts and inquiries could be referred. The result was that litigious business requiring accounts or inquiries tended to find its home there; and this is still the position today. In addition, of course, the Courts of Equity dealt with all matters concerning trusts, equitable interests in land and equitable remedies such as injunctions, rectification of deeds and specific performance of contracts relating to land. In modern times, all actions relating to Companies and to insolvency (both corporate and individual) have naturally been included within the Chancery jurisdiction, as being matters which are likely to involve the detailed consideration of accounts.

The distribution of business amongst the Divisions of the High Court is now expressly dealt with by section 61 and Schedule 1 to the Supreme Court Act 1981, paragraph 1 of which assigns the following specific causes or matters to the Chancery Division:

(1) The sale, exchange or partition of land, or the raising of charges on land;

(2) The redemption or foreclosure of mortgages[3];

(3) The execution of trusts;

(4) The administration of the estates of deceased persons;

(5) Bankruptcy;

(6) The dissolution of partnerships or the taking of partnership or other accounts;

(7) The rectification, setting aside or cancellation of deeds or other instruments in writing;

(8) Probate business,[4] other than non-contentious or common form business (which are dealt with in the Family Division);

---

[1] s.5(5) of the Supreme Court Act 1981.

[2] See, *e.g.* s.21 of the County Courts Act 1984 which gives the county court exclusive jurisdiction in relation to most mortgage actions for possession of dwelling-houses.

[3] See Ord. 88.

[4] See Ord. 76 which deals with contentious probate business.

(9) Patents, trade marks, registered designs or copyright;
(10) The appointment of a guardian of a minor's estate[5]; and
(11) All causes or matters involving the exercise of the High
     Court's jurisdiction under the Companies Acts.[6]

In addition, certain other business is expressly assigned to
the Chancery Division, of which the most important are:

(12) The Revenue List[7];
(13) Applications under the Trustee Act 1925[8];
(14) Applications under the Variation of Trusts Act 1958[9];
(15) Applications under the Landlord and Tenant Acts 1927
     and 1954[10];
(16) Applications concerning the management of the prop-
     erty and affairs of persons incapable by reason of mental
     infirmity of managing their own affairs; this jurisdiction,
     previously known as the jurisdiction in Lunacy, was
     transferred in 1956 from the Lords Justices to the judges
     of the Chancery Division,[11] who are now the nominated
     judges under the Mental Health Act 1983, s.93; in that
     capacity they exercise powers in addition to and also on
     appeal from the Court of Protection.

Generally speaking, any action principally concerning one or
more of the above matters should be begun in the Chancery
Division; and if it is brought in any other Division it is liable to
be transferred to the Chancery Division, on the application of
any party or by the Court of its own motion; and any costs
thereby thrown away may be ordered to be paid by the
plaintiff.[12]

The Conduct of Business in the Chancery Division

The Judges:

The judges of the Chancery Division normally sit in London;
but there is a long-standing jurisdiction, derived from that of
the old Palatine Courts of Lancaster and Durham,[13] for Chancery actions to be heard in the district registries at Liverpool,

---

[5] Proceedings concerning the wardship of minors, which used to be the province of the
   Chancery Division, are now assigned to the Family Division: Supreme Court Act 1981,
   Sched. 1, para. 3, and see Ord. 90.
[6] See Ord. 102.
[7] Redistribution of Business (Revenue Paper) Order 1962; and see Ord. 91.
[8] See Ord. 93, r. 4.
[9] See Ord. 93, r. 6.
[10] See Ord. 97.
[11] See [1956] 2 All E.R. 248.
[12] See *Re Pollard* (1888) 20 Q.B.D. 656 (C.A.).
[13] The old Palatine Courts of Lancaster and Durham were merged into the High Court by
   the Courts Act 1971, s.41.

Manchester and Preston and, time permitting, at Newcastle and Leeds, by judges assigned by the Lord Chancellor for that purpose; and, with effect from October 1, 1982, the jurisdiction to hear Chancery actions outside London has been extended to the district registries at Cardiff, Birmingham and Bristol.[14]

The result is that Chancery actions may now be heard in each of those cities,[15] as well as in London, although it remains the case that the great majority of Chancery actions continue to be heard in London. In any event, the jurisdiction to hear Chancery actions outside London is always subject to questions of practicality, and any party may, on the hearing of the Summons for Directions or at any other convenient time, apply for an action proceeding in a district registry to be transferred[16] to another district registry or to London, or for an action proceeding in London to be transferred to one of the district registries having jurisdiction to hear Chancery actions.

A Chancery writ (other than in a probate action[17]) may be issued out of any district registry.[18] But the action, if and when it comes to trial, cannot be heard except in London or one of the district registries having Chancery jurisdiction; nor can accounts or inquiries be conducted outside London or one of those district registries, unless the order for the account or inquiry expressly directs that the account or inquiry be conducted in some other district registry.[19]

The distribution of business amongst the Judges:

There are at present 13 judges of the High Court assigned to the Chancery Division, all of whom sit in London except one (to whom is given the ancient title Vice-Chancellor of the County Palatine of Lancaster) who sits as the Chancery judge in the district registries of the Northern Area.[20] Chancery actions in the district registries of Cardiff, Birmingham and Bristol are heard by two Circuit judges.

During term, there are also three or four deputy judges of the Chancery Division (usually senior members of the practis-

---

[14] See *Practice Direction (Chancery Chambers)* [1982] 1 W.L.R. 1189.

[15] For the general practice relating to Chancery actions proceeding outside London, see *Practice Direction (Chancery: Proceedings outside London)* [1972] 1 W.L.R. 1 and [1984] 1 W.L.R. 417; *Practice Direction (Chancery Chambers)* [1982] 1 W.L.R. 1189; and *Practice Direction (Chancery: Trial and hearing of Chancery Causes and Matters out of London)* No. 1 of 1988, [1988] 1 W.L.R. 630.

[16] For the procedure and practice on transfers between district registries or between district registries and London, see Ord. 4, r. 5.

[17] Ord. 76, r. 2.

[18] Ord. 6, r. 7(2).

[19] *Re Smith* (1877) 6 Ch.D. 692.

[20] *i.e.* Liverpool, Manchester, Preston, Newcastle and Leeds.

ing Bar) appointed temporarily to sit in London, and to whom are generally assigned the less "weighty" Chancery actions or who may assist in dealing with the business of the motions judge (for motions, see below). The Vice-Chancellor of the County Palatine of Lancaster is assisted in the conduct of Chancery business in the Northern Area by two Circuit judges, while the judges dealing with Chancery business in the Cardiff, Birmingham and Bristol district registries are from time to time assisted by one or more deputies.

The Vice-Chancellor of the Chancery Division[21] as vice-president of the Division is responsible for the distribution of business amongst the Chancery judges in London. Generally speaking, so many of the judges as are from time to time required will sit during term for the disposal of the Witness and the Non-Witness Lists (for an explanation of the Witness and Non-Witness Lists, see p. 373 below). But there are two patent judges whose functions are normally restricted to patent and registered trade mark work. In addition, two judges are assigned each term (the Easter and Trinity terms being treated as one) to hear motions. One of them ("the motions judge") will hear all motions every day for a period of two weeks; in the meantime, the second judge hears such of the other work of the Division as may be required, usually any short non-witness work. If the volume of business requires it, any other judge then available will assist with motions and hear such motions as the motions judge directs. At the end of the two weeks, the motions judge and the second judge exchange functions for the ensuing two weeks and so on until the end of the term.[22] Of the other judges, one is assigned to hear the Revenue List, and one to deal with companies business ("the Companies Court judge"). The remaining judges of the Division hear the Witness or Non-Witness Lists as the pressure of business demands.

The former practice of assigning the Judges of the Chancery Division to Group A or Group B, and dividing all actions proceeding in the Division to one Group or the other, was abolished with effect from October 1, 1982.

The Chancery Masters:

As in the Queen's Bench Division, a good deal of the business of the Chancery Division is undertaken by the

---

21 Who is not to be confused with the Vice-Chancellor of the County Palatine of Lancaster.
22 See *Practice Direction (Chancery Division: Motions Procedure)* [1980] 1 W.L.R. 751 as updated by *Practice Direction (Chancery Division: Motions Procedure) (No. 2)* [1985] 1 W.L.R. 244.

Masters. There are currently five Masters of the Division, presided over by the Chief Master. All the Masters of the Chancery Division are former solicitors (the Masters of the Queen's Bench Division are all former barristers). They sit every day during term in rooms in the Thomas More Building (which is also where most of the Chancery Division judges sit) in the Royal Courts of Justice.

The masters have the initial conduct of every action commenced in or transferred to the Chancery Division in London, other than Companies Court and bankruptcy business. Business was formerly distributed amongst the masters by use of the Group A and B system and then by reference to the first letter of the plaintiff's name (each master being assigned certain letters of the alphabet). But the Group A and B system was abolished with effect from October 1, 1982, and today all business is distributed simply by action number—as each successive writ or other originating process is issued, it is given an action number; upon issue of the first summons of the action, it is assigned to one or other of the masters by reference to the last digit of the action number.

The duties of the Chancery masters are to oversee the course of each action assigned to them and, when called upon to do so, to assist the parties in reaching a conclusion to their business in Court. A great many Chancery actions involve, because of the nature of the business assigned to the Division, the taking of accounts, the making of inquiries and the working out of judgments. This work is done or supervised by the masters and can be (though by no means always is) difficult and time-consuming, invariably (in the case of accounts and inquiries) requiring the consideration of affidavit evidence and may even require the hearing of oral evidence. The masters are supported by a staff of officials, from whom assistance (particularly in relation to the taking of accounts) may be sought by the parties themselves, as well as by the masters.

As well as dealing with administrative matters, and with accounts, inquiries and the working out of judgments, the Chancery masters are often called upon to make judicial decisions, not just in interlocutory matters such as applications for summary judgment or striking out applications, but also (at any rate where neither party objects) by way of final judgment in matters which are sufficiently straightforward not to require the attention of a judge (for further comments on the jurisdiction of the Chancery masters, see under Interlocutory Proceedings at pp. 366–367, below).

Chancery Chambers:

With effect from October 1, 1982, the administration of business in the Chancery Division was extensively revised.[23] All originating process issued in the Chancery Division in London, other than Companies Court and bankruptcy business, is now issued out of an office in the Royal Courts of Justice called Chancery Chambers. The business of Chancery Chambers is distributed amongst four Sections, namely:

—**The Chancery Chambers (Registry)**, which deals with court files, masters' summons and the issue of process;

—**The Drafting Section**, whose officers (called associates) deal with the drafting of orders;

—**The Listing Section**, which deals with (i) the setting down of all cases except motions and (ii) the listing of all cases except motions and patent actions;

—**The Accounts Section**, which deals with the examination of accounts and any certificates arising as a result of an account or inquiry.

A full list of the various types of business done in Chancery Chambers, and which Section deals with it, is set out in the Schedule to Practice Direction (Chancery Chambers) [1982] 1 W.L.R. 1189.

Nothing in the new arrangements affected the conduct of proceedings in the Companies Court or in bankruptcy; those are still dealt with in the separate offices of the companies' registrar and the bankruptcy registrars respectively.

Commencement of an action

As in the Queen's Bench Division, an action may be commenced in the Chancery Division by writ, by originating summons, by originating motion or by petition. Actions begun by originating motion or by petition (other than in the Companies Court and in bankruptcy) are exceedingly rare. In the Queen's Bench Division, most actions are begun by writ. Business in the Chancery Division, on the other hand, is more or less evenly divided, because of the nature of the work done in the Division, between actions begun by writ and actions begun by originating summons. All originating process in the Chancery Division in London (other than Companies Court and bankruptcy business) is issued out of Chancery Chambers.

Although most of the Rules of the Supreme Court applicable to an action begun by writ apply equally to an action begun by

[23] For full details of the administrative arrangements which came into force on October 1, 1982, see *Practice Direction (Chancery Chambers)* [1984] 1 W.L.R. 1189.

some other originating process, it is convenient to deal in the
rest of this Chapter with the procedure in the Chancery
Division on the basis (save where the contrary appears) that
the relevant action has been begun by writ, and then to deal in
the following Chapter (Chapter 22) with the particular features
of actions begun by originating summons, originating motion
and by petition.

Actions by Writ in the Chancery Division

Generally, and save as mentioned above, the procedure for
issue and service of the writ, acknowledgement of service and
on default of notice of intention to defend (which is, however,
frequently to move a motion for judgment) follows the same
rules as those applicable in the Queen's Bench Division.

A writ may be issued in the Chancery Division out of any
district registry,[24] except in a contentious probate action (in
which case the writ must be issued out of Chancery Chambers)[25]; and the district registrar has the same powers and
duties in relation to the action as the Chancery masters would
have had if the writ had been issued in London.[26]

The general rule (contrary to the former practice) in the
Chancery Division is that the title to the writ or any other
originating process should contain only the names of the
parties to the action, but there are two exceptions. (1) Where
the proceedings relate to the administration of an estate or a
probate action, they should be entitled "In the estate of AB
deceased"; and (2) Where the proceedings relate to the construction of a document they should be entitled "In the Matter
of [describe document briefly] dated . . . between AB and CD,"
or if there were numerous parties to the document, " . . .
between AB and others"; and if there is more than one
document, only the main document need be referred to.[27]
Although probate actions are invariably begun by writ, it will
in the nature of things be rare that an action relating to the
construction of a document will be begun by writ, so that
exception (2) above will normally only apply to actions begun
by originating summons.

Where there is more than one Plaintiff, or more than one
Defendant, the practice in the Chancery Division is to prefix
each party's name in the title to the action with a number, *e.g.*

---

[24] Ord. 6, r. 7(2).
[25] Ord. 76, r. 2.
[26] Ord. 32, r. 23.
[27] See *Practice Direction* [1983] 1 W.L.R. 4.

IN THE HIGH COURT OF JUSTICE   CH 1990
CHANCERY DIVISION

BETWEEN

(1) ARTHUR BOGGIS	
(2) MARY BOGGIS	*Plaintiffs*
and	
(1) CHRISTOPHER DAVIDSON	
(2) SUSAN DAVIDSON	*Defendants*

It is also the practice in the Chancery Division to refer to companies in the singular, using the singular neuter pronoun ("it") rather than the plural "they."

Summary Judgment (Order 14; Order 86)

Whilst the procedure of applying for summary judgment under Order 14 in actions commenced by writ is perfectly applicable to the Chancery Division, in practice, from the very nature of the actions dealt with, it is much less frequently resorted to than in the Queen's Bench Division. There is, however, a corresponding procedure under Order 86, only applicable to the Chancery Division, under which summary judgment may be obtained in any action commenced by a writ indorsed with a claim for specific performance of an agreement, whether or not in writing, for the sale, purchase or exchange of any real or personal[28] property, or for the grant or assignment of a lease of any property, or for rescission of such an agreement, or for the forfeiture or return of any deposit made under such an agreement.[29]

In contrast to Order 14, an Order 86 summons may be issued as soon as the action is commenced; the plaintiff need not have served a statement of claim, nor need he wait for the defendant to acknowledge service of the writ.[30]

Where there is no real defence to the action, the plaintiff may in such cases, on affidavit made by any person who can swear positively to the facts verifying the cause of action and stating that in his belief there is no defence, apply by summons for an order for the appropriate judgment; as in all interlocutory applications, the affidavit may include hearsay evidence pro-

---

[28] *Woodlands* v. *Hinds* [1955] 1 W.L.R. 688.
[29] Whether or not there is also a claim for damages: Ord. 86, r. 1(1)(*a*).
[30] Ord. 86, r. 1.

vided that the source of the information is given—the usual
formula is "I am informed by . . . and believe that . . ." The
summons must be accompanied by full minutes of the order to
which the plaintiff considers himself to be entitled: we shall
have something to say later about the minutes of Chancery
orders in general (*post*, pp. 374–375: a copy of the affidavit in
support and any exhibits must be served upon the defendant
together with the summons, which is returnable not less than
four clear days after service.[31]

Thereupon, unless the defendant by affidavit, by his own
viva voce evidence, or otherwise, can satisfy the master (or
judge, if the matter has been referred or appealed to him[32]) that
he has a good defence to the action on the merits, or discloses
such facts as entitle him to a hearing, judgment will be given
for the plaintiff.[33] Leave to defend may be given unconditionally or subject to such terms as to giving security or time or
mode of trial or otherwise as the master or judge may think fit,
and where such leave is given, further directions must be given
as to the further conduct of the action, as if the application for
judgment was a summons for directions.[34]

The Order 86 procedure must not, of course, be resorted to
where the plaintiff knows that there is in fact a substantial
issue to be tried: if he does resort to it in such a case, his
summons will be dismissed and in all probability with costs,
which may be ordered to be paid forthwith.[35] The procedure is,
in any event, not available against the Crown.[36]

Another procedure frequently resorted to in the Chancery
Division for obtaining what is in effect summary judgment is
that provided by Order 43, where the writ is indorsed with a
claim for an account. This enables orders for the taking of
accounts and inquiries to be obtained speedily in clear cases.[37]

Pleadings

All the rules of pleading which we have already elaborated[38]
apply just as much to the statement of claim and subsequent

---

[31] Ord. 86, r. 2.
[32] See as to the general procedure before the master in the Chancery Division, *post*.
[33] Ord. 86, r. 3.
[34] Ord. 86, rr. 4, 5.
[35] Ord. 86, r. 6.
[36] Ord. 77, r. 7(1).
[37] The procedure can also be, and frequently is, used in proceedings begun by Originating
Summons such as an application under section 30 of the Law of Property Act 1925 for
the sale of real property held jointly, or for the winding-up of the affairs of a partnership
(other than an insolvent partnership).
[38] See Chaps. 6 to 9, *ante*.

pleadings in a Chancery action as they do to one in the Queen's Bench Division. On the whole, however, pleadings in the Chancery Division tend to be longer and more detailed. The reason is not far to seek; for in general one or other of the parties will be seeking some equitable relief, or relying upon some equitable defence, which involves the exercise of the court's discretion. Such exercise always necessitates the consideration of the whole of the surrounding circumstances, many of which would not be material in an action at law. Thus specific performance may be refused upon the ground of unilateral mistake[39]; or an injunction upon the ground of hardship[40]; or any remedy because the plaintiff does not come to the court "with clean hands."[41] Both the plaintiff and the defendant must therefore plead very much more of the surrounding circumstances than is either necessary or desirable in a common law action.

The biggest difference lies, however, in the nature of the relief claimed, which is normally much more complicated than that sought at common law,[42] and frequently involves, because of the nature of the business assigned to or commonly dealt with in the Chancery Division, an account or an inquiry of some sort. As equitable relief can always be moulded to suit the facts disclosed in any particular case, it often happens that precisely the right relief is not sought in the first instance; thus, it is a Chancery tradition that the heads of relief claimed invariably end up with two heads of "Further or other relief" and "Costs."[43]

Interlocutory Proceedings

The summons for directions,[44] discovery[45] (which originated in Courts of Chancery), applications for particulars,[46] service of

---

[39] *Weston* v. *Bird* (1853) 2 W.R. 145.

[40] *Behrens* v. *Richards* [1905] 2 Ch. 614. And consider the facts a careful pleader would have needed to plead in *Redland Bricks Ltd.* v. *Morris* [1970] A.C. 652 to have obtained the relief which the House of Lords said might properly have been granted in that case (limited mandatory injunction).

[41] *Davis* v. *Symonds* (1787) 1 Cox Eq.Cas. 402.

[42] See, *e.g. Redland Bricks Ltd.* v. *Morris, supra.*

[43] Costs need not be specifically claimed: Ord. 18, r. 15. Despite the wide phrasing of "further or other relief," it is limited to relief consistent with what is expressly asked for:— *Cargill* v. *Bower* (1878) 10 Ch.D. at p. 508; and if the defendant is in default of pleading or fails to appear at the trial no relief other than that expressly claimed can be granted: *Faithfull* v. *Woodley* (1889) 43 Ch.D. 287.

[44] See Chap. 18.

[45] See Chap. 16.

[46] See Chap. 10.

interrogatories,[47] and other cognate interlocutory matters follow the same course as in an action in the Queen's Bench Division, and any necessary applications to the court (other than those made by notice under the summons for directions) will be by summons. The master, whose powers are governed by different provisions from those governing a Queen's Bench master's,[48] will deal with any such application in the first instance.[49] Indeed, subject to the limitations on his powers contained in Order 32, rule 14, the master has power to transact all such business and exercise all such authority and jurisdiction as may be transacted and exercised by a judge in chambers.[50]

But if the parties invite the master, instead of hearing the summons himself, immediately to refer it to the judge, of if the master himself feels that the application is one which ought to be determined by a judge rather than by a master, he may adjourn the summons to come before the judge in chambers, either on a Monday morning or, if it appears that the hearing is likely to take longer than about 15 minutes, on a date to be fixed through "the usual channels" (*i.e.* the Clerk of the Lists).[51]

If the master (as is usually the case) himself hears the summons and makes an order on it, any party aggrieved may appeal his decision in the same way as he would appeal a decision of a Queen's Bench master. The time for appealing is within five days of the order.[52]

Interlocutory Relief

It is principally in the matter of obtaining interlocutory relief that the form of a Chancery action before judgment differs from that in the Queen's Bench Division. Most interlocutory relief is obtained by means of a motion, made to the judge in open court, upon two clear days' notice.[53] This affords an extremely speedy way of obtaining relief with a minimum of

---

[47] See Chap. 19.
[48] A Chancery Master's powers are in general regulated by Ord. 32, r. 14(1) and the directions given thereunder (as to which see *Practice Direction* [1990] 1 W.L.R. 52); a Queen's Bench Master's by Ord. 32, r. 11.
[49] See Ord. 32, r. 14(1).
[50] Ord. 32, r. 14(1). The master's powers are subject to any limitations imposed by the direction of the Vice-Chancellor, and the present practice is governed by directions contained in *Practice Direction* [1990] 1 W.L.R. 52. Where the master's jurisdiction is limited by reference to the size of the fund in question, it is generally assimilated to the equity jurisdiction of the county court.
[51] *Practice Direction (Summonses)* [1974] 1 W.L.R. 1659.
[52] Ord. 58, rr. 1 and 2.
[53] Ord. 8, r. 2(2).

delay, and accordingly is universally followed in contentious matters. But where the parties are agreed upon the desirability of some form of interlocutory relief—for example, the appointment of a receiver—the application can as well be made by summons unless speed is essential.

Motions normally should be, and usually are, made upon notice to the party against whom the order is sought, but where delay would be fatal ("I never wait till the axe is laid to the root of the tree," said Lord Eldon), or where the purpose of the motion is to obtain, for example, an order for the seizure of documents likely to be destroyed or an injunction restraining assets from being dissipated or removed from the jurisdiction, motions may be made *ex parte*,[54] and, in extreme cases, before the issue of the writ.[55]

Normally, however, even in a case of extreme urgency there is still time to issue a writ, and the notice of motion can be served together with the writ.[56] The difficulty in the way of bringing an urgent motion on notice is that it must be a two clear days' notice. Accordingly, an application will be made *ex parte* to the motions judge at the afternoon resumption of the sitting of the court for leave to serve short notice of motion.[57] This enables service to be effected for the next motion day (at present every weekday save the last day of each sittings[58]). The court is also often asked to grant an interim injunction over that day in order to preserve the status quo in the meantime. If granted, such an interim injunction is upon such terms as to costs, and subject to such undertaking, if any, as the court may think fit to impose. The party restrained is theoretically at liberty to move the court to discharge any order so made,[59] but, from the nature of the situation, it is not often a right of which he can take advantage in time.

The notice of motion itself must be in writing,[60] addressed to the party or parties against whom the order is sought, and must state on its face on whose behalf it will be made. If leave

---

[54] Any relief obtainable by summons in the Chancery Division can equally well be obtained by motion: *Heywood* v. *B.D.C. Properties Ltd.* [1964] 1 W.L.R. 971, *per* Harman L.J. at p. 974.

[55] *Carr* v. *Morice* (1873) 16 Eq. 125. An *ex parte* order for the seizure of documents is known as an "Anton Piller Order" (see *Anton Piller KG* v. *Manufacturing Processes Ltd.* [1976] Ch. 55; an *ex parte* injunction restraining the dissipation of assets or their removal out of the jurisdiction is known as a "Mareva Injunction" (see *Mareva Compania Naviera SA* v. *International Bulk Carriers SA* [1980] 1 All E.R. 213 (C.A.). See Chap. 4.

[56] Ord. 8, r. 4.

[57] Ord. 8, r. 2(2).

[58] See *Practice Direction (Chancery Division: Motions Procedure)* [1980] 1 W.L.R. 751.

[59] Ord. 8, r. 2(1).

[60] Ord. 8, r. 3(1).

to serve short notice of the motion has been obtained from the judge, this must be stated on its face,[61] and a defendant is at liberty to disregard a short notice of motion which does not show that such leave has been obtained.[62] A single notice of motion may include claims for several different species of relief and the separation of claims will be actively discouraged in costs.[63] It is impossible to list all the types of relief which can be obtained; the two commonest are injunctions and the appointment of receivers; but the validity of the writ can also be attacked in this way, the defendant may be made to bring money into court, an order of committal (usually for disobedience to an order of the court) may be obtained,[64] and so on.

The notice of motion should be settled by counsel—the cost of this will always be allowed upon taxation[65]—and should specify the relief sought, whatever it is, in precise terms. Evidence upon the motion will in the first instance be given by affidavit,[66] usually drafted by counsel at the same time as the notice of motion; and, since the relief sought is interlocutory, evidence upon information and belief may be received, provided the sources and grounds thereof are given[67]—a qualification often forgotten. The court may, and in a proper case will, make an order for the attendance of the deponents for cross-examination.

The notice of motion is served in the same way as any other document requiring service during the course of an action, unless its object is to commit to prison for contempt of court the person to whom it is addressed, in which case personal service must be made if at all possible.[68] In such cases, copies of the affidavit evidence must be served together with the notice.[69]

Motions are heard in open court.[70] They are listed so far as possible. For this purpose the necessary documents, namely

---

[61] Ord. 8, r. 3(1).

[62] *Moggridge* v. *Thomas* (1847) 2 Coop., temp.Cott. 166.

[63] *Hawke* v. *Kemp* (1840) 3 Beav. 288.

[64] Ord. 52, r. 4(1).

[65] *Practice Note* [1929] W.N. 105.

[66] Ord. 38, r. 2(3).

[67] Ord. 41, r. 5(2).

[68] Ord. 52, rr. 4(2) and 4(3).

[69] Ord. 52, r. 4(2).

[70] The procedure described is new, and was introduced with effect from October 1, 1980: see *Practice Direction (Chancery Division: Motions Procedure)* [1980] 1 W.L.R. 751 and [1985] 1 W.L.R. 244. The previous procedure was that motions were heard on Tuesdays and Fridays and were not listed. They were moved in order of seniority of counsel (*Soltau* v. *De Held* (1851) 15 Jur. 1151), "ineffective" or unopposed motions being disposed of first time through, and "effective" or opposed motions being heard second time round.

two copies of the writ and of the notice of motion and counsel's estimate of the length of the hearing, are lodged with the clerk of the lists in Chancery Chambers by 12 noon on the weekday before the hearing day. If the motion is "short" (five minutes or less), it is so marked in the motions book. In the daily list motions are heard, subject to the judge's overriding discretion, in the following order: (a) motions affecting the liberty of the subject, which take absolute priority over other business,[71] (b) motions marked "short," (c) motions which have been listed, in the listed order and (d) motions which are not listed, in the order of the seniority (or juniority[72]) of the counsel moving them. If the hearing of the motion is likely to take more than two hours, it will immediately be stood over by the motions judge to come on to be heard on a date to be fixed (a "motion by order"). If motions business is heavy, the motions judge may call on other judges of the Division (and deputies if any are sitting) to assist if available. Unfinished business is put at the head of the following day's list. It frequently happens that a defendant appears by counsel before having acknowledged service of the writ. In such cases it is the duty of counsel to inform the court of this fact, and undertake on his behalf that service of the writ will be acknowledged forthwith, and to see that his instructing solicitors understand that this must be done.[73]

Frequently it is necessary to adjourn the motion from time to time in order to enable the opposition to file evidence in answer, or for the party moving to file evidence in reply. Justice is usually served in such cases by putting the party moved against upon terms when adjourning, in order to preserve the status quo.[74] Usually all that is required is a suitable undertaking on his behalf; it rarely proves necessary actually to obtain an injunction, but if the party moved against is not willing to assist in preserving the position, whilst at the same time he desires time to answer the evidence (to which he is, of course, clearly entitled), the party moving may move *ex parte*, immediately after the motion has been stood over, for the same relief.

Where there are no undertakings to be given for the first time (as opposed to merely being continued) and the motion is

---

[71] *Ashton* v. *Shorrock* (1880) 29 W.R. 117.

[72] The tradition has developed that on the last motion day of the sittings unlisted motions are moved in order of juniority of counsel, not their seniority. This practice is now formally recognised.

[73] *Practice Note* [1934] W.N. 228.

[74] Ord. 8, r. 5.

to be stood over for not more than 14 days, this may now be done by the solicitors or counsel for the parties or one of them appearing before the associate and producing the written consent (usually a letter) of the parties. Not more than three successive adjournments may be applied for in this manner and no such adjournment may be made to the last two motion days of the sittings. The procedure is entirely optional, but if adopted the parties must notify the clerk to the motions judge of the date to which the motion has been stood, as otherwise he will not list the motion for that day.[75]

Sometimes the hearing of the motion is, in simple cases, by consent treated as the trial of the action or as a motion for judgment, and an immediate order in the usual form taken. Thus in, say, a partnership dispute, where one partner moves for a receiver and manager, the other partner may clearly realise that the partnership must be dissolved. Accordingly, in such a case by consent of both parties an immediate order for the dissolution of the partnership would be made, and the usual accounts and inquiries directed, thus saving any further pleadings; and so also in many others.

Often the action is compromised on the hearing of the motion: and here, as at any other stage of the action, the usual form of order (colloquially known as a "Tomlin Order," see Practice Note [1927] W.N. 290) is to stay all further proceedings upon the terms scheduled to the order except for the purpose of carrying such terms into effect, with liberty to apply for that purpose.

It frequently happens that the nature or subject-matter of the action will make its final determination a clear matter of urgency. In such a case the judge will, either on the parties' application or when deciding the motion before him, give directions for a speedy trial, as if there were a summons for directions before him. The directions will impose a strict timetable for pleadings and other interlocutory matters and will specify a date for the matter to be restored before the master, with liberty to proceed to set down for trial notwithstanding any of the directions may not have been complied with.[76]

If, for any reason, the applicant does not desire to move his motion, he may save it, either by agreement or by mentioning it to the court. But, if it is not so moved or saved to be heard at the trial, it is treated as abandoned, and the costs thereof will be the respondent's in any event.[77]

---

[75] *Practice Direction (Chancery Division: Motions Procedure)* [1980] 1 W.L.R. 751 and [1985] 1 W.L.R. 244.
[76] *Practice Direction* [1974] 1 W.L.R. 339.
[77] *Harrison* v. *Leutner* (1881) 16 Ch.D. 559.

Where, on the final disposal of the motion, the judge makes no express order as to the incidence of costs, the well-settled rules (which have survived the introduction of The Supreme Court Costs Rules 1969, now Order 62) are as follows:

(a) The party making a successful motion is entitled to his costs as costs in the cause; but the party opposing it is not entitled to his costs as costs in the cause.

(b) The party making a motion which failed is not entitled to his costs as costs in the cause; but the party opposing it is entitled to his costs as costs in the cause.

(c) If a motion was made by one party and not opposed by the other, the costs of both parties are costs in the cause.

The order will be drawn accordingly. If costs are explicitly dealt with, it will usually be on the same principles, although in some contested cases "costs in cause" may be awarded as more appropriate.

Motions for Judgment

So far we have been speaking of motions for interlocutory relief in the course of an action. In a large number of cases the mode of obtaining judgment is by motion for judgment; and the types of action in which this procedure is necessary (See Chapter 4) are in general precisely the types which find their natural forum in the Chancery Division. In addition, in this Division this is the correct procedure where judgment is sought upon admissions of fact.[78]

Such motions are set down in the cause book and are listed. If it is considered that they will not take more than 10 minutes, then upon production of a certificate of counsel to this effect they will be marked as a short cause and come into the list on the next short cause day.[79] If this certificate cannot be given, they will be entered in the Non-Witness List[80] and come on for hearing in the ordinary way.

In all such cases the notice of motion for judgment must either set out the exact order sought in the body thereof,[81] or, more usually, be accompanied by minutes of order. This is so even when all that is asked for is a "common form" order. It must also state that it has been marked short if this is the case.

The defendant must be given two clear days' notice of the motion.[82] If it is moved in default of his notice of intention to

---

[78] *Cook* v. *Heynes* [1884] W.N. 75.
[79] At present this is Wednesday.
[80] See *Practice Direction* [1983] 1 W.L.R. 436, para. 8.
[81] *De Jongh* v. *Newman* (1887) 56 L.T. 180.
[82] Ord. 8, r. 2(2).

defend, there having been no acknowledgment of service, then
following the previous practice,[83] there will be no necessity for
the production of a certificate to this effect at the hearing, but
one will have to be produced to the associate before the order
is drawn up.

Upon the hearing of a motion for judgment no evidence is
receivable and the plaintiff will be granted only the relief to
which he is clearly entitled on the facts pleaded in his statement of claim.[84] The frequent need to resort to this procedure is
another reason why the claim in a Chancery action tends to be
fully and meticulously pleaded.

Trial and Judgment

Chancery actions which are to be heard in London are set
down for trial, at the request of either party (usually the
plaintiff) by the cause clerk in Chancery Chambers[85]; Chancery
actions which are to be heard in one of the District Registries
having jurisdiction to hear Chancery[86] actions are set down in
that District Registry.

The Chancery cause list in London is divided into the
Witness List and the Non-Witness List. Actions commenced by
writ will almost invariably be set down in the Witness List. The
Witness List is again divided into two parts. Actions estimated
to last more than three days are set down in Part I of the
Witness List and those estimated to last three days or less in
Part II. Actions are initially set down on the basis of the
master's provisional estimate of length.[87]

Within 10 days of setting an action down for trial the
solicitors for each party must lodge with the cause clerk a
certificate signed by counsel stating the length of time which
the trial is expected to occupy. Where practicable, there should
be a single certificate signed by all the counsel concerned. Any
action is, in theory, liable to come on for trial at any time after
28 days from setting down. However, a party to a Part I action
may, within such time, apply to the Clerk of the Lists for a
fixed date, or a marking that the action shall not come on
before a particular date, or without a specified period of notice.
In special circumstances, for example where the attendance of

---

[83] *Re Thomas* [1940] W.N. 319.
[84] *Young v. Thomas* [1892] 2 Ch. 134.
[85] *Practice Direction (Chancery Chambers)* [1982] 1 W.L.R. 1189.
[86] *i.e.* Leeds, Liverpool, Manchester, Newcastle-upon-Tyne and Preston, Birmingham, Cardiff and Bristol.
[87] *Practice Direction (Chancery Lists)* [1983] 1 W.L.R. 436.

several witnesses is required, such an application may be made in respect of a Part II case. If the estimated length of trial changes at any time, it is the solicitor's duty to inform the Clerk of the Lists immediately, and, if appropriate, the action will be transferred from Part I to Part II of the Witness List or *vice versa.*[88]

The actual course of the trial will follow the course of a normal trial without a jury in the Queen's Bench Division. We have already noted the usual form of order if the action is compromised.[89] Because the calculation of damages in Chancery matters is often complicated (for example, assessing the loss of profits of a business in a passing-off action), it is common for the plaintiff to seek, as part of his relief, an inquiry as to damages. It is then unnecessary to plead or adduce evidence of lengthy details of the alleged loss, so that the trial is kept shorter. If the plaintiff succeeds on the merits it is the Chancery practice that, provided he proves some loss to himself as a result, he will be entitled to an inquiry as to precisely what damage he has suffered.[90]

When the judge has given his judgment, either at the conclusion of the hearing or after *curia advisari vult* (commonly abbreviated to c.a.v. and meaning that the court takes time to consider its decision), the question often arises as to the precise form in which the result of that judgment should be embodied in an order. In such cases, junior counsel are often directed by the judge to settle and sign a minute, or settle and circulate a minute, in order that proper consideration can be given to the exact terms in which it should be framed. If, as not infrequently happens, counsel cannot agree, the action must be mentioned again to the judge on the form of the minutes ("speaking to the minutes"), and he will then settle any items in dispute.

The forms of Chancery judgments, following the form of the relief sought, often differ greatly from the form of the normal Queen's Bench judgment. Indeed, whilst in the latter division the whole of the litigation is normally finished as soon as judgment is pronounced, in the Chancery action it has often barely begun: the terms of the judgment have yet to be worked out.

The traditional storehouse of this branch of the law is the three volumes of *Seton on Judgments and Orders,*[91] where prece-

---

88 [1983] 1 W.L.R. 436 *supra.*

89 *Ante,* p. 371.

90 *Rightside Properties Ltd.* v. *Gray* [1975] Ch. 72 at p. 89.

91 (7th ed.), 1912. Atkin's *Court Forms* (2nd ed.), *current*, contains the more modern forms.

dents appropriate to many actions may be found. There is, however, a very great art in drawing such judgments and orders with precision, and the ultimate arbiters are the Chancery associates, who are finally responsible for the form of orders in all cases, though if the judge has directed the signature of a minute by counsel[92] their task is rendered comparatively simple.

Working Out of the Judgment

It is impossible in the space available to follow up all the different possible types of action which can be brought, and consider all the various types of judgments and the working out which they necessitate. But the typical Chancery judgment directs an account, or an inquiry, or involves the settlement of some document, or the sale of some property. In all such cases the matter is referred back to chambers for the master to take the account, hold the inquiry, or do whatever else is necessary in order to make the judgment effective. The further consideration of the action by the judge is postponed until after the result of the proceedings before the master is known.

Let us assume that the order has directed some form of accounts and inquiries. In such a case, unless the judgment contains directions as to the manner in which the accounts and inquiries are to proceed[93] the next step is for the party in whose favour the order was made (usually the plaintiff) to issue a summons to proceed returnable before the master.

The summons to proceed must be served on all parties to the action. On the return of the summons, the master will decide whether all the persons interested in the result of the action are before the court or bound by the action. If not—for example, though *one* beneficiary under a trust may have an order against the trustees for the carrying of the trusts into execution, clearly *all* beneficiaries will be interested parties—he may give directions for the service of notice of the judgment or order on the interested parties. After such notice, they will be bound by the judgment as if they had originally been parties and equally will be at liberty to move upon notice to set the judgment aside or apply by summons to vary or add to it.[94]

---

[92] See *Practice Direction (Chancery Chambers)* [1982] 1 W.L.R. 1189. The Chancery associates perform the same duties as the associates in the Queen's Bench Division so far as proceedings in court are concerned, but their principal functions are to act as watchdogs in all matters of practice and to draw up all judgments and orders.

[93] Ord. 44, r. 3; and see the note to Ord. 44, r. 1.

[94] Ord. 44, r. 2.

As soon as the master is satisfied that all the interested parties are accounted for, he will give directions as to the way in which each account or inquiry is to proceed, the evidence which he will require upon each, who is to attend the proceedings under each, and fix any necessary time limits for carrying out such directions.[95] Thus in an action for the administration of an estate, advertisements for creditors and beneficiaries will normally be directed,[96] and if the next-of-kin of the deceased are unknown, one of the parties may be directed to bring in a pedigree of the deceased; in an action for dissolution of a partnership various accounts are normally directed and the accounting party will be directed to bring in a properly vouched account.

The course of the proceedings in front of the master follows as near as may be that of a motion in open court, except that in general it will be conducted by the parties' solicitors, and counsel will only be brought in on points of difficulty or perhaps of principle. Thus the evidence is all given by affidavit in the first instance. If during the course of taking the account or inquiry any point of principle arises upon which the parties cannot agree, the master will direct the issue of a summons raising the point in question; the master will then adjudicate on the summons or, if the question is more appropriate for decision by the judge, he will refer the summons to the judge in the usual way. Alternatively, questions of disputed fact may arise, or of mixed fact and law, which need to be determined after the hearing of oral evidence; in such a case, the master will direct the service of Points of Claim, Points of Defence and so forth, which have the same purpose as ordinary pleadings in an action and to which, broadly speaking, the same rules apply. If appropriate, the master will hear the evidence and adjudicate on the issue himself; if not, he will refer it to the judge.

When the accounts and inquiries have finally been answered, the master makes his report of the result in the form of an order which is drawn up in Chancery Chambers.[97] Every order of the master whether made during the course of the accounts and inquiries or as his final order, has immediate binding effect on all parties,[98] although subject to appeal. Any appeal must be made by issuing notice of appeal in the usual

---

[95] Ord. 44, r. 3.
[96] Ord. 44, r. 5.
[97] Ord. 44, r. 11.
[98] Ord. 44, r. 11(4).

way, within five clear days (or longer if leave is given and it is a proper case for extending time) after the order is made.[99]

Further Consideration

It sometimes happens that questions raised in the action are left over for further consideration once the results of the accounts and inquiries are known; or that those results show (for example, because the inquiry reveals new information not previously known to the parties) that further questions arise in the action, or further accounts or inquiries need to be ordered.

Apart from the further consideration of (i) debenture holders' actions, or for the distribution of an insolvent estate, or the estate of an intestate, (ii) an order made in chambers and (iii) when the original judgment or the master by order[1] directs the further consideration to take place in chambers, all of which take place in chambers, all further consideration of the action is heard in open court. The action must be set down for further consideration in the cause book, and notice given to all parties affected thereby, in accordance with the directions given in that respect by the judge in the original judgment or by the master on making his order.

The order on further consideration will be drawn up by the associate in the normal way.[2] If it, in its turn, as sometimes happens, directs further accounts and inquiries, or the settlement of documents, the further consideration of the action will again be adjourned and the procedure in chambers which we have already outlined will recommence in connection with such further inquiries.

Costs

The costs of and incidental to all proceedings in the Supreme Court, including the administration of estates and trusts, are in the discretion of the court[3] (see Chapter 25 for general principles on costs). But it is expressly provided that where a person is or has been a party to any proceedings in the capacity of trustee, personal representative or mortgagee, he is to be entitled to his costs (so far as they are not recovered from or

---

[99] Ord. 44, r. 12; Ord. 58, r. 1.

[1] Ord. 44, r. 11(3).

[2] An interlocutory order may now be drawn up by solicitors on their request and subject to the master's discretion. Ord. 42, r. 6.

[3] Ord. 62, r. 3.

paid by any other person) out of the trust fund, estate, or the mortgaged property, as the case may be. And the court can only deprive him of these costs on the ground that the person concerned has acted unreasonably, or, in the case of a trustee or personal representative, has in substance acted for his own benefit rather than for the benefit of the fund.[4] Moreover on any taxation of costs of a trustee or personal representative which are payable out of the trust fund or estate, he is entitled to be paid his costs taxed on the "indemnity basis" (*i.e.* all his costs except in so far as they are of an unreasonable amount or have been unreasonably incurred, all doubts being resolved in his favour[5]), although costs shall be presumed to have been unreasonably incurred if incurred contrary to his duty as trustee or personal representative.[6]

Execution and Appeals

The method of enforcement of an order, whether interlocutory or final, or a judgment, in the Chancery Division is the same as that of enforcing a judgment in the Queen's Bench Division[7]; and, except that many of the possible grounds of appeal will not apply, the procedure on appeal to the Court of Appeal and the House of Lords is also the same.[8]

---

[4] Ord. 62, r. 6(2).
[5] Ord. 62, r. 12(2).
[6] Ord. 62, r. 14.
[7] See Chap. 24.
[8] See Chap. 23.

CHAPTER 22

OTHER CAUSES AND MATTERS IN THE CHANCERY DIVISION

In Chapter 21, we dealt with the way in which business is organised in the Chancery Division, and the procedure in the Chancery Division in actions begun by writ. In this chapter, we deal with the other three forms of originating process, namely originating summonses, originating notices of motion and petitions, prefacing such consideration with the observation that in many cases there is a choice of the method of approach to the court, although that most frequently encountered is the choice between an approach by writ and originating summons.

Originating Summonses

This is one of the four originating procedures.[1] Where an application is to be made to the High Court under any Act, then this is the appropriate originating procedure, unless under the Rules or the Act the application is expressly required or authorised to be commenced in some other fashion.[2] Except in the case of proceedings which must be commenced by writ, either as a result of the provisions of the Rules or any Act, proceedings may be begun either by writ or originating summons as the plaintiff thinks fit.[3]

Where the main point at issue is one of construction of a document or statute, or is one of pure law, then this is the appropriate procedure. It is not, however, appropriate where there is likely to be any substantial dispute of fact. It is also inappropriate if the plaintiff thinks that the action is one in which summary judgment can be obtained under Order 14 or Order 86.[4]

Before 1964, there was no general right to proceed by originating summons; but its simplicity and speed had led to a great and growing number of rules and statutes prescribing this procedure. It is now, as we have seen above, available generally. Its merits lie in the fact that there are no pleadings or (in general) witnesses, the question for decision being raised directly by the summons itself, and the evidence being given

---

[1] Ord. 5, r. 1.
[2] Ord. 5, r. 3.
[3] Ord. 5, r. 4(1).
[4] Ord. 5, r. 4(2).

by affidavit, and that often there is no necessity to resort to any interlocutory proceedings such as discovery.

There are no less than three different types of originating summons in common use[5]: the general form, the expedited form and an *ex parte* form.[6] Service of the first two has to be acknowledged, but on the expedited form, which is used only where prescribed, an appointment may be fixed on the issue of the summons itself.

Where the originating summons relates to the administration of an estate, it should be headed "In the Matter of AB deceased"; where it relates to the construction of a document, it should be headed "In the Matter of [describe document briefly, *e.g.* the Lease] dated —— between AB and CD"; in either case followed by the names of the parties to the action, as in a writ. Otherwise, there is no distinction between the heading to an originating summons and that to a writ.[7]

The general form of summons will be used in all cases unless it is taken out under the provisions of an Act or order which provides that the expedited form shall be used[8]; the *ex parte* form will be used only upon applications where there are no opponents (*e.g.* an application by all the beneficiaries under a trust for the appointment of a new trustee upon the death of a sole trustee). The Rules, and if necessary the appropriate Act, must be consulted to see if there are any special rules as to parties. If not, the normal rules as to parties apply,[9] including the usual rules as to parties under a disability.[10] Where, however, as frequently happens, the rights *inter se* of beneficiaries under a trust or will are in question, as under the common "construction summons" under Order 85, r. 2, there can obviously be no following of the general rule that the trustees or executors sufficiently represent the estate and the beneficial interests, and all the beneficiaries interested in the questions in debate must be made parties to the application, either as plaintiffs or defendants. This may result in very large numbers of parties (as always in Chancery actions, if there are

---

[5] There is a fourth, specifically prescribed only for use when claiming possession against "squatters" under Ord. 113. The form is R.S.C., Appx. A, Form 11a.

[6] See R.S.C., Appx. A, Forms Nos. 8, 10 and 11. Form 9, previously used in a District Registry, was deleted as from June 3, 1980.

[7] Practice Direction [1983] 1 W.L.R. 4.

[8] See Ord. 57 (Divisional Court Proceedings): Ord. 94(5) (proceedings under the Representation of the People Acts): Ord. 106 (proceedings under the Solicitors Act 1974): and Ord. 99 (proceedings under the Inheritance (Provision for Family and Dependants) Act 1975).

[9] See Ord. 15 generally.

[10] Ord. 80.

two or more plaintiffs, or two or more defendants, each must be given a number in the heading to the action). If, however, persons who have the same interest are very numerous, or difficult or expensive to discover, a representation order appointing one of the class to represent the whole will often be ordered.[11]

An originating summons is prepared in the same way as a writ, and must bear an indorsement of address. It must in the body thereof raise the exact questions which it is desired to have determined, ideally in such a form that the court will be able merely to pronounce for one of the alternatives propounded. The court will in general only determine the exact points raised, and will not determine anything not specifically raised unless the plaintiff or applicant agrees,[12] but in a suitable case it is now possible for a defendant to make a counterclaim.[13]

Unless the action is brought in a District Registry,[14] a Chancery Division summons will be issued and sealed at Chancery Chambers, and at the same time it will be given an action number and assigned to one or other of the five Chancery masters. The assignment is made by reference to the last digit of the action number.[15]

Service of an originating summons is required to be effected in the same way as service of a writ,[16] including the time-limit for service.[17] Orders for substituted service,[18] or service out of the jurisdiction,[19] may be obtained in proper cases. If an acknowledgment of service is required it should be given in the normal way within 14 days after service, for although service may be acknowledged at any time prior to the hearing, no extra time will be allowed at any stage on account of such delay.[20]

As soon as all defendants have acknowledged service—or sufficient time has elapsed to enable this to be done[21]—an

---

[11] Ord. 15, rr. 12 and 13.
[12] *Re Carter* (1893) 41 W.R. 140. See Ord. 7, r. 3.
[13] Ord. 28, r. 7.
[14] The District Registries which have Chancery jurisdiction are those at Liverpool, Manchester, Preston, Newcastle and Leeds (the Northern Area); and since October 1, 1982, Birmingham, Cardiff and Bristol.
[15] Ord. 4, r. 1(1).
[16] Ord. 10, r. 5.
[17] Ord. 6, r. 8; Ord. 7, r. 6.
[18] Ord. 65, r. 4. *Re Conan Doyle's Will Trust* [1971] Ch. 982.
[19] Ord. 11, r. 9.
[20] Ord. 12, r. 6(2).
[21] Ord. 28, r. 2: Ord. 28 constitutes a complete code of the procedure upon originating summons.

appointment will be taken before the master to whom the matter has been assigned (or if the summons is proceeding in a District Registry, before the district registrar), and notice of this appointment, in the prescribed form, must be served upon the defendants or respondents, at the address given for service in the acknowledgment of service, at least four clear days before the return day. In the case of summonses in the expedited form, the return day may be fixed on the issue of the summons and is stated in the body thereof: in the case of *ex parte* summonses it is fixed in chambers on the production of the original summons and is indorsed in the margin.[22]

Hearing of Summons

When the summons first comes before him the master (or district registrar) will give all necessary directions as to the further conduct of the proceedings as he thinks best adapted to secure the just, expeditious[23] and economical disposal thereof.[24] Normally, the initial directions will be as to the filing of evidence. Such evidence is invariably given by affidavit in the first instance, and an affidavit on behalf of the plaintiff or applicant supporting the summons is normally sworn and filed[25] shortly after issue. Very often no further evidence will be required, but all the other parties will require to take advice on the point, and the master will accordingly adjourn the appointment from time to time until the evidence is completed. The master does not merely act as a ring-keeper, but may and frequently does require of his own motion the filing of further evidence which he thinks he will require (if the summons is one which he has power, and proposes, to deal with himself)[26] or which he thinks may be of assistance to the judge, and the joinder of additional parties. Or, indeed, he may at any time give any directions which could have been given if the proceedings had been commenced by writ and a summons for directions therein were before him[27] (for example, an order for

---

[22] Ord. 28, r. 2(2).
[23] Special directions have been given as to the conduct of business in chambers with a view to avoiding delay: Practice Direction (Ch.D.). (Interlocutory Proceedings: Avoidance of Delay) [1970] 1 W.L.R. 95; [1970] 1 All E.R. 11.
[24] Ord. 28, r. 4(2).
[25] Notwithstanding Ord. 28, r. 4(4) the present practice is not to file evidence but to lodge it in Chambers at least two clear days before the hearing: see also Ord. 41, r. 10.
[26] See Ord. 32, r. 14, in particular the notes thereto.
[27] Ord. 28, r. 4(4); see Chap. 18. But it is noteworthy that while the plaintiff's action may be dismissed for default in complying with an order or for want of prosecution (Ord. 28, r. 10), no order can be made in originating summons procedure penalising the defendant or respondent for his default. *Isaac* v. *Isaac* [1972] 1 W.L.R. 921, 924.

discovery, which is not automatic in the originating summons procedure).

Indeed, with the introduction of a choice, in many cases, of a writ or summons as the originating process, it may well turn out that a wrong choice was made: accordingly, the master can, if it appears that the proceedings ought properly to continue as if commenced by writ, so order.[28] He may at the same time order that any affidavits[29] shall stand as pleadings, and give (or refrain from giving) liberty to any of the parties to add thereto or apply for particulars thereof. This procedure applies even where the proceedings could not have been commenced by writ in the first place.[30] Thereafter, of course, the action will continue along the lines noted in the preceding chapter.

Where no such order has been made, then when the evidence is complete, the master may himself deal with the matter if he has, under the rules and the direction of the Vice-Chancellor from time to time,[31] power so to do. Some matters must always be dealt with by the judge in person, for example, questions as to the construction of documents or questions of law[32]; others can be dealt with by the master, for example, an order for general administration in a creditor's administration action where the estate appears to be insolvent. Even, however, when the master has the power, he may refuse to exercise it himself and send the matter to the judge; and he will usually do so if there is an amount in dispute significantly in excess of £30,000. If, however, he can and does deal with it himself, any party has the same right to appeal his order to the judge as in the case of interlocutory proceedings in an action (see Chapter 21) and under the same conditions.

In a typical case, however, the master will adjourn the summons to the judge without first expressing any opinion upon the matter, and may either adjourn it into open court, when it will take its turn in the Non-Witness List (if it is to be heard without cross-examination of witnesses, or if it is adjourned "into court with witnesses, to go into the Non-Witness List," as happens when the proposed cross-examination will be short), Part I or Part II[33] of the Witness List (if either

[28] Ord. 28, r. 8; *Re Deadman dec'd.* [1971] 1 W.L.R. 426.
[29] This power is used sparingly, as affidavits are rarely suitable to take the place of pleadings and anyway cannot (being on oath) easily be amended.
[30] Ord. 28, r. 8(3); *Re 462 Green Lane, Ilford* [1971] 1 W.L.R. 138.
[31] Ord. 32, r. 14; and the notes thereto.
[32] Ord. 32, r. 14(1). See also *Re Beaumont dec'd.* [1979] 3 W.L.R. 818 at 831.
[33] See Chap. 21.

party wishes to cross-examine the deponents at length) or into chambers. It is entirely in the discretion of the judge whether he hears any matter in court or chambers, although he will normally adhere to the well-settled practice of the court as to the matters suitable for hearing in chambers, basically those which raise questions of pure administration. Matters can be adjourned if necessary, from court to chambers and vice versa.[34] If the summons is adjourned into chambers, it will be entered in the Non-Witness List.

It will be apparent from this sketch of the procedure that it is primarily designed to deal with questions of law or discretion arising upon facts substantially not in dispute, and, indeed, where there is any choice in the matter, it is wrong to bring proceedings by originating summons if it is known that the facts are disputed.[35] But, as we have already noticed, sometimes the procedure is obligatory even in cases where there may be very substantial disputes of fact; for example, in a case under the Inheritance (Provision for Family and Dependants) Act 1975[36] the question whether the testator has made reasonable provision for his family and dependants may be bitterly fought by those who inherit under his will. The evidence in chief is still given in such cases by affidavit; but upon the request of any opposite party the deponents will be ordered to attend for cross-examination, and the master will adjourn the summons into court to be heard with witnesses. In that case the matter will still be set down in the Non-Witness List unless it is estimated that the length of the hearing will exceed one day, in which case it is appropriate to go into the Witness List.[37]

Whilst it also follows from the above that interlocutory applications are not normal in proceedings commenced by originating summons, yet, if necessary, applications can be made for the appointment of receivers,[38] and for discovery,[39] or for any other interlocutory relief which could be granted in an action commenced by writ.

Further, the summons may be amended to the same extent as a writ, and not therefore so as to include a claim to a right which was not in existence at the date when it was issued.[40]

---

[34] Ord. 32, r. 18.
[35] *Re Powers* (1885) 30 Ch.D. 291; Ord. 5, r. 4(2).
[36] Ord. 99.
[37] Practice Direction (Chancery Lists) [1983] 1 W.L.R. 436.
[38] *Re Francke* (1888) 57 L.J.Ch. 437.
[39] See Ord. 24, r. 3.
[40] *Coutts & Co.* v. *Duntroon Investment Corpn. Ltd.* [1958] 1 W.L.R. 116.

There are special Chancery rules as to the costs. In general, the costs of the proceedings are, like the costs of any other proceedings, in the discretion of the court or judge.[41] But where the summons is not hostile in spirit (*e.g.* a summons to determine the true construction of an obscure will or trust instrument) and there is a common fund (residuary estate, trust fund, etc.), the general rule is that the costs, on the standard or indemnity basis, as the case may be, of all proper parties,[42] whether successful or unsuccessful in the issue, will come out of such common fund in a due course of administration. But all parties having a common interest should arrange for their joint representation, as unless the circumstances justify separate representation only one set of costs of the hearing may be allowed.[43] In cases where the litigation is hostile in spirit, however, costs, as between party and party, normally follow the event.[44]

Appeals

If the judge makes a final order on the Originating Summons in Chambers, any appeal lies to the Court of Appeal in the ordinary way. Leave to appeal is not required.[45] Order 58, r. 6 was amended in 1988 so as to remove the necessity for leave which had previously been required in most cases.

Originating Motions

Proceedings may be commenced by originating motion if, but only if, this procedure is permitted by the Rules or a statute.[46] This procedure is extremely rare in the Chancery Division, otherwise than in the Companies Court (see Chapter 21). Such a motion may or may not be *ex parte*. Its heading will be in the same form as the title to a writ or originating summons; and it

---

[41] Ord. 62, r. 3(2).
[42] But see *Re Preston, Raby* v. *Port of Hull Society's Sailors' Orphans' Home* [1951] 2 All E.R. 421.
[43] Ord. 85, r. 3; *Re Amory* [1951] 2 All E.R. 947n.
[44] *Re Buckton* [1907] 2 Ch. 406.
[45] Ord. 58, r. 6.
[46] Ord. 5, r. 5. In the Chancery Division it is compulsory for many applications under the Companies Act 1985, *e.g.* for an order declaring that a company's affairs ought to be investigated under s.432 of the Act or for an order setting aside a dissolution (s.651 of the Act). For other examples, see Ord. 102, r. 3. In the Q.B.D., the same process is mandatory for applications to the Divisional Court (i) for an application for judicial review (Ord. 53, r. 5) or for determination of a case stated (Ord. 56, r. 10); (ii) in appeals from lower courts or tribunals under a statute (Ord. 55, r. 3); and (iii) for leave to commit for contempt where there are no pending proceedings (Ord. 52).

will be prepared in the normal way as for an ordinary motion.[47] As with an ordinary motion, it must contain a concise statement of the relief sought.[48]

When prepared, it must be taken to the Registry Section of Chancery Chambers, where it will be issued, unless the motion is to be heard in one of the District Registries having Chancery jurisdiction, in which case it should be issued in that District Registry. Once issued, it must be indorsed and served in the same way as a writ of summons. Substituted service or service out of the jurisdiction may be ordered in a proper case.[49] The rule or statute must be consulted as to the length of notice required: in default of any such provision it is two clear days.[50] A respondent to a notice of originating motion is not required to acknowledge service, but he cannot be heard by the court until he has done so.[51]

The motion will be heard in open court by the motions judge on the day named in the notice. It will then be moved by counsel as in the case of any other motion. Evidence will normally be given by affidavit, and the respondents will be entitled to have the motion adjourned in the first instance in order to enable them to put in evidence in reply. The court can if necessary order the attendance of the deponents for cross-examination. In other words, the ordinary motion procedure will apply.[52]

Petitions

A petition is a written application, in the nature of a pleading, setting out a party's case in detail and made in open court. Formerly it might or might not have been an originating process; now it is originating only.[53] It is only available where the Rules or a statute expressly prescribe this method of procedure.[54] Its most frequent use in the Chancery Division is upon applications under the Insolvency Act 1986 for the winding-up of insolvent companies or partnerships ("winding-up petitions") or for the making of bankruptcy orders against insolvent individuals ("bankruptcy petitions").[55] Special rules of procedure apply.[56]

---

[47] See Chap. 21.
[48] Ord. 8, r. 3(2).
[49] Ord. 65, r. 4; Ord. 11, r. 9; Ord. 73, r. 7.
[50] Ord. 8, r. 2(2).
[51] Practice Note (1934) W.N. 228.
[52] See Chap. 21.
[53] Ord. 9, r. 5.
[54] Ord. 5, r. 5.
[55] Also certain applications under the Companies Act 1985; see Ord. 102, r. 4.
[56] Insolvency Rules 1986.

There are no prescribed forms which a petition should follow, but the form is in fact well settled by long usage.[57] The title follows that of an originating summons or notice of motion. It is addressed to Her Majesty's High Court of Justice, and states by whom it is presented, and his address. It then sets out the facts upon which the petitioner relies in consecutively numbered paragraphs in the manner of a statement of claim.

The petition then concludes with a prayer asking for the relief to which the petitioner considers himself entitled, if necessary in the alternative, and also asking for such other order as the court thinks fit to make. It concludes with the words "And your petitioner will ever pray, etc.," the abbreviation being found thus in even the oldest books of Chancery precedents.

The persons who are to be the respondents to the petition and upon whom it will be necessary to serve it, are set out in a footnote. If it is not intended to serve it on anybody—as, for example, in the case of the presentation by a company of a petition to wind itself up—this must also be stated.[58] All the normal rules as to parties apply, and the petitioner must make respondents to his petition all the persons who will be affected by the order he wishes to have made.

Subject to any special provisions under the rules or any Act, a petition must be presented by leaving it at Chancery Chambers[59] or in one of the district registries having Chancery jurisdiction, but not elsewhere[60]; and it will also then be given a reference number. Petitions in the Companies Court are presented and dealt with in the office of the Registrar of the Companies Court.

All petitions require answering. This is a purely formal matter, and consists in the proper officer of the court endorsing upon the petition an order fixing a day for the hearing of the petition.[61]

Except with special leave, service must be effected at least seven clear days before the day fixed for the hearing.[62] It must be served as near as possible in the same way as a writ, substituted service[63] and service out of the jurisdiction[64] being permitted in proper cases.

---

[57] See Precedent No. 52.
[58] Ord. 9, r. 2(2).
[59] Ord. 9, r. 3(2).
[60] Ord. 9, r. 3(1).
[61] Ord. 9, r. 4.
[62] Ord. 9, r. 4(2).
[63] Ord. 65, r. 4.
[64] Ord. 11, r. 9(1).

A respondent to a petition does not need to acknowledge service. He may simply appear on the hearing, which is normally on a Tuesday, or, in the case of a petition under the provisions of the Insolvency Act 1986, on a Wednesday morning. Petitions are listed and taken in rotation, unopposed petitions normally being taken first, although (apart from the Companies Court) there are now very few petitions presented. It must be borne in mind that a petition is as much a litigious procedure as any other, and that accordingly the petitioner can properly be considered a plaintiff for the purposes of interrogatories, and discovery can be had if requisite.[65] Applications will in such cases be made by summons before the appropriate master or, in company matters, the Registrar of the Companies Court.

The evidence follows the normal Chancery procedure, and is usually given by affidavit, though attendance for cross-examination can be had if desired.

The hearing of a petition may be adjourned from time to time either to complete the evidence, or to allow the respondent to put in his evidence.[66] If, on any adjournment, the petitioner is not represented, the respondents present are entitled to have the petition dismissed with costs against the petitioner. Apart from this, the costs normally follow the event in a hostile petition.

---

[65] *Re Credit Co.* (1879) 11 Ch.D. 256.
[66] Ord. 8, r. 5.

CHAPTER 23

APPEALS

An appeal is an application to set aside or vary the decision of another tribunal on the ground that it was wrongly made. There is no inherent common law right to appeal. Such rights as are available are creatures of statute.[1]

Jurisdiction

In ordinary litigation there is a right of appeal to the Court of Appeal against any judgment or order[2] of the High Court. This right is conferred by section 16 of the Supreme Court Act 1981, except as otherwise provided.

In matters where a point of law of general public importance arises, an appeal may lie direct to the House of Lords from the High Court. This "leap frog" procedure was created by section 4 of the Appellate Jurisdiction Act 1876 and extended by section 12 of the Administration of Justice Act 1969.[3]

Appeals from the county courts lie to the Court of Appeal by virtue of section 77(1) of the County Courts Act 1984, though this is subject to certain exceptions.[4]

There is a statutory right to require a case to be stated by, *inter alia*, the Lands Tribunal for determination by the Court of Appeal. The relevant procedures are to be found in Order 61.[5] An appeal on a point of law lies from the Restrictive Practices Court to the Court of Appeal under the Restrictive Practices Court Act 1976, s.10 and is governed by Order 60. Appeals from certain decisions of Ministers of the Crown, government departments and tribunals, the Crown Court and justices may be taken to the High Court (rather than the Court of Appeal) by way of case stated. The procedural requirements are to be found in Order 56.

In all cases of contempt of court a defendant may appeal against any order made, and so also may any person applying for committal, by virtue of section 13 of the Administration of Justice Act 1960. The appeal may be heard by the Divisional

---

[1] *Att.-Gen.* v. *Sillem* (1864) 10 H.L.C. 704.
[2] See *Lake* v. *Lake* [1955] P. 336.
[3] Introduced pursuant to the recommendations of the Evershed Committee on Supreme Court Practice and Procedure, Final Report (Cmnd. 8878, 1953 paras. 483–508), and taking effect on January 1, 1970.
[4] *e.g.* County Courts Act 1984, s.77(6); Supreme Court Act, s.18(1).
[5] R. 2 deals with other tribunals and r. 4 with the Special Commissioners.

Court, the Court of Appeal or the House of Lords. Broadly speaking this will depend upon the general rule governing appeals from the court in question. The procedure is dealt with under Order 59, r. 20.

An appeal lies to the Court of Appeal from the decision of an official referee under Order 58, r. 4 on a question of law, or with leave of the official referee or of the Court of Appeal, on any question of fact.[6]

But where a matter is proceeding as official referees' business, it is open to the official referee, of his own motion or on an application by the parties, to transfer the matter to the Queen's Bench Division or the Chancery Division if he considers that it may more appropriately be tried by a master or a judge.[7] Essentially, leave to appeal is required against decisions of official referees in the same circumstances as in the case of appeals against the orders of High Court judges.[8]

An appeal from any judgment, order or decision of a Queen's Bench or Chancery master on the final determination of any issue tried before or referred to him under Order 36, r. 11 (*i.e.* with the consent of the parties), or on an assessment of damages under Order 37 or otherwise, lies direct to the Court of Appeal.[9] But on any matter which has not resulted in a "final determination," the appeal lies to a judge in chambers.[10]

An appeal lies from a judge in Chambers to the Court of Appeal (Order 58, r. 6) subject to the exceptions described below and to the requirement of leave for any appeal in an interlocutory matter. A further exception specified by rule 6 is Order 53, r. 13, which prevents appeal from the refusal of a judge in Chambers to grant leave to move for judicial review in cases where the applicant has the right under Order 53, r. 3(4) to renew the application in open court or to the Divisional Court. Order 58, r. 6 is stated to be without prejudice to section 13 of the Administration of Justice Act 1960, which provides for an appeal in cases of contempt of court.

In the following cases, no appeal lies to the Court of Appeal at all:

---

[6] R. 4 was amended in 1988 to permit appeals on questions of fact with leave.
[7] Order 36, r. 3.
[8] See *Giles (Electrical Engineers) Ltd.* v. *Plessey Communications Systems Ltd.* [1985] 1 W.L.R. 243 in which C.A. held that the earlier decision in *Technistudy Ltd.* v. *Kelland* [1976] 1 W.L.R. 1042, had been rendered obsolete by changes in legislation and in the R.S.C.
[9] Order 58, r. 2.
[10] Order 58, r. 1 which must be read subject to Order 58, r. 2 and Order 59.

(a) from any judgment of the High Court in any criminal cause or matter (Supreme Court Act 1981, s.18(1)(a))[11];

(b) from a judgment of the High Court in civil proceedings after leave to appeal direct to the House of Lords has been given by that House (Administration of Justice Act 1969, s.13(2)(a));

(c) from an order extending time for appeal (Supreme Court Act 1981, s.18(1)(b));

(d) from any decision of the High Court or a judge thereof declared by statute to be final (*ibid.* s.18(1)(c));

(e) from an order refusing leave to one who has been identified as a vexatious litigant to institute or continue legal proceedings (*ibid.* s.42(4));

(f) from an order arising from an appeal to the High Court under the Arbitration Act 1979, except as provided in that Act. (*ibid.* s.18(1)(g));

(g) from a judgment or order of the High Court sitting as a Prize Court (*ibid.* s.16(2)). In such circumstances, an appeal will lie to the Judicial Committee of the Privy Council;

(h) where the parties have, by agreement excluded their right of appeal and such agreement is embodied formally in an order (see Order 25, r. 5).[12] In County Court actions a similar rule applies (County Courts Act 1984, s.77(6)) except that the waiver of the right to appeal may be by written agreement, and need not be included in a formal order;

(i) where a party takes the benefit of a judgment, he cannot afterwards be heard to appeal against it[13];

(j) seemingly, where the appeal concerns a matter which is no longer a live issue between the parties.[14]

In some cases, an appeal to the Court of Appeal lies only if leave is given. Where leave may be given either by the court below or by the Court of Appeal, application should be made in the first instance to the lower court (Order 59, r. 14(4)). This requirement will be varied only where there are special circumstances which make it impossible or impracticable to fulfil it. If

---

[11] In fact, any matter arising in a case, which is criminal in nature will invoke this prohibition (see Lord Esher M.R. in *ex p. Woodhall* (1888) 20 Q.B.D. at 836) and this includes cases which *may* end in the imprisonment of the defendant (*Seaman* v. *Burley* (1896) 2 Q.B. 344). Also, see *Carr* v. *Atkins* [1987] Q.B. 963.

[12] *Re Hull & County Bank* (1880) 13 Ch.D. 261.

[13] *Harris* v. *Minister of Munitions* (1924) 124 L.T. 489; *Evans* v. *Monmouthshire, etc., Indemnity Society* (1937) 30 B.W.C.C. 196; but see *Evans* v. *Bartlam* [1937] A.C. 473.

[14] See *National Coal Board* v. *Ridgeway* [1987] 3 All E.R. 582.

the lower court refuses leave to appeal, a further application for leave to appeal may be made to the Court of Appeal. In the first instance this should be an *ex parte* application in writing, setting out the reasons why leave should be granted (rule 14(2)). The appeals referred to are:

(a) from the determination by a Divisional Court of any appeal to the High Court (Supreme Court Act 1981, s.18(1)(*e*)). Leave may be given by the Divisional Court or by the Court of Appeal;

(b) from an order of any court or tribunal (i) made with the consent of the parties or (ii) as to costs only. Leave may be given by the court or tribunal which makes the order[15] (*ibid.* s.18(1)(*f*));

(c) from an interlocutory[16] order or judgment of a judge, with certain exceptions (see *ibid.* s.18(1)(*h*)). Leave may be given by the judge[17] of the tribunal which made the order or of a court or tribunal of the same category or by the Court of Appeal. The question whether a judgment is treated as final or interlocutory is to be determined according to the provisions of Order 59, r. 1A, which defines a final judgment or order and sets out a list of specific types of orders which are to be treated as final and another list of types of orders which are to be treated as interlocutory;

(d) from the summary decision of a judge against a claimant in an interpleader matter (Order 58, r. 7). Leave may be given by the judge, or by the Court of Appeal;

(e) from a decision of the High Court on any question of law, whether on appeal or otherwise, under Part III of the Representation of the People Act 1983 (*ibid.* s.157(1)). Special leave must be obtained from the High Court;

(f) from certain orders of judges of the county court where the claim in issue is for an amount not exceeding one half of the current county court limit (County Courts Act

---

15 The Court of Appeal may entertain an appeal on costs, notwithstanding the absence of leave from the lower tribunal, where the judge in that tribunal has failed properly to exercise his discretion to grant leave: see *Scherer* v. *Counting Systems Ltd.* [1986] 1 W.L.R. 615. In these circumstances, the appellant must establish that the judge has failed to exercise his discretion, or that he has exercised it otherwise than judicially; see *Infafabrics* v. *Jaytex Ltd.* [1987] F.S.R. 529. The decision in *Scherer* was approved by the House of Lords in *Bankamerica Finance Ltd.* v. *Nock* [1988] A.C. 1002.

16 The distinction between interlocutory and final orders has presented some historical difficulty. R. 1A is an attempt to avoid this difficulty and was made pursuant to the specific power conferred by Supreme Court Act 1981, s.60.

17 *i.e.* a judge of the tribunal which gave the order below, or a judge in a tribunal of the same category, see *Warren* v. *T. Kilroe & Sons Ltd. & Another* (1988) 1 W.L.R. 516. The Courts and Legal Services Act 1990, s.7, amends s.18 of the Supreme Court Act 1981.

1984, s.77(2)) and County Courts Appeals Order 1981 S.I. 1981 no. 1749). Leave may be given by the County Court judge or by the Court of Appeal;

(g) from an appeal on a question of law from a Social Security Commissioner under the Social Security Act 1980, s.14. (Order 59, r. 21). Leave of the Commissioner or of the Court of Appeal is required;

(h) from orders in bankruptcy matters (Insolvency Act 1986, s.375(2)). Leave must be obtained from a judge of the Chancery Division or the Court of Appeal.

Following the substantial amendments made to Order 59 in 1982, most of the above applications are now heard by a single judge of the Court of Appeal who may refer the matter to the full court. (Supreme Court Act 1981, s.54(6) and Order 59, r. 14(10)). The enhanced competence of the single judge and of the Registrar[18] of Civil Appeals are a strong feature of the 1982 amendments.

In one case an appeal lies only if a certificate *and* leave is given. On application by any of the parties, and provided that certain conditions are satisfied, a High Court judge may grant a certificate (with the consent of all the parties) at the conclusion of the trial giving, as it were, leave to apply for leave to appeal direct to the House of Lords. (Administration of Justice Act 1969, s.12). Having obtained such a certificate any party may apply[19] to the House of Lords for leave to appeal (*ibid.* s.13(1)). The judgment to be appealed *must* involve a point of law of general public importance *either* relating to the construction of a statute or statutory instrument which was fully argued and fully considered in the court below *or* being one which the High Court felt itself bound by precedent to follow, and the point of law was fully considered by the court in that preceding decision (*ibid.* s.12(3)).

Additionally, the trial judge *must* be satisfied that a sufficient case for a direct appeal has been made out to justify the exercise of his discretion to grant the certificate. Ideally, the application for such a certificate should be made at the end of the trial itself, but it may be made within 14 days thereof. There is no appeal against the grant or refusal of a certificate (section 12(5)) but in the event of a refusal the disappointed party may still go to the Court of Appeal in the ordinary way.

---

[18] See Order 59 generally and Practice Statement Court of Appeal (New Procedure) at [1982] 1 W.L.R. 1313.

[19] For the detailed procedure, see Practice Note [1970] 1 W.L.R. 97; and *Inland Revenue Commissioners* v. *Church Commissioners* [1975] 1 W.L.R. 251.

If a certificate has been granted, application for leave to appeal may be made to the House of Lords within 30 days. The application will be dealt with without a hearing. The House of Lords has a wide discretion in the matter, and may grant leave if it appears to be expedient to do so (*ibid*. s.13(2)). If the House grants leave, the Court of Appeal will have been "leapfrogged." This happens only rarely. The procedure is useful in cases which seem to the trial judge to be destined to go to the House of Lords in any event, or where novel circumstances, or some previous oversight seem to necessitate a final and authoritative ruling on an issue.

Interlocutory Appeals

There is a right of appeal to a judge in chambers from any order made by a master or district registrar (except in the cases mentioned, *ante* (Order 58, r. 1). Notice to attend before the judge (without a fresh summons) must be given, in writing, within five days[20] of the order which is to be the subject of the appeal. The appeal is dealt with by way of an actual rehearing of the application which led to the order under appeal and the master's order need not be drawn up. The judge is in no way fettered by any exercise of discretion by the master.[21]

In addition, there are circumstances in which an appeal will lie direct to the Court of Appeal from an order of a master of the Queen's Bench or Chancery Division. Such an appeal will lie from an order made:

    (a) on the hearing of an issue tried before the master under Order 36, r. 11, (*i.e. trial* by master with the consent of the parties);

    (b) on an assessment of damages made by a master under Order 37 or otherwise. (Order 58, r. 2). It will be appreciated that this order covers circumstances in which the master has made a final, rather than interlocutory order.

In all other cases, the Order 58, r. 1 procedure is to be used. In that case, access to the Court of Appeal is possible. We have seen that an appeal lies from the judge to the Court of Appeal—but as a rule only by leave of the judge or the Court of Appeal or after an application to set aside or discharge the judgment of the judge in chambers has been made to the judge sitting in court, and has been refused. Such an appeal will not

---

[20] Seven days if the appeal is from an order of a district registrar (Order 58, r. 3).
[21] *Evans* v. *Bartlam* [1937] A.C. at p. 478.

otherwise lie, but this rule is subject to some exceptions. In the following cases, among others, leave is not necessary:

(a) where the liberty of the subject or the custody, education or welfare of minors is at stake (Supreme Court Act 1981, s.18(1)(*h*));

(b) where an injunction or the appointment of a receiver is granted or refused (*ibid.*);

(c) where unconditional leave to defend an action has been refused (*ibid.* s.18(2)).[22]

Procedure

The procedures adopted by the Court of Appeal were a matter of some controversy at the time when the previous edition of this book was published in 1981. During the 1970s the problems of delay in the Court of Appeal had become acute. In February 1978 a committee was set up under the chairmanship of Lord Scarman to examine ways of alleviating the problem of delay in civil appeals. The committee seems to have recognised that, in an adversarial system which places substantial reliance on oral advocacy, some of the time variables are difficult to control. The Scarman Committee was not prepared to challenge the pre-eminence of oral advocacy, but it did suggest the adoption of certain techniques designed to make the hearing process less lengthy. It contemplated the use of "perfected grounds of appeal" on the lines of those used in the Criminal Division of the Court of Appeal, the aim being to identify the major issues in advance of the hearing. General changes in the administration of the appeals system were also suggested.[23]

The Supreme Court Act 1981 introduced some reforms designed to bring greater efficiency to the Civil Division. For example, as we have seen, section 54(6) of the Act creates an important role for the single judge of the Court of Appeal. In addition, very important procedural changes were made by the amendment of Order 59, also in 1981.[24] Among the reforms were the tightening of time limits and of the rules as to provision of bundles of documents by the parties, and a new

---

[22] Similarly under this subsection, leave is not required by either party to appeal against an order granting leave to defend on conditions (*Gordon* v. *Craddock* [1964] 1 Q.B. 503). Since 1981, it has also been possible to appeal against an order granting unconditional leave to defend, but as this order is interlocutory in nature, it is not within the scope of s.18(2). See also Courts and Legal Services Act 1990, s.7.

[23] Donaldson M.R. discusses the committee's conclusion in a Practice Note: Court of Appeal (New Procedure) [1982] 1 W.L.R. 1312 especially at p. 1316.

[24] Rules of the Supreme Court (Amendment No. 2) 1981 (S.I. 1981 No. 1734 (L.21)).

jurisdiction in the Registrar of Civil Appeals to make directions as to the conduct of the appeal to secure the "just, expeditious and economical disposal of the appeal."[25]

In 1982 Lord Denning retired as Master of the Rolls and was replaced by Sir John Donaldson, as he then was. In October 1982, only a month after taking office, the new Master of the Rolls issued a Practice Note designed to explain the amended Order 59. The note is a fascinating indication of the Master of the Rolls' approach to the management of the Civil Division and can be read with profit at [1982] 1 W.L.R. 1312. These reforms have been augmented by the introduction of the use of skeleton arguments, among other changes.[26] The process of reform has not been uncontroversial. Some commentators have expressed the concern that the current emphasis on efficiency and saving time tend to undermine the traditional reliance upon oral advocacy.[27]

Every appeal to the Court of Appeal from a final judgment or order must be heard, except by consent of all parties, by not less than three judges of the Court of Appeal (Supreme Court Act 1981, s.54). However, appeals from interlocutory decisions and from the County Court, among others may be heard by two judges (section 54(4)).[28] The procedure is mainly governed by Order 59.[29] An appeal to the Court of Appeal is said to be "by way of rehearing" (Order 59, r. 3) unless the application is for a new trial or the setting aside of a verdict, finding or judgment (Order 59, r. 2). The words "by way of rehearing" do not mean that the Court of Appeal hears all of the witnesses afresh. Instead, the rehearing is "on the documents" giving the court the power to draw any inferences of fact and to give any judgment or make any order which it thinks ought to have been made when the matter was heard in the lower court (Order 59, r. 10(3)). The court has wide powers in this regard, and is not even limited to consideration of matters raised in the notice of appeal.[30]

The appeal is brought by notice of motion,[31] hereafter referred to as a "notice of appeal," which may be given in

---

[25] Order 59, r. 9(3).
[26] See Practice Note (Court of Appeal—Skeleton Arguments) [1983] 1 W.L.R. 1055.
[27] See, *e.g.* F. A. Mann [1983] 2 C.J.Q. 320 at p. 325 who remarks upon a tendency to "Americanise" the procedure.
[28] Also note that an application for leave to appeal to the Court of Appeal may be heard by a single judge thereof (s.54(6)). See Courts and Legal Services Act 1990, s.7
[29] Special rules apply to appeals in matrimonial causes, patent actions, from county courts and from the Lands Tribunal and certain other tribunals, as to which, except where specially noted herein, see Order 59, rr. 16–20 and Orders 60 and 61.
[30] And see *Curwen* v. *James* [1963] 1 W.L.R. 748 and *Purnell* v. *G.W.R.* [1876] 1 Q.B.D. 636.
[31] To which Order 8 applies.

respect of the whole or any specified part of the judgment appealed from (Order 59, r. 3). It must specify the grounds of appeal and the precise form of the order which the appellant proposes to ask the Court of Appeal to make.[32] Except with the leave of the Court of Appeal, or a single judge thereof, the appellant will not be entitled to rely upon any grounds or to apply for any relief not specified in the notice (r. 3(3)). However, as noted above, the Court is not precluded from acting on matters extraneous to the notice of appeal.[33] Obviously, a full and accurate notice of appeal is desirable, but rule 7 allows it to be amended without leave by supplementary notice[34] at any time before the appeal first appears on the "List of Forthcoming Appeals" (see r. 9(1)). Thereafter, leave will be required and application should be made to the Registrar of Civil Appeals. The Master of the Rolls has indicated that such leave will be granted only where the Registrar is satisfied that there are good reasons for it, and that the application has been made at the earliest possible date.[35]

The main function of the notice of appeal is to "define and confine the area of controversy."[36] Thus, the broad issues should be raised, rather than the detailed arguments that support them. The notice of appeal should be short and fairly simple; as a rule it should not be drafted as elaborated as pleadings. The aim is to save time and costs, and to enable the court to familiarise itself with the major issues of the appeal in advance of the hearing, thus enabling Counsel to come at once to those major issues without prolonged opening speeches. The Master of the Rolls has made it clear that failure to provide the Court with a carefully drawn notice of appeal may lead to penalties in costs.[37] On the other hand, it is not enough for the appellant merely to say for example, that he complains of a "misdirection"; the notice must state in what manner the judge misdirected himself or the jury, and if improper admission or rejection of evidence is alleged, that must be specified.[38] Fur-

---

[32] Including any amendment of the pleadings (*G.L. Baker Ltd.* v. *Medway Building & Supplies Ltd.* [1958] 1 W.L.R. 1216–1242.

[33] Orders 59, r. 10(4) and see *Curwen* v. *James* [1963] 1 W.L.R. 748.

[34] Which may be in the form of a letter (*Sansom* v. *Sansom* [1956] 1 W.L.R. 945). Two copies of the supplementary notice must be provided to the registrar within two days of its service on the other parties.

[35] Practice Note (Court of Appeal: New Procedure) [1982] 1 W.L.R. 1312 at 1313, *per* Donaldson M.R.

[36] *Per* Donaldson M.R. in Practice Note (Court of Appeal: New Procedure) [1982] 1 W.L.R. 1312. Also see *Sansom* v. *Sansom* [1956] 1 W.L.R. 945.

[37] Practice Note [1982] 1 W.L.R. 1312 at 1312.

[38] *Murfett* v. *Smith* (1887) 12 P.D. 116, *Taylor* v. *John Summers & Sons Ltd.* [1957] 1 W.L.R. 1182.

ther, the notice must specify the list of appeals in which the appellant proposes that the appeal shall be set down (*e.g.* Queen's Bench Division, Queen's Bench Division (Admiralty), Queen's Bench Division (Commercial) County Courts, Chancery Division, Chancery Division (in Bankruptcy)).[39] A notice may be struck out if it is plain that there is no right to appeal in the circumstances.[40]

The title of the notice in the Court of Appeal remains the same as in the court of trial. The parties appear on the face of the notice as "Plaintiff" and "Defendant," although the usual practice at the hearing is to call the party appealing "Appellant" and his opponent "Respondent."

Cross appeal.—If a respondent desires to contend on the hearing of the appeal that the decision of the court below should be varied, either in any event, or in the event of the appeal being allowed in whole or in part, he need not enter a substantive motion of his own but must, within 21 days after being served with the notice of appeal serve a notice called a "respondent's notice" on the appellant and any other party directly affected (Order 59, r. 6). Two copies thereof should be provided to the Registrar of Civil Appeals within four days (r. 6(4)). This he must also do if he wishes to contend that the decision of the court below was wrong in whole or in part or that the original decision should be affirmed on grounds other than these relied on by the court below. The notice must specify the grounds of the respondent's contentions, and if he asks for a variation of the order of the court below, he must specify the precise form of the order for which he proposes to ask. In default of notice he will not be entitled to raise any such contentions without leave of the Court of Appeal, the single judge or the Registrar.[41] The notice may be amended in the same way as a notice of appeal (see Order 59, r. 7).

Service of notice.—A notice of appeal must be served on all parties to the proceedings in the court below who are directly affected by the appeal (r. 3(5)). The court may, however, direct that it or a respondent's notice be served on any other person, whether a party or not (r. 8). In that event, the appeal may be adjourned if necessary and an order may be made as though the person served had originally been a party. In the case of a

---

[39] Appeals from the Commercial Court and the Queen's Bench Divisional Court now have their own final and interlocutory lists. Formerly, they came under the aegis of the Queen's Bench Division lists.

[40] *Aviagents Ltd.* v. *Balstravest Investments Ltd.* [1966] 1 W.L.R. 150.

[41] Order 59, r. 6(2) and see, *e.g. Thomas* v. *Marconi's Wireless Telegraph Co. Ltd.* [1965] 1 W.L.R. 850.

county court appeal, the notice must also be served on the county court registrar.

Any party served with notice of appeal is prima facie entitled to attend the hearing and, if the appeal fails, to be paid his costs (subject to the discretion of the court under Order 62), but not where his attendance is obviously unnecessary or useless.[42]

Time for appeal.—Until the substantial amendments in Court of Appeal procedure in 1981/82, the time for serving notice of appeal varied according to the nature of the appeal. There is now a single, blanket time limit of four weeks which runs from the date on which the judgment or order of the court below was sealed or otherwise perfected.[43] (Order 59, r. 4(1) and Order 3, r. 5(4)). An application for leave to serve notice out of time will normally be heard by the Registrar and must be made by way of summons supported by an affidavit deposing to any facts relied upon by the applicant. Leave will be granted only in exceptional cases.[44] Apart from this, there are few other exceptions to the four week time limit. Appeals from decisions of the Social Security Commissioners constitute one exception. In that case, notice of appeal may be served within six weeks of the order below (rule 21). Where leave to appeal is required, and is granted by the Court of Appeal and an application for such leave is made within four weeks of the sealing or perfection of the order of the court below, the time limit for service of the notice of appeal is extended by seven days (rule 4(3)). Similarly, where an appellant has sought to appeal directly to the House of Lords by way of the leapfrog procedure pursuant to section 12 of the Administration of Justice Act 1969, and the House of Lords has refused leave to appeal, the appellant may seek to appeal to the Court of Appeal. In those circumstances, the four week period for service of notice of appeal runs from the date on which the House of Lords refused to grant leave to appeal (rule 4(2)). In other cases, the normal four week time limit can be extended by the court below in cases where application is made to it before the four week period has expired (rule 15).

---

[42] *Ex p. Webster* (1882) 22 Ch.D. 136; *Re New Callas* (1882) *ibid.* 484.

[43] A restriction on the pre-1982 rule by which the relevant period could run from date of entry of the order. Now the *seal* and date thereof must be plainly visible on the face of the order or copy thereof which is provided to the Registrar under r. 5(1)a.

[44] *Per* Donaldson M.R. in Practice Note (Court of Appeal: New Procedure) [1982] 1 W.L.R. 1312. Leave is discretionary. The factors which should be taken into account include the length of the delay and the reasons for it, the prospects of the appeal succeeding, and any prejudice to the respondent which may result from the granting of such leave (see *C.M. Van Stillevoldt B.V.* v. *E.L. Carriers Inc.* [1983] 1 W.L.R. 207).

Setting down.—Within seven days after the latter of either service of the notice of appeal, or the sealing or perfecting of the order of the court below the appellant must apply to the registrar to "set down" the appeal. This is the process by which the appeal is entered in the court records, and is effected by lodging certain documents with the Registrar, *i.e.* a copy of the judgment or order of the court below and two copies of the notice of appeal.[45] (Order 59, r. 5(1)). The registrar then files the relevant documents and enters the appeal on the appropriate list, giving it a serial number. The appeals on the list will come on to be heard in order of appearance thereon, unless otherwise ordered (rule 5(2)).

Within four days after the appeal has been set down, the appellant must give notice to that effect to all parties concerned, specifying the list in which the appeal has been entered (rule 5(4)). Two copies of any supplementary notice of appeal must be sent to the registrar within two days of service.

Notice has been given that the above time limits are to be strictly enforced,[46] but jurisdiction to abridge or extend them lies with the Registrar, the single Lord Justice and the full Court of Appeal (Order 3, r. 5(4)).[47]

The listing of the appeal at this stage should not be confused with the entry of the appeal on the List of Forthcoming Appeals which occurs at a later stage in the procedure. This is purely a matter of setting the matter down on the court's records.

The "list of forthcoming appeals."—As soon as is reasonable after the setting down of the appeal as described above, the appeal will be set down in a List of Forthcoming Appeals. Since the Warned List of appeals has now been abolished, this is now the sole list of pending appeals. Once the appeal has been entered on the records, a letter will be sent to the appellant's solicitor informing him of the date when the appeal will appear on the List of Forthcoming Appeals (rule 9).[48] This element of the appeals procedure is particularly significant[49]

---

[45] A fee is payable (currently £30).

[46] Practice Note (Court of Appeal: New Procedure) [1982] 1 W.L.R. 1312 at 1313, *per* Donaldson M.R. and see *Columbus Dixon Ltd.* v. *Dingle Belles (Ormskirk) Ltd.* 131 S.J. 1188.

[47] Extension is within the discretion of the Court. The factors to be taken into account are set out by Griffiths L.J. in *C.M. Van Stillevoldt B.V.* v. *E.I. Carriers Inc.* [1983] 1 W.L.R. 207 and approved and re-emphasised in *Hollis* v. *R.B. Jenkins*, 81 L.S.Gaz. 3342, C.A.

[48] Practice Statement [1987] 1 W.L.R. 1422.

[49] Explained by Donaldson M.R. in Practice Note (Court of Appeal: New Procedure) [1982] 1 W.L.R. 1312 at 1314 and Practice Statement (List of Forthcoming Appeals and Warned List) [1987] 1 W.L.R. 1422.

because once an appeal appears in the List of Forthcoming Appeals, the appellant has 14 days in which to lodge (or cause to be lodged) the following documents with the registrar:

> The notice of the appeal (together with any supplementary or respondents notices).
>
> The judgment or order of the court below.
>
> The originating process by which proceedings were instituted in the court below, the pleadings and any other related documentation.
>
> The transcript of the official shorthand note or record, if any, of the judge's reasons for making his order in the court below. Failing that counsel's note of the said reasons as approved by the judge may be acceptable.
>
> Such parts of the record of the evidence adduced in the court below as may be available, to the extent that it is relevant together with all relevant affidavits and exhibits. (Order 59, r. 9(1)).
>
> Counsel's estimate of the likely length of the hearing. Naturally, this may differ as between appellant and respondent.[50]

An official shorthand writer still attends the trial of many witness actions in the High Court and will take a note of the evidence, summing up or judgment (Order 68). The practice of the Court of Appeal is to insist on proper transcription unless the case is of such urgency that this is impossible. Transcription must be bespoken and paid for by the appellant.[51] The registrar will not accept photocopies. It should be noted that the Court of Appeal has shown great concern that its rules as to documents should be adhered to strictly. Bundles of documents must be properly bound and paginated.[52] Failure to observe the requirements may lead to the appeal being struck out.[53] Again the emphasis is upon efficiency and expedition in the treatment of appeals. Practice Notes which interpret and refine the effects of Order 59, r. 9 are issued frequently and must be followed closely.[54]

---

[50] This device, used on an experimental basis previously has now been formalised, and the estimate must be certified—see Practice Statement [1987] 1 W.L.R. 1422.

[51] See Order 59, r. 9(1)f and g and r. 2A and Practice Direction [1943] W.N. 30 and Practice Statement [1986] 1 W.L.R. 1318.

[52] Practice Note [1983] 2 All E.R. 416.

[53] Practice Statement: Documentation [1986] 1 W.L.R. 1318.

[54] Especially in the light of the new procedures set out in Practice Statement [1987] 1 W.L.R. 1422. Because the appellant or his solicitor has advance notice of the matter's appearance in the List of Forthcoming Appeals, it is thought that there is no excuse for tardiness in lodging bundles of documents. Accordingly, a very serious view will be taken of any default. Practice Note (Court of Appeal: New Procedure) [1982] 1 W.L.R. 1312 at 1315.

One of the most significant reforms in Court of Appeal procedure has been the introduction of a power in the Registrar of Civil Appeals to issue directions regarding the documents to be produced, the manner of their presentation and such other matters incidental to the conduct of the appeal as appear to him to be necessary. Such directions are to be issued so as to make the conduct of the appeal "just, expeditious and economical." (Order 59, r. 9(3)).

Lord Donaldson M.R. has described this as "perhaps the most important single change in the rules."[55] It allows the Registrar some opportunity to individualise some procedural matters, according to the different needs of various kinds of appeals. Such directions are normally handed down without the need for a hearing, but the Registrar can require the parties to attend by summons, and he can be consulted, by appointment, at any time. On the face of r. 9(3) it is apparent that the aim of this reform is efficiency and expedition. The Master of the Rolls has explained that:

> "What needs to be said now, and said with all possible emphasis, is that the better use of time is in the interests of everyone—the parties to the appeal, their advisers, parties to other appeals which will be delayed if time is not used to the best advantage and to the public at large which has the interest in the efficient administration of justice."[56]

One of the most important illustrations of this attitude is to be found in the introduction of "skeleton arguments." The Scarman Committee had noticed that use of "perfected grounds of appeal" (as in criminal appeals) must enhance the efficiency of the Court of Appeal (Civil Division). The new Order 59, r. 9(3) afforded an opportunity to experiment with this device, and in 1982 the Master of the Rolls recommended that advantage should be taken of that opportunity.[57] In 1983, the court issued a practice note explaining and propounding the use of skeleton arguments.[58] At that stage, it was thought inappropriate to direct their use in all appeals, as the need for skeleton arguments would vary from case to case. In 1985, the court affirmed its belief in the value of skeleton arguments, and

---

[55] Practice Note (Court of Appeal: New Procedure) [1982] 1 W.L.R. 1312.
[56] *Ibid.* at p. 1315.
[57] *Ibid.*
[58] Practice Note (Court of Appeal: Skeleton Arguments) [1983] 1 W.L.R. 1055.

exhorted their use, stating that the appellant's side should also furnish the court with a written chronology of the events relevant to the appeal. In 1989 skeleton arguments were made compulsory for all appeals to the Court of Appeal except those heard as a matter of great urgency and any individual case where the Court otherwise directs. Practice Directions have been issued prescribing in detail the procedures and timetables to be followed.[59]

The purpose of skeleton arguments is to identify, not to argue, the issues. They must be lodged 14 days before the date fixed for the hearing. They will be read by the judges and in consequence it will not normally be necessary for counsel to open the facts at the oral hearing. Instead he can proceed immediately to the ground of appeal.[60]

Powers of the Court of Appeal

The Court of Appeal has all the powers, authority and jurisdiction of the High Court over any action or matter brought before it on appeal (Supreme Court Act 1981, s.15) and all the powers and duties as to amendment and otherwise of the High Court (Order 59, r. 10(1)). It has full discretionary powers to receive further evidence upon questions of fact, either orally or by affidavit or deposition; but where there has been a hearing below upon the merits, no further evidence except as to matters which have occurred since the hearing below, may be admitted, save on special grounds (r. 10(2)).[61] It may draw inferences of fact and give any order which ought to have been given or made or such further or other order as the case may require (r. 10(3)). There is a qualification to that rule in cases where there has been a trial by jury. Then such inferences should not be inconsistent with the jury's findings unless the latter are such as no reasonable men could have arrived at:[62] "the Court of Appeal is not at liberty to usurp the province of a jury, yet if the evidence be such that only one conclusion can properly be drawn the court may enter judgment."[63] It may direct issues to be tried, accounts to be taken and inquiries to be held and it may refer any question or issue of fact to an official referee (rule 10(1)). It has the usual powers and duties

---

[59] Practice Note [1989] 1 W.L.R. 281; [1990] 2 All E.R. 318.
[60] Practice Note (Court of Appeal: Skeleton Arguments) [1989] 1 W.L.R. 281.
[61] See *Ladd* v. *Marshall* [1954] 1 W.L.R. 1489 (approved in *Skone* v. *Skone* [1971] 1 W.L.R. 812 (H.L.) for the meaning of "special grounds."
[62] *Mechanical Inventions Co. Ltd.* v. *Austin* [1935] A.C. 346.
[63] *Per* Lord Loreburn L.C. in *Paquin Ltd.* v. *Beauclerk* [1906] A.C. 148 at 161.

as to costs in Order 62[64] and may, in special circumstances[65] order security to be given (rule 10(5)). It may stay execution, but an appeal does not of itself have that effect. Generally, the court has no desire to deprive a successful litigant of the benefit of the order below pending an appeal. Such a stay of execution is only available by way of an order of the Court below or the Court of Appeal or a single judge thereof (rule 13). Interest for such time as execution has been delayed by an appeal is allowed unless otherwise ordered (*ibid.*).

New Trial

Where a judgment has been obtained by fraud, the appropriate procedure is to bring an action to set it aside, giving full particulars of the fraud alleged,[66] but a motion in the Court of Appeal for a new trial may be made in special cases provided that the charge of fraud is made out with a high degree of particularity.[67] Leave to bring such an action is not required.[68] The Court of Appeal has expressed the view that a court of first instance generally should be regarded as the most appropriate forum in such cases, because of the particularity of proof that is required.[69] Such an action will also lie in cases where, since judgment, fresh material evidence has been obtained which could not previously have been procured,[70] alternatively, an application may be made to the Court of Appeal for a new trial.[71]

A new trial may be ordered on any question without interfering with the decision on any other question; and if some miscarriage of justice affects only a part of the matter in controversy or only some of the parties, an appropriate order can be made.[72]

The main grounds[73] on which an application for a new trial may be founded are:

(i) That the judge misdirected the jury.

---

[64] See Chap. 25.
[65] See *Weldon* v. *Maples, Teesdale & Co.* [1887] 20 Q.B.D. 331; *Hills* v. *LPTB* [1937] W.N. 339.
[66] *Jonesco* v. *Beard* [1930] A.C. 298.
[67] *Hip Foong Hong* v. *H. Neotia & Co.* [1918] A.C. 888.
[68] *Isherwood, Foster & Stacey Ltd.* v. *Miglio* [1938] W.N. 189.
[69] *Robinson* v. *Robinson* [1982] 2 All E.R. 699.
[70] *Charles Bright & Co.* v. *Sellar* [1904] 1 K.B. 6; *Ladd* v. *Marshall* [1954] 1 W.L.R. 1489; and *Crook* v. *Derbyshire* [1961] 1 W.L.R. 1360.
[71] See Order 59, r. 10(2) and *Piotrowska* v. *Piotrowski* [1958] 1 W.L.R. 797.
[72] Order 59, r. 11(3); *Marsh* v. *Isaacs* (1876) 45 L.J.C.P. 505.
[73] The Court of Appeal must be presented with solid grounds before it will exercise its discretion (see *Watt* v. *Watt* [1905] A.C. 115; *Automatic Woodturning Co.* v. *Stringer* [1957] A.C. 544).

(ii) That the judge wrongly received or wrongly rejected evidence.

(iii) That there was no evidence to go to the jury.

(iv) That the verdict was against the weight of the evidence.

(v) That fresh evidence has been newly discovered.

(vi) Surprise.

(vii) Misconduct of the jury generally.

(viii) That the damages are excessive or inadequate.

As to (i) and (ii), "Misdirection" for this purpose included non-direction and the wrongful withdrawal from the jury of matters which ought to have been left to them. The general principle here is that the litigant has the right to have his evidence and his arguments fairly submitted to the tribunal.[74] The Court of Appeal is not, however, bound to order a new trial on the grounds of misdirection, or the improper admission or rejection of evidence or because the verdict of the jury was not taken upon a question which the judge was not asked to leave them, unless in the opinion of the court some substantial wrong or miscarriage has been thereby occasioned.[75] But where, through misdirection, the jury have never had the opportunity to address their minds to the question of damages at all, that amounts to a miscarriage of justice in any event. In that case, the Court of Appeal will not speculate as to what amount the jury, if properly directed, would have awarded.[76]

Neither the wrongful withholding of a document by a third party who has been *subpoenaed* to produce it, nor his failure to attend on his *subpoena* is by itself sufficient ground for granting a new trial.[77] Nor is the wrong ruling of the judge admitting a document after a stamp objection.[78]

The court will not grant a new trial if it is satisfied that the jury, if rightly directed, would still have returned the same verdict.[79] Indeed, the test that the Court of Appeal will apply in deciding whether there has been "some substantial wrong or miscarriage" is to ask whether, had the error in the court below not been made, the verdict must have been the same.[80] If this is answered affirmatively, there will have been no miscarriage. It should be noted, however, that each case will depend upon its

---

[74] See *Bray* v. *Ford* [1896] A.C. 44 at 49.

[75] Order 59, r. 11(2): *Bray* v. *Ford* [1896] A.C. 44; *Tait* v. *Beggs* [1905] 2 Ir.R. 525; *Lionel Barber & Co.* v. *Deutsche Bank* [1919] A.C. 304.

[76] *Farmer* v. *Hyde* [1938] 1 K.B. 728, 740.

[77] *Rowell* v. *Pratt* [1930] A.C. 101, 116; 106 L.J.K.B. 790.

[78] Order 59, r. 11(5).

[79] *Per* Lord Esher M.R. in *Merivale* v. *Carson* (1887) 20 Q.B.D. at p. 281.

[80] See, *e.g.* *Bray* v. *Ford* [1896] A.C. 44.

own circumstances. In that sense, Order 59, r. 11(2) parallels the similar wording of the proviso which may be involved in criminal appeals, by virtue of section 2 of the Criminal Appeals Act 1968.

As to (iii) and (iv), an objection that there was no evidence to go to the jury on a particular issue is an objection on a point of law; it means that there was no evidence worthy of being considered by the jury—in the technical language of the courts, there must be more than a mere scintilla of evidence if a party is to discharge his evidential burden of proof. On the other hand the objection that the verdict was against the weight of the evidence raises a question of fact, *i.e.* did the jury reach the "right" conclusion on the evidence? Traditionally, this is considered to be a somewhat improper question. Generally, in jury trials it is the jury that acts as exclusive tribunal of fact. The Judge and jury below who saw the witnesses and saw them cross examined are the best judges of the weight of their evidence. It does not matter how many witnesses swore one way, and how few the other. Where there is any evidence on both sides which is proper to be submitted to a jury, their verdict once found must stand.[81] If it is obvious that on all the available evidence no verdict for the plaintiff could be supported and a new trial would therefore be a waste of time, the Court of Appeal may order judgment to be entered for the defendant.[82] In the absence of any misdirection, the court will not interfere to set aside a verdict or grant a new trial on the ground that the verdict was against the weight of the evidence, unless the verdict was one which no reasonable man could have found.[83] "If reasonable men might find the verdict which has been found, I think no court has jurisdiction to disturb a decision of fact which the law has confided to juries, not to judges."[84]

(v) A new trial may be granted on the ground that fresh evidence has been discovered, but only when it could not with reasonable diligence had been discovered before trial and when it is so conclusive that it would probably have led to a different verdict if it had been adduced.[85]

---

81 *Commissioner for Railways* v. *Brown* (1887) 13 App.Cas. 133.
82 *Mechanical Inventions Co. Ltd.* v. *Austin* [1935] A.C. 346.
83 *Winterbotham, Gurney & Co.* v. *Sibthorp & Cox* [1918] 1 K.B. 625; *Mechanical Inventions Co. Ltd.* v. *Austin, ante.*
84 *Per* Lord Halsbury in *Metropolitan Ry.* v. *Wright* (1886) 11 App.Cas. at p. 156. But see the judgments of Lopes L.J. in *Spencer* v. *Jones* (1897) 13 T.L.R. 174 and the speeches of the Lords in *Jones* v. *Spencer* (1897) 77 L.T. 536.
85 *Phosphate Sewage Co.* v. *Molleson* (1879) 4 App.Cas. 801; *Meek* v. *Fleming* [1961] 2 Q.B. 366; *Ellis* v. *Scott (No. 2)* [1965] 1 W.L.R. 276.

(vi) "Surprise" is the term used to cover those cases in which either party has been prevented from having a fair trial through no fault of his own; *e.g.* if the case was unexpectedly called on when he was reasonably absent; if his opponent misled him as to time or place of trial; if the case took a wholly unexpected turn which could not reasonably have been anticipated; or if a material witness was kept away, by his opponent.[86] Whenever a new trial is moved for on the grounds of surprise the applicant must show that he was in fact taken by surprise, that he is not simply invoking the surprise rule in order to set aside an unfavourable verdict in the court below, and that a substantial miscarriage of justice has resulted from the surprise. Accordingly, there must be an affidavit setting out the facts. "Surprise is a matter extrinsic to the record and the judge's notes, and consequently can only be made to appear by affidavit."[87]

(vii) The "misconduct" of the jury, or of an officer of the court,[88] or the counsel,[89] or even the judge,[90] is ground for a new trial, if it really prevented either party having a fair trial. A new trial will not be granted merely on the ground that the jury expressed an opinion during the judge's summing up which is inconsistent with its final verdict,[91] or on the ground that either judge or jury have expressed a strong opinion on the case either way after having the evidence,[92] or that the jury separated after the summing up and before giving their verdict.[93] It would be otherwise if a juror before being sworn expressed his determination to give his verdict a certain way[94]; or if the jury arrive at their verdict by drawing lots, or in any other way made an improper compromise without really trying the issues submitted to them[95]; or if the handbills abusing the plaintiff were distributed in court, and show to the jury on the day of the trial.[96]

(viii) Where the damages are unliquidated, the court seldom grants a new trial on the grounds that the amount awarded by the jury is either too small or too great.[97] The verdict will only

---

[86] See *Isaacs* v. *Hobhouse* [1919] 1 K.B. 398.
[87] *Per* Maule J. in *Hoare* v. *Silverlock* (No. 2) [1850] 9 C.B. 22.
[88] *Coby* v. *Wetherill* [1915] 2 K.B. 674.
[89] *Beevis* v. *Dawson* [1957] 1 Q.B. 195.
[90] *Jones* v. *National Coal Board* [1957] 2 Q.B. 55.
[91] *Napier* v. *Daniel* (1836) 3 Bing N.C. 77.
[92] *Allum* v. *Boultbee* (1854) 9 Ex. 738; *De Freville* v. *Dill* [1927] W.N. 133.
[93] *Fanshaw* v. *Knowles* [1916] 2 K.B. 538.
[94] *Ramadge* v. *Ryan* (1832) 9 Bing. 333.
[95] *Falvey* v. *Stanford* (1874) L.R. 10 Q.B. 54.
[96] *Coster* v. *Merest* (1882) 3 B. & B. 272; *Harvey* v. *Hewitt* (1840) 8 D.P.C. 598.
[97] *Davis* v. *Shepstone* (1886) 11 App.Cas. at p. 191.

be set aside (and a new trial ordered) where the figure awarded
is one at which no reasonable jury could have arrived, considering those matters which ought to have been taken into
account (and them alone) and applying the correct measure of
damages. Put more briefly, a new trial will be ordered on this
ground only if the award must have been arrived at
"capriciously, unconscionably or irrationally."[98] In these circumstances, the new trial which is ordered should normally be
limited to consideration of quantum of damages. Applying
these principles in *Sutcliffe* v. *Pressdram Ltd.*[99] the Court of
Appeal ordered a new trial on the question of damages against
a jury's award of damages of £600,000 for libel, on the ground
that this amount was so substantially in excess of any sum
which could reasonably be thought appropriate to compensate
the plaintiff that it must have included a very large exemplary
element even though the case did not fall into the categories in
which exemplary damages could be awarded. By Order 59,
r. 11(4) the Court of Appeal may increase or reduce the amount
of damages awarded by the jury, provided that the parties
consent to such a substitution. The inadequacy of this power in
the light of recent awards by juries in libel cases is recognised
by the Courts and Legal Services Act 1990. Section 8 will
permit rules to be made conferring power on the Court of
Appeal to substitute for the sum awarded by the jury "such
sum as appears to the court to be proper" in cases where the
court now only has power to order a new trial.

Similarly, where the appeal is from the decision of a judge
alone, the Court of Appeal will not interfere, although they
might themselves have awarded a different amount, unless
satisfied that he acted upon a wrong principle of law or
misapprehended the facts or that the amount awarded was so
extremely high or low as to make it an entirely erroneous
estimate.[1]

Questions of Law and of Fact

An appeal on a matter of law has, as a rule, a greater chance of
success than an appeal on any question of fact. If matters of
fact only are involved, the judges of the Court of Appeal are
naturally very reluctant to disturb the finding of the judge or

---

[98] *Per* Lord Kilbrandon in *Cassell & Co. Ltd.* v. *Broome* [1972] A.C. 1027 at 1135.
[99] [1990] 1 All E.R. 269 C.A. The parties later reached agreement on damages in the sum of
£60,000 plus interest (one tenth of the jury's award).
[1] See *Davies* v. *Powell Duffryn Assd. Collieries Ltd.* [1942] A.C. 617.

jury below, who saw and heard the witnesses and had the opportunity of judging their demeanour in the box.[2] If the action was tried by a judge without a jury, the Court of Appeal must decide whether, not having those advantages, they are in a position to say that the judge was plainly wrong.[3] If the appellant convinces them of that, the decision will be reversed[4]—even though the judge has clearly relied on the demeanour of the witnesses in deciding the facts[5]; if the matter is left in doubt, the Court of Appeal will not alter it.[6] In particular, when a party has been acquitted of fraud the decision should not be displaced on appeal except on the clearest grounds.[7] And when the action was tried by a judge with a jury, it is still more difficult to disturb an adverse finding of fact.

The great growth in recent years of the practice of trying cases with a judge alone has led to a substantial increase in appeals (many of them successful) on points of fact. As was pointed out by Lord Sumner in *S.S. "Hontestroom"* v. *S.S. "Sagaporack,"*[8] where the trial judge's estimate of the witness as a man and his assessment of his credit enter substantially into the process of arriving at his finding of fact, the appellate court ought not as a rule to disturb such a finding. But once findings of fact pass beyond simple direct testimony and become inferential in character, then the Court of Appeal is at no particular disadvantage compared with the trial judge and may reverse his conclusions, though it will give due weight to his views. In short, a distinction must be drawn between "the perception and evaluation of facts" (*per* Viscount Simonds in *Benmax* v. *Austin Motor Co. Ltd.*).[9] The reasons given by a judge alone for arriving at conclusions which could be matters for the jury, if there were a jury, are not to be treated as citable propositions of law.[10]

Appeals may be brought on points of law or mixed law and fact, either alone or in conjunction with appeals on fact. A common ground of appeal, which in strictness is one of law, is

---

[2] *Clarke* v. *Edinburgh, etc. Tramways Co.*, 1919 S.C. (H.L.) 35.
[3] *Powell* v. *Streatham Manor Nursing Home* [1935] A.C. 243; *Watt* v. *Thomas* [1947] A.C. 484.
[4] *Hicks* v. *British Transport Commission* [1958] 2 All E.R. 39, 50.
[5] *Yuill* v. *Yuill* [1945] P. 15.
[6] *Colonial Securities Trust Co.* v. *Massey* [1896] 1 Q.B. 38; *Coghlan* v. *Cumberland* [1898] 1 Ch. 704.
[7] *Akerhielm* v. *de Mare* [1959] A.C. 789.
[8] [1927] A.C. 37 at p. 47.
[9] [1955] A.C. 370; and see the observations of Denning L.J. on primary facts and the conclusions to be drawn from them in *British Launderers' Research Assn.* v. *Hendon Rating Authority* [1949] 1 K.B. at pp. 471–472.
[10] *Qualcast (Wolverhampton) Ltd.* v. *Haynes* [1959] A.C. 743, 744.

that there was no evidence entitling the judge to decide as he did. Where a point of law is relied on it must be one which was raised at the trial below, unless the appellant was taken by surprise or there are other special circumstances which excuse the omission.[11] If either party at the trial deliberately elects to fight one question only, on which he is beaten, he cannot afterwards on appeal raise another question, although that question was at the trial open to him on the pleadings and on the evidence.[12] The respondent, however, may as a rule support the finding of the court below on any ground, whether raised at the trial or not, provided he has given due notice. It is the duty of every court to prevent any abuse of its process; hence it may at any stage of the proceeding raise of its own motion the question of the illegality of the contract sued on, although the point had not been pleaded nor raised in the argument before it.[13] Also it is the duty of counsel to prevent any court from enforcing an illegal transaction; it seems that he ought, therefore, to inform the court of such illegality even though it has not been pleaded.[14]

Where a discretionary jurisdiction is given to the trial judge, the Court of Appeal will not ordinarily interfere with his decision except on a point of law, unless it is shown that on other grounds (for example, that he has not given adequate weight to considerations which ought to have weighed with him) injustice will result.[15]

Appeal as to Costs

By section 18(1) of the Supreme Court Act 1981 "No appeal shall lie to the Court of Appeal without the leave of the Court or tribunal in question, from any order of the High Court or any other Court or tribunal made with the consent of the parties or relating only to costs which are by law left to the discretion of the court or tribunal."

The section embodies the basic principle upon which a discussion of appeals as to costs must proceed, but it should be noted that what follows must be read in conjunction with the

---

[11] *Clouston & Co. Ltd.* v. *Corry* [1906] A.C. 122; *Wilson* v. *United Counties Bank Ltd.* [1920] A.C. 102, 106. In appeals from county courts the rule is inflexible (*United Dominions Trust Ltd.* v. *Bycroft* [1954] 1 W.L.R. 1345).

[12] *Martin* v. *G.N. Ry.* (1855) 16 C.B. 179; *Gloucester Union* v. *Gloucester Industrial Society* (1907) 96 L.T. 168; 5 L.G.R. 493.

[13] *Snell* v. *Unity Finance Co. Ltd.* [1964] 2 Q.B. 203, and earlier cases there cited.

[14] See *Mercantile Credit Co. Ltd.* v. *Hamblin* [1964] 1 W.L.R. 423.

[15] *Evans* v. *Bartlam* [1937] A.C. 473, 481; *Phillips* v. *A. Lloyd & Sons* [1938] 2 K.B. 282, 288; see also *Maxwell* v. *Keun* [1928] 1 K.B. 645.

most recent version of Order 62 which deals with costs generally.

The effect of the percursor of this section and the many cases decided under it was considered by the House of Lords in *Donald Campbell & Co. Ltd.* v. *Pollack*,[16] and a more recent discussion of the jurisdiction to hear appeals on the issues of costs without leave is to be found in *Scherer* v. *Counting Instruments*.[17] The following basic principles may be distilled from these cases, among others. Essentially, where a judge has exercised his discretion as to costs in a proper and judicial manner, the Court of Appeal will not entertain an appeal as to costs without the leave of the court below. It follows that if a party wishes to appeal on the issue of costs without leave, he must show that the judge below did not exercise his discretion at all or, at least, that he exercised it a non-judicial manner. This places a substantial burden on the party seeking to appeal as to costs, especially as the Court of Appeal will inquire into the matter in some depth in order to decide whether it has jurisdiction to hear the appeal. First, the appellant will have to make out a prima facie case of abuse of judicial discretion at an *ex parte* hearing before the full Court of Appeal. If such a case is made out, the Court will determine the jurisdictional issue. If the Court decides that the order of the court below lies within the *Scherer* principle (and therefore outside of the four corners of section 18(1)(f))[18] the matter can be listed for appeal in the usual way.

It is clear from the words of Viscount Cave in *Donald Campbell & Co. Ltd.* v. *Pollack* at p. 812 that—

> "If a judge were to refuse to give a party his costs on the ground of some misconduct wholly unconnected with the cause of action, or of some prejudice due to his race or religion, or (to quote a familiar illustration) to the colour of his hair, then the Court of Appeal might well feel itself compelled to intervene. But when a judge, deliberately intending to exercise his discretionary powers, has acted on facts connected with or leading up to the litigation, which have been proved before him or which he himself has observed during the progress of the case, then it seems to me that a Court of Appeal, although it may deem his reasons insufficient and may disagree with his

---

[16] [1927] A.C. 732.
[17] [1977] F.S.R. 569; [1986] 1 W.L.R. 615. *Infabrics Ltd.* v. *Jaytex Ltd.* [1987] F.S.R. 529.
[18] See *Marshall* v. *Levine* [1985] 1 W.L.R. 814. Courts and Legal Services Act 1990, s.7.

conclusions, is prohibited by the statute from entertaining an appeal from it."

Additionally, if an appeal clearly touches and concerns the merits of the case in general as well as costs, the Court of Appeal has jurisdiction to take the appeal, notwithstanding section 18(1)(*f*). This may be so even if the appellant failed on these other aspects of the case. However, if this exception is to apply there must be a genuine appeal as to those other aspects, they must not be used as a smokescreen to evade the rigours of section 18(1)(*f*).[19] The issue of costs must be incidental, at least in theory.

The above discussion assumes that the jurisdiction of the court below to make an order as to costs is not an issue. However, where that matter is in issue it seems that an appeal will lie without leave of the court below.

It should also be borne in mind that the questions of use and abuse of discretion which are dealt with here relate specifically to the issue of costs and are a result of section 18(1)(*f*) of the Supreme Court Act 1981. The propositions laid down do not necessarily apply to other instances of discretionary powers, many of which are governed by the rule in *Evans* v. *Bartlam*.[20]

Appeal to a Divisional Court

Divisional Courts may be held in any Division under section 66 of the Supreme Court Act 1981 for the transaction of any business assigned to them by the Rules. They have jurisdiction in numerous matters other than appeals, such as proceedings for contempt of court under Order 52. But since 1981 applications for a writ of *habeas corpus ad subjiciendum* under Order 54 and for leave to apply for judicial review under Order 53 must be made in the first instance to a judge.[21]

Divisional courts retain jurisdiction to hear appeals from certain inferior courts of civil jurisdiction, but since county court appeals were transferred to the Court of Appeal in 1934 few occasions now arise for its exercise. In such cases notice of motion must be served and the appeal entered within 28 days (see Order 55, r. 4).

Appeals from orders made by county courts in insolvency matters lie to a divisional court of the Chancery Division

---

[19] See *Wheeler* v. *Somerfield* [1966] 2 Q.B. 94.
[20] [1937] A.C. 486.
[21] Rules of the Supreme Court (Amendment No. 4) 1980.

(Order 55, r. 1(3)) and in these circumstances the procedural rules of Order 59 will apply, subject to the necessary modifications.

An appeal lies to a divisional court of the Queen's Bench Division under the Tribunals and Inquiries Act 1971, on points of law from the decisions of certain tribunals including Rent Tribunals, National Health Service Tribunals and from Agricultural Land Tribunals. The procedure, including the persons to be served and the time for appeal, is regulated by Orders 55, 56 and 94.

Appeal to the House of Lords

An appeal may lie from the Court of Appeal to the House of Lords, but only with the leave of the Court of Appeal or the House of Lords (Administration of Justice (Appeals) Act 1934). The practice on such an appeal is regulated by the Appellate Jurisdiction Acts 1876 and 1887 and by certain standing orders and practice directions which may be consulted in the second volume of the Supreme Court Practice. Accurate information may be obtained from a document supplied free of charge by the House of Lords (The "Blue Book").

Since 1974, petitions for leave to appeal and appeals to the House of Lords carry the same title as in the court of first instance. The plaintiff's name is therefore shown first in the title, whether he is the appellant of the respondent in the House of Lords.[22]

Recently, changes have been made in the procedure for applying to the House of Lords for leave to appeal thereto.[23] As in the case of the reforms in the Court of Appeal, the aim of the revision is to enhance efficiency. This is to be achieved by dispensing with the need for an oral hearing upon the application in a majority of cases.

Initially, a petition for leave to appeal to the House of Lords will be referred to an Appeal Committee, consisting of three Lords of Appeal. At this stage the Committee will examine the petition and decide on the threshold issue of its competence.

A petition will be regarded as incompetent if it falls within one of the following categories:

(a) A petition asking for leave to appeal to the House of Lords against a refusal by the Court of Appeal to grant leave to appeal to that court from the decision of a lower court.

[22] Practice Direction [1974] 1 W.L.R. 305.
[23] House of Lords, Practice Direction [1988] 2 All E.R. 831.

(b) A petition asking for leave to appeal to the House of Lords from certain decisions from which an appeal is barred by the Housing Act 1985.

(c) A petition asking for leave to appeal to the House of Lords brought by a petitioner who is the subject of an order to restrict vexatious legal proceedings, made by the High Court pursuant to section 42 of the Supreme Court Act 1981, unless the High Court has granted leave to present such a petition.

If the Appeal Committee determines that the petition is competent, it may arrive at one of three conclusions—

(i) That the petition should be dismissed.
(ii) That the petition should be allowed.
(iii) That the petition should be referred to an oral hearing.

If the Appeal Committee is unanimously of the view that the petition is incompetent, or that it is competent, but should be dismissed the Principal Clerk will inform the parties accordingly.

If the Appeal Committee is unanimously of the view that the petition should be allowed, the parties will be informed of this, on the basis that it is a provisional conclusion. The Respondent then has the opportunity to lodge any objections to the petition, or any suggestions as to the conditions upon which leave to appeal should be granted. These should be lodged within fourteen days of the date upon which the respondent is informed of the Appeal Committee's provisional determination. Copies should be served on all other parties to the proposed appeal.

The Appeals Committee will then consider the Respondent's arguments. If it remains unanimous that leave to appeal should be granted, the Principal Clerk will inform the parties of the decision.

In all cases where the view of the Appeal Committee is not unanimous, the petition will be referred for an oral hearing, in which case the Respondent should not lodge written objections, as he will be heard at that hearing after which a final decision will be made.

The practice on appeals from the High Court direct to the House of Lords under Part II of the Administration of Justice Act 1969 has already been dealt with above. If the requisite certificate is granted in the High Court (*ibid.* s.12(4)), the application for leave to appeal should be made to the House of Lords within one month, subject to any extension that may be granted (*ibid.* s.13(1)).

Appeals are heard in the presence of not less than three (usually five) Lords of Appeal—a body consisting of the Lord

Chancellor, the ten Lords of Appeal in Ordinary and such other peers as hold or have held high judicial office. In practice, lay peers do not vote on judicial questions.

Where leave has been refused by the Court of Appeal, it may nevertheless be possible to seek leave from the House of Lords. The appeal must be lodged within three months of the last order appealed from. A petition for leave to appeal must be lodged within one month. The documents and contentions of each party are set out in a printed "Case" which performs a similar function to the "Skeleton Arguments" which are used in the Court of Appeal.[24] The appellant is normally required to give security for costs by lodgment of cash in the amount of £4,000 unless the respondent waives this requirement, or unless Legal Aid has been made available.

---

[24] See *M.V. Yorke Motors* v. *Edwards* (1982) 1 W.L.R. 444, in which the written "Case" is compared to the written "briefs" submitted in the appellate proceedings in the United States.

CHAPTER 24

EXECUTION AND ENFORCEMENT OF JUDGMENTS

We now come to the process by which a judgment of the court
is enforced.[1] It is always advisable for a successful plaintiff to
act promptly, lest he lose the fruits of his victory. Unlike the
county court the High Court has no officers of its own for the
purpose of executing its judgments or orders.[2] They are
enforced either by one of the various writs of execution
directed to the sheriff of a county[3] commanding him to take the
appropriate steps; or by charging the debtor's property,
appointing a receiver, or attaching debts due to him; or, when
the law permits, by committing him to prison. Another potent
weapon in the hands of a judgment creditor is the threat or
issue of a bankruptcy notice. A money judgment of the High
Court may be enforced in a county court as if it were a county
court judgment (County Courts Act 1984, s.105); but if for any
reason this is not appropriate, the judgment creditor may
obtain from a master an order under Order 48 that the debtor
be examined as to his means, which may lead to the issue of
whatever form of execution may be appropriate. Under the
Attachment of Earnings Act 1971 the High Court may make an
attachment of earnings order to secure payment of a High
Court maintenance order, but not to enforce other judgment
debts.[4]

Enforcement of Money Judgments

The essential words of a money judgment under the existing
rules are "that the defendant do pay the plaintiff £——."[5] The
judgment need not, though it may, specify a time for payment,[6] and a time may be added or altered by a subsequent
order made on a summons which must be served on the
person ordered to pay.[7]

---

[1] See generally, Report of the Committee on the Enforcement of Judgment Debts (the
Payne Committee) 1969, Cmnd. 3909. Civil Justice Review, Chap. 9.
[2] Except the tipstaff, who conducts to prison anyone committed under an order of
committal for contempt committed in the face of the court (and whose authority may
now extend to other types of contempt).
[3] Or sometimes to other persons as sequestrators.
[4] See Ord. 105, Pt. V. A county court may make an attachment of earnings order to secure
payment of a judgment debt of £5 or more and to secure payment of maintenance and
administration orders (Attachment of Earnings Act 1971, s.1(2)).
[5] In its full form it is accompanied by such recitals and ancillary provisions as circumstances demand (see Ord. 42, r. 1).
[6] Ord. 42, r. 2(2).
[7] Ord. 45, r. 6.

A judgment or order for the payment of money may ordinarily be enforced in various ways,[8] each of which will be explained in this chapter. The judgment creditor may issue a writ of *fieri facias* (commonly abbreviated to *fi. fa.*) against the debtor's goods under Order 45, r. 1, or apply for a charging order under Order 50; or, in some cases, he can apply under Orders 51 and 30 for equitable execution by means of a receiver. If he knows of anyone who owes money to the judgment debtor, he can attach the debt by what are known as garnishee proceedings under Order 49. If the judgment specifies a time for payment and the defendant disobeys, it may, with the leave of the court, also be enforced by a writ of sequestration against his property and (subject to the provisions of the Debtor's Acts 1869 and 1878 and section 11 of the Administration of Justice Act 1970) by committal.

Fi. fa.—The most ordinary form of execution is by writ of "*fieri facias.*"[9] This writ commands the sheriff to *cause to be made* out of the goods and chattels of the judgment debtor the sum recovered by the judgment, together with interest and costs of execution, and immediately after the execution of the writ to pay the money and interest to be paid to the judgment creditor. The writ may not be indorsed to levy the costs of execution where the judgment is for less than £600 and does not carry costs (Order 47, r. 4). Immediately after execution the sheriff must make an indorsement on the writ showing how it has been executed and send a copy to the plaintiff. By the authority thus given him the sheriff may enter the house of the execution debtor and seize what goods can be found there belonging to the debtor[10]; he must not seize goods which are the property of someone else. He may also enter the house of a third person, if the goods of the debtor are to be found there; but in this case there is always the risk that the house may contain nothing belonging to the debtor and then the sheriff would be liable to an action of trespass.

Under a *fi. fa.* the sheriff may seize and sell all the personal goods and chattels belonging to the execution debtor which he can find and which can be sold, with the exception of the wearing apparel and bedding of the judgment debtor or his family up to £100 in value and the tools and implements of his trade worth up to £150[11] or such larger amount as the Lord

---

[8] See Ord. 45, r. 1.
[9] See Form No. 53 in App. A to the R.S.C. There are also special writs which go, under Ord. 47, r. 5, against the incumbent of a benefice who has no goods in the county except ecclesiastical property. They are executed by the diocesan officers of the bishop.
[10] But he may not use force to gain entry: see *Vaughan* v. *McKenzie* [1969] 1 Q.B. 557, D.C.
[11] But see Courts and Legal Services Act 1990, s.13.

Chancellor may prescribe.[12] The sheriff cannot take goods which are already in the custody of the law, *e.g.* by distress; but if he may seize *choses in action*, such as bank-notes, cheques, bills of exchange, bonds and other securities for money[13]; and the goods so seized he may safely proceed to sell unless he receives notice that a third person claims them as his property.[14]

It often happens, however, that when a sheriff seizes goods under an execution some third person intervenes and claims that the goods are his, or that he has a charge on them under a bill of sale or otherwise. In such cases the sheriff applies to a master for protection by means of an interpleader summons (Chapter 13) which he serves on both the claimant and the execution creditor. All three parties then appear before the master, who generally by consent disposes of the case summarily, if the amount in dispute is not large and no difficult question of law or fact arises. In other cases,[15] he may direct an issue between the claimant and the execution creditor, which is tried like an ordinary action. If the claimant will pay into court a reasonable amount to abide the event of the issue, the sheriff will be ordered to withdraw from possession of the goods; if not, the master may order so many of the goods to be sold as will realise the amount of the judgment. If the value of the goods does not exceed the county court limit he may transfer the proceedings to a county court. The procedure on a sheriff's interpleader is regulated by Order 17. The legal position is regulated by section 138 of the Supreme Court Act 1981 which provides that a writ of *fieri facias* or other writ of execution against goods issued from the High Court shall bind the property in the goods of the execution debtor as from the time when the writ is delivered to the sheriff to be executed. The writ shall not prejudice the title to any goods of the execution debtor acquired by a person in good faith and for valuable consideration unless he had notice of the writ or of a county court warrant at the time he acquired his title.

Charging order.—Order 50 gives effect to the Charging Orders Act 1979 and vests in the High Court jurisdiction to make a charging order for the purpose of enforcing a judgment of the court.[16] If made, the order imposes on such property of the

---

[12] Small Debts Act 1845, s.8; Administration of Justice Act 1956, s.37.
[13] Judgments Act 1838, s.12.
[14] Bankruptcy and Deeds of Arrangement Act 1913, s.15. *Curtis* v. *Maloney* [1951] 1 K.B. 736 (C.A.). *The Observer Ltd.* v. *Gordon* [1983] 1 W.L.R. 1008.
[15] In a difficult case, summary disposal is inappropriate even if the parties consent: see *Fredericks, etc.* v. *Wilkins, Read (Claimant)* [1971] 1 W.L.R. 1197 (C.A.).
[16] The act is based on the Report of the Law Commission on Charging Orders (Cmnd. 6412, 1976). See also *National Westminster Bank Ltd.* v. *Stockman* [1981] 1 W.L.R. 67.

judgment debtor as may be specified, a charge for the purpose of securing the payment of any money due or to become due under the judgment.

The Order applies to any judgment, order, decree or award of any court or arbitrator, including any foreign court or arbitrator which has become enforceable in whole or in part as if it were a High Court judgment (Charging Orders Act 1979, s.6(2)). By section 3 of the Act a charging order may be made either absolute or subject to conditions as to notifying the debtor or as to the time when the charge is to become enforceable or as to other matters.

A charging order gives the judgment creditor security over the property of the debtor which is subject to the charge. The creditor will have to enforce the charge if he wishes to obtain the proceeds in order to satisfy his judgment. The Act provides (s.3) that a charge imposed by a charging order will have effect and will be enforceable in the same courts and in the same manner as an equitable charge created by the debtor by writing under his hand.

The High Court has jurisdiction to make a charging order in three cases only. They are: first, where the property to be charged is a fund which is lodged in the High Court; secondly, where the order to be enforced is a maintenance order (as defined in s.2(a) of the Attachment of Earnings Act 1971) of the High Court; and thirdly, where the judgment or order to be enforced is a judgment or order of the High Court for a sum exceeding £5,000 (which is the present monetary jurisdiction of the county courts in actions founded on contract or tort). In all other cases the jurisdiction to make a charging order is vested in the county courts, where a High Court maintenance order may also be enforced.

The Act gives the court a wide discretion whether to make a charging order. Section 1(5) provides that:

> "the court shall consider all the circumstances of the case and, in particular, any evidence before it as to (a) the personal circumstances of the debtor, and (b) whether any other creditor of the debtor would be likely to be unduly prejudiced by the making of the order"

when deciding whether to make a charging order. The creditor is under a duty to make full disclosure of all relevant circumstances of which he knows and in particular rule 1(3)(b) requires him to state the name of any other creditor of the debtor whom the creditor can identify. The court may then direct service of the relevant documents on the other creditor and on any other interested party.

The assets of the debtor which may be made the subject of a charging order are defined in section 2. They are any interest held by the debtor beneficially in (a) any land or (b) any securities including government stock and units in a unit trust but excluding stock in a building society and (c) any funds in court. An order may also be made in respect of any interest held by the debtor beneficially under any trust and certain other trust interests.

Application for an order *nisi* is made *ex parte* to the Practice Master and must be supported by an affidavit which, in accordance with rule 1(3), must identify the order to be enforced and state the amount unpaid at the date of the application, give the name of the judgment debtor and of any other creditor of his whom the applicant can identify, give full particulars of the subject-matter of the intended charge including full details of any securities and the account number in respect of any funds in court, and verifying that the interest to be charged is owned beneficially by the judgment debtor. The affidavit may contain statements of information or belief with the sources and grounds thereof, unless the court otherwise directs.

If the court exercises its discretion to make the order, it will be an order to show cause, imposing the charge but specifying the time and place for further consideration of the matter. The order *nisi* and affidavit must, unless the court otherwise directs, be served on the judgment debtor in accordance with rule 2(1) at least seven days before the time fixed for further consideration of the matter. On the return hearing, the court must exercise its discretion either to make the order absolute with or without modifications, or to discharge it.[17] If made absolute, it will be open to the creditor to enforce his charge in the manner described above. Proceedings for the enforcement of a charging order by sale of the property charged must be begun by originating summons issued out of Chancery Chambers or out of one of the Chancery district registries (rule 9A).

Equitable execution.—In some cases in which execution could not be had at law, equitable relief could be obtained by the appointment of a receiver. Though called equitable execution, "it is not execution, but a substitute for execution."[18] Thus, a

---

[17] See *Roberts Petroleum Ltd.* v. *Bernard Kenny Ltd.* [1982] 1 W.L.R. 301 at p. 307 *per* Lord Brandon (C.A.).
[18] *Per* Bowen L.J. in *Re Shephard* (1889) 43 Ch.D. at p. 137.

receiver will be appointed to receive a fund in court, or a legacy not yet payable, or a share of the proceeds of the sale of land not yet sold. The appointment of such a receiver operates as an injunction to restrain the judgment debtor from himself receiving the moneys and prevents his dealing with them to the prejudice of the execution creditor.[19] In this way, too, an execution creditor can sometimes secure payment of his debt out of an equity of redemption or any other interest in land which could not be reached by the ordinary process of execution at law.

The appointment of a receiver is one of the three ways in which a judgment or order for the payment of money into court may be enforced, the others being committal and sequestration (Order 45, r. 1(2)).

The Supreme Court Act 1981, s.37(4) provides that the power of the High Court to appoint a receiver by way of equitable execution shall operate in relation to all legal estates and interests in land whether or not a charge has been imposed on the land under the Charging Orders Act 1979. In determining whether such appointment would be just or convenient regard is to be had to the amount of the judgment debt, the amount which will probably be obtained by the receiver and the probable costs of his appointment (Order 51, r. 1). The receiver may be required to give security and must render periodical accounts; the machinery is provided by Order 30, rr. 2–8.

The judgment creditor of a person who is a partner in a firm can, under section 23 of the Partnership Act 1890, obtain an order charging that partner's interest in the partnership property and profits with payment of the amount of the judgment debt and interest thereon, and by the same or a subsequent order a receiver may be appointed of that partner's share of profits (whether already declared or accruing) and of any other money which may be coming to him in respect of the partnership (and see Order 81, r. 10).

Attachment of debts.—Any debt owing to the judgment debtor from any other person within the jurisdiction of the court can be recovered by the judgment creditor towards the satisfaction of his judgment, by a process known as "attachment of debts." In order to ascertain what debts are owing to the debtor, it is often necessary to obtain an order for his examination (see Order 48, r. 1). If the judgment debtor disobeys the order, he is liable to be committed to prison. Either before or after any oral examination of the judgment debtor, the judgment creditor

---

[19] *Re The Marquis of Anglesey* [1903] 2 Ch. 727.

may apply *ex parte* to a master for an order, which is technically known as a "Garnishee Order *nisi*." He must present an affidavit showing that judgment has been recovered,[20] and is still unsatisfied, and to what amount, and that a person named and within the jurisdiction owes the judgment debtor money. The master thereupon may make an order attaching the debt "due or accruing due"[21] to the judgment debtor from such person (who is henceforth called "the garnishee"), and ordering the garnishee to appear and show cause why he should not pay such debt to the judgment creditor, or so much of it as may suffice to satisfy his claim (Order 49, rr. 1–3).[22] This order must be served personally upon the garnishee; and, as soon as it is served on him, it binds the debt in his hands[23]; he must not, therefore, after service pay any money to the judgment debtor. The garnishee must appear as the order directs, if he wishes to dispute the debt or his liability to be thus garnished. If the garnishee does not appear in obedience to the order *nisi*, or does not dispute his liability, the master may make the order absolute, so that unless the garnishee pays over the amount due from him, or so much thereof as may be sufficient to satisfy the judgment debt, execution can issue against him forthwith (rule 4). If the garnishee appears and disputes his liability, the master, instead of ordering that execution shall issue, may direct that any issue or question necessary for determining his liability be tried (rule 5). Payment by, or execution levied on, the garnishee under any such order is a valid discharge to him of his debt to the judgment debtor, to the amount paid or levied, even though such an order be subsequently set aside, or the judgment reversed (rule 8). In *Choice Investments Ltd.* v. *Jeromnimon*[24] the Court of Appeal held that a sum in foreign currency standing to the credit of a judgment debtor in a deposit account in a bank within the jurisdiction was attachable in garnishee proceedings notwithstanding that the judgment debt was expressed in sterling. The

---

[20] Or that the judgment debtor has given an undertaking to the court, which has been incorporated in a written order: *Gandolfo* v. *Gandolfo (Standard Chartered Bank Ltd. Garnishee)* [1980] 2 W.L.R. 680.

[21] See *Dunlop & Ranken Ltd.* v. *Hendall Steel Structures Ltd.* [1957] 1 W.L.R. 1102. The words of the former rule were "owing or accruing."

[22] The order will not normally be made if its effect would be to prefer one creditor over another, as where an estate is insolvent. If the solvency of an estate is in doubt, the money in the hands of the garnishee should be paid into court pending an inquiry: *George Lee & Sons (Builders) Ltd.* v. *Olink* [1972] 1 W.L.R. 214 (C.A.).

[23] Rule 3; *Edmunds* v. *Edmunds* [1904] P. 362. By this method the debtor's bank balance (if any) may be attached, which is how the process if most often used.

[24] [1981] Q.B. 149. The judgment of Lord Denning M.R. contains an informative discussion of garnishee proceedings and the machinery for enforcement.

Supreme Court Act 1981, s.40 provides that a sum standing to the credit of a person in a deposit account in a bank shall be deemed to be a sum due or accruing to that person and attachable accordingly notwithstanding conditions relating to personal application, notice of withdrawal, production of deposit book, or other conditions. The section applies also to deposit accounts and withdrawable share accounts with other deposit-taking institutions as defined by the Banking Act 1979 but the Lord Chancellor may by order include other types of account. An institution on which a garnishee order is served may deduct administrative and clerical expenses of compliance (section 40A).

Bankruptcy notice.—It is beyond the scope of this work to describe in detail this method of enforcing judgments but, broadly speaking, the procedure is to serve on the judgment debtor a notice which requires him to pay the judgment debt within a specified time and if he does not do so a petition may be presented and he may be adjudged bankrupt.

Enforcement of other Judgments

The commonest judgments other than for the payment of money are for possession of land and for delivery of goods. The form of judgments for possession is prescribed by R.S.C. Appendix A, (see Order 42, r. 1). The plaintiff either gets a judgment, following nearly the form of order common in the Chancery Division in mortgage cases, "that the defendant do give the plaintiff possession" of the land,[25] or, in summary proceedings under Order 113, a judgment "that the plaintiff do recover possession" of the land "and the defendant do give possession of the said land on. . . . "[26] In actions relating to the detention of goods the plaintiff ordinarily gets a judgment that the defendant do deliver to the plaintiff the goods described or pay their value to be assessed and, if claimed, damages for their detention to be assessed.[27] As in the case of a money judgment, these judgments may contain or be supplemented by a time for performance (Order 42, r. 2). There may be other judgments or orders requiring the defendant to do an act, and in those cases the time for performance must be specified (*ibid.*).

---

[25] See form in R.S.C., App. A, No. 42 (Ord. 42, r. 1).
[26] Form 42A, amended by R.S.C. (Amendment No. 3) 1980 (S.I. 1980 No. 1908).
[27] *Ibid.* Form No. 41. But except in the case of judgment by default the judgment need not necessarily provide the alternative of paying the assessed value (see Ord. 45, r. 4(1)).

Judgments for possession of land and delivery of goods are enforceable, respectively, by writ of possession and writ of delivery. If a time of performance is fixed they may also, by leave, be enforced by sequestration and in some circumstances by committal.

Writ of possession.—This writ commands the sheriff to enter the land and cause the plaintiff to have possession of it.[28] It may be combined with a writ of *fi. fa.* It will not issue without leave except in mortgage actions and after a final order for possession made in summary proceedings under Order 113.[29] To obtain leave the plaintiff should first give notice of the judgment to the defendant and all persons in actual occupation (other than members of the defendant's family living with him), so that they may have an opportunity of applying for relief if so advised. The application is then made *ex parte* to the practice master on an affidavit showing that notice has been given to all such persons and that there is no obstacle to execution, *e.g.* that the defendant has some statutory protection.[30] Where a suspended order for possession is made, as it may be under section 36 of the Administration of Justice Act 1970[31] in an action for possession of a dwelling-house by a mortgagee, the defendant must be allowed an opportunity of being heard before leave to issue execution is given[32]; and if the defendant fails to acknowledge service the plaintiff must follow the prescribed procedure as to service.[33] If the defendant gets in again after the sheriff has notionally restored possession to the plaintiff, a writ of restitution may issue; but leave is necessary for the issue of any supplementary writ in aid of execution.[34]

Writ of delivery.—If a plaintiff has obtained judgment for the delivery of goods, his precise remedy depends upon the form of his judgment. If it makes no alternative provision for the payment of assessed value he may enforce it without leave by a writ of specific delivery,[35] or, if it specifies a time, he may get leave to enforce it by committal or sequestration (Order 45, r. 4(1)). If it does make such alternative provision, a summons must be issued for an order of the court before a writ of specific delivery will issue, and sequestration may be allowed if a time

---

[28] See R.S.C., App. A, Forms Nos. 66 and 66A.

[29] Ord. 45, r. 3; Ord. 113, r. 7.

[30] Ord. 46, r. 4. See *Peachey Property Corpn. Ltd.* v. *Robinson* [1966] 2 W.L.R. 1386.

[31] See also Administration of Justice Act 1973, s.8.

[32] *Fleet Mortgage and Investment Co. Ltd.* v. *Lower Maisonette, 46 Eaton Place Ltd.* [1972] 1 W.L.R. 765.

[33] See Practice Direction (Possession Order: Issue of Execution) [1972] 1 W.L.R. 240.

[34] Ord. 46, r. 3. And see R.S.C., App. A, Form No. 68.

[35] R.S.C., App. A, Form No. 64 (Ord. 45, r. 12).

is specified (rule 4(2)). A supplementary order may also be obtained requiring the delivery of the goods within a limited time, and if this is disobeyed, an application for committal may follow (rule 5(3)). The only remedy open *without leave* to a plaintiff where the judgment gives the alternative is to issue an ordinary writ of delivery[36] to recover the goods or their assessed value (rule 5(3)). Either form of writ may be combined with a *fi. fa.* for any sum of money payable under the judgment in respect of damages or otherwise.

Writ of sequestration.—If a time for performance is specified in or has been added to a judgment or order, whether it orders payment of money, giving possession of land, delivery of goods or any other act (such as the abatement of a nuisance or the delivery of an account), and the defendant refuses or neglects to obey within the time limit, a writ of sequestration may by leave be issued against his property (or against the property of any director or officer of a corporate defendant) (Order 45, r. 5). So also if a person disobeys a judgment or order requiring him to abstain from doing an act (*ibid.*). Leave may only be obtained by motion to a judge (Order 46, r. 5).

Before sequestration can issue, a copy of the judgment or order indorsed with a penal notice to the effect that if the party neglects to obey or disobeys he is liable to process of execution, must be served personally on him before any time for compliance expires[37]; but such service may be dispensed with if the court thinks it just, *e.g.* when he has already had notice of the judgment or order and is evading formal service.[38]

Such a writ[39] is directed to commissioners, not less than four in number, called sequestrators, giving them authority to enter on the lands of the person in contempt and sequester and receive into their hands the rents and profits of all his real and personal estate, and to detain them until the contempt be cleared. All moneys that come into the hands of the sequestrators may be applied by them to meet the demand of the party prosecuting the writ. But they must apply for leave before they

---

[36] *Ibid.* Form No. 65. This form commands the sheriff to cause the goods to be delivered to the plaintiff and, *if possession cannot be obtained*, to levy the assessed value. If strictly enforceable this would seem not to give the defendant the alternative contemplated by the judgment. The extent of the sheriff's powers must therefore be regarded as open to question if the defendant has the goods and will not hand them over. (The old form commanded the sheriff to distrain all the defendant's goods until those the subject of the judgment were found.) The plaintiff's remedy in such a case is to apply for an order for a writ of specific delivery, and leave may, if necessary, be given to supplement this by a writ of assistance (Form No. 69; Ord. 46, r. 1).

[37] Ord. 45, r. 7; but note sub-rule (6).

[38] *Ibid.*

[39] See R.S.C., App. A, Form No. 67.

sell any of the goods and chattels sequestered, and the proceeds of such a sale will be dealt with as the court may direct.

Committal.[40]—The court has a general power to punish contempt by committing the offender to prison.[41] In this chapter we are concerned in particular with disobedience to a judgment or order. With a money judgment there is an independent power, now limited, under the Debtors Acts 1869–78 to commit a person who wilfully refuses to pay when he has or has had the means to do so (see "Debtors Acts and Judgment Summons" *post* and Order 45, r. 1(3)). Apart from this, committal may be ordered under the Rules of the Supreme Court, Order 45, rr. 1(1)(2) and 5, but in the case of a money judgment this power is subject to the provisions of the Debtors Acts (rule 5(1)(iii)). These Acts, as we shall see, prevent imprisonment for default in payment of money save in the excepted cases. Committal, like sequestration, may be ordered for refusal or neglect to obey a judgment or order when a time for performance is specified, or for disobedience to a prohibitive order.

The procedure is governed by Order 52. The application is made by motion to a judge, supported by an affidavit. A copy of the judgment or order indorsed with a penal notice must first have been served as already described under "sequestration."[42] The notice of motion, stating the grounds of the application, and a copy of the supporting affidavit must also be served personally unless the court dispenses with such service.[43] A committal order may be suspended for such period or on such terms as the judge may specify[44]; and after committal the court may, on the application of the person committed, discharge him,[45] although it is unlikely while he continues in disobedience unless he has been sufficiently punished and it is plain that further imprisonment will not secure obedience.[46]

General Rules

If judgment has been recovered against a firm, execution can ordinarily issue without leave against all property of the firm

---

[40] The analogous process of "attachment" has been abolished.

[41] It also has power to fine him (see Ord. 52, r. 9).

[42] Ord. 45, r. 7. In the case of an order for discovery or production of documents or to answer interrogatories, service upon his solicitor is sufficient to cast on a party the burden of showing that he had no notice or knowledge of the order (Ord. 24, r. 16(3); Ord. 26, r. 6(3)).

[43] Ord. 52, r. 4.

[44] *Ibid.* r. 7.

[45] *Ibid.* r. 8.

[46] See *Re Barell Enterprises* [1973] 1 W.L.R. 19.

within the jurisdiction, and also against the goods of any person who has acknowledged service of the writ in the action as a partner, or who was served with the writ as a partner and failed to acknowledge service, or has admitted on the pleadings that he is, or who has been adjudged to be a partner. But the plaintiff cannot without leave issue execution against any other person. Thus, for example, if the writ was served not on a partner but on the person in control, and judgment was entered in default of notice of intention to defend leave must be obtained before execution can be levied on the private goods of the partners. If such person disputes his liability, an issue will probably be directed to determine whether he was a partner or held himself out as a partner at the date of the contract (Order 81, r. 5).[47]

A writ of execution, if unexecuted, remains in force for a year from its issue[48] and may be renewed from year to year thereafter (Order 46, r. 8). Execution may not be effected on a Sunday except, in case of urgency, with leave (Order 65, r. 10). Leave to issue execution is also required under Order 46, r. 2 in the following cases:

    (a) where six years or more have elapsed since the judgment or order;

    (b) where any change has taken place, whether by death or otherwise, in the parties entitled or liable to execution;

    (c) where judgment is against the assets of a deceased;

    (d) where under the judgment any person is entitled to relief subject to the fulfilment of any condition which it is alleged has been fulfilled; and

    (e) where any of the goods sought to be seized are in the hands of a receiver appointed by the court or a sequestrator.

Leave is also necessary pursuant to the Reserve and Auxiliary Forces (Protection of Civil Interests) Act 1951 if the defendant is performing a service described in the First Schedule.

Debtors Act and Judgment Summons

Before the Debtors Act 1869 a judgment debtor who failed to pay even through poverty was liable to indefinite imprisonment. Section 4 of that Act provided that with certain excep-

---

[47] *Davis* v. *Hyman & Co.* [1903] 1 K.B. 854.

[48] If an interpleader summons is issued during the validity of the writ, the validity is extended until the expiry of 12 months from the conclusion of the interpleader proceedings (Ord. 46, r. 8(6)).

tions no person should be arrested or imprisoned for making default in payment of a sum of money. Within the exceptions are penalties other than under a contract, sums recoverable summarily before justices, sums ordered to be paid by defaulting trustees, costs payable personally by a solicitor for misconduct and money which he has been ordered to pay as an officer of the court, salary or income which a bankrupt has been ordered to pay for the benefit of his creditors, and sums which the court orders a debtor to pay under section 5 (*infra*). Section 4 of the Debtors Act 1869 also applies to protect the debtor in respect of sums of money payable and debts due to the Crown.[49] Furthermore, that section provides that even in the excepted cases imprisonment shall not exceed one year. It was at one time held that in the case of defaulting trustees and solicitors the court was bound to order imprisonment if it was asked for. Since the Debtors Act 1878 such an order is discretionary. Under the Debtors Act 1869, s.5, a person who defaults in payment after an order or an instalment order has been made for payment of a debt may be ordered to be imprisoned for a term not exceeding six weeks (subject to earlier release if he pays) if it is proved that he has, or since the date of the order, has had, the means to pay.[50] But the Administration of Justice Act 1970, s.11, provides that jurisdiction to commit to prison under this section shall be exercisable by the High Court only in respect of a High Court maintenance order. The jurisdiction is therefore limited in the High Court to the Family Division.[51]

The debtor's means are established by the procedure of a judgment summons, requiring the debtor to appear and be examined on oath as to his means.[52] If the judge comes to the conclusion that he has not paid as much as he could have done, he may commit him to prison then and there; but he usually orders him to pay by stated instalments, making an order that he be committed on failure to do so.

Enforcement of Foreign and Dominion Judgments

The Administration of Justice Act 1920 provides for the enforcement in many of H.M. Dominions of judgments of our courts

---

[49] Crown Proceedings Act 1947, s.26(2).
[50] Debtors Act 1869, s.5, proviso (2); *Buckley* v. *Crawford* [1893] 1 Q.B. 105. Such imprisonment does not extinguish the debt (s.5, proviso (2)).
[51] The county court may commit in respect of a High Court or county court maintenance order and in respect of a judgment for the payment of certain taxes, national insurance contributions and redundancy fund contributions.
[52] See Matrimonial Causes Rules 1977, rr. 86–91.

and vice versa. The Foreign Judgments (Reciprocal Enforcement) Act 1933 contains similar provisions with regard to such foreign countries as give corresponding facilities. The procedure in each case is governed by the provisions of Order 71, Pt. I.

Order 71, Pt. II governs the machinery for the registration and enforcement of decisions, judgments and orders of European Community Institutions under the treaties establishing the European Communities, and for the enforcement of Euratom inspection orders.[53]

Order 71, Pt. III provides the machinery for the reciprocal enforcement of judgments pursuant to the Civil Jurisdiction and Judgments Act 1982.

Staying Execution

Although the court will not without good reason delay a successful plaintiff in obtaining the fruits of his judgment, it has power to stay execution if justice requires that the defendant should have this protection. Ancient arguments as to the extent of this power have now become academic.[54] Apart from a general power to stay proceedings under the Supreme Court Act 1981, s.49,[55] and the power to make instalment orders under the Debtors Act 1869 (*ante*), the court has wide powers under the Rules of the Supreme Court.

Under Order 47, r. 1, if a judgment is given or an order made for the payment of money the debtor may apply then or later for a stay. The judge or master, if satisfied that there are special circumstances which render it inexpedient to enforce the judgment or that the judgment debtor is unable from any cause to pay the money, may stay execution by *fi. fa.* either absolutely or for such period and subject to such conditions as he thinks fit. The order may subsequently be varied or revoked. If the application is not made when judgment is given, it may be made later by summons, even though the defendant may not have acknowledged service of the writ or originating summons or did not state in his acknowledgment of service that he intended to apply for a stay of execution. The summons must be supported by an affidavit showing the

---

[53] See European Communities (Enforcement of Community Judgments) Order 1972 (S.I. 1972 No. 1590).

[54] A number of cases were referred to in the eighteenth edition of this work, to which reference could be made if necessary.

[55] The extent of which in relation to execution is not clearly defined, but is presumably exercisable in accordance with rules of court.

grounds and relevant facts; in case of inability to pay, the applicant's income, property and liabilities must be disclosed.

Again, in the case of any judgment or order to do an act, whether it be to pay money or not, the court has an indirect power to postpone its operation by fixing a time for performance or extending a time already fixed.[56] Or if matters have occurred since judgment which would make it just to stay execution, the court may do so under Order 45, r. 11. A master who gives summary judgment against a defendant under Order 14 is expressly empowered to stay execution pending a counterclaim.[57]

The Court of Appeal or the court below may stay execution pending an appeal, but the mere service of a notice of appeal does not operate as a stay (Order 59, r. 13(1)). Interest for such time as execution has been delayed by an appeal from the High Court shall be allowed unless the court orders otherwise (r. 13(2)).

[56] Ord. 42, r. 2; Ord. 45, r. 6.
[57] Ord. 14, r. 3(2).

CHAPTER 25

COSTS

Lastly comes the important question of "Costs." The term refers to the sum of money which a solicitor will charge his client for services and other expenses incurred in connection with legal proceedings. In this chapter, however, we are mainly concerned with the issue of *inter partes* costs, that is to say where the court orders or considers ordering one party to pay the other party's costs. This order is usually made in favour of the successful party but it is unlikely to compensate that party in full for the expenditure which he has had to make in connection with the action.

In a typical case the solicitor will draw up a bill of costs at the end of the action. This will include the solicitor's fees (known as "profit costs") and disbursements which are the expenses incurred in connection with the action (court fees, barristers' fees, expenses of witnesses, etc.).

If the court has ordered that the losing party shall pay the successful party's costs then there will be a taxation[1] which is assessment and evaluation by the court[2] of the contents of the bill which the successful party's solicitor submits. The taxation will largely be an adversarial procedure with each side making submissions as to what should be allowed or disallowed in the bill. The amount allowed on taxation is called "taxed costs" and this, as a rule, is all that the unsuccessful party has to pay to his opponent. The difference between "taxed costs" and the amount which the successful party is liable to pay to his own solicitor is sometimes called "extra costs" and this the successful party must pay out of his own pocket. There are different bases on which costs may be taxed which are explained hereafter.

Power to Order Costs

The Court of Chancery assumed from its earliest days an inherent power to deal with all questions of costs.[3] By contrast, in the common law courts the right to award costs arose solely from statute and was, at least in the earlier statutes, made to depend entirely on the result of the litigation (or, in legal

---

[1] Unless the parties can agree on the costs.
[2] Undertaken by a taxing master.
[3] See *Andrews* v. *Barnes* (1888) 39 Ch.D. 133.

language, the costs followed the event). Whichever party had
judgment recorded in his favour recovered costs; and the judge
had no discretion in the matter until the seventeenth century,
and then only of a very limited kind.[4]

Now, however, every Division of the High Court has complete discretion over the costs of proceedings subject to the
express provisions of the rules of court or of any statute. This
jurisdiction is conferred on the court by section 51 of the
Supreme Court Act 1981.[5]

> "Subject to the provisions of this or any other Act and to
> rules of court, the costs of and incidental to all proceed-
> ings in the civil division of the Court of Appeal and in the
> High Court, including the administration of estates and
> trusts, shall be in the discretion of the court, and the court
> shall have full power to determine by whom and to what
> extent the costs are to be paid."

By Order 62, r. 2(4) the powers and discretion of the court
under section 51 are to be exercised "subject to and in
accordance with" Order 62.[6]

Except as otherwise provided in the rules one party can only
recover costs from another party to the proceedings under an
order of the court (Order 62, r. 3(2)). There are however a
number of exceptions to this rule contained in rule 57.[7]

Generally, a party to proceedings has no right to have his
costs taxed before the conclusion of the proceedings (rule
8(1)).[8] The court can, exceptionally, make an order that costs
should be taxed earlier unless the person against whom the
order is being made is a legally aided person (rule 8(2) and
(3)).[9]

The costs which are usually allowable in any case are taxed
costs. However, the court may instead direct the payment of a

---

[4] Originally, except in very limited circumstances, costs could only be awarded to
successful plaintiffs. It was not until the mid-sixteenth century that the common law
courts had power to award costs more generally to successful defendants.

[5] Derived from the Judicature Act 1925, s.50.

[6] But see *Re Gosscott (Groundworks) Ltd.* (1988) 4 B.C.C. 372.

[7] *e.g.*, where a summons is taken out to set aside any proceedings on the ground of
irregularity and the summons is dismissed, the party who issued the summons shall pay
the costs of every party or where a party by notice in writing and without leave
discontinues an action against any party that other party shall be entitled to his costs of
the action which he has incurred up to the time of receipt of the notice of
discontinuance.

[8] This new rule which was introduced in 1986 alters the previous position whereby costs
could be taxed at any stage of the proceedings.

[9] The order should be in the form "costs to be taxed forthwith."

gross sum, thus saving the parties the delay and expense of taxation, or may order a specified proportion[10] of the taxed costs from or up to a particular stage in the proceedings to be paid (rule 7(4)).[11]

The judge generally deals expressly with costs in his judgment; if he does not, the successful party should ask for them, not forgetting to ask also for any special costs which might not otherwise be allowed (see Chapter 20).

Exercise of Discretion

The basic jurisdiction conferred on the court under section 51(1) is in the widest possible terms giving the court freedom of action.[12] The exercise of discretion is, however, subject to two considerations. First, as the power is given expressly subject to the rules of court the rule-making authority can impose such controls as it thinks right.[13] Secondly, the appellate courts can establish principles upon which the discretionary power may be exercised.[14]

The judge may, in his discretion, expressly state that he makes "no order as to costs." In that case each party must pay his own.[15] If the judge does make an order as to costs the general rule is that he shall order the costs to follow the event[16]

---

[10] See *Bourne* v. *Swan and Edgar Ltd.* [1903] 1 Ch. 211.

[11] See *Silva* v. *C. Czarnikow Ltd.* (1960) 104 S.J. 369; and *Leary* v. *Leary* [1987] 1 W.L.R. 72 where it was held that the power to award a gross sum in lieu of taxed costs under r. 7(4) was not subject to any formal restrictions but was a discretionary power which must be exercised judicially considering each case on its merits. There is no statutory obligation on the judge to receive submissions from counsel on whether a gross sum should be ordered or if so how much it shall be but obviously this would be of assistance in many cases. Also, in an appropriate case the judge can make an order without hearing submissions from the party against whom the order is to be made.

[12] Lord Goff in *Aiden Shipping Ltd.* v. *Interbulk Ltd.* [1986] A.C. 965 rejecting the notion that there are any implied limitations on the jurisdiction of the court to award costs under s.51 and in particular, any implied limitation on the persons by whom costs may be ordered to be paid.

[13] *e.g.* Ord. 62, r. 3(3), 9 (*post*). See also Ord. 62, r. 6.(2) which provides that where a person is or has been a party to proceedings in the capacity of trustee, personal representative or mortgagee he shall be entitled to the costs of those proceedings out of the fund held by him in that capacity insofar as they are not recovered from or paid by any other party. But the court may order otherwise if such a person has acted unreasonably or in the case of a trustee or personal representative has acted for his own benefit rather than for the benefit of the fund.

[14] See the propositions laid down by Buckley L.J. in *Scherer* v. *Counting Instruments Ltd.* [1986] 2 All E.R. 529 at 536 and cited by O'Connor L.J. in *Smiths Ltd.* v. *Middleton (No. 2)* [1986] 2 All E.R. 539 and approved by the House of Lords in *Bankamerica Finance Ltd.* v. *Nock* [1988] 1 All E.R. 81.

[15] If so intended this may be equivalent to an order that a trustee shall not be entitled to retain his costs out of the estate (*Re Hopkinson* [1895] 2 Ch. 190). But the judge cannot make such an order in the case of a trustee, personal representative or mortgagee, except on special grounds.

[16] As to the meaning of "the event" see *Reid, Hewitt & Co.* v. *Joseph* [1918] A.C. 717. The term may have to be construed distributively as between separate issues.

except when it appears to him that in the circumstances of the case some other order should be made as to the whole or any part of the costs (Order 62, r. 3(3)).

The discretion exercised by the judge "like any other discretion, must, of course, be exercised judicially, and the judge ought not to exercise it against the successful party except for some reason connected with the case."[17] It is not therefore a judicial exercise of the judge's discretion to order a party, who has been completely successful and against whom no misconduct is even alleged, to pay costs.[18] To exercise his discretion judicially, the judge will have to act in accordance with the established principles and taking into account the facts of the case, the parties' conduct in the litigation, the circumstances leading to the litigation and other relevant factors connected with it.[19] If there is no ground justifying a departure from the normal rule of costs following the event,[20] or even if there is such a ground but the judge is known to have acted not on this ground but on an extraneous ground, then there will effectively have been no exercise of discretion and an appeal against an order for costs will be allowed.[21]

Similarly, if it can be shown that the judge wrongly applied a rule or principle excluding the exercise of his discretion[22] or sought to exercise his discretion at a time when relevant information and materials were not before him,[23] then there will not have been a proper exercise of discretion.

The court is specifically empowered to take into account any misconduct or neglect in the conduct of the proceedings by any party. If it appears to the court that anything has been done or omitted unreasonably or improperly by any party then the court may order that the costs of that party in respect of the

---

[17] *Per* Viscount Cave in *Donald Campbell & Co. Ltd.* v. *Pollak* [1927] A.C. 732 at 811, 812.
[18] *Kierson* v. *Joseph L. Thompson & Sons* [1913] 1 K.B. 587.
[19] See also A. L. Smith L.J. in *Bostock* v. *Ramsay U.D.C.* [1900] 2 Q.B. 616 at 622.
[20] In order to determine whether the facts of the case justify a departure from the normal rule it was said by Bowen L.J. that,
> "The judge should look, in the first place, at the result of the action itself, namely, the verdict of the jury, and he should look also at the conduct of the parties to see whether either of them had in any way involved the other unnecessarily in the expense of litigation, and beyond that he should consider all the facts of the case so far as no particular fact was concluded by the finding of the jury."
> *per* Bowen L.J. in *Jones* v. *Curling* (1884) 13 Q.B.D. 262 at 272.
[21] *Scherer* v. *Counting Instruments Ltd.* [1986] 2 All E.R. 529. But see *Smiths Ltd.* v. *Middleton (No. 2)* [1986] 1 W.L.R. 598 where it was held that even if the judge had taken into account extraneous matters in considering his order for costs, the Court of Appeal could not interfere with the order unless the extraneous reasons were the overriding or only reason for the exercise of the discretion.
[22] *Bew* v. *Bew* [1899] 2 Ch. 467.
[23] *Civil Service Co-operative Society* v. *General Steam Navigation Co.* [1903] 2 K.B. 756.

unreasonable or improper act or omission shall not be allowed.[23a] In addition, where any costs are incurred as a result of the act or omission of any other party the court may order that these shall be paid by that party. (Order 62, r. 10).

An example of a situation in which the court might well exercise its powers under rule 10 would be where there was unnecessary delay in the proceedings. Further, the court can even make an order that a solicitor should personally bear the costs of proceedings. This power originates from the inherent jurisdiction of the court over solicitors which, in relation to costs, is now to be found in Order 62, r. 11. Where the court is of the opinion that costs have been incurred unreasonably or improperly in proceedings or have been wasted by a failure to conduct proceedings with reasonable competence and expedition, the court may order that the solicitor responsible repay his client any costs which the client has been ordered to pay any other party in the proceedings. Alternatively, the court can order that the solicitor personally indemnify any parties for costs which they have been ordered to pay and order that the costs as between the solicitor and his client be disallowed.[24] A successful party may sometimes be deprived of an order for costs where for instance he has acted oppressively, wasted the court's time or given false evidence.[25] A successful plaintiff may moreover be ordered to pay the costs of the defendant.[26] But a defendant who is wholly successful is unlikely to be ordered to pay the plaintiff's costs of the action unless it is an exceptional

---

[23a] See Ord. 62, r. 28; *Sekhon* v. *British Airways plc* [1990] 3 All E.R. 23; Practice Direction [1990] 3 All E.R. 24.

[24] See, *e.g. Batten* v. *Wedgwood Coal and Iron Co.* (1886) 31 Ch.D. 346; *Shorter* v. *Tod Heatley* [1894] W.N. 21; *Harbin* v. *Masterman* [1896] 1 Ch. 351; *Wilkinson* v. *Wilkinson* [1963] P.1; *Davy-Chiesman* v. *Davy-Chiesman* [1984] Fam. 48; *Countrywide Properties* v. *Moore, The Times,* January 30, 1987.

[25] See, *e.g. Baylis Baxter Ltd.* v. *Sabath* [1958] 1 W.L.R. 528 where judgment was given for the plaintiff company but the judge rejected most of the evidence given by the principal witness for the plaintiff (who was also the controller of the plaintiff) and accordingly made no order for costs. See also *Jones* v. *McKie* [1964] 1 W.L.R. 960 where the judge declined to make an order for the plaintiff for a successful defendant's costs where this defendant had allowed a situation to exist in which a co-defendant negligently caused damage to the plaintiff. See also *Celsteel Ltd.* v. *Alton House Holdings Ltd.* [1986] 1 All E.R. 608; *Anglo-Cyprian Trade Agencies Ltd.* v. *Paphos Wine Industries Ltd.* [1951] All E.R. 873. In a case where a plaintiff is successful on the issue of liability but fails to substantiate alleged special damage he may be ordered to pay the costs occasioned by the claim for the items of special damage: *Forster* v. *Farquhar* [1893] 1 Q.B. 564. And see *Gupta* v. *Kilbank, The Times,* November 23, 1989, the plaintiff appeared in person.

[26] *London Welsh Estates Ltd.* v. *Phillip* (1931) 100 L.J.K.B. 449.

case.[27] The fact that the defendant won the action by relying on a mere technical defence is no ground for depriving him of costs.[28]

In certain circumstances the court can make an order that the costs of proceedings are to be paid by persons who are not parties to the proceedings but have some other connection with them. For instance, where there are two or more separate sets of proceedings which are heard together because they share common features and one or more of the parties in one set differs from the parties in another set, it may be difficult or unfair to attribute the costs of presenting evidence on a common feature to one set of proceedings rather than another.[29] Again, an order may be made against a person who is providing the financial support for a plaintiff's action where that person is not a party to the proceedings and has no interest in the litigation, since it would be contrary to justice to allow someone to wholly maintain an action in these circumstances if that person would not otherwise be liable for any of the other party's costs if the action failed.[30]

Appeals from Orders as to Costs

If either party desires to appeal from the judge's decision as to costs and from that only, his counsel must ask for leave to appeal; otherwise the Court of Appeal will not entertain an appeal as to costs only, nor will it as a rule hear an appeal against the refusal of the trial judge to give the necessary leave.[31]

---

[27] *Knight* v. *Clifton* [1971] 1 Ch. 700; *Ottway* v. *Jones* [1955] 1 W.L.R. 706 (special case of actions under the Rent Acts). The old rule which prevented the court making an order in these circumstances (*e.g. Re Foster* v. *Great Western Railway* (1882) 8 Q.B.D. 515) can no longer be regarded as good law.

It has also been said that a county court judge does have power "to order a successful defendant to pay such part of the plaintiff's costs as has been caused by the defendant's misconduct in the action" *Andrew* v. *Grove* [1902] 1 K.B. 625 at 628.

[28] *Granville & Co.* v. *Frith* (1903) 72 L.J.K.B. 152.

[29] *Aiden Shipping Ltd.* v. *Interbulk Ltd.* [1986] A.C. 965. See also *Davies (Joseph Owen)* v. *Eli Lilly & Co.* [1987] 1 W.L.R. 1136 where the Court of Appeal approved an order made by Hirst J. that the costs incurred by particular plaintiffs while pursuing "lead actions" against a defendant for damages for personal injury should be shared by other plaintiffs bringing similar actions for personal injuries against the same defendant. There were approximately 1,500 plaintiffs (some 1,000 of whom were legally aided) and the order was to the effect that each plaintiff should contribute on a per capita basis. Sir John Donaldson M.R. stated that this type of order would have been impossible before *Aiden Shipping*.

[30] *Singh* v. *Observer Ltd.* [1989] 2 All E.R. 751 although an appeal against the judge's order was successful after the Court of Appeal heard further evidence: [1989] 3 All E.R. 777.

[31] Supreme Court Act 1981, s.18(1)(*f*) "No appeal shall lie to the Court of Appeal without the leave of the court or tribunal in question, from any order of the High Court or any other court or tribunal made with the consent of the parties or relating only to costs which are by law left to the discretion of the court or tribunal."

However, cases where the judge arrives at a decision following an exercise of his discretion based on the relevant facts and appropriate considerations, however wrong the decision appears to be, have to be distinguished from those cases where the judge fails to exercise his discretion at all by taking into account extraneous matters or by reaching his decision without the proper material being available to him, or where there are no grounds for departing from the general rule that costs should follow the event. In the second group of cases an appeal as to costs can be made without leave.[32]

If the appeal involves other matters besides costs, the Court of Appeal can deal with the question of costs, even though the appeal as to the other matters fails and no leave has been obtained from the trial judge.[33] Also, if the appeal is in relation to the issue of the jurisdiction of the court to award costs it does not fall within section 18(1)(*f*) of the Supreme Court Act 1981 and therefore leave is not required.[34]

There are some instances in which the judge's discretion in relation to costs is affected by statute and these are dealt with below.

Review of Taxation

Any party who is dissatisfied with a taxing master's decision may apply to the master to review his decision (Order 62, r. 33(1)). This must be done within 21 days[35] and the party

---

[32] " . . . in order to justify an appeal as to costs only, this court must be able to say that the judge in the court below, however much he may have been purporting to exercise his discretion, has not really exercised his discretion at all. This court can say that . . . if it is satisfied that the judge in the court below has taken into consideration wholly extraneous and irrelevant matters." *per* Willmer L.J. in *Jones* v. *McKie* [1964] 1 W.L.R. 960. See *Scherer* v. *Counting Instruments Ltd.* [1986] 2 All E.R. 529. Where a party wishes to appeal against an order as to costs only asserting that his case falls within the "Scherer principle," the proper course is for the Registrar of Civil Appeals to allow the appeal to be entered. However, if it appears to the Registrar to be a case where there is no prima facie right of appeal, the matter should be referred to a full Court of Appeal where the appellant, in the absence of the respondent, has to satisfy the court that he has an arguable case and that his case on its facts might come within the "Scherer principle." If the court is so satisfied then the appeal is heard with the respondent present and here the issue is whether the case actually does fall within the "Scherer principle." *Marshall* v. *Levine* [1985] 1 W.L.R. 814.

[33] *Wheeler* v. *Somerfield* [1966] 2 Q.B. 94. An order under Ord. 62, r. 11 that a solicitor pay a party's costs personally is not an order "relating only to costs" within s.18(1)(*f*); therefore the leave of the judge making the order is not necessary before an appeal can be made against it: *Thompson* v. *Fraser* [1986] 1 W.L.R. 17.

[34] *Aiden Shipping Co. Ltd.* v. *Interbulk Ltd.* [1985] 1 W.L.R. 1222 C.A. (but in view of the House of Lords' wide interpretation of s.51(1) jurisdictional points will not often arise).

[35] " . . . or within such other period as may be fixed by the taxing officer." (Ord. 62, r. 33(2)).

must deliver his objections in writing stating concisely the nature or grounds of his objection (rule 33(3)). A copy of the objections has to be delivered to any other party to the taxation and a party who has had a copy of objections sent to him under this rule may, within 21 days, deliver to the taxing master written answers to the objections (rule 33(4)). A copy of the answers to objections also has to be delivered to the objecting party.

The review is carried out by the same taxing master who carried out the original taxation. (rule 34(1)).

On this review further evidence can be considered and the taxing master can exercise all the powers which he could exercise on an original taxation (rule 34(2)). This includes the power to award costs of the review. Other parties to the taxation to whom objections were delivered have the right to be heard on the review even if they did not deliver answers to the objections. (rule 34(3)).

At the conclusion of the review the master may issue a certificate pursuant to Order 62, r. 22(1)(*a*) which sets out the costs which are to be allowed. Any party to the review can request, within 14 days, that he include in the certificate or state in writing the reasons for his decision (rule 34(4) and (5)).

Any party who is dissatisfied with the decision of a taxing master on a review may, within 14 days, apply by summons to a judge for an order to review that decision (rule 35(1)). An application of this sort will normally be held in chambers.

The judge may make any order that is necessary having regard to the circumstances and this includes ordering that the taxing master's certificate be amended (rule 35(6)). In addition, if he thinks fit he can appoint assessors (not fewer than two) under the Supreme Court Act 1981, s.70 to hear or dispose of the matter (rule 35(5)). Normally no further evidence will be allowed on this application (rule 35(4)).

Statutes Affecting Discretion

By far the most important instance of statutory restriction on the court's jurisdiction over costs is to be found in sections 19 and 20 of the County Courts Act 1984. These sections apply where an action which is founded on contract or tort and is commenced in the High Court could have been commenced in the county court.[36] In the case of such an action if the plaintiff

---

[36] *Solomon* v. *Miller* [1901] 1 K.B. 76. That is to say the action must be of the kind which is within the county court limit despite the fact that the amount claimed may exceed it. These provisions do not apply to proceedings brought by the Crown.

recovers[37] a sum less than £3,000[38] he will not be entitled to recover any more costs of the action than those to which he would have been entitled if the action had been brought in the county court.[39] In addition, if a plaintiff in an action recovers less than £600 he is not entitled to recover any costs at all.[40] These provisions do not apply however,

(a) if it appears to the High Court that there were reasonable grounds for supposing the amount recoverable in respect of the plaintiff's claim to be in excess of the amount recoverable in an action commenced in the county court[41]; or

(b) if the High Court is satisfied either that there was sufficient reason for bringing the action in the High Court, or that the defendant or one of the defendants objected to the transfer of the action to a county court.[42]

A plaintiff is to be treated for the purposes of section 20 as recovering the full amount recoverable in respect of his claim without taking into account any deduction for contributory negligence when determining whether action could have been commenced in the county court.[43] For the purposes of these sections and in deciding whether the plaintiff has recovered more than £3,000, the word "recovered" is wider than simply money awarded in a judgment. So, for instance, money which the plaintiff accepts which has been paid into court by the defendant is money which is "recovered."[44] Also money is "recovered" which is received by the plaintiff following an out-of-court compromise during the action.[45]

---

[37] Money paid into court and accepted is "recovered": *Parr* v. *Lillicrap* (1862) 1 H. & C. 615; *Parkes* v. *Knowles* [1957] 1 W.L.R. 1040; *Cotton* v. *McCaughey* [1970] 1 W.L.R. 63.

[38] In the case of an action for the recovery of goods it is the *aggregate* amount which is recovered which is relevant: s.20(2). An "action for the recovery of goods" means for the purpose of this section "an action brought to enforce a right to recover possession of goods or to enforce such a right and to claim payment of a debt or other demand or damages": s.20(7).

[39] s.20, *i.e.* he will only be able to recover on the county court scales.

[40] s.20(4) and (5).

[41] County Courts Act 1984, s.19(2). *Hopkins* v. *Rees & Kirby Ltd.* [1959] 1 W.L.R. 740. Would it be obvious to a reasonable man in the plaintiff's position at the time of issue of the writ that no judge would award more than £5,000 damages? If this was not the case then the plaintiff can recover High Court costs notwithstanding the fact that he has recovered less than £3,000. See also *Chic-Grit Ltd.* v. *Weatherhead Ltd.* (1982) 126 Sol.Jo. 658.

[42] s.19(3). See *The Katcher I (No. 2)* [1969] P. 72. A sufficient reason may be that the case raises difficult points of law and fact and that the case itself is not trivial despite the fact that the claim might not be worth £5,000.

[43] s.20(6).

[44] *Parkes* v. *Knowles* [1957] 1 W.L.R. 1040.

[45] *Colton* v. *McCaughey* [1970] 1 W.L.R. 63. *Lamb Bros.* v. *Keeping* (1914) 111 L.T. 527 (payment made to plaintiff out of court after writ was issued was money "recovered" even though it was made by the defendant in ignorance of the writ).

If a plaintiff's award is reduced below £3,000 as a result of a successful set-off then the provisions will apply and he will only be entitled to county court costs at best.[46] However, if his award is so reduced by a counterclaim he will not be affected by the provisions.[47] Moreover, if the plaintiff, in addition to recovering only nominal damages, obtains an injunction or other relief claimed as a matter of substance, he will be entitled to High Court costs in spite of these sections.[48]

The defendant is always entitled to the costs of his counterclaim regardless of the amount which he has recovered under it.[49] Nor do the sections apply as between the defendant and a third party whom he has brought in.[50]

When one or more of the parties to an action is an assisted person under the Legal Aid Act 1988 the court should not take this into account when it is considering the exercise of its discretion.[51] If, however, the court in the exercise of its discretion makes an order against an assisted person, his liability by virtue of this order cannot exceed an amount (if any) which is a reasonable one for him to pay having regard to all the circumstances of the case including the means of all the parties and their conduct in connection with the dispute.[52] The amount of any damages awarded to him at this stage may be taken into consideration.[53]

An unassisted person may sometimes be justified in making an application for an order under the Legal Aid Act 1988 for his own costs on the standard basis to be paid out of the Legal Aid fund if he is successful in an action against an assisted party. But no order can be made in favour of an unassisted party unless the proceedings in the court of first instance were instituted by the party receiving legal aid *and* the court is satisfied that the unassisted party will suffer "severe financial hardship" if the order is not made.[54] Then the court can make

---

[46] Since in substance the set-off is a defence to the action and so the plaintiff has not "recovered" the full amount he claimed. *Lovejoy* v. *Cole* [1894] 2 Q.B. 861; *Lund* v. *Campbell* (1885) 14 Q.B.D. 82.

[47] *Stooke* v. *Taylor* (1880) 5 Q.B.D. 569; *Goldhill* v. *Clarke* (1892) 68 L.T. 414.

[48] *Keates* v. *Woodward* [1902] 1 K.B. 532; *Marine & General Mutual Life Assurance Society* v. *Venn* (1973) 117 S.J. 914.

[49] *Blake* v. *Appelyard* (1878) 3 Ex.D. 195; *Amon* v. *Bobbett* (1889) 22 Q.B.D. 543.

[50] *Per* Field J. in *Bates* v. *Burchell* (1884) W.N. 108.

[51] *Re Saxton, Johnson* v. *Saxton* [1962] 1 W.L.R. 968.

[52] Legal Aid Act 1988. See Megaw J. in *Cope* v. *United Dairies (London) Ltd.* [1963] 2 Q.B. 33.

[53] *Nolan* v. *C. & C. Marshall Ltd.* [1954] 2 Q.B. 42. See also *McDonnell* v. *McDonnell* [1977] 1 W.L.R. 34.

[54] Legal Aid Act 1988, s.18. On the meaning of "severe financial hardship," see *Hanning* v. *Maitland (No. 2)* [1970] 1 Q.B. 580; *Kelly* v. *London Transport Executive* [1982] 1 W.L.R. 1055; *R. & T. Thew Ltd.* v. *Reeves* [1982] Q.B. 172. *Adams* v. *Riley* [1988] 1 All E.R. 89.

an order under this section, if it is satisfied that it is just and equitable in all the circumstances to do so[55] and also that if the unsuccessful party had not been assisted an order for costs would have been made against him.[56]

There is no need for an unassisted party to show severe financial hardship in respect of costs incurred in an appellate court.[57] Appeal costs have been awarded to a building society[58]; to an insurance company[59]; to an unassisted party whose costs were met by an association of which he was a member[60]; and to others who were insured and whose costs would be met by the insurers.[61] In the last two cases costs are "incurred" by the unassisted party and an award may be "just and equitable" because the unassisted party may wish to repay his association or insurers and the unassisted party is still the person legally responsible. The existence of an indemnity does not relieve the unassisted party from "incurring" costs.[62]

By section 1 of the Slander of Women Act 1891 in any action for words spoken and made actionable by that Act, "a plaintiff shall not recover more costs than damages, unless the judge shall certify that there was reasonable ground for bringing the action." Hence, in this case the plaintiff's counsel must ask at the conclusion of the trial[63] for a certificate, unless the verdict is so large that it clearly exceeds the amount at which the costs of the action will be taxed.

Section 141(4) of the Rent Act 1977 provides that if a person takes proceedings under the Act in the High Court which he could have taken in the county court, he shall not be entitled to recover any costs.

There are other statutes which contain special provisions as to costs, but these do not always necessarily deprive the judge of his power in a proper case to make a discretionary order as to costs.

Bases of Taxation

In 1986 a new Order 62 came into force and one of the main aims of the revised order was to rationalize the basis of

---

[55] See *Hanning* v. *Maitland (No. 2)* [1970] 1 Q.B. 580; *Saunders* v. *Anglia Building Society* [1971] A.C. 1039; *Lewis* v. *Averary (No. 2)* [1973] 1 W.L.R. 510 for consideration of the phrase "just and equitable."

[56] Legal Aid Act 1988, s.18. *Hanning* v. *Maitland (No. 2), supra.*

[57] *Parker* v. *Thompson* [1967] 1 W.L.R. 28.

[58] *Gallie* v. *Lee (No. 2)* [1971] A.C. 1039.

[59] *General Accident, Fire and Life Assurance Corporation* v. *Foster* [1973] Q.B. 50.

[60] *Lewis* v. *Averary (No. 2), supra.*

[61] *Davies* v. *Taylor (No. 2)* [1974] A.C. 225.

[62] *O'Brien* v. *Robinson (No. 2)* [1973] 1 W.L.R. 515.

[63] Although a later application can be made to the trial judge if necessary: *Russo* v. *Cole* [1966] 1 W.L.R. 248.

taxation. The court has a discretion which basis to award when making an order for costs. On taxation the number of items which the litigant in whose favour the order was made will be able to claim will depend on which basis the order was made.[64] Before the revised order came into force there were five main bases of taxation.[65] These bases were:

(i) Party and party;
(ii) Common fund;
(iii) Trustee;
(iv) Solicitor and own client;
(v) Indemnity.

The party and party basis was the ordinary basis and was the basis which applied unless a special order was made. For instance, the court might have ordered that costs should be paid on the common fund basis in which case the receiving party would have been entitled to a slightly more generous award.[66] The old Order 62, however, attracted some heavy criticism for its obscurities and complications especially in relation to the bases of taxation.[67] Therefore a committee was set up, the Horne Committee, in the wake of the Royal Commission on Legal Services report in 1979 to work on the simplification of costs. The eventual result was the present Order 62.

There are now only two bases of taxation, the standard basis and the indemnity basis (Order 62, r. 12). The party and party basis has disappeared and the common fund basis has become the standard basis. This is defined by rule 12(1) as follows:

> "On a taxation of costs on the standard basis there shall be allowed a reasonable amount in respect of all costs

---

[64] With some exceptions, *e.g.* legally aided matrimonial proceedings, and certain Court of Protection work, there is no general High Court scale which prescribes specific amounts for certain items of work, as there is for the county court. Instead, the amount to be allowed on each item is in the discretion of the taxing master and Ord. 62, App. 2, Pt. I sets out a number of circumstances which the taxing master should have regard to when exercising his discretion, *e.g.* the complexity of the item, the skill and specialised knowledge and responsibility required.

[65] See Sir Robert Megarry V.-C. in *E.M.I. Records* v. *Ian Cameron Wallace Ltd.* [1982] 2 All E.R. 980 at 983.

[66] It was estimated that on average a common fund taxation would only produce an award about 5 to 10 per cent. higher than a party and party taxation: Sir Robert Megarry V.-C. in *E.M.I. Records* v. *Ian Cameron Wallace Ltd.* (*supra*).

[67] *e.g.*: "The process of reading through the main body of the order, even without the appendices, is one that brings to mind Oliver Cromwell's phrase 'an ungodly jumble.' Matters of principle and substance lie cheek by jowl with details of procedure; and if one day there is to be a rewritten order, there will be little difficulty in achieving an improvement on the present drafting."
per Sir Robert Megarry in *E.M.I. Records* v. *Ian Cameron Wallace Ltd.* (*supra*).

reasonably incurred and any doubts which the taxing officer may have as to whether the costs were reasonably incurred or were reasonable in amount shall be resolved *in favour of the paying party*. . . . "

The other basis of taxation is the indemnity basis[68] which is defined by rule 12(2) as follows:

"On a taxation on the indemnity basis, all costs shall be allowed except insofar as they are of an unreasonable amount or have been unreasonably incurred and any doubts which the taxing officer may have as to whether the costs were reasonably incurred or were reasonable in amount shall be resolved *in favour of the receiving party.* . . ."

Where the court makes an order for costs but either does not specify a basis of taxation or specifies a basis other than the standard or indemnity bases then the costs shall be taxed on the standard basis (Order 62, r. 12(3)).

So, for the successful party in hostile litigation the normal basis will be the lower, standard basis and it will only be in exceptional circumstances that the court will order costs on the indemnity basis. In this respect the new rules are a radical rationalisation rather than a complete restatement fundamentally altering what a successful party is entitled to.[69]

Costs of Separate Issues

Although the judge may award one party the general costs of the action, he may yet order him to pay the costs of any separate issues on which he has failed. In any litigation there may be a number of issues to be determined but:

"[a]n isolated question of fact is not an 'issue.' An 'issue' is that which results in a determination or adjudication in favour of one party or the other."[70]

There was formerly a rule which provided that the costs of separate issues should follow their own event but this was

---

[68] This basis is derived partly from the old rules and partly from the judgment of Sir Robert Megarry V.-C. in *E.M.I. Records Ltd.* v. *Ian Cameron Wallace Ltd.* [1981] 2 All E.R. 980.

[69] *Bowen-Jones* v. *Bowen-Jones* [1986] 3 All E.R. 163 (Knox J.).

[70] Per Buckley L.J. in *Howell* v. *Dering* [1915] 1 K.B. at 63; see also *Reid, Hewitt & Co.* v. *Joseph* [1981] A.C. 717; *Williams* v. *Stanley Jones & Co.* [1926] 2 K.B. 37.

revoked in 1929. So, while the cases cited before that date have therefore lost much of their former importance, they are still useful as a guide for the exercise of judicial discretion in deciding whether or not a special order should be made. Thus a party against whom judgment is entered may yet fairly expect to be awarded the costs of any separate issues upon which he has succeeded, or that some equivalent order will be made.[71] The general costs of the action will be found as a rule to exceed the costs of any number of issues, but the taxing master will divide any items of costs which are attributable to more than one issue. A judge sometimes makes a special order giving one party the costs of the action, except in so far as they have been increased by some particular issue having been raised.[72] Or, he will in some cases direct that the whole of the successful party's costs of the action be taxed, and that he shall receive only a certain proportion of the amount at which they are taxed—a course held in *Cinema Press Ltd.* v. *Pictures and Pleasures Ltd.*[73] to be the simplest method—or he may award any party a lump sum in lieu of taxed costs (Order 62, r. 7(4)).

When the plaintiff sues on two distinct *causes of action*, fails on one and wins on the other, the defendant is entitled, subject to the judge's discretion, to all his costs referable solely to the first cause of action, the plaintiff to all his costs referable solely to the second cause of action, the costs common to both causes of action being apportioned between them.[74]

Payment into Court

If the defendant pays a sum of money into court, and the plaintiff accepts it in satisfaction of the cause of action or all the causes of action in respect of which he claims, the plaintiff is entitled to his costs up to the time of receipt of the notice of payment in however small the sum paid in may be.[75] If the plaintiff does not accept the sum paid into court, but continues his action in the hope of recovering more, the judge must take the payment in and its amount into consideration when exercising his discretion as to costs. (Order 62, r. 9(1)(*b*)).

Ordinarily the plaintiff will be entitled to the whole of his costs in the action if the amount of the ultimate judgment is

---

[71] *Adamson* v. *Birkenhead Corporation* [1937] Ch. 279.
[72] *The Adams* (1919) 88 L.J.P. 129.
[73] [1945] 1 K.B. 356.
[74] *Todd* v. *N.E. Ry.*, (1903) 88 L.T. 112. See also *Brown* v. *Houston* [1901] 2 K.B. 855; *Sparrow* v. *Hill* (1881) 7 Q.B.D. 362 and 8 Q.B.D. 479; *Smyth* v. *Wilson* [1904] 2 Ir.R. 40.
[75] *M'Sheffery* v. *Lanagan* (1887) 20 L.R.Ir. 528.

larger than the sum paid into court. If, however, he recovers an amount not greater than the sum paid into court, the plaintiff is, subject to the judge's discretion, entitled to have his costs of the action up to the time when the money was paid into court, and the defendant to have his costs incurred after that time, less any severable costs subsequent to the payment into court in respect of any issue on which the plaintiff has succeeded.[76] The matter is, however, discretionary, so that in a personal injuries case for example, where the defendant pays a sum into court having denied liability, the plaintiff who succeeds at the trial but is awarded less than the amount paid in may be denied his costs after the date of payment in, even those incurred on the issue of liability.[77]

Offer to Settle and Calderbank Letters

In an action where the claim is not simply for "debt or damages"[78] if one party makes an "open" offer to settle which is rejected by his opponent and it is one which the court considers should have been accepted then the court can make an order relieving the offering party from liability for costs incurred after the date of the offer.

Many offers of course are made "without prejudice" but in certain circumstances one party can make a written offer to his opponent in the form of what has become known as a "Calderbank Letter." The name derives from the case in which the Court of Appeal considered and gave recognition to this procedure[79] although it was codified in 1986 by the addition of a new rule to Order 22 (Order 22, r. 14).

A party can make a written offer to his opponent to settle any issue in the proceedings and the offer can be expressed to be "without prejudice save as to costs." If the offer is rejected its existence is not made known to the court until the court considers the question of costs. The court then, when exercising its discretion as to costs, takes into account any offer made

---

[76] *Powell* v. *Vickers, Sons & Maxim Ltd.* [1907] 1 K.B. 71; *Fitzgerald* v. *Thomas Tilling Ltd.* (1907) 96 L.T. 718; *The Blanche* [1908] P. 259; *Findlay* v. *Railway Executive* [1950] 2 All E.R. 969.

[77] *Hultquist* v. *Universal Pattern and Precision Engineering Co. Ltd.* [1960] 2 Q.B. 467 (C.A.); *Griffen* v. *C.V. (Sales & Repairs)* (1983) C.A.T. 246.

[78] Where a payment into court under Ord. 22, r. 1 is appropriate to protect the parties' position as to costs.

[79] *Calderbank* v. *Calderbank* [1976] Fam. 93. The procedure originated in the context of matrimonial proceedings but was utilised in other areas: see, *e.g.* *Computer Machinery Co. Ltd.* v. *Drescher* [1983] 1 W.L.R. 1379.

under Order 22, r. 14 (rule 9(1)(*d*)).[80] However, as the rule clearly states the court cannot take this type of offer into account if a payment into court under Order 22, r. 1 would have been appropriate[81] and therefore the action in question has to be for something more than just "debt or damages."

Several Parties

When several persons join in one action as plaintiffs and some succeed and others fail, the defendant should ask for an order for any special costs occasioned by the joinder of those who failed. Before 1959 a defendant was entitled to them automatically unless the judge otherwise ordered.

Where a plaintiff sues two defendants who defend jointly by the same solicitor, and judgment is given in favour of one defendant and against the other, the successful defendant is, in the absence of any agreement between him and his co-defendant as to how their costs are to be borne *inter se*, entitled to recover from the plaintiff half the costs of the defence.[82]

Where a plaintiff brings an action against two defendants and his claim against them is in the alternative, if the judge is satisfied that it was a reasonable and proper course for the plaintiff to join both defendants[83] he may order the plaintiff to pay the costs of the successful defendant and then to add that amount to the costs which the unsuccessful defendant is ordered to pay to the plaintiff. This is known as a "Bullock order."[84] The judge may do so whether one defendant has blamed the other or not[85]; it is a matter of discretion.[86] In some cases the unsuccessful defendant is ordered to pay the successful defendant's costs to him directly. This is known as a "Sanderson order."[87] Where the judge has power to make a

---

[80] This is a departure from the strong general authority of *Walker* v. *Wilsher* (1889) 23 Q.B.D. 335 that the court cannot take into account "without prejudice" negotiations in order to decide the question of costs. In a case decided before the "codification" of the procedure Ormrod L.J. said that a Calderbank letter "should influence but not govern the exercise of discretion": *McDonnell* v. *McDonnell* [1977] 1 W.L.R. 34. See also *Corby D.C.* v. *Holst & Co. Ltd.* [1985] 1 W.L.R. 427.

[81] This accords with the limitation imposed on the Calderbank letter by Oliver L.J. in *Cutts* v. *Head* [1984] 1 All E.R. 597.

[82] *Beaumont* v. *Senior and Bull* [1903] 1 K.B. 282; *Ellingsen* v. *Det Skandinavishe Co.* [1919] 2 K.B. 567.

[83] *e.g.* where the plaintiff is a passenger in a vehicle and is injured in a collision between that vehicle and another.

[84] After the case *Bullock* v. *London General Omnibus Co.* [1907] 1 K.B. 264.

[85] *Besterman* v. *British Motor Cab Co. Ltd.* [1914] 3 K.B. 181.

[86] *Hong* v. *A. & R. Brown Ltd.* [1948] 1 K.B. 515.

[87] After the case *Sanderson* v. *Blythe Theatre Co.* [1903] 2 K.B. 533, and see *The Esrom* (1914) W.N. 81; *Parkes* v. *Knowles* [1957] 1 W.L.R. 1040.

Bullock or a Sanderson order the choice between them is a matter for his discretion.[88]

Where several co-defendants are ordered to pay the plaintiff's costs and one of the co-defendants pays the whole of such costs, he is entitled to obtain contribution from the others without an independent proceeding.[89]

The court has a complete discretion in regard to the costs of third or subsequent parties.[90]

Costs of Proceedings in Chambers

The combined effect of Order 62, r. 8(1) and (2) is that the costs of any proceedings will not be taxed until the conclusion of the proceedings unless the court makes a special order that they should be taxed earlier.[91] However, on the conclusion of any hearing in chambers the court can make an order as to who shall ultimately bear the costs of that hearing.[92] The provision in Order 62, r. 3(3) that costs will be ordered to follow the event except when it appears to the court that in the circumstances of the case some other order should be made is applicable to proceedings in chambers no less than to a trial. If the application was a proper one, the normal and just order to make is "costs in the cause."

Although the costs of the proceedings will not be taxed until the conclusion of the cause or matter unless exceptionally a specific order is made under Order 62, r. 8(2), where it appears to a taxing master on an application to him that there will be no further order made in the cause or matter he may tax the costs of any interlocutory proceedings forthwith (Order 62, r. 8(9)). This situation is likely to arise, for instance, where an application for an interlocutory injunction has effectively disposed of or settled a dispute.

No costs are allowed in respect of counsel attending before a master or registrar in chambers unless the master or registrar certifies that the attendance was proper in the circumstances. Before a judge in chambers one counsel is allowed without

---

[88] *Mayer* v. *Harte* [1960] 1 W.L.R. 770; *Goldsworthy* v. *Brickell* [1987] 2 W.L.R. 133 at 166. In many cases the eventual outcome will be the same; the choice between the orders could, however, be crucial where, for instance, the unsuccessful defendant is insolvent at the date of the judgment: see *Bankamerica Finance Ltd.* v. *Nock* [1988] 1 All E.R. 81.

[89] *Newry Salt Works Co.* v. *Macdonnell* [1903] 2 Ir.R. 454.

[90] *Edginton* v. *Clark* [1964] 1 Q.B. 367.

[91] See also Ord. 14, r. 7(1). There is no jurisdiction to make the special order where the person against whom the order for costs is to be made is an assisted person within the meaning of the Legal Aid Act 1988.

[92] "The court" here includes judges in chambers, masters and district registrars.

certificate, but for more than one the judge must be asked to certify that the attendance was proper (Order 62, App. 2, Part I, para. 2(2)).

An appeal from an order as to costs made by a master or district registrar lies to a judge in chambers.[93]

Where the plaintiff makes an application for summary judgment under Order 14 the costs are still in the discretion of the court and prima facie a successful plaintiff will be entitled to the costs of the proceedings and the Order 14 application. If, however, the plaintiff makes an Order 14 application where the case does not fall within the Order or if the court is of the opinion that the plaintiff knew that the defendant relied on a contention which would entitle him to unconditional leave to defend, then the court may dismiss the application and may require the costs to be paid by the plaintiff forthwith.[94] Where leave to defend is given and it is ordered that the costs of the Order 14 application be "costs in cause" the judge who tries the action has no power to interfere or vary the order as to costs.[95]

Where an application is made under Order 24, r. 7A or Order 29, r. 7A for an order under section 33 or 34 of the Supreme Court Act 1981, the person against whom the order is sought shall be entitled, unless the court otherwise directs, to his costs of and incidental to the application and of complying with any order made (Order 62, r. 6(9)).[96]

Costs in the Court of Appeal

In the Court of Appeal costs ordinarily follow the event[97]; and if nothing is said by the court as to costs, the order will be so drawn up. Thus, if the appeal is dismissed, the respondent retains his order for costs in the court of trial and gets his costs of resisting the appeal. However, if the court allows the appeal and reverses the decision of the trial judge, including his

---

[93] Ord. 58, r. 1. The right to appeal on a question of costs from a master's decision to a judge in chambers is unfettered and does not depend on a master giving leave and is not subject to the restriction contained in s.18(1) of the Supreme Court Act 1981: *Hall* v. *Wandsworth Health Authority* (1985) 129 Sol.Jo. 188.

[94] Ord. 14, r. 7. See Ord. 86, r. 6 for the equivalent provision in that Order. See also *Marshall* v. *Levine* [1985] 1 W.L.R. 814.

[95] *Koosen* v. *Rose* [1897] 76 L.T. 145.

[96] *Hall* v. *Wandsworth Health Authority* (*supra*) shows that where it is delay on the part of the party against whom the order is made which results in the issuing of s.33 proceedings then that party may be deprived of an order for costs and in exceptional circumstances that party may be ordered to pay the costs of the applicant.

[97] *Ex p. Masters* (1875) 1 Ch.D. 113.

award of costs to the now unsuccessful respondent, the normal order in the Court of Appeal will be "Appeal allowed with costs here and below" and the court should be asked to make such an order. The Court of Appeal, however, has full discretion over the costs of an appeal, and in the court below, and can make such order as to the whole or any part of them as may be just.[98] Hence it may, in a proper case, refuse costs to the successful party. For instance, an appellant has been deprived of his costs where he succeeded on a point not raised in the court below,[99] or on fresh evidence,[1] or on a mere point of law, after having failed to prove allegations of fraud.[2]

Similarly, a successful respondent may be deprived of his costs where, for instance, his defence is discreditable[3]; and in one case where the appellants were innocent persons, who had used due diligence, but had been made the victims of a forgery, although their appeal was dismissed it was dismissed without costs.[4] However, the mere omission by the respondent to inform his opponent that he has a preliminary objection which proves fatal to the appeal is not a sufficient reason for depriving him of costs.[5]

The costs of an appeal may include the cost of the transcript of the judgment of the court below whether taken down and transcribed by an official shorthand writer or transcribed from a mechanical recording. Formerly the cost of a transcript of the evidence was only allowed in special circumstances.[6] Nowadays where such a transcript is a document required for use on appeal the cost of relevant portions would normally be allowable.

If the Court of Appeal orders a new trial, the costs of the first trial follow the event of the second, unless any special order be made when the new trial is granted, or at the second trial.[7] And by "the event" of the second trial is meant the result of that trial as to costs.[8] The costs of a successful application for a new trial will, as a rule, be given to the applicant.[9]

---

[98] Supreme Court Act 1981, s.51 and Ord. 62, r. 8(4).
[99] *Hussey* v. *Horne-Payne* (1878) 8 Ch.D. 870; *Dye* v. *Dye* (1884) 13 Q.B.D. 147.
[1] *Arnot's Case* (1887) 36 Ch.D. 710; *Ex p. Hauxwell* (1883) 23 Ch.D. 643; *Chard* v. *Jervis* (1882) 9 Q.B.D. 178.
[2] *Ex p. Cooper* (1878) 10 Ch.D. 313.
[3] *Jones* v. *Merionethshire Permanent Benefit Building Society* [1892] 1 Ch. 173.
[4] *Cooper* v. *Vesey* (1881) 20 Ch.D. 611.
[5] *Ex p. Shead* (1885) 15 Q.B.D. 338.
[6] *Pilling* v. *Joint Stock Institute* (1896) 73 L.T. 570; *Castner Kellner* v. *Commercial, etc., Corp.* [1899] 1 Ch. 803.
[7] *Creen* v. *Wright* (1877) 2 C.P.D. 354; *Field* v. *G.N. Ry.* (1878) 3 Ex.D. 261.
[8] *Brotherton* v. *Metropolitan District Ry., Joint Committee* [1894] 1 Q.B. 666; but see *Dunn* v. *S.E. & C. Ry.*, [1903] 1 K.B. 358.
[9] *Hamilton* v. *Seal* [1904] 2 K.B. 262.

Interest on Costs

A party who is awarded costs is entitled to interest thereon pursuant to the Judgments Act 1838. In *Hunt* v. *R. M. Douglas (Roofing) Ltd.*[10] the House of Lords considered the question whether "a litigant who has been awarded costs is entitled to interest on the amount of the costs from the date on which judgment is pronounced (. . . the incipitur rule) or from the date on which the taxation of costs is completed by the issue of the taxing master's certificate (the allocatur rule)."[11] The House, overruling two earlier decisions of the Court of Appeal[12] to the contrary, held that the incipitur rule prevails, and that interest on costs runs from the date of judgment.

The court only has power to award interest on costs under a judgment or order so that if a plaintiff accepts money paid into court by the defendant under Order 22 in full settlement of his claim the court has no jurisdiction to make an order for the payment of interest on his costs. This is because his entitlement to costs in these circumstances arises under the Rules of the Supreme Court and not by virtue of any judgment or order of the court.[13]

---

[10] [1988] 3 All E.R. 823.
[11] *Ibid. per* Lord Ackner at p. 824.
[12] *K.* v. *K.* [1977] Fam. 39 and *Erven Warnink BV* v. *J. Townend & Sons (Hull) Ltd. (No. 2)* [1982] 3 All E.R. 312.
[13] *Legal Aid Board* v. *Russell* [1990] 3 All E.R. 18.

APPENDIX 1

PRECEDENTS

I. Indorsements on Writ

II.—Statements of Claim

In Actions for Breach of Contract

In Actions of Tort

In Actions for the Possession of Land

In Actions in the Chancery Division

III.—Defences

In Actions for Breach of Contract

In Actions of Tort

IX.—Appeal

I.—INDORSEMENTS ON WRIT

No. 1

Writ of Summons Specially Indorsed with Claim for Debt[1]

[Royal Arms]

In the High Court of Justice   1990 S. No. 1234
   Queen's Bench Division
     [DISTRICT REGISTRY]

BETWEEN	John Smith	PLAINTIFF
AND	David Jones	DEFENDANT

TO THE DEFENDANT David Jones
of 555 Fleet Street, in the City of London.

THIS WRIT OF SUMMONS has been issued against you by the above-named Plaintiff in respect of the claim set out on the back.

Within 14 days after the service of this Writ on you, counting the day of service, you must either satisfy the claim or return to the Court Office mentioned below the accompanying ACKNOWLEDGEMENT OF SERVICE stating therein whether you intend to contest these proceedings.

If you fail to satisfy the claim or to return the Acknowledgment within the time stated, or if you return the Acknowledgment without stating therein an intention to contest the proceedings, the Plaintiff may proceed with the action and judgment may be entered against you forthwith without further notice.

---

[1] See R.S.C., Appendix A, Form No. 1 (the composite form of writ of summons). The specimen writ set out here is issued in the Queen's Bench Division out of the Central Office, hence the name of the District Registry has been left blank.

Issued from the Central Office [or   District Registry] of the High Court this 4th day of June 1990.

Note.—This Writ may not be served later than 4 calendar months (or, if leave is required to effect service out of the jurisdiction, 6 months) beginning with that date unless renewed by order of the Court.

Important

Directions for Acknowledgment of Service are given with the accompanying form.

[Back of the writ]

STATEMENT OF CLAIM

The Plaintiff's claim is for £5,500, balance of the price of goods sold and delivered by the Plaintiff to the Defendant.

Particulars

	£	p
1988—June 12—Invoice No. AB456, 60 rolls denim cloth @ £100 per roll	6,000	00
1988—July 5—less cheque	500	00
Balance	5,500	00

The Plaintiff further claims interest pursuant to section 35A of the Supreme Court Act 1981 at the rate of 15% per annum from the 12th June 1988 to the date hereof, namely £___ and thereafter at the daily rate of £2.26 until judgment or sooner payment.

(Signed) Francis Bacon

[*Where the Plaintiff's claim is for
a debt or liquidated demand only:*
If, within the time for returning the Acknowledgment of
Service, the Defendant pays
the amount claimed and £____
for costs and, if the Plaintiff
obtains an order for substituted service, the additional
sum of £____ , further proceedings will be stayed. The
money must be paid to the
Pliantiff, his Solicitor or
Agent].

[*If this Writ was issued out of a
District Registry, indorsement as
to place where cause of action
arose:*
The cause [One of the causes]
of action in respect of which
the Plaintiff claims relief in
this action arose wholly or in
part at   in the district
of the District Registry named
overleaf].

THIS WRIT was issued by F. W. Williams of 666 Fleet Street
London E.C.4.
        [Agent for   of   ]
Solicitor for the said Plaintiff whose address is 145 Grand Park
Gardens, Hampstead, London N.W.3.
        [*or where the Plaintiff sues in person*]

THIS WRIT was issued by the said Plaintiff who resides at

and (*if the Plaintiff does not reside within the jurisdiction*) whose
address for service is

Acknowledgment of Service of Writ of Summons

Directions for Acknowledgment of Service

1. The accompanying form of ACKNOWLEDGMENT OF SERVICE
should be detached and completed by a Solicitor acting on
behalf of the Defendant or by the Defendant if acting in

person. After completion it must be delivered or sent by post to the Central Office, Royal Courts of Justice, Strand, London WC2A 2LL [*or, if the Writ was issued out of a District Registry*, to the District Registrar, (*address*)].

2. A Defendant who states in his Acknowledgment of Service that he intends to contest the proceedings MUST ALSO SERVE A DEFENCE on the Solicitor for the Plaintiff (or on the Plaintiff if acting in person).

If a Statement of Claim is indorsed on the Writ (*i.e.* the words "Statement of Claim" appear at the top of the back of the first page), the Defence must be served within 14 days after the time for acknowledging service of the Writ, unless in the meantime a summons for judgment is served on the Defendant.

If a Statement of Claim is not indorsed on the Writ, the Defence need not be served until 14 days after a Statement of Claim has been served on the Defendant.

If the Defendant fails to serve his defence within the appropriate time, the Plaintiff may enter judgment against him without further notice.

3. A STAY OF EXECUTION against the Defendant's goods may be applied for where the Defendant is unable to pay the money for which any judgment is entered. If a Defendant to an action for a debt or liquidated demand (*i.e.* a fixed sum) who does not intend to contest the proceedings states, in answer to Question 3 in the Acknowledgment of Service, that he intends to apply for a stay, execution will be stayed for 14 days after his Acknowledgment, but he must, within that time, ISSUE A SUMMONS for a stay of execution, supported by an affidavit of his means. The affidavit should state any offer which the Defendant desires to make for payment of the money by instalments or otherwise.

4. IF THE WRIT IS ISSUED OUT OF A DISTRICT REGISTRY but the Defendant does not reside or carry on business within the district of the registry and the writ is not indorsed with a statement that the Plaintiff's cause of action arose in that district, the Defendant may, in answer to Question 4 in the Acknowledgment of Service, apply for the transfer of the action to some other District Registry or to the Royal Courts of Justice.

Notes for Guidance

1. Each Defendant (if there are more than one) is required to complete an Acknowledgment of Service and return it to the appropriate Court Office.

2. For the purpose of calculating the period of 14 days for acknowledging service, a writ served on the Defendant personally is treated as having been served on the day it was delivered to him and a writ served by post or by insertion through the Defendant's letter box is treated as having been served on the seventh day after the date of posting or insertion.

3. Where the Defendant is sued in a name different from his own, the form must be completed by him with the addition in paragraph 1 of the words "sued as (*the name stated on the Writ of Summons*)."

4. Where the Defendant is a FIRM and a Solicitor is not instructed, the form must be completed by a PARTNER by name, with the addition in paragraph 1 of the description "partner in the firm of (. . . . .)" after his name.

5. Where the Defendant is sued as an individual TRADING IN A NAME OTHER THAN HIS OWN, the form must be completed by him with the addition in paragraph 1 of the description "trading as (. . . . .)" after his name.

6. Where the Defendant is a LIMITED COMPANY the form must be completed by a Solicitor or by someone authorised to act on behalf of the Company, but the Company can take no further step in the proceedings without a Solicitor acting on its behalf.

7. Where the Defendant is a MINOR or a MENTAL Patient, the form must be completed by a Solicitor acting for a guardian *ad litem*.

8. A Defendant acting in person may obtain help in completing the form either at the Central Office of the Royal Courts of Justice or at any District Registry of the High Court or at any Citizens' Advice Bureau.

9. A Defendant who is NOT a Limited Company or a Corporation may be entitled to Legal Aid. Information about the Legal Aid Scheme may be obtained from any Citizens' Advice Bureau and from most firms of Solicitors.

10. These notes deal only with the more usual cases. In case of difficulty a Defendant in person should refer to paragraphs 8 & 9 above.

[Heading as in No. 1 to be completed by plaintiff]

ACKNOWLEDGMENT OF SERVICE
OF WRIT OF SUMMONS

If you intend to instruct a Solicitor to act for you, give him this form IMMEDIATELY

If you intend to instruct a Solicitor to act for you, give him this form IMMEDIATELY

Important, Read the accompanying directions and notes for guidance carefully before completing this form. If any information required is omitted or given wrongly, THIS FORM MAY HAVE TO BE RETURNED.

Delay may result in judgement being entered against a Defendant whereby he or his Solicitor may have to pay the costs of applying to set it aside.

See Notes 1, 3, 4 and 5

1. State the full name of the Defendant by whom or on whose behalf the service of the Writ is being acknowledged.

---

2. State wether the Defendant intends to contest the proceedings (*tick appropriate box*)

☐ yes   ☐ no

See Direction 3

3. If the claim against the Defendant is for a debt or liquidated demand, AND he does not intend to contest the proceedings, state if the Defendant intends to apply for a stay of execution against any judgment entered by the Plaintiff (*tick box*)

☐ yes

---

4. If the Writ of Summons was issued out of a District Registry and

    (*a*) the Defendant's residence, place of business or registered office (if a limited company) is NOT within the district of that District Registry AND (*b*) there is no indorsement on the Writ that the Plaintiff's cause of action arose wholly or in part within that district,

state if the Defendant applies for the transfer of the action

(*tick box*)   yes ☐

If YES, state—

(*tick appropriate box*) ☐ to the Royal Courts of Justice, London: OR

☐ to the   District Registry
(*state which Registry*)

---

* *Where words appear between square brackets delete if inapplicable*

Service of the Writ is acknowledged accordingly

*(*Signed*) [Solicitor] [Agent for   ]
[Defendant in person]
Address for service

Notes as to Address for Service

Solicitor, Where the Defendant is represented by a Solicitor, state the Solicitor's place of business in England or wales. If the Solicitor is the Agent of another Solicitor, state the name and the place of business of the Solicotor for whom he is acting.

Defendant in person. Where the Defendant is acting in person, he must give his residence OR, if he does not reside in England or Wales, he must give an address in England or Wales were communications for him should be sent. In the case of a limited company "residence" means its registered or principal office.

INDORSEMENT BY PLAINTIFF'S SOLICITOR (OR BY PLAINTIFF IF SUING IN PERSON) OF HIS NAME, ADDRESS AND REFERENCE, IF ANY.

No. 2

Writ of Summons Indorsed with Claim for Unliquidated Demand[2]

In the High Court of Justice   1990 R. No. 5678
    Queen's Bench Division
        Manchester DISTRICT REGISTRY
BETWEEN   Michael Robinson   PLAINTIFF
                (A minor, suing by his father and
                    next friend Charles Robinson)
AND   Speedwell Traction Company Ltd.   DEFENDANTS
TO THE DEFENDANTS Speedwell Traction Company Ltd. whose registered office is situate at Enterprise House, Rotten Row,

---

[2] R.S.C., Appendix A, Form No. 1, appropriately modified. In this precedent the accompanying forms for Acknowledgment of Service have been omitted.

London S.W.1.
THIS WRIT, etc. [as in No. 1].

Within, etc. [as in No. 1].

If you fail, etc. [as in No. 1].

Issued from the Manchester District Registry of the High Court this 17th day of September 1990.

Note.—This Writ, etc. [as in No. 1].

The Plaintiff is a minor who sues by his father and next friend Charles Robinson.

The Plaintiff's claim is for:
  (1) Damages for personal injuries, loss and damage caused by the negligent driving of the Defendant's servant or agent on December 24, 1989, at Deansgate in the City of Manchester;
  (2) An order for provisional damages pursuant to section 32A of the Supreme Court Act 1981.
  (3) Interest thereon pursuant to section 35A of the Supreme Court Act 1981.
      (Signed) Ardwick & Co.
The cause of action in respect of which the Plaintiff claims relief in this action arose wholly or in part at Manchester in the district of the District Registry named overleaf.

THIS WRIT was issued, etc. [as in No. 1].

No. 3

The Plaintiff's claim is for damages for breach of a written contract dated January 28, 1989, made between the Plaintiff and the Defendant together with interest thereon pursuant to section 35A of the Supreme Court Act 1981.

No. 4

The Plaintiff's claim is for:
  (1) Specific performance of a contract for the sale of a picture made orally on September 17, 1989, between the Plaintiffs and the Defendants;
  (2) Further or in the alternative; damages for breach of contract;

(3) Interest pursuant to section 35A of the Supreme Court Act 1981;

(4) Further or other relief.

No. 5

The Plaintiff's claim is for:

(1) Rescission of an agreement in writing dated May 12, 1989 and made between the Plaintiff and the Defendant on the ground of the Defendant's fraudulent misrepresentation with all proper consequential directions;

(2) Repayment of the sum of £24,000 paid by the Plaintiff to the Defendant pursuant to the said agreement;

(3) Further or in the alternative; damages for fraudulent misrepresentation and/or breach of warranty whereby the Plaintiff was induced to enter into the said agreement and make the said payment pursuant thereto.

(4) Interest pursuant to section 35A of the Supreme Court Act 1981 at the rate of 15 per cent. per annum on the sum of £24,000 from May 12, 1989 to the date hereof namely £— and thereafter at a daily rate of £— until judgment or sooner payment.

No. 6

The Plaintiffs' claim is for:

(1) Damages for breach of a written contract of service dated October 31, 1988, made between the Plaintiffs and the Defendant;

(2) A declaration that the technical designs and information concerning the development and production of an electric toothbrush communicated by the Plaintiffs to the Defendant between November 1, 1988 and June 4, 1989, were and are trade secrets and/or constituted confidential information the property of the Plaintiffs which was communicated to the Defendant in confidence;

(3) An order for the delivery-up to the Plaintiffs of all documents and other records containing any such confidential information whether such documents or records were made by the Plaintiffs or by the Defendant;

(4) An injunction restraining the Defendant whether by himself or by his servants or agents or otherwise from making any use of such confidential information as aforesaid or any part thereof for any purpose whatsoever;

(5) An inquiry into what damages have been and may be suffered by the Plaintiffs by reason of the Defendant's breach of confidence in making use of such confidential information as aforesaid;

(6) Further or in the alternative an account of profits made by the Defendant by the use of such confidential information as aforesaid or any part thereof;

(7) Payment of the amount certified in answer to such inquiry or account as aforesaid;

(8) Interest pursuant to section 35A of the Supreme Court Act 1981;

(9) Further or other relief.

No. 7

The Plaintiff's claim is for £5,000 money lent by the Plaintiff to the Defendant at the Defendant's request on May 9, 1990 and/or for the said sum as money paid to the Defendant upon a consideration that has wholly failed and for interest thereon pursuant to section 35A of the Supreme Court Act 1981, etc. (as in No. 1).[3]

No. 8

The Plaintiff's claim is for:

(1) Damages for libel contained in a letter dated July 10, 1990, written and published by the Defendant[4];

(2) An injunction restraining the Defendant by himself, his servant or agent or otherwise from further publishing the said or any similar libel of and concerning the Plaintiff.

No. 9

The Plaintiff's claim is for:

(1) Damages for personal injuries, loss and damage, the said injuries having been sustained on November 16, 1988, while the Plaintiff was a visitor at the Defendants' premises at 777 Anson Street, London N. 28, and caused by the negligence and breach of statutory duty of the Defendants as occupiers of such premises;

---

[3] Although a claim for interest must be specifically pleaded in the Statement of Claim (Ord. 18, r. 8) it does not have to be claimed on a generally indorsed writ. As a matter of practice it usually is claimed on the writ.

[4] See Ord. 82, r. 2.

(2) Interest thereon pursuant to section 35A of the Supreme Court Act 1981.

No. 10

The Plaintiff's claim is as Administratix of the estate of Terence Rivers deceased for:
(1) Damages under the Fatal Accidents Act 1976 (as amended) for the death following an accident on December 4, 1989 of the said deceased caused by the negligence and/or breach of statutory duty of the Defendants as occupiers of premises at 1 Smog Lane, Wolverhampton, in the County of Staffordshire;
(2) Damages under the Law Reform (Miscellaneous Provisions) Act 1934 for the benefit of the estate of the said deceased for funeral expenses and loss caused to the said estate by the negligence and/or breach of statutory duty of the Defendants as occupiers of the said premises.
(3) Interest, etc. (as in No. 9).

No. 11

The Plaintiff's claim is for:
(1) An injunction restraining the Defendants, their servants or agents or otherwise from doing the following acts or any of them, that is to say, carrying on or permitting to be carried on upon their premises the business or undertaking of manufacturers of chemical products so as to cause or permit noxious vapours to escape to the Plaintiff's said land and/or so as by the discharge of the said noxious vapours to cause a nuisance to the Plaintiff's said land or to the Plaintiff or the members of his family or his servants occupying the same.
(2) Damages for nuisance and for damage to the Plaintiff's land at 99 Acacia Avenue, Grove Park, in the County of Kent, by the escape of noxious vapours from the Defendants' premises at 1 Back Street, Grove Park, in the County of Kent, caused by the nuisance of the Defendants, their servants or agents.
(3) Interest, etc. (as in No. 9).

No. 12

The Plaintiff's claim is:

(1) Against the First Defendant for damages for wrongful interference with the Plaintiff's motor-car on or about May 1, 1990.

(2) Against the Second Defendant for an order for the delivery up of the said motor-car or £5,800 its value[5] and for damages for its detention.

(3) Interest, etc. (as in 9 above).

No. 13

The Plaintiff's claim is for:

(1) Possession of premises which do not constitute or comprise a dwelling-house, known as 77 Endsleigh Gardens, London W.C.1.[6]

(2) Damages for breach of covenant to repair the premises.

(3) Interest, etc. (as in 9 above).

(4) Further or other relief.

(5) Costs.

No. 14

The Plaintiff's claim is for:

(1) Execution of the trusts of the above-mentioned Settlement dated February 1, 1990 and made between John Lloyd of the one part and Andrew Gibson of the other part.

(2) All such accounts, inquiries, directions and other relief as may be just.

(3) Further or other relief.

(4) Costs.

No. 15

The Plaintiff's claim is for:

(1) An inquiry whether any and if so what moneys subject to the trusts of the above-mentioned Will have been invested by the Defendants in the purchase of ordinary shares of Mammoth Investment Properties Limited and whether and if so when any such shares were sold by the Defendants and whether any and if so what sum has been lost to the estate subject to the said trusts by reason of the said investment.

[5] See Ord. 6, r. 2(1)(*d*).
[6] See Ord. 6, r. 2(1)(*c*).

(2) An order that the Defendants be charged with interest at the rate of 15 per cent. per annum[7] on the amount invested by them in the said purchase.

(3) An account of the moneys due to the said estate in respect of any such loss and interest as aforesaid.

(4) Payment of the amount found due on taking the said account.

(5) Further or other relief.

(6) Costs.

The Defendants are sued as the trustees of the above-mentioned Will and personally.

II.—STATEMENTS OF CLAIM
IN ACTIONS FOR BREACH OF CONTRACT

No. 16

Agency—Liability to Account

In the High Court of Justice   1990 S. No. 5678
Queen's Bench Division
                    Writ issued the 29th day of May 1990
BETWEEN   Steven Smiles   PLAINTIFF
                    (trading as Smiles and Son)
                    and
          Universe Collections Limited   DEFENDANTS

STATEMENT OF CLAIM

1. The Plaintiff is a bookseller carrying on business at 25 Worm Street, London E.C.1. The Defendants are debt collectors carrying on business at 76 Universe Buildings, London W.C.1.

2. By an agreement in writing contained in a letter dated August 12, 1989, from the Plaintiff to the Defendants and a letter dated August 16, 1989, from the Defendants to the Plaintiff, the Defendants agreed to act as the Plaintiff's agent for the collection of debts due to the Plaintiff from the Plaintiff's customers and the Plaintiff agreed to pay to the Defendants a commission of 10 per cent. on all such debts collected by the Defendants.

3. It was an express term of the agreement that at the end of each calendar month beginning on September 1, 1989, the

[7] The rate of interest on judgments entered on or after April 16, 1985 was increased to this amount by the Judgment Debts (Rates of Interest) Order 1985 (S.I. 1985 No. 437).

Defendants would deliver to the Plaintiff a statement of the accounts of the customers and of the sums collected by the Defendants in such month and that the Defendants would thereupon pay to the Plaintiff a sum representing the total sums collected as aforesaid less the Defendants' commission.

4. In breach of that term the Defendants have failed to deliver to the Plaintiff the statements or any of them and the Defendants have not paid to the Plaintiff the sums or any part thereof.

And the Plaintiff claims:
- (1) An account of what sums, if any, have been received by the Defendants for and on account of the Plaintiff.
- (2) An order for the payment by the Defendants to the Plaintiff of the sum, if any, found due to the Plaintiff from the Defendants on the taking of such account.
- (3) Interest on such sum pursuant to section 35A of the Supreme Court Act 1981 at the rate of 15 per cent. per annum.
- (4) Further or alternatively; Damages for breach of contract.
- (5) Further or other relief.

(signed) Edward Coke

Served on the 6th day of July 1990 by Doolittle & Co. of 225 Worm Street, London E.C.1., Solicitors for the Plaintiff.

No. 17

Employment—Wrongful Dismissal

1. By an agreement in writing dated July 12, 1989, made between the Plaintiff and the Defendants the Plaintiff agreed to serve and the Defendants agreed to employ the Plaintiff as assistant sales manager from August 1, 1989, at a salary of £15,000 per annum.

2. The agreement contained no stipulation as to notice of termination. There was therefore an implied term of the agreement that the Plaintiff was entitled to reasonable notice to determine the employment. In the premises reasonable notice would have been 6 months' notice.

3. By a letter dated November 8, 1989, in breach of the term the Defendants gave the Plaintiff one week's notice to determine the employment and they wrongfully refused to employ the Plaintiff from and after November 15, 1989.

4. In the circumstances the Plaintiff has suffered loss and damage and has been unable to obtain employment elsewhere.

Particulars of Loss and Damage[8]

                    £   p

Loss of Salary for 6 months at £ ____ per month
net after tax
Less credit one week's salary

5. The Plaintiff claims interest pursuant to section 35A of the Supreme Court Act 1981 on the amount found to be due to the Plaintiff at such rate and for such period as the Court thinks fit.

And the Plaintiff claims:
    (1) Damages.
    (2) Interest as pleaded.
Served, etc.

No. 18

Employment—Breach of Duty of Confidence

(Statement of Claim for No. 6)

1. By an agreement in writing dated October 31, 1988, made between the Plaintiffs and the Defendant the Plaintiffs agreed to employ and the Defendant agreed to serve the Plaintiffs as a research engineer from November 1, 1988, at a salary of £16,000 per annum.

2. It was an express; alternatively an implied term of the agreement that the Defendant should keep secret all records, knowledge and information which might from time to time be communicated to him by the Plaintiffs in the course of his employment and that he should not make use of the same or any part thereof other than in the furtherance of the business of the Plaintiff company.

3. Between about November 1, 1988, and about June 4, 1989, the Plaintiffs communicated to the Defendant certain technical designs and information concerning the development and production of an electric toothbrush.

4. The technical designs and information were and are confidential to the Plaintiffs and were and are trade secrets of the Plaintiffs and were communicated to the Defendant, as the Defendant well knew, in confidence.

[8] *Ante*, Chap. 12.

5. On or about June 4, 1989, the Defendant orally terminated his employment with the Plaintiffs and on or about that date or shortly thereafter set up his own laboratory and business as a research and development engineer.

6. In or about July 1989 the Defendant commenced to manufacture and market an electric toothbrush using in breach of the term and/or in breach of the duty of confidence, the technical designs and information communicated by the Plaintiffs to the Defendant as aforesaid.

7. By reason of the premises the Plaintiffs have suffered loss and damage.

8. Further, the Plaintiff claims interest, etc., as in No. 17.

Particulars of Loss and Damage

Full particulars will be supplied after discovery herein.
And the Plaintiffs claim:
(1) Damages for breach of contract;
(2) Interest as pleaded.
    [Then as set out in No. 6]
Served, etc.

No. 19

Sale of Goods—Breach of Implied Conditions

1. The Plaintiff is and was at all material times a grower of orchids. The Defendants are and were at all material times in the business of selling fertilisers.

2. On May 25, 1989, the Defendants in the course of the said business sold to the Plaintiff 5 cwt. of "X" fertiliser for the sum of £200.

3. At the time of the sale the Plaintiff expressly and/or impliedly made known to the Defendants that the fertiliser was required for the Plaintiff's business as a grower of orchids and it was an implied condition of the contract of sale that the fertiliser was reasonably fit for the purpose of fertilising orchids. Further or alternatively it was an implied condition of the contract of sale that the fertiliser was of merchantable quality.

4. In breach of the implied conditions and each of them, the fertiliser was not of merchantable quality and was not reasonably fit for the said purpose in that it contained chemical impurities which caused orchids treated by the Plaintiff with the fertiliser to wither and die.

5. In consequence of the matters referred to in paragraph 4 hereof the Plaintiff has suffered loss and damage.

Particulars of Loss and Damage

		£	p
Loss of "Hothouse" orchids:	Cost		
	Loss of Profit	___	__
Loss of "Tropicana" orchids:	Cost		
	Loss of Profit	___	__

6. Interest, etc., as in No. 17.

And the Plaintiff claims:
    (1) Damages.
    (2) Interest as pleaded.
Served, etc.

No. 20

Sale of Goods—Specific Performance

(Statement of Claim for No. 4)

    1. The Plaintiffs and the Defendants are and were at all material times dealers in oil paintings.
    2. By an oral agreement made by telephone on September 17, 1989, between James Lovelace on behalf of the Plaintiffs and Cecil Wycherley on behalf of the Defendants the Defendants agreed to sell to the Plaintiffs and the Plaintiffs agreed to buy an oil painting known as "Four Cubist Nudes" painted by Pablo Picasso for a price of £100,000.
    3. In breach of the agreement the Defendants have refused and still refuse to deliver the painting to the Plaintiffs in spite of repeated requests, oral and in writing, by the Plaintiffs to the Defendants to do so.
    And the Plaintiffs claim:
    (1) Specific performance of the said agreement.
    (2) Further or in the alternative damages for breach of the said agreement.
    (3) Interest thereon pursuant to s.35A of the Supreme Court Act 1981.
    (4) Further or other relief.
Served, etc.

No. 21

Sale of a Business—Misrepresentation—Collateral Warranty

(Statement of Claim for No. 5)

1. In or about March 1988 the Defendant advertised for sale freehold premises situate at 75 Woburn Avenue, London W.C.1., and the goodwill of the tobacconist's business carried on thereat. The Plaintiff entered into negotiations with the Defendant with a view to purchasing the same.

2. During the negotiations on or about April 10, 1988, in order to induce the Plaintiff to purchase the premises and business, the Defendant orally represented and/or warranted to the Plaintiff that the business had made a profit of £4,500 in the preceding six months.

3. In reliance upon the representation and/or in consideration of the warranty, the Plaintiff, by a written agreement dated May 12, 1989, purchased the premises and business from the Defendant for the sum of £24,000.

4. The representation was false and/or the Defendant was in breach of the warranty in that the business had not made the said or any profit in the preceding six months but had made a loss in that period.

5. The Defendant made the representation fraudulently in that he knew the same was false alternatively he was reckless in not caring whether the same was true or false.

6. In the premises the Plaintiff has suffered loss and damage.

Particulars

	£	p
Value of the business as represented and/or warranted	24.000	00
Value of the business as purchased by the Plaintiff	17,500	00
Difference in value	6,500	00

7. Interest, etc., as in No. 17.

And the Plaintiff claims:

(1) Under paragraphs 4 and 5 hereof rescission of the agreement referred to in paragraph 3 hereof on the ground of fraudulent misrepresentation with all proper consequential directions.

(2) Under paragraphs 4 and 5 hereof repayment of the sum of £24,000 paid by the Plaintiff to the Defendant pursuant to the said agreement.

(3) Further or in the alternative under paragraphs 4, 5 and 6, hereof, damages for fraudulent misrepresentation and/or breach of warranty.

(4) Interest as pleaded.

Served, etc.

No. 22

Work and Services—Quantum Meruit

1. The Plaintiff is a member of the Society of Chartered Accountants and carries on practice as an accountant at 7 Capitalist Buildings, Rotten Row, London S.W.1.

2. On or about May 30, 1989, the Defendants orally instructed the Plaintiff to prepare the accounts of the Defendant company for the trading year 1988–9 and to compile a report of the financial position of the Defendant company for presentation to the next annual general meeting of the Defendant company.

3. Pursuant to those instructions the Plaintiff prepared the accounts and compiled the report in or about July 1989.

4. It was an implied term of the contract between the Plaintiff and the Defendants that on completion of the instructions the Defendants should pay to the Plaintiff a reasonable fee in consideration of the work.

5. A reasonable fee for the work is £7,500.

6. The Defendants have failed to pay the Plaintiff the said sum of £7,500 or any sum.

7. Further, the Plaintiff claims interest, etc. (as in No. 16).

And the Plaintiff claims:

(1) £7,500 or alternatively such sum as is found reasonable.

(2) Interest as pleaded.

No. 23

Money Paid—Total Failure of Consideration

1. By an agreement partly oral and partly in writing made on or about June 4, 1990, between the Plaintiff and George Herbert on behalf of the Defendants, the written part of the agreement being contained in the Defendants' acknowledgment of order dated June 5, 1990, the Defendants agreed to deliver to one Henry Vaughan on June 12, 1990, certain goods, full particulars whereof were set out in a letter dated July 16, 1990, from solicitors for the Plaintiff to the Defendants, in

consideration whereof the Plaintiff agreed to pay to the Defendants the sum of £6,000.

2. On June 10, 1990, the Plaintiff paid to the Defendants the sum of £6,000.

3. The Defendants have failed to deliver to Henry Vaughan the goods or any part thereof.

4. In the premises the consideration for the said agreement has wholly failed.

And the Plaintiff claims:

(1) £6,000.

(2) Interest thereon pursuant to section 35A of the Supreme Court Act 1981.

Served, etc.

IN ACTIONS OF TORT

No. 24

Negligence—Personal Injuries in a Collision—Provisional Damages

(Statement of Claim for No. 2)

1. At all material times the Plaintiff was a pedestrian in Deansgate, Manchester and the Defendants were the owners of a bus, registration number XYZ 789, which was being driven by their servant or agent Sidney James Allen in the course of his employment.

2. On December 24, 1989 at about 3.00 pm the Plaintiff was crossing Deansgate from the southside to the northside at the junction with King Street when the bus, which was being driven west along Deansgate, collided with the Plaintiff.

3. The accident was caused by the negligence of the Defendants, said servant or agent.

Particulars of Negligence

Sidney James Allen was negligent in that he:

(i) Collided with the Plaintiff.

(ii) Drove too fast.

(iii) Failed to keep any or any proper lookout.

(iv) Failed to see and/or to heed the Plaintiff crossing the road.

(v) Failed to give any or any adequate warning of the approach of the bus.

(vi) Failed to stop, to slow down, to swerve or in any other way so to control the bus as to avoid colliding with the Plaintiff.

4. On March 22, 1989 at Corporation Street Magistrates' Court, Manchester, Sidney James Allen was convicted of driving without due care and attention pursuant to section 3 of the Road Traffic Act 1972. Those proceedings arose out of the aforesaid collision. The conviction is relevant to these proceedings and the Plaintiff will rely upon it as prima facie evidence of negligence on the part of Sidney James Allen for himself and as servant or agent of the Defendants.[9]

5. By reason of the matters aforesaid the Plaintiff, who was born on May 2, 1979, suffered injury, loss and damage.

Particulars of Injury

Pain and shock

Contusions to the right leg, right arm & back

A fracture of the right tibia

A closed head injury which required brain surgery.

There is continuing pain and instability in the right leg which is likely to be permanent.

The Plaintiff has been placed at a disadvantage on the labour market because it is unlikely that he will ever be able to engage in work involving prolonged standing or walking.[10]

A medical report is annexed to this pleading pursuant to Order 18, r. 12(1A)(*a*).

Particulars of the Claim for Provisional Damages

There is a chance that at some definite or indefinite time in the future the Plaintiff will, as a result of the Defendant's negligence, develop a disease or suffer a serious deterioration in his physical condition, namely; epilepsy.

If the Plaintiff's claim for provisional damages is refused then the Plaintiff will contend that there is a risk of epilepsy in the future of 5 per cent.

Particulars of Loss and Damage

A schedule of special damages is served herewith pursuant to Order 18, r. 12(1A)(*b*).

---

[9] See Ord. 18, r. 7A.
[10] See *Smith* v. *Manchester Corporation* (1974) 17 K.I.R. 1 (C.A.) and *Moeliker* v. *A. Reyrolle & Co. Ltd.* [1977] 1 W.L.R. 132 (C.A.).

6. The Plaintiff claims interest pursuant to section 35A of the Supreme Court Act 1981.

AND the Plaintiff claims against the Defendants:

(1) An order for provisional damages pursuant to section 32A of the Supreme Court Act 1981 on the assumption that the Plaintiff will not develop epilepsy.

(2) An order that if at a future date the Plaintiff does develop epilepsy he shall be entitled to apply for further damages.

(3) Directions in relation to any such application for further damages.

(4) Alternatively to (1), (2) and (3); Damages.

(5) Interest as pleaded.

Served, etc.

No. 25

Negligence—Breach of Statutory Duty—Liability of an Occupier

[Statement of Claim for No. 9]

1. The Defendants are and were at all material times the owners and occupiers of premises known as Vericheap Discount Stores at 777 Anson Street, London N.28, where they carry on the business of retailers of electrical equipment.

2. On or about November 16, 1988, the Plaintiff entered the premises as a customer for the purpose of purchasing electrical equipment from the Defendants and while examining an item of electrical equipment fell through an open and unguarded trap-door or hole in the floor of the premises.

3. The matters complained of were caused by the negligence and/or breach of statutory duty under section 2 of the Occupiers' Liability Act 1957 of the Defendants, their servants or agents.

Particulars of Negligence and/or Breach of Statutory Duty

(a) Causing or permitting the trap-door or hole to be and/or to remain open and unguarded and a danger to persons lawfully using their premises.

(b) Failing to take any or any reasonable care to see that the Plaintiff would be reasonably safe in using their premises.

(c) Failing to warn the Plaintiff adequately or at all of the presence of the trap-door or hole and/or that the same was open and unguarded.

(*d*) Failing to illuminate their premises adequately or at all so as to enable the Plaintiff to see and/or avoid the trap-door or hole.

The Plaintiff will rely upon the maxim *res ipsa loquitur*.[11]

4. In the circumstances the Plaintiff who was born on the   day of   19   sustained injuries and has suffered loss and damage.

Particulars of Injuries

[As in No. 24]

Particulars of Loss and Damage

5. Interest, as in No. 24.

And the Plaintiff claims:

   (1) Damages.

   (2) Interest, etc. [as in No. 24].

Served, etc.

No. 26

Negligence—Breach of Statutory Duty—Liability of an Employer—Fatal Accident Claim

[Statement of Claim for No. 10]

1. The Plaintiff is the widow and administratrix of Terence Rivers (hereinafter called "the deceased"). Letters of administration were granted to the Plaintiff on February 11, 1990. The Plaintiff brings this action for the benefit of the deceased's estate under the Law Reform (Miscellaneous Provisions) Act 1934 and for the benefit of the dependants of the deceased under the Fatal Accidents Act 1976.

2. At all material times the deceased was employed by the Defendants as a fitter at their premises at 1 Smog Lane, Wolverhampton, in the County of West Midlands, which premises were a factory within the meaning of the Factories Act 1961.

3. On or about December 4, 1989, in the course of his employment and pursuant to an instruction by the Defendants

---

[11] The doctrine of *res ipsa loquitur* need not be expressly pleaded: (*Bennett* v. *Chemical Construction (G.B.) Ltd*. [1971] 1 W.L.R. 1571), but it is common practice to plead an intention to rely on the maxim.

to repair a machine in a store-room of the premises, the deceased was descending a flight of stairs to the store-room when his foot slipped on the second step of the stairs in consequence whereof he fell to the bottom of the stairs sustaining severe injuries from which he died immediately.

4. The deceased's fall and death were caused by the breach of statutory duty of the Defendants, their servants or agents.

Particulars of Breach of Statutory Duty

(*a*) Failing to keep the stairs free from a substance, namely lubricating oil, which was likely to cause the deceased to slip, contrary to section 28(1) of the Factories Act 1961.

(*b*) Failing to provide and maintain safe means of access to a place at which the deceased had to work at the material time, namely the store-room, contrary to section 29(1) of the Factories Act 1961.

5. Further or in the alternative, the deceased's fall and death were caused by the negligence of the Defendants, their servants or agents.

Particulars of Negligence

(*a*) Failing to take any or any adequate measures to keep the stairs free from oil.

(*b*) Failing to clean adequately or at all the oil from the stairs.

(*c*) Failing to provide any or any sufficient safe means of access to the store-room and/or causing or permitting the deceased to use the means of access when they knew or should have known that the same was unsafe.

(*d*) In the premises failing to provide and/or maintain a safe system of working in the factory.

6. The estate of the deceased has suffered loss and damage.

Particulars

Funeral expenses: £593

7. Further as a result of the death of the deceased his dependants have suffered loss and damage.

Particulars Pursuant to the Fatal Accidents Act[12]

A. The persons on whose behalf the claim is brought are:

[12] See the Fatal Accidents Act 1976 as amended by the Administration of Justice Act 1982.

(1) The Plaintiff, the widow of the deceased, born on the   day of   19 and now aged 27.

(2) Anthony Rivers, the son of the deceased, born on the   day of   19 and now aged six.

(3) Kate Rivers, the daughter of the deceased, born on the   day of   19 and now aged 18 months.

B. The deceased was born on the   day of   19 and was aged 30 at the date of his death. He was in good health. At the time of his death the deceased had been employed by the Defendants for 10 years and earned £219 per week net on average.

C. The deceased was the sole support of the Plaintiff and the children and the Plaintiff will claim a dependency of 75% of the deceased's earnings.

D. The Plaintiff has lost the benefit of the deceased's household services.

E. The Plaintiff claims damages for bereavement in the sum of £3,500 pursuant to section 1A of the Fatal Accidents Act 1976.

8. [Interest as in No. 24].

AND the Plaintiff claims against the Defendants:

(1) Damages under the Law Reform (Miscellaneous Provisions) Act 1934.

(2) Damages under the Fatal Accidents Act 1976.

(3) Interest as pleaded.

Served, etc.

No. 27

Nuisance—Claim Under the Rule in Rylands v. Fletcher

[Statement of Claim for No. 11]

1. The Plaintiff is and was at all material times the owner and occupier of a dwelling-house at 99 Acacia Avenue, Grove Park, in the County of Kent. The Defendants are and were at all material times the owners and occupiers of land and premises situate at 1 Back Street, Grove Park, in the County of Kent, and adjoining the Plaintiff's house. At all material times the Defendants have carried on the business of manufacturers of chemical products at their premises.

2. Since about November 1989 in the course of carrying out their business the Defendants have wrongfully caused to issue and proceed from their land noxious and offensive fumes and vapours which spread and were diffused over the Plaintiff's

land and into his house and the Defendants have thereby committed nuisance to the Plaintiff.

3. In the circumstances the Plaintiff's house and land has been rendered unhealthy and dangerous and the Plaintiff and his family have been caused annoyance and discomfort and the Plaintiff has suffered loss and damage.

Particulars of Loss and Damage

	£	p
Damage to paintwork and chromium of Plaintiff's car		
Damage to the trees, grass, plants and flowers growing on the Plaintiff's land		
Loss in value of the Plaintiff's house		

4. Further or in the alternative the matters complained of in paragraph 2 hereof constituted a non-natural user of the Defendants' land and the Defendants failed to prevent the escape of the said fumes and vapours to the Plaintiff's land.

5. The Defendants threaten and intend unless restrained by injunction to continue to commit the nuisance aforesaid.

6. The Plaintiff claims interest, etc. [as in No. 17].

And the Plaintiff claims:

(1) An injunction restraining the Defendants by themselves, their servants or agents or otherwise from continuing the said nuisance.

(2) Damages.

(3) Interest, etc. [as in No. 24].

Served, etc.

No. 28

Liability for Fire

1. The Plaintiff is and was at all material times the owner and occupier of a dwelling-house at 88 Laurel Road, London S.W.77. The First Defendant is and was at all material times the owner and occupier of the dwelling-house at 90 Laurel Road adjacent to the Plaintiff's said house. The Second Defendant at all material times carried on the business of a decorator.

2. On or about April 23, 1990, the First Defendant employed the Second Defendant to burn off old paint in the dining-room of the First Defendant's house and to redecorate the room. On

April 24, 1990, the Second Defendant when using a blow-lamp
to burn off the paint set fire to dust-sheets covering furniture in
the room and the fire spread to the Plaintiff's house.

3. The matters complained of were caused by the negligence
of the Second Defendant while acting in the course of his
employment with the First Defendant.

Particulars of Negligence

The Second Defendant was negligent in that he:
    (1) Applied the blow-lamp to or near the dust-sheets so as
        to set fire thereto.
    (2) Failed to prevent the blow-lamp from setting fire to the
        dust-sheets.
    (3) Failed to extinguish the fire in time or at all or to prevent
        the same from spreading to the Plaintiff's house.

4. Further or alternatively the use of the blow-lamp by the
Second Defendant in the First Defendant's house was a non-
natural user caused or permitted by the First Defendant. In
consequence of such user the fire broke out as aforesaid and
the Defendants and each of them failed to prevent the spread
of the same to the Plaintiff's house.

5. By reason of the premises the Plaintiff has suffered loss
and damage.

Particulars of Loss and Damage

	£	p
Cost of repairs to structure of house	___	
Cost of replacing furniture and fittings	___	

6. The Plaintiff claims, interest, etc., as in No. 17.
And the Plaintiff claims against the Defendants and each of
them:
    (1) Damages.
    (2) Interest, etc. [as in No. 24].
Served, etc.

No. 29

Libel

[Statement of Claim for No. 8]

1. The Plaintiff is a chartered accountant. The Defendant is a
travel agent.

2. On or about July 10, 1990, in a letter addressed to the Society of Travel Agents, the Defendant falsely and maliciously wrote and published of and concerning the Plaintiff the following words: "I refer to the letter you have recently received from Mr. Smith" (meaning thereby the Plaintiff) "complaining about the holiday I arranged for him in Majorca. Mr. Smith is nothing but a troublemaker, and I can assure you there is no need to waste time investigating his so-called complaints."

3. By the words complained of in their natural and ordinary meaning the Defendant meant and was understood to mean that the Plaintiff had no or no adequate grounds for complaint concerning the holiday and/or that he was insincere in making such complaint and/or that his object in making the complaint was solely to cause annoyance, inconvenience and distress to the Defendant and/or to damage the Defendant's reputation and business as a travel agent.[13]

4. The Defendant sent the letter by post in an envelope addressed to the Society of Travel Agents. The Defendant well knew at the time he sent the letter that it was likely in the ordinary course of business to be opened and read by some person or persons in the employment of the Society. The letter was in fact opened and read in the ordinary course of business by Mr. George Euripides, Assistant Liaison Officer of the Society.

5. By reason of the premises the Plaintiff has been severely injured in his credit and reputation and has been brought into scandal, odium and contempt.

And the Plaintiff claims:

1. Damages for libel.
2. An injunction restraining the Defendant by himself, his servants or agents or otherwise from further publishing the said or any similar libel of and concerning the Plaintiff.

Served, etc.

---

[13] Where a plaintiff relies on the natural and ordinary meaning of the words complained of and those words were capable of more than one ordinary meaning, it is necessary to plead by way of a "false" or "popular" innuendo the meanings which the words are claimed to bear: *D.D.S.A. Pharmaceuticals Ltd.* v. *Times Newspapers Ltd.* [1973] 1 Q.B. 21 (C.A.).

No. 30

Interference with Goods (Conversion)

[Statement of Claim for No. 12]

1. The Plaintiffs are and were at all material times the owners of and entitled to possession of a Ford Escort motor-car, registration number C789 XYZ, of the value of £5,800.
2. The First Defendant was an employee of the Plaintiff company until April 30, 1990. During the course of such employment the Plaintiffs permitted the First Defendant to have custody of and to use the car.
3. On or about May 1, 1990, the First Defendant wrongfully pledged and delivered the car to the Second Defendant and thereby wrongfully interfered with the same to her own use.
4. By a letter dated May 28, 1990, the Plaintiffs demanded the return of the car from the Second Defendant but the Second Defendant has not returned the car and wrongfully detains the same from the Plaintiffs.
5. In the circumstances the Plaintiffs have been deprived of the said motor-car and have suffered damage.

Particulars of Damage

1. Value of the car	£5,800
2. Loss of use of the car for 10 days at £15 per day	£150
	£5,950

6. Interest, etc., as in No. 17.

And the Plaintiffs claim:
  (1) Against the First Defendant, damages for wrongful interference with goods.
  (2) Against the Second Defendant an order for the delivery up of the said motor-car or its value, namely £5,800, and damages for its detention.
  (3) Interest as in No. 24.

Served, etc.

IN ACTIONS FOR THE POSSESSION OF LAND

No. 31

Possession of a Dwelling-House—Non-payment of Rent

(COUNTY COURT)

In the Barchester County Court   Case No. 1234

BETWEEN   Foulstream Properties Limited   PLAINTIFFS
AND   Isaac McGregor   DEFENDANT

PARTICULARS OF CLAIM[14]

1. The Plaintiff is the freehold owner of and is entitled to possession of a dwelling-house at 88 Hambledon Road, Barchester, in the County of Dorset.

2. The net annual value for rating of the premises is within the county court limit.

3. By an agreement in writing date March 1, 1988, the Plaintiff let the dwelling-house to the Defendant from March 26, 1988, at the yearly rent of £1,000, payable in arrear by four equal quarterly instalments of £250 each on the usual quarter days, subject to a proviso for re-entry by the Plaintiff in the event of any such instalment of rent or any part thereof remaining unpaid for 28 days after becoming payable whether legally demanded or not.

4. The instalments of rent due for the quarters ending March 25, 1990, and June 24, 1990, have not been paid by the Defendant to the Plaintiffs and the Defendant's tenancy has become forfeited.

5. The premises are premises to which the Rent Acts apply and possession is claimed pursuant to the provisions of Case 1 of Schedule 15 to the Rent Act 1977.

6. The Plaintiff claims interest pursuant to section 69 of the County Courts Act 1984 for such period and at such rate as the court shall decide.

And the Plaintiff claims:

 (1) Possession of the said premises.

 (2) £500 arrears of rent due on March 25 and June 24, 1990.

 (3) Rent at the rate of £2.74 per day from June 24, 1990, to the date of the service of the summons and mesne profits at the rate of £2.74 per day from the date of service of the summons until possession of the said premises is delivered up.[15]

 (4) Interest on the arrears of rent pursuant to section 69 of the County Courts Act 1984.

Dated this twenty-fifth day of July 1990.

---

[14] See the County Court Rules, Ord. 6, r. 3.

[15] It is the service of the proceedings which is equivalent to re-entry and which effects a forfeiture, and the lease is therefore determined from the date of service. Rent is payable to date of service and mesne profits thereafter: *Canas Property Co. Ltd.* v. *K.L. Television Services Ltd.* [1970] 2 Q.B. 433 (C.A.). Mesne profits are payable up to the date of obtaining possession of the land: *Southport Tramways Co.* v. *Gandy* [1897] 2 Q.B. 66.

No. 32

Forfeiture—Breach of Covenants in a Lease

[Statement of Claim for No. 13]

1. The Plaintiff is the freehold owner and is entitled to possession of the premises known as 66 Endsleigh Gardens, London W.C.1 therein after called "the premises").

2. By a lease dated January 4, 1980, made between Colin Cameron of the one part and Richard Robertson of the other part Colin Cameron demised the premises to Richard Robertson for the term of 21 years from January 4, 1980 at the yearly rent of £400. The lease contained a proviso for re-entry in case of any breach of the covenants referred to in paragraph 3 hereof or any of them.

3. By the lease Richard Robertson covenanted for himself, his executors, administrators and assigns as follows:

   (1) During the term to keep the inside of the premises together with the fixtures and fittings in as good and tenantable repair and decorative condition as they were in on January 4, 1980.

   (2) Within three calendar months after notice in writing of any defects of repair should have been given to the lessee, to repair decorate and amend the same accordingly.

   (3) To paint the exterior of the premises in every third year of the term and the interior of the same in every seventh year of the term.

4. By a conveyance dated June 3, 1985, made between Colin Cameron of the one part and the Plaintiff of the other part the reversion immediately expectant upon the determination of the term became and is now vested in the Plaintiff.

5. During the term the same became and was vested in the Defendant as assignee of the term and he took and now holds possession thereof.

6. In breach of the covenants set out in paragraph 3 hereof the Defendant while assignee of the term as aforesaid has:

   (1) Failed to repair or paint the premises.

   (2) After notice in writing of all defects of repair was given by the Plaintiff to the Defendant on July 21, 1989, failed within three calendar months from the delivery thereof, to repair, decorate or amend the said premises.

7. On January 5, 1990, the Plaintiff served on the Defendant a notice in writing specifying the said breaches of the covenants full particulars whereof were contained in a schedule of dilapidations annexed to the notice and requiring the Defendant to remedy the same and to make compensation in money therefor.[16] The Defendant has failed within a reasonable time or at all to remedy the breaches or any of them or to make compensation therefor and the lease has become forfeited to the Plaintiff.

8. The Defendant retains possession of the premises.

9. By reason of the breaches the Plaintiff has been injured in his reversion and the value of the same has diminished and he has thereby suffered damage.

10. Interest as in No. 17.

And the Plaintiff claims:

(1) Possession of the premises.
(2) Mesne profits at the rate of £400 per annum namely £   per day from the date of service of the writ herein until possession is delivered up.
(3) Damages for breach of covenant.
(4) Interest as in No. 24.
(5) Further or other relief.
(6) Costs.

Served, etc.

IN ACTIONS IN THE CHANCERY DIVISION

No. 33

Breach of Trust—Unauthorised Investment

[Statement of Claim for No. 14]

In the High Court of Justice   CH 1990 A. No. 9876
     Chancery Division
        Writ issued the 3rd day of June 1990.

BETWEEN	(1) Paul Ashton	
	(2) Michael Ashton (a minor)	PLAINTIFFS
AND	(1) Robert Harley	
	(2) Stephen John Ashworth	DEFENDANTS

STATEMENT OF CLAIM

1. The second Plaintiff is a minor who sues by his brother and next friend the first Plaintiff.

---

[16] See the Law of Property Act 1925, s.146(1).

2. By his will dated September 17, 1985, Joseph Ashton deceased ("the Testator") appointed the Defendants executors and trustees thereof and devised and bequeathed the residue of his estate to his said trustees upon trust for sale and to stand possessed of the proceeds of such sale on trust for his two sons, the Plaintiffs in this action, absolutely in equal shares.

3. By clause 7 of the said will the Testator directed that the trust money should be invested in the names of his trustees in or upon investments for the time being authorised by law for the investment of trust money.

4. The Testator died on April 19, 1987, without having altered or revoked his said will which was duly proved by the Defendants as the executors therein named on May 4, 1987, in the Sandford District Probate Registry.

5. In or about August or September 1989 the Defendants invested certain moneys representing proceeds of sale of the Testator's residuary estate, full particulars whereof cannot be given before discovery herein, in or towards the purchase of ordinary shares of Mammoth Investment Properties Limited and thereby invested and dealt with money subject to the trust of the said will in breach of trust.

Particulars

The said ordinary shares of Mammoth Investment Properties Limited were not an investment for the time being authorised by law for the investment of trust money in that:

(a) the total issued and paid up share capital of the said company was less than one million pounds, being only one hundred thousand pounds; and

(b) the said company had not in the five years immediately preceding the year 1987 or in each or any of the said five years paid a dividend on all or any of the shares issued by the said company.[17]

6. Further or alternatively the Defendants invested and dealt with trust money in breach of trust in that they failed to obtain and/or to consider proper advice as to whether the said investment was satisfactory before making the same and/or in that they made the same without regard to the suitability to the said trust of investments of that description and/or to the suitability of the said investment as an investment of that description.[18]

[17] See the Trustee Investments Act 1961, s.1 and Sched. 1, Pts. III and IV.
[18] See the Trustee Investments Act 1961, s.6(1) and (2).

And the Plaintiffs claim:
[Set out claim for relief as in Precedent No. 15.]
Served, etc.

No. 34

Breach of Trust—Improper Advancement—Constructive Trust

In the High Court of Justice   CH 1990 G. No. 1289
    Chancery Division
        Writ issued the 10th day of June 1990

BETWEEN   (1) Margaret Green
                 (2) Sylvia Green   PLAINTIFFS
AND   (1) Frank Green
                 (2) George White
                 (3) Harold Brown   DEFENDANTS

STATEMENT OF CLAIM

1. The Plaintiffs are the persons beneficially interested under the trusts of the Settlement next mentioned herein and the Second and Third Defendants are the Trustees thereof.

2. By a Settlement dated October 31, 1985, and made between the First Defendant of the one part and the Second and Third Defendants of the other part, certain property therein described which was then or thereupon vested in the said Trustees of the Settlement was settled upon trust to sell the same and to invest the proceeds of sale in or upon investments authorised by law for the investment of trust money and to stand possessed of the same upon trust for the First Plaintiff for life and after her death upon trust for the Second Plaintiff absolutely.

3. The Second and Third Defendants have dealt with money subject to the trusts of the said Settlement in breach of trust.

Particulars

In or about September 1988 the Trustees sold for the sum of £100,000, 5,000 preference shares in Associated Biscuit Factors Limited, part of the property subject to the trusts, and purported to advance the said sum to the Second Plaintiff, who had just attained the age of 18 years and who had no adequate independent advice, under the powers conferred upon the Second and Third Defendants by section 32 of the Trustee Act

1925. As the Trustees well knew and intended, the said advance was made in order that the money should be applied in reduction of debts incurred by the First Defendant, the father of the Second Plaintiff, and the said sum was upon receipt handed by the Second Plaintiff to the First Defendant, who utilised the same in reduction of his said debts.

4. Further or alternatively the First Defendant is accountable to the Plaintiffs in respect of the said sum as a constructive trustee on the ground that he knowingly participated in the misapplication of the sum in breach of trust. Particulars of knowledge will be served separately.

And the Plaintiffs claim:

(1) As against the First Defendant:

(a) A declaration that the First Defendant is liable as constructive trustee to pay the sum of £100,000 to the Trustees of the said Settlement.

(b) An order that the said sum be paid together with interest thereon at such rate as the court shall think fit.

(c) Such other accounts, inquiries, directions or relief as may be just.

(d) Costs.

(2) As against the Second and Third Defendants:

(a) A declaration that the said advancement purported to be made by the Second and Third Defendants as trustees of the above-mentioned trust under the powers conferred on them by the Trustee Act 1925 was improper and a breach of trust.

(b) An order that David Cubitt and Richard Bailey both of 77 South Square, Gray's Inn, London W.C.1., solicitors, or some other fit and proper persons may be appointed to be trustees of the said trusts in place of the Second and Third Defendants.

(c) An inquiry as to the dividends which would have been received by the Second and Third Defendants as such trustees as aforesaid if they had not sold the said investment but had retained the same from the date of sale thereof.

(d) An order for payment to the said new trustees when so appointed as aforesaid of the amount certified in answer to the said inquiry.

(e) An order that the Second and Third Defendants do purchase and transfer to the said new trustees when so appointed as aforesaid 500 shares in Associated Biscuit Factors Limited to represent the said investment sold as aforesaid.

(f) Such other accounts, inquiries, directions or relief as may be just.

(g) If and so far as may be necessary execution of the said trusts under the direction of this Honourable Court.

(h) Costs.

Served, etc.

III.—DEFENCES
IN ACTIONS FOR BREACH OF CONTRACT

No. 35

Employment—Wrongful Dismissal

[Defence to No. 17]

1. Paragraph 1 of the Statement of Claim is admitted.

2. In the course of his employment under the said agreement between about September 2, 1989, and November 7, 1989, the Plaintiff was guilty of misconduct in and about the said employment in that he was habitually drunk and thereby failed to perform the duties of the said employment with due care and attention.[19]

3. By reason of the matters set out in paragraph 2 hereof, the Defendants were entitled to terminate the Plaintiff's employment without giving him any notice of their intention to do so.

4. In the premises the Defendants deny that they dismissed the Plaintiff in breach of contract as alleged or at all.

5. No admissions are made as to the alleged or any loss and damage suffered by the Plaintiff nor as to his entitlement to interest.

Served, etc.

No. 36

Sale of Goods—Implied Conditions

[Defence to No. 19]

1. Paragraphs 1 and 2 of the Statement of Claim are admitted.

2. The Defendants deny that at the time of the sale the Plaintiff expressly and/or impliedly made known to the Defen-

---

[19] See *Clouston and Co. Ltd*. v. *Corry* [1906] A.C. 122.

dants that the fertiliser was required for use in the Plaintiff's business. Further or alternatively if, which is denied, such purpose was made known expressly and/or impliedly to the Defendants, the Plaintiff did not rely on the Defendants' skill and judgment in relation to the sale but relied solely on his own skill and judgment and expressly requested the supply of "X" fertiliser.[20]

3. The Defendants deny that the fertiliser contained chemical impurities or was otherwise unsuitable for use in the Plaintiff's business or was unmerchantable. Further or alternatively if, which is denied, the fertiliser contained the alleged or any chemical impurities the same would not and did not cause orchids treated with the fertiliser to wither and die.

4. No admissions are made as to the numbers or types of orchids treated by the Plaintiff with the fertiliser and paragraph 5 of the Statement of Claim is not admitted.

5. Further and in any event it was an express term of the said sale or alternatively was to be implied as a term of the said sale by reason of a course of dealing between the Plaintiff and the Defendants that the Defendants should not be liable for any loss or damage howsoever caused arising out of the use of fertiliser bought from the Defendants unless notice in writing of such loss or damage was given to the Defendants within 3 months of the date of purchase of the fertiliser. The Plaintiff did not notify the Defendants in writing or at all of the alleged loss and damage until October 1, 1989, which date is more than 3 months after May 25, 1989, being the date of purchase of the said fertiliser.

6. No admissions are made as to the alleged or any loss and damage suffered by the Plaintiff nor as to his entitlement to interest.

7. Further, the Plaintiff failed to mitigate his loss.

Particulars of Failure to Mitigate

The Defendants will rely upon the fact that on June 15, 1989, Interorchid Limited made a written offer to the Plaintiff to purchase all those orchids which were healthy and had not yet flowered (over 40%) for £2,000, which offer was unreasonably refused by the Plaintiff.[21]
Served, etc.

---

[20] See the Sale of Goods Act 1979, s.14(3).
[21] See Ord. 18, r. 12(1)(c) which requires that any claim in mitigation or reduction of damages must be pleaded.

No. 37

Misrepresentation—Restitutio in Integrum

[Defence to No. 21]

1. Paragraph 1 of the Statement of Claim is admitted.

2. The Defendant admits that he made the representation set out in paragraph 2 of the Statement of Claim. It is denied that the representation was intended by the Defendant to be a warranty or was so understood by the Plaintiff and save for the said admission paragraph 2 of the Statement of Claim is denied.

3. The Defendant admits that by a written agreement dated May 12, 1989, he sold the premises and business to the Plaintiff for the sum of £24,000. Save for this admission paragraph 3 of the Statement of Claim is denied.

4. It is admitted that the representation was unfounded as set out in the Statement of Claim but the Defendant denies that the same was made fraudulently or recklessly. The Defendant had reasonable ground to believe and did believe up to the time the agreement was made that the said representation was true.[22]

Particulars

(1) In the Defendant's trading year 1987–88 ending August 31, 1988, the said business had made a net profit of £3,740.

(2) In the six months from September 1, 1988, until February 28, 1989, following the end of the said trading year the turnover of the said business increased by 5 per cent.

5. No admissions are made as to the alleged or any loss and damage.

6. Further and in any event the Plaintiff has materially changed the subject-matter of the agreement in that in or about July 1989 he ceased to carry on the business of a tobacconist and commenced to carry on the business of a seller of magazines.

7. In the circumstances the Plaintiff is unable to return the goodwill of the tobacconist's business in the same condition as

[22] See the Misrepresentation Act 1967, s.2(1).

he received it from the Defendant or in any condition and by reason thereof is not entitled to rescind the agreement.
Served, etc.

No. 38

Work and Services—Set-off

[Defence to No. 22]

DEFENCE AND COUNTERCLAIM

DEFENCE

1. Paragraph 1 of the Statement of Claim is admitted.
2. The Defendants admit that the Plaintiff carried out accountancy work for the Defendants and at their request as alleged in the Statement of Claim and it is admitted that a reasonable fee for the said work is £7,500, and that the Defendants have not paid the said sum or any part thereof.
3. The Defendants claim to be entitled to set off against the Plaintiff's claim the sum of £2,400 counterclaimed herein.

COUNTERCLAIM

4. On or about August 14, 1989, the Defendants paid the sum of £2,400 to Messrs. Cranshaw and Sons, solicitors, of 444 Piccadilly, London W.1, in partial satisfaction and discharge of the Plaintiff's claim pursuant to a request made orally on the telephone by the Plaintiff to the Defendants on August 10, 1989, to pay such sum to Messrs. Cranshaw as aforesaid.
And the Defendants counterclaim £2,400.
Served, etc.

No. 39

Sale of Goods—Counterclaim for Breach of Implied Condition

[Defence and Counterclaim to No. 1]

DEFENCE AND COUNTERCLAIM

DEFENCE

1. The Plaintiff carries on the business of a cloth dealer.

2. The Defendant admits that by an agreement in writing made between the Plaintiff and the Defendant and contained in the Defendant's Order dated April 4, 1988, and the Plaintiff's Acknowledgment of Order dated April 5, 1988, he agreed to buy and the Plaintiff agreed to sell 60 rolls of blue denim cloth at a price of £100 per roll.

3. At the time of the agreement the Defendant orally by telephone made known to the Plaintiff that the cloth was required for making up into jackets and trousers and in order to fulfil contracts made or to be made with the Defendant's customers and it was an implied condition of the agreement that the cloth should be reasonably fit for the purpose of being made up as aforesaid.

4. In breach of the implied condition the bulk of the cloth, namely 55 rolls thereof, was not fit for making up into jackets and trousers in that the colour was uneven and the material was too thin.

5. By a letter dated May 1, 1988, the Defendant gave notice to the Plaintiff that he rejected the said 55 rolls of cloth, as he was entitled to do by reason of the matters set out in paragraph 4 hereof, and that he refused to accept the same.

6. Alternatively in so far as may be necessary the Defendant will seek to set off against the Plaintiff's claim so much of the sum counterclaimed herein as will wholly extinguish the claim.

COUNTERCLAIM

7. The Defendant repeats paragraphs 1 to 6 inclusive of the Defence.

8. In the circumstances the Defendant has suffered loss and damage.

Particulars of Damage

The 55 rolls of cloth would have been sufficient to make up 200 jackets and 300 pairs of trousers. The Defendant's losses are calculated as follows:

(1) Loss of profit on contract with Europatogs Limited for 100 jackets and 100 pairs of trousers cancelled on May 10, 1988—£825.00.

(2) Loss of profit on contract with the Government of Ruritania for 100 battledress jackets and 200 pairs of battledress trousers cancelled on May 10, 1988—£4,400.00.

9. Further the Defendant counterclaims interest, etc., as in No. 17.

And the Defendant counterclaims:
(1) Damages.
(2) Interest, etc. [as in No. 24].
Served, etc.

No. 40

Employment—Duty of Confidence—Counterclaim for Inducement of Breach of Contract

[Defence and Counterclaim to No. 18]

DEFENCE AND COUNTERCLAIM

DEFENCE

1. Paragraph 1 of the Statement of Claim is admitted.
2. The Defendant denies that the agreement contained any such express or alternatively implied term or terms as alleged in paragraph 2 of the Statement of Claim or any term to the like effect.
3. The Defendant admits paragraph 3 of the Statement of Claim.
4. Paragraph 4 of the Statement of Claim is denied. The Defendant denies that the technical designs and information were or are confidential to the Plaintiffs and/or that they were communicated to the Defendant in confidence and/or that they were or are trade secrets of the Plaintiffs. The technical designs and information were public property particulars whereof were set out in the issues of the magazine "New Frontiers" for December 1987 and January 1988 at pages 117–142 and 63–70 respectively.
5. Paragraph 5 of the Statement of Claim is admitted.
6. The Defendant denies paragraphs 6 and 7 of the Statement of Claim. The electric toothbrush manufactured and marketed by the Defendant was based on an independent design of the Defendant and in the design the Defendant made no use of the matters and information communicated to him by the Plaintiffs or any part thereof.
7. The Defendant makes no admissions as to paragraph 8 of the Statement of Claim.
8. In so far as may be necessary the Defendant will seek to set off against the Plaintiff's claim so much of the sum counterclaimed herein as will wholly extinguish the claim.

COUNTERCLAIM

9. The Defendant repeats paragraphs 1 to 6 inclusive of the Defence.

10. By an agreement in writing dated August 2, 1989, made between the Defendant and Development Associates Limited, Development Associates Limited agreed to provide financial assistance to the Defendant for the purpose of marketing the Defendant's said toothbrush and the Defendant agreed to pay to Development Associates Limited a percentage of the profits from sales of the said toothbrush.

11. On or about August 15, 1989, Eric Jarvis on behalf of the Plaintiffs orally threatened Development Associates Limited that if they did not repudiate the said or any agreement made or to be made with the Defendant the Plaintiffs would have no further dealings with that company and thereby induced and procured Development Associates Limited wrongfully to repudiate their said agreement with the Defendant which repudiation was communicated by that company to the Defendant by a letter dated August 16, 1989.

12. In the circumstances the Defendant has suffered loss and damage. Particulars of damage will be served separately.

And the Defendant counterclaims:

(1) Damages.
(2) Interest thereon pursuant to s.35A of the Supreme Court Act 1981.
(3) An injunction restraining the Plaintiffs by themselves, their servants or agents or otherwise from further inducing or procuring any breach of any contract made by the Defendant or otherwise hindering or interfering in any manner whatsoever with the performance of such contract.

Served, etc.

IN ACTIONS OF TORT

No. 41

Negligence—Personal Injuries—Contributory Negligence

[Defence to No. 24]

1. Paragraphs 1 and 2 of the Statement of Claim are admitted.

2. The Defendants deny that they were negligent by their servant or agent as alleged in Paragraph 3 of the Statement of Claim or at all or that such injury, loss and damage as the Plaintiff may prove was caused thereby.

3. The Defendants admit the conviction of Sidney James Allen and the particulars relating thereto set forth in paragraph

4 of the Statement of Claim but no admissions are made as to the relevance of the same to any issue in this action.

4. If, which is not admitted, the Plaintiff did suffer the alleged or any personal injuries, loss and damage, the same were caused or contributed to by the negligence of the Plaintiff.

Particulars

The Plaintiff was negligent in that he:
  (1) Attempted to cross the road without ascertaining whether it was safe for him to do so.
  (2) Failed to keep any or any proper look-out.
  (3) Failed to see and/or to heed the approach of the Defendants' bus.

5. No admissions are made as to the injury, loss, damage or entitlement to interest alleged in Paragraph 5 or 6 of the statement of claim.

6. It is denied that the Plaintiff is entitled to claim provisional damages pursuant to section 32A of the Supreme Court Act 1981 whether as alleged or at all.

Served, etc.

No. 42

Negligence—Liability of an Occupier

[Defence to No. 25]

1. Paragraph 1 of the Statement of Claim is admitted.

2. The Defendants admit that the Plaintiff entered their premises as a customer and that the Plaintiff fell through a trap-door in the floor of the premises. Save as aforesaid no admissions are made as to paragraph 2 of the Statement of Claim.

3. The trap-door is situated in the rear of the premises through a door marked "STORES. PRIVATE." The Plaintiff was not invited or permitted by the Defendants or any of their servants or agents to enter such part of the premises and the Plaintiff was at all material times a trespasser therein.

4. The Defendants deny that they were negligent and/or in breach of statutory duty as alleged in Paragraph 3 of the Statement of Claim or at all or that such injury, loss and damage as the Plaintiff may prove was caused thereby.

5. No admissions are made as to the alleged or any injury loss and damage.

6. The accident was caused or contributed to by the negligence of the Plaintiff.

Particulars

(1) Entering a part of the premises which, as he knew or ought to have known by reason of the words on the door, was private and into which he had no invitation or licence, express or implied, to enter.
(2) Failing to observe or avoid the trap-door.
(3) Failing to look where he was walking.

7. Further or alternatively the matters complained of were caused by the negligence of Superquick Repairs Ltd. who were independent contractors engaged by the Defendants to repair the floor of the said part of the premises. Superquick Repairs Ltd. are experts in such work and the Defendants acted reasonably in entrusting to them the repair of the floor. On November 16, 1988, Superquick Repairs Ltd. were working in the said part of the premises.[23]

Particulars of Negligence of Superquick Repairs Ltd.

(1) Causing or permitting the trap-door to be and/or to remain open and/or failing to provide a guard for the same.
(2) Failing to warn the Plaintiff adequately or at all of the presence of the trap-door and/or that the same was open and unguarded.
(3) Failing to prevent the Plaintiff from falling through the said trap-door.

Served, etc.

No. 43

Negligence—Liability of an Employer—Volenti Non Fit Injuria

[Defence to No. 26]

1. Paragraphs 1, 2 and 3 of the Statement of Claim are admitted.

---

[23] See the Occupiers' Liability Act 1957, s.2(4)(*b*). Rather than merely denying negligence and breach of statutory duty, this defence should be specifically pleaded to avoid the possibility of taking the plaintiff by surprise at the trial. (See *Davie* v. *New Merton Board Mills Ltd.* [1956] 1 W.L.R. 233).

2. The instruction referred to in paragraph 3 of the Statement of Claim was given to the deceased by one Matthew Edwards a foreman employed by the Defendants. At the time of giving the instruction, Matthew Edwards informed the deceased that lubricating oil had been spilt on the flight of stairs and that it would be cleaned away as soon as possible. In the circumstances the deceased knew or ought to have known that the stairs were slippery and unsafe and by using the same before the oil had been cleaned away, impliedly consented to run the risk of injury arising therefrom.

4. The Defendants deny that they were in breach of statutory duty and/or negligent as alleged in Paragraph 4 or 5 of the Statement of Claim or at all, or that the fall and death of the deceased were caused thereby.

5. Further or alternatively the fall and death of the deceased were caused or contributed to by his own negligence.

Particulars of Negligence

(a) Failing to heed his instructions.

(b) Failing to heed the oil.

(c) Failing to avoid the oil.

(d) Failing, in the premises, to have sufficient regard for his own safety.

6. No admissions are made as to any of the matters set out in paragraph 6, 7 or 8 of the Statement of Claim.

Served, etc.

No. 44

Nuisance—Prescription

[Defence to No. 27]

1. Paragraph 1 of the Statement of Claim is admitted.

2. The Defendants deny that they have caused or permitted any fumes and vapours to come on to the Plaintiff's land and/ or into his house or that they were guilty of the alleged or any nuisance and paragraph 2 of the Statement of Claim is denied.

3. Paragraph 3 of the Statement of Claim is denied.

4. If, which is denied, the Defendants have committed the alleged or any acts of nuisance, the Defendants have for a period of 23 years before the commencement of this action openly enjoyed as of right and without interruption the right to do the said acts and the Defendants have accordingly a prescriptive right to do those acts.

5. Paragraph 4 of the Statement of Claim is denied. The manufacture of chemical products constituted a natural and reasonable use of the Defendants' land and the emission of fumes and vapours is a natural and inevitable incident of such user. The Defendants deny that the said or any fumes and vapours have escaped on to the Plaintiff's land and/or into his house.

6. Save that the Defendants intend to continue to conduct their said business in a lawful manner at their premises as heretofore, paragraph 5 of the Statement of Claim is denied. Served, etc.

No. 45

Libel—Justification—Qualified Privilege

[Defence to No. 29]

1. Paragraph 1 of the Statement of Claim is admitted.

2. The Defendant admits that on or about July 10, 1990, he wrote the letter set out in paragraph 2 of the Statement of Claim and sent the same in an envelope addressed to the Society of Travel Agents. The Defendant does not admit that George Euripides or any other person read the same.

3. The words complained of did not bear and were not understood to bear and were not capable of bearing the meanings alleged in paragraph 3 of the Statement of Claim or any of the alleged meanings or any meaning defamatory of the Plaintiff.

4. The words complained of in their natural and ordinary meaning are true in substance and in fact. Particulars will be served separately.[24]

5. If and in so far as may be necessary the Defendant will rely on section 5 of the Defamation Act 1952.[25]

6. Save as aforesaid no admissions are made as to paragraph 4 of the Statement of Claim.

7. If, which is not admitted, the said letter was published to the George Euripides and/or to any other person in the employment of the Society the same was published on an occasion of qualified privilege.

---

[24] It must be made clear in the particulars of justification the meaning to be attributed to the words that the Defendant is seeking to justify: *Lucas-Box* v. *News Group Newspapers Ltd.* [1986] 1 W.L.R. 147.

[25] If the defendant intends to rely on this defence, he must expressly plead it even if only in the alternative: *Moore* v. *News of the World Ltd.* [1972] 1 Q.B. 441 (C.A.).

Particulars

(1) The Defendant is a member of the Society of Travel Agents.

(2) On or about June 10, 1990, the Plaintiff wrote a letter to the Society in which he complained about the arrangements made by the Defendant in connection with the Plaintiff's holiday in Majorca in May 1990 and requested the Society to investigate his complaints. The Defendant will refer to the letter at trial for its full terms and effects.

(3) On or about June 26, 1990, the Society wrote a letter to the Defendant in which they informed him of the Plaintiff's letter and requested or alternatively invited the Defendant to reply to and comment upon the complaint.

(4) In the premises the Defendant had a duty and/or interest in writing and sending the letter to the Society and the Defendant wrote and sent the letter pursuant to that duty and/or interest and the Society had a corresponding duty and/or interest in receiving the letter and the matters set out therein.

8. Paragraph 5 of the Statement of Claim is denied.

Served, etc.

IN ACTIONS FOR THE POSSESSION OF LAND

No. 46

Breach of Covenant—Counterclaim for Relief Against Forfeiture

[Defence and Counterclaim to No. 32]

DEFENCE

1. Paragraphs 1 to 5 inclusive of the Statement of Claim are admitted save that the Defendant denies that the Plaintiff is entitled to possession of the premises.

2. The Defendant denies that he is in breach of covenant as alleged in paragraph 6 of the Statement of Claim or at all and denies that the Plaintiff gave to him the notice referred to in the said paragraph as therein alleged or at all.

3. The Defendant admits that the Plaintiff served on him the notice referred to in paragraph 7 of the Statement of Claim. Save as aforesaid the said paragraph 7 is denied.

4. If, which is denied, the Defendant has committed the said breaches of covenant or any of them, a reasonable time for

remedying the same after service of the said notice had not elapsed before the issue of the writ herein.

5. The Defendant admits that he retains possession of the premises.

6. Paragraph 9 of the Statement of Claim is denied.

7. No admissions are made as to paragraph 10 of the Statement of Claim.

COUNTERCLAIM

7. The Defendant repeats paragraphs 1 to 6 inclusive of the Defence.

8. If, contrary to the Defendant's contention, it should be found that he has committed and/or failed to remedy before the issue of the writ herein, the alleged or any breach or breaches of the said covenants, the Defendant claims to be relieved from the alleged forfeiture under section 146 of the Law of Property Act 1925 on such terms as the Court shall think fit.

Served, etc.

IN ACTIONS IN THE CHANCERY DIVISION

No. 47

Breach of Trust—Consent—Impounding of Beneficial Interest

[Defence and Counterclaim to No. 34]

DEFENCE AND COUNTERCLAIM OF SECOND AND THIRD DEFENDANTS

DEFENCE

1. The Second and Third Defendants admit paragraphs 1 and 2 of the Statement of Claim.

2. The Second and Third Defendants admit that they raised the sum of £100,000 by the sale of shares as alleged, such shares being part of the property subject to the said trusts, and that they advanced the said sum to the Second Plaintiff pursuant to the powers conferred upon them by section 32 of the Trustee Act 1925. The said advancement was made with the knowledge and consent of the First Plaintiff and pursuant to a request made orally by the Second Plaintiff in or about August 1988 to the Second and Third Defendants to provide her with the said sum in order that she might be able to clear

up certain debts and make a start in life. In the premises the Second and Third Defendants deny that they dealt with money subject to the said trusts in breach of trust and save as aforesaid each and every allegation contained in paragraph 3 of the Statement of Claim is denied.

3. If, which is denied, the said sum was dealt with by the Second and Third Defendants in breach of trust, the acts alleged in paragraph 3 of the Statement of Claim to constitute such breach of trust were done with the knowledge and consent of the Plaintiffs and each of them.

4. No admissions are made by the Second and Third Defendants as to paragraph 4 of the Statement of Claim.

COUNTERCLAIM

5. The Second and Third Defendants repeat paragraphs 1 to 3 of the Defence.

6. On diverse occasions in or about August 1988, the First Plaintiff orally requested the Second and Third Defendants as trustees of the said Settlement to comply with the Second Plaintiff's said request well knowing and intending that the Second Plaintiff would or was likely to hand over the said sum to the First Defendant and well knowing that by reason of such handing over the said advancement would or might be rendered a breach of trust.[26]

And the Second and Third Defendants counterclaim as trustees of the said Settlement against the First Plaintiff:

(1) Such order as shall be just for impounding all or any part of the interest of the First Plaintiff under the trusts of the above-mentioned Settlement by way of indemnity to the Second and Third Defendants if, contrary to their contention, it should be found that they dealt with money subject to the above-mentioned trusts in breach of trust.

(2) Further or other relief.

(3) Costs.

Served, etc.

---

[26] See the Trustee Act 1925, s.62(1).

IV.—REPLIES

No. 48

Sale of Goods—Counterclaim—Damage too Remote

[Reply and Defence to Counterclaim to No. 39]

REPLY AND DEFENCE TO COUNTERCLAIM

REPLY

1. The Plaintiff joins issue with the Defendant upon his Defence save in so far as the same consists of admissions and save for any admissions contained herein.

2. The Plaintiff denies that the facts pleaded entitled the Defendant to reject the said 55 rolls of cloth as alleged or at all. Further or alternatively the Plaintiff denies that the letter dated May 1, 1988, referred to in paragraph 5 of the Defence amounted to a rejection of the cloth and the Plaintiff will refer at trial to the letter for its full terms and effects.

DEFENCE TO COUNTERCLAIM

3. The Plaintiff admits that he entered into an agreement with the Defendant as alleged in paragraph 7 of the Counterclaim and that he knew that the cloth was required by the Defendant for making up into jackets and trousers. The Plaintiff denies that he had the alleged or any knowledge of the existence and/or terms of any contracts made or to be made by the Defendant with his customers by reason whereof the damages claimed by way of Counterclaim are too remote.

4. Save for any matters expressly stated herein to be admitted, the Plaintiff denies each and every allegation contained in the Counterclaim.

Served, etc.

No. 49

Libel—Qualified Privilege—Malice

[Reply to No. 45]

1. The Plaintiff joins issue with the Defendant upon his Defence save in so far as the same consists of admissions, and save for any admissions contained herein.

2. In publishing the words set out in paragraph 2 of the Statement of Claim the Defendant was actuated by express malice.

Particulars

(1) At the end of the said holiday on May 21, 1990, the Plaintiff presented to one Michael Seneca, a servant or agent of the Defendant then acting as courier on the holiday, a list of the Plaintiff's complaints concerning the holiday. Michael Seneca then stated to the Plaintiff that the Plaintiff's complaints were justified and that the Plaintiff would receive a refund on the cost of the holiday. The Plaintiff has not received the said or any refund.

(2) The Defendant did not honestly believe in the truth of the words.

Served, etc.

V.—PETITIONS

No. 50

Winding up of a Company

In the High Court of Justice   No. 579 of 1990
    Chancery Division
    Companies Court
    In the Matter of Gooddeals Limited
    And in the Matter of the Insolvency Act 1986
    To Her Majesty's High Court of Justice

The Humble Petition of Gilbert Moriarty of 2 Madison Avenue, London W.1, advertising agent, showeth as follows:

1. Gooddeals Limited (hereinafter called "the Company") was incorporated in the month of July 1968 under the Companies Act 1948 as a company limited by shares.

2. The registered office of the Company is situated at Enterprise House, Rotten Row, London S.W.1.

3. The nominal capital of the Company is £100 divided into one hundred shares of £1 each. The amount of the capital paid up or credited as paid up is £50.

4. The objects for which the Company was established are to carry on business as general wholesalers of consumer goods and other objects set forth in the Memorandum of Association thereof.

5. The Company is indebted to your Petitioner in the sum of £5,112, the cost of work done and services rendered by your Petitioner to the Company pursuant to an agreement in writing dated March 22, 1990, made between the Company and your Petitioner.

6. Your Petitioner has made repeated applications to the Company for payment of the said debt but the Company has failed and neglected to pay or satisfy the same or any part thereof.

7. The Company is insolvent and unable to pay its debts.

8. In the circumstances it is just and equitable that the Company should be wound up.

Your Petitioner therefore humbly prays as follows:
(1) that Gooddeals Limited may be wound up by the Court under the provisions of the Insolvency Act 1986; or
(2) that such other Order may be made in the premises as to the court shall seem just.

And your Petitioner will ever pray, etc.

Note: It is intended to serve this Petition on Gooddeals Limited.

VI.—SUMMONSES, ORDERS AND NOTICES

No. 51

Originating Summons (Chancery Division)[27]

In the High Court of Justice   CH 1990 S. No. 7654
Chancery Division
In the matter of the Trusts of the Will dated August 8, 1984, of Roger Smythe deceased.

BETWEEN	(1) Harold Smythe	
	(2) Charlotte Smythe	PLAINTIFFS
AND	(1) Nicholas Wilson	
	(2) Serena Fish (Married Woman)	
	(3) Her Majesty's Attorney-General[28]	DEFENDANTS

---

[27] See R.S.C., Appendix A, Form No. 8 (the general form of originating summons which has been appropriately modified for this precedent. The accompanying form for acknowledgment of service has been omitted).

[28] The Attorney-General is generally a necessary party to all actions relating to charities (5 *Halsbury's Laws* (4th ed.), pp. 538 *et seq.*).

To Nicholas Wilson of High Trees House, Brighton, Sussex (who claims to be beneficially interested under the trusts of the above-mentioned Will), Serena Fish of (address), (who is sued on behalf of the Dunroamin Home of Rest for Maladjusted Primates, which claims to be beneficially interested under the said trusts) and to Her Majesty's Attorney-General.

Let the Defendants within 14 days after service of this summons on them respectively, counting the day of service, return the accompanying Acknowledgment of Service to the appropriate Court Office.

By this summons, which is issued on the application of the Plaintiffs Harold Smythe and Charlotte Smythe of (address), who are the trustees of the above-mentioned trusts and who sue as such trustees, and who are beneficially interested as next-of-kin in the said Will, the Plaintiffs seek the determination of the Court on the following questions and the following relief, namely:

1. Whether upon the true construction of the above-mentioned Will and in the events which have happened the Plaintiffs hold the legacy of £50,000 bequeathed to them by the said Will:

    (1) for themselves beneficially; or

    (2) on trust for the First Defendant in accordance with the paper writing which forms exhibit "H.S.1" to an affidavit of Harold Smythe intended to be sworn herein.

2. Whether upon the true construction of the above-mentioned Will and in the events which have happened the Plaintiffs hold the residuary estate of the Testator devised and bequeathed to them by the said Will:

    (1) on trust for the Dunroamin Home of Rest for Maladjusted Primates; or

    (2) on trust for such other charitable trust as the court may determine; or

    (3) on resulting trust for themselves beneficially as next-of-kin of the Testator as aforesaid; or

    (4) on some other and if so what trusts.

3. That if the answer to question 2 above be in terms of subparagraph 2(2) the court may so far as is necessary give directions as to a scheme for the application of the said residuary estate pursuant to the provisions of the Charities Act 1960.

4. That provision may be made for the costs of this application.

5. Further or other relief.

If a Defendant does not acknowledge service such judgment may be given or order made against or in relation to him as the court may think just and expedient.

Dated the 26th day of January 1990.

[The remaining parts of the general form are similar to those of the general form of a writ of summons: see Precedent No. 1]

No. 52

Summons Under Order 14[29]

[Summons for No. 22]

[Title as in action—see Precedent No. 1]

Let all parties concerned attend the Master in Chambers in Room No. 105, Central Office, Royal Courts of Justice, Strand, London, on Wednesday the 5th day of June 1990 at 11 o'clock in the forenoon on the hearing of an application on the part of the Plaintiff for final judgment in this action against the Defendant for the amount claimed in the statement of claim with interest, if any, and costs.

Take notice that a party intending to oppose this application or to apply for a stay of execution should send to the opposite party or his solicitor, to reach him not less than three days before the date above-mentioned, a copy of any affidavit intended to be used.

Dated the 2nd day of May 1990.

This summons was taken out by Wilson Edwards of 750 Cheapside, London, solicitors for the above-named Plaintiff.

To the above-named Defendants and to Evans and Rees, their solicitors.

No. 53

Affidavit on Application Under Order 14[30]

[Affidavit for No. 52]

[Title as in action—see Precedent No. 1][31]

I, Fergus Milne, of 7 Capitalist Buildings, Rotten Row, London S.W.1, the above-named Plaintiff, make oath and say as follows:

---

[29] See R.S.C., Practice Form No. PF 11.

[30] See R.S.C., Practice Form No. PF 10.

[31] All affidavits must bear in the top right hand corner of the first page the name of the deponent, the party on whose behalf the affidavit is filed, whether the affidavit is the first or subsequent affidavit by that party in the action, and the date of the affidavit. In Precedent No. 53 the top right hand corner of the affidavit should read:

> "Fergus Milne
> Plaintiff
> First Affidavit
> Sworn the   day of   19 "

1. The Defendants are and were at the commencement of this action justly and truly indebted to me in the sum of £5,500 as the price of work done and services rendered by me to the Defendants. The particulars of the claim appear by the statement of claim in this action.
2. It is within my own knowledge that the debt was incurred and is still due and owing as aforesaid.
3. I verily believe that there is no defence to this action.

Sworn, etc.

This affidavit is filed on behalf of the Plaintiff.

No. 54

Order Under Order 14

[Title as in action—see Precedent No. 1]

Upon hearing counsel for the Plaintiff and the Defendants, and upon reading the affidavits of the Plaintiff and Peter Smith on behalf of the Defendants filed herein.

It is ordered that:

The Plaintiff may enter final judgment against the Defendants for the sum of £7,800 of the amount indorsed on the writ with interest, if any, and costs.

The Defendants may defend the action as to the residue of the Plaintiff's claim.

The Defendants shall have 14 days in which to serve their defence.

The Plaintiff and the Defendants do respectively, within seven days of service of the defence, serve upon each other a list stating what documents are or have been in their possession, custody or power relating to any matter in question in this action and there shall be inspection thereof within two days thereafter.

The action shall be tried in London without a jury and be set down within 14 days in the Short Cause List, the estimated length of the trial being two hours.

The costs of and occasioned by this application shall be the Plaintiff's costs in cause.

Dated the 5th day of June 1990.

No. 55

Summons for Directions Pursuant to Order 25[32]

(General Form)

[Title as in action]

Let all parties attend the Master in Chambers in Room No.   , Royal Courts of Justice, Strand, London, on Friday the   th   day   of   19   at   o'clock   in   the noon on the hearing of an application for directions in this action:

1. This action be consolidated with actions(s) 19   ,   , No.   and 19   ,   No.   .

2. The action be transferred for trial to an Official Referee and that the costs of this application be costs in the cause.

3. The action be transferred to   County Court, under section 40 of the County Courts Act 1984 and that the costs of the action, including this application, be in the discretion of the County Court.

4. The Plaintiff have leave to amend the writ by   and that service of the writ and the defendants' acknowledgment of service do stand, and that the costs incurred and thrown away by the amendment be the Defendant's in any event.

5. The Plaintiff have leave to amend the statement of claim [*or* the Defendant have leave to amend the Defence (and Counterclaim) *or* the Plaintiff have leave to amend the Reply (and Defence to Counterclaim)] as shown in the document initialled by the Master, and to re-serve the amended pleading within   days and that the opposite party have leave to serve an amended consequential pleading, if so advised, within   days thereafter and that the costs of and occasioned and thrown away by the amendments be the Defendant's (*or* the Plaintiff's) in any event.

6. The Plaintiff serve on the Defendant [*or* the Defendant serve on the Plaintiff] within   days the Further and Better Particulars of his pleading specified in the document initialled by the Master.

7. The Plaintiff within   days serve on the Defendant and the Defendant within   days serve on the Plaintiff a list of documents (and file an affidavit verifying such list) (limited to

---

[32] See R.S.C., Practice Form No. PF 50.

the documents relating to the special damages claimed *or as may be*).

8. There be inspection of the documents within   days of the service of the lists [and filing of the affidavits].

9. The Plaintiff [Defendant] [retain and preserve pending the trial of the action] [upon   days' notice to give inspection of]   [the subject-matter of the action to the Defendant] [Plaintiff] and to his legal advisers [and experts].

10. *Set out fully and precisely any other directions intended to be applied for (e.g. adducing expert evidence, etc.):—*

11. Trial.   Place: Mode: Listing Category: A or B or C.

Estimated length:—To be set down within   days [and to be   listed with and tried immediately after (before) action 19   ,   , No.   ].

12. The costs of this application be costs in the cause.
Dated the   day of   19 .

To the Defendant(s) and to his (their) solicitors.

This summons was issued by   of   solicitors for the Plaintiff.

No. 56

Notice of Motion[33]

[For interlocutory injunction: Chancery Division—Nos. 6 and 18]

[Title as in action]

Take notice that the Court will be moved on Tuesday the 11th day of October 1990 at 10.30 o'clock, or so soon thereafter as Counsel can be heard, by Counsel for the above-named Plaintiff for an order that the Defendant whether by himself or his agents or servants or any of them or otherwise be restrained by injunction until judgment in this action or further order from doing the following acts or any of them that is to say (1) making any use whatsoever of any confidential information of whatsoever kind the property of the Plaintiff in any technical designs and information concerning the development and production of an electric toothbrush (2) manufacturing, offering for sale, selling or supplying any such toothbrushes made

---

[33] See R.S.C., Appendix A, Form No. 38.

according to or with the assistance of the Plaintiffs' said confidential information or any of the same.

And that the costs of this application be provided for. Dated the 2nd day of October 1990.

(Signature)

Messrs. Bowdler and Co. of (address)
Solicitors for the Plaintiffs

To the Defendant and to
Savage and Cross of (address)
his Solicitors.

No. 57

Third Party Notice[34]

[See Nos. 25 and 42]

In the High Court of Justice   1990 P. No. 4567
   Queen's Bench Division

BETWEEN	Arthur Ponsonby	PLAINTIFF
AND	Vericheap Discount Stores Limited	DEFENDANTS
AND	Superquick Repairs Limited	THIRD PARTY

THIRD PARTY NOTICE

[Issued pursuant to the order of Master Goodman dated November 27, 1990.][35]

To Superquick Repairs Limited, etc.

Take notice that this action has been brought by the Plaintiff against the Defendants. In it the Plaintiff claims against the Defendants damages for negligence and/or breach of statutory duty as appears from the writ of summons a copy whereof is served herewith together with a copy of the statement of claim.

The Defendants claim against you to be indemnified against the Plaintiff's claim and the costs of this action or contribution to the extent of the Plaintiff's claim on the grounds that:

---

[34] See R.S.C., Appendix A, Form No. 20.
[35] See Ord. 16, r. 1(2).

1. By an agreement in writing dated November 1, 1988, made between you and the Defendants you agreed to undertake repairs to the floor of the Defendants' premises known as 777 Anson Street, London N.28, at a total cost of £500.
2. It was an express term of the agreement that you should be solely liable for and should indemnify the Defendants in respect of any liability, loss or claim arising under statute or at common law in respect of personal injury to any person whomsoever, arising out of or in connection with the said work of repair, provided always that the same should be due to any negligence or omission of yourselves, your servants or agents.
3. The matters complained of by the Plaintiff, the alleged personal injuries, loss and expense thereof being not admitted by the Defendants, were caused or contributed to by the negligence of you, your servants or agents, in carrying out the work of repair.

Particulars

(a) Causing or permitting the trap-door to be and/or to remain open and/or failing to provide a guard for the same;
(b) Failing to warn the Plaintiff adequately or at all of the presence of the trap-door and/or that the same was open and unguarded;
(c) Failing to prevent the Plaintiff from falling through the trap-door.
4. Alternatively the Defendants claim a contribution pursuant to the Civil Liability (Contribution) Act 1978.

And take notice that within 14 days after service of this Notice on you, counting the day of service, you must acknowledge service and state in your Acknowledgment whether you intend to contest the proceedings. If you fail to do so, or if your Acknowledgment does not state your intention to contest the proceedings, you will be deemed to admit the Plaintiff's claim against the Defendants and the Defendants' claim against you and your liability to indemnify the Defendants or contribute to the extent claimed and will be bound by any judgment or decision given in the action, and the judgment may be enforced against you in accordance with Order 16 of the Rules of the Supreme Court 1985.

Dated the 8th day of December 1990.

(Signature)

Solicitors for the Defendants

Important
Directions for Acknowledgment of Service are given with the accompanying form.

VII.—DISCOVERY OF DOCUMENTS

No. 58

List of Documents[36]

[Plaintiff's List of Documents for No. 23]

[Heading as in action]

LIST OF DOCUMENTS

The following is a list of the documents relating to the matters in question in this action which are or have been in the possession, custody or power of the above-named Plaintiff and which is served in compliance with Order 24, rule 2.

1. The Plaintiff has in his possession, custody or power the documents relating to the matters in question in this action enumerated in Schedule 1 hereto.

2. The Plaintiff objects to produce the documents enumerated in Part 2 of the said Schedule 1 on the ground that they are privileged. They consist of professional communications of a confidential character made to the plaintiff by his legal advisers for the purpose of giving him legal advice, cases for the opinion of counsel, opinions of counsel and instructions to counsel prepared and given in anticipation of and during the progress of this action, letters and copies of letters passing between the Plaintiff and his solicitors and memoranda made by the Plaintiff's solicitors for the purposes of this action.

3. The Plaintiff has had, but has not now, in his possession, custody or power the documents relating to the matters in question in this action enumerated in Schedule 2 hereto.

4. Of the documents in the said Schedule 2, those numbered 1 and 2 in that Schedule were last in the Plaintiff's possession, custody or power in June 1990 and the other in July 1990.

---

[36] See R.S.C., Appendix A, Form No. 26.

5. Neither the Plaintiff, nor his solicitors nor any other person on his behalf, has now, or ever had, in his possession, custody or power any document of any description whatever relating to any matter in question in this action, other than the documents enumerated in Schedules 1 and 2 hereto.

Schedule 1

Part 1

1. Memorandum made by the Plaintiff of telephone call made by him on June 4, 1990, to George Herbert.
2. Memorandum made by the Plaintiff of telephone call made to him on June 4, 1990, by Henry Vaughan.
3. Defendant's acknowledgment of order dated June 5, 1990.
4. Copy of letter dated June 10, 1990, from the Plaintiff to the Defendants.
5. Copy of letter dated July 16, 1990, from solicitors for the Plaintiff to the Defendants.

Part 2

Letters, drafts, memoranda, cases for the opinion of counsel, opinions of counsel and instructions to counsel prepared and given in anticipation of and during the progress of this action.

Schedule 2

1. Letter dated June 10, 1990, from the Plaintiff to the Defendants.
2. Cheque dated June 9, 1990, signed by the Plaintiff and made out to the Defendants in the sum of £2,500 sent by the Plaintiff to the Defendants with the letter referred to in 1 of this Schedule on June 10, 1990.
3. Letter dated July 16, 1990, from solicitors for the Plaintiff to the Defendants.

Dated the 1st day of December 1990.

NOTICE TO INSPECT

Take notice that the documents in the above list, other than those listed in Part 2 of Schedule 1 [and Schedule 2] may be inspected at the office of the solicitors for the above-named Plaintiff at 50 South Square, Gray's Inn, London W.C.1, between the hours of 9 a.m. and 5 p.m. by appointment.

To the defendants and their solicitor.

Served, etc.

No. 59

Affidavit Verifying List of Documents[37]

[for No. 58]

[Heading as in action][38]

I, the above-named Plaintiff, Nicholas Huntington, make oath and say as follows:
1. The statements made by me in paragraphs 1, 3 and 4 of the list of documents now produced and shown to me marked "NH 1" are true.
2. The statements of fact made by me in paragraph 2 of the said list are true.
3. The statements made by me in paragraph 5 of the said list are true to the best of my knowledge, information and belief.

Sworn, etc.
This affidavit is filed on behalf of the Plaintiff.

VIII.—PARTICULARS AND INTERROGATORIES

No. 60

Request for Further and Better Particulars of the Statement of Claim (No. 19)

Under paragraph 2
Of the allegation that the Plaintiff bought fertiliser from the Defendants on May 25, 1989, giving full particulars of the sale; stating whether the sale was made orally or in writing; if orally stating between whom and where such sale was made and giving the full terms relied on; and if in writing identifying documents.

Under paragraph 3
Of the allegation that the Plaintiff expressly and/or impliedly made known to the Defendants that the fertiliser was required for use in the Plaintiff's business as a grower of orchids giving full details of all facts and matters relied on in support of that allegation; stating whether such express communication was

---

[37] See R.S.C., Appendix A, Form No. 27.
[38] See n. 31, *ante.*

made orally or in writing and giving like particulars to those requested under paragraph 2 hereof; and stating all facts and matters relied on in support of the implication of such communication.

Under paragraph 4
Of the allegation that the fertiliser contained chemical impurities which caused orchids treated by the Plaintiff with the fertiliser to wither and die, identifying the said chemical impurities and stating how many and which types of orchids were treated with the fertiliser and stating how many and which types of the treated orchids are alleged to have withered and died as a result of the impurities being present in the fertiliser.
Served, etc.

No. 61

Further and Better Particulars of the Statement of Claim (No. 19) Served Pursuant to a Request Dated the 16th Day of March 1990 (No. 60)

Under paragraph 2
[Repeat the request under paragraph 2 of Precedent No. 60]

Answer:
The sale was made orally at the Defendants' premises at Lewes in East Sussex between the Plaintiff and Nathaniel Giles on behalf of the Defendants and was evidenced by a delivery note dated May 26, 1989, made out to the Plaintiff and signed by Nathaniel Giles on behalf of the Defendants.

Under paragraph 3
[Repeat the request under paragraph 3 of Precedent No. 60]

Answer:
At the time of the sale the Plaintiff stated to Nathaniel Giles that he wanted 5 cwt. of "Brand X" fertiliser for immediate delivery in order to commence the cultivation of his 1989 orchids. The Plaintiff will further rely in support of the allegation that the communication was express and/or implied upon a course of dealing between himself and the Defendants evidenced by delivery notes from the Defendants to the Plaintiff, full particulars whereof will be supplied on discovery herein.

Under paragraph 4

[Repeat the request under paragraph 4 of Precedent No. 60]

Answer:

Full particulars of the chemical impurities are contained in a report on the composition of the fertiliser made by Messrs. Parkinson, consultant agricultural chemists of Lewes, a copy whereof has been supplied to the Defendants.

The Plaintiff used the fertiliser to treat 500 "Hothouse" orchids and 300 "Tropicana" orchids. All the treated orchids withered and died as a result of the presence of the impurities in the fertiliser.

Served, etc.

No. 62

Interrogatories

[Interrogatories for No. 31]

[Heading as in No. 31]

INTERROGATORIES

On behalf of the above-named Plaintiffs for the examination of the above-named Defendant.

1. Have you ever paid any and if any what sum in part or complete payment of the rent which is the subject of the Plaintiffs' claim in this action?

2. If the answer to the preceding interrogatory is yes—state:
   (1) to whom the said sum was paid;
   (2) when the said sum was paid;
   (3) in what form the said sum was paid;
   (4) whether a receipt for the said sum was given and if so;
   (5) by whom.

The Defendant is required to answer all the interrogatories.

(Signature of counsel if settled by him)

Served this 16th day of October 1990 by Rattle and Rolle of 1 Wall Street, London W.1., the Plaintiffs' solicitors.

To the above-named Defendant.

IX.—APPEAL

No. 63

Notice of Appeal

[Against the grant of an interlocutory injuction—see No. 56

In the Court of Appeal

1990 E. No. 285

On Appeal from the High Court of Justice
Chancery Division

BETWEEN   Electronic Novelties Limited   PLAINTIFFS

AND   Arnold Thompson   DEFENDANT

NOTICE OF APPEAL

Take notice that the Court of Appeal will be moved so soon as Counsel can be heard on behalf of the Defendant.

On appeal from the order herein of the Honourable Mr. Justice Bracton, made on the 11th day of October 1990, ordering in favour of the Plaintiffs that the Defendant whether by himself his servants or agents or any of them or otherwise be restrained until trial of his action or further order from doing the following acts or any of them that is to say (1) making any use whatsoever of any confidential information of whatsoever kind the property of the Plaintiffs in any technical designs and information concerning the development and production of an electric toothbrush (2) manufacturing, offering for sale, selling or supplying any such toothbrushes made according to or with the assistance of the Plaintiffs' said confidential information or any of the same and ordering that the costs of the application be the Plaintiffs' in any event.

For an Order that the issue of the said injunction be set aside and for an Order that the costs of this Appeal and below be the Defendant's costs in any event.

And further take notice that the grounds of this appeal are:

1. The learned judge was wrong in holding that the Plaintiffs had discharged the burden of proof on them to show that the technical designs and information in question were trade secrets of and/or confidential to the Plaintiffs and that they were communicated to the Defendant in confidence.

2. The learned judge was wrong in holding that the toothbrush designed, manufactured and marketed by the Defendant was not based on an independent design of the Defendant, but was based on a design incorporating and making use of some or all of the drawings, technical data and instructions in question.

3. The learned judge was wrong in holding (i) that on the facts damages would not be an adequate remedy to compensate the Plaintiffs for any loss sustained by them pending trial of this action, and (ii) that in law such finding was sufficient in itself to justify the issue of the said injunction.

And further take notice that the Defendant proposes to apply to set down this Appeal in the Chancery Division (Interlocutory) List.

Dated the 25th day of October 1990.
(Signature)
of (address) Solicitors for the Defendant.
To the Plaintiffs and to
Messrs. Bowdler and Co. their solicitors.
To the above-named Plaintiffs and their Solicitors:

No notice as to the date on which this appeal will be in the list for hearing will be given: it is the duty of solicitors to keep themselves informed as to the state of the list. A respondent intending to appear in person should inform the office of the Registrar of Civil Appeals, Royal Courts of Justice, Strand, London WC2A 2LL, of that fact and give his address; if he does so he will be notified by telemessage to the address he has given of the date when the appeal is expected to be heard.

APPENDIX 2

OPINIONS AND ADVICE

AT any stage of a case, counsel may be asked by his instructing solicitor to give his views in writing. The statement of such views when delivered is called an "opinion" or an "advice." For all practical purposes these terms are synonymous, although it is conventional to use "opinion" to refer to counsels' initial consideration of the whole matter, and "advice" when dealing with particular aspects of procedure and evidence once proceedings are under way. In theory there are many occasions on which counsel could be asked to advise in writing; in practice the two most common are the first time that counsel sees the papers, when he is usually asked to advise as to the case generally, and at some time after the close of pleadings, when he will be asked to advise on the detailed preparation of the case for trial—this is called the advice on evidence.

Opinions

There are no rules as such for the writing of an opinion. Consequently there are as many different styles of opinion writing as there are practising barristers. It is quite likely that one of the first things a new pupil in chambers will be told is to forget what he or she has been taught before, and to start again by adopting his master's style. However, with this qualification in mind, there are certain matters of presentation, content and style which are generally accepted.

An opinion should bear on the back the name of the client being advised, or the title of the action if proceedings have already been commenced. It is usually headed "Opinion" and is often divided into numbered paragraphs for ease of reference.

The first paragraph may well contain a brief statement of the nature of the case and the material facts in summary form. Such an introduction should help concentration on the essentials of the case, but the student should beware of making an opening paragraph too long. The solicitor will not be interested in reading counsel's re-writing of his own instructions.

The issues in the case should then be dealt with. Clearly, the number and combination of these is infinite, and much will depend on the precise wording of the instructions, and the matters counsel is asked to consider. Whether he is simply asked to advise on liability or the merits of a claim, as is often the case, then a simple and logical approach is to deal with the issues of fact and law in the order in which they are necessary to establish liability or other grounds for relief. For example, in a case where it is fairly clear that the only cause of action is negligence, the first issue would be whether on the facts as they appear from the instructions, a duty of care was owed by one party to the other. In many cases of course, *e.g.* a collision between two cars on a public highway, this will be such an obvious proposition that its existence can be assumed. The next issue would then be whether the party against whom a claim is or might be made was in breach of that duty. This is a question of fact, and counsel may find that his instructions are insufficiently detailed to enable him to come to a conclusion on the point. In that event, he should state his provisional view in the opinion and indicate to the solicitor the further documents or information he needs to advise fully. The third issue, assuming the duty and the breach to be established, would be the damage suffered by the party injured, and whether such damage can be said to have been caused by the party in breach. Under this heading any issues of causation and remoteness of damage may be considered.

At this point, if satisfactory conclusions have been reached on those issues, counsel may be able to say that a prima facie case can be made out. Remaining issues would be any reduction or avoidance of liability, *e.g.* by contributory negligence or the application of the maxim *volenti non fit injuria*, and the claim for relief. In the majority of cases the claim will be for damages.[1] In advising on quantum, counsel should consider whether he has all the necessary particulars of special damage; if not, further details should be requested. General damage may take many forms, depending on the nature of the case. In many cases further information and reports will be necessary, *e.g.* information as to future loss of profits in a breach of contract action, medical reports on the prognosis of a personal injuries case and so on. Advice on quantum, therefore, may often be provisional at this early stage, but nonetheless counsel should indicate roughly the sort of figure he would expect to be recovered in an action. Such an estimate is obviously crucial in any attempt at settlement, or in determining whether a payment into court should be accepted. In dealing with the claim for relief, counsel should also consider whether any alternative or additional remedies ought to be claimed, *e.g.* an

---

[1] See Chap. 12.

injunction, or specific performance of a contract, etc., and advise accordingly.

Finally, advice may be required as to the future course of the actual or contemplated litigation. Several matters might be relevant here, and again, it will largely depend on the particular case as to which need to be considered. If counsel is acting for a plaintiff for example, he may need to consider whether the action should be brought in the High Court or the county court, who are the appropriate parties to the action,[2] whether it is a suitable case for Order 14 proceedings[3] and so on. If he is acting for a defendant he might advise a payment into court in respect of the whole or a part of the claim,[4] attempting to obtain security for costs from the plaintiff,[5] making a counterclaim,[6] requesting further and better particulars of the statement of claim,[7] issuing a third party notice[8] and so on.

At the end of their opinion, many barristers write a summary of their conclusions on the case. This is entirely a matter of personal style. It is suggested that a short paragraph of conclusion on the whole matter is a convenient and elegant way of rounding off an opinion, and it may be that busy solicitors find such a practice useful.

A final point of style concerns the citation of authorities in an opinion. Again this is a question of personal taste and depends very much on the problem being advised upon. In so far as it is possible to suggest any guidelines, it is submitted that if a general principle of law is stated in the opinion, no authorities are necessary. Where a specific proposition is relied on, the particular case or section of a statute establishing that proposition may be cited. Facts of cases are not usually set out unless they are directly relevant to the matter in hand, and where there may be a question of distinguishing a previous case.

Advice on Evidence

The best time for sending the papers to counsel for his advice on evidence is when discovery has been completed and preferably before the summons for directions is issued. Both sides should do this, even in cases apparently simple; otherwise the

[2] Chap. 2.
[3] Chap. 5.
[4] Chap. 17.
[5] Chap. 18.
[6] Chap. 14.
[7] Chap. 10.
[8] Chap. 8.

action may be lost for want of some certificate or other formal piece of proof.[9] Every document in the case should be sent to counsel; especially, if there has been discovery, the lists of documents, the answers to interrogatories, and the draft notices (if any) to admit and produce documents. Also the statements of all witnesses who have been interviewed during the preparation of the case.

If counsel has been instructed before the summons for directions or any adjourned hearing thereof, he should first consider whether any interlocutory application of whatever nature ought to be made at the hearing and advise accordingly; he should also cast his mind forward to the trial on the lines set out later in this chapter, so that the master may be asked to make all such orders as to the mode of proof of his case as may be calculated to save expense at the trial. Even if the hearing of the summons for directions has already been concluded, further directions may always be asked for by notice thereunder.

Before writing his advice on evidence counsel should, therefore, consider whether everything is in proper order for the trial. Answers to interrogatories or documents disclosed by the other party may throw a new light on the matters in dispute. Is any amendment of the pleadings or particulars necessary to enable his client's case to be properly presented at the trial? If so, he must promptly apply for leave to add such new matter. Are his opponent's answers to interrogatories sufficient? Should not more documents be disclosed or produced? Is it desirable for some surveyor or other agent to inspect the *locus in quo*, or take samples of the goods in dispute? If so, an order can be applied for under Order 29, r. 3 (see Chapter 18). Should an application be made under the Bankers' Books Evidence Act 1879? Should any notice, or further notice, be given under Order 38, r. 21? Then, when counsel is satisfied that all preliminaries are in order, and that all material questions are properly raised on the pleadings, he can proceed to write his advice.

Advising on evidence is an extremely important part of the work of a junior barrister; success at the trial so much depends on the care with which the case is got up beforehand; and the solicitor, who may have had but little experience in litigious work, will look to counsel for advice on every necessary detail. As appears earlier there are no rules for the writing of such an advice; it is entirely a matter of personal style. However, most advices on evidence do conform more or less to the pattern of

---

[9] See, *e.g. Collins* v. *Carnegie* (1834) 1 A. & E. 695.

first setting out briefly the issues in the action and on whom the burden of proving each issue lies; then stating seriatim the evidence by which each issue is to be proved or rebutted; then giving a list of the witnesses to attend court to give evidence; then a list of the documents which will be required, and finally advice on any other matters necessary for the preparation of the case for trial, such as amendment of pleadings,[10] notices under the Civil Evidence Act 1968[11] and so on.

Burden of Proof

What the issues are appears, or ought to appear, clearly from the pleadings. From the pleadings also it can at once be ascertained on which party lies the initial burden of proof on each issue. The "burden of proof" is the duty which lies on a party to establish his case. It will lie on A, whenever A must either call some evidence or have judgment given against him. As a rule (but not invariably) it lies upon the party who has in his pleading maintained the *affirmative* of the issue; for a *negative* is in general incapable of proof. *Ei incumbit probatio qui dicit, non qui negat.* The affirmative is generally, but not necessarily, maintained by the party who first raises the issue. Thus, the onus lies, as a rule, on the plaintiff to establish every fact which he has asserted in the statement of claim, and on the defendant to prove all facts which he has pleaded by way of confession and avoidance, such as fraud, performance, release, rescission, etc. It is important to distinguish between the legal burden which rests on a party by law to satisfy the court upon the whole of the evidence that he has proved his case, the "evidential" burden of adducing evidence on particular issues, and a provisional burden which is raised by the state of the evidence. The burden of adducing enough evidence to raise particular issues for the court to consider generally follows the legal burden, but may sometimes fall on the other party, as when a rebuttable presumption of law arises. As the case proceeds and as a prima facie case is established (the evidential burden thus being discharged), then a provisional burden is effectively cast on the party disputing the issue to challenge the case thus established. At the end of the day, when all the evidence from all parties has been heard, the court will decide whether the legal burden has been discharged.[12]

---

10 Chap. 11.
11 Order 38, rr. 21 *et seq.*
12 For a full explanation of these terms, see *Cross on Evidence* (6th ed., 1985), Chap. 4.

Illustrations

The precise form into which the pleading is cast does not matter; the judge will look at the substance of the allegation. Thus in a plea of privilege, it is immaterial whether the defendant pleads that he published the words bona fide, or that he published them without malice; in either case the plaintiff must prove malice, if the occasion be held one of qualified privilege.

In some cases a party will have to establish a negative. For example the plaintiff in an action for malicious prosecution must show that there was no reasonable and probable cause for the prosecution (*Abrath* v. *N.E.Ry.* (1886) 11 App.Cas. 247); and where the defendant had sold a book or newspaper which, unknown to him, contains a libel, the onus lies on him to prove that it was not through any negligence on his part that he was unaware of the existence of the libel.

Vizetelly v. *Mudie's Select Library Ltd.* (1900) 2 Q.B. 170.

Having determined what facts your client has to prove at the trial, you may proceed to state how they are to be proved, what witnesses must be called, and what documents must be put in on each issue. Each party must be prepared with evidence not only to prove the issues which lie upon him, but also to rebut his adversary's case. But remember:

1. There are some matters which need not be proved at all, *e.g.* the law of England, public statutes, private statutes passed since 1850, official seals and certain facts of which the court can take judicial notice.[13] But foreign law (including the law of Scotland, Ireland or the Channel Islands), or the custom of any particular county, or of a city such as London or Bristol, the practice of an inferior or foreign court, resolutions of the House of Commons,[14] or the existence of a war between foreign countries, or the internal constitution or economy of a foreign state,[15] must be proved as facts.[16] All these may be proper subjects for a special order under the summons for directions as to mode of proof.

2. Again neither party need prove that which the law already presumes in his favour, *e.g.* the plaintiff in an action of libel need not prove that the words are false; the holder of a bill of exchange need not prove that he gave value for it.

3. But even where there is no presumption of law in your favour, it is often only necessary for you to give prima facie evidence. You need not prove any fact up to the hilt. The circumstances, though unexplained, may in themselves be sufficient to establish a prima facie case; or some letter may

---

[13] See Cross, *op. cit.*, Chap. 5.

[14] *Stockdale* v. *Hansard* (1837) 7 C. & P. 731, 736.

[15] *Rendal* v. *Arcos Ltd.* [1936] 1 All E.R. 623.

[16] Except where a party intends to rely, under the provisions of s.4 of the Civil Evidence Act 1972, on a previous finding or decision on a question of foreign law. He must give notice of such intention. (See Order 38, r. 7).

contain an admission which will effectively shift the onus of proof on to your opponent.

Illustrations

Where a document, for example a notice, is authorised by statute to be served by post, then service will generally be presumed on proof of proper addressing, pre-paying and posting the document.

See the Interpretation Act 1978, s.7.

In some negligence actions the mere fact that the Plaintiff's injuries were caused by a thing under the control of the defendant may enable the Plaintiff to invoke the maxim *res ipsa loquitur*, and to argue that the injury could not have happened but for negligence by the defendant in his management of the thing.

See, *e.g. Ward* v. *Tesco Stores Ltd.* [1976] 1 All E.R. 219. However this authority needs to be treated with care.

Witnesses

Counsel must decide what witnesses his client should subpoena to attend the court to give evidence. It is as well to name them in the advice on evidence. If it be necessary to bring up a prisoner to give evidence, an order may be obtained from the Home Office under the Criminal Justice Act 1961, section 29; alternatively an application may be made *ex parte* to the judge at chambers for an order under the Criminal Procedure Act 1853, section 9. For the latter purpose an affidavit must be sworn, stating where the prisoner is confined, and for what crime, and when and where his attendance will be required. In the case of a person confined upon civil process, the latter statute does not apply, but a writ of *habeas corpus ad testificandum* may be obtained upon application on affidavit to a judge at chambers. A patient may be brought up from a mental hospital under such a writ, if he is fit for examination. A witness residing in Scotland or Northern Ireland can be compelled to attend by *subpoena ad testificandum* issued under the Supreme Court Act 1981, s.36, by the special leave of a master.

It is sometimes erroneously assumed that a witness who has given a statement to or has been subpoenaed by one party may not be approached by the solicitor on the other side with a view to giving a statement. There is no property in a witness and so long as there is no question of tampering with him or seeking to persuade him to change his story it is permissible to interview him and to take a statement from him. Great discretion should be exercised in order to avoid even the suspicion of irregularity in the approach. Any attempt to intimidate or influence a witness would amount to contempt of court. It is contrary to professional etiquette to interview the *client* of another solicitor, particularly in pending proceedings, without that solicitor's consent.

It may be necessary to apply to postpone the trial, *e.g.* to secure the attendance of witnesses who are ill or absent abroad. Or it may be necessary to apply for the examination before trial of a witness who is abroad or about the leave the country or who is dangerously ill. (Order 39, r. 1).[17] The old procedure of obtaining evidence out of the jurisdiction by writ of commission is obsolete. The appropriate procedure is different for different countries and will be found in the notes to Order 39 in *The Supreme Court Practice*. In some cases the evidence may be ordered to be taken before a special examiner or before a British consul. But several foreign governments object to commissions being issued and to examiners administering oaths to witnesses within their dominions. Consequently the Foreign and Commonwealth Office, at the request of the Senior Master, often sends through diplomatic channels a "letter of request" addressed to the tribunal of such other country asking the judges of that tribunal to order the required evidence to be taken and remitted to the English court. The English High Court returns the compliment, and will on request take evidence for a foreign tribunal under Order 70.

A defendant will obtain an order for the examination of witnesses more readily than a plaintiff who has chosen his own *forum*.[18] The affidavit filed in support of such an application must state the name of at least one witness whom it is desired to examine, and the general nature of the evidence which he is expected to give. If such evidence is not directly material to some issue in the cause, but only incidentally useful in corroboration of other evidence, the application will almost certainly not be granted. The plaintiff himself will not be allowed to give his evidence before an examiner save on very exceptional grounds, it should be given before the court. But a defendant, if resident abroad, will be allowed this indulgence.[19] The application is not usually made till the pleadings are closed; but it may be made earlier, if there be special reasons for such urgency. The application will fail if it can be shown that the witnesses could be brought to England without much greater expense, or that witnesses now in England could give

---

[17] Where the circumstances render it expedient in the interests of justice to do so, the court has power, instead of making an order for the examination of a witness (*e.g.* an elderly person) under Order 39, r. 1, to adjourn the trial of an action under Order 35, r. 3, to the place where the witness is, so as to hear the oral examination of the witness as upon the trial itself: *St. Edmundsbury and Ipswich Diocesan Board of Finance* v. *Clark* [1973] 2 W.L.R. 1042.

[18] *Ross* v. *Woodford* [1894] 1 Ch. 38.

[19] *New* v. *Burns* (1894) 64 L.J.Q.B. 104.

the same evidence. Sometimes the mere delay, which will thus necessarily be caused, is a sufficient reason for refusing the application. The costs of the examination must be borne by the party who applied for it, unless the judge at the trial makes some other order in respect of them. It is in every way a misfortune not to have the evidence of an important witness given orally in court. The deposition, when read aloud at the trial, produces but a faint effect; if there is a jury, they like to see the man and hear him examined and cross-examined. Moreover, your opponent learns beforehand exactly what your case is, and has plenty of time to prepare his answer to it.

Consideration should also be given to whether it is appropriate to apply to the Court for an order requiring the parties to exchange witness statements (Order 38, r. 2A). This provision now applies to all High Court actions.

Documentary Evidence

Counsel must next consider what documents will be required to prove his client's case, whether leave should be asked to prove particular facts by documentary rather than by oral evidence, and also what documents will be needed for the cross-examination of the witnesses called by the other side. On this several questions arise: Are such documents still in existence? In whose handwriting are they? Are they within the jurisdiction? If the originals cannot be produced, is any secondary evidence of their contents procurable? If so, is it admissible?

Much needless expense would be incurred at the trial if it were necessary formally to prove all the documents intended to be read. Hence the opposing party may be called upon beforehand to admit their authenticity. Furthermore a copy cannot strictly be put in evidence unless a notice (or the equivalent) has been given to the other side to produce the original at the trial and the original is not produced. Thus an important step in preparing for trial was always to give proper notices to admit and to produce documents under Order 27, r. 5. However, Order 27, r. 4 (see Chapter 16) has in some cases made such notices unnecessary and in nearly all cases has reduced their scope, since a party who serves a list of documents under Order 24 is put in much the same position as if he had served his opponent with a notice to admit and had himself been served with a notice to produce the documents in his list. Nevertheless there will still be many cases where such notices must be served.

Unless your opponent within a limited time—usually 21 days after inspection—serves you with a notice stating that he does not admit the authenticity of any particular documents in your list and requires them to be proved at the trial, he is deemed to admit them all (in the sense indicated below). This is subject to any special order of the master or to any extension of time which he may grant. The admission deemed to be made is that any document described in the list as an original is an original and was printed, written, signed or executed as it purports to have been, and that any document described as a copy is a true copy; but it does not prejudice his right to object to the admissibility of the document in evidence at the trial (Order 27, r. 4(1) and (2)). Since a party can hardly be expected to admit the authenticity of documents which he has not seen, it may often be prudent to serve a notice of non-admission of the documents for which privilege has been claimed.

If you have not had to serve a list of documents upon any particular party and wish to put some documents in evidence at the trial, or if you wish to put in any document not included in your list (*e.g.* because they are in someone else's possession), you can within 21 days after the action is set down for trial serve a notice to admit their authenticity, and if a notice of non-admission is not served within 21 days thereafter, they are deemed to be admitted (r. 5(1)–(3)).

If you refuse to admit a document you should ask the master or the trial judge to certify that your refusal was reasonable, otherwise you will have to pay your opponent's costs of proving it, whatever the result of the trial (Order 62, r. 6(8)).

Again, if you have served a list of documents on any party, you are *ipso facto* deemed to have been served by him with a notice to produce them at the trial and vice versa. (Order 27, r. 4(3)). In cases not covered by that sub-rule a written notice to produce particular documents may be served (r. 5(4)). The effect of giving a notice to produce, whether express or implied, is to enable a party to give secondary evidence of the contents of any document referred to in the notice if it is not produced at the trial. It does not of itself oblige your opponent to produce the document, even though he has it; when it is called for in court, his counsel may say that he does not produce it, in which case it is open to you to put in a copy or give oral evidence of its contents if you can.

When advising on evidence you should therefore carefully consider in the light of the above rules whether it is necessary to serve any notice or counter-notice, or to ask for any extension of time or other order of a master.

If the correspondence is voluminous it will be necessary to have an agreed bundle for the use of the judge, the paging of which should be identical with that of the bundles for counsel on both sides. In default of a special agreement, only such letters in the bundle as are actually read at the trial will be taken to be in evidence, and agreeing a bundle does not constitute an admission that all the letters contained in it are admissible in evidence.

Subject to certain statutory exceptions, the rule is that the originals of documents must be available to be produced in court, if they still exist and can be found within the jurisdiction. If they are in the possession of the other side, notice to produce them should, if necessary, be given a reasonable time before the trial; if in the possession of a third person within the jurisdiction, he should be served with a *subpoena duces tecum*[20]; if in the possession of a third person out of the jurisdiction, all that you can do is to impress upon him the importance of his attending the trial or sending the document and offer him such inducements as may be necessary. If the original document is produced, it may be necessary to call witnesses to handwriting: as to this, see Chapter 20. If it is not produced, there may be considerable difficulty in proving a copy.

In addition to the provisions of the common law as to the admissibility in certain cases of secondary evidence, several statutes have been passed which make copies of registers and other public and offical documents admissible in evidence, if duly authenticated, although the originals are still in existence, so as to save the necessity for conveying ancient records up and down the country. Such copies are of three kinds:

  (i) An examined copy, *i.e.* a copy which someone, who is called as a witness, swears he has compared with the original, and found to be correct and complete.

 (ii) A certified copy, *i.e.* a copy which some public officer, officially in charge of the original, certifies to be a true copy; he need not be called as a witness if he has properly sealed or stamped or otherwise authenticated the copy.

(iii) An office copy, *i.e.* a copy made in the office of the High Court of Justice by an officer having custody of the original; this, in the same court, is accepted as equivalent to the original.

[20] The court can always set aside a subpoena, if it has not been obtained bona fide for the purpose of the trial: *R. v. Baines* [1909] 1 K.B. 258. See also *Morgan v. Morgan* [1977] Fam. 122 (subpoena set aside as an oppressive invasion of privacy of a non-party to the proceedings).

Counsel must be careful to advise the solicitor to obtain the proper kind of copy which is made admissible by the particular Act.

Illustrations

"Office copies of writs, records, pleadings and documents filed in the High Court shall be admissible in evidence in any cause or matter and between all parties to the same extent as the original would be admissible."
Order 38, r. 10(1).
As to foreign judgments, public registers, etc., see Evidence (Foreign, Dominion and Colonial Documents) Act 1933 at present of limited application.
An affidavit verifying a list of documents or an answer to interrogatories made in the cause can be proved either by an office copy, or by producing the copy of the affidavit received from the deponent's solicitor, whose act in forwarding it to his opponent amounts to an admission that it is a correct copy.
See *Slatterie* v. *Pooley* (1840) 6 M. & W. 664.
Order 41, r. 10.
Under the provisions of the Civil Evidence Act 1968, s.11, a conviction may be admissible.

Five matters affecting the strict rules of evidence deserve special attention.

(i) By the Bankers' Books Evidence Act 1879, a copy of an entry in the book of any banker or any company carrying on the business of bankers is in all legal proceedings made prima facie evidence of such entry, and of the matters, transactions and accounts therein recorded, provided that (1) the book was at the time of the making of the entry one of the ordinary books of the bank, and (2) the entry was made in the usual and ordinary course of business,[21] and (3) the book is in the custody or control of the bank. The copy must be verified by an affidavit of a partner or officer of the bank, who must state that a copy has been examined with the original entry, and is correct. On the application of any party to an action, an order may be made that he shall be at liberty to inspect and take copies of entries in the books of any bank for the purposes of the litigation (Bankers' Books Evidence Act 1879, s.7), provided the case be one in which the applicant could, before the Act, have compelled the banker to attend at the hearing and produce his books.[22] Such an order will be made, although the bank be in Scotland or Northern Ireland.[23] It can be made

---

[21] It is sufficient if the book be kept for reference, though it may not be in daily use: *Asylum for Idiots* v. *Handysides* (1906) 22 T.L.R. 573.
[22] *Arnott* v. *Hayes* (1887) 36 Ch.D. 731.
[23] See *Kissam* v. *Link* [1896] 1 Q.B. 574. *MacKinnon* v. *Donaldson, Lufkin and Jenrette Securities Corporation* [1986] Ch. 482 concerning a bank in New York where the Court held that only in exceptional circumstances could it require a foreigner, not party to the action, and in particular a foreign bank, to produce documents outside the jurisdiction concerning business transacted outside it. Such orders are unusual and should be made on notice to the bank.

although the account to which the entries relate is kept in the name of a stranger, provided the entries would be evidence in the action; but in this case the jurisdiction will be exercised with the greatest caution. No banker or officer of a bank can in any proceedings to which the bank is not a party be compelled to produce books, or to give evidence of the contents of books, which may be proved by copies under the Act, unless by the order of a judge for special cause (s.6).

(ii) Where production of any business books for inspection is applied for, the master may, instead of ordering production of the original books, order a copy of any entries thererin to be supplied and verified by the affidavit of some person who has examined the copy with the original books; such affidavit must state whether or not there are in the original book any and what erasures, interlineations or alterations (Order 24, r. 14). And such copies will be evidence against the party supplying them. But the master may always order the book from which the copy was made to be produced for inspection. If there are numerous alterations, photographic copies are likely to be most convenient.

(iii) By Order 38, rr. 2 and 3 the master on the hearing of the summons for directions or otherwise, or the judge at the trial, may order evidence to be given by affidavit, or facts to be proved in some special manner, *e.g.* by production of documents or copies thereof. (See Chapter 18).

(iv) By the Civil Evidence Act 1968[24] certain out-of-court statements tending to establish relevant facts are admissible in evidence in civil proceedings either by agreement of the parties or subject to certain conditions. The Act defines a statement to include any representation of fact whether made in words or otherwise, and deals specifically with statements made out-of-court by any person (s.2), previous statements made by a person called as a witness (s.3), statements contained in a document being, or forming part of, a record (s.4), and statements contained in a document produced by a computer (s.5). Documents are defined to include not only a document in writing but (*inter alia*) any map, plan, photograph, disc or tape (s.10). Thus counsel must consider a variety of matters when advising on evidence having the provisions of the Act and the rules made thereunder in mind. Note that under section 6 the

---

[24] See principally ss.2–5 inclusive. See also the Civil Evidence Act 1972, s.1, which extends the provisions of Pt. I of the Act of 1968 (with the exception of s.5) to hearsay statements of opinion with the necessary modification that any reference in Pt. I of the Act of 1968 to a fact stated in a statement shall be construed as a reference to a matter dealt with therein.

court can allow in many cases the production of a copy whether or not the original document is still in existence.

Order 38, rr. 21 to 31 inclusive[25] provide the procedures to be adopted where it is intended to adduce "hearsay evidence" under the Act by any one of the several methods authorised. The rules themselves are of some complexity whereas the actual procedure to be followed in any given situation appears to be relatively simple. The party wishing to take advantage of the procedure by adducing hearsay or secondary evidence at the trial must accept the disadvantage of disclosing that evidence to the other side in advance. He must give notice of his intention (r. 21), stating his reasons (if any), for not calling the maker of the statement as a witness (r. 25), and he must give all the necessary particulars of the evidence he is seeking to adduce (see rr. 22, 23 and 24). Unless objection is taken he will be allowed to adduce that evidence at the trial provided it is relevant and otherwise admissible. If objection is taken he should in due course receive a counter-notice (r. 26) giving the reason (if any) why the witness should attend to give oral evidence. Any dispute whether a witness is available to testify or can be expected to recollect the facts must be determined, if possible, before the trial by a master whose decision is subject to review on fresh evidence but will normally be final (r. 27(3)). If it is found to have been unreasonable to require the attendance of a witness named in the counter-notice the party seeking to secure his attendance may be penalised in costs (r. 32; and see Order 62, r. 10(1)). Where it is desired to give in evidence a statement made in previous legal proceedings (r. 28) notice under r. 21 must still be given, but, instead of serving a counter-notice your opponent must, if he objects to its admissibility, apply to the court for directions (r. 26(3)).

Under rule 29 the court has an overriding discretion to allow a statement to be given in evidence at the trial by a party applying to do so notwithstanding his non-compliance with the rules. The court can only exercise its discretion under this rule in favour of a defaulting party if it is in possession of all the relevant facts. Therefore, there can be no valid exercise of discretion if for any reason there has been a deliberate withholding from the court of the reason for non-compliance with the rules.[26] Furthermore, the discretion cannot be properly exercised where the judge knows that the non-compliance with

<hr>

[25] Order 38, r. 34 extends the provisions of rr. 20–23 and 25–33 to a hearsay statement of opinion which a party desires to give in evidence.
[26] *Ford* v. *Lewis* [1971] 1 W.L.R. 623.

the rules was the result of a deliberate decision made for tactical reasons,[27] or where there is ground to suppose that injustice will be caused to the other party, or that he will be materially prejudiced or embarrassed.[28] On the other hand if that party has complied with the rules and no counter-notice has been served (or he can show his witness cannot attend) he must ordinarily be allowed to put the statement in evidence (see section 8(3)(*a*) of the Civil Evidence Act 1968).

Remember that sometimes your opponent may have in his possession material with which to attack the credibility of your witness, or another and inconsistent statement made by him, in which case (subject to the conditions mentioned in rr. 30 and 31 respectively) he may be allowed to adduce this evidence. You will normally, but not necessarily be forewarned that such attack is to be made, though your opponent ought at least to have served a counter-notice requiring the attendance of the witness; but even if he has not done so he may get leave from the judge at the trial to adduce the evidence he desires.

Subject to the above qualifications,[29] an order providing for the proof of particular facts by means of a document without producing the original or calling the maker of the statement may be made by the master or the trial judge. The weight which the court will attach to any such statement[30] depends upon the circumstances in which and the time at which it was made, and a statement by an interested person[31] *post litem motam* will almost certainly be excluded.

(v) Order 38, rr. 35–44, made pursuant to the powers given by section 2 of the Civil Evidence Act 1972 contains provisions relating to expert evidence.[32] These rules restrict the right of the parties to adduce expert evidence in civil proceedings, and they also provide procedures for the pre-trial disclosure by each part to the other of the expert evidence intended to be relied on at the trial. These procedures are, however, entirely subject to the direction of the court. They do not affect the rule of substantive law that reports of experts prepared for the purpose or pending or contemplated civil proceedings or in connection with the obtaining or giving of legal advice are

---

[27] *Ibid.*

[28] *Morris* v. *Stratford-on-Avon R.D.C.* [1973] 1 W.L.R. 1059.

[29] Whether and to what extent the powers of the court have been enlarged by Order 38, r. 3 may be a matter for judicial decision.

[30] And any statement admitted under the Act (s.6).

[31] See, for example, *Kelleher* v. *T. Wall & Sons Ltd.* [1958] 2 Q.B. 346; *Constantinou* v. *Frederick Hotels Ltd.* [1966] 1 W.L.R. 75.

[32] Rules 36 and 37 must be read in conjunction with Ord. 25, r. 8 (automatic directions in personal injury cases).

privileged from disclosure.[33] One party will still be unable to compel the disclosure of such reports by the other party unless the privilege is waived.

The effect of section 2 and the rules is that a party will not be allowed to adduce any expert evidence at the trial except with the leave of the court, or where all parties agree, or where it is permitted to be given by affidavit (see Order 38, rr. 2 and 3), or where the conditions specified in Order 38, r. 36 are satisfied.

For the purposes of the disclosure and admission of expert evidence the rules distinguish sharply between actions for personal injuries and other actions. In personal injury cases Order 25, r. 8 provides for automatic disclosure of any expert evidence intended to be relied on at trial in the form of a written report, which, if possible, should be agreed. If such reports cannot be agreed the experts whose evidence has been disclosed may be called as witnesses, their numbers being limited to two medical experts and one expert of any other kind. Since this procedure is automatic it would appear unnecessary to make separate application to the court under Order 38, r. 36 for directions to be given under rule 37 (which applies to exactly the same actions as Order 25, r. 8). However, where different directions or orders are sought in a personal injuries case, the provisions of Order 38 will be applicable. Rule 37 provides that where an application is made in respect of oral expert evidence, the court shall direct that the substance of the evidence be disclosed to such other parties and within such period as the court may specify, unless the court considers that there is sufficient reason for not so directing. The burden of proof is thus on the party resisting disclosure to show why it should not be ordered. He may be able to do this in the case of medical evidence by showing that the pleadings allege medical negligence or malpractice, or that the evidence contains an opinion as to the origin of the injuries or an opinion as to whether the injured party is malingering (rule 37(2)). For non-medical expert evidence he may be able to set up one of the circumstances in rule 38(2) as a sufficient reason for non-disclosure. Rule 38 deals with expert evidence other than in personal injury cases. Disclosure of such evidence will only be ordered in an application under rule 36 where the court is satisfied that it is desirable to make such a direction.[34] Thus

---

[33] *Worrall* v. *Reich* [1955] 1 Q.B. 296; *Causton* v. *Mann Egerton (Johnsons) Ltd.* [1974] 1 W.L.R. 162.

[34] Where an order is made under r. 38 for the disclosure of the *substance* of experts' reports, that means both the expert's description of the facts and circumstances of the accident and his opinion in relation to the accident, since it is the opinion which is the very justification for admitting expert evidence: *Ollett* v. *Bristol Aerojet Ltd. (Note)* [1979] 1 W.L.R. 1197.

in cases under rule 38 the burden of proof is reversed. The party claiming disclosure must satisfy the court of the need to make such an order, and rule 38(2) sets out particular circumstances which the court should take into account as affording a sufficient reason for not giving such a direction.[35] Under rule 38(3) the Court may direct that, either before or after disclosure, the experts meet for the purpose of identifying which parts of their evidence are in issue; after that, they may prepare a joint statement which indicates those areas of agreement or disagreement.

This machinery in intended to operate on the basis of fairness and mutuality between the parties, and one party should not in general be able to obtain an advantage by securing the disclosure of the other party's expert evidence without at the same time disclosing his own. Thus in personal injuries cases, mutual exchange of reports is required by Order 25, r. 8(2); under Order 38, in the case of medical reports, mutual disclosure will normally be ordered within a specified period; for non-medical experts, any order for disclosure will normally be by way of exchange.[36] In general therefore reciprocity will be the normal practice, but in exceptional circumstances and to save costs, disclosure by one party only may be ordered and the other party permitted to defer disclosure of any report.[37] The sanctions for failure to comply with any direction under rule 36 are that the party in default will be precluded from adducing expert evidence at the trial, and in addition the directions of the court may be enforced under any other provisions of the R.S.C. with the exception of orders for committal or sequestration.

One party may put in evidence any expert report disclosed to him by any other party under the rules,[38] but not where such report has been disclosed voluntarily, unless the parties have agreed to put it in evidence. Where the maker of a report disclosed under the rules is called as a witness, his report may be put in evidence at the commencement of his examination-in-chief or at such other time as the Court may direct (r. 43).

---

[35] However, it has been stated that, despite the difference in wording in r. 38, the court should ordinarily make an order for the exchange of non-medical expert reports, since this will enable the true nature of any dispute on expert evidence to be clarified and surprise thereby avoided, and will assist in saving expense by dispensing with the calling of expert witnesses if there is no real dispute: *Ollett* v. *Bristol Aerojet, supra*. See also *Sullivan* v. *West Yorkshire Passenger Transport Executive* [1985] 2 All E.R. 134 C.A., (order for exchange of reports of actuaries).

[36] *Practice Direction* [1974] 1 W.L.R. 904.

[37] *Ibid.*

[38] Ord. 38, r. 42.

There is power to revoke or vary at or before the trial any direction given under the rules on sufficient cause being shown (r. 44).

Varying Mode or Place of Trial

The master will have dealt with these matters when giving directions; but his decision then is not final; it may be varied without appeal by a subsequent order made at or before the trial (Order 33, r. 4). Circumstances may have changed since then; matters may have arisen which alter the complexion of the case. Counsel should therefore now consider whether it would be better for his client to apply[39] that the action should be tried at a different trial centre, or by a judge alone, or by judge and jury, or as official referee's business. An application under section 69 of the Supreme Court Act 1981 for a jury as a right cannot, however, be made after the mode and place of trial have been fixed (r. 5).[40] If the trial is to be by judge and jury, counsel should consider whether it is necessary for the jury to have a preliminary "view" of the *locus in quo*. The master will alter the place of trial if he is satisfied that there is no probability of a fair trial in the place originally fixed. Such extraneous facts must be proved by affidavit.

[39] If doubt arises whether a belated application of this kind should be made to the judge in charge of the list or to a master (as to which see Chapter 20), the Clerk of the Lists or the Practice Master should be consulted.
[40] See *Cropper v. Chief Constable of the South Yorkshire Police and another* [1990] 2 All E.R. 1005, C.A.; *Beta Construction Ltd. and another v. Channel Four Television Ltd. and another* [1990] 2 All E.R. 1012, C.A.

APPENDIX 3

CIVIL JUSTICE REVIEW
LIST OF RECOMMENDATIONS

The Review Body on Civil Justice was appointed by the Lord Chancellor in 1985, and reported in June 1988 (Cm. 394). Its recommendations are set out below.

THE CIVIL JUSTICE SYSTEM
High Court and County Court

(1.) The High Court and the County Court should remain separate courts, subject to the adoption of new measures providing for an increase in the upper limit of County Court jurisdiction, selective introduction of a single point of entry at County Court level and improved transfer of cases between the two courts.

The work appropriate to each court

(2.)

(i) The High Court should handle and try:—
(a) public law cases;
(b) other specialist cases; and
(c) general list cases of importance, complexity and substance.

(ii) Cases of substance mean those where the amount in issue exceeds £25,000.

(iii) There should be a flexible financial band between £25,000 and £50,000 within which cases may be tried in the County Court or the High Court.

Jurisdiction limits: the County Court upper limit

(3.) There should be no upper limit of County Court jurisdiction.

The management of personal injury cases

(4.) There should be a single point of entry in the County Court for personal injury cases.

Other general list cases

(5.) The costs sanction system should be reviewed in due course.

Jurisdiction of registrars and Circuit judges

(6.) The general trial jurisdiction of County Court registrars, concurrent with Circuit judges, should be increased to £5,000.

(7.) The upper limit of the automatic small claims jurisdiction should be £1,000.

The transfer system: non-personal injury cases

(8.)

(i) Applications to set down for trial in the High Court, other than applications in public law cases, should be examined to see that they comply with the criteria of substance (minimum £25,000), importance or complexity.

(ii) Those which do not comply should be transferred to the County Court.

(iii) Under the supervision of Presiding Judges, cases within a band above £25,000, but not exceeding £50,000, should be allocated flexibly between High Court and County Court.

Transfer up: personal injury and other cases

(9.) Applications to transfer cases from the County Court to the High Court should be made to a High Court master or a district registrar at a provincial High Court centre, acting in each case under the guidance of Presiding Judges or judges nominated by them.

Changing the limit

(10.) The minimum figure of £25,000 regulating eligibility for High Court trial should be fixed, and subject to change, by practice direction.

Transitional arrangements

(11.) Cases commenced in the High Court under the old system should be scrutinised on setting down for trial or earlier interlocutory application in accordance with the new criteria with a view to transfer to the County Court.

County Court trial centres

(12.) (i) County Court trials should be concentrated at centres at which continuous trial facilities are made available.

(ii)   Additional   centres
should, in the first
instance, be estab-
lished at High Court
centres where they do
not already exist.

(iii) An immediate estimate should be made
of the need for further
County   Court   trial
facilities   in   Central
London and the prov-
inces.   Appropriate
steps should be taken
to see that the need is
met.

(iv) In London, County
Council trial facilities
should be available at
the Royal Courts of
Justice and other Cen-
tral London County
Courts.

The Circuit bench   (13.)   There should be an upper tier
of Circuit judges who take respon-
sibility for heavier civil work, with
appropriate remuneration.

County Court   (14.)   Barristers as well as solicitors
registrars   should be eligible for appointment
as County Court and district regis-
trars. Registers should be given the
title of judge.

Common remedies (15.)   (i)   Subject to (iii) the same remedies should be available in the County Court as in the High Court, including remedies by way of injunction and summary judgment.

(ii)   County Court registrars should have jurisdiction to exercise all the powers of the court, subject to the limitations proposed in the text.

(iii) The power to grant Mareva and Anton Piller orders should be reserved to High Court judges, with special provision for County Court cases.

The High Court Sittings by Circuit judges and deputy judges (16.)   (i)   Deputy judges should only be appointed to give them experience or to cover peaks of work or temporary shortages of judge power.

(ii)   Circuit judges and deputies should hear their cases in the County Court.

PROCEDURE **Delay before** **proceedings are** **commenced**	(17.)	(i)	The normal permitted period between issue and service of process should be 4 months. This period should be reviewed from time to time with a view to seeing whether it should be further shortened. The plaintiff's statement of claim should be served not later than the end of the period permitted for service.
		(ii)	The Limitation Act 1980 should be amended so as to provide that an action is brought for the purposes of that Act at the time when process is served.
Standards of practice **and specialisation**	(18.)	(i)	The Bar and the Law Society should issue specific written professional standards relating to the conduct of all principal types of litigation.
		(ii)	Schemes fostering specialisation by practitioners should be based on objective criteria of competence and experience.

Methods of commencing legal proceedings

(19.) Subject to a very few essential exceptions, all civil proceedings should be commenced by a document called a writ. The writ should state that it is issued either in the High Court or the County Court. Where a special method of procedure is to apply the writ should be endorsed with an appropriate indication of that procedure, in a prescribed form.

Place of commencement

(20.)

(i) Subject to (ii), and to the court's powers of transfer, a plaintiff should be free to start a High Court or a County Court case wherever he chooses.

(ii) Housing possession cases and liquidated claims for not over £5,000 in the County Court should, as now, be commenced in the defendant's local court or the court with whose district the case is most closely connected.

Court management of litigation

(21.) A system of court control of case progress should be introduced.

Exchange of information between parties

(22.) There should be provision for exchange of witness statements.

Other changes to encourage openness

(23.) Other steps to encourage openness should be adopted.

Pre-trial handling by the court (24.)   (i) Automatic directions should be introduced generally for trial in the High Court and County Court.

  (ii) The system of pre-trial review in the High Court should be expanded on an experimental basis under the aegis of one or more High Court judges.

Proceedings at trial (25.) New arrangements should be laid down for trials generally.

Hearsay evidence (26.) The Lord Chancellor is invited to commission an enquiry by one of the law reform agencies into the usefulness of the hearsay rule and the current machinery for rendering hearsay admissible.

Class actions (27.) The Lord Chancellor is invited to institute a separate study by one of the law reform agencies of the case for extending the availability of representative or class actions, or establishing other procedures, to be available in cases where there are large numbers of litigants whose claims or defences have a common basis. The study should extend to the funding of such cases.

Rules of court (28.) There should be a common core of procedural rules in the High Court and the County Court.

Making rules (29.) The statutory rule committees and the Supreme Court Procedure Committee should continue to exist as separate bodies. Heads of Divisions should be able to nominate other judges to attend the Supreme Court Rule Committee on their behalf. If there is to be a common code of procedure there should be a single rule committee to include Circuit judge members.

Costs (30.) There should be a single costs regime for High Court and County Court, subject to an exception for County Court cases below £3,000.

Interest on judgments (31.) The existing statutory power to provide for interest on judgment debts in the County Court should be exercised.

Waiting for trial (32.) Existing County Court targets aimed at reducing delay should be maintained and reduced where possible. Targets for the High Court should be adopted and published.

Information for the public and the press (33.) (i) Where a witness statement is relied upon in court but is not read out in full, members of the public should be entitled, for a limited period, to inspect the statement.

(ii) There should be a public right to inspect summonses, judgments and orders in County Court proceedings and to obtain copies of them.

Excessive use of documents

(34.) In heavy cases there should be a core bundle of key documents. Abuse should be checked by sanctions in costs.

JUDICIAL ADMINISTRATION

(35.) Judicial teams handling civil business on circuit should be strengthened, under the leadership of Presiding Judges, and should include resident judges at individual County Courts or groups of courts.

Implementing the changes

(36.) Arrangements should be made on circuit for practitioners to express their views on the new system particularly during the transitional period.

Objectives for court staff

(37.) There should be published objectives for court staff setting out the standard of service required.

Staff training

(38.) A detailed civil justice training plan should be drawn up for court staff.

County Court resources

(39.) Resources allocation to the County Court should reflect the proposed changes in volume of work and standard of service.

Listing   (40.) Listing officers, either full-
time or part-time, should be trained
and appointed in all County Courts
as well as High Court centres and
should have appropriate stability in
post.

New technology   (41.) Computer facilities for the
management of lists and individual
cases should be made available as a
matter of priority.

Management   (42.) Steps should be taken to
information   improve the availability of management information, to lead to better
communication between the Department and the judiciary at all levels
and to promote arrangements for
setting up joint action, at the appropriate level, when this is needed.

Judicial training (43.)   (i) There should be a
substantial expansion
of judicial training in
civil business, to be
set up by the Judicial
Studies Board.

(ii) The preparation of
manuals on civil
adjudication should
also be set in hand by
the Judicial Studies
Board.

Sitting hours   (44.) A five-hour sitting day, five
days a week should be the normal
objective.

Sitting days (45.) The number of days sat by High Court judges should continue as at present.

Long vacation (46.) The long vacation in the High Court should be limited to August, without any curtailment of judicial leave.

ACCESS TO JUSTICE
Conduct of
proceedings (47.) Cases in which individual litigants tend not to be represented should be conducted on an interventionist basis.

Advice and
representation (48.) Litigants in small claims cases and in debt and housing cases which are proceeding in a County Court should have a statutory right to be assisted or represented by a lay representative of their choice, subject to the discretion of the court.

Forms and guides (49.) All forms should be produced centrally and standardised to avoid local variation. They should be written in plain English, where necessary paraphrasing the requirements of rules and avoiding technical legal terminology. The main forms should be piloted before introduction into general use.

(50.) The information provided to litigants in small claims, debt, housing and personal injury cases should be reviewed and simplified or expanded as appropriate. A list of local advice agencies should be sent out with each summons in these types of cases.

Advice by court staff (51.) Staff training should be designed to enable staff to give direct assistance to members of the public in the handling of their cases.

Advice agencies (52.) The following steps should be taken in relation to advice agencies:—

(i) Registrars and court officials should be available to advise advice agency staff on court procedures. To assist in this procedure each court should have a nominated link officer from whom agencies may obtain information and guidance.

(ii) Agencies should seek more training and greater experience for their staff in assisting litigants to present their cases.

(iii) Advice agencies should be encouraged, wherever business justifies it, to have duty representatives either permanently or occasionally available at courts and accommodation should be provided for this purpose.

(iv) Those agencies whose staff maintain a regular presence at courts, and which provide representation and other services to litigants, should be eligible for funding by the new Legal Aid Board in respect of such services.

Court facilities (53.) The programme of improvements to facilities in court buildings, providing for better waiting areas and interview arrangements, refreshments and information to the public, should be maintained as a matter of priority.

Evening hearings for small claims (54.) There should be carefully monitored experiments in conducting early evening arbitrations at a small number of trial centres.

Paper adjudication (55.) Some registrars should be invited to take part in a carefully prepared experiment to test the wider use of paper adjudication in selected small claims cases.

Legal aid (56.) As a matter of priority the Legal Aid Board should take early action to reduce the time taken to handle applications for civil legal aid.

Information about costs

(57.) Solicitors and barristers should be encouraged and expected to provide information to the public by way of stated rates per case or per hour and should be entitled to free publicity about those rates in lawyers' referral lists.

Contingency fees

(58.) The prohibition on contingency fees and other forms of incentive scheme should be open to re-examination.

PERSONAL INJURIES
Early release of accident reports

(59.) Arrangements should be made in personal injury cases to expedite release of accident reports by the police.

Other changes to encourage early exchange of information

(60.)

(i) Arrangements should be made in personal injury cases to expedite release of medical reports by hospitals.

(ii) Plaintiffs should serve such reports as soon as possible after issue of a writ. The court should have power under rules of court to prescribe in an order for production of such reports the time by which such an order is to be complied with.

| | (iii) | Rules of court should provide for medical reports to be supported wherever possible by up-to-date statements of special damages and statements of future earnings loss. |

Split trials   (61.) The court should have the power to order a split trial of its own motion as well as on application by a party.

Alternatives to tort liability   (62.) The Lord Chancellor should consider, in consultation with the insurance industry, the feasibility of a no-fault scheme, restricted to less serious road accidents and financed by private insurance.

SMALL CLAIMS
Identity of the small claims jurisdiction   (63.)

| | (i) | Small claims cases should continue to be heard in the County Court. |
| | (ii) | In rules, forms, literature available to litigants and notices within court buildings, specific reference should be made to 'small claim' or 'the small claims court'. |

    (iii) Courts should be encouraged to make special arrangements for handling small claims cases and wherever possible should maintain separate lists for them.

(64.) Small claims cases should be the subject of a self-contained set of small claims rules.

Increasing the scope of the small claims jurisdiction

(65.) (i) For all unliquidated County Court claims the plaintiff should be required to state, if it be the case, that the amount involved exceeds £1,000.

    (ii) In the absence of such a statement the case should, where it becomes defended, proceed as a small claim.

    (iii) If the statement, if any proves to be unfounded, the plaintiff should lose his entitlement to costs.

Transfer for trial

(66.) The registrar should have power of his own motion to rescind a reference to arbitration. The current grounds for rescission should apply.

Preliminary hearings

(67.) Small claims cases should normally be disposed of at a single substantive hearing which should be fixed by the court upon receipt of a defence.

Conduct of hearing (68.)   (i)   At the hearing, the registrar should:—

    (a) conduct the hearing according to the circumstances of each case and adopt an interventionist role, dispensing with the formal rules of evidence and procedure, and assuming control of the questioning of the parties and their witnesses;

    (b) give short reasons for his decision;

    (c) explain the legal terms he finds it necessary to use.

   (ii)   The rules should be clarified so as to make it plain that the registrar may require questions to be directed through him.

   (iii)   Hearings should normally be in private.

Expenses (69.)   There should be specific guidance on the award of expenses recoverable for small claims.

DEBT ENFORCEMENT
Responsibility for enforcement

(70.) (i) Responsibility for executing County Court judgment debts should be as follows:—

(a) All judgments below £5,000 and those arising out of regulated agreements under the Consumer Credit Act 1974 should continue to be enforced by County Court bailiffs.

(b) Above that figure, judgment debts should automatically be transferred to the Sheriffs for enforcement.

(ii) High Court judgments, of whatever value, should continue to go to the Sheriffs and it should also continue to be possible to transfer County Court judgments over £2,000 to the Sheriffs provided they are of a commercial nature.

The management of the bailiff service

(71.) Steps should be taken to ensure that County Court bailiffs are fully integrated into the court service.

County Court bailiffs' enforcement duties

(72.) The duties of County Court bailiffs should be redefined and set out in one manual which should be publicly available.

High Court enforcement officers

(73.) The law governing execution by Under Sheriffs and Sheriff's Officers should be the subject of detailed reform.

Administration orders

(74.) The administration order should be the subject of detailed reforms.

Exemptions from seizure

(75.) The current provisions which exclude certain items from seizure and sale should be revised to bring them in line with bankruptcy.

Terminology

(76.) Plain modern terms should be substituted for those now used in connection with enforcement.

**HOUSING CASES
Forum for dealing with housing cases**

(77.) There should be no separate housing court but the systematic handling of housing cases should be actively encouraged. In particular, courts should maintain distinctive lists for housing cases.

Possession procedure

(78.) In housing possession cases, there should be reforms in procedure and forms to provide the court with fuller evidence on the basis of the claim and the circumstances of the defendant.

(79.) The only reference in the title appended to lists of possession cases should be to the name of the local County Court.

Rent action (80.) There should be a new form of rent action.

Housing action (81.) There should be a new form of housing action.

High Court jurisdiction (82.) Subject to an early survey there should be an effective shift of housing possession cases from High Court to County Court.

Judicial training (83.) Judges and registrars should receive specific and systematic training in housing work. Training should be organised by the Judicial Studies Board and should include training in social security systems, local authority management practices and the relevant legislation.

Mortgage posessions (84.) Details of the new procedures should be publicised to local authorities, housing associations, banks and building societies.

Information for litigants (85.) The practice of adding mortgagees' costs to security without specifying an amount should be discontinued.

Rent Assessment Committee (86.) Rent Assessment Panels should be integrated into the national structure for courts and tribunals administered by the Lord Chancellor.

THE COMMERCIAL COURT
A programme to reduce delay

(87.)

(i) The waiting time for trial in the Commercial Court should within 3 years be reduced to 12 months from the time when a trial date is given.

(ii) Commercial actions should be redefined in modern language with a lower limit of £50,000 for the amount claimed or involved, subject to special exceptions for complex or difficult cases below that amount.

(iii) The lower limit should be increased if necessary to enable the waiting time objective to be met.

(iv) One extra judge should be made available in the first year and, if need be, two judges in the second year.

Fees

(88.) In the Commercial Court, court fees should be raised to a level which reflects the cost of handling the business, including the cost of hearings.

Handling of interlocutory business

(89.)

(i) Judges should continue to be responsible for interlocutory business.

(ii)   Formal and uncontested business should normally be dealt with by consent, or, where an application is necessary, on paper.

Case management   (90.) Directions for the future conduct of a commercial action including the date when the case should be set down for trial, should continue to be given at the hearing of a summons for directions.

Special handling   (91.) There should be a mechanism for identifying especially complex cases and, where special handling is merited, a named Commercial judge or judges should be nominated to deal with such a case throughout.

INDEX

[References in heavy type are to numbers of the Precedents which appear on pp. 451–560.]